Contents

KT-161-318

INTRODUCTION   4

What to see	6	Things not to miss	12
Where to go	8	Itineraries	22
Author picks	11		

BASICS   24

Getting there	25	Outdoor activities	38
Getting around	26	National parks and reserves	42
Accommodation	30	Health	43
Food and drink	32	Culture and etiquette	44
The media	35	Shopping	45
Festivals	35	Travel essentials	45
Spectator sports	36		

GUIDE   52

1 Santiago and around	52	7 Chiloé	314
2 Valparaíso, Viña and the Central Coast	96	8 Northern Patagonia	344
3 El Norte Chico	122	9 Southern Patagonia	380
4 El Norte Grande	166	10 Tierra del Fuego	414
5 The Central Valley	216	11 Easter Island and the Juan Fernández Archipelago	438
6 The Lake District	262		

CONTEXTS   462

History	463	Books	500
Landscape and the environment	488	Chilean Spanish	505
Chilean music: nueva canción	493		

SMALL PRINT & INDEX   512

Introduction to
CHILE

A long, narrow sliver of land, clinging to the edge of a continent, Chile has often drawn attention to itself for its wholly implausible shape. Seen in the pages of an atlas, the country's outline strikes you as aberrant and fantastical; 4300km in length (the equivalent of Norway to Nigeria), and with an average width of just 175km, the very idea of it seems absurd. Once you're on Chilean soil, however, these boundaries make perfect sense, and visitors quickly realize that Chile is a geographically self-contained unit. The Andes, the great mountain range that forms its eastern border, are a formidable barrier of rock and ice that cuts the country off from Argentina and Bolivia. The Atacama Desert, a 1000km stretch of parched wasteland, separates it from Peru to the north. And to the west, only a few islands dotted in the Pacific Ocean break the waves that roll onto Chile's coast from Australasia.

All this has created a country distinct from the rest of South America and one that defies many people's expectations of an Andean country. It is developed, relatively affluent and non-corrupt, and – with the exception of the infamous military regime of the 1970s and 1980s – boasts a long tradition of **political stability** and orderly government. It is, without doubt, one of the safest and most relaxing South American countries to travel in. Its buses are comfortable and run on time; its people polite, respectful and discreet; and its **indigenous minorities**, in the main, coexist peacefully alongside the rest of the population.

A country of geographical extremes, Chile's diversity is reflected both in its people – from the alpaca herders of the altiplano and the gauchos of Patagonia to the businessmen of Santiago – and its cuisine, which encompasses the tropical fruit of the arid north as well as king crab from the southern fjords. Above all, though, it is for its remote and dizzyingly beautiful landscapes that visitors head to Chile. With its population of fifteen million largely confined to a handful of major cities, much of Chile is made up of vast tracts of scarcely touched wilderness – places where you can be days from the nearest tarred road.

ABOVE CUERNOS DEL PAINE, PARQUE NACIONAL TORRES DEL PAINE

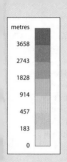

metres	
3658	
2743	
1828	
914	
457	
183	
0	

▲ *Easter Island (Chile)*

PERU

Arica

Iquique

BOLIVIA

PARAGUAY

Calama

San Pedro
de Atacama

Antofagasta

Copiapó

La Serena   Vicuña

ARGENTINA

Los Vilos

Viña del Mar

Valparaíso   SANTIAGO

Rancagua

*Juan Fernández
Archipelago (Chile)*

Talca

Chillán

Concepción

**PACIFIC
OCEAN**

Temuco   Pucón

Valdivia

Osorno

Puerto Varas

N

Puerto Montt

Ancud

Chiloé   Castro

Quellón

Chaitén

*Arch. de los
Chonos*

**ATLANTIC
OCEAN**

Puerto Aisén

Coyhaique

Cochrane

Golfo de Penas

Villa O'Higgins   El Chaltén

Isla Wellington   El Calafate

Puerto Natales   *Straits of Magellan*

Punta Arenas   *Tierra
del Fuego*

Porvenir

Ushuaia

Puerto
Williams

Cape Horn

0	250
kilometres	

What to see

Few countries, moreover, can match Chile for the **sheer diversity of scenery and range of climatic zones** – from the driest desert in the world to immense ice fields and glaciers. Spread between these extremes is a kaleidoscope of panoramas, taking in sun-baked scrubland, lush vineyards and orchards, virgin temperate rainforest, dramatic fjords and endless **Patagonian steppes**. Towering over it all is the long, jagged spine of the Andes, punctuated by colossal peaks and **smouldering volcanoes**. Given this geographical spread and dearth of population, it's not unusual to stumble on steaming hot springs, gleaming white salt flats or emerald lakes, and have them all to yourself.

Lovers of the great outdoors will likewise be seduced by the almost endless possibilities for **outdoor activities**, whether it be jeep rides, birdwatching, skiing, horse trekking, hiking, volcano climbing, sea kayaking, whitewater rafting or fly-fishing – all offered by a large number of local outfitters, with the possibility of designing unique itineraries to suit your tastes. If you have less active plans in mind, you can sit back and take in Chile's scenery from multi-day boat cruises through the southern fjords or jaw-dropping topography from the comfort of a plane or hot air balloon. Wilderness aside, Chile's wine-growing regions are second to none and connoisseurs can sample a wide range of tipples, including Carmenère, Chile's signature grape, while cultural exploration may take you from Santiago's Salvador Allende memorial to to the Mapuche *reducciones* of the Lake District, the gold rush remains in Tierra del Fuego, the Chinchorro mummies in Arica's best museum or the remains of nitrate mines around Iquique. However you do it, Chile will not disappoint you, and you can experience its diversity in whatever style you choose – this is not a developing country, and you don't have to slum it while you're here. There are plenty of modest, inexpensive **accommodation** options and camping facilities up and down the country, while those on a more generous budget will find increasing numbers of luxurious, beautifully designed boutique lodges in spectacular locations, particularly in the south.

FACT FILE

• Though Chile lives and breathes **football**, the national team has not had much luck against its mightier neighbour, Argentina. The first ever win over its rivals in 2008 was a cause for national jubilation.

• **17.2 million people** live in Chile, consisting of a fairly homogenous mestizo population with a few indigenous groups: Mapuche in the Lake District (around 650,000), Aymara in the far north (around 54,000), Easter Island's Rapa Nui (around 4300), Yámana (around 1800) and Kawéskar (around 2800) in Patagonia and Tierra del Fuego.

• Chile's **motto** is *'Por la razón o la fuerza'* meaning 'By right or by might'.

• One of the most **developed** countries in Latin America, Chile has the steadiest growth in the region and the lowest level of corruption in Latin America.

• In the longest recorded dry spell in Chile's **Atacama Desert**, it didn't rain for over 40 years.

• Chile only legalized **divorce** in 2004.

• Although notorious for the **Pinochet's** infamous **military dictatorship** during the 1970s and 1980s, Chile otherwise has a long history of parliamentary democracy.

Where to go

Given Chile's great length, and the huge distances that separate the main attractions, it's important to give careful thought to your **itinerary** before you go. Chile splits roughly into two halves, with Santiago the jumping-off point for both the sunny north, all vineyards, beaches and desert, and the capricious south, comprised of glaciers, mountains and steppe. Many travellers choose to focus on one half or another rather than spread themselves too thin, especially if time is a factor. If, however, you want to hit both extremes, a LAN air pass (see p.25) or inexpensive Sky Airline flights should aid you in your quest.

Santiago, though boasting some fine monuments, museums and restaurants, with its ceaseless noise and traffic and heavy pollution, is not a destination city like Río or Buenos Aires, and two or three days here is enough for most visitors. The capital is handy for visiting some of the country's oldest **vineyards**, while both a string of splendid beaches and the fashionable if rather bland seaside resort of **Viña del Mar** sit on its doorstep. Nearby, the quirky port of **Valparaíso** – Chile's other major city – provides an interesting contrast, with its snaking alleyways decorated by local street artists, its gritty vibe and the funiculars allowing splendid views of the bay from its many hills.

North of Santiago, highlights include the handsome colonial city of **La Serena** and the lush, deeply rural **Elqui Valley**, with hills ideal for horse treks. The valley is also home to pisco – a drink that's the source of great dispute between Chile and Peru. Another succession of idyllic **beaches** lies spread out along the dazzling fringe of the **Norte Chico**, a region comprising semi-arid landscapes and hardy vegetation that takes all the moisture it needs from the mist rising from the sea. At the northern edge of this region, the tidy little mining city of **Copiapó** serves as a springboard for excursions to the white sands and turquoise waters of **Bahía Inglesa**, one of the country's most attractive seaside resorts, and east into the barely trodden cordillera, where you'll find the mineral-streaked volcanoes of **Parque Nacional Nevado de Tres Cruces** and the almost impossibly turquoise **Laguna Verde**.

Further north, the parched **Atacama Desert**, stretching over 1000km into southern Peru, presents an unforgettable, moonlike landscape, whose sights number ancient petroglyphs (indigenous rock art), abandoned nitrate ghost towns and a scattering of fertile, fruit-filled oases. Up in the Andes, the vast plateau known as the **altiplano**, as high and remote as Tibet, encompasses snowcapped volcanoes, bleached-white salt flats, lakes speckled pink with flamingoes, grazing llamas, alpacas and vicuñas, tiny whitewashed churches and native Aymara communities. The best points to head for up here are **Parque Nacional Lauca** – the highest of Chile's many national parks, and accessible from the city of Arica – and **Parque Nacional Volcán Isluga**, near the busy seafront city of Iquique, popular with surfers and paragliders.

South of Santiago, the lush **Central Valley**, with its swaths of orchards and vineyards, dotted with stately haciendas, invites you to find Chile's best vintage by sampling the offers of the various vineyards. Further south, the famous, much-visited **Lake District**

CHILE'S WILDLIFE

Chile's diverse **animal kingdom** inhabits a landscape of extremes. The country's formidable natural barriers – the immense Pacific, lofty Andes and desolate Atacama – have resulted in an exceptional degree of **endemism**, with a third of Chile's mammals, such as the shy pudú (pygmy deer) not found anywhere else in the world.

Four species of **camelid** alone are found in Chile's barren altiplano, namely the shaggy, domesticated **llama** and **alpaca** in the north, and their wild cousins – the Patagonia-dwelling **guanaco** and the delicate **vicuña** with its highly prized fur, restricted to the high altitudes. Chile's biggest cat is the elusive **puma**, another Patagonia resident, while smaller wildcats, from the **colo-colo** to the **guiña**, also stalk these grasslands. Endemic rodents, such as the mountain **vizcacha**, are found in the northern highlands, while several species of **fox** can be spotted in the desert, altiplano and coastal forest.

A country seemingly made for birdwatchers, Chile is home to a curious mix of the small and beautiful, such as **hummingbirds** (including the firecrown, endemic to the Juan Fernández islands), while at the other end of the scale is the mighty Andean **condor**, soaring over the mountains. High in the Andes near the Bolivian border, the **Chilean and James's flamingo** gather at remote saltwater lakes, while the long-legged **ñandú** propels itself over the Patagonian steppe. Equally impressive sea birds include the **Humboldt**, **Magellanic** and **king penguins**, and Chile's coastal waters host some spectacular mammals, such as the **blue whale** and several species of **dolphins**.

presents a picture-postcard of perfect, conical volcanoes (including the exquisite **Volcán Osorno**), iris-blue lakes, rolling pastureland and dense native forests, perfect for hiking. A short ferry ride from Puerto Montt, at the southern edge of the Lake District, the **Chiloé** archipelago is a quiet, rural backwater, famous for its rickety houses on stilts, unique wooden churches, rich local mythology and a Polynesian-style regional dish.

Back on the mainland south of Puerto Montt, the **Carretera Austral** – a 1000km-long unpaved "highway" – carves its way through virgin temperate rainforest and past dramatic fjords, one of which is the embarkation point for a 200km boat trip out to the

ABOVE LLAMA, ALTIPLANO

ADVENTURE SPORTS

If you're looking to experience an adrenaline rush in the great outdoors, you've come to the right place. Chile features some of the best **skiing** in the southern hemisphere and the finest resorts lie just 40km from Santiago, in Valle Nevado and Portillo, while the Termas de Chillán ski centre in the middle of the country allows you to combine the longest run in South America with steaming thermal pools for après-ski relaxation.

Eventually due to span the 4320km length of the country, the hugely ambitious **Sendero de Chile** (Chile Trail; ⓦsenderodechile.cl) currently consists of numerous sections running through spectacularly varied scenery and skirting some splendid volcanoes. **Volcanoes** are in fact a defining feature of Chile's geography. In the Far North, experienced trekkers can tackle behemoths such as Volcán Parinacota and Volcán Ojos del Salado – the tallest active volcano in the world – while the Lake District's Volcán Villarica and Volcán Osorno make spectacular day climbs for novices. The most challenging vertical ascents are the giant granite towers at the heart of Torres del Paine National Park. If the mountains aren't high enough, climb aboard a hot-air balloon or **paraglide** above Iquique's giant sand dune – a favourite with sandboarders.

Water junkies will undoubtedly be tempted by Chile's veritable playground of rivers and seas. While Río Trancura and Río Petrohue cater to beginners, Río Futaleufú remains Chile's most challenging river for **whitewater rafting** and **kayaking**, while the northern sector of Parque Pumalín, the Gulf of Ancud, the southern fjords and the turbulent Magellan Strait are all prime **sea-kayaking** territory.

sensational **Laguna San Rafael glacier** – a fast-disappearing landmark. Beyond the Carretera Austral, cut off by the **Campo de Hielo Sur** (Southern Ice Field), lies **Patagonia**, a country of bleak windswept plains bordered by the magnificent granite spires of the **Torres del Paine** massif, Chile's single most famous sight, and a magnet for hikers and climbers. Just over the easily crossed border in Argentina are two of the region's star attractions: the **Fitz Roy Sector** in the north of the **Parque Nacional Los Glaciares**, a favourite for trekkers, and, to the south, the awe-inspiring **Glaciar Perito Moreno** – South America's most spectacular (and most accessible) glacier. Across the Magellan Strait, **Tierra del Fuego**, shared with Argentina, sits shivering at the bottom of the world, a remote land of harsh, desolate beauty, steeped in dreams of a gold rush past.

Finally, there are Chile's two Pacific possessions: **Easter Island** – one of the most remote places on earth, famed for its mysterious statues and fascinating prehistoric culture – and the little-visited **Isla Robinson Crusoe**, part of the Juan Fernández Archipelago, Chile's largest marine reserve, sporting dramatic volcanic peaks covered with dense vegetation and a wealth of endemic wildlife.

MOAI AT SUNSET, EASTER ISLAND

Author picks

Scaling the breathless heights of its lofty national parks, driving some of Chile's most challenging and isolated roads, and enduring the heat of the desert, Rough Guides authors have covered every nook and cranny of this impossibly-shaped country – from the wilds of southern Isla Navarino to the Atacama Desert in the north. Here are their personal favourites:

Best sunrise Chile has numerous contenders for this title, but the mesmerizing sight of the sun rising up behind the fifteen colossal *moai* of Ahu Tongariki (p.450) on Easter Island is hard to beat.

Dawn by canoe Paddle your canoe through Chepu Valley's sunken forest at dawn – the best time to see the varied birdlife. p.326

Drive that sled Step into the snow-shoes of a musher and bond with your own husky team during a multi-day expedition in the Andes. p.273

Put your trip in context Santiago's thought-provoking Museo de la Memoria y los Derechos Humanos (Museum of Memory and Human Rights) is dedicated to the many victims of the Pinochet dictatorship. p.70

Stargazing Make the most of clear night skies and see the universe like you've never seen it before with potent telescopes and engaging astronomers at the mountaintop Del Pangue observatory. p.146

Hit the road For the ultimate driving challenge, take on Chile's Carretera Austral (p.346) through the land of cowboys and pioneers, admiring the waterfalls plunging down from the mountains around you.

Glacier fun Glacier Perito Moreno (p.441) and Glacier Viedma (p.412) in the Parque Nacional Los Glaciares (p.408) are the best places to strap on crampons and get up close and personal with the ice.

Our author recommendations don't end here. We've flagged up our favourite places – a perfectly sited hotel, an atmospheric café, a special restaurant – throughout the guide, highlighted with the ★ symbol.

24

things not to miss

It's not possible to see everything Chile has to offer in one trip – and we don't suggest you try. What follows is a selective taste of the country's highlights: outstanding scenery, picturesque villages and dramatic wildlife. All highlights have a page reference to take you further into the guide, where you can find out more.

1 SOUTHERN PATAGONIA
Pages 382
Explore the tip of the Americas, where the country splinters into granite towers, glaciers and fjords.

2 TELEFÉRICO OVER SANTIAGO
Page 73
Dangle high above the sprawling capital, surrounded by the snowcapped Andes.

3 LAGUNA VERDE
Page 160
Massive active volcanoes surround these richly hued waters, making for an almost surreal landscape – the perfect spot to enjoy the bubbling lakeside hot springs.

4 PARQUE NACIONAL LAUCA
Page 211

Behold Chile's highest national park, with altitudes between 4000m and 6000m, herds of llamas, remote geysers and altiplano lakes.

5 RODEOS AND HUASOS
Page 223

Witness expert horsemanship and a slice of national culture at the rodeos in the Central Valley.

6 PARAGLIDING IN IQUIQUE
Page 190

Soar over Iquique, one of South America's top paragliding destinations, and enjoy incredible views of the giant sand dune of Cerro Dragón far below.

7 PENGUINS
Page 394

Head to the thriving sanctuaries at Isla Magdalena and Seno Otway for an up-close look at penguins.

8 VALPARAÍSO
Page 98

This remarkable city sits perched by the sea, draped over a jumble of steep hills around a wide bay.

12

9 CURANTO
Page 324

In Chiloé, tuck into this delicious concoction of shellfish, smoked meat and potato dumplings, traditionally cooked in a pit in the ground.

10 CHINCHORRO MUMMIES
Page 210

Gape at these prehistoric, remarkably intact mummies, pulled from a seven-thousand-year-old burial site near Arica.

11 HIKING VOLCÁN VILLARRICA
Page 282

Take a guided hike up this active volcano, the focal point of a park with excellent opportunities for trekking and camping.

12 TRACKING PABLO NERUDA
Pages 72, 106 & 111

The Nobel Prize-winning poet is one of Chile's best-known literary exports. Visit any of the three houses he lived in: La Chascona in Santiago, La Sebastiana in Valparaíso, or the museum on Isla Negra.

13 THE NIGHT SKY
Page 146

Chile's northern skies are the most transparent in the southern hemisphere, as testified by the many international observatories stationed here. Head to the Elqui Valley's Cerro Mamalluca observatory to play astronomer and gaze up at the stars.

13

14 SEA LIONS IN THE BEAGLE CHANNEL
Page 434

If you make it all the way down to Tierra del Fuego, a trip through the Channel to see these delightful creatures is a near requisite.

15 TERMAS DE PUYUHUAPI
Page 361

Isolated and largely inaccessible, the resort here is home to steaming hot springs, and is one of the great getaways along the Carretera Austral.

16 TAPATI, EASTER ISLAND
Page 448

Partake in the remote island's liveliest festival, complete with traditional dancing, woodcarving and surfing competitions, all amid the mysterious *moai* stone statues.

17 PARQUE NACIONAL TORRES DEL PAINE
Page 400

Without a doubt, this spectacular park is what draws most visitors to southern Chile, and it does not disappoint even after all the photos and build-up.

18 BAHÍA INGLESA
Page 163

Dip into turquoise waters and soak up rays on the relatively unspoilt beach.

19 FLY-FISHING
Page 362
The gin-clear rivers of the
Carretera Austral feature
some of the world's best
spots for fly-fishing.

20 PISCO ELQUI
Page 151
Take a tour of a distillery,
followed by a taste of a pisco
sour, Chile's national cocktail.

21 LAPIS LAZULI
Page 45
For a lovely Chilean souvenir,
pick up jewellery made from
lapis, the cool blue stone
mined throughout the
country and sold in local
crafts markets.

**22 CHURCHES OF
CHILOÉ**
Pages 321 & 328
The archipelago's beautiful
wooden churches rise over
the heart of almost every
small village.

23 VALLE DE LA LUNA
Page 185
Trek across this aptly named
moonscape, just south of
San Pedro de Atacama.

**24 SAN RAFAEL
GLACIER**
Page 369
Embark on an exhilarating
boat ride alongside this
stunning ice formation.

20

21

Itineraries

The following itineraries span the entire length of this incredibly diverse country, taking you from the icy fjords and snow-tipped mountains of the south to the fertile wine-growing valleys in the centre and parched desert and highland lagoon of the north. Given the vast distances involved, you may not be able to cover every highlight, but even picking a few from the itineraries below will give you a thrilling window onto Chile's geographical and cultural wonders.

THE GRAND TOUR

Allow at least three weeks if you wish to cover Chile from top to bottom; flying between some of the destinations will allow you to cover vast distances quickly.

❶ Atacama desert Visit erupting geysers, crinkly salt plains and emerald lakes in the morning, and deep, mystical valleys by sunset in the driest desert on earth. **See p.168**

❷ Elqui Valley/stargazing near Vicuna Take advantage of some of the clearest skies in Chile and look at the universe through some of the world's most powerful telescopes. **See p.143**

❸ Santiago Chile's rapidly evolving capital city boasts a vibrant eating out and nightlife scene, several fascinating museums, numerous cultural pursuits and a selection of excellent places to stay. **See p.54**

❹ Valparaíso One of South America's most enchanting cities, Valparaíso has a tangle of colourful houses, cobbled streets and bohemian hang-outs spread across a series of undulating hills overlooking the Pacific. **See p.98**

❺ Isla Negra Pablo Neruda's house has been turned into a beguiling museum with an evocative collection of the Nobel Prize-winning

poet's kitsch and often bizarre trinkets and knick-knacks. **See p.111**

❻ Wineries Visit the numerous traditional bodegas around San Fernando and Santa Cruz, and sample some of Chile's finest vintages. **See p.239 & 232**

❼ Parque Nacional Torres del Paine Hike the trails of Chile's most popular – and most spectacular – national park or climb the granite towers that give the park its name. **See p.400**

ISLAND HOPPING

Since you're very likely to linger on one of Chile's enchanted isles, and given some of the distances involved, allow at least three weeks for this trip.

❶ Easter Island Gazing down into the giant crater of the extinct Rano Kau volcano and visiting the magical *moai* at Ahu Tongariki and Rano Raraku are once-in-a-lifetime experiences. **See p.441**

❷ Isla Robinson Crusoe Although badly damaged by the 2010 tsunami, Isla Robinson Crusoe still has the end-of-the-world castaway feel that inspired Daniel Defoe's famous book. **See p.456**

❸ Chiloé Sample one of Chile's most memorable dishes, admire the *palafitos*

ABOVE BARRIO BELLAVISTA, SANTIAGO; PARAGLIDING, IQUIQUE

(traditional houses on stilts) or hike through temperate rainforest on Chile's mist and legend shrouded island. **See p.316**

❹ Patagonian islands Lose yourself in this veritable maze of fjords and tiny islets by taking to the water in a sea kayak, or take a boat trip in search of the elusive blue whale. **See p.390**

❺ Tierra del Fuego Explore the deserted roads running through steppe and dotted with guanacos and rheas, or fish in the pristine lakes and rivers of Chile's remotest region. **See p.416**

❻ Isla Navarino Chile's southernmost inhabited territory (barring Antarctica), where the warmth of the locals contrasts with the harshness of the landscape. **See p.422**

❼ Cape Horn Fly over some of the world's most treacherous waters or brave a sailing trip to Chile's southernmost group of islands – the biggest nautical graveyard in the Americas. **See p.426**

THE GREAT OUTDOORS

With the exception of the treks, all items on this itinerary are do-able as day excursions, so a couple of weeks should be sufficient.

❶ Paragliding/surfing in Iquique Ilquique's perfect climate makes it one of the best places in the world to soar the skies or dance through waves. **See p.187**

❷ Skiing at Portillo Take to the slopes at Chile's top ski resort, famous for its powder snow and with plenty of challenges for expert skiers. **See p.90**

❸ Parque Nacional La Campana Follow in the footsteps of Charles Darwin by hiking up to the 1880m summit of Cerro La Campana, where you'll be rewarded by some of the best views in the country. **See p.94**

❹ Kayaking in Parque Pumalin Explore the maze of tiny islands in the isolated fjords of Chile's largest private nature reserve as part of a challenging multi-day expedition. **See p.301**

❺ A boat trip around the San Rafael glacier Take a boat trip to the ice-filled lagoon that is Chile's fastest shrinking glacier and get close to the ice in a Zodiac speedboat. **See p.369**

❻ Trekking the Dientes de Navarino Take up the challenge of one of South America's toughest hikes at the very end of the world. **See p.425**

PERU

BOLIVIA

PARAGUAY

ARGENTINA

THE GRAND TOUR

ISLAND HOPPING

THE GREAT OUTDOORS

ROAD IN THE ALTIPLANO

Basics

25 Getting there

26 Getting around

30 Accommodation

32 Food and drink

35 The media

35 Festivals

36 Spectator sports

38 Outdoor activities

42 National parks and reserves

43 Health

44 Culture and etiquette

45 Shopping

45 Travel essentials

Getting there

Most people fly into Chile, arriving at Santiago's modern international airport, though some travel by land from neighbouring countries, and a handful arrive by sea.

Airfares depend on the **season**. You'll pay the highest fares in the December to February and June to August periods, the southern and northern hemisphere's summer holiday months, respectively. Fares drop slightly during the "shoulder" months – March and November – and you'll get the best prices during the low seasons: April, May, September and October.

Flights from the US and Canada

US travellers shouldn't find it too hard to get a fairly convenient flight to Santiago. American Airlines (Ⓦaa.com), Delta (Ⓦdelta.com) and LAN (Ⓦlan .com) offer **non-stop flights** from airports such as **Miami, Dallas-Fort Worth** and **Atlanta**. It is also possible to travel via other Latin American countries such as Peru and Brazil. **Typical fares are around** US$1000–1200 in the high season.

LAN and Air Canada (Ⓦaircanada.com) both have flights from Toronto to Santiago; high season fares are around C$1600–1900.

Flights from the UK and Ireland

There are currently no direct flights from either London or Dublin to Chile, so you'll have to travel via **a European, Latin American or US city**; LAN (Ⓦlan .com), Iberia (Ⓦiberia.com), British Airways (Ⓦbritish airways.com), Air France (Ⓦairfrance.com) and Varig (Ⓦwww.varig.com) are all options. In general, high-season fares cost around £900–1100. In addition to price, it's also worth paying attention to the routes used by the different airlines; even the shortest and most convenient ones via Madrid or Buenos Aires entail a total travelling time of over 16 hours. Flying via the US is longer still (though sometimes cheaper).

Flights from Australia, New Zealand and South Africa

Qantas (Ⓦqantas.com), Air New Zealand (Ⓦairnewzealand.com), LAN (ⓌLAN.com) and – via Buenos Aires – Aerolíneas Argentinas (Ⓦaerolineas .com) offer flights from Sydney and Auckland to Santiago. In the high season, expect to pay from around Aus$2100/NZ$1700.

ARRIVAL TAX

Chile levies an **arrival tax** for **US, Canadian, Australian, Mexican and Albanian** citizens in reciprocation for similar taxes levied on Chilean citizens arriving in these countries. This means you must pay **US$131, US$132, US$61, US$23 or US$30 respectively** on arrival at Santiago or Easter Island airports (check with a Chilean consulate for the latest amount). However, the payment is valid for the lifetime of the passport and is not levied when crossing land borders.

From South Africa, South Africa Airways (Ⓦflysaa .com) has flights from Johannesburg to Sao Paulo, Brazil, from where there are regular connections to Santiago. It is cheaper to buy the main flight separately – expect to pay around R8000–9000 – and then book your flight on to Chile.

Round-the-world flights

If Chile is only one stop on a longer journey, you might want to consider a round-the-world (RTW) ticket. "An off-the-shelf" ticket will have you touching down in about half a dozen cities. An itinerary including Santiago costs from around £1000. Alternatively, you can have a travel agent custom-make a RTW ticket for you, though this is more expensive. Trailfinders (Ⓦtrailfinders.com) and STA Travel (Ⓦstatravel.com) both sell RTW tickets.

Air passes

Air passes are another alternative if you plan to visit several destinations in South America. The **Visit South America** pass (Ⓦoneworld.com) is operated by the Oneworld alliance (which includes LAN, British Airways and American Airlines). It allows you to plan your own itinerary, with set flight prices depending on the distance travelled between (or within) countries; note that you must use a minimum of three flights. LAN's **South America Airpass** is similar, though generally a little cheaper. However, you may find that promotional fares within Chile are a better option than either of the passes.

If you plan to visit Easter Island, your flight there from Santiago will be far cheaper if it is bought in conjunction with a LAN international flight.

Trains

Chile has **international rail links** between Arica and Tacna in Peru and between Uyuni in Bolivia

A BETTER KIND OF TRAVEL

At Rough Guides we are passionately committed to travel. We feel that travelling is the best way to understand the world we live in and the people we share it with – plus tourism has brought a great deal of benefit to developing economies around the world over the last few decades. But the growth in tourism has also damaged some places irreparably, and climate change is exacerbated by most forms of transport, especially flying. All Rough Guides' trips are carbon-offset, and every year we donate money to a variety of charities devoted to combating the effects of climate change.

and Calama; at the time of writing, however, the latter route was suspended. There are also plans to construct a railway line between Arica and La Paz in Bolivia.

Buses

Several roads **connect Chile with Argentina** – from Santiago or Valparaíso to Mendoza via Los Andes; from Osorno and Puerto Montt to Bariloche and from Puntas Arenas to Río Gallegos – all of which are served by buses. There are other routes, including the Ruta 41 from La Serena, one of the most dramatic, which leads over the mountains from the Elqui Valley before joining other roads to San Juan. The route only opens in the warmer months between October/November and April. All Andean routes, even the road to Mendoza, can be blocked by snow from April onwards. A decent road and regular buses link Chile to Peru from Arica through to Tacna. You can also catch buses from Arica to La Paz in Bolivia; this takes you through the stunning scenery of the Lauca National Park (see pp.211–213), but it does mean travelling from sea level up to 4500m in just a few hours so take plenty of water and expect to feel pretty uncomfortable.

AGENTS AND OPERATORS

Adventure Associates Australia ☎ 02 8916 3000, adventureassociates.com.au. Established operator with tours and cruises to Antarctica, Chile and South America as a whole.

Adventures Abroad ☎ 1-800 665 3998, Ⓦ adventures-abroad .com. Adventure specialists offering two-week tours to Patagonia, and extended trips throughout Chile and Argentina.

Anglatin Ltd ☎ 1-800 918 8580, Ⓦ anglatin.com. A range of tours focusing on topics such as rural life, birdwatching, ancient cultures and even llamas.

Austral Tours UK ☎ 020 7233 5384, Ⓦ latinamerica.co.uk. Small company offering a 16-day tour in northern and southern Chile, plus tailor-made itineraries based around wine, fishing, trekking or archeology.

Dragoman UK ☎ 01728 861 133, Ⓦ www.dragoman.com. Overland journeys in purpose-built vehicles; shorter camping and hotel-based safaris, too.

Exodus UK ☎ 0845 240 5550, Ⓦ exodus.co.uk. Adventure tour operator taking small groups for specialist programmes including hiking, biking, overland and cultural trips.

Explore Worldwide UK ☎ 0870 333 4001, Ⓦ explore.co.uk. Small-group tours, treks, expeditions and safaris throughout Chile.

Intrepid Travel UK ☎ 0800 781 1660, Ⓦ intrepidtravel.com. Small-group tours with the emphasis on cross-cultural contact and low-impact tourism.

Journey Latin America UK ☎ 020 8747 3108, Ⓦ journeylatinamerica.co.uk. Long-established Latin America specialists, with a huge choice of trips (both package and tailor-made) across Chile.

Mountain Travel Sobek ☎ 1-888 831 7526, Ⓦ mtsobek.com. Trips include a "Patagonia Explorer" package, featuring hiking and sailing.

Nature Expeditions International ☎ 1-800 869 0639, Ⓦ naturexp.com. The 15-day Chile tour takes in Torres del Paine and the Atacama desert.

REI Adventures ☎ 1-800 622 2236, Ⓦ rei.com/adventures. Climbing, cycling, hiking, cruising, paddling and multi-sport tours.

Ski.com ☎ 1-800 908 5000, Ⓦ ski.com. Package skiing trips to Portillo and Valle Nevado.

South America Travel Centre Australia ☎ 03 9642 5353, Ⓦ satc.com.au. Large selection of tours and accommodation packages throughout the region.

Tucan Travel UK ☎ 020 8896 1600, Ⓦ tucantravel.com. Backpacker group trips in Chile and neighbouring countries.

Wilderness Travel ☎ 1-800 368 2794, Ⓦ wildernesstravel.com. Specialists in hiking, cultural and wildlife adventures.

Wildlife Worldwide UK ☎ 020 8667 9158, Ⓦ wildlifeworldwide .com. Customised trips for wildlife and wilderness enthusiasts.

World Expeditions Australia ☎ 02 8270 8400, Ⓦ worldexpeditions.com.au, New Zealand ☎ 09 368 4161, Ⓦ worldexpeditions.co.nz. Offers a range of adventure holidays.

Getting around

Travelling in Chile is easy, comfortable and, compared with Europe or North America, inexpensive. Most Chileans travel by bus, and it's such a reliable, affordable option that you'll probably do likewise. However, internal flights are handy for covering long distances in a hurry. The country has a good road network, and driving is a quick, relatively stress-free way of getting around. Chile's rail network has fallen into decline and only limited services are available. South of Puerto Montt, ferry services provide a slow but scenic way of travelling as far as Puerto Natales.

By air

Chile is a country of almost unimaginable distances (it's more than 5000km by road from Arica to Punta Arenas), which makes **flying** by far the quickest and most convenient way of taking in both its northern and southern regions in a single trip. Fares are quite high, though you can find good promotions from time to time.

The leading airline is **LAN** (☎600 526 2000, ⓦLAN .com), which besides offering the widest choice of domestic flights, is Chile's principal long-haul carrier and the only one with flights to Easter Island. **Sky Airline** (☎2 352 5600, ⓦskyairline.cl) has more limited routings but usually lower prices.

Air taxis and regional airlines operate regular services to smaller destinations between Puerto Montt and Puerto Williams, but they are susceptible to weather delays and won't fly without a minimum number of passengers (usually six). Two companies also fly out from Santiago to Isla Robinson Crusoe (see p.461).

By bus

Chile's **long-distance buses** offer an excellent service, far better than their European or North American counterparts – thanks mainly to the enormous amount of legroom, frequent departures and flexible itineraries. Facilities depend less on individual companies than on the class of bus you travel on, with prices rising according to comfort level. A **pullman** (not to be confused with the large company of the same name) or **clásico** contains standard semi-reclining seats; a **semicama** has seats with twice the amount of legroom that recline a good deal more; and a **salon cama**, at the top of the luxury range, has wide seats (just three to a row) that recline to an almost horizontal position à la first class on a plane. All buses have toilets. Some include meals or snacks, while others stop at restaurants where set meals might be included in the ticket price. Videos, piped music and bingo games are also common attractions (or irritations). Check out the locations of video screens first and seat yourself appropriately.

Thanks to the intense competition and price wars waged between the multitude of bus companies, **fares** are low. As a rule of thumb, reckon on around CH$1500 per hour travelled on standard inter-city buses; the most luxurious services are at least four times that. It always pays to compare fares offered by the different companies serving your destination, as you'll almost certainly find one offering a special deal. This price comparing is easily done at the central terminal used by long-distance buses in most cities, where you'll find separate booking offices for each company (though Tur Bus and Pullman Bus, the two largest companies, often have their own separate terminals). Some towns, however, don't have a **central terminal**, in which case buses leave from their company offices.

Try to buy your ticket at least a few hours in advance, and preferably the day before travelling, especially if you plan to travel on a Friday. An added advantage of buying ahead is that you'll be able to choose a seat away from the toilets, either by the aisle or window and, more importantly, the side of the bus you sit on. Even with a/c, seats on the sunny side can get extremely hot. There is little reason to buy a round-trip ticket unless you are travelling at peak season.

When it comes to **boarding**, make sure that the departure time on your ticket corresponds exactly to the time indicated on the little clock on the bus's front window, as your ticket is valid only on the bus it was booked for. Your luggage will be safely stored in lockers under the bus and the conductor will issue you a numbered stub for each article.

If you're travelling north of Santiago on a long-distance route, or crossing an international border, the bus and all luggage may be searched by Ministry of Agriculture officials at checkpoints, and all sandwiches, fresh fruit and vegetables will be destroyed.

By local bus, colectivo and taxi

Local buses, often called micros, connect city centres with suburbs and nearby villages. These buses are often packed, and travelling with a large rucksack can be difficult. The main points of the route and final destination are displayed on the inside of the front window, but it always helps to carry a street map and be able to point to your intended destination. Buses that leave the city for the countryside normally depart from their own *terminal rural*, usually close to the Mercado Municipal (market building).

Colectivos, which are shared taxis operating along a set route with fixed fares, are normally only slightly more expensive than local buses. Most *colectivos* look exactly like regular taxis (apart from being all black, not black and yellow) and have their route or final destination marked on a board on the roof, but in some cities *colectivos* are bright yellow cars, often without a roof-board.

Taxis are normally black with a yellow roof. Foreigners are often overcharged, so check that the meter has been turned on before you start a journey and get an estimate for the fare, if possible in Spanish. Fares should be shown in the windscreen.

By car

While Chile's towns and cities are linked by plenty of buses, most visitors are here for the country's wilderness areas, which are often difficult, and sometimes impossible, to reach on public transport. Many remote attractions are visited by tour companies, but for more independence, your best bet is to **rent a car**. To do this, you need to be at least 21 years old and have a major credit card so you can leave a blank voucher as a guarantee. You're allowed to use your national driver's licence, but you're strongly advised to bring, in addition, an **inter-national licence**. Chile's *carabineros* (police officers), who frequently stop drivers to check their documents, are often suspicious of unfamiliar foreign licences and are always happier when dealing with international ones. Traffic regulations are rarely enforced, except for speeding on the highways. The **speed limit** is 50km per hour or less in urban areas and 100km per hour on highways, and radar speed traps are commonplace. If an oncoming vehicle flashes its headlights, you're being warned of *carabineros* lurking ahead. If you do get pulled over, exercise the utmost courtesy and patience, and under no circumstances do or say anything that could possibly be interpreted as bribery.

Rental outlets and costs

Several international car-rental companies have offices throughout Chile. In addition to these, you'll find an abundance of local outlets which are often, but by no means always, less expensive than the international firms. Rates can vary quite a lot from one company to another, and it's always worth phoning as many as possible to compare prices. **Basic saloon cars** go from around US$400–500 per week. Make sure the quoted price includes IVA (the

19 percent Chilean value added tax), insurance and unlimited mileage. Your rental contract will almost certainly be in (legal and convoluted) Spanish – get the company to take you through it. In most cases your liability, in the event of an accident, is around the US$500 mark; costs over this amount will be covered in total by the company. Petrol, at the time of writing, cost around US7–9 a gallon.

CAR RENTAL AGENCIES

Avis Ⓦ avis.com.
Budget Ⓦ budget.com.
Dollar Ⓦ dollar.com.
Hertz Ⓦ hertz.com.
Thrifty Ⓦ thrifty.com.

Driving in towns

Most Chilean towns are laid out on a grid plan, which makes navigating pretty easy. However, the country is obsessed with **one-way traffic** systems, and many streets, even in the smallest towns, are one-way only, the direction of traffic alternating with each successive street. The direction is usually indicated by a white arrow above the street name on each corner; if in doubt, look at the direction of the parked cars. **Parking** is normally allowed on most downtown streets (but on one side only), and around the central square. You'll invariably be guided into a space by a wildly gesticulating *cuidador de autos* – a boy or young man who will offer to look after your car (quite unnecessarily) in return for a tip. In larger towns there's a small half-hourly charge for parking on the street, administered by eagle-eyed traffic wardens who slip tickets under your wipers every thirty minutes then pounce on you to collect your money before you leave (a small tip is expected, too). If you can't find a space, keep a look-out for large *"estacionamiento"* signs, which indicate private car parks.

Driving on highways

The **Panamerican** highway, which runs through Chile from the Peruvian border to the southern tip of Chiloé, is known alternately as Ruta 5, la *Panamericana*, or *el longitudinal*, with *sur* (south) or *norte* (north) often added on to indicate which side of Santiago it's on. Thanks to a multi-billion dollar modernization project, it is quickly becoming a divided highway, with two lanes in each direction and a toll booth every 30km. This is undoubtedly a major improvement over most single-lane highways in Chile, which are prone to head-on collisions involving buses and trucks.

Backcountry and altiplano driving

You'll probably find that many places you want to get to are reached by dirt road, for which it's essential to rent a suitable vehicle, namely a **Jeep** or **pick-up truck**. On regular dirt roads you rarely need a 4WD vehicle. For **altiplano driving**, however, you should pay extra to have 4WD (with the sturdiest tyres and highest clearance), as you can come across some dreadful roads, hundreds of kilometres from the nearest town. Make sure, too, that you take two spare tyres, not one, and that you always carry a funnel or tube for siphoning, and more than enough petrol. Also pick up several five-litre water jugs – it may be necessary for either the passengers or the engine at some point. It can be difficult to navigate in the *altiplano*, with so much open space and so few landmarks – make a careful note of your kilometre reading as you go along, so you can chart your progress over long roads with few markers. A compass is also helpful. Despite this tone of caution, it should be emphasized that *altiplano* driving is among the most rewarding adventures that Chile offers.

Finally, a general point on **tyre punctures**. This is such a common occurrence in Chile that even the smallest towns have special workshops (bearing signs with a tyre painted white) where they are quickly and cheaply repaired.

Hitching

While we don't recommend hitching as a safe way of getting about, there's no denying that it's widely practised by Chileans themselves. In the summer it seems as though all the students in Chile are sitting beside the road with their thumb out, and in rural areas it's not uncommon for entire families to hitch a lift whenever they need to get into town.

By ferry

South of Puerto Montt, where the mainland breaks up into an archipelago, a network of ferries operates through the fjords, inlets and channels of Chile's far south, providing a more scenic and romantic alternative to flights and long-distance buses. Two ferries in particular are very popular with tourists: one from Puerto Montt to Chacabuco and the San Raphael glacier, the other between Puerto Montt and Puerto Natales. In addition, there are ferry links with Quellón on Chiloé, and with Chaitén, on the Carretera Austral, as well as a number of shorter routes forming a bridge along various points of the Carretera Austral (see p.346). There's also a ferry trip across Lago Todos Los Santos, in the

ADDRESSES

These are nearly always written with just the street name (and often just the surname, if the street is named after a person) followed by the number; for example, Prat 135. In the case of avenues, however, the address usually starts with the word *avenida*, eg Avenida 21 de Mayo 553. Buildings without a street number are suffixed by s/n, short for *sin número* ("without a number").

Lake District, connecting Petrohué with Peulla, near the Argentine border (see p.301).

MAIN FERRY ROUTES

Petrohué–Peulla, across Lago Todos Los Santos Five hours; daily crossings (year-round) with Andina del Sud (ⓦ www .andinadelsud.com). See p.308.

Puerto Montt–Chacabuco 24 hours; one sailing per week with Navimag (year-round; ⓦ www.navimag.com) and TransMarChilay (year-round; ⓦ www.transmarchilay.cl). See p.311 & p.368.

Puerto Montt–Chacabuco–Laguna San Rafael Five days, four nights (returning to Puerto Montt); one sailing per week with Navimag (year-round) and two, three or four with TransMarChilay (year-round). See p.312 & p.369.

Puerto Montt–Chaitén Ten hours; one sailing per week with Navimag (Jan& Feb); three or four per week with TransMarChilay (year-round). See p.312 & p.354.

Puerto Montt–Puerto Natales Four days, three nights; one sailing per week with Navimag (year-round). See p.312 & p.396.

Quellón–Chaitén Five hours; three sailings per week with Navimag (Jan & Feb). See p.340 & p.354.

By bike

With the right amount of time and energy, travelling by bike can be incredibly rewarding. Your time is your own and you won't find yourself stuck to rigid timetables or restricted to visiting destinations only served by public buses.

Supplies in Chile can be unreliable so it's best to bring as much as you can from home. A good, sturdy mountain bike is a must, along with the usual locks and chains, strong racks, repair kit, lights, waterproof panniers, jackets and over-trousers. All equipment and clothes should be packed in plastic to protect from dust and moisture. Your major problem will be getting hold of **spares** when you need them – bike shops tend to be found only in Santiago and a few major cities. When on the road, bear in mind that long stretches are bereft of accommodation options and even the most basic services, so you must be completely self-sufficient and prepared for a long wait if you require assistance. Some bus companies will not transport bicycles unless you wrap frame and wheels separately in cardboard. When you enter the country, you may well find that customs officials enter details of your bicycle in your passport to prevent you from selling it.

The main danger when cycling on Chile's roads are drivers. Make sure you stand out in the traffic by wearing bright colours, good reflective gear and lights when the vision is poor. It goes without saying that you should **wear a helmet**; it's actually illegal to ride in Chile without one. Before you set off get your hands on one of the many good guidebooks available on long-distance cycling. Alternately contact the **Cyclists Touring Club** in the UK (☎0844 736 8450, ⓦctc.org.uk).

By train

Chile once possessed a huge network of **railways**, particularly in the far north where hundreds of kilometres of lines transported the region's nitrate ore down to the ports to be shipped abroad. Now the nitrate days are over, no national railway lines operate north of Santiago, and what lines are left south of the capital are unable to compete with the speed, prices and punctuality offered by buses.

Accommodation

On the whole, the standard of accommodation in Chile is reasonable, though many visitors feel prices are high for what they get, especially in mid- and top-range hotels. Bottom-end accommodation starts at around CH$8000 (US$16) for a dorm room, CH$20,000–25,000 (US$40-50) for a double. You'll have to pay around CH$35,000–45,000 (US$70-90) for a double or twin with a private bathroom in a decent mid-range hotel, and anything from CH$50,000–70,000 (US$100-140) for a smarter hotel. There's usually a wide choice in the major tourist centres and the cities on the Panamericana, but in more remote areas you'll invariably have to make do with basic *hospedajes* (modest rooms, often in family homes). Most places include a small breakfast in their rates.

ACCOMMODATION ALTERNATIVES

Useful websites that provide alternatives to standard hotel and hostel accommodation:
Airbnb ⓦairbnb.com.
CouchSurfing ⓦcouchsurfing.org.
Crashpadder ⓦcrashpadder.com.
onefinestay ⓦonefinestay.com.
Vacation Rentals by Owner ⓦvrbo.com.

The price of accommodation often increases dramatically in **high season** – January and February – particularly in seaside resorts, where it can be as much as double or even triple. Outside high season it's always worth trying to negotiate a discount. A simple *"¿tiene algo un poco mas económico?"* ("do you have anything a little cheaper?") or *"¿me puede dar un descuento?"* ("could you give me a discount?") will often get you a lower price on the spot. It's rarely necessary to make reservations, unless you've got your heart set on a particular hotel, in which case it can be a good idea to phone a few days in advance – especially at weekends, even more so if it's within striking distance of Santiago.

Room rates are supposed to be quoted inclusive of IVA (a Chilean goods and services tax of 19 percent), but you should always check beforehand (*¿está incluido el iva?*). Many mid- and most upper-range hotels give you the opportunity to pay for your accommodation in US dollars, which exempts you from paying IVA. However, hotels are not always eager to offer this discount – they need to be reminded forcefully. Often, though, if they can't take off IVA, they'll offer you a discount of ten percent if you pay cash.

Hotels

Chilean hotels are given a one- to five-star rating by Sernatur (the national tourist board), but this only reflects facilities and not standards, which vary widely. In practice, then, a three-star hotel could be far more attractive and comfortable than a four-star and even a five-star hotel; the only way to tell is to go and have a look, as even the room rates aren't a reliable indication of quality.

In general, **mid-range hotels** fall into two main categories: large, old houses with spacious, but sometimes tired, rooms; and modern, purpose-built hotels, usually with smaller rooms, no common areas and better facilities. You'll always get a private bathroom with a shower (rarely a bath), hot water and towels, and generally cable TV. As the price creeps up there's usually an improvement in decor and space, and at the upper end you can expect room service, a mini-bar (*frigobar*), a safe, a hotel restaurant, private parking and sometimes a swimming pool. The standards of top end **hotels** can still vary quite dramatically, however – ranging from stylish boutique hotels or charming *haciendas* to grim, impersonal monoliths catering for businessmen.

Motels, incidentally, are usually not economical roadside hotels, but places where couples go to have sex (rooms are generally rented for three-hour periods).

Residenciales

Residenciales are the most widely available, and widely used, accommodation option. As with hotels, standards can vary enormously, but in general they offer simple, modestly furnished rooms, usually off a corridor in the main house, or else in a row arranged around the backyard or patio. They usually contain little more than a bed, a rail for hanging clothes and a bedside table and lamp, though some provide additional furniture, and a few more comforts such as a TV or a thermos for making tea or coffee. Most, but not all, have shared bathrooms.

Where places differ is in the upkeep or "freshness" of the rooms: some are dank and damp, others have good bed linen, walls that are painted every summer, and a clean, swept, feel to them. Some of

the slightly more expensive *residenciales* are very pleasant, particularly the large, nineteenth-century houses. While some *residenciales* cater exclusively to tourists, many, especially in the mining towns of the north, fill mainly with workmen.

Hospedajes and casas de familia

The distinction between a *residencial* and a *hospedaje* or *casa de familia* is often blurred. On the whole, the term **hospedaje** implies something rather modest, along the lines of the cheaper *residenciales*, while a **casa de familia** (or *casa familiar*) offers, as you'd expect, rooms inside a family home. The relationship between the guest and the owner is nevertheless no different from that in a *residencial*. *Casas de familia* don't normally have a sign at the door, and if they do it usually just says "*Alojamiento*" ("lodging"); more commonly, members of the family might go and meet tourists at the bus stations. These places are perfectly safe and you shouldn't worry about checking them out. Sometimes you'll find details of *casas de familia* at tourist offices, as well.

Cabañas

Cabañas are very popular in Chile, and you'll find them in tourist spots up and down the country, particularly by the coast. They are basically holiday chalets geared towards families, and usually come with a kitchen, sitting/dining area, one double bedroom and a second bedroom with bunks. They range from the very rustic to the distinctly grand, complete with daily maid service. Note that the price is often the same for two people as it is for four: i.e. charged by cabin rather than per person. That said, as they're used predominantly by Chileans, their popularity tends to be limited to January and February and sunny weekends, and outside these times demand is so low that you can normally get a very good discount. Many *cabañas* are in superb locations, right by the ocean, and it can be wonderfully relaxing to self-cater for a few days in the off-season.

Refugios

Many of the ranger stations in the national parks have a limited number of bunk beds available for tourists, at a charge of around CH$5000 (US$10) per person. Known as **refugios**, these places are very rustic – often a small, wooden hut – but they usually have toilets, hot running water, clean sheets and woollen blankets. Some of them, such as those at the Salar de Surire and Lago Chungará, are in stunning locations. Most *refugios* are open year-round, but if you're travelling in winter or other extreme weather conditions it's best to check with the regional forestry (Conaf) office in advance. While you're there, you can reserve beds in the *refugio*. This is highly advisable if you're relying solely on the *refugio* for accommodation, but if you're travelling with a tent as a back-up, it's not really necessary to book ahead.

Hostels

Hostels are increasingly banding together to provide a link between Chile´s major cities. What was until recently a score of isolated bargain spots is now starting to resemble a highly developed hostelling operation such as the one, for example, in New Zealand; some are pretty smart, and a few even style themselves as "boutique hostels". In addition to dorms, most also have a selection of private rooms. Hostels also tend to be among the best informal networks for information about local guides and excursions.

Many hostels are affiliated to Hostelling International (Ⓦhihostels.com), and offer discounts for members.

Camping

There are plenty of opportunities for **camping** in Chile, though it's not always the cheapest way to sleep. If you plan to do a lot of camping, equip yourself with the annual Spanish-language camping guide, **Turistel Rutero Camping**, which has maps, prices and information. Even those who don't speak Spanish will find plenty of helpful information, ranging from trail maps to cabins. Official campsites range from plots of land with minimal facilities to swanky grounds with hot showers and private barbecue grills. The latter, often part of holiday complexes in seaside resorts, can be very expensive (around CH$15,000–20,000/US$30–40), and are usually only open between December and March.

It's also possible to camp wild in the countryside, but you'll really need your own transport to do this in remote areas. Most national parks don't allow camping outside designated areas, in order to protect the environment. Instead they tend to have either rustic camping areas administered by Conaf (very common in northern Chile), costing about CH$5000 (US$10) per tent, or else smart, expensive sites run by *concessionaires* (more common in the south) that charge about CH$20,000 (US$40) for two to four people. As for beaches, some turn into informal, spontaneously erected campsites in the summer; on others, camping is strictly forbidden.

If you do end up camping wild on the beach or in the countryside, bury or pack up your excrement, and take all your refuse with you when you leave. Note that butane gas and sometimes Camping Gaz are available in hardware shops in most towns and cities. If your stove takes white gas, you need to buy *bencina blanca*, which you'll find either in hardware stores or, more commonly, in pharmacies.

For details of **camping in Chile's national parks**, see p.43.

Food and drink

Chile boasts a vast range of quality raw produce, but many restaurants lack imagination, offering the same limited menu. That's not to say, however, that you can't eat well in Chile, and the fish and seafood, in particular, are superb. There are also various traditional dishes, often called *comida típica* or *comida criolla*, still served in old-fashioned restaurants known as picadas. Furthermore, most cities have increasing numbers of smarter restaurants.

On the whole, eating out tends to be inexpensive. In local restaurants you can expect to pay around CH$3500–5500 for a main course. If you're aiming to keep costs way down, rather than resort to the innumerable **fast-food outlets**, you could head for the **municipal markets** found in most towns; besides offering an abundance of cheap, fresh produce, they are usually dotted with food stalls. The best trick is to join the Chileans and make lunch your main meal of the day; many restaurants offer a fixed-price *menú del día*, always much better value than the à la carte options.

As for the other meals of the day, **breakfast** at most *residenciales* and hotels is usually a disappointing affair of toasted rolls, jam and tea or coffee, though if your hosts are inclined to pamper you, this will be accompanied by ham, cheese and cake. The great tradition of *onces* – literally "elevenses" but served, like afternoon tea, around 5 o'clock – is a light snack consisting of bread, ham, cheese and biscuits when taken at home, or huge fruit tarts and cakes when out in a *salon de té*. Except during annual holidays or at weekends, relatively few Chileans go out to dinner, which leaves most restaurants very quiet through the week. Note, also, that most places don't open for dinner before 8 or 9pm.

Fish and seafood

Chile's fish and seafood rank among the best in the world. To sample the freshest offerings, head to one of the many *marisquerías* (fish restaurants), particularly those along the coasts of the Litoral Central and the Norte Chico.

A note of caution: you should never collect shellfish from the beach to eat unless you know for sure that the area is free of red tide, an alga that makes shellfish toxic, causing death within a few hours of consumption (see p.00). There is little danger of eating shellfish contaminated by red tide in restaurants.

Meat dishes

Chileans are also tremendous carnivores, with beef featuring prominently on most restaurant menus and family dinner tables. The summertime *asado* (barbecue) is a national institution. Always slow, leisurely affairs, accompanied by lots of Chilean wine, *asados* take place not only in back gardens, but also in specially equipped picnic areas that fill to bursting on summer weekends. In the south, where the weather is less reliable, large covered grills known as *quinchos* provide an alternative venue for grilling; animals such as goats are often sliced in half and cooked in *quinchos* on long skewers, Brazilian-style. The restaurant equivalent of an *asado* is the *parrillada* – a mixture of grilled steaks, chops and sausages, sometimes served on a hot grill by your

---

POTATOES

The **potato**, a staple in the Chilean diet, has long been the subject of numerous traditions and superstitions. Nowhere is this truer than in Chiloé, where potatoes must be sown during a waning moon in August or September, unless large *macho* specimens are required for seeds, in which case they are sown at the full moon. Neighbours help each other in every aspect of cultivation, a communal labouring tradition known as a *minga*. There are three main *mingas*: *quechatún*, the turning of the earth; *siembra de papa*, the planting; and *cosecha* or *sacadura*, the harvest.

Among the mythology and traditional customs associated with the potato are "magic stones" (*piedras cupucas*), which are found on Cerro Chepu, a hill near Ancud in Chiloé. Believed to have been hidden by witches (*brujos*), these porous silicone stones are carefully guarded until the potato plants bloom, and then the flowers are placed on them and burnt as a sacrifice.

Another potato myth holds that a small silver lizard, *el Lluhay*, feeds on potato flowers, and anyone who can catch one is guaranteed good fortune. Still another maintains that a maggot, *la coipone*, which lives in the potato root ball, will prevent babies from crying when placed under their pillows.

MASH IT UP: POPULAR AND TRADITIONAL POTATO DISHES

Chuchoca Mashed potato mixed with flour and pig fat, plastered onto a long, thick wooden pole (*chuchoquero*) and cooked over an open fire.

Colao Small cakes made from potato, wheat, pork fat and crackling, cooked in hot embers.

Mallo de papas Potato stew.

Mayo de papas Peeled, boiled potatoes mashed with onions, chillies, pepper and pig fat.

Mayocan A potato, seaweed and dried-shellfish stew traditionally eaten for breakfast.

Milcao Small cakes of grated and mashed potato that are steamed like dumplings, baked or deep fried.

Pan de papas Baked flat round cakes of mashed potato mixed with flour, eggs and pig fat.

Papas rellenas Sausage-shaped rolls of mashed potato mixed with flour and filled with meat or shellfish.

Pastel de papas A baked dish with alternating layers of mashed potato and meat or shellfish topped with more potato.

table. Following beef in the popularity stakes is **chicken**, which is usually served fried, but can also be enjoyed oven- or spit-roasted. Chilean chickens are nearly all corn-fed and are delicious when well cooked. Succulent, spit-roasted chicken is widely available and inexpensive in Arica, in the far north, owing to the locally based chicken breeding industries. In central Chile, *pollo al coñac* is a popular, and very tasty, chicken casserole, served in large clay pots with brandy and cream. Pork also features on many restaurant menus, but lamb (*cordero*) is hardly ever available, except in the Lake District.

Traditional food

There's a wide range of older, traditional dishes – usually a fusion of indigenous and Hispanic influences – that are still very much a part of Chilean home cooking and can, with a little luck, be found in the small, old-fashioned restaurants that survive in the hidden corners of town or out in the countryside. Though recipes vary from region to region, depending on the local produce available, there are a few core staples, including sweetcorn and potatoes. **Sweetcorn** forms the basis of two of the most traditional Chilean dishes: *humitas* – mashed corn, wrapped in corn husks and steamed – and **pastel de choclo**, a pie made of mince or chicken topped by pureed sweetcorn and sugar and then baked in the oven. The **potato**, meanwhile, is such an important staple in the Chilean diet that it has acquired its own mythology and folklore (see box, p.00).

Another great traditional dish (or snack) is the *empanada*, as symbolic as the national flag, although it was introduced by the Spanish and is popular throughout South America. Baked or fried, large or small, sweet or savoury, *empanadas* (which are not unlike Cornish pasties) can be filled with almost anything, but the most traditional filling is *pino*, a mixture of minced beef, loads of onions, a slice of hard-boiled egg, and an olive, with the pit (beware, as this is a good way to leave a tooth in Chile!).

Also very typical are **soups** and **broths**. There are numerous varieties, of which the most famous, cropping up as a starter on many a set meal, is *cazuela*. Named after large Spanish saucepans, *cazuela* is celebrated as much for its appearance as for its taste, with ingredients carefully chosen and cooked to retain their colour and texture: pale yellow potato, orange pumpkin, split rice, green beans, peas and deep yellow sweetcorn swimming in stock, served in a large soup plate with a piece of meat on the bone, and sprinkled with parsley and coriander. Other favourite one-pot broths include *caldillo*, very similar to *cazuela* but with fish instead of meat, and *escabechado*, a stew made with fish steaks that have been fried then soaked in vinegar. Doubtless because it is so economical, offal enjoys a long (though waning) history in Chilean cookery.

Fast food

All of Chile's towns are well endowed with greasy-spoon cafés and snack bars – usually known as *fuentes de soda* or *schoperías* – serving draught beer and cheap fast food. This usually consists of **sandwiches**, which are consumed voraciously by Chileans – indeed, one variety, the **Barros Luco** (beef and melted cheese), is named after a former president who is said to have devised the combination. **Barros Jarpa** (ham and cheese), is another dietary staple. The choice of fillings is firmly meat-based, with most options revolving around **churrasco** – a thin cut of griddle-fried beef, rather like a minute steak.

Chile is also the unlikely home of a variety of **hot dogs**. Sitting all by itself in a bun, the hot dog is simply called a *vienesa*, but it's called an *especial* when mayonnaise is squeezed along the top, and the addition of tomato, sauerkraut and avocado makes it a *dinámico*. The most popular version is the *italiano* – tomato, mayonnaise and avocado, which together resemble the colours of the Italian flag. It is not until the sausage is buried under extra sauerkraut and chopped tomato that it becomes completely *completo*.

Drinking

Soft **fizzy drinks** can be found everywhere in Chile. Bottled **mineral water**, too, is widely available, both sparkling (*con gas*) and still (*sin gas*). **Coffee**, in Chile, is usually instant Nescafé, although it's getting easier to find good, real coffee (ask for *café de grano*). **Herbal teas** are widely available and come in countless flavours. The most popular varieties are *manzanilla* (camomile), *menta* (mint) and *boldo* (a fragrant native plant). Where Chile really comes into its own, though, is with the delicious, freshly squeezed **fruit juices** (*jugos naturales*) available in many bars, restaurants and roadside stalls, especially in the Central Valley, and a few northern oases like Pica. Another home-grown drink is *mote con huesillo*, sold at numerous roadsides throughout the Central Valley and Lake District in summer. *Mote* is boiled or soaked barley grain, and *huesillos* are sun-dried peaches, though this sweet, gooey drink can be made with any fresh soft fruit.

Chilean **beer** doesn't come in many varieties, with Cristal and Escudo dominating the choice of bottled lagers, and Kunstman the only speciality brand to make a national mark.

There's always a good selection of **wine**, on the other hand, though the choice on restaurant lists rarely reflects the vast range of wines produced for export. Regarded as the Chilean national drink, **pisco sour** is a tangy, refreshing aperitif made from pisco (a white brandy created from distilled Moscatel grapes, freshly squeezed lemon juice and sugar). You may also come across a number of **regional specialities**, including *chicha de manzana* (apple cider), made at home by every *huaso* in the Central Valley. Further south, in the Lake District, a traditional element of many drinks is *harina tostada* (toasted maize flour), used by the Mapuche since pre-Spanish days. Today it's still common to see Mapuche sitting around a table with a large jug of frothy coffee-coloured liquid, which is dark beer mixed with *harina tostada*. The flour is also mixed with cheap wine, among other drinks, and is usually stocked by the sackful at local Lake District bars.

The media

Media output in Chile is nothing to get excited about. If you know where to look, journalistic standards can be high but you might find yourself turning to foreign TV channels or papers if you want an international view on events.

Newspapers and magazines

The Chilean **press** has managed to uphold a strong tradition of editorial freedom ever since the country's first newspaper, *La Aurora*, was published by an anti-royalist friar in 1812, during the early days of the independence movement. One year before *La Aurora* folded in 1827, a new newspaper, *El Mercurio*, went to press in Valparaíso, and is now the longest-running newspaper in the Spanish-speaking world. Emphatically conservative, and owned by the powerful Edwards family, *El Mercurio* is considered the most serious of Chile's dailies, but still has a minimal international coverage. The other major daily is *La Tercera*, which tends to be more sensationalistic. The liberal-leaning *La Nación* is the official newspaper of the state. The online English-language *Santiago Times* (W santiagotimes.cl) is a good read, though you'll need to subscribe to get full access.

Chile also produces a plethora of racy **tabloids** as well as ¡Hola!-style clones. For a more edifying read, try the selection of *Private Eye*-style satirical papers, such as *The Clinic* and the weekly magazine *Siete más 7*.

In Santiago you can usually track down a selection of foreign papers, though elsewhere you'll generally have to rely on online editions.

Television and radio

Cable TV is widespread, offering innumerable domestic and international channels. CNN is always on offer, and BBC World is widely available. Of the five terrestrial channels, top choice is Channel 7, the state-owned Televisión Nacional, which makes the best programmes in Chile. Generally, however, soap operas, game shows and, of course, football, predominate.

Voice of America (W voa.gov) and Radio Canada (W rcinet.ca) can both be accessed but unfortunately the BBC no longer broadcasts its World Service in Chile.

Festivals

Most of Chile's festivals are held to mark religious occasions, or to honour saints or the Virgin Mary. What's fascinating about them is the strong influence of pre-Spanish, pre-Christian rites, particularly in the Aymara communities of the far north and the Mapuche of the south. Added to this is the influence of colourful folk traditions rooted in the Spanish expeditions of exploration and conquest, colonization and evangelism, slavery and revolution.

In the *altiplano* of the **far north**, Aymara herdsmen celebrate Catholic holy days and the feasts of ancient cults along with ritual dancing and the offering of sacrificial llamas.

In **central Chile**, you'll witness the influence of colonial traditions. In the days of the conquest, an important ingredient of any fiesta was the verbal sparring between itinerant bards called *payadores*, who would compose and then try to resolve each other's impromptu rhyming riddles. The custom is kept alive at many fiestas in the Central Valley, where young poets spontaneously improvise *lolismos* and *locuciones*, forms of jocular verse that are quite unintelligible to an outsider. These rural fiestas always culminate in an energetic display of *cueca* dancing, washed down with plenty of wine and *chicha* – reminiscent of the entertainment organized by indulgent hacienda-owners for their peons.

In the **south**, the solemn Mapuche festivals are closely linked to mythology, magic and faith healing, agricultural rituals, and supplications to gods and spirits. Group dances (*purrún*) are performed with gentle movements; participants either move round in a circle or advance and retreat in lines. Most ceremonies are accompanied by mounted horn players whose four-metre-long bamboo instruments, *trutrucas*, require enormous lung power to produce a note. Other types of traditional wind instruments include a small pipe (*lolkiñ*), flute (*pinkulwe*), cow's horn (*kullkull*) and whistle (*pifilka*). Of all Mapuche musical instruments, the most important is the sacred drum (*kultrún*), which is only used by faith healers (*machis*).

For more on *altiplano* fiestas and ceremonies, see p.000.

A FESTIVAL CALENDAR

January 20 San Sebastián. Spaniards brought the first wooden image of San Sebastián to Chile in the seventeenth century. After a Mapuche raid on Chillán, the image was buried in a nearby field, and no one was able to raise it. The saint's feast day has become an important Mapuche festival, especially in Lonquimay, where it's celebrated with horse racing, feasting and drinking.

February 1–3 La Candelaria. Celebrated throughout Chile since 1780, when a group of miners and muleteers discovered a stone image of the Virgin and Child while sheltering from an inexplicable thunderstorm in the Atacama. Typical festivities include religious processions and traditional dances.

End of February Festival Internacional de la Canción. This glitzy and wildly popular five-day festival is held in Viña del Mar's open-air amphitheatre, featuring performers from all over Latin America and broadcast to most Spanish-speaking countries.

Easter Semana Santa (Holy Week). Among the nationwide Easter celebrations, look out for Santiago's solemn procession of penitents dressed in black habits, carrying crosses through the streets, and La Ligua's parade of mounted *huasos* followed by a giant penguin.

First Sunday after Easter Fiesta del Cuasimodo. In many parts of central Chile, *huasos* parade through the streets on their horses, often accompanied by a priest sitting on a float covered in white lilies.

May 3 Santa Cruz de Mayo. Throughout the *altiplano*, villages celebrate the cult of the Holy Cross, inspired in the seventeenth century by the Spaniards' obsession with crosses, which they carried everywhere, erected on hillsides and even carved in the air with their fingers. The festivities have strong pre-Christian elements, often including the sacrifice of a llama.

May 13 Procesión del Cristo de Mayo. A huge parade through the streets of Santiago bearing the *Cristo de Mayo* – a sixteenth-century carving of Christ whose crown of thorns slipped to its neck during an earthquake, and which is said to have shed tears of blood when attempts were made to put the crown back in place.

June 13 Noche de San Juan Bautista. An important feast night,

celebrated by families up and down the country with a giant stew, known as the *Estofado de San Juan*. In Chiloé, an integral part of the feast are roasted potato balls called *tropones*, which burn the fingers and make people "dance the *tropón*" as they jig up and down, juggling them from hand to hand.

June 29 Fiesta de San Pedro. Along the length of Chile's coast, fishermen decorate their boats and take the image of their patron saint out to sea – often at night with candles and flares burning – to pray for good weather and large catches.

July 12–18 Virgen de la Tirana. The largest religious festival in Chile, held in La Tirana in the Far North, and attended by over 80,000 pilgrims and hundreds of costumed dancers (see p.196).

July 16 Virgen del Carmen. Military parades throughout Chile honour the patron saint of the armed forces; the largest are in Maipú, on the southern outskirts of Santiago, where San Martín and Bernardo O'Higgins defeated Spanish Royalists in 1818.

August 21–31 Jesús Nazareno de Caguach. Thousands of Chilotes flock to the archipelago's tiny island of Caguach to worship at a two-metre-high figure of Christ, donated by the Jesuits in the eighteenth century.

September 18 Fiestas Patrias. Chile's Independence Day is celebrated throughout the country with street parties, music and dancing.

First Sunday of October Virgen de las Peñas. Each year, numerous dance groups and more than 10,000 pilgrims from Chile, Peru, Bolivia and Argentina make their way along a tortuous cliff path to visit a rock carving of the Virgin in the Azapa valley, near Arica. There are many smaller festivals in other parts of Chile, too.

November 1 Todos los Santos (All Saints' Day). Traditionally, this is the day when Chileans tend their family graves. In the north, where Aymara customs have become entwined with Christian ones, crosses are often removed from graves and left on the former bed of the deceased overnight. Candles are kept burning in the room, and a feast is served for family members, past and present.

November 2 Día de los Muertos (All Souls' Day). A second vigil to the dead is held in cemeteries, with offerings of food and wine sprinkled on the graves. In some far north villages, there's a tradition of reading a liturgy, always in Latin.

December 8 La Purísima. Celebrated in many parts of Chile, the festival of the Immaculate Conception is at its liveliest in San Pedro de Atacama, where it's accompanied by traditional Aymara music and dancing.

December 23–27 Fiesta Grande de la Virgen de Andacollo. More than 100,000 pilgrims from all over the north come to Andacollo, in Norte Chico, to worship its Virgin and watch the famous masked dancers (see p.132).

Spectator sports

The Chileans are not a particularly exuberant people, but passions are roused by several national enthusiasms – chiefly football and rodeo, which at their best are performed with electrifying skill and theatricality.

Football

El **fútbol** reigns supreme as Chile's favourite sport. Introduced by British immigrants in the early 1800s, football in Chile can trace its history back to the playing fields of the Mackay School, one of the first English schools in Valparaíso, and its heritage is reflected in the names of the first clubs: Santiago Wanderers, Everton, Badminton, Morning Star and Green Cross.

Everton and Wanderers are still going strong, but the sport is now dominated by the Santiago teams of Colo Colo, Universidad Católica and Universidad de Chile. Matches featuring any of these teams are guaranteed a good turn-out and a great atmosphere. There's rarely any trouble, with whole families coming along to enjoy the fun. If you can't make it to a match, you'll still see plenty of football on the huge TVs that dominate most cafés and bars, including European games shown on cable channels (you may notice, too, that widespread exposure to English football has led many young Chileans to refer to an Englishman as a *húligan* rather than a gringo).*

Football hardly has a season in Chile. In addition to the league games played between March and December, there are numerous other competitions of which the Copa de Libertadores is the most important. So you'll generally be able to catch the action whatever time of year you visit.

Horse racing

There are two very different types of horse racing in Chile: conventional track racing, known as *hípica*, and the much rougher and wilder *carreras a la chilena*. Hípica is a sport for rich Santiaguinos, who don their tweeds and posh frocks to go and watch it at the capital's Club Hípico and Hipódromo Chile, which have races throughout the year. The most important of these are the St Leger at the Hipódromo Chile on December 14, and the Ensayo at the Club Hípico on the first Sunday in November.

Carreras a la chilena are held anywhere in the country where two horses can be found to race against each other. Apart from the organized events that take place at village fiestas, these races are normally a result of one *huaso* betting another that his horse is faster. Held in any suitable field, well away from the prying eyes of the *carabineros*, the two-horse race can attract large crowds (who bet heavily on the outcome).

Rodeo

Rodeos evolved from the early colonial days when the cattle on the large estancias had to be rounded up and branded or slaughtered by *huasos* (see p.37). The feats of horsemanship required to do so soon took on a competitive element, which eventually

---

THE CHILEAN HUASO

"Of the many cowboys of the Americas, none remains as shrouded in mystery and contradiction as Chile's *huaso*," says Richard Slatta in *Cowboys of the Americas*. Certainly the *huaso* holds a special place in Chile's perception of its national identity. But the definition of the *huaso* is somewhat confused and subject to differing interpretations. The one you're most likely to come across is that of the "gentleman rider", the middle-class horseman who, while not a part of the landed elite, is a good few social rungs up from the landless labourer. This is the *huaso* you'll see in *cueca* performances (see p.38) and at rodeos.

These gentlemen riders are part of a romanticized image of the Chilean countryside and a far cry from the much larger and perhaps more authentic group who carried out the real horse-work on the land. More akin to the Argentine gaucho and the Mexican *vaquero*, this other type of *huaso* was a landless, badly paid and poorly dressed ranch-hand who worked on the large haciendas during the cattle round-up season. Despite the harsh reality of his lifestyle, the lower-class *huaso* is also the victim of myth-making, frequently depicted as a paragon of virtue and happiness.

All types of *huasos*, whatever their social status, were renowned for outstanding **horsemanship**, marvelled at for their practice of training their horses to stop dead in their tracks at a single command (*la sentada*). A skill mastered in the southern Central Valley was that of the *bolas* – three stones or metal balls attached to long leather straps, which were hurled at animals and wrapped around their legs, bringing them to the ground. Huasos also developed a host of equestrian contests including the *juego de cañas* (jousting with canes), the *tiro al gallo* (a mounted tug-of-war) and *topeadura* (a side-by-side pushing contest). Today these displays have a formal outlet in the regular **rodeos** (see p.223) in the Central Valley. As for the working *huaso*, you'll still come across him in the back roads of rural central Chile.

THE CUECA

Huasos are the chief performers of *cueca*, Chile's national dance – a curious cross between English morris dancing and smouldering Sevillanas. Its history can, in fact, be traced to the African slave dances, which were also the basis of the Brazilian samba and Peruvian *zamacueca*, and were introduced to Chile by a battalion of black soldiers in 1824. During the War of Independence, Chileans adopted their own forms of these dances known as la Chilena, la Marinera and el Minero, which eventually became a national victory dance known simply as the *cueca*. Although there are regional variations, the basic elements remain unchanged, consisting of couples strutting around each other in a courtship ritual, spurs jingling and handkerchiefs waving over their heads. The men are decked out in their finest *huaso* gear, while the women wear wide skirts and shawls. In the background, guitar-strumming musicians sing romantic ballads full of patriotic sentiments. If you are going to a fiesta and want to take part in a *cueca*, remember to take along a clean white handkerchief.

found an expression in the form of rodeos. Even though ranching has long declined in Chile, organized rodeos remain wildly popular, with many free competitions taking place in local stadiums (known as *medialunas*) throughout the season, which runs from September to April. Taking in a rodeo not only allows you to watch the most dazzling equestrian skills inside the arena, but also to see the *huasos* decked out in all their traditional gear: ponchos, silver spurs and all. Added to this, the atmosphere is invariably loads of fun, with lots of whooping families and excited kids, and plenty of food and drink afterwards.

Outdoor activities

Chile offers an enormous range of outdoor activities, including volcano-climbing, skiing, surfing, white-water rafting, fly-fishing and horseriding. An increasing number of operators and outfitters have wised-up to the potential of organized adventure tourism, offering one- or multi-day guided excursions.

Many of these companies are based in Pucón, in the Lake District, with a good sprinkling of other outfitters spread throughout the south. There are fewer opportunities for outdoor activities in the harsh deserts of the north, where *altiplano* jeep trips and mountain biking are the main options. If you plan to do take part in adventurous activities, be sure to check that you're covered by your travel insurance, or take out specialist insurance where necessary.

Rafting and kayaking

Chile's many frothy rivers and streams afford incomparable rafting opportunities. Indeed, the country's top destinations, the mighty **Río Bío Bío** and the **Río Futaleufú**, entice visitors from around the globe. Rafting trips generally range in length from one to eight days and, in the case of the Bío Bío, sometimes include the option of climbing 3160m Volcán Callaquén. In addition to these challenging rivers, gentler alternatives exist on the **Río Maipo** close to Santiago, the **Río Trancura** near Pucón, and the **Río Petrohue** near Puerto Varas. The Maipo makes a good day-trip from Santiago, while excursions on the latter two are just half-day affairs and can usually be arranged on the spot, without advance reservations. In general, all rafting trips are extremely well organized, but you should always take great care in choosing your outfitter – this activity can be very dangerous in the hands of an inexperienced guide.

Chile's white-water rapids also offer excellent **kayaking**, though this is less developed as an organized activity – your best bet is probably to contact one of the US-based outfitters that have camps on the Bío Bío and Futaleufú (see p.247, 357). **Sea kayaking** is becoming increasingly popular, generally in the calm, flat waters of Chile's southern fjords, though people have been known to kayak around Cape Horn. Note that the Chilean navy is very sensitive about any foreign vessels (even kayaks) cruising in their waters, and if you're planning a trip through military waters, you'd be

FIVE GREAT OUTDOOR ACTIVITIES
Dog sledding near Villarica. See p.273.
Hiking in Torres del Paine. See p.400.
Paragliding over Iquique. See p.190.
Skiing at Portillo. See p.90.
White-water rafting on the Río Futaleufú. See p.357.

wise to inform the Chilean consulate or embassy in your country beforehand.

Hiking

For the most part, Chile is a very empty country with vast tracts of wilderness offering potential for fantastic hiking. Chileans, moreover, are often reluctant to stray far from their parked cars when they visit the countryside, so you'll find that most trails without vehicle access are blissfully quiet. However, the absence of a national enthusiasm for hiking also means that, compared with places of similar scenic beauty like California, British Columbia and New Zealand, Chile isn't particularly geared up to the hiking scene, with relatively few long-distance trails (given the total area) and a shortage of decent trekking maps. That said, what is on offer is superb, and ranks among the country's most rewarding attractions.

The **north** of Chile, with its harsh climate and landscape, isn't really suitable for hiking, and most walkers head for the lush native forests of Chile's **south**, peppered with waterfalls, lakes, hot springs and volcanoes. The best trails are nearly always inside **national parks** or reserves, where the *guardaparques* (rangers) are a good source of advice on finding and following the paths. They should always be informed if you plan to do an overnight hike (so that if you don't come back, they'll know where to search for you). The majority of trails are for half-day or day hikes, though some parks offer a few long-distance hikes, sometimes linking up with trails in adjoining parks. The level of path maintenance and signing varies greatly from one park to another, and many of the more remote trails are indistinct and difficult to follow.

Hardly any parks allow wild **camping**, while the few others that now allow it have a series of rustic camping areas that you're required to stick to – check with the *guardaparque*. If you do camp (the best way to experience the Chilean wilderness) note that **forest and bush fires** are a very real hazard. Take great care when making a campfire (having checked beforehand that they're allowed). Also, never chop or break down vegetation for fuel, as most of Chile's native flora is endangered.

By far the most popular destination for hiking is **Torres del Paine** in the far south, which offers magnificent scenery but fairly crowded trails, especially in January and February. Many quieter, less well-known alternatives are scattered between Santiago and Tierra del Fuego, ranging from narrow paths in the towering, snow-streaked central Andes to hikes up to glaciers off the Carretera Austral.

If you go hiking, it's essential to be well prepared – always carry plenty of water, wear a hat and sun block for protection against the sun and carry extra layers of warm clothing to guard against the sharp drop in temperature after sundown. Even on day hikes, take enough supplies to provide for the eventuality of getting lost, and always carry a map and **compass** (*brújula*), preferably one bought in the southern hemisphere or adjusted for southern latitudes. Also, make a conscious effort to help preserve Chile's environment – where there's no toilet, bury human waste at least 20cm under the ground and 30m from the nearest river or lake; take away or burn all your **rubbish**; and use specially designed **eco-friendly detergents** for use in lakes and streams.

Climbing

The massive Andean cordillera offers a wide range of climbing possibilities. In the far north of Chile, you can trek up several volcanoes over 6000m, including Volcán Parinacota (6330m), Volcán Llullaillaco (6739m) and Volcán Ojos del Salado (6950m). Although ropes and crampons aren't always needed, these ascents are suitable only for experienced climbers, and need a fair amount of independent planning, with only a few companies offering guided excursions.

In the central Andes, exciting climbs include Volcán Marmolejo (6100m) and Volcán Tupungato (6750m), while in the south, climbers head for Volcán Villarrica (2840m) and Volcán Osorno (2652m), both of which you can tackle even with little mountaineering experience.

Throughout Chile there's a lot of tedious bureaucracy to get through before you can climb. To go up any mountain straddling an international border (which means most of the high Andean peaks), you need advance **permission** from the **Dirección de Fronteras y Límites** (DIFROL), Fourth Floor, Bandera 52, Santiago (❶2 671 4110, ⓦdifrol.cl). To get this, write to, fax or email DIFROL with the planned dates and itinerary of the climb, listing full details (name, nationality, date of birth, occupation, passport number, address) of each member of the climbing team, and your dates of entry and exit from Chile. Authorization will then be sent to you on a piece of paper that you must present to Conaf before ascending (if the peak is not within a national park, you must take the authorization to the nearest *carabineros* station). If your plans change while you're in Chile, you can usually amend the authorization or get a new one at the *Gobernación* of each provincial capital. You can also apply through a Chilean embassy in advance of your departure, or print and send a form from their website. There's further information on climbing in Chile online at ⓦescalando.cl or ⓦtrekkingchile.com.

Fly-fishing

Chile has an international, and well-deserved, reputation as one of the finest fly-fishing destinations in the world. Its pristine waters teem with rainbow, brown and brook trout, and silver and Atlantic salmon. These fish are not native, but were introduced for sport in the late nineteenth century; since then, the wild population has flourished and multiplied, and is also supplemented by generous numbers of escapees from local fish farms. The fishing season varies slightly from region to region, but in general runs from November to May.

Traditionally, the best sport-fishing was considered to be in the Lake District, but while this region still offers great possibilities, attention has shifted to the more remote, pristine waters of Aisén, where a number of classy fishing lodges have sprung up, catering mainly to wealthy North American clients. Fishing in the Lake District is frequently done from riverboats, while a typical day's fishing in Aisén begins with a ride in a motor dinghy through fjords, channels and islets towards an isolated river. You'll then wade upstream to shallower waters, usually equipped with a light six or seven weight rod, dry flies and brightly coloured streamers. Catches weigh in between 1kg and 3kg – but note that many outfitters operate only on a catch and release basis.

Skiing

Chile offers the finest and most challenging **skiing** in South America. Many of the country's top slopes and resorts lie within very easy reach of Santiago, including **El Colorado**, **La Parva**, **Valle Nevado** and world-renowned **Portillo**. A bit further south, but no less impressive, stands the popular **Termas de Chillán**.

Horse-trekking

Exploring Chile's dramatic landscapes on horseback is a memorable experience. The best possibilities are **around Santiago**, and in the **Central Valley**, where riding has been a way of life for centuries. In addition to the spectacular scenery, you can also expect to see condors and other birds of prey. Trips are usually guided by local *arrieros*, who herd cattle up to high pastures in springtime and know the mountain paths intimately. You normally spend about five or six hours in the saddle each day; a lingering *asado* (barbecue), cooked over an open fire and accompanied by plenty of Chilean wine, will be part of the pleasure. At night, you sleep in tents transported by mules, and you'll be treated to the most breathtaking display of stars.

The only disadvantage of riding treks in the central Andes is that, due to the terrain, you're unlikely to get beyond a walk, and cantering is usually out of the question. If you want a faster pace, opt for the treks offered by some companies in Patagonia, where rolling grasslands provide plenty of opportunity for gallops – though the weather can often put a dampener on your trip.

Mountain biking

For most of Chile's length, there are extremely good and little-used dirt roads perfect for **cycling** – although the numerous potholes mean it's only worth attempting them on a **mountain bike**. For a serious trip, you should bring your own bike or buy one in Santiago – **renting** a bike of the quality required can be difficult to arrange. An alternative is to go on an organized biking excursion, where all equipment, including tents, will be provided. Note that during the summer, cycling in Patagonia and Tierra del Fuego is made almost impossible by incessant and ferociously strong winds.

Surfing

Chile's beaches are pulling in an increasing number of surfers, who come to ride the year-round breaks that pound the Pacific shore. By unanimous consent, the **best breaks** – mainly long left-handers – are concentrated around Pichilemu, near Rancagua, which is the site of the annual National Surfing Championships. Further north, the warmer seas around Iquique and Arica are also increasingly popular.

Adventure tourism operators and outfitters

Below is a selection of operators and outfitters for various outdoor activities. The list is by no means comprehensive, and new companies are constantly springing up to add to it – you can get more details from the relevant regional Sernatur office.

ALL-ROUNDERS

Altue Active Travel General Salvo 159, Providencia, Santiago ☎ 2 235 1519, Ⓦ altue.com. Reliable, slick operation whose options include rafting the Río Maipo, Aconcagua and Ojos del Salado expeditions, and horse treks.

Azimut 360 General Salvo 159, Providencia, Santiago ☎ 2 235 1519, Ⓦ azimut360.com. Franco–Chilean outfit with a dynamic team of guides and a wide range of programmes, including mountain biking, Aconcagua expeditions and climbs up Chile's highest volcanoes.

Cascada Expediciones Don Carlos 3219, Las Condes, Santiago ☎ 2 232 9878, Ⓦ cascada.travel. One of the pioneers of adventure tourism in Chile, with a particular emphasis on activities in the Andes close to Santiago, where it has a permanent base in the Cajón del Maipo. Programmes include rafting and kayaking the Río Maipo, horse treks in the high cordillera and hiking and mountain biking.

Sportstour Av El Bosque Norte 500, 15th Floor, Santiago ☎ 2 549 5260, Ⓦ sportstour.cl. This well-run operation offers balloon rides and flights, among other tours.

CLIMBING

See also Azimut 360 and Altue Active Travel in "All-rounders" above for details of tours up Volcán Osorno and Volcán Villarrica.

Mountain Service Paseo Las Palmas 2209, Providencia, Santiago ☎ 2 234 3439. An experienced, specialist company, dedicated to climbing Aconcagua, the major volcanoes and Torres del Paine.

FLY-FISHING

For a list of guides and lodges on and around the Carretera Austral, see p.362.

Bahía Escocia Fly Fishing Lago Rupanco ☎ 64 197 4731, ⓔ lodgepuntiagudo@gm,ail.cl. Small, beautifully located lodge with fly-fishing excursions run by a US–Chilean couple.

Cumilahue Lodge PO Box 2, Llifen ☎ 2 196 1601, Ⓦ anglingtours.com. Very expensive packages at a luxury Lake District lodge run by Adrian Dufflocq, something of a legend on the Chilean fly-fishing scene.

Off Limits Adventures Av Bernado O'Higgins 560, Pucón ☎ 45 442681, Ⓦ offlimits.cl. Half-day and full-day excursions, plus fly-fishing lessons. One of the more affordable options.

HORSE-TREKKING

See also Altue Active Travel and Cascada Expediciones in "All-rounders".

Chile Nativo Casilla 42, Puerto Natales ☎ 2 717 5961, Ⓦ chilenativo.com. Dynamic young outfit specializing in five- to twelve-day horse-trekking tours of the region, visiting out-of-the-way locations in addition to the Parque Nacional Torres del Paine.

Hacienda de los Andes Río Hurtado, near Ovalle ☎ 53 691822, Ⓦ haciendalosandes.com. Beautiful ranch in a fantastic location in the Hurtado valley, between La Serena and Ovalle, offering exciting mountain treks on some of the finest mounts in the country.

Pared Sur Juan Esteban Montero 5497, Las Condes, Santiago ☎ 2 207 3525, Ⓦ paredsur.cl. In addition to its extensive mountain-biking programme, Pared Sur offers a one-week horse trek through the virgin landscape of Aisén, off the Carretera Austral.

Rancho de Caballos Casilla 142, Pucón ☎ 09 8346 1764, Ⓦ rancho-de-caballos.com. Ranch offering a range of treks from three to nine days.

Ride World Wide Staddon Farm, North Tawton, Devon, UK ☎ 01837 82544, Ⓦ rideworldwide.com. UK-based company that hooks up with local riding outfitters around the world. In Chile, it offers a range of horseback treks in the central cordillera, the Lake District and Patagonia.

KAYAKING

Al Sur Expediciones Aconcagua corner of Imperial, Puerto Varas ☎ 65 232300, Ⓦ alsurexpeditions.com. One of the foremost adventure tour companies in the Lake District, and the first one to introduce sea kayaking in the fjords south of Puerto Montt.

Bío Bío Expeditions PO Box 2028, Truckee, CA 96160, US ☎ 562 196 4258, Ⓦ bbxrafting.com. This rafting outfitter also rents out kayaks to experienced kayakers, who accompany the rafting party down the Bío Bío or Futaleufú.

¡ecole! Urrutia 592, Pucón ☎ 45 441675, Ⓦ ecole.cl. Ecologically focused tour company offering, among other activities, sea kayaking classes and day outings in the fjords south of Puerto Montt, and around Parque Pumalín, from its Puerto Montt branch.

Expediciones Chile Gabriela Mistral 296, Futaleufú ☎ 65 721386, Ⓦ exchile.com. River kayaking outfitter catering to all levels of experience, especially seasoned paddlers. Operated by former Olympic kayaker Chris Spelius.

Onas Patagonia Blanco Encalada 211, Puerto Natales ☎ 61 614300, Ⓦ onaspatagonia.com. Sea kayaking excursions in the bleak, remote waters of Patagonia.

MOUNTAIN BIKING

See also Azimut 360 and Cascada Expediciones in "All-rounders".

Pared Sur Juan Esteban Montero 5497, Las Condes, Santiago ☎ 2 207 3525, Ⓦ paredsur.cl. Pared Sur has been running mountain bike trips in Chile for longer than anyone else. It offers a wide range of programmes throughout the whole country.

SKIING

Full details of the resorts near Santiago are given in Chapter 1.

Sportstour Av El Bosque Norte 500, 15th Floor, Santiago ☎ 2 549 5260, Ⓦ sportstour.cl. Among a wide-ranging national programme, including hot-air balloon rides and flights on cockpit biplanes and gliders, this travel agent offers fully-inclusive ski packages at the resorts near Santiago, and the Termas de Chillán ski centre.

WHITE-WATER RAFTING

See also Cascada Expediciones.

Bío Bío Expeditions PO Box 2028, Truckee, CA 96160, US ☎ 562 196 4258, Ⓦ bbxrafting.com. Headed by Laurence Alvarez, the captain of the US World Championships rafting team, this experienced and friendly outfit offers ten-day packages on the Bío Bío and Futaleufú, plus one- to three-day excursions down the latter.

Trancura O'Higgins 211-C, Pucón ☎ 45 401189, ⓦ trancura.com. Major southern operator with high standards and friendly guides, offering rafting excursions down the Río Trancura and the Bío Bío.

National parks and reserves

Some eighteen percent of Chile's mainland territory is protected by the state under the extensive Sistema Nacional de Areas Silvestres Protegidas (National Protected Wildlife Areas System), which is made up of thirty national parks, thirty-eight national reserves and eleven natural monuments. These inevitably include the country's most outstanding scenic attractions, but while there are provisions for tourism, the main aim is always to protect and manage native fauna and flora. Given Chile's great biodiversity, these vary tremendously, and park objectives are as varied as protecting flamingo populations and monitoring glaciers. All protected areas are managed by the Corporación Nacional Forestal, better known as Conaf.

Definitions and terms

National parks (*parques nacionales*) are generally large areas of unspoilt wilderness, usually featuring fragile endemic ecosystems. They include the most touristy and beautiful of the protected areas, and often offer walking trails and sometimes camping areas too. **National reserves** (*reservas nacionales*) are areas of ecological importance that have suffered some degree of natural degradation; there are fewer regulations to protect these areas, and "sustainable" commercial exploitation (such as mineral extraction) is allowed to take place. **Natural monuments** (*monumentos naturales*) tend to be important or endangered geological formations, or small areas of biological, anthropological or archeological significance.

In addition to these three main categories, there are a few **nature sanctuaries** (*sanctuarios de la naturaleza*) and **protected areas** (*areas de protección*), usually earmarked for their scientific or scenic interest. It is not difficult for the government to

change the status of these areas, and it has been known for national parks to be downgraded so that their resources could be commercially exploited. In addition to these state-owned parks, there are several important private initiatives, including **Parque Pumalín** (see p.352–354).

Park administration

The administration of Chile's protected areas is highly centralized with all important decisions coming from **Conaf's head office** in Santiago (see p.78). This is a good place to visit before heading out of the capital, as you can pick up brochures, books and basic maps. In addition, each regional capital has a Conaf headquarters, which is useful for more practical pre-visit information. The parks and reserves are staffed by **guardaparques** (park wardens), who live in ranger stations (called *guárderías*). Most parks are divided into several areas, known as "sectors" (*sectores*), and the larger ones have a small *guardería* in each sector.

Visiting the parks

No permit is needed to visit any of Chile's national parks; you simply turn up and pay your **entrance fee** (usually CH$1000–4000), though some parks are free. Alternatively, Conaf's Annual Pass (CH$10,000) allows unlimited access to all of Chile's national parks and reserves – except Torres del

> ### HIKING IN CHILE'S PARKS AND RESERVES
>
> Chile boasts some outstanding hiking trails, with plenty of options for both novice and experienced hikers. Most are found in the following national parks and reserves:
> **Monumento Nacional El Morado** (p.89)
> **Parque Nacional Chiloé** (p.334–337)
> **Parque Nacional Huerquehue** (p.278)
> **Parque Nacional La Campana** (p.94)
> **Parque Nacional Queulat** (p.359)
> **Parque Nacional Tolhuaca** (p.258)
> **Parque Nacional Torres del Paine** (pp.400–407)
> **Parque Nacional Vicente Pérez Rosales** (pp.305–309)
> **Parque Pumalín** (pp.352–354)
> **Reserva Nacional Radal Siete Tazas** (p.234)
> **Reserva Nacional Río de los Cipreses** (p.224)

Paine and Easter Island – for a year; it can be purchased from Conaf offices.

Ease of **access** differs wildly from one park to the next – a few have paved highways running through them, while others are served by dirt tracks that are only passable for a few months of the year. Getting to them often involves renting a vehicle or going on an organized trip, as around two-thirds of Chile's national parks can't be reached by public transport.

Arriving at the park boundary, you'll normally pass a small hut (called the Conaf control) where you pay your entrance fee and pick up a basic map. Some of the larger parks have more than one entrance point. The main ranger station is always separate from the hut; it contains the rangers' living quarters and administrative office, and often a large map or scale model of the park. The more popular parks also have a **Centro de Información Ambiental** attached to the station, with displays on the park's flora and fauna. A few parks now have **camping** areas. These are often rustic sites with basic facilities, run by Conaf, which charge around CH$5000–10,000 per tent. In other parks, particularly in the south, Conaf gives licences to concessionaires, who operate campsites and *cabañas*, which tend to be very expensive. Some of the more remote national parks, especially in the north, have small **refugios** attached to the ranger stations – these are usually rustic, stone-built huts (from CH$5000 per person) containing around eight to ten bunk beds, hot showers and gas stoves. Some of them are in stunning locations, overlooking the Salar de Surire, for example, or with views across Lago Chungará to Volcán Parinacota. Sadly, however, they are increasingly unreliable.

Health

Chile is a fairly risk-free country to travel in as far as health problems are concerned. No inoculations are required, though you might want to consider a hepatitis A jab, as a precaution. Check, too, that your tetanus boosters are up to date. Many travellers experience the occasional stomach upset, and sunstroke is also quite common, especially at high altitudes.

Chile is well endowed with **pharmacies** (*farmacias*) – even smaller towns usually have at least a handful. If you need to see a **doctor**, make an appointment at the outpatient department of the nearest hospital, usually known as a *clínica*. The majority of *clínicas* are private, and expensive, so make sure your **travel insurance** provides good medical cover.

Rabies

Rabies, though only a remote risk, does exist in Chile. If you get bitten or scratched by a dog, you should seek medical attention *immediately*. The disease can be cured, but only through a series of stomach injections administered before the onset of symptoms, which can appear within 24 hours or lie dormant for months, and include irrational behaviour, fear of water and foaming at the mouth. There is a vaccine, but it's expensive and doesn't prevent you from contracting rabies, though it does buy you time to get to hospital.

Altitude sickness

Anyone travelling in Chile's northern *altiplano*, where altitudes commonly reach 4500m – or indeed anyone going higher than 3000m in the cordillera – needs to be aware of the risks of **altitude sickness**, locally known as *soroche* or *apunamiento*. This debilitating and sometimes dangerous condition is caused by the reduced atmospheric pressure and corresponding reduction in oxygen that occurs around 3000m above sea level. **Basic symptoms** include breathlessness, headaches, nausea and extreme tiredness, rather like a bad hangover. There's no way of predicting

---

MAREA ROJA

Chile's **shellfish** should be treated with the utmost caution. Every year, a handful of people die because they inadvertently eat bivalve shellfish contaminated by red tide, or *marea roja*, algae that becomes toxic when the seawater temperature rises. The government monitors the presence of this algae with extreme diligence and bans all commercial shellfish collection when the phenomenon occurs. There is little health risk when eating in restaurants or buying shellfish in markets, as these are regularly inspected by the health authorities, but it's extremely dangerous to collect shellfish for your own consumption unless you're absolutely certain that the area is free of red tide. Note that red tide affects all shellfish, cooked or uncooked.

whether or not you'll be susceptible to the condition, which seems to strike quite randomly, affecting people differently from one ascent to another. You can, however, take steps to avoid it by ascending slowly and allowing yourself to acclimatize. In particular, don't be tempted to whizz straight up to the *altiplano* from sea level, but spend a night or two acclimatizing en route. You should also avoid alcohol and salt, and drink lots of water. The bitter-tasting coca leaves chewed by most locals in the *altiplano* (where they're widely available at markets and village stores), can help ease headaches and the sense of exhaustion.

Although extremely unpleasant, the basic form of altitude sickness is essentially harmless and passes after about 24 hours (if it doesn't, descend at least 500m). However, in its more serious forms, altitude sickness can be dangerous and even life-threatening. One to two percent of people travelling to 4000m develop HAPO (high-altitude pulmonary oedema), caused by the build-up of liquid in the lungs. Symptoms include fever, an increased pulse rate, and coughing up white fluid; sufferers should descend immediately, whereupon recovery is usually quick and complete. Rarer, but more serious, is HACO (high-altitude cerebral oedema), which occurs when the brain gets waterlogged with fluid. Symptoms include loss of balance, severe lassitude, weakness or numbness on one side of the body and a confused mental state. If you or a fellow traveller display any of these symptoms, descend immediately and get to a doctor; HACO can be fatal within 24 hours.

Sunburn and dehydration

In many parts of Chile, **sunburn** and **dehydration** are threats. They are obviously more of a problem in the excessively dry climate of the north, but even in the south of the country, it's easy to underestimate the strength of the summer sun. To prevent sunburn, take a **high-factor sunscreen** and wear a wide-brimmed hat. It's also essential to drink plenty of fluids before you go out, and always carry large quantities of water with you when you're hiking in the sun. As you lose a lot of salt when you sweat, add more to your food, or take a rehydration solution.

Hypothermia

Another potential enemy, especially at high altitudes and in Chile's far southern reaches, is **hypothermia**. Because early symptoms can include an almost euphoric sense of sleepiness and disorientation, your body's core temperature can plummet to danger level before you know what has happened. Chile's northern deserts have such clear air that it can drop to -20ºC (-4ºF) at night, which makes you very vulnerable to hypothermia while sleeping if proper precautions aren't taken. If you get hypothermia, the best thing to do is take your clothes off and jump into a sleeping bag with someone else – sharing another person's body heat is the most effective way of restoring your own. If you're alone, or have no willing partners, then get out of the wind and the rain, remove all wet or damp clothes, get dry, and drink plenty of hot fluids.

MEDICAL RESOURCES

Canadian Society for International Health ☎ 613 241 5785, ⓦ csih.org. Extensive list of travel health centres.

CDC ☎ 1-800 232 4636, ⓦ cdc.gov/travel. Official US government travel health site.

Hospital for Tropical Diseases Travel Clinic UK ☎ 0845 155 5000, ⓦ thehtd.org.

International Society for Travel Medicine US ☎ 1-404/373-8282, ⓦ istm.org. Has a full list of travel health clinics.

MASTA (Medical Advisory Service for Travellers Abroad) UK ⓦ masta.org for the nearest clinic.

Tropical Medical Bureau Ireland ☎ 1850 487 674, ⓦ tmb.ie.

The Travel Doctor – TMVC ☎ 1300 658 844, ⓦ tmvc.com.au. Lists travel clinics in Australia, New Zealand and South Africa.

Culture and etiquette

Chile's social mores reflect the European ancestry of the majority of its population, and travellers from the West will have little trouble fitting in, especially if they have a good grasp of Spanish. Chileans are not especially ebullient and high-spirited – particularly when compared with their Argentine neighbours – and are often considered rather formal.

However, they are also known for their quick wit and wordplay, and considering its relatively small population, Chile has produced an impressive array of writers, poets, artists and musicians. The overwhelming majority of Chileans identify themselves as Catholic, and the church still has significant – though waning – influence in the country. Unsurprisingly, then, this is a rather conservative country: divorce was only legalised in 2004 and attitudes towards homosexuality, though improving, are generally far from enlightened. Chileans are very family-oriented: children are popular and travelling families can expect special treatment and friendly attention. Although stereotypical Latin American machismo undoubtedly exists, it is not as strong as in some other countries in the region.

Shopping

While Chile's handicrafts (*artesanía*) are nowhere near as diverse or colourful as in Peru or Bolivia, you can still find a range of beautiful souvenirs, which are usually sold in *ferias artesanales* (craft markets) on or near the central squares of the main towns. As for day-to-day essentials, you'll be able to locate just about everything you need, from sun block to contact lens solution, in the main towns across the country.

Artesanía and other souvenirs

The finest and arguably most beautiful goods you can buy in Chile are the items – mainly jewellery – made of **lapis lazuli**, the deep-blue semi-precious stone found only in Chile and Afghanistan. The best place to buy these is in Bellavista, Santiago: note that the deeper the colour of the stone, the better its quality. Though certainly less expensive than lapis exports sold abroad, they're still pricey.

Most *artesanía* is considerably less expensive. In the **Norte Grande**, the most common articles are alpaca sweaters, gloves and scarves, which you'll find in *altiplano* villages like Parinacota, or in Arica and Iquique. The quality is usually fairly low, but they're inexpensive and very attractive all the same. In the **Norte Chico**, you can pick up some beautiful leather goods, particularly in the crafts markets of La Serena. You might also be tempted to buy a bottle of pisco there, so that you can recreate that pisco sour experience back home –

> **TIPPING**
>
> It's customary to leave a ten percent tip in restaurants – service is rarely included in the bill. You are not, however, expected to tip taxi drivers.

though you're probably better off getting it at a supermarket in Santiago before you leave, to save yourself carting it about. The **Central Valley**, as the agricultural heartland of Chile, is famous for its *huaso* gear, and you'll find brightly coloured ponchos and stiff straw hats in the numerous working *huaso* shops. The highlight in the **Lake District** is the traditional Mapuche silver jewellery, while the **far south** is a good place to buy chunky, colourful knitwear.

A range of these goods can also be bought in the major crafts markets in **Santiago**, notably Los Dominicos market. Also worth checking out are Santiago's little **flea markets** (see p.86).

Hard **haggling** is neither commonly practised nor expected in Chile, though a bit of bargaining is in order at many markets. It's also worth trying to bargain down the price of hotel rooms, especially outside the peak months of January and February.

Travel essentials

Climate

As you might expect given its incredibly long, thin shape, Chile encompasses a wide range of climates (and micro climates). Its seasons are the reverse of those in Europe and North America, with, broadly speaking, winter falling in the June to September period and summer in the December to March period.

Costs

Chile is an expensive country compared with most of South America. Accommodation is relatively expensive, but eating out is relatively good value if you avoid the flashier restaurants and take advantage of set lunch menus. Transport is relatively inexpensive.

In general, per week, you'll need to allow US$250 to get by on a tight budget; around US$600 to live a little more comfortably, staying in mid-range hotels and eating in restaurants most days; and upwards of US$1000 to live in luxury.

The most widespread hidden cost in Chile is the **IVA** (Impuesto al Valor Agregado), a tax of 19 percent added to most goods and services. Although most prices include IVA, there are many irritating exceptions. Hotel rates sometimes include IVA and sometimes don't; as a tourist, you're

CLIMATE

	Jan	Feb	Mar	Apr	May	Jun	Jul	Aug	Sep	Oct	Nov	Dec
Arica												
Max (°C)	26	27	25	24	22	19	18	18	19	20	22	24
Max (°F)	79	80	78	75	71	67	65	65	66	69	72	76
Min (°C)	20	20	19	17	15	14	14	14	15	15	17	18
Min (°F)	68	68	66	63	60	58	57	58	59	60	62	65
rainfall (mm)	1	0	0	0	0	0	0	3	0	0	0	2
Punta Arenas												
Max (°C)	15	14	12	10	7	5	4	6	8	11	12	14
Max (°F)	59	57	54	50	45	41	39	43	46	52	54	57
Min (°C)	7	7	5	4	2	1	-1	1	2	3	4	6
Min (°F)	45	45	41	39	36	34	30	34	36	37	39	43
rainfall (mm)	38	23	33	36	33	41	28	31	23	28	18	36
Santiago												
Max (°C)	29	29	27	23	18	14	15	17	19	22	26	28
Max (°F)	84	84	81	73	64	57	59	63	66	72	79	82
Min (°C)	12	11	9	7	5	3	3	4	6	7	9	11
Min (°F)	54	52	48	45	41	37	37	39	43	45	48	52
rainfall (mm)	3	3	5	13	64	84	76	56	31	15	8	5

supposed to be exempt from IVA if you pay for your accommodation in US dollars. Car rental is almost always quoted without IVA. If in doubt, you should always clarify whether a price quoted to you includes IVA.

Once obtained, various official and quasi-official **youth/student ID cards** soon pay for themselves in savings. Full-time students are eligible for the International Student ID Card (ISIC; @isiccard .com).

Crime and personal safety

Chile is one of the safest South American countries, and violent crime against tourists is rare. The kind of sophisticated tactics used by thieves in neighbouring Peru and Bolivia are extremely uncommon in Chile, and the fact that you can walk around without being gripped by paranoia is one of the country's major bonuses.

That's not to say, of course, that you don't need to be careful. Opportunistic pickpocketing and petty theft is common in Santiago and major cities such as Valparaíso, Arica and Puerto Montt, and you should take all the normal precautions to safeguard your money and valuables, paying special attention in bus terminals and markets – wear a money belt, and keep it tucked inside the waistband of your trousers or skirt, out of sight, and don't wear flashy jewellery, flaunt expensive cameras or carry a handbag. It's also a good idea to keep photocopies of your passport, tourist card, driving licence, air tickets and credit card details separate from the originals – whether it's safer to carry the originals with you or leave them in your hotel is debatable, but whatever you do, you should always have some form of ID on you, even if this is just a photocopy of your passport.

Chile's police force, the **carabineros**, has the whole country covered, with stations in even the most remote areas, particularly in border regions. If you're robbed and need a police report for an insurance claim, you should go to the nearest *retén* (police station), where details of the theft will be entered in a logbook. You'll be issued a slip of paper with the record number of the entry, but in most cases a full report won't be typed out until your insurance company requests it.

Electricity

220V/50Hz is the standard throughout Chile. The sockets are two-pronged, with round pins (as opposed to the flat pins common in neighbouring countries).

Entry requirements

Most foreign visitors to Chile do not need a visa. The exceptions are citizens of Cuba, Russia, Middle Eastern countries (except Israel) and African counties (except South Africa).

Visitors of all nationalities are issued with a 90-day **tourist entry card** (*Tarjeta de Turismo*) on arrival in Chile, which can be extended once for an additional 90 days. It will be checked by the International Police at the airport or border post when you leave Chile – if it's expired you won't be allowed to leave the country until you've paid the appropriate fine at the nearest *Intendencia* (up to US$100, depending on the number of days past the expiry date). If this happens when you're trying to fly out of the international airport in Santiago, you'll have to go back downtown to Moneda 1342 (Mon–Fri 9am–1pm; ☎2 672 5320).

If you lose your tourist card, ask for a duplicate immediately, either from the Fronteras department of the Policía Internacional, General Borgoño 1052, Santiago (☎2 698 2211) or from the Extranjero's department of the Intendencia in any provincial capital. There's no charge for replacing lost or stolen cards.

If you want to **extend** your tourist card, you can either pay US$100 at the Intendencia of Santiago or any provincial capital, or you can simply leave the country and re-enter, getting a brand-new 90-day *Tarjeta de Turismo* for free.

A tourist card does not allow you to undertake any **paid employment** in Chile – for this, you need to get a work visa before you enter the country, which can either be arranged by your employer in Chile or by yourself on presentation (to your embassy or consulate) of an employment contract authorized by a Chilean public notary. You can't swap a tourist card for a work visa while you're in Chile, which means that legally you can't just go out and find a job – though many language schools are happy to ignore the rules when employing teachers. Other points to note are that **under-18s** travelling to Chile without parents need written parental consent authorized by the Chilean Embassy, and that minors travelling to Chile with just one parent need the written, authorized consent of the absent parent.

CHILEAN EMBASSIES ABROAD

Australia 10 Culgoa Circuit, O'Malley, Canberra ACT 2606 ☎02 6286 2098, ⓦchileabroad.gov.cl/australia/.
Canada 50 O'Connor St, suite 1413, Ottawa, ON K1P 6L2 ☎613 235 4402, ⓦchile.ca.
New Zealand 19 Bolton St, Wellington ☎04 471 6270, ⓦembchile.co.nz.
South Africa 169 Garsfontein Rd Ashlea, Delmondo Office Park Block C, Gardens, Pretoria ☎012 460 1676, ⓦchileabroad.gov.cl /sudafrica/.
UK 12 Devonshire St, London W1N 2DS ☎020 7580 1023, ⓦchileabroad.gov.cl/reino-unido/en.

> ### EMERGENCY NUMBERS
> **Air rescue** 138
> (for mountaineering accidents)
> **Ambulance** 131
> **Carabineros** 133
> **Coast Guard** 137
> **Fire** 132
> **Investigaciones** 134 (for serious crimes)

US 1732 Massachusetts Ave NW, Washington, DC 20036 ☎202 785 1746, ⓦchile-usa.org.

Gay and lesbian travellers

Chilean society is extremely **conservative**, and homosexuality is still a taboo subject for many Chileans. Outside Santiago – with the minor exceptions of some northern cities such as La Serena and Antofagasta – there are no gay venues, and it is advisable for same-sex couples to do as the locals do and remain discreet, especially in public. Machismo, while not as evident here as in other Latin American countries, is nevertheless deeply ingrained and mostly unchallenged by women, despite a growing feminist movement. That said, gay-bashing and other homophobic acts are rare and the government has passed anti-discrimination legislation. The International Gay and Lesbian Association (ⓦiglta.org) has information of gay- and lesbian-friendly travel companies in Chile (and around the world). ⓦsantiagogay.com is another good source of information.

Insurance

You'd do well to take out an insurance policy before travelling to cover against theft, loss and illness or injury. Before paying for a new policy, however, it's worth checking whether you are already covered: some all-risks home insurance policies may cover your possessions when overseas, and many private medical schemes include cover when abroad.

After checking out the possibilities above, you might want to contact a **specialist travel insurance company**, or consider the travel insurance deal we offer (see box, p.48). A typical travel insurance policy usually provides cover for the loss of baggage, tickets and – up to a certain limit – cash or cheques, as well as cancellation or curtailment of your journey. Most exclude so-called dangerous sports unless an extra premium is paid; in Chile this can mean scuba-diving, white-water rafting, windsurfing and trekking, though probably

---

ROUGH GUIDES TRAVEL INSURANCE

Rough Guides has teamed up with WorldNomads.com to offer great travel insurance deals. Policies are available to residents of over 150 countries, with cover for a wide range of adventure sports, 24hr emergency assistance, high levels of medical and evacuation cover and a stream of travel safety information. Roughguides.com users can take advantage of their policies online 24/7, from anywhere in the world – even if you're already travelling. And since plans often change when you're on the road, you can extend your policy and even claim online. Roughguides.com users who buy travel insurance with WorldNomads.com can also leave a positive footprint and donate to a community development project. For more information go to ⓦ roughguides.com/shop.

---

not kayaking or jeep safaris. If you take medical coverage, ascertain whether benefits will be paid as treatment proceeds or only after you return home, and if there is a 24-hour medical emergency number. When securing baggage cover, make sure that the per-article limit will cover your most valuable possession. If you need to make a claim, you should keep receipts for medicines and medical treatment, and in the event you have anything stolen, you must obtain an official statement from the police.

Internet

Chile is one of the most wired Latin American nations. Cybercafés are everywhere, and broadband (*banda ancha*) access is quite common. Most hotels and many cafes and restaurants provide wi-fi access, often for free.

Living and/or working in Chile

There are plenty of short-term work opportunities for foreigners in Chile; the difficulty lies in obtaining and maintaining a work visa. You can only apply for one once you have a firm job offer, with the result that many people enter on a tourist visa and hold off on applying until they've actually found work.

If you're pre-planning a longer stay, consult the websites of the **Overseas Jobs Express** (ⓦ overseas jobs.org) and the **International Career and Employment Center** (ⓦ internationaljobs.org); both list internships, jobs and volunteer opportunities across the world.

Many students come to Chile taking advantage of semester or **year-abroad programmes** offered by their universities. Go to ⓦ studyabroad.com for links and listings to study programmes worldwide.

Teaching English

Demand for native-speaking English teachers in Chilean cities is high and makes **language teaching**

an obvious work option. Though it can be competitive, it's relatively easy to find work either teaching general English in private language schools or business English within companies. A lucky few get by with minimal teaching experience, but with an **EFL** (English Language Teaching)/**TEFL** (Teaching English as a Foreign Language) qualification you're in a far better position to get a job with a reputable employer. **CELTA** (Certificate in English Language Teaching to Adults) courses are among the best and you can qualify before you leave home or even while you're abroad. The most lucrative work is private, one-to-one lessons, which are best sought through word-of-mouth or by placing an ad in a local newspaper. The British Council website (ⓦ british council.org/work/jobs.htm) has a list of vacancies.

Volunteering

Opportunities for work need not be limited to language teaching. You can easily become a **volunteer** in Chile, but you'll often have to pay for the privilege. Many organizations target people on gap years (at whatever stage in their lives) and offer placements on both inner city and environmental projects. For free or low-cost volunteer positions have a look at the excellent ⓦ volunteersouthamerica.net.

STUDY AND WORK PROGRAMMES

AFS Intercultural Programs ⓦ afs.org. Intercultural exchange organization with programmes in over 50 countries.'

Amerispan ⓦ amerispan.com. Highly rated educational travel company that specializes in language courses, but also runs volunteer programmes all over Latin America.

British Council ⓦ britishcouncil.org. Produces a free leaflet which details study opportunities abroad. The website has a list of current job vacancies for recruiting TEFL teachers for posts worldwide.

Council on International Educational Exchange (CIEE) ⓦ ciee.org. Leading NGO offering study programmes and volunteer projects around the world.

Earthwatch Institute ⓦ earthwatch.org. Scientific expedition project that spans over 50 countries with environmental and archeological ventures worldwide.

Rainforest Concern ⓦ rainforestconcern.org. Volunteering opportunities protecting threatened habitats in South and Central America. The Chilean project is based in the Nasampulli Reserve in the south of the country.

Raleigh International ⓦ raleigh.org.uk. Volunteer projects across the world for young travellers.

Mail

The Chilean **postal service** is very reliable for international items, but can be surprisingly erratic for domestic items. A letter from Santiago takes about five days to reach Europe, a little less time to reach North America and usually no more than a couple of weeks to more remote destinations. Allow a few extra days for letters posted from other towns and cities in Chile. Do not send any gifts to Chile using regular post; theft is extremely common for incoming shipments. For important shipping to Chile try express services such as FedEx and DHL.

Post offices are marked by a blue Correos sign, and are usually on or near the Plaza de Armas of any town; postboxes are blue, and bear the blue Correos symbol.

Maps

No two **road maps** of Chile are identical, and none is absolutely correct. The bulk of errors lie in the representation of dirt roads: some maps mark them incorrectly as tarred roads, some leave out a random selection of dirt roads altogether, and some mark them quite clearly where nothing exists at all.

You'll find a number of reliable country maps, including the **Rough Guides**' detailed, waterproof Chile map. The comprehensive **TurisTel** map is printed in the back of its guides to Chile and also published in a separate booklet. Sernatur produces a good fold-out map of the whole of Chile, called the Gran Mapa Caminero de Chile, on sale at the main office in Santiago, and an excellent map of the north, called the Mapa Rutero Turístico Macroregión Norte, free from Sernatur offices in Santiago and the north. Other useful maps include **Auto Mapa's** Rutas de Chile series, distributed internationally. Outside Chile, also look for the **Reise Know-How Verlag** and **Nelles Verlag** maps of Chile, which combine clear road detail along with contours and colour tinting.

You can pick up free and usually adequate street plans in the tourist office of most cities, but better by far are those contained in the Turistel guidebooks, with a map for practically every town and village you're likely to want to visit. Bookshops and kiosks sell street-indexed maps of Santiago, but the most comprehensive A–Z of Santiago appears in the back of the CTC phone directory.

The best ones to use for **hiking** are the series of **JLM** maps, which cover some of the main national parks and occasionally extend into Argentina. They're produced in collaboration with Conaf and are available in bookshops and some souvenir or outdoor stores.

Money

The basic unit of currency is the peso, usually represented by the $ sign (and by CH$ in this book, for clarity). Many hotels, particularly the more expensive ones, accept US dollars cash (and will give you a discount for paying this way; see p.30). Apart from this, you'll be expected to pay for everything in local currency. You may, however, come across prices quoted in the mysterious "UF". This stands for *unidad de fomento* and is an index-linked monetary unit that is adjusted (every minute) daily to remain in line with inflation. The only time you're likely to come across it is if you rent a vehicle (your liability, in the event of an accident, will probably be quoted in UFs on the rental contract). You'll find the exchange rate of the UF against the Chilean peso in the daily newspapers, along with the rates for all the other currencies.

Credit and debit cards can be used either in **ATM**s or over the counter. MasterCard, Visa and American Express are accepted just about everywhere, but other cards may not be recognized. Alternatively, pick up a pre-paid debit card such as Travelex's Cash Passport (ⓦ travelex.co.uk).

Travellers' cheques should always be in US dollars, and though most brands are accepted, it's best to be on the safe side and take one of the main brands such as American Express, Citibank or Thomas Cook. You will have to change them in a **casa de cambio** (exchange bureau), usually for a small commission.

Opening hours and public holidays

Most **shops and services** are open Monday to Friday from 9am to 1pm and 3pm to 6pm or 7pm, and on Saturday from 10am or 11am until 2pm. Supermarkets stay open at lunchtime and may close as late as 11pm on weekdays and Saturdays in big cities. Large shopping malls are often open all day on Sundays. **Banks** have more limited hours, generally Monday to Friday from 9am to 2pm, but *casas de cambio* tend to use the same opening hours as shops.

Museums are nearly always shut on Mondays, and are often free on Sundays. Many tourist offices only open Monday to Friday throughout the year, with a break for lunch, but in summer (usually between Dec 15 and March 15) some increase their weekday hours and open on Saturday and sometimes Sunday; note that their hours are subject to frequent change. Post offices don't close at lunchtime on weekdays and are open on Saturdays from 9am to 1pm.

February is the main holiday month in Chile, when there's an exodus from the big cities to the beaches or the Lake District, leaving some shops and restaurants closed. February is also an easy time to get around in Santiago, as the city appears half-abandoned.

MAJOR HOLIDAYS

January 1 New Year's Day (*Año nuevo*)
Easter Good Friday, Easter Saturday and Easter Sunday are the climax to Holy Week (*Semana Santa*)
May 1 Labour Day (*Día del Trabajo*)
May 21 *Combate Naval de Iquique*. A Remembrance Day celebrating the end of the War of the Pacific after the naval victory at Iquique
June 15 Corpus Christi
June, last Monday San Pedro and San Pablo
August 15 Assumption of the Virgin
September 18 National Independence Day (*Fiestas Patrias*), in celebration of the first provisional government of 1810
September 19 Armed Forces Day (*Día del Ejército*)
October 12 Columbus Day (*Día de la Raza*), marking the discovery of America
November 1 All Saints' Day (*Todos los Santos*)
December 8 Immaculate Conception
December 25 Christmas Day (*Navidad*)

Phones

Landline **telephone numbers** are six or seven digits long, depending on where you are in the country. If you are making a long-distance call you need to first dial a "carrier code" (for example "188" for Telefónica or "181" for Movistar), then an area code (for example "2" for the Santiago metropolitan region or "32" for the Valparaíso region) and finally the number itself. Mobile phone numbers have eight digits. When calling from a landline to a mobile, dial "09" and then the rest of the number (for mobile to mobile calls, the "09" is not necessary).

> ### CALLING HOME FROM ABROAD
> Note that the initial zero is omitted from the city code when dialling numbers in the UK, Ireland, Australia and New Zealand from abroad.
>
> **US and Canada** international access code + 1 + area code.
>
> **Australia** international access code + 61 + city code.
>
> **New Zealand** international access code + 64 + city code.
>
> **UK** international access code + 44 + city code.
>
> **Republic of Ireland** international access code + 353 + city code.
>
> **South Africa** international access code + 27 + city code.

Using **phonecards** is a practical way to phone abroad, and it's worth stocking up on them in major cities, as you can't always buy them elsewhere. Alternatively there are dozens of call centres or **centros de llamadas** in most cities. Another convenient option is to take along an **international calling card**. The least expensive way to call home, however, is via Skype.

The cheapest way to use your mobile is to pick up a local sim card, though you may also have to get your phone unlocked to ensure it works. The main operators are Movistar, Entel and Claro, and you'll find several branches of each in the larger cities.

Time

From the end of October to late March, Chile observes Daylight Saving Time and is three hours behind GMT; the country is four hours behind GMT the rest of the year. Easter Island is two hours behind the mainland.

Tourist information

Chile's government-run tourist board is called **Sernatur**. There's a large office in Santiago, plus branches in every provincial capital. It produces a huge amount of material, including themed booklets on camping, skiing, national parks, beaches, thermal springs and so on. In smaller towns you're more likely to find a municipal **Oficina de Turismo**, sometimes attached to the Municipalidad (town hall) and usually with a very limited supply of printed information to hand out. If there's no separate tourist office it's worth trying the Municipalidad itself. Another source of information is the excellent series of TurisTel guidebooks, published annually by the Chilean phone company CTC, and available at numerous pavement kiosks in Santiago, and CTC offices in Chilean cities. They come in three volumes, covering the north, the centre and the south, and give extremely detailed information on even the tiniest of places, with comprehensive street plans and road maps. The English translation, available at many kiosks, however, suffers from infrequent updating.

GOVERNMENT WEBSITES

Australian Department of Foreign Affairs Ⓦ dfat.gov.au.
British Foreign & Commonwealth Office Ⓦ fco.gov.uk.
Canadian Department of Foreign Affairs Ⓦ international .gc.ca.
Irish Department of Foreign Affairs Ⓦ foreignaffairs.gov.ie.
New Zealand Ministry of Foreign Affairs Ⓦ mfat.govt.nz.
South African Department of Foreign Affairs
Ⓦ www.dfa.gov.za.
US State Department Ⓦ travel.state.gov.

OTHER USEFUL WEBSITES

Chilean Patagonia Ⓦ chileaustral.com. Website dedicated to tourism in Chilean Patagonia, including city guides, national parks, hotels and weather forecasts.
Chile Hotels Ⓦ chile-hotels.com. A long list of Chilean hotels, with online booking facilities, plus brief descriptions of the towns and cities.
El Mercurio Ⓦ emol.com. The long-established, rather conservative daily newspaper, online in Spanish.
Foody Chile Ⓦ foodychile.com. Well-written blog on what and where to eat in Chile.
I Love Chile Ⓦ ilovechile.cl. Useful website with news, features, music and blogs, plus its own online radio station.
South American Explorers Ⓦ saexplorers.org. Useful site of the long-established travel NGO. Offers travel advisories and warnings, trip reports, a bulletin board and links with other sites.
Turismo Chile Ⓦ turismochile.cl. Descriptions of the major attractions in each region, with some historical and cultural background.

Travellers with disabilities

Chile makes very few provisions for people with disabilities, and travellers with mobility problems will have to contend with a lack of lifts, high curbs, dangerous potholes on pavements and worse. However, Chileans are courteous people and are likely to offer assistance when needed. Spacious, specially designed toilets are becoming more common in airports and the newer shopping malls, but restaurants and bars are progressing at a slower pace. New public buildings are legally required to provide **disabled access**, and there will usually be a full range of facilities in the more expensive hotels. It is worth employing the help of the **local tourist office** for information on the most suitable place to stay. Public transport on the other hand is far more of a challenge. Most bus companies do not have any dedicated disabled facilities so, given that reserved disabled parking is increasingly common, travelling with your **own vehicle** might be the easier option.

Travelling with children

Families are highly regarded in Latin American societies, and Chile is no exception. Chile's **restaurants** are well used to catering for children and will happily provide smaller portions for younger mouths. In hotels, you should try to negotiate cheaper rates. The main health hazards to watch out for are the heat and sun. Very high factor suncream can be difficult to come by in remote towns so it is best to stock up on **sunblock** at pharmacies in the bigger cities. Always remember that the sun in Chile is fierce, so hats and bonnets are essential; this is especially true in the south where the ozone layer is particularly thin. **High altitudes** may cause children problems and, like adults, they must acclimatize before walking too strenuously above 2000m. If you intend to travel with babies and very young children to high altitudes, consult your doctor for advice before you leave.

Long-distances buses charge for each seat so you'll only pay less if a child is sitting on your knee. On **city buses**, however, small children often travel for free but will be expected to give up their seat for paying customers without one. Airline companies generally charge a third less for passengers under 12 so look out for last-minute **discount flights** – they can make flying an affordable alternative to an arduous bus ride.

Santiago
and around

56 Santiago
88 Around Santiago

FUNICULAR, CERRO SAN CRISTÓBAL,
SANTIAGO

1

Santiago and around

Set on a wide plain near the foot of the Andes, **Santiago** boasts one of the most dazzling backdrops of any capital city on earth. The views onto the towering cordillera after a rainstorm clears the air are magnificent, especially in winter, when the snow-covered peaks rise behind the city like a giant white rampart against the blue sky (though smog, unfortunately, often obscures such vistas). The city itself is a rapidly expanding metropolis of around seven million people, and though long in the shadow of Buenos Aires and Rio de Janeiro has its own proud identity.

Santiago is divided into 32 autonomous *comunas*, most of them squat, flat suburbs stretching out from the centre. The historic centre, in contrast, is compact, manageable, and has a pleasant atmosphere. Part of the appeal comes from the fact that it's so green: tall, luxuriant trees fill the main square, and there are numerous meticulously landscaped parks. Above all, though, it's the all-pervading sense of energy that makes the place so alluring, with crowds of Santiaguinos constantly milling through narrow streets packed with shoe-shiners, fruit barrows, news kiosks and sellers of everything from coat hangers to pirated DVDs.

Architecturally, the city is a bit of a hotchpotch, thanks to a succession of earthquakes and a spate of undisciplined rebuilding in the 1960s and 1970s. Ugly office blocks and *galerías* compete for space with beautifully maintained colonial buildings, while east of the centre Santiago's economic boom is reflected in the glittering new commercial buildings, skyscrapers and luxury hotels of the *comunas* of Vitacura, Providencia and Las Condes. These different faces are part of a wider set of contrasts – between the American-style shopping malls in the barrios altos, for example, and the old-fashioned shops in the historic centre; between the modish lounge bars and the greasy *fuentes de soda*; and, in particular, between the sharp-suited professionals and the scores of street sellers scrambling to make a living. It's not a place of excesses, however: homelessness is minimal compared with many other cities of its size, and Santiago is pretty safe.

Santiago is also a great base for exploring the surrounding region. With the **Andes** so close and accessible, you can be right in the mountains in an hour or two. In winter people go **skiing** for the day; in warmer months the **Cajón del Maipo** offers fantastic trekking, horseriding and rafting. Heading west towards Valparaíso (see pp.98–111) you'll also find good hiking opportunities in the **Parque Nacional La Campana**. Nearby villages such as **Los Andes** and **Pomaire** can provide a relaxing antidote to Santiago's bustle. Still more tempting are the many **vineyards** within easy reach. There are also a number of excellent **beaches** (see Chapter 2) less than two hours away.

The legend of the slipping crown p.64
Palacios of the Alameda p.68
Hiking in the Monumento Nacional El Morado p.89
Top 5 hostels p.79

Top 5 places to eat traditional Chilean food p.81
Wine tours near Santiago p.88
Skiing near Santiago p.92
Hiking in Parque Nacional La Campana p.94

CATEDRAL METROPOLITANA, PLAZA DE ARMAS, SANTIAGO

Highlights

❶ **Plaza de Armas** Gaze at the colonial architecture surrounding Santiago's lively central plaza – or sit on a bench and take in the hustle and bustle. **See p.57**

❷ **Museo Chileno de Arte Precolombino** This exquisite collection of artefacts from dozens of pre-Hispanic civilizations features fine tapestries, intricate ceramics and dazzling jewels. **See p.61**

❸ **Mercado Central and La Vega** The city's two main markets are great places to explore and sample excellent fresh fish and seafood. See **p.70 & p.71**

❹ **Bellavista** The traditional bohemian quarter offers great theatres, restaurants and bars, as well as one of poet Pablo Neruda's eccentric homes. **See p.71**

❺ **Cerro San Cristóbal** Ride the elevator to the top of this steep hill where, on a clear day, you have great views of the snowcapped Andes towering over the city. **See p.73**

❻ **Andean skiing** Skiers and snowboarders will delight in the world-class ski areas near Santiago, including the world-famous Portillo resort. **See p.92**

HIGHLIGHTS ARE MARKED ON THE MAPS ON P.56 & P.58–59

1

Santiago

Although it is not Chile's most dazzling highlight, **SANTIAGO** is a cultural, economic and educational hub, and the best place to get a handle on the country's identity. Dipping into the city's vibrant cultural scene, checking out its museums, and dining at its varied restaurants will really help you make the most of your time in this kaleidoscopic country.

You can get round many of Santiago's attractions on foot in two to three days. A tour of the compact core, centred on the bustling **Plaza de Armas**, should include visits to the **Palacio de la Moneda**, the excellent **Museo Chileno de Arte Precolombino** and the evocative **Museo Colonial**, followed by a climb up **Cerro Santa Lucía**. Less strenuous options include lunch at the colourful **mercados Central** or **La Vega**.

North of downtown, on the other side of the Río Mapocho, it's an easy funicular ride up **Cerro San Cristóbal**, whose summit provides unrivalled views. At its foot, **Barrio Bellavista** is replete with cafés, restaurants, bars and clubs, plus the former home of **poet Pablo Neruda**, now a wonderful museum. West of the centre, the once glamorous barrios that housed Santiago's moneyed classes at the beginning of the twentieth century make for rewarding, romantic wanders, and contain some splendid old mansions, including **Palacio Cousiño**. Moving east into the barrios altos of Providencia and Las Condes, the tone is newer and flasher. Apart from shiny malls, there's less to draw you out here, with the notable exception of the crafts market at **Los Dominicos**.

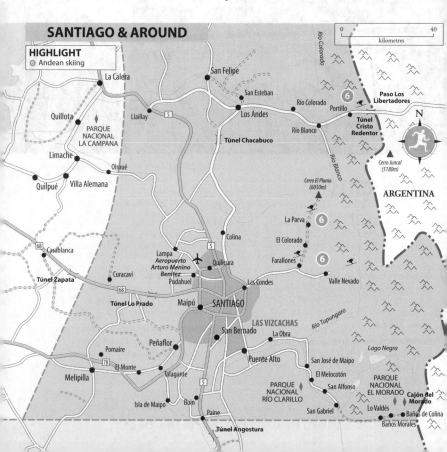

1

Brief history

Some seven years after Francisco Pizarro conquered Cuzco in Peru, he dispatched **Pedro de Valdivia** southwards to claim and settle more territory for the Spanish crown. After eleven months of travelling, Valdivia and his 150 men reached what he considered to be a suitable site for a new city, and, on February 12, 1541, officially founded "Santiago de la Nueva Extremadura", wedged into a triangle of land bounded by the Río Mapocho to the north, its southern branch to the south and the rocky Santa Lucía hill to the east. A native population of **Picunche** was scattered around the region, but this didn't deter Valdivia from getting down to business: with great alacrity the main square was established and the surrounding streets were marked out with a string and ruler, a fort was built in the square (thus named "Plaza de Armas") and several other buildings were erected. Six months later they were all razed in a Picunche raid.

The town was doggedly rebuilt to the same plans, and Santiago began to take on the shape of a new colonial capital. But nine years after founding it, the Spaniards, in search of gold, shifted their attention to Arauco in the south, and Santiago became something of a backwater. Following the violent Mapuche uprising in 1553, however, the Spaniards were forced to abandon their towns south of the Bío Bío, and many returned to Santiago. Nonetheless, growth continued to be very slow: settlers were never large in number, and what opportunities the land offered were thwarted by strict trade restrictions. Moreover, expansion was repeatedly knocked back by regular **earthquakes**.

Independence

Santiago started to look like a real capital during the course of the eighteenth century, as trade restrictions were eased, more wealth was created, and the population increased. However, it wasn't until after **independence** in 1818 that expansion really got going, as the rich clamoured to build themselves glamorous mansions and the state erected beautiful public buildings such as the Teatro Municipal.

Santiago today

As the city entered the twentieth century it began to push eastwards into the new barrio alto and north into Bellavista. The horizontal spread has gone well beyond these limits since then, gobbling up outlying towns and villages at great speed; Gran Santiago now stretches 40km by 40km. Its central zones have shot up vertically, too, particularly in Providencia and Las Condes, where the showy high-rise buildings reflect the country's rapid economic growth over the past decade. Despite this dramatic transformation, however, the city's central core still sticks to the same street pattern marked out by Pedro de Valdivia in 1541, and its first public space, the Plaza de Armas, is still at the heart of its street life.

Plaza de Armas

The **Plaza de Armas** is the centre of Santiago and the country, both literally – all distances to the rest of Chile are measured from here – and symbolically. It was the first public space laid out by Pedro de Valdivia when he founded the city in 1541 and quickly became the nucleus of Santiago's administrative, commercial and social life. This is where the young capital's most important seats of power – the law courts, the governor's palace, and the cathedral – were built, and where its markets, bullfights (no longer allowed), festivals and other public activities took place. Four and a half centuries later, this is still where the city's pulse beats loudest, and half an hour's people watching here is perhaps the best introduction to Santiago.

These days the open market space has been replaced by flower gardens and numerous trees; palms, poplars and eucalyptus tower over benches packed with giggling schoolchildren, gossiping old men, lovers, tourists, indulgent grandmothers and packs

1

of uniformed shop girls on their lunch break. Thirsty dogs hang around the fountain; shoe-shiners polish the feet of dour businessmen clutching *El Mercurio*; and ancient-looking chess players hold sombre tournaments inside the bandstand. Against this is a backdrop of constant noise supplied by street performers, singers and evangelical preachers. Meanwhile, a constant ebb and flow of people march in and out of the great civic and religious buildings enclosing the square.

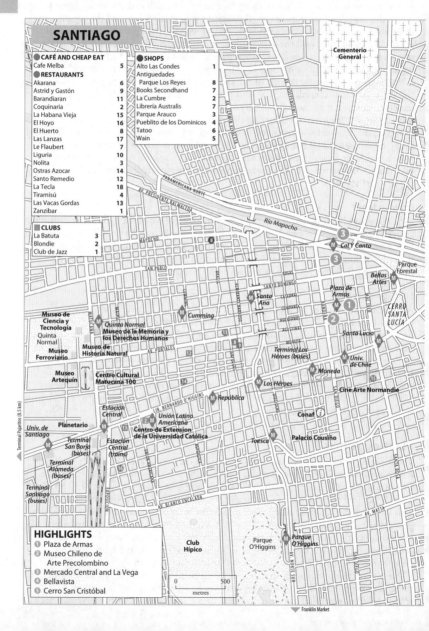

SANTIAGO

● CAFÉ AND CHEAP EAT	
Cafe Melba	5
● RESTAURANTS	
Akarana	6
Astrid y Gastón	9
Barandiaran	11
Coquinaria	2
La Habana Vieja	15
El Hoyo	16
El Huerto	8
Las Lanzas	17
Le Flaubert	7
Liguria	10
Nolita	3
Ostras Azocar	14
Santo Remedio	12
La Tecla	18
Tiramisú	4
Las Vacas Gordas	13
Zanzibar	1

● SHOPS	
Alto Las Condes	1
Antiguedades	
Parque Los Reyes	8
Books Secondhand	7
La Cumbre	2
Librería Australis	7
Parque Arauco	3
Pueblito de los Dominicos	4
Tatoo	6
Wain	5

■ CLUBS	
La Batuta	3
Blondie	2
Club de Jazz	1

HIGHLIGHTS
❶ Plaza de Armas
❷ Museo Chileno de
 Arte Precolombino
❸ Mercado Central and La Vega
❹ Bellavista
❺ Cerro San Cristóbal

Correo Central

Plaza de Armas 559 • Mon–Fri 8.30am–7pm, Sat 8.30am–1pm

On the northwest corner of the Plaza de Armas stands the candyfloss-coloured **Correo Central** (central post office), whose interior, with its tiered galleries crowned by a beautiful glass roof, is every bit as impressive as its elaborate facade. It was built in 1882 on the foundations of what had been the Palacio de los Gobernadores (governors' palace) during

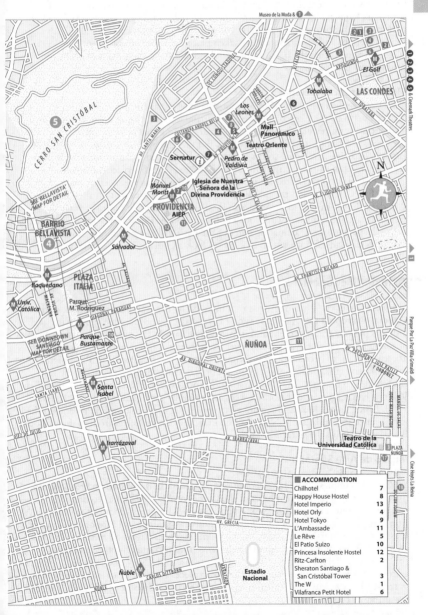

■ ACCOMMODATION	
Chilhotel	7
Happy House Hostel	8
Hotel Imperio	13
Hotel Orly	4
Hotel Tokyo	9
L'Ambassade	11
Le Rêve	5
El Patio Suizo	10
Princesa Insolente Hostel	12
Ritz-Carlton	2
Sheraton Santiago & San Cristóbal Tower	3
The W	1
Vilafranca Petit Hotel	6

1

colonial times, and the Palacio de los Presidentes de Chile (presidential palace) after independence. Now given over to more mundane affairs, this is where you can come to send postcards home and pick up poste restante.

Municipalidad

Plaza de Armas s/n

On the northeast corner of the Plaza de Armas is the pale, Neoclassical edifice of Santiago's **Municipalidad**. The first *cabildo* (town hall) was erected on this site back in the early seventeenth century and also contained the city's prison. Several reconstructions and restorations have taken place since then, most recently in 1895. A curious feature is that the basement is still divided into the original cells of the old prison, now used as offices.

Museo Histórico Nacional

Plaza de Armas • Tues–Sun 10am–5.30pm • CH$600, free on Sun • ☎ 2 411 7000, ⓦ dibam.cl/historico_nacional

Wedged between the Correo and the Municipalidad is the splendid **Palacio de la Real Audiencia**, an immaculately preserved colonial building that's borne witness to some of Santiago's most important turns of history. Built by the Spanish Crown between 1804 and 1807 to house the royal courts of justice, it had served this purpose for just two years when Chile's first government junta assembled here to replace the Spanish governor with its own elected leader. Eight years later it was the meeting place of Chile's first Congress, and the building was the seat of government until 1846, when President Bulnes moved to La Moneda. The Palacio's grand old rooms, arranged around a large central courtyard, today house the **Museo Histórico Nacional**, crammed with eclectic and often fascinating relics of the past, including furniture, sewing machines and ladies' clothes – all of it fun to look at, but too chaotic to be really illuminating.

Cathedral Metropolitana

Plaza de Armas • Mon–Sat 9am–7pm, Sun 9am–noon

The west side of the Plaza de Armas is dominated by the grandiose stone bulk of the **Catedral Metropolitana**. A combination of Neoclassical and Baroque styles, with its orderly columns and pediment and its ornate bell towers, the cathedral bears the mark of **Joaquín Toesca,** who was brought over from Italy in 1780 to oversee its completion. Toesca went on to become the most important architect of colonial Chile, designing many of Santiago's public buildings, including La Moneda. This is actually the fifth church to be built on this site; the first was burnt down by Picunche just months after Valdivia had it built, and the others were destroyed by earthquakes in 1552, 1647 and 1730. Inside, take a look at the main altar, carved out of marble and richly embellished with bronze and lapis lazuli. Note also the intricately crafted silver frontal, the work of Bavarian Jesuits in the sixteenth century.

Museo de Arte Sagrado

Plaza de Armas • Mon–Sat 9am–7pm, Sun 9am–noon • Free

You'll find examples of the Jesuits' exquisite silverwork in the **Museo de Arte Sagrado** tucked away behind the main body of the Cathedral Metropolitana. To find the entrance, go down the passage belonging to the bookshop next door to the cathedral. A gate at the bottom takes you back into the cathedral grounds and into one of Santiago's most evocative courtyards, where languid palm trees brush against crumbling colonial architecture. From here, signs point to the three rooms containing the museum's collection of religious paintings, sculpture, furniture and silverwork, including a finely crafted silver lectern and tabernacle. These two pieces aside, none of it is as impressive as the stuff in the Museo Colonial in the Iglesia San Francisco (see p.67), but it is still rewarding to browse here.

Casa Colorada – Museo de Santiago

Merced 860 • Mon–Fri 10am–5.45pm, Sat 10am–4.45pm, Sun 11am–1.45pm • CH$500, free on Sun

Just off the southeast corner of the Plaza de Armas is the **Casa Colorada**, built in 1769 and generally considered to be Santiago's best-preserved colonial house. With its clay-tiled roof, row of balconied windows giving onto the street and distinctive, deep-red walls, the two-storey mansion certainly provides a striking example of an eighteenth-century town residence. The house is built around two large patios, one of which you walk through to get to the **Museo de Santiago**, which occupies five of the Casa Colorada's rooms. This rather humble museum is dedicated to the history of the city from pre-Columbian to modern times, using scale models, maps and paintings.

The Ex Congreso Nacional

Morandé and Compañía

North of Plaza de la Constitución are another couple of impressive public buildings. The most beautiful, from the outside, is the white, temple-like **Ex Congreso Nacional**, set amid lush gardens. This is where Congress used to meet, until it was dissolved on September 11, 1973, the day of the coup d'état. In 1990, following the end of the military regime, a new congress building was erected in Valparaíso; since this one currently houses the Cancillería (foreign ministry), unfortunately public access to the inside is extremely limited.

Tribunales de Justicia

Compañía

On the southern side of Compañía, spanning the whole block, is the Tribunales de Justicia, an imposing Neoclassical building housing the highest court in Chile, the Corte Suprema. You'd never guess it from the outside, but this austere building conceals one of the most beautiful interiors in the city. Topped by a stunning glass-and-metal vault three floors above, the hall is flooded with natural light. If you want to take photos, you need to get permission from the *secretaría* on the first floor.

Museo Chileno de Arte Precolombino

Compañía and Bandera • Previously Tues–Sun 10am–6pm • CH$3000, free on Sun • ☎ 688 7348, ⓦ precolombino.cl

Just off the southwest corner of the Plaza de Armas is the beautifully restored 1807 Real Casa de la Aduana (the old royal customs house), which now houses the **Museo Chileno de Arte Precolombino**. Unquestionably Chile's best museum, it is unfortunately currently **closed** for major renovations and is not due to reopen until 2013.

The museum's collection spans a period of about ten thousand years and covers regions from present-day Mexico down to southern Chile, brilliantly illustrating the artistic wealth and diversity of Latin America's many cultures. The items were selected primarily on the basis of their artistic merit, rather than on their scientific or anthropological significance.

The museum's rooms take you on a north-to-south geographical tour of different areas of Latin America, starting with **Mesoamérica,** corresponding to present-day Mexico, Guatemala, Honduras, El Salvador and parts of Nicaragua; moving on to the **Area Intermedia**, covering what is now Ecuador, Colombia, Panama, Costa Rica and Nicaragua; followed by the **Andes Centrales**, or central Andean region (today's Peru and western Bolivia); and ending in the **Andes del Sur** (Chile and parts of Argentina).

Area Mesoamérica

The first section of the museum has one of the most startling pieces in the collection: a statue of **Xipé-Totec,** the god of spring, represented as a man covered in the skin of a monkey, exposing both male and female genitalia. At the time of the Spanish conquest, the cult of Xipé-Totec was widespread throughout most of Mesoamérica, and was

DOWNTOWN SANTIAGO

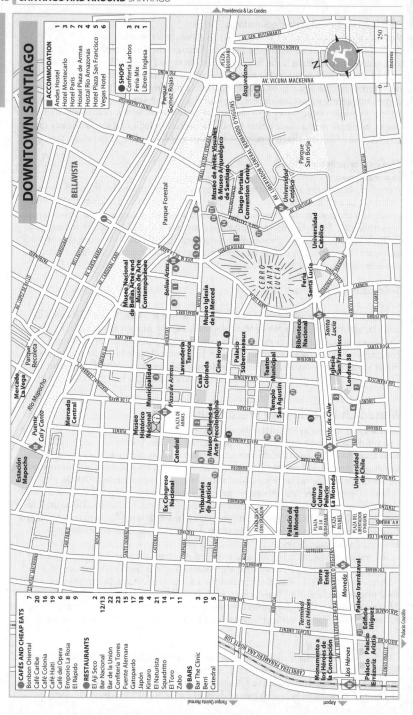

▲ Providencia & Las Condes

■ ACCOMMODATION

Andes Hostel	1
Hotel Montecarlo	3
Hotel Paris	7
Hostel Plaza de Armas	2
Hostal Río Amazonas	4
Hotel Plaza San Francisco	5
Vegas Hotel	6

● SHOPS

Confitería Larbos	3
Feria Mix	2
Librería Inglesa	1

● CAFÉS AND CHEAP EATS

Bonbon Oriental	7
Café Caribe	20
Café Colonia	16
Café Haiti	19
Café del Opera	6
Emporio La Rosa	8
El Rápido	9

● RESTAURANTS

El Ají Seco	2
Bar Nacional	12/13
Bar de la Unión	22
Confitería Torres	23
Fuente Alemana	15
Gatopardo	17
Japón	18
Kintaro	4
El Naturista	21
Squadritto	14
El Toro	1
Zabo	11

● BARS

Bar The Clinic	3
Berri	10
Catedral	5

▲ Parque Quinta Normal

▲ Airport

celebrated in a bizarre ritual in which a young man would cover himself with the skin of a sacrificial victim and wear it until it rotted off, revealing his young, fresh skin and symbolizing the growth of new vegetation from the earth.

Another eye-catching object, further up the room on the left, is the elaborately ornamented **incense burner**, used by the Teotihuacán culture (300–600 AD) to pray for rain and good harvests. The face carved in the middle represents a rain god, and when the incense was burning, the smoke would escape from his eyes. Standing at the far end of the room, by the exit, a huge slab of stone features **bas-relief carvings** depict a hulking, armed warrior with two small figures at his feet. It originally formed part of an immense Maya structure, built between 600 and 900 AD.

Area Intermedia

In this region the continent's oldest pottery was produced, along with some exquisite goldwork. Pottery made its first appearance in the Americas around 3000 BC on the coast of Ecuador, where it was created by the Valdivia culture. Among the museum's best examples of **Valdivia pottery** is the gorgeous little female figurine with a round belly and childlike face, thought to have been used for fertility rites carried out at harvest time. Note also the wonderful **coca-leaf-chewing figures** known as *coqueros*, carved with a telltale lump in their mouth by the Capulí culture (500 BC to 500 AD). As well as pottery, this *sala* contains beautiful **gold objects,** such as the miniature, finely worked carvings produced by the Veraguas and Diquis cultures (700–1550 AD) featuring images of frightening monsters and open-jawed, long-fanged felines.

Area Andes Centrales

The next room is distinguished by its **masks** and **copper figurines**, many of which were retrieved from ancient graves. Among the collection are examples of the highly expressive work of the Moche culture (100 BC to 800 AD), including copper figurines and masks, now a lustrous jade-green colour, and a series of polished ceremonial pots decorated with images of animals, faces and houses. The room also features some noteworthy **textiles**. Hanging by the door as you go in is a fragment of painted cloth depicting three human figures with fanged jaws – this is the oldest textile in the museum, produced by the Chavín culture almost three thousand years ago, and still in astonishingly good condition.

Area Andes del Sur

Among the most striking pieces on display in the final room are the huge **ceramic urns** of the Aguada culture (600–900 AD), painted with bold geometric designs incorporating fantastic, often feline, images. Look out too for the wooden and stone **snuff trays**, carved by the San Pedro people of northern Chile between 300 and 1000 AD, and used with small tubes to inhale hallucinogenic substances. The curious thing on the wall that looks like a grass skirt is a relic from the Inca, who made it all the way down to central Chile during their expansion in the fifteenth century. Known as a **quipú**, it consists of many strands of wool attached to a single cord, and was used to keep various records by means of a complex system of knots tied in the strands.

Ahumada

The southeast corner of downtown Santiago contains one of the city's busiest pedestrian thoroughfares, **Ahumada**. Running south from the west side of the Plaza de Armas to the Alameda, the paseo is a seething mass of people at every moment of the day. Walking down, you'll pass sombre doorways leading into labyrinthine shopping arcades, *confiterías* and, between Agustinas and Moneda, the famous **Café Caribe** and **Café Haiti** (see p.80). Take a moment to pop into the **Banco de Chile**, between Huérfanos and Agustinas; its vast hall, polished counters and beautiful old clock have barely changed since the bank opened in 1925.

1

Huérfanos and around

One of the city's busiest pedestrian streets, **Huérfanos** crosses Ahumada at right angles, one block south of the plaza, and is lined with numerous banks and cinemas. Several places of interest are dotted among the shops, office blocks and *galerías* of the surrounding streets.

Museo Iglesia de la Merced

Mac Iver 341 • Museum Tues–Fri 10am–2pm & 3–6pm • CH$1000

The **Basilica de la Merced** is a towering, Neo-Renaissance structure just off Huérfanos, on the corner of Merced and Mac Iver, with a beautifully carved eighteenth-century pulpit. Attached to the church is a small **museum** where you'll find a collection of Easter Island artefacts, including a wooden **rongo rongo tablet**, carved in the undeciphered Easter Island script – one of just 29 left in the world.

Teatro Municipal and around

Agustinas 749 • ☎ 800 471 000, ⓦ www.unicipal.cl

From the Basilica de la Merced, head south for two blocks and turn right at Agustinas, to find the dazzling white facade of the **Teatro Municipal**, a splendid French-style Neoclassical building, all arches and columns and perfect symmetry. This has been the capital's most prestigious ballet, opera and classical music venue since its inauguration in 1857. It's worth asking to have a look around inside; the main auditorium is quite a sight, with its sumptuous red upholstery and crystal chandeliers. See p.85 for ticket information. Opposite the theatre is the **Mansión Subercaseaux**, built at the beginning of the twentieth century for one of Santiago's wealthiest families, and now occupied by a bank.

Templo de San Agustín

Agustinas and Estado

A short walk along Agustinas from the Teatro Municipal takes you to the looming green walls and yellow columns of the **Templo de San Agustín**, dating from 1608 but extensively rebuilt since then. The chief interest within its highly decorative interior is the wooden carving of Christ, just left of the main altar as you face it (see box, below).

Palacio de la Moneda

Plaza de la Ciudadanía 26 • Inner courtyards Mon–Fri 10am–6pm; changing of the guard 10am on alternate days • Free, but bring your passport for identification

The best approach to the **Palacio de la Moneda** is from the northern side of the vast, paved Plaza de la Constitución, three blocks west and south of the Plaza de Armas. From here you can appreciate the perfect symmetry and compact elegance of this low-lying Neoclassical building, spread across the entire block. The inner courtyards are open to the public.

It was built between 1784 and 1805 by the celebrated Italian architect Joaquín Toesca for the purpose of housing the royal mint. After some forty years it became the residential palace for the presidents of Chile, starting with Manuel Bulnes in 1848 and

---

THE LEGEND OF THE SLIPPING CROWN

Known as the *Cristo de Mayo*, the wooden carving of Christ in the Templo de San Augustín (see above) is the subject of an intriguing local legend. The story goes that the crown of thorns around the figure's head slipped down to its neck during the 1647 earthquake, and that when someone tried to move the crown back up to its head, the carved face of Christ began to bleed. For this reason, the crown has remained untouched ever since, still hanging around the neck.

1

ending with Carlos Ibáñez del Campo in 1958. At this point it stopped being used as the president's home, but it continues to be the official seat of government. One ceremony worth watching is the **changing of the guard**. In front of the Justice Ministry is one of Chile's few monuments to President Salvador Allende, with his arm outstretched.

Centro Cultural Palacio La Moneda

Plaza de la Ciudadania 26 • Daily 9am–9pm, exhibitions 9am–7.30pm • CH$1000, free Mon–Fri before noon • ☎ 2 355 6500, ⓦ ccplm.cl

The **Centro Cultural Palacio La Moneda**, on the Alameda side of the Palacio de la Moneda, opened in 2006 as an early part of Chile's 2010 bicentennial celebrations. This flagship underground art gallery and cultural space has a vast modernist concrete central hall, which houses ever-changing exhibitions. The permanent displays in the adjacent galleries feature an eclectic array of artwork, jewellery, pottery, textiles and photography from across Chile (none of the exhibits are signed in English). There's also an art cinema, film archive, craft store, bookshop, *Confiteria Torres* branch (see p.80), restaurant and café.

Along the Alameda

Officially the Avenida del Libertador General Bernardo O'Higgins, Santiago's most vital east–west artery is universally known as the **Alameda**, a poplar-lined avenue used for strolling and recreation, and found in many Latin American cities. This one began life as *La Cañada* (or "channel"), when a branch of the Mapocho was sealed off shortly before independence, and a roadway was created over the old riverbed. A few years later, when the Supreme Director Bernardo O'Higgins decided that Santiago required an alameda, La Cañada was deemed the best place to put it: "There is no public boulevard where people may get together for honest relief and amusement during the resting hours, since the one known as Tajamar, because of its narrowness and irregularity, far from being cheerful, inspires sadness. La Cañada, because of its condition, extension, abundance of water and other circumstances, is the most apparent place for an alameda." Three rows of poplars were promptly planted along each side, and the Alameda was born, soon to become *the* place to take the evening promenade.

Since those quieter times the boulevard has evolved into the city's biggest, busiest, noisiest and most polluted thoroughfare. Still, it's an unavoidable axis and you'll probably spend a fair bit of time on it or under it: the main metro line runs beneath it, and some of Santiago's most interesting landmarks stand along it.

Cerro Santa Lucía and around

The lushly forested **Cerro Santa Lucía** is Santiago's most imaginative and exuberant piece of landscaping. Looking at it now, it's hard to believe that for the first three centuries of the city's development this was nothing more than a barren, rocky outcrop, completely ignored despite its historical importance – it was at the foot of this hill that Santiago was officially founded by Valdivia, on February 12, 1541. It wasn't until 1872 that the city turned its attention to Santa Lucía once more, when the mayor of Santiago, Vicuña Mackenna, enlisted the labour of 150 prisoners to transform it into a grand public park.

Quasi-Gaudíesque in appearance, with swirling pathways and Baroque terraces and turrets, this is a great place to come for panoramic views across the city. If slogging up the steps doesn't appeal, use the free lift on the western side of the park, by the junction with Huérfanos. While it's always busy and safe by day, muggings have been reported in the Cerro Santa Lucía after dark.

Immediately west of the hill stands the massive **Biblioteca Nacional**, one of Latin America's largest libraries.

Barrio Lastarria

Ⓦ barriolastarria.com

Just east of Cerro Santa Lucía, set back from the Alameda, is the quiet, arty **Barrio Lastarria** neighbourhood centred on **Plaza Mulato Gil**, at the corner of Merced and Lastarria. This small cobbled square is enclosed by old buildings housing artists' workshops, galleries, an antiquarian bookshop, a bar-restaurant and the Museo de Artes Visuales (see p.67). The rest of the neighbourhood is well known for its sparkling restaurant scene (see p.80).

Museo de Artes Visuales

Jose Victorino Lastarria 307 • Tues–Sun 10.30am–6.30pm • CH$1000 • ☎ 2 638 3502, Ⓦ mavi.cl

The **Museo de Artes Visuales** features some of the best new sculptures, painting and photography by Chile's emerging artists. It also houses the small but well-stocked **Museo Arqueológico de Santiago** (same hours and entry fee), with hats, bags, jewellery, baskets and other items from all over the country.

Iglesia San Francisco

Av O'Higgins 834 • Mon–Sat 11am–6pm, Sun 10am–1pm • Free

Looking west from the Biblioteca Nacional, you can't miss the **Iglesia San Francisco**, with its towering red walls jutting out into the street. This is Santiago's oldest building, erected between 1586 and 1628. Take a look inside at the **Virgen del Socorro**, a small polychrome carving (rather lost in the vast main altar) brought to Chile on the saddle of Pedro de Valdivia in 1540 and credited with guiding him on his way, as well as fending off Indian attackers by throwing sand in their eyes. For all its age and beauty, the most remarkable feature of this church is its deep, hushed silence; you're just metres from the din of the Alameda but the traffic seems a million miles away.

Museo Colonial

Londres 4 • Tues–Sat 10am–1pm & 3–6pm, Sun 10am–2pm • CH$1000

The monastery adjacent to the Iglesia San Francisco houses the **Museo Colonial**, which has a highly evocative collection of paintings, sculpture, furniture, keys and other objects dating from the colonial period, most of it religious and a good deal of it created in Peru, the seat of colonial government. Note the immense eighteenth-century **cedar door** of the first room you come to off the cloisters; carved into hundreds of intricately designed squares, this is one of the museum's most beautiful possessions. Inside the room, you'll find another arresting sight: a gigantic painting of the **genealogical tree of the Franciscan Order** consisting of 644 miniature portraits.

Barrio París-Londres

Turn left out of the Museo Colonial and you'll find yourself on Calle Londres, which intersects Calle París to form **Barrio París-Londres**, tucked behind the Iglesia San Francisco on what used to be the monastery's orchards. These sinuous, cobbled streets lined with refurbished mansions, stylish hotels and busy hostels, look like a tiny piece of Paris's Latin Quarter. Created in 1923 by a team of architects, the barrio is undeniably attractive but feels incongruous to its surroundings. There is, however, a dark side to the area, at Londres 38.

Londres 38

Londres 38 • Mon–Fri 10am–1pm & 3–6pm, Sat 10am–2pm • Free • Guided tours Mon–Fri noon & 4pm, Sat noon • ☎ 2 325 0374 • Ⓦ londres38.cl

The seemingly innocuous building at Calle Londres 38 was one of the four main torture and detention centres in Santiago during the Pinochet dictatorship – and the only one not subsequently destroyed. Between September 1973 and September 1974,

1

96 people – considered opponents of the dictatorship – were killed here by the Dirección de Inteligencia Nacional (DINA). After a long battle by survivors, victims' families and human rights groups, the building was taken over and opened to the public in an effort to highlight the grave human rights abuses of the Pinochet years and the ongoing fight for justice. As well as displays on the building's history, Londres 38 also serves as a space for exhibitions, workshops and talks.

Universidad de Chile and around

West of Barrio París-Londres, on the Alameda, is the **Universidad de Chile**, a fine French Neoclassical building dating from 1863. Opposite is the **Bolsa de Comercio**, Santiago's stock exchange, housed in a flamboyant, French Renaissance-style building that tapers to a thin wedge at the main entrance. One block further along you reach Plaza Bulnes, flanked by the **tomb** and massive **equestrian statue of Bernardo O'Higgins** to the south (often chained off to keep the public away), and to the north by the grey stone outline of the **Palacio de la Moneda** (see p.64), sitting with its back to the Alameda. Just west of here is a 128m telecommunications tower, known as the **Torre Entel**, the focus of New Year's Eve fireworks displays.

South of the Alameda: Palacio Cousiño

Dieciocho 438 • Mon–Fri 9.30am–1.30pm & 2.30–5pm, Sat & Sun 9.30am–1.30pm; obligatory 45min tour included in price • CH$2100

The **Palacio Cousiño** remains the most magnificent of the historic palaces, the one that dazzled Santiago's high society by the sheer scale of its luxury and opulence. It was built between 1870 and 1878 for Doña Isidora Goyenechea, the widow of Luis Cousiño, who had amassed a fortune with his coal and silver mines. All the furnishings and decoration were shipped over from Europe, especially France, and top European craftsmen were brought here to work on the house. The first floor was burnt to ashes in 1968, but the ground floor remains totally intact, and provides a wonderful close-up view of late-nineteenth-century craftsmanship at its best: Italian hand-painted tiles; Bohemian crystal chandeliers; mahogany, walnut and ebony parquet floors; a mosaic marble staircase; and French brocade and silk furnishings are just a few of the splendours of the palace. Visitors must take the 30–45-minute guided **tour** (included in the entry fee), available in Spanish or English.

PALACIOS OF THE ALAMEDA

Walk west of Torre Entel along the Alameda and you enter what was once the preserve of Santiago's moneyed elite, with several glorious mansions built around 1900 serving as reminders. The first to look out for is the French-style **Palacio Irarrázaval**, on the south side of the Alameda between San Ignacio and Dieciocho; built in 1906 by Cruz Montt, it now houses an old-fashioned restaurant. Adjoining it at the corner of Dieciocho, the slightly later and more ornate **Edificio Iñíguez**, by the same architect in league with Larraín Bravo, houses *Confitería Torres* (see p.80), said to be where the "national" sandwich, the Barros Luco, was invented in honour of a leading politician.

Then check out the 1917 **Palacio Ariztía**, headquarters in Santiago for the nation's deputies, a little further on in the next block; a fine copy of an Art Nouveau French mansion, again by Cruz Montt, it is set off by an iron-and-glass door canopy. Next door, the late-nineteenth-century **Palacio Errázuriz**, the oldest and finest of these Alameda mansions, is now the Brazilian Embassy. Built for Maximiano Errázuriz, mining mogul and leading socialite, it is a soberly elegant two-storey building in a Neoclassical style – the architect was Italian Eusebio Chelli. You're now standing opposite the triumphant **Monumento a los Héroes de la Concepción**, an imposing statue which borders the junction of the Alameda with the Avenida Norte Sur (the Panamericana); this is where metro Lines #1 and #2 intersect at Los Héroes station.

Parque Bernardo O'Higgins

Three blocks from Parque O'Higgins metro

Perhaps the best reason to come to **Parque Bernardo O'Higgins**, a few blocks southwest of Palacio Cousiño, is to soak up the Chilean family atmosphere, as it's one of the most popular green spaces in the city. It was originally the Parque Cousiño, commissioned by Luis Cousiño, the entrepreneurial millionaire, in 1869, and the place to take your carriage rides in the late nineteenth century. These days working-class families and groups of kids flock here on summer weekends to enjoy the picnic areas, outdoor pools (very crowded), roller rink, basketball court and gut-churning rides of **Fantasilandia**, an outdoor amusement park (ⓦwww.fantaslandia.cl), and **El Pueblito**, a collection of adobe buildings typical of the Chilean countryside and housing several cheap restaurants, some craft stalls and a handful of small museums, the best of which is the **Museo del Huaso**.

Museo del Huaso

Parque Bernardo O'Higgins • Tues–Sat 10am–5pm • Free • ⓣ 2 555 0054

The **Museo del Huaso** is dedicated to the Chilean cowboy, or horseman (see p.37), with displays of spurs, saddles, ponchos and hats, and a big photo of Pope John Paul II decked out in a poncho when he visited the museum in April 1987 (he came to offer Mass at the chapel next door).

West to Estación Central

West of Los Héroes, the Alameda continues through the once-wealthy neighbourhoods abandoned by Santiago's well-heeled a few decades ago, when the moneyed classes shifted to the more fashionable east side of town. After falling into serious decline, these areas are finally coming into their own again, as a younger generation has started renovating decaying mansions, opening up trendy cafés and bookshops and injecting a new vigour into the streets.

Barrios Concha y Toro, Brasil and Yungay

One of the most beautiful neighbourhoods on the northern side of the Alameda, between Avenidas Brasil and Ricardo Cumming, is **barrio Concha y Toro**, a jumble of twisting cobbled streets leading to a tiny round plaza with a fountain in the middle. Further north you'll find **barrio Brasil**, one of the liveliest of the newly revived neighbourhoods, centred on the large, grand Plaza Brasil, full of children playing at the amusing cement sculpture playground and among the old silk-cotton and lime trees. Bordering barrio Brasil to the west and stretching over to Parque Quinta Normal, **barrio Yungay** has a growing number of bohemian restaurants and bars, many housed in attractively crumbling buildings.

Estación Central

Twelve blocks west of Plaza Brasil stands one of the Alameda's great landmarks: the stately **Estación Central**, featuring a colossal metal roof that was cast in the Schneider-Creuzot foundry in France in 1896. It's the only functioning train station left in the city, with regular services to the south.

Parque Quinta Normal

About 1km north of the Estación Central, **Parque Quinta Normal** is perhaps the most elegant and peaceful of Santiago's parks. It was created in 1830 as a place to introduce and acclimatize foreign trees and plants to the city – Chileans from the nineteenth century onwards have been very fond of filling their public squares with a variety of different trees, many of them imported. Today the park is packed with some beautifully mature examples: Babylonian willows, Monterey pine, cypress, Douglas fir and poplars, to name just a few. Additional attractions include a pond with rowing

1

boats for hire, and several **museums**. Often deserted during the week, the park is packed on summer weekends.

Museo de Historia Natural

Parque Quinta Normal • Previously Tues–Sat 10am–5.30pm, Sun 11am–5.30pm • CH$600, free on Sun • ☎ 2 680 4600, ⓦ www.dibam .cl/historia_natural/

The grand, Neoclassical building near the entrance of Parque Quinta Normal houses the **Museo de Historia Natural**. Founded in 1830 and occupying its present building since 1875, this is Latin America's oldest natural history museum and still one of the most important. It has a colossal blue whale skeleton, and an Easter Island collection that features a *moai*, an upturned topknot or hat, and the famous Santiago Staff, inscribed with the mysterious, undeciphered *rongo rongo* script (see p.444). The museum was badly damaged in the 2010 earthquake and was closed at the time of research, though there are plans to reopen it.

Museo de Ciencia y Tecnología

Parque Quinta Normal • Tues–Fri 10am–6pm, Sat & Sun 11am–6pm • CH$800 • ☎ 2 681 6022, ⓦ corpdicyt.cl

A short distance west of the natural history museum is the **Museo de Ciencia y Tecnología**. Far more modern and high-tech than the natural history museum, it's geared primarily towards kids, demonstrating the basic principles of physics with entertaining, hands-on gadgets and displays.

Museo Ferroviario

Parque Quinta Normal • Tues–Sun 10am–6pm • CH$800 • ☎ 2 681 4427, ⓦ corpdicyt.cl

Follow the road down towards the southern park gate, on Avenida Portales, and you'll reach the shiny black steam engines belonging to the outdoor **Museo Ferroviario**. The museum consists of fourteen pristine locomotives dating from 1893 to 1940, including a splendid Kitson-Meyer, manufactured in England in 1909.

Museo Artequín

Avenida Portales 3530 • Tues–Fri 9am–5pm, Sat & Sun 11am–6pm • CH$800, free Sun • ☎ 2 681 8656, ⓦ artequin.cl

The wildly colourful glass and metal building standing opposite Parque Quinta Normal's Avenida Portales entrance was originally the Chilean pavilion in the Universal Exhibition in Paris, 1889. It now contains the engaging **Museo Artequín** – short for Arte en la Quinta – which aims to bring people, especially schoolchildren, closer to art by exposing them to reproductions of the world's greatest paintings in a relaxed, less intimidating environment. They're all here, from El Greco and Delacroix through to Andy Warhol and Jackson Pollock.

Museo de la Memoria y los Derechos Humanos

Matucama 501 • Tues–Sun 10m–6pm • Free • ☎ 2 365 1165, ⓦ museodelamemoria.cl

The **Museo de la Memoria y los Derechos Humanos** (Museum of Memory and Human Rights), housed in an eye-catching glass building just outside Parque Quinta Normal, is dedicated to the victims of human rights abuses during the years of the Pinochet dictatorship, a period in which over three thousand people were killed or "disappeared", and one hundred thousand tortured or detained. A powerful combination of multimedia displays, exhibits, photos, art, poetry and literature are used to tell the story of the military coup and its enduring impact. Not to be missed.

Mercado Central

Daily 7am–5/6pm

If you follow Calle Puente north from the Plaza de Armas you'll reach the **Mercado Central**, close to the southern bank of the Río Mapocho. This huge metal structure, prefabricated in England and erected in Santiago in 1868, contains a very picturesque fruit, vegetable and fish market. The highlight is the fish stalls, packed with glistening eels, sharks and salmon, buckets of oysters, mussels and clams, and unidentifiable shells out of which live things with tentacles make occasional appearances. The best time to come here is at lunchtime, when you can feast at one of the many **fish restaurants** dotted around the market; the cheapest and most authentic are on the outer edge, while those in the centre are touristy and pricier. Keep an eye on your belongings, as pickpockets are not unknown here.

Feria Municipal La Vega

Mon–Sat 5.30am–6pm, Sun 6am–3pm

The gargantuan **Feria Municipal La Vega** is a couple of blocks back from the riverbank opposite the Mercado Central. There's no pretty architecture here, and few tourists; just serious shoppers and hundreds of stalls selling the whole gamut of Central Valley produce, from cows' innards and pigs' bellies to mountains of potatoes and onions, at a fraction of the price charged in the Mercado Central. There is also a gallery of economical **seafood restaurants**, popular with locals and rarely visited by tourists. Few have alcohol licences, but if you ask for an "iced tea" ("*te helado*") you'll be served either white wine in a Sprite bottle or red wine in a Coca-Cola bottle.

Estación Mapocho

Just west of the Mercado Central, right by the river, is the immense stone and metal **Estación Mapocho**, built in 1912 to house the terminal of the Valparaíso–Santiago railway line. With the train service long discontinued, the station is now a cultural centre, housing exhibitions, plays and throbbing concerts. Take a look inside at the great copper, glass and marble roof. One of the continent's most important book fairs is also held here during the last week of November, the **Feria Nacional del Libro**.

Parque Forestal

The **Parque Forestal**, stretching along the southern bank of the Mapocho between Puente Recoleta and Puente Pío Nono, was created at the end of the nineteenth century on land that was reclaimed from the river after it was channelled. Lined with long rows of trees and lampposts, it provides a picturesque setting for the **Palacio de Bellas Artes**, built to commemorate the centenary of Chilean independence.

Museo Nacional de Bellas Artes

Tues–Sun 10am–6.50pm • CH$600, free on Sun

The **Palacio de Bellas Artes** houses the **Museo Nacional de Bellas Artes,** featuring predominantly Chilean works from the beginning of the colonial period onwards, and the **Museo de Arte Contemporáneo**. The quality of the work is mixed, and none of the paintings equals the beauty of the building's vast white hall with its marble statues bathing in the natural light pouring in from the glass-and-iron ceiling.

Barrio Bellavista

There's no metro in Bellavista itself, but it's a short walk from Baquedano station

Originally – and sometimes still – known as *La Chimba*, which means "the other side of the river" in Quichoa (the Inca language), **Barrio Bellavista** grew first into a residential area when Santiago's population started spilling across the river in the nineteenth century. Head across the Pío Nono bridge at the eastern end of the Parque Forestal and you'll find yourself on Calle Pío Nono, Bellavista's main street. Nestling

1

between the northern bank of the Mapocho and the steep slopes of Cerro San Cristóbal, Bellavista is a warren of leafy streets and a centre for restaurants, bars and pubs. An evening handicraft market that spreads along the length of Pío Nono is held at weekends.

You might also be tempted by the dozens of lapis lazuli outlets running along Avenida Bellavista, between Puente Pío Nono and Puente del Arzobispo, though there are few bargains to be found. **Patio Bellavista**, Pío Nono 73, is a shopping and dining complex – and a popular gringo hangout.

La Chascona

Marquéz de la Plata 192 • Jan & Feb Tues–Sun 10am–7pm; March–Dec Tues–Sun 10am–6pm • Guided tour CH$2500 in Spanish, CH$3500 in English; reserve in advance • ☎ 2 737 8712, ⓦ fundacionneruda.org

Tucked away in a tiny street at the foot of Cerro San Cristóbal is **La Chascona**, the house the poet Pablo Neruda shared with his third wife, Matilde Urrutia, from 1955 until his death in 1973. It was named *La Chascona* ("tangle-haired woman") by Neruda, as a tribute to his wife's thick red hair. Today it's the headquarters of the

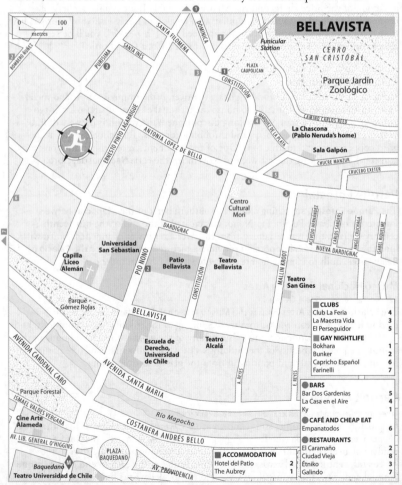

BELLAVISTA

CLUBS	
Club La Feria	4
La Maestra Vida	3
El Perseguidor	5

GAY NIGHTLIFE	
Bokhara	1
Bunker	2
Capricho Español	6
Farinelli	7

BARS	
Bar Dos Gardenias	5
La Casa en el Aire	4
Ky	1

CAFÉ AND CHEAP EAT	
Empanatodos	6

RESTAURANTS	
El Caramaño	2
Ciudad Vieja	8
Étniko	3
Galindo	7

ACCOMMODATION	
Hotel del Patio	2
The Aubrey	1

1

Fundación Neruda, which has painstakingly restored this and the poet's two other houses – La Sebastiana in Valparaíso (see p.106) and Isla Negra, about 90km down the coast (see p.111) – to their original condition, opening them to the public.

This house, split into three separate sections that climb up the hillside, is packed to the rafters with objects collected by Neruda, illuminating his loves, enthusiasms and obsessions. Beautiful African carvings jostle for space with Victorian dolls, music boxes, paperweights and coloured glasses; the floors are littered with old armchairs, stools, a rocking horse, exotic rugs and a sleeping toy lion. There are numerous references to Neruda's and Matilde's love for each other, such as the bars on the windows, in which their initials are entwined and lapped by breaking waves, and the portrait of Matilde by Diego Rivera, which has the profile of Neruda hidden in her hair. The third and highest level houses Neruda's library, containing more than nine thousand books, as well as the diploma he was given when awarded the Nobel Prize for Literature in 1971, and a replica of the medal.

Cerro San Cristóbal

Funicular Mon 1–8pm, Tues–Sun 10am–8pm • CH$1800 return

A trip to the summit of **Cerro San Cristóbal** – which includes parkland, botanical gardens, a dismal zoo and two swimming pools (see below) - is one of the city's highlights, particularly on a clear, sunny day when the views are stunning. The hill is, in fact, an Andean spur, jutting into the capital's heart and rising to a peak of 860m, a point marked by a 22m-high statue of the *Virgen de la Inmaculada*. The easiest way to get up is via the **funicular** from the station at the north end of Pío Nono in Bellavista, which takes you up to the Terraza Bellavista. From here it's a short but steep walk up to the huge white Virgin, where you'll be rewarded with fine views over Santiago's suburbs vanishing into hazy mountains. If you are fortunate enough to be in Santiago after a rain in the winter, this view includes rows of snowy mountain peaks. A new **teleférico** (cable car) system is currently under construction; when completed it will take you from close to Terraza Bellavista to other parts of the park.

Piscina Tupahue and Piscina Antilén

Mid-Nov to mid-March Tues–Sun 10am–7.30pm • CH$6000–75000 • A *colectivo* from the bottom of the hill costs CH$700–800 one-way

For an afternoon picnic and **swimming** in the summer months, there is no better place in Santiago than the two huge pools atop the Cerro San Cristóbal. The jointly run Piscina Tupahue and Piscina Antilén offer cool, clean swimming and, at 736m above the city, wonderful views.

Los barrios altos

The barrios east of the city centre spreading into the foothills of the Andes are home to Santiago's moneyed elite; the farther and higher you get, the richer the people, the bigger the houses and the higher the gates. It's hard to believe that up until the beginning of the twentieth century there was virtually no one here; it was for its isolation and tranquillity that the Sisters of Providencia chose to build their convent on what is now Avenida Providencia in 1853 (the parallel street running in the other direction, Avenida 11 de Septiembre, takes its name from the date of the 1973 military coup, not the 2001 terrorist attacks in the US). Later, following a slow trickle of eastbound movement, there was a great exodus of wealthy families from their traditional preserves west of the city over to the new barrio alto in the 1920s, where they've been entrenched ever since.

The barrio you're most likely to visit is Providencia, home to Sernatur, and various hotels, restaurants and travel agencies. Further east in Las Condes the atmosphere is

1

more residential, and apart from a few notable exceptions such as Los Dominicos market, there's less to pull you out here. If you've access to a car, however, it can be quite fun to drive around the fabulously wealthy uptown barrios of El Arrayán, La Dehesa and Vitacura (home to numerous art galleries and a fashion museum). You could even just sit on a bus to the end of Avenida Las Condes to watch the Andes get closer and closer and feel the city creep higher and higher.

Providencia

Providencia, northeast of the city centre, takes its name from its oldest building, the yellow-washed **Iglesia de Nuestra Señora de la Divina Providencia**, founded in 1853 – the interior is disappointingly dull. Opposite, occupying a former fruit and vegetable market, is **Sernatur** (see p.78), and a few blocks east of here you're into the commercial heart of the barrio, with its stylish stores and elegant cafés. Bland and faceless for some, Providencia is nonetheless convenient for its modern retail, buzzing nightlife and compact size.

Las Condes

As you head east from Providencia towards **Las Condes**, the shops and office blocks gradually thin out into a more residential district, punctuated with the occasional giant shopping mall, such as **Alto Las Condes** (see p.86). Of a quite different nature, the Pueblito de los Dominicos is well worth a visit.

Pueblito de los Dominicos

Apoquindo 9085, near Los Dominicos metro • Daily: summer 10.30am–8pm, winter 10am–7pm • ☎ 2 248 2295

The best collection of arts and crafts in Santiago is found at the **Pueblito de los Dominicos** market, a large, lively and expensive craft fair held in a mock village in Las Condes. You'll find a wide range of beautiful handicrafts, as well as antiques, books, fossil shark teeth, a decent restaurant, and a quiet respite from the noise and grime of the city.

Museo de la Moda

Avenida Vitacura 4562 • Tues–Thurs 10am–6pm, Sat & Sun 11am–7pm • CH$3500, Wed & Sun CH$1800 • ☎ 2 218 5500, Ⓦ museodelamoda.cl • Bus #112, 425, 425e, 419e or C22 from the Escuela Militar metro

The **Museo de la Moda** is an essential stop-off for fashionistas, with a collection of over ten thousand exhibits, dating from the 5th century BC to the present day. Dresses worn by Princess Diana and Marilyn Monroe, Madonna's bra from her Blond Ambition tour, and a jacket used by Arnold Schwarzenegger in Terminator, are among the items on display.

Peñalolén

On Santiago's outskirts, southwest of Las Condes, is Peñalolén. This neighbourhood was the site of Villa Grimaldi, one of the main torture and interrogation centres during the Pinochet years. The buildings have since been knocked down, and the grounds are now home to the thought-provoking **Parque por la Paz Villa Grimaldi**.

Parque por la Paz Villa Grimaldi

Av José Arrieta 8401, Peñalolén • Daily 10am–6pm • Free • ☎ 2 292 5229, Ⓦ villagrimaldi.cl • Bus #513 or #D09 from Plaza Egaña metro

From mid 1974 to mid 1978, Villa Grimaldi – a privately owned country house that was taken over by the secret police – was used for the interrogation and torture of those deemed political opponents of the Pinochet regime. Around five thousand people were detained here; at least 240 were killed. The buildings have since been knocked down, and the grounds turned into the **Parque por la Paz Villa Grimaldi** (Peace Park Villa Grimaldi), as both a memorial to the victims and to educate future generations about the dictatorship.

ARRIVAL AND DEPARTURE   SANTIAGO

Santiago is one of the easiest and least intimidating South American capitals to arrive in. Connections from the airport, bus terminals and train station to the city centre are frequent and straightforward, and while you should take normal precautions, you're unlikely to be hassled or feel threatened while you're finding your feet.

BY AIR
AEROPUERTO ARTURO MERINO BENÍTEZ
International and domestic flights arrive at Arturo Merino Benítez airport in Pudahuel (the commune the airport is sometimes named after; ☎ 2 690 1752, ⓦ aeropuertosantiago .cl), 26km northwest of Santiago. The smart international terminal has a tourist information desk, bureaus de change (rates are fairly poor) and ATMs. There are flights from here throughout Chile and South America; most are operated by LAN (central office Av Providencia 2006 ☎ 600 526 2000, ⓦ lan.com).

The cheapest way to get to the city centre is by bus, with two companies offering frequent services from just outside the arrivals gate: Centropuerto (6am–11.30pm; every 10min; CH$1400), which drops you off at Los Héroes; and Tur Bus (6am–midnight; every 30min; CH$1700), which takes you to Terminal de Buses Alameda. A couple of minibus companies, operating from the row of desks by the airport exit, offer door-to-door services from the airport to your hotel, charging around CH$4000–5000 per person. The only disadvantages are that you have to wait around until the bus is full, and you'll probably get an unwanted city tour as other passengers are dropped off before you reach your own hotel. Alongside the minibus counters there's a desk where you can book official airport taxis, which cost around CH$15,000. If you bargain with the private taxi drivers touting for business outside the exit, you can usually pay less, but taking these taxis is at your own risk.

CAR RENTAL
For car rental at the airport there's Avis (☎ 2 795 3990, ⓦ avis.com) and Rosselot (also at Bilbao 2045; ☎ 2 381 3695, ⓦ rosselot.cl). In town try Dollar, Av Kennedy 8292 (☎ 2 202 5510, ⓦ dollar.com), or Lys, Miraflores 537 (☎ 2 633 7300, ⓦlys.cl).

BY BUS
By far the greatest majority of transport services are provided by buses, run by a bewildering number of private companies. These operate out of four main terminals. While you can normally turn up and buy a ticket for travelling the same day, it's better to get it in advance, especially at weekends. For travel on the days around Christmas, New Year's Eve and Easter, you should buy your ticket at least a week ahead.

TERMINAL DE BUSES SANTIAGO
The Terminal de Buses Santiago, more often known as Terminal de Estación Central (☎ 2 376 1750, ⓦ terminaldebusessantiago.cl), just west of the Universidad de Santiago metro station, is the largest (and most chaotic) of the terminals, with more than a hundred bus companies operating out of here. Services south down the Panamericana from this terminal are provided by all the major companies, including Andimar (☎ 2 779 3810, ⓦ andimar.cl), Cóndor Bus (☎ 2 680 6900, ⓦ condorbus .cl), Inter Sur (☎ 2 779 6312, ⓦ www.busesinter.cl) and Tas Choapa (☎ 2 779 4694, ⓦ www.taschoapa.cl). Buses to the coastal resorts of the Litoral Central are run by Cóndor Bus (☎ 2 680 6900, ⓦ condorbus.cl) and Pullman Bus (☎ 2 779 2026, ⓦwww.pullman.cl), though you can also reach these destinations from the Alameda and San Borja terminals (less frequent services from the latter).
Destinations Chillán (20 daily; 5hr); Concepción (every 30min; 6hr); Curicó (every 30min; 2hr 45min); Osorno (hourly; 10hr); Puerto Montt (every 30min; 14hr); Talca (every 15min; 3hr 30min); Valdivia (hourly; 11hr).

TERMINAL DE BUSES ALAMEDA
This terminal (☎ 2 270 7500), just east of the Terminal de Buses Santiago, is used only by Tur Bus (☎ 2 270 7500, ⓦ turbus.cl) and Pullman Bus (☎ 2 560 3781, ⓦwww .pullman.cl), Chile's largest and most comprehensive bus companies.
Destinations Valparaíso (every 15min; 1hr 30min–1hr 45min); Viña del Mar (every 15min; 1hr 30min–1hr 45min).

TERMINAL SAN BORJA
San Borja (☎ 2 776 0645) is at the back of a shopping mall behind the Estación Central (from the metro, follow the signs carefully to exit at the terminal). This is the main departure point for buses to the north of Chile. There are several regional buses, as well, and some services to the coastal resorts. Bus companies going north include Elqui Bus (☎ 2 778 7045, ⓦ buselquibus.cl), Pullman Bus (☎ 2 560 3821, ⓦ pullman.cl) and Tas Choapa (☎ 2 778 6827, ⓦ taschoapa.cl). Tur Bus (☎ 2 778 7338, ⓦ turbus.cl) also runs services to the Litoral.
Destinations Antofagasta (hourly; 19hr); Arica (hourly; 30hr); Calama (hourly; 22hr); Iquique (hourly; 24hr); La Serena (hourly; 6hr 30min).

LOS HÉROES
The fourth terminal, **Los Héroes** (☎ 2 420 0099), is located on Tucapel Jiménez, just north of the Plaza de Los Héroes, near the metro stop of the same name. It hosts a mixture of northbound, southbound and international

1

buses (to destinations in Argentina) and is used by eight companies: Buses Ahumada (☎ 2 696 9798, ⓦ www .busesahumada.cl), Cruz del Sur (☎ 2 696 9324, ⓦ www .pullmansur.cl), Fenix (☎ 2 696 9321), Flota Barrios (☎ 2 696 9311), Los Héroes (☎ 2 441 0343), Libac (☎ 2 698 5974, ⓦ buseslibac.cl), Pullman del Sur (☎ 2 673 1967, ⓦ pdelsur .cl) and Tas Choapa (☎ 2 696 9326, ⓦ www.taschoapa.cl).
Destinations Bariloche (several daily; 16hr); Buenos Aires (several daily; 22hr); Mendoza (several daily; 7hr).

PAJARITOS TERMINAL
The much smaller **Pajaritos** terminal (☎ 2 250 3464), next to the metro station of the same name at General

Bonilla 5600, around 12km west of the centre, is useful for travelling to and from the airport, as it allows you to bypass the city- centre traffic.

BY TRAIN
The only train services are between Santiago and destinations in the central valley to the south, with all trains departing from the Estación Central, next to the metro stop of the same name. For train information, call ☎ 600 585 5000 or check ⓦ efe.cl.
Destinations Chillán (3 daily; 4hr 50min); Curicó (5 daily), 2hr 10min); Rancagua (5 daily; 1hr); San Fernando (5 daily; 1hr 30min–1hr 55min); Talca (5 daily; 2hr 50min).

GETTING AROUND

You'll probably spend most time in the city centre, which is entirely walkable, but for journeys further afield public transport is inexpensive, safe and abundant.

BY METRO
Santiago's spotless metro system (most lines Mon–Fri 6.30am–11pm, Sat, Sun & public holidays 8.30am–10.30pm; ⓦ www.metro.cl) is modern and efficient, though packed solid at rush hour. Many stations are decorated with huge murals, and often offer free wi-fi. Fares are the same regardless of the length of your journey, but vary according to time of day (CH$530–680). Alternatively buy a Tarjeta Bip! card (CH$1300, plus credit), a rechargeable multi-trip ticket from which each journey's fare is deducted until it runs out. It gives you slightly cheaper travel, less waiting in ticket queues and is also needed on the buses.

METRO LINES
Line #1 is the most useful, running east–west under the Alameda and Avenida Providencia. Line #2 runs north–south from Vespucio Norte down to La Cisterna, crossing Line #1 at Los Héroes. Line #4 (there's no Line #3) runs from Tobalaba to Plaza de Puente Alto, while the shorter Line #4A connects La Cisterna to Vicuña Mackenna; these two lines mainly travel through residential areas. Line #5 runs from Plaza de Maipú to Vicente Valdés.

BY BUS
Santiago has one of the highest densities of buses in the world. The buses don't take cash; instead you have to use a Tarjeta Bip! card (see p.75), which makes them considerably less convenient than the metro. Buses are useful for going east or west, along the Alameda – as a general rule, buses displaying Estación Central will take you west, while those displaying Providencia or Apoquindo are going east.

BY TAXI
Santiago has more taxis than New York, and in the centre you'll have no trouble flagging one down. Taxis are black

with yellow roofs and have a small light in the top right-hand corner of the windscreen that's lit to show the cab is available. Taxi drivers aren't tested on their knowledge of the city's streets in order to get a licence; if you're going somewhere out of the way, it's best to check where it is beforehand (there's a good A–Z in the back of the yellow pages).

FARES
Fares are relatively low and displayed on the window – usually CH$250 when the meter's started and CH$100 for every 200m; you're not expected to tip. Drivers are allowed to charge more at night, so try to verbally confirm an estimate to your location. Scams are frequent, and include drivers taking extra-long routes, and rip-offs on large bills. Be firm and pay with exact change (you supply the small bills).

BY COLECTIVO
Santiago's *colectivos* (shared taxis) look like ordinary taxis except they're black all over and cram in as many as four passengers at a time. They travel along fixed routes, mostly from the centre out to the suburbs; a sign on the roof indicates the destination. Plaza Baquedano (usually called Plaza Italia) is the starting point for many *colectivo* routes. Prices vary along the route, but *colectivos* generally cost around CH$400–500.

BY BIKE
The city authorities are expanding the network of cycle lanes in Santiago, and offer a (so far fairly limited) public bike rental scheme; La Bicicleta Verde, Loreto 6 (☎ 2 570 9338, ⓦ labicicletaverde.com), rents far better bikes (with helmets) from CH$9000 a day.

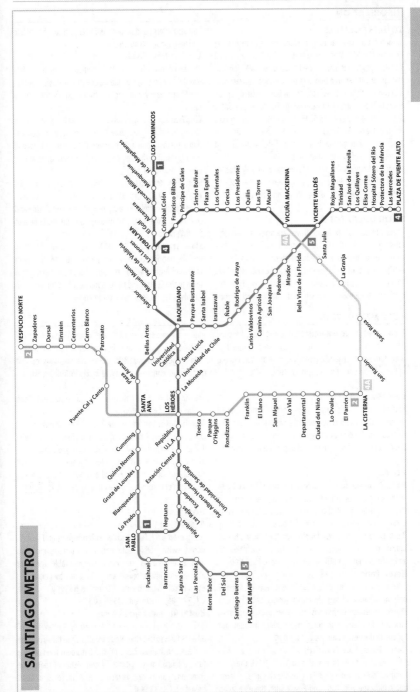

SANTIAGO METRO

1

INFORMATION

TOURIST OFFICES

Sernatur, the national tourist board, has an office at Av Providencia 1550 (Mon–Fri 9am–6pm, Sat 9am–2pm; ☎2 731 8336, ⊕sernatur.cl), as well as a much smaller kiosk at the airport. It has free booklets on Santiago's attractions, accommodation and restaurants, and staff usually speak English. The Oficina de Turismo (Mon–Fri 9am–6pm, Sat & Sun 10am–4pm; ☎2 713 6745, ⊕turismo@munistgo.cl), on the Plaza de Armas next to the Museo Histórico Nacional, is run by the Municipalidad de Santiago, and offers a range of free walking tours.

Conaf, the body responsible for Chile's national parks, has an office at Presidente Bulnes 265 (Mon–Thurs 9.30am–5.30pm, Fri 9.30am–4.30pm; ☎2 663 0125, ⊕conaf.cl).

TOUR OPERATORS

There are several excellent travel agencies in Santiago offering an electric range of tours of the city, the surrounding area, Chile and South America as a whole.

Andina del Sud Av El Golf 99, 2nd floor ☎2 484 8444, ⊕www.andinadelsud.com. This agency is good for booking inexpensive domestic and International flights, and also offers holidays and guided trips throughout Chile and neighbouring countries.

La Bicicleta Verde Loreto 6 ☎2 570 9338, ⊕labicicletaverde.com. This well-run company offers excellent cycling trips, including one that visits vineyards in the Maipo valley and another that explores the city by night.

ChipTravel Santa Maria 227, ☎2 737 5649, ⊕chiptravel.cl. Chip Travel runs interesting human-rights-themed tours that examine the enduring legacy of the 17-year Pinochet regime, as well as more general city, wine, bike and golf tours.

Santiago Adventures Guardia Vieja 255, office 406 ☎2 244 2750, ⊕santiagoadventures.com. A well-respected, comprehensive agency offering cycle, wine and city tours, skiing trips and holidays throughout Chile and South America.

Slow Travel ☎2 417 7039, ⊕slowtravel.cl. Offers flexible, personalized wine, food and nature tours in both Chile and Argentina. The culinary tour of Santiago, which takes in the Central and La Vega markets, and finishes with a cookery lesson, is highly recommended.

ACCOMMODATION

There's plenty of **accommodation** to suit most budgets, though really inexpensive places are scarce. Most of the city's low-cost rooms are small, simple and sparsely furnished, often without a window but usually fairly clean; the many hostels with dorms make a good alternative. There are numerous good mid-range hotels and B&Bs, plus several luxurious top-end options. Prices don't fluctuate much, though a few hotels charge more November–February. All prices include breakfast.

CENTRAL SANTIAGO

East of the Plaza de Armas is the tidier, better-restored section of the historic centre, with the easiest walking access to most of the central attractions. There are some good budget places and many mid- and upper-range options.

HOTELS

Hotel Montecarlo Victoria Subercaseaux 209 ☎2 633 9905, ⊕www.hotelmontecarlo.cl; map p.62. Location is the main selling point of this hotel: it overlooks Cerro Santa Lucia, the Alameda is a couple of blocks away, and lively Barrio Lastarria is just around the corner. The building has an unusual modernist shape, and the small rooms could do with a freshen-up, but overall it's a decent choice. **CH$41,000**

Hotel París París 813 ☎2 664 0921, ⊕carbott @latinmail.com; map p.62. Decent low-cost hotel offering a range of slightly musty rooms, with TVs and shared or private bathrooms; the older ones sometimes lack outside windows so unless pesos are really tight, opt for one in the newer annexe. **CH$20,000**

Hotel Plaza San Francisco Alameda 816 ☎2 639 3832, ⊕plazasanfrancisco.cl; map p.62. This is the most luxurious downtown top-end choice: the en suites are large and handsome with tubs and easy chairs; there's also an indoor pool, mini art gallery and quality restaurant. Good online deals. **CH$72,000**

Vegas Hotel Londres 49 ☎2 632 2514, ⊕hotelvegas .net; map p.62. A national monument, in the quiet París-Londres neighbourhood, the Vegas is a good mid-range choice, with spacious en suites, friendly service, and thoughtful touches like secondhand novels to read and a collection of umbrellas for use on rainy days. **CH$46,200**

HOSTELS

Andes Monjitas 506 ☎2 632 9990, ⊕andeshostel .com; map p.62. Funky hostel with tidy four- and six-bed dorms, swish marble bathrooms, a roof terrace, and a bar area featuring a big-screen TV and a pool table. There are also decent private rooms and – in a nearby building – economical apartments. Dorm **CH$8900**, double **CH$22,000**, apartment **CH$36,600**

Hostal Río Amazonas Vicuña Mackenna 47 ☎2 635 1631, ⊕hostalrioamazonas.cl; map p.62. Travellers of all ages flock to this charming hostel, next to the Argentine embassy. Each room has a private bathroom (and often a tub), colourful decor, phone, TV and plenty of space. The communal areas are attractive, and there is a good breakfast. **CH$33,000**

TOP 5 HOSTELS

Andes p.62
Happy House Hostel p.58–59
Hostel Plaza de Armas p.62
Hostal Río Amazonas p.62
El Patio Suizo p.58–59

Hostel Plaza de Armas Compañía 960, apartment 607 ☎2 671 4436, ⓦplazadearmashostel.com; map p.62. This gem, on the sixth floor of a building hidden within an alleyway filled with fast-food joints, has a prime location on the Plaza de Armas. There are bright dorms, colourful if compact private rooms, ample communal space, and a terrace with fine views. Dorm CH$7800, double CH$29,000

BARRIO BRASIL

Bohemian Barrio Brasil, to the north of the Alameda, is growing in popularity, thanks to its ever-increasing supply of cool cafés, restaurants and bars.

HOTELS

Hotel Imperio Av Lib Bernardo O'Higgins 2876 ☎2 592 6000, ⓦhotelimperio.cl; map pp.58–59. A functional, well-equipped hotel on the Alameda popular with business travellers; while the rooms are beginning to show their age, they are decorated in warm, soothing colours and remain good value. CH$30,000

Hotel Tokyo Almirante Barroso 160 ☎6 698 4500, ⓦhoteltokyo.cl; map pp.58–59. Tucked away on a little side street just west of the Panamerican highway, the *Tokyo* has simple en suites with bright colour schemes. Pieces of antique furniture and Japanese collectables decorate the place, and you can take breakfast in the flower garden. CH$27,000

HOSTELS

★ **Happy House** Moneda 1829 ☎2 688 4849, ⓦhappyhousehostel.cl; map pp.58–59. Now in a new location, Happy House is still a cut above most other hostels. This restored early twentieth-century town house has stylish six- to eight-bed dorms, beautiful, airy rooms (with shared or attached bathrooms) that put many mid-range hotels to shame as well as a bar, terrace and pool table. Dorm CH$8000, double CH$25,000

Princesa Insolente Moneda 2350 ☎2 671 6551, ⓦprincesainsolentehostel.cl; map pp.58–59. This popular and sociable hostel has clean and economical private rooms, three- to ten-bed dorms, free internet, TV lounge and patio. The cheerful staff members host regular barbecues. Dorm CH$7500, double CH$30,000

PROVIDENCIA

As the glitzy commercial heart of Santiago, Providencia has a number of pricey hotels, as well as a range of B&Bs and small mid-range hotels.

HOTELS AND B&BS

Chilhotel Cirujano Guzmán 103 ☎2 264 0643, ⓦchilhotel.cl; map pp.58–59. This small hotel, located on a quiet street in central Providencia, is a good choice. The rooms are comfortable and good value, though the decor is a bit twee; all of them come with private bathrooms, TVs and fridges; a/c costs extra. CH$39,000

Hotel Orly Pedro de Valdivia 27 ☎2 231 8947, ⓦorlyhotel.com; map pp.58–59. Welcoming and cosy, *Orly* almost seems out of place in the heart of Providencia. The immaculate en suites have wood fittings, colourful throws, mini fridges and TVs; they can range quite considerably in size, however, so ask to see a few. CH$69,000

Hotel del Patio Pio Nono 61 ☎2 732 7571, ⓦhappyhousehostel.com/hotel-del-patio-about-us -en-hdp.html; Baquedano metro; map pp.58–59. Part of the Patio Bellavista complex (see p.86), this somewhat overpriced hotel has slightly tight but attractive rooms with wooden floors, marble bathrooms, flat-screen TVs and lamps shaped like exotic fruits. Noise, however, can be an issue. CH$60,000

L'Ambassade Av Suiza 2084 ☎2 761 9711, ⓦambassade.cl; map pp.58–59. Run by a very welcoming Franco–Chilean family, this intimate and peaceful boutique B&B has tasteful en-suite doubles, an artwork-filled lounge, a small outdoor pool and a sauna. The breakfast is excellent. CH$58,000

Le Rêve Orrego Luco 23 ☎2 757 6000, ⓦlerevehotel .cl; map pp.58–59. An excellent addition to Santiago's luxury accommodation options, Le Rêve is a welcoming boutique hotel with plenty of French touches in both the architecture and the furnishings. The en suites are elegant (though a bit overpriced), and service is welcoming and efficient. CH$135,000 (US$259)

Sheraton Santiago and San Cristóbal Tower Santa María 1742 ☎2 233 5000, ⓦstarwoodhotels.com; map pp.58–59. Two hotels in one, but rooms in the *San Cristóbal Tower* are significantly better and only a little more expensive than those in the original 1970-built *Sheraton*. Tucked alongside Cerro San Cristóbal, the hotel has impressive views, spacious rooms and a huge pool. One of Santiago's more affordable top end hotels, though it's a bit removed from things. CH$98,000 (US$189)

The Aubrey Constitución 317 ☎2 940 2800, ⓦtheaubrey.com; map pp.58–59. Nestling beside Cerro San Cristóbal, with Bellavista's restaurants and bars just a stone's throw away, The Aubrey is based in two beautifully restored 1920s mansions, and boasts some of Santiago's

1

most stylish en suites: swish bathrooms, Tom Dixon lamps, and docks for MP3 players are just a few of the features. The hotel also has a pool, piano lounge and a fine restaurant. CH$125,000 (US$240)

★ **Vilafranca Petit Hotel** Pérez Valenzuela 1650 ☎ 2235 1413, ⦿ vilafranca.cl; map pp.58–59. A charming eight-room B&B in a 1940s-era home on a peaceful street: each room is unique, but all are supremely tasteful, service is personalized, black and white photos of historic Santiago cover the walls and there's a sunny patio area. CH$49,000

HOSTELS

El Patio Suizo Condell 847 ☎ 2 474 0634, ⓔ elpatiosuizo@gmail.com; map pp.58–59. Pretty Swiss-owned hostel with a dorm and a handful of modern rooms, bordering on the minimalist; the more expensive ones are en suite and have their own access to the garden. It's very popular, so make sure you book ahead. Dorm CH$10,000, double CH$24,000

LAS CONDES

Las Condes is Santiago's burgeoning luxury hotel neighbourhood. The city's two largest shopping centres and many art galleries are nearby, but you'll need to take the metro to the central attractions.

Ritz-Carlton El Alcade 15 ☎ 2 470 8500, ⦿ ritzcarlton .com; map pp.58–59. One of Santiago's top 5-stars, the Ritz-Carlton has classically styled en suites, attentive but not overbearing service, excellent restaurants and bars, and a fifteenth-floor swimming pool, gym and spa sheltered from the elements by a glass dome. CH$222,000 (US$428)

The W Isidora Goyenechea 3000 ☎ 2 770 0000, ⦿ starwoodhotels.com; map pp.58–59. In an eye-catching skyscraper, *The W* is a glamorous, achingly hip hotel. Highlights include the über-modern en suites with floor-to-ceiling windows, and the rooftop (21st-floor) pool and bar with superlative views. Service, however, can be inconsistent. CH$192,000 (US$369)

EATING AND DRINKING

Santiago has a wide range of **places to eat**, from humble *picadas* serving traditional favourites to slick modern restaurants offering cuisines such as Japanese, Southeast Asian, Spanish, Peruvian, French and Italian. Some are modestly priced but most are fairly expensive, although at lunchtime many offer a good-value fixed-price *menú del día* or *menú ejecutivo*. In most places there's no need to **book**. There are also innumerable fast food joints and (generally) unappealing *fuentes de soda*. The bar scene is fast developing, with the historic centre enjoying something of a renaissance. Barrio Brasil (and neighbouring Barrio Yungay) boasts a growing number of cool, idiosyncratic bars and there are plenty options in Bellavista, plus several bar-restaurants elsewhere in Providencia (there are also dozens of dispiriting American-style bars, particularly around the junction of Suecia and Holley, which should be avoided at all costs). Las Condes, unsurprisingly, has a few suitably expensive joints.

CAFÉS AND SNACKS

Santiago is not a café city, but a number of places cater to the great tradition of *onces* (afternoon tea). There are also some great ice-cream parlours and innumerable joints specialising in *empanadas*. An unusual (and politically incorrect) feature of the city is the tradition of **stand-up coffee bars**, known as *cafés con piernas*; they're staffed by micro-skirted or scantily dressed waitresses serving inexpensive, generally decent coffee. While mainly patronized by men, there's no taboo against women entering, and plenty of people do go just for the coffee, which is often better than anywhere else.

HISTORIC CENTRE

Café Caribe Ahumada 120 (one of several branches), ⦿ www.cafecaribe.cl; map p.62. Traditional *café con piernas* where male members of Chile's ageing business class stand around for what seems like hours, ogling the waitresses and talking on their mobile phones. Coffee from CH$1000. Mon–Fri 8am–9pm.

Café Colonia Mac Iver 161 ☎ 2 639 7256, ⦿ cafecolonia .cl; map p.62. At this cute little café, which has been going for over 50 years, matronly waitresses serve the best cakes,

tarts, *küchen* and strudel (all from CH$500 per slice) in Santiago. Mon–Fri 8am–9pm, Sat & Sun 10am–8pm.

Café Haiti Ahumada 140 (one of several branches); map p.62. Another of the timewarp *cafés con piernas*; casual, stand-up cafés serviced by tightly clad waitresses – but the coffee (from CH$1000) is not to be sniffed at. Mon–Fri 8am–9pm.

El Rápido Bandera 347 ☎ 2 672 2375; map p.62. For decades, El Rápido has lived up to its name, with a brisk turnover in excellent empanadas (from CH$850). Call out your order as you enter and by the time you reach the counter your food will be waiting for you. Mon–Fri 9am–9pm, Sat 9am–3.30pm.

BARRIO LASTARRIA

Bonbon Oriental Merced 355 ☎ 2 639 1069; map p.62. Photos of regular customers cover the walls of this tiny Middle Eastern café, which serves cardamom-scented Arabic coffee (CH$1000), falafel sandwiches and sticky-sweet baclavas; there's also a sister joint a few doors down. Daily 9am–9pm.

Café del Opera Corner of Merced and Jose Miguel de la Barra ☎ 2 664 3048, ⦿ operacatedral.cl; map p.62. This slick *heladería* (ice-cream parlour) has a great range of flavours including the wonderful *maracujá* (passion fruit), served in cones, cups or in sundaes (CH$2800-6800), as well as coffee, sandwiches and snacks. Mon–Fri 9am–9pm, Sat & Sun 10.30am–10pm.

Emporio La Rosa Merced 291, Barrio Lastarria ☎ 2 638 0502, ⓦ www.emporiolarosa.com; map p.62. This café/ *heladería*, popular with students, has delicious, inventive ice cream flavours, such as green tea with mango, and banana with palm honey (from CH$2600), as well as fine croissants and pain au chocolats. There are several other branches too. Daily noon–10pm.

BELLAVISTA

Empanatodos Pio Nono 153; map p.72. There are 33 types of *empanada* (CH$900–1100) here, from the savoury (such as chicken and mushroom) to the sweet (such as apple), which you can take away or eat on the plastic chairs and tables outside. Tues–Thurs 11.30am–1am, Fri & Sat 12.30pm–6am.

RESTAURANTS

Most of Santiago's **restaurants** are concentrated in the historic centre, Barrio Lastarria, Bellavista, Barrio Brasil, Providencia, and Las Condes. There are also some imaginative places springing up around Plaza Ñuñoa in the southeast part of town, and in pricey Vitacura. A memorable place for lunch is the Mercado Central (see p.70), whose central hall is lined with *marisquerías*. Alternatively follow the locals to the cheaper joints across the river in the Feria Municipal La Vega.

HISTORIC CENTRE

El Aji Seco San Antonio 530 ☎ 2 638 8818, ⓦ elajiseco .cl; map p.62. A hectic Peruvian joint serving sizeable portions of ceviche, fried chicken, seafood and *lomo saltado* (a heaped plate of beef, onions, tomatoes, chips and rice), which you can wash down with an Inca Cola or a Cusqueña beer. Mains CH$4300–7500, set lunch CH$4400. There are several other branches. Mon–Thurs & Sun 12.30–11pm, Fri & Sat 12.30pm–1am.

Bar Nacional Paseo Huérfanos 1151 ☎ 2 696 5986; map p.62. This unpretentious stalwart of the Santiago dining scene serves hearty Chilean staples such as *pastel de choclo* with the minimum of fuss. There's another branch at Bandera 317. Mains CH$3500–7000. Mon–Sat 8am–11pm.

Bar de la Unión Nueva York 11; map p.62. Old wooden floors, shelves of dusty wine bottles and animated, garrulous old men make this an atmospheric place to pop in for a cheap glass of wine or a leisurely meal. Mains from CH$3000. Mon–Fri 10am–10.30pm, Sat 10am–5pm.

Confitería Torres Alameda and Dieciocho ☎ 2 688 0751, ⓦ confiteriatorres.cl; map p.72. Open since 1879,

this is one of Santiago's oldest restaurants. While the food is a little overpriced (mains around CH$4000–8000), the wood-panelled walls, old mirrors and sagging chairs provide a fabulous atmosphere. There are a few other branches, including one at the Centro Cultural Palacio La Moneda. Mon–Sat 10.30am–midnight.

La Habana Vieja Tarapaca 755 ☎ 2 638 5284; map pp.58–59. Large hall containing a restaurant, dance floor and a stage, best at the weekend when there's live salsa, son and bolero. The menu includes Cuban staples (CH$4000–7000) like cassava, yellow rice and black beans, and fried plantains. Mon 12.30–4pm, Tues & Wed 12.30–4pm & 7.30pm–1am, Thurs 12.20–4pm & 7.30pm–2.30am, Fri 12.30–4pm & 7.30pm–4am, Sat 7.30pm–3am.

★ **Kintaro** Monjitas 460 ⓦ kintaro.cl; map p.62. A busy – particularly at lunch time – Japanese canteen serving a delicious range of sushi, sashimi, tempura and yakisoba (mains CH$3200–8200). If you sit at the counter you can even watch the chefs at work. Mon–Fri 12.30–3pm & 7.30–11pm, Sat 7.30–11.30pm.

El Naturista Moneda 846 ☎ 2 390 5940, ⓦ elnaturista .cl; map p.62. The original pioneer of vegetarian food in Santiago, this large, inexpensive restaurant attracts a huge, frenetic crowd at lunch time. Dishes (CH$2680–3780) include *huevos rancheros*, potato and onion soufflé, and quinoa risotto. There are a couple of other branches around town. Mon–Fri 8am-9pm, Sat 9am–4pm.

BARRIO BRASIL AND ESTACIÓN CENTRAL

Interesting, off-beat cafés, restaurants and bars are springing up all the time in Barrio Brasil, with seafood a particular speciality. The area just south of Estación Central, meanwhile, has a classic Chilean eatery. Reservations are recommended for all the establishments listed below.

★ **El Hoyo** San Vicente 375, just south of Estación Central ☎ 2 689 0339, ⓦ elhoyo.cl; map pp.58–59. Travelling gastronome Anthony Bourdain said the best food he ate in Chile was at El Hoyo, and the hearty, pork-focused dishes (CH$4950–8900) don't disappoint. Specialities include *pernil* (leg of pork) and *arrollado* (rolled pork). The restaurant is also the originator of the *terremoto* (earthquake), an earth-tremblingly potent mix of young

---

> ## TOP 5 PLACES TO EAT TRADITIONAL CHILEAN FOOD
> **Bar Liguria** pp.58–59
> **El Caramaño** p.72
> **Fuente Alemana** p.62
> **Galindo** p.72
> **El Hoyo** pp.58–59

white *pipeño* wine, pisco and pineapple ice cream. Mon–Fri 11am–11pm, Sat 11am–9pm.

Ostras Azocar General Bulnes 37, Barrio Brasil ☎ 2 681 6109, ⊚ ostrasazocar.cl; map pp.58–59. This seafood restaurant has been serving king crab, lobster, squid and more since 1945. The house speciality is baked razor clams in a cheese sauce. Sadly the waiting staff can be a bit slack. Mains CH$7000–14,000. Mon–Wed 1.30–4.30pm & 7.30–11.30pm, Thurs–Sat 12.30–11.30pm, Sun 12.30–4.30pm.

★ **Las Vacas Gordas** Cienfuegos 280, Barrio Brasil ☎ 2 697 1066; map pp.58–59. This superior steakhouse has earned a well-deserved reputation for top-quality meat (from CH$6500) – try the melt-in-the-mouth *wagyu* beef or the flavoursome *entrecôte*. Service is sharp, and the large, airy dining room has a pleasantly relaxed ambience. Mon–Sat 12.30pm–12.30am, Sun 12.30–5pm.

BARRIO LASTARRIA AND AROUND

Reservations are recommended here in the evenings, as many of the restaurants have fewer than ten tables. Parking is easy, and the barrio is just a two-minute walk from the Universidad Católica metro stop. This neighbourhood generally is safe, but Cerro Santa Lucia park should be avoided at night.

Fuente Alemana Alameda 58 ☎ 2 639 3231; map p.62. This fun Santiago institution feels a bit like a Germanic take on an American-style diner. Grab a seat at the counter, order a draft beer, and watch your vast *lomito* (CH$3300), *churrasco* or other artery-clogging meal being prepared before you. There are a couple of other branches. Mon–Sat 10am–10.30pm.

Gatopardo Jose V. Lastarria 192 ☎ 2 633 6420; map p.62. Sturdy oak trunks dominate the dining room at this Mediterranean restaurant, whose CH$7000 set lunch includes a trip to the salad bar, main course, desert, pisco sour, glass of wine and a coffee. Mon–Fri 11am–midnight, Sat 7.30pm–1am.

Japón Baron Pierre de Coubertin 39 ☎ 2 222 4517; map p.62. Tucked away on a quiet side street close to the Argentine embassy is Santiago's oldest and best Japanese restaurant. The sushi, in particular, is outstanding, making full-use of Chile's wonderful range of seafood. Mains CH$3400–12,000. Mon–Sat noon–3pm & 8–11pm.

Squadritto Rosal 332 ☎ 2 632 2121, ⊚ squadrittoristorante.cl; map p.62. This long-running Italian restaurant serves superb, though rather pricey, pizzas, pastas and other traditional dishes – the risottos are a particular highlight. Staff are welcoming, though the atmosphere is somewhat formal. Mains CH$5750–9200. Mon–Sat 1–4pm & 7pm–midnight, Sun 1–4pm.

Zabo Plaza Mulato Gil de Costa, just off Lastarria ☎ 2 639 3604; map p.62. This Japanese cocktail bar is a great place for an early evening drink (happy hour Mon–Fri 5–9pm) and a

teriyaki, sushi or sashimi snack (CH$3000–6000). Sit outside in the cobbled courtyard or in the intimate bar area. Mon–Wed 9am–midnight, Thurs–Sat 9am–1am.

BELLAVISTA

Bellavista – particularly Calle Constitución, which runs parallel with the area's main drag, Pio Nono – is the epicentre of Santiago's eating-out scene, with a wide range of excellent, and often innovative, restaurants.

El Caramaño Purisima 257 ☎ 2 737 7043, ⊚ caramano .tripod.com; map p.72. Graffiti-covered walls, soft live guitar music, amiable waiters, excellent, wallet-friendly Chilean food like *pastel de choclo*, and frequently a free aperitif make this restaurant a stand-out choice. Mains CH$3000–6000. Daily 2pm–midnight.

★ **Ciudad Vieja** Constitución 92 ☎ 2 248 9412, ⊚ ciudadvieja.cl; map p.72. This cool *sanguchería* turns sandwich-making into an art form: varieties (CH$3400–4700) include teriyaki chicken, suckling pig, fried *merluza* (hake) and the *chivito*, Uruguay's take on the steak sandwich. Deliciously salty chips (French fries) come on the side, and there's an extensive range of artisanal beers too. Mon 12.30pm–midnight, Tues 12.30pm–1am, Wed 12.30pm–1.30am, Thurs 12.30pm–2am, Fri & Sat 12.30pm–2.30am.

Étniko Constitución 172, at Lopez de Bello ☎ 2 732 0119, ⊚ www.etniko.cl; map p.72. The blue neon-lit, Japanese-inspired interior attracts a cool 20s–30s crowd drawn by more than 40 types of sushi and sashimi, plus numerous other Southeast Asian dishes, and excellent ceviche. It turns into a bar-club (with a focus on house/electro) later on – try the knockout sake-based cocktails. You have to ring the doorbell to enter. Mains CH$5000–9000. Mon–Thurs 8pm–midnight, Fri & Sat 8pm–2am.

Galindo Corner of Constitución and Dardignac ☎ 2 777 0116, ⊚ galindo.cl; map p.72. Classic Bellavista hangout, busy at all hours for hearty dishes like beef casserole and *longaniza* (spicy sausage) and chips. During the summer the tables spill out onto the street. Mains CH$3000–5500. Mon–Sat 10am–2am.

★ **El Toro** Loreto 33 ☎ 2 737 5937; map p.72. An effortlessly trendy restaurant with an appealing whimsical air – pots of crayons are left on each table so that you can doodle while you wait for your food – and an array of tempting dishes such as shrimp crêpes. Mains CH$5000–9000. Mon–Sat 1–4pm & 7pm–midnight.

PROVIDENCIA AND ÑUÑOA

Conveniently located on the metro, Providencia offers many lunch and dinner options. Nearby, though less accessible, Ñuñoa has trendier eateries, often with good music thrown in.

Astrid y Gastón Antonio Bellet 201, Providencia ☎ 2 650 9125, ⊚ astridygaston.cl; map pp.58–59.

Highly regarded fusion restaurant (although some contend it's lost a little of its sparkle in recent times). The owners' Peruvian origins show through in the menu, but you can also find European and Asian influences. Dishes (CH$8000–15,000) include heart of palm *panna cotta*, duck confit with chilli and orange sauce, and chocolate soufflé. Reservations are a must. Mon–Fri 1–3pm & 8pm–midnight, Sat 8pm–midnight.

Barandiaran Manuel Montt 315, Providencia ☎2 236 6854, ⓦbarandiaran.cl; map pp.58–59. Some of the best Peruvian food in Santiago is served here: ceviche, sea bass and the more leftfield choice of Patagonian lamb in a coriander sauce are all on offer. There are also branches in Patio Bellavista and Ñuñoa. Mains CH$7000–11,000. Tues–Thurs 1–4pm & 8pm–midnight, Fri & Sat 1–4pm & 8pm–1am, Sun 1–4pm.

El Huerto Orrego Luco 54, Providencia ☎2 233 2690, ⓦelhuerto.cl; map pp.58–59. The best vegetarian restaurant in Santiago, with a mouthwatering range of inventive, seasonal dishes (CH$4900–6100); asparagus and ricotta strudel, paneer tikka masala, and vegetable quesadillas all feature on the menu. The freshly squeezed juices and artisan beers are also well worth a try. Daily noon–midnight.

Las Lanzas Humberto Trucco 25, Plaza Ñuñoa ☎2 225 5589; map pp.58–59. This traditional bar-restaurant, with tables spilling onto the pavement, is *the* classic drinking spot in Ñuñoa, with beer from CHS1000. It also offers a range of meat and fish dishes at amazingly low prices (mains CH$2400–4600). Mon–Thurs 10am–1am, Fri & Sat 10am–3am.

★ **Le Flaubert** Orrego Luco 125, Providencia ☎2 231 9424, ⓦleflaubert.cl; map pp.58–59. This exemplary Chilean–French bistro and *salon de thé* has an ever-changing menu marked up on chalkboards. Dishes (around CH$5000–7000) could include country pate, coq au vin and *tarte tatin*. There are also 30 different varieties of tea, and home-made cheeses and preserves for sale too. Set lunch CH$7200. Mon 10.30am–8pm, Tues–Fri 10.30am–11.30pm, Sat noon–11.30pm, Sun noon–8pm.

Liguria Av Providencia 1373, Providencia ☎2 235 7914, ⓦliguria.cl; map pp.58–59. Portraits, film posters, flower designs and football pennants adorn the walls of this legendary Santiago restaurant-bar, which has outdoor tables, a bar area, main dining area and several back rooms, so you can normally find a seat. Dishes include pork ribs in mustard sauce, sea bass with capers, and pot roast. There are two other branches, but this one is the best. Mains from CH$5000. Mon–Sat 2pm–2am.

Santo Remedio Roman Diaz 152, Providencia ☎2 235 0984, ⓦsantoremedio.cl; map pp.58–59. The idiosyncratic decor has a surreal edge – including high-backed wooden chairs and a zebra print sofa – and the food

is billed as "an aphrodisiacal experience", with pastas, Thai curries, steaks and seafood all featuring on the menu. It's also *the* place for a Sunday night out, as well as a good stopover for drinks any night of the week. Mains CH$6300–7900, set lunches CH$3990–5990. Mon–Fri 1–3.30pm & 6.30pm–late, Sat & Sun 8.30pm–late.

La Tecla Doctor Johow 320, south side of Plaza Ñuñoa ☎2 475 1673; map pp.58–59. A curvaceous piano keyboard design on the outside, shaded courtyard garden, some of the city's best pancakes (from CH$2500), potent cocktails and vaguely Spanish–French fare make *La Tecla* a great choice. Mon–Thurs 12.30–3.30pm & 7pm–midnight, Fri & Sat 12.30pm–2am.

LAS CONDES AND VITACURA

As you'd expect in these exclusive neighbourhoods, restaurants are often more about money than taste, but those listed below are well worth the extra outlay.

★ **Akarana** Reyes Lavalle 3310 ☎2 231 9667, ⓦwww.akaranarestaurant.cl; map pp.58–59. This hugely popular New Zealand-run restaurant offers everything from hearty lamb dishes to creations made with Chile's wealth of seafood on its menu (mains CH$4900–11,500, set weekday lunch CH$11,500), which changes with the seasons. There's live music Wed–Fri (except in the winter). Daily noon–midnight.

Cafe Melba Don Carlos 2898 ☎2 232 4546; map pp.58–59. Brunch (CH$4200–6000), complete with eggs Benedict, French toast and fine coffee, is a Sunday ritual for many expats. Under the same management as Akarana, *Melba* also offers free wi-fi and English-language message boards. Mon–Fri 7.30am–7pm, Sat & Sun 8am–3.30pm.

Coquinaria Isidora Goyenechea 3000 ☎2 245 1934, ⓦcoquinaria.cl; map pp.58–59. This British-run gourmet food store-cum-restaurant is an appealing place at any time of day. The menu features a host of breakfast, brunch, lunch and dinner options – if you're feeling decadent, try the wagyu beef burger with foie gras. Mains CH$6950–11,950. Mon–Fri 8.30am–11.30pm, Sat 9.30am–11.30pm, Sun 9.30am–9.30pm.

Nolita Isidora Goyenechea 3456 ☎2 232 6114, ⓦnolita .cl; map pp.58–59. Self-consciously aping the style of the eponymous New York district, *Nolita* produces top-quality, artfully presented Italian cuisine (mains CH$7900–14,900), with the seafood dishes, pastas and desserts all outstanding. Mon–Thurs 1–3.30pm & 8–11pm, Fri & Sat 1–3.30pm & 8pm–midnight, Sun 1–3.30pm.

Tiramisú Isidora Goyenechea 3141 ☎2 519 4900, ⓦtiramisu.cl; map pp.58–59. Long-running Italian restaurant with a vast array of salads, thin-crust pizzas (CH$3900–6950), pastas and desserts, all at – considering the location – reasonable prices. The *calzones* are particularly good. Daily 12.45–4pm & 7pm–midnight.

1

Zanzibar Monseñor Escriva de Balaguer 6400, inside the Borde del Río complex, Vitacura ☎ 2 218 0120, ⓦ zanzibar.cl; map pp.58–59. One of Santiago's most beautiful restaurants, with a host of dining rooms, including a rooftop Moroccan-style tented lounge. The global menu has an eclectic range of dishes including lamb tagine and conger eel with a black olive crust. Check out the monthly full moon parties. Mains CH$7200–13,500. Daily noon–midnight.

BARS

Santiago's bars range from dusty, mahogany-panelled corner bars full of ancient regulars to ultra-trendy spaces. They are often good places to catch up on some musical entertainment too.

HISTORIC CENTRE

Bar The Clinic Monjitas 578 ☎ 2 639 9548, ⓦ bartheclinic.cl; map p.62. Run by the people behind satirical magazine *The Clinic*, this restaurant-bar maintains an appealingly irreverent air, from the quote of the day chalked up on a blackboard outside to the regular stand-up shows (in Spanish). There are also inexpensive snacks and meals (CH$3100–3900). Mon–Sat 2pm–3am, Sun 2pm–2am.

★ **Berri** Rosal 321; map p.62. Small bar, hidden away on a side street east of Sana Lucía with an understated, bohemian feel. Friendly staff and a loyal local following give this place a great atmosphere, even during the week. Mon–Thurs 7pm–3am, Sat 7pm–4am.

Catedral Corner of Merced and Jose Miguel de la Barra ☎ 2 664 3048, ⓦ operacatedral.cl; map p.62. This second-floor bar is a swish, modern space with a roof terrace ideal for a summer evening. There's a good menu of drinks (from CH$3000), and a small selection of dishes (CH$6200–8800) such as fried *tilapia* if you get peckish. Alternatively try the attached, and very swanky, *Opera* restaurant downstairs (mains CH$9600–13,000) or the adjacent *Café de Opera* (see p.62). Mon–Thurs 12.30pm–3am, Fri & Sat 12.30pm–5am.

BELLAVISTA

Bar Dos Gardenias Antonia López de Bello 199; map p.72. A chilled-out and welcoming Cuban bar, with a faded red and yellow exterior, the obligatory Che picture, live Latin music and refreshing drinks (a mojito will set you back CH$3000). It's always lively on Fri and Sat nights and there's a sister café at no. 104. Opening hours vary.

La Casa en el Aire Antonia López de Bello 125 ☎ 2 735 6680, ⓦ lacasaenelaire.cl; map p.72. Named after Neruda's poem *Voy a hacerte una casa en el aire*, this bar-café is one of the nicest places in Bellavista to enjoy a drink and live folk music, with occasional poetry recitals thrown in. There's also a newer, much less atmospheric branch in Patio Bellavista. Daily 8pm–2/3am.

Ky Av Peru 631 ☎ 2 777 7245; map p.72. From the outside this old house appears to have been abandoned, but once inside you find a beautifully renovated "resto-bar" kitted out with an eclectic array of knick-knacks. It's great for a late-night drink or a Southeast Asian meal. Tues–Sat 8pm–2am.

NIGHTLIFE AND ENTERTAINMENT

Santiago is not a 24/7 party town, but Thursday, Friday and Saturday nights are lively, and the club scene is constantly evolving. Live music – from folk to heavy metal – is popular, and you'll find venues everywhere from the historic centre to bohemian Ñuñoa, in bars, jazz clubs and concert venues. Bellavista, in particular, has many "resto-bars" with live music, as well as a number of (generally unappealing) clubs on Pío Nono; this area can be a bit unsafe at night, so take care. Arts-wise, Chile is noted in Latin America for the quality of its **theatre**, and Santiago is the best place to see it. **Classical music** is performed in a number of venues, including theatres, cultural centres and churches. **Cinema** is very popular: most films shown are Hollywood imports, but **arts cinemas** have more varied offerings. The Friday newspapers include comprehensive entertainment listings.

CLUBS

La Batuta Jorge Washington 52, Plaza Ñuñoa ☎ 2 724 4037, ⓦ batuta.cl; map pp.58–59. There's a wonderful grungy atmosphere at this dark, packed club just off Plaza Ñuñoa, which hosts rock bands, hip hop groups and heavy metal outfits. Wed & Thurs 10pm–2am, Fri & Sat 10pm–4.30am.

Blondie Alameda 2879, north side, near ULA metro ☎ 2 681 7793, ⓦ blondie.cl; map pp.58–59. A popular student hangout with loud – and often live – music (lots of techno, dance, electro and indie), and dancing. Generally Thurs–Sat midnight–4/5am, though it sometimes hosts events on other nights too.

Club La Feria Constitución 275, Bellavista ☎ 09 9591 2775, ⓦ clublaferia.cl; map pp.58–59. The best place in Santiago for electro, Club La Feria – which has been running since 1996 – plays host to an illustrious cast of Chilean and international DJs. Wed–Sat 10pm–4/5am.

La Maestra Vida Pío Nono 380, Bellavista ☎ 2 777 5325, ⓦ maestravida.cl; map pp.58–59. One of Santiago's oldest *salsatecas* and popular with dancers of all ages, giving it a friendly vibe – there's no need to feel shy about practising your steps here. It also runs salsa classes. Tues 10pm–3.30am, Wed & Thurs 10.30pm–3.30am, Fri 10.30pm–4.30am, Sat 11.30pm–4.30am, Sun 10pm–3.30am.

LIVE MUSIC

Club de Jazz Santa Rita 1153, La Reina, around 700m east of Simón Bolívar metro ⓦ clubdejazz.cl; map pp.58–59. Founded in 1943 and still going strong, the Club de Jazz is currently based at the Centro Cultural de la Reina, after the 2010 earthquake damaged its original base. Though currently only open one night a week, there's invariably an excellent line-up of Chilean and international jazz musicians. Fri 9pm–3/4am.

El Perseguidor Antonia López de Bello 126, Bellavista ☎ 2 777 6763, ⓦ elperseguidor.cl; map p.72. Acts at *El Perseguidor* tend to play more contemporary and experimental jazz than at *Club de Jazz*; check the website to see the line-up. It's an intimate, welcoming place, and you can get a decent bite to eat too. Mon–Sat 7pm–late; live music from 10pm.

CINEMA

Most of the best cinemas are in the east of the city. **Huérfanos** is the main cinema street in the historic centre. Tickets start at around CH$3000–3500.

MAINSTREAM

Cine Hoyts Huérfanos 735, historic centre ☎ 600 500 0400, ⓦ cinehoyts.cl; map p.62. In a convenient location in the historic centre of Santiago, this cinema has six screens.

Cine Hoyts La Reina Av Ossa 655, La Reina, near Simón Bolívar metro ☎ 600 500 0400, ⓦ cinehoyts.cl; map pp.58–59. Chile's largest movie complex, with sixteen screens, including a couple reserved for non-commercial art films or recent Chilean releases. Way out in La Reina, an eastern suburb.

Cinemark Theatres Av Kennedy 9001, Mall Alto Las Condes ☎ 2 580 1420, ⓦ www.cinemark.cl; map pp.58–59. Modern multiplex offering Hollywood's latest flicks.

ARTHOUSE

AIEP Miguel Claro 177, Providencia ☎ 2 570 4000, ⓦ aiep.cl; map pp.58–59. University cinema screening off-beat European documentaries and art films.

Centro Arte Alameda Alameda 139, historic centre ☎ 2 664 8821, ⓦ www.centroartealameda; map p.62. Comfy cinema with a regularly changing and wide-ranging choice of foreign films.

Centro Cultural Matucana 100 Matucana 100, near Parque Quinta Normal ☎ 2 682 4502, ⓦ m100.cl; map pp.58–59. Runs regular film seasons, sometimes in English, plus art exhibitions and concerts.

Centro de Extensión de la Universidad Católica Alameda 390, historic centre ☎ 2 354 6516, ⓦ uc.cl /extension; map p.62. Especially good for older films, often presented as part of themed programmes. Many free showings for students with ID.

Cine Arte Normandie Tarapacá 1181, near Universidad de Chile metro ☎ 2 697 2979, ⓦ normandie.cl; map p.62. Cinema with a reputation for showing obscure contemporary European films.

THEATRE

The best time to experience Chilean theatre is in January, when Santiago hosts "*Santiago a Mil*" (ⓦ stgoamil.cl), an enormous international **festival of theatre** (plus dance and other arts). During the rest of the year, many theatres are only open Thursday to Saturday. Ticket prices are usually reasonable, from around CH$4000–5000.

Centro Cultural Mori Constitución 183, Bellavista ☎ 2 777 6246, ⓦ centromori.cl; map p.72. A cutting-edge theatre, dance and arts venue.

Sala Galpón 7 Chucre Manzur 7, Bellavista ☎ 2 735 5484; map p.72. This venue has a consistently strong line-up of edgy Chilean performances, both leading actors and up-and-comers.

Teatro Alcalá Bellavista 97, Bellavista ☎ 2 732 7161, ⓦ teatroalcala.showare.cl; map p.72. Theatre with leading actors and great performances virtually guaranteed.

Teatro Bellavista Dardignac 110, Bellavista ☎ 2 735 2395; map p.72. This long-established and reliable theatre usually stages modern foreign plays, often comedies.

Teatro San Gines Mallinkrodt 76, Bellavista ☎ 2 738 2159, ⓦ sangines.cl; map p.72. Top Chilean productions are staged here, as are fine children's shows on weekend afternoons.

Teatro de la Universidad Católica Jorge Washington 26, Ñuñoa ☎ 2 205 5652, ⓦ teuc.cl; map pp.58–59. This university-run venue offers classic shows and adaptations of international works.

CLASSICAL MUSIC, DANCE AND OPERA

In addition to the three main venues listed below, classical music concerts are also performed in many churches (often for free) and cultural centres – look under "*música selecta*" in the listings papers. Traditionally, the season lasts from March to December. Tickets start from around CH$4000–5000.

Teatro Municipal Agustinas 749, historic centre ☎ 800 471 000, ⓦ municipal.cl; map p.62. Santiago's most prestigious performing arts venue, offering a menu of classical concerts, ballet and opera in a splendid old building.

Teatro Oriente Pedro de Valdivia 99, Providencia ☎ 2 231 2173, ⓦ teatrooriente.com; map pp.58–59. Here you can enjoy classical music performed by Fundación Beethoven and visiting theatre and musical groups.

Teatro Universidad de Chile Providencia 43, Providencia ☎ 2 634 5295, ⓦ teatro.uchile.cl; map pp.58–59. Established venue for ballet and classical music, featuring national groups (principally the Orquésta Sinfónica de Chile and the Ballet Nacional Chileno) and touring artists.

1

GAY SANTIAGO

Santiago is the only city in Chile with anything resembling an organized gay community. The scene, such as it is, centres around **Bellavista**, and consists of a small collection of bars, restaurants, discos and saunas; visit ⊛ santiagogay.com for more info. Chile's Gay Pride Parade takes place in September, and there is a gay and lesbian film festival every January or February at the Centro Arte Alameda (see p.85).

Bokhara Pío Nono 430 ☏ 2 732 1050; map p.72. A legendary, multi-storey club with a mixed gay and lesbian crowd, and shows featuring drag artists and Brazilian dance troupes. The queues to get in, however, can be long. Daily 10pm–4/5am.

Bunker Bombero Nuñez 159 ☏ 2 737 1716, ⊛ bunker.cl; map.72. This refurbished theatre is one of the most popular gay clubs in Santiago, thanks mainly to its dance and techno policy. There's a cavernous back room, filled with large crowds. The same owners run the nearby Femme. Fri & Sat 11pm–4/5am.

Capricho Español Purísima 65 ☏ 2 777 7674;

map p.72. Spanish and international cuisine (mains around CH\$50000–8000) served by an all-male wait staff in an atmospheric, neo-colonial building. Try to grab the cow-print sofa on the terrace. Free passes to *Bokhara* are often handed out. Mon–Thurs 8pm–2.30am, Fri & Sat 8pm–3am.

Farinelli Bombero Nuñez 68 ☏ 2 732 8966, ⊛ farinelli .cl; map p.72. This gay version of a *café con piernas* (the waiters wear nothing but sequin waistcoats and G-strings), lays on nightly shows every evening, some of them hilarious comic drag acts requiring a decent level of Spanish to fully appreciate. Tues–Sat noon–4am.

SHOPPING AND MARKETS

Santiago is a curious place to go **shopping**. The historic centre is packed with small, old-fashioned shops and a warren of arcades (*galerías*) that seem to lurk behind every other doorway. Providencia and Las Condes, on the other hand, sport a slick array of fashionable boutiques and modern, American-style malls – better shopping, perhaps, but far less interesting.

CRAFTS, KNITWEAR AND LAPIS LAZULI

Avenida Bellavista Between Puente Pío Nono and Puente del Arzobispo, Bellavista; map p.72. A string of workshops and salesrooms selling jewellery and other objects made of lapis lazuli.

Feria Santa Lucía Opposite Cerro Santa Lucía, historic centre; map p.62. Fairly large market selling crafts, clothes and lapis lazuli. Daily 11am–9pm.

Patio Bellavista Pio Nono 73, Bellavista ☏ 2 249 8700, ⊛ patiobellavista.cl; map p.72. Pricey collection of crafts, jewellery and clothes; there are more economical stalls nearby on Pio Nono and Santa Maria. Mon–Wed & Sun 10am–2am, Thurs–Sat 10am–4am.

Pueblito de los Dominicos Apoquindo 9085, Las Condes ☏ 2 248 2295; map pp.58–59. Excellent market with over 200 stalls selling knitwear, ceramics, glass objects, books, antiques and lots more (see also p.74). Daily: summer 10.30am–8pm; winter 10am–7pm.

BOOKS, MAGAZINES AND CDS

Books Secondhand Providencia 1652, in courtyard next to Phone Box Pub, Providencia; map pp.58–59. As the name suggests, a good range of used English-language books (mainly novels) to buy or exchange. Mon–Fri 11am–2pm & 4–8pm, Sat 11am–3pm.

Feria Mix Ahumada 286, historic centre ☏ 2 592 8921 ⊛ www.feriamix.cl; map p.62. One of the best places to buy Chilean and world music. This branch also sells concert tickets. Mon–Fri 10am–9pm, Sat & Sun 10am–8pm.

Libreria Australis Providencia 1652, in courtyard next to Phone Box Pub, Providencia; map pp.58–59. A decent selection of English-language travel guides and maps. Summer Mon–Fri 10am–8pm, Sat 10.30am–3pm; winter Mon–Fri 10am–7pm, Sat 10am.30am–3pm.

Librería Inglesa Huérfanos 669, local 11, historic centre ☏ 2 632 5153, ⊛ libreriainglesa.cl; map p.62. Fairly good choice of Penguin paperbacks and other English-language books. Expensive. Mon–Fri 10am–7pm, Sat 10am–1.30pm.

SHOPPING MALLS

Alto Las Condes Av Kennedy 9001, Las Condes ☏ 2 299 6965, ⊛ cencosudshopping.cl/altolascondes; map pp.58–59. Huge, modern shopping mall with 240 shops. Connected to central Santiago by free shuttle buses (call for times). Daily 10am–10pm.

Parque Arauco Av Kennedy 5413, Las Condes ☏ 2 299 0629, ⊛ parquearauco.cl; map pp.58–59. Gets insanely busy at weekends as this is regarded as the best mall in town (it also has some unexpectedly good restaurants, plus cinemas and a theatre). Frequent shuttle buses from Estación Militar metro. Daily 11am–9pm.

FLEA MARKETS AND ANTIQUES

Antiguedades Parque Los Reyes Brasil 1157, Barrio Brasil ☏ 2 688 1348, ⊛ www .antiguedadesparquelosreyes.cl; map pp.58–59. Lots

1

of antique furniture, musical instruments, books and bric-à-brac. A wonderful place to browse. Daily 10am–mid-afternoon.

Franklin Market Near Franklin metro, south of the historic centre; map pp.58–59. Enormous and very lively market running the length of two parallel streets, Franklin and Bío Bío. There's a lot of rubbish at the bottom end, near the metro, but if you walk about five blocks up to the junction with Victor Manual, there's a great flea market, and lots of antiques stalls. Sat & Sun 9am–mid-afternoon.

FOOD AND DRINK

Don't miss the stalls at the Mercado Central and the Feria Municipal La Vega (see p.71 and 72), which are great places to explore and eat at. Coquinaria (see p.83) also has a great selection of Chilean and imported food and drink.

Confiteria Larbos Estado 26, historic centre ☎2 639 3434, ⓦlarbos.cl; map p.62. A lovely, old-fashioned shop selling fine wines, spirits (such as pisco) and fancy foodstuffs including chocolates. Mon–Sat 10am–8pm, Sun 10am–5pm.

Wain Nueva Costanera 3955, Vitacura ☎2 953 6290, ⓦwain.cl; map pp.58–59. Well-informed staff guide you through an extensive range of quality wine from across Chile; the shop also produces its own wine magazine. Mon–Sat 10am–6pm.

MOUNTAIN CLIMBING AND OUTDOOR EQUIPMENT

La Cumbre Av Apoquindo 5258, Las Condes ☎2 220 9907, ⓦlacumbreonline.cl; map pp.58–59. Run by friendly Ivo and Katja, this shop has world-class boots, eyewear and climbing accessories as well as a small library of books about exploring the Andes. Mon–Fri 11am–8pm, Sat 11am–4pm.

Tatoo Los Leones 81, Providencia ☎2 946 0008, ⓦtatoo.ws; map pp.58–59. Hiking, climbing and camping equipment at competitive prices. Mon–Fri 10.30am–8pm, Sat 10.30am–7pm.

DIRECTORY

Banks and currency exchange Most banks are open 9am–2pm only; almost all have ATMs – look for the maroon and white Redbanc sign. Many commercial establishments (particularly pharmacies) also have ATMs. The best place to change cash and travellers' cheques is the cluster of change houses on Agustinas between Ahumada and Bandera in the historic centre. Few Chilean banks are useful for changing dollars, but Citibank (many branches, including Huérfanos 770, Ahumada 40, Teatinos 180 and La Bolsa 64) charges no commission for changing US dollars into pesos.

Embassies Argentina, Miraflores 285 ☎2 633 1076; Australia, Isidora Goyenechea 3621 ☎2 550 3500; Brazil, Alonso Ovalle 1665 ☎2 698 2486; Canada, 12th floor, World Trade Centre, Nueva Tajamar 481 ☎2 652 3800; France, Condell 65 ☎2 470 8000; Germany, Agustinas 785 ☎2 463 2500; Israel, San Sebastián 2812 ☎2 750 0500; Netherlands, Apoquindo 3500 ☎2 756 9200; New Zealand, Office 703, El Golf 99 ☎2 290 9800; Peru, Av Andrés Bello 1751 ☎2 235 6451; South Africa, 16th floor, Av 11 de Septiembre 2353 ☎2 231 2862; Spain, Av Andrés Bello 1895 ☎2 235 2754; UK, Av El Bosque Norte 0125 ☎2 370 4100; US, Av Bustos 2800 ☎2 232 2600.

Emergencies Ambulance ☎131; fire department (*bomberos*) ☎132; police (*carabineros*) ☎133.

Hospitals Clínica Las Condes, Lo Fontecilla 441 ☎2 210 4000, ⓦwww.clinicalascondes.cl; Clínica Indisa, Av Santa María 1810 ☎2 362 5555, ⓦwww.indisa.cl; Clínica Las Lilas, Eliodoro Yáñez 2087 ☎2 410 6666, ⓦclinicalaslilas .cl; Clínica Santa María, Av Santa María 0410 ☎2 410 2000, ⓦwww.clinicasantamaria.cl; Clínica Universidad Católica, Lira 40 ☎2 676 7000, ⓦredsalud.cl.

Internet Most hostels and hotels provide computers with internet access and (generally free) wi-fi; the latter you can also access inside many metro stations. There are innumerable internet cafés throughout the city.

Language courses BridgeChile, Los Leones 439 ☎2 233 4356, ⓦbridgechile.com; Centro Chileno Canadiense, Office 601, Luis Thayer Ojeda 191 ☎2 334 1090, ⓦcanadiense.cl; Instituto Chileno Británico, Miraflores 123 ☎2 413 2000, ⓦwww.britanico.cl; and Instituto Chileno Norteamericano, Moneda 1467 ☎2 677 7070, ⓦnorteamericano.cl.

Laundry Most hostels and hotels offer a laundry service, and there are also numerous laundries throughout the city. Lavandería Tarroca, Mac Iver 490, is conveniently located in the historic centre.

Maps Topographical maps on all parts of Chile are available at the Instituto Geográfico Militar, Calle Dieciocho 369, near Toesca metro (☎2 410 9463, ⓦwww.igm.cl). For tourist and walking maps, go to Sernatur (see p.78). See also "Books, magazines and CDs" section (p.86).

Newspapers There are numerous newspaper kiosks around town; those at the corner of Huérfanos and Ahumada sell a reasonable range of foreign newspapers, including *Die Welt*, the *Financial Times* and *The New York Times*, and magazines.

Pharmacies Farmacias Ahumada (☎2 222 4000, ⓦfarmaciasahumada.cl) has a number of 24hr branches, including Portugal 155, in the historic centre, and El Bosque 164, Providencia; they'll deliver for a small charge.

Post offices Correo Central, Plaza de Armas 559 (Mon–Fri 8.30am–7pm, Sat 8.30am–1pm). Other branches at Moneda 1155, near Morandé; Local 17, Exposición 57 Paseo Estación; Av 11 de Septiembre 2092.

1

Around Santiago

Santiago is close to some fine, and frequently overlooked, attractions, from national parks and thermal springs to sleepy villages and lush vineyards.

The obvious main attraction is the **Andes**, with the **Cajón del Maipo** river valley providing good access into the cordillera, leading to the small but spectacular **Monumento Nacional El Morado**. In winter, **skiing** is a terrific possibility, several excellent resorts are just a 90min drive from the capital and increasingly offer year-round activities like hiking and mountain biking. **Wineries** are another of the area's highlights, with some of Chile's oldest and most famous vineyards within easy striking distance.

Towards the coast, **Parque Nacional La Campana** offers excellent hiking, while **Pomaire**, west of the capital, is a picturesque village known for its ceramics. North of Santiago, head for the colonial town of **Los Andes**, surrounded by picturesque villages and mountain scenery.

Cajón del Maipo

The **CAJÓN DEL MAIPO** is a beautiful river valley carved out of the Andes by the Río Maipo. Served by a good paved road and punctuated by a string of hamlets offering tourist facilities, it's one of the most popular weekend escapes from the capital. The potential for outdoor adventures is enormous, with organized **hiking**, **rafting** and **mountain biking** trips all on offer.

Start at the mouth of the *cajón,* just 25km southeast of Santiago, at Las Vizcachas. Here the scenery is lush and gentle, and as you climb into the valley you'll pass vineyards, orchards, roadside stalls selling locally produced fruit, and signs advertising home-made *küchen, miel* (honey), *pan amasado* (fresh oven-baked bread) and *chicha* (cider).

Note that there are no banks or ATMs in the valley, so bring cash.

San José de Maipo

Twenty-five kilometres on from Las Vizcachas is the administrative centre of the valley, **SAN JOSÉ DE MAIPO**. It's quite attractive, with single-storey adobe houses and an old,

---

WINE TOURS NEAR SANTIAGO

Santiago is within easy reach of some of Chile's oldest **wineries**, several of which offer tours and tastings. Those by the Río Maipo, in particular, are beautifully located, with large swaths of emerald-green vines framed by the snowcapped cordillera and bright-blue skies. Harvesting takes place in March, and if you visit during then you'll see the grapes being sorted and pressed. If you want to visit a vineyard you should book at least a day beforehand. We've listed three, relatively easily reached wineries below; most are accessible by public transport. All the tours include free tastings.

Viña Concha y Toro Virginia Subercaseaux 210, Pirque ⊕ 2 476 5269, ⓦ conchaytoro.com; metro to Las Mercedes, from where it's a short taxi ride to the vineyard. This handsome vineyard was founded in 1883 by Don Melchor Concha y Toro, and in 1994 became the first-ever winery to trade on the New York Stock Exchange. It is now the largest wine producer in Latin America. Bilingual tours CH$8000. Daily 10am–5pm.

Viña Cousiño Macul 7100 Av Quilin ⊕ 2 351 4175, ⓦ cousinomacul.com; metro to Quilin station and then a taxi or walk 30min east along Avenida Quilin. The main estate and park of Chile's oldest winery (dating from 1550) make a nice quick trip from central

Santiago. Bilingual tours CH$7000. Mon–Fri 11am, noon, 3pm and 4pm, Sat 11am & noon.

Viña Undurraga Old road to Melipilla, Km 34 ⊕ 2 372 2850, ⓦ www.undurraga.cl; bus to Talagante from Terminal San Borja (every 15min; 30min), and ask to be dropped off at the vineyard. Still run by the Undurraga family, the vineyard was established in 1885, complete with mansion and park. It's now a large, modern winery, and you're likely to be shown around by someone who's directly involved in the wine-making process. Bilingual tours CH$8000. Mon–Fri 10.15am, noon, 2pm and 3.30pm, Sat & Sun 10.15am, noon & 3.30pm.

HIKING IN THE MONUMENTO NACIONAL EL MORADO

A path from the bus stop in Baños Morales crosses a bridge and leads to the Conaf hut at the entrance to **Monumento Nacional El Morado** (Oct–April daily 8.30am–6pm; CH$1700), where you should get the latest hiking and climbing information as landslides, snowmelts and the glaciers change the terrain from year to year. The park's single 8km trail follows the Río Morales through a narrow valley that ends at the glacier that feeds the river. Towering above the glacier, and visible from almost all points along the trail, is the magnificent silhouette of El Mirador del Morado (4320m) and, just behind, El Morado itself (5060m).

Apart from the first half-hour, the path is fairly level and not hard going, though you may find yourself feeling breathless as you gradually climb in altitude. About 5km beyond the Conaf hut – after roughly two to three hours of hiking – you reach a small **lake**, Laguna de Morado, where there is free camping, a toilet and water pump. Once past the lake, the path is less defined, but it's easy enough to pick your way through the stones to the black, slimy-looking **glacier** 3km beyond, at an altitude of 2500m. Don't enter the tempting ice caves – they are unstable. This is a good place for day-trekkers to turn around and head back. An alternative way to arrive is on **horseback**; Cascada de las Animas (see below) offers guided rides from CH$15,000.

colonial church. The town is also the last place along the road where you can fill up with petrol.

San Alfonso

Some 15km beyond San José is **SAN ALFONSO** (1100m altitude), a lovely place if you just want to unwind for a few hours in beautiful mountain scenery. Former nineteen-century horse ranch Cascada de las Animas (see p.90) offers **horseriding**, **kayaking** and **whitewater rafting**. You can also arrange similar trips through Altué Expediciones in Santiago (☎2 232 1103, ⓦaltue.com). There's a good ninety-minute walk from here up to the 20m **waterfall** (the "**Cascada de las Animas**") on the other side of the river; ask at the complex's reception for permission to cross the bridge.

San Gabriel and El Volcán

Moving on from San Alfonso, the scenery becomes increasingly rugged and wild as you climb higher into the Andes. By the time you reach **San Gabriel**, 50km from the start of the valley road at Las Vizcachas, the steep walls of the valley are dried-out reds and browns, and you are at 1300m. This uninteresting village marks the end of the asphalt road, which continues as a very poor dirt track for another 20km to Lo Valdés. To carry on, you have to go through a *carabineros* (police) checkpoint, so make sure you've got all your driving documents and passport with you. Unless you're in a 4WD you should expect to go *very* slowly from this point onwards. The village of **El Volcán**, at Km 56, was practically wiped out by a landslide some years ago. By now the scenery is really dramatic as you snake between 4000m mountains coloured with jagged mineral-patterns of violet, cream and blue.

Baños Morales and around

About 12km on, a short track branches left across a rudimentary bridge to **BAÑOS MORALES**, the site of an uninviting thermal pool. Despite its spectacular location, the village is a bit tacky, with lukewarm pools and a half-finished feel. It is, however, the closest base to the beautiful, jagged-peaked **Monumento Nacional El Morado** (see box, above). From here the road deteriorates into an even poorer track, but continues for another 11km to **Baños de Colina**, a series of natural thermal pools carved into the mountainside; for all their remoteness they can get horribly crowded in summer weekends, but otherwise are blissfully empty. This is also the embarkation for multi-day **horse treks** into the Andes. Up to week-long excursions often leave in packed caravans that snake into the mountains. For less arduous trips, many locals rent out horses by the hour or afternoon.

Cajón del Morado

The **CAJÓN DEL MORADO**, which runs parallel to the Río Morales, a few kilometres east of Monumento Nacional El Morado, leads to a huge glacier towering over a chocolate-coloured lake full of great chunks of ice. You can take a guided horseriding trip, or walk independently; take a good map and compass, and have a word with the Conaf ranger first, as the route isn't obvious. For information on other guided trips to the park, contact Cascada de las Animas (see below), Turismo Arpue (☎ 2 211 7165) or Manzur Expeditions (☎ 2 777 4284).

ARRIVAL AND DEPARTURE   CAJÓN DEL MAIPO

By bus Getting to Cajón del Maipo is easy from Santiago: buses to San José de Maipo (every 10–20min; 1hr 30min) run from Avenida Concha y Toro, outside Las Mercedes metro station. There are less frequent services from Santiago to Baños Morales (daily mid-Dec to Feb; weekends only March to mid-Dec; 2hr 30min) and El Volcán (several daily; 2hr). From Plaza Italia, Tursmontaña (☎ 2 850 0555) runs minivans to Baños Morales (1hr 30min; call ahead for

reservations. Shared taxis and minibuses connect San José de Maipo with San Alfonso and other places in the *cajón*.
By car For private vehicles the road from Santiago is fine until San Gabriel, where it may be filled with rocks and landslides. Weekend traffic can be horrendous, with two-to three-hour backups. To avoid the traffic, make sure you enter the *cajón* well before 10am and leave before 3pm (or, if necessary, late at night).

ACCOMMODATION AND EATING

SAN ALFONSO

★ **Cascada de las Animas** By the river ☎ 2 861 1303, ⓦ cascada.net. Set in a park, this highly recommended lodge has a wide range of accommodation including camping spots, cosy rooms in a renovated 1930s building, and lovely wooden cabins, as well as a fabulous outdoor pool, a restaurant overlooking the steep river gorge and a good **bar**. An extensive range of activities are on offer including trekking, horseriding, rafting and ziplining. Camping CH$10,000 per person, double CH$30,000, cabin CH$50,000
Residencial España By the road ☎ 2 861 1543. There are just five rooms at this simple B&B; all are clean, homely

and share bathrooms. Rates include breakfast, and there's an excellent attached restaurant that serves – among other dishes – a very tasty paella. CH$18,000

LO VALDÉS

Refugio Lo Valdés About 1km beyond the fork to Baños Morales ☎ 2 220 8525, ⓦ refugiolovaldes.com. This atmospheric Alpine-style hotel, dating back to 1932, has comfortable rooms and dorm-style accommodation in the attic, plus a restaurant-bar. Numerous activities – such as horseriding, trekking and mountain biking – are on offer too. Dorm CH$15,000, double CH$48,000

Pomaire

Some 50km southwest of Santiago, the dusty, quaint village of **POMAIRE** was one of the *pueblos de indios* created by the Spanish in the eighteenth century in an attempt to control the native population. Its inhabitants quickly developed a reputation for their **pottery** and the village consists of one long street packed with dozens of workshops selling a vast range of pots, bowls and kitchenware. Pomaire also has several good, traditional restaurants, some of them specializing in giant 1.5kg *empanadas*.

ARRIVAL AND DEPARTURE   POMAIRE

Buses Melipilla runs regular services from Terminal San Borja; ask to be set off at the side road to Pomaire (1hr–1hr

30min from Santiago). From here, it's a 30min walk into the village, or take a *colectivo* or taxi.

Los Andes and around

There's nothing wildly exciting about **LOS ANDES**, but this old colonial town, with its narrow streets and lively main square, makes a convenient base for day-trips to the ski

1

resort of Portillo (see p.92). Eighty kilometres north of Santiago, on the international road to Mendoza, Argentina, it's set in the beautiful Aconcagua valley; the first ridge rises to 3500m and then soars to 6959m Aconcagua, the highest peak outside the Himalayas, just across the border in Argentina. The surrounding region is fertile, and as you approach Los Andes from Santiago you'll pass vineyards and numerous peach and lemon orchards.

Monasterio del Espíritu Santo
Av Santa Teresa s/n • Museum Mon–Sat 9am–1pm & 3–6.30pm, Sat & Sun 10am–7pm • CH$600

You can find out more about Santa Teresa in the **Monasterio del Espíritu Santo**, a simple brick building where she lived until her death in 1920, at the age of 19. A small museum upstairs exhibits an assortment of memorabilia, including photos and clothes.

Museo Arqueológico
Av Santa Teresa s/n • Tues–Sun 10am–6.30pm • CH$600

The **Museo Arqueológico**, based in a lovely old house, has an impressive collection of

---

SKIING NEAR SANTIAGO

Santiago is close to some of the best **skiing** in South America. **Sunshine is abundant** and queues for lifts are practically nonexistent during weekdays. The season normally lasts from mid-June to early October, with snow virtually guaranteed from mid-July to the first week in September.

Sitting high in the Andes at the foot of Cerro Colorado, a 90min drive from Santiago, **Farellones** is a straggling collection of hotels and apartments, connected by roads to the resorts of El Colorado (4km north), La Parva (2km further on), and Valle Nevado (a winding 14km east). Alternatively, a 2hr drive from Santiago takes you to posh **Portillo**.

TRANSPORT AND EQUIPMENT RENTAL

The least expensive way to go skiing is to stay in Santiago and visit for the day. A number of **minibus** companies offer daily services to the resorts, including Ski Total, Apoquindo 4900 (☎ 2 246 0156, ⊛ skitotal.cl). Buses leave 8am–8.30am daily for El Colorado, La Parva (return ticket to either CH$10,000) and Valle Nevado (CH$12,000), and on Wednesdays and Saturdays to Portillo (CH$20,000); buses return from the resorts at 5pm. Ski/snowboard equipment rental starts at CH$18,000 for the full kit.

If you intend to drive up yourself, note traffic is only allowed up the road to Farellones until noon, and back down to Santiago from 2pm onwards; tire chains are often required but seldom used; they can be rented on the way up.

Each resort has its own **lift ticket** costing CH$34,000 in high season and CH$26,000 in low.

THE RESORTS

All of the resorts have ski schools, English-speaking instructors, and equipment rental outlets.

El Colorado ⊛ elcolorado.cl. Linked to Farellones by ski lift, as well as by road, El Colorado has 15 lifts and 22 runs, covering a wide range of levels. Elevations range from 2430m to 3333m. The resort's base is known as Villa El Colorado, and includes several apart-hotels, restaurants and pubs.

La Parva ⊛ laparva.cl. La Parva has moderate terrain, huge areas of backcountry skiing and a classy feel. The skiing here is excellent, with some very long intermediate cruising runs and a vertical drop of nearly 1000m. The resort has thirty pistes and fourteen lifts, but limited accommodation facilities.

Portillo ⊛ www.skiportillo.com. Just off the international road from Los Andes, 7km short of the border with Argentina, Portillo is a sophisticated place, with no condominiums and just one hotel – the restored 1940s-vintage *Hotel Portillo* (see opposite). The ski-runs are world-class, and off-piste options are endless, with elevation ranges from 2510m to 3350m. There are 12 lifts, plus extensive snow-making equipment. Portillo is avidly kid-friendly and its ski school is routinely ranked one of the world's best.

Valle Nevado ⊛ vallenevado.com. Connected to both El Colorado and La Parva by ski runs, Valle Nevado is a luxury resort with first-class hotels and some good restaurants. It has 27 runs, eight lifts and is the clear favourite for snowboarders.

pre-Columbian pottery, petroglyphs and skulls, and an astonishing mummy from the Atacama Desert, as well as more recent exhibits from the Independence period.

Cerro de la Virgen

If you're feeling energetic, climb **Cerro de la Virgen**, the hill rising behind the town. It takes about an hour to reach the top following the path from the picnic site on Independencia. The views are wonderful, especially just before sunset when the whole valley is bathed in a clear, golden light.

Santuario de Santa Teresa de los Andes

About 10km outside of Los Andes • Daily 7.30am–8pm • Free • ☎ 34 401900, ⦿ santuarioteresadelosandes.cl

The **Santuario de Santa Teresa de los Andes** is a huge, modern church built in 1987 to house the remains of **Santa Teresa**, who became Chile's first saint when she was canonized in 1993. Her shrine attracts thousands of pilgrims each year, especially on July 13, her feast day.

ACCOMMODATION

Alongside the hotels listed below, you can also rent an apartment/*condo* – this is often a more economical option, particularly if you negotiate with private owners. Cecilia Wilson Propiedades (☎ 2 342 4269, ⦿ www.ceciliawilsonpropiedades.cl) can put you in touch.

Condominio Nueva La Parva La Parva ☎ 2 964 2100, ⦿ laparva.cl. The only commercial place to stay in La Parva with a range of apartments – each featuring a kitchen – sleeping up to eight people. Note that you must book for at least a week. CH$470,000 (US$900) per person per week

Hotel Portillo Portillo ☎ 2 361 7000, ⦿ skiportillo.com. The only hotel in Portillo, perched by the shores of the Laguna del Inca, offers the hippest ski scene in South America. There are a wide range of (very expensive) accommodation options, from simple bunks in the Inca Lodge to suites with stunning views. All rates are per person and include seven nights' accommodation and full board. Inca Lodge CH$516,000 (US$990), double CH$1,750,000 (US$3350)

Hotel Posada de Farellones El Colorado ☎ 2 248 7672, ⦿ farellones.cl. The best place to stay near El Colorado, this hotel has smart en suites, a Jacuzzi and a good restaurant. Prices include half board and transport to the slopes. CH$167,000 (US$320)

Hotel Valle Nevado Valle Nevado ☎ 2 206 0027, ⦿ vallenevado.com. This hotel, renovated in 2010, has classy en suites with panoramic mountain views, a gym and spa, and the excellent La Fourchette restaurant. You have direct "ski-in, ski-out" access to the slopes, and heli-skiing is also on offer. Rates include half board. CH$260,000 (US$500)

Lodge Andes Camino La Capilla 662, Farellones ☎ 2 264 9899, ⦿ lodgeandes.cl. A sociable lodge with simple private rooms and shared bathrooms, as well as four-, six- and eight-bed dorms (including a women-only one) with bunk beds and lockers; both rooms and dorms have central heating. There is also a decent restaurant and bar, a pool table, free internet access, multilingual staff, and a lounge with a TV and a log fire. Rates include half board. Dorm CH$34000, double CH$80,000

BACKCOUNTRY SKIING

There are some great backcountry options for skiers who want to escape the resorts. **Ski Arpa**, near the city of San Esteban, a 2hr drive from Santiago, offers cat skiing (off-trail skiing accessed via a snowcat vehicle, rather than a ski lift) and snowboarding in two beautiful valleys, el Arpa and la Honda, which lie to the west of Argentina's Cerro Aconcagua, the highest mountain in the Andes. Note, that the season at Ski Arpa generally opens slightly later than the other resorts in the region, and that there is no equipment hire available. A full-day here (featuring four runs with a guide) costs CH$122,000–135,000 (US$235–260). Santiago Adventures (☎ 244 2750, ⦿ santiagoadventures.com, ⦿ santiagoadventures.com) can organize transport and accommodation nearby; the company also offers (pricey) heli skiing trips in the Tres Valles, Cajon del Maipo and Aconcagua areas.

ARRIVAL AND INFORMATION   LOS ANDES

By bus Frequent buses (1hr 20min) depart from Terminal Los Héroes in Santiago, dropping you at the bus station on Membrillar, one block east of the main square; most of them stop at the Santuario de Santa Teresa en route.

Tourist information The Oficina de Turismo (Mon–Fri 9am–2pm & 3–5pm) is next door to the Municipalidad at Esmeralda 526.

ACCOMMODATION AND EATING

Hotel Plaza Manuel Rodriguez 368 ☏34 421929, ⊚hotelplazalosandes.cl. If you want to stay the night, Hotel Plaza is a decent choice. The rooms – which have private bathrooms and TVs – are comfortable, if nothing to write home about. There's also wi-fi access and a restaurant. **CH$35,000**

Parque Nacional La Campana

Daily 9am–5.30pm • CH$1500

Set in the dry, dusty mountains of the coastal range, **PARQUE NACIONAL LA CAMPANA** is a wonderful place to go hiking and offers some of the best views in Chile. From the 1880m-high summit of Cerro La Campana you can see the Andes on one side and the Pacific Ocean on the other – in the words of Charles Darwin, who climbed the mountain in 1834, Chile is seen "as in a map". Another draw is the chance to see a

---

HIKING IN PARQUE NACIONAL LA CAMPANA

There are about a dozen very scenic **walks** in the park, most of them along good, well-maintained trails and many of them interconnected. The maps given away at the Conaf hut are very useful. If you plan to do some serious walking, try to get hold of a more detailed **map** from Sernatur before you come. If you're on a day-hike you must get back to the Conaf control before it closes (5.30pm); if you want to camp in the park, talk to the *guardaparque* when you sign in. Finally, there aren't many water sources along the trails so bring plenty with you. Also take **sunblock**; the summer sun combined with the high altitude make it easy to get burned.

SECTOR GRANIZO

The well-marked 9km **Sendero el Andinista**, up Cerro La Campana, is the most popular and rewarding trek in the park. It's quite hard going, especially the last ninety minutes, when it's more a climb than a hike, but the views from the top are breathtaking – and this is where Darwin climbed. Allow at least four and a half hours to get up and three to get down. **Sendero Los Peumos** is a pretty, 4km walk (about three hours) up to the Portezuelo Ocoa, through gentle woodland for the first half, followed by a fairly steep climb. Three paths converge at the Portezuelo; you can either go back the way you came; take the right-hand path (Sendero Portezuelo Ocoa; see p.94) down through the Cajón Grande to that sector's Conaf hut (about three hours); or follow the left-hand path (Sendero El Amasijo) through Sector Ocoa to the northernmost park entrance (another four hours; best if you're camping as there's no accommodation at the other end).

SECTOR CAJÓN GRANDE

The **Sendero Portezuelo Ocoa**, also known as **Sendero Los Robles**, is a 7km trail (about three hours) through beautiful woods with natural *miradores* giving views down to the Cuesta La Dormida. From the Portezuelo Ocoa, at the end of the path, you can link up with other paths as described above.

SECTOR OCOA

Sendero La Cascada makes a lovely day-hike through lush palm groves to a 35m-high waterfall, most impressive in early spring. The 8km path is mainly flat; allow about seven hours there and back. It has eight well-marked *estaciones* that describe local flora. **Sendero El Amasijo** is a 7km trail (3hrs) following the Estero Rabuco (a stream) through a scenic canyon before climbing steeply to the Portezuelo Ocoa. Most walkers make this a cross-park trek, continuing to Granizo or Cajón Grande (see p.95). Fast, fit walkers should be able to do it in a day, but it's more relaxing if you camp overnight.

profusion of **Chilean palms** in their natural habitat; this native tree was all but wiped out in the nineteenth century, and the Palmar de Ocoa, a grove in the northern section of the park, is one of just two remaining places in the country where you can find wild palms. You can also expect to see eagles and giant hummingbirds and, if you're lucky, mountain cats and foxes.

The park is located 110km northwest of Santiago, and about 60km east of Valparaíso. It's divided into three "sectors" – Ocoa, Granizo and Cajón Grande – each with its own entrance. **Sector Ocoa**, on the northern side of the Park, is where you'll find the palm trees – literally thousands of them. **Sector Granizo** and **Sector Cajón Grande** are both in the south of the park, close to the village of **Olmué**; this is the part to head for if you want to follow Darwin's footsteps and climb **Cerro La Campana**. While it's possible to get to Parque Nacional La Campana on a day-trip from Valparaíso, Viña or even, at a push, Santiago, you should count on spending a couple of nights here.

ARRIVAL AND DEPARTURE   PARQUE NACIONAL LA CAMPANA

SECTOR GRANIZO AND SECTOR CAJÓN GRANDE

By bus For these sectors, aim for the gateway village of Olmué: Pullman runs buses (hourly; 1hr 30min–2hr) from Santiago's San Borja and Alameda terminals; Ciferal Express runs buses (every 2hr; 1hr) from Playa Ancha in Valparaíso. From Olmué it's a further 9km to the park; regular buses (every 15min) run from the main square to Granizo; the last bus stop is a 15min walk from the Conaf hut in Sector Granizo, and a 40min walk from Sector Cajón Grande.

By car If you're coming from Santiago by car, the quickest route is via Casablanca, Villa Alemana and Limache. Don't

be tempted to take the short route from Tiltil to Olmué across the Cuesta La Dormida – this is very scenic but unsuitable unless you're in a 4WD.

SECTOR OCOA

By bus Sector Ocoa is approached on a gravel road branching south from the Panamericana about halfway between Llay-Llay and Hijuelas; coming from Llay-Llay, it's the left turn just before the bridge across the Río Aconcagua. Any northbound bus along the Panamericana will drop you at the turn-off, but from here it's a 12km hike to the park entrance, with minimal hitching opportunities.

ACCOMMODATION

A lovely village in a fertile valley, **Olmué** (w olmueturistico .cl) has a good choice of **places to stay**. It is also possible to camp in the park itself – ask at the Conaf hut at the park entrance for more information.

Centro Turístico La Campana Blanca Encalada 4651 t 33 441515, w campana.cl. The friendly La Campana has the feel of a motel: pink buildings house clean, slightly gaudy but good-value en suites with TVs, and there's a

garden, pool and a children's play area. Rates include breakfast. CH$30,000

Hostería El Copihué Portales 2203 t 33 441544, w copihue.cl. The top place in town, with comfortable en suites, a nice pool, spa, beautiful gardens full of vines and flowers, and a good restaurant. Rates include breakfast and wi-fi access is available. CH$76,000

Valparaíso, Viña and the Central Coast

98 Valparaíso

111 South of Valparaíso

113 Viña del Mar

119 North of Viña

Valparaíso, Viña and the Central Coast

2

Of Chile's 4000km-plus **coastline**, the brief central strip between Rocas de Santo Domingo and Los Vilos is the most visited and developed. Known as the Litoral Central, this 250km stretch boasts bay after bay lined with gorgeous, white-sand beaches, and a string of coastal resort towns. **Valparaíso** ("Valpo" for short) and **Viña del Mar** (or "Viña") sit next to each other near the middle of the strip. They are geographical neighbours, but poles apart in appearance and atmosphere.

Viña is Chile's largest beach resort and one of its ritziest. With its high-rises, casino, and seafront restaurants, as well as the beaches and clubs in nearby **Reñaca**, Viña typifies modern hedonism. Valparaíso, on the other hand, has far more personality, with ramshackle, colourful houses spilling chaotically down the hills to the sea (but no decent beaches). For stretches of sand, you'll need to head south or north.

Closest to Santiago, via the "Autopista del Sol" (Ruta 78), are the resorts **south of Valparaíso**, which are busier and more developed. Further south, there's an almost uninterrupted string of *cabañas*, villas and small, unappealing resorts. Even so, it's still possible to find places with charm and soul, especially where Pablo Neruda found them, at **Isla Negra** – though it, too, is fast being swallowed up by development.

Heading **north of Viña** you leave most of the concrete behind at **Concón**, and from **Horcón** up, the coast begins to look more rugged and feels distinctly wild and windswept by the time you reach **Maitencillo**, where sandstone cliffs tower above a huge, white beach. The stretch from here to **Papudo** is easily the most beautiful of the region. Not even the new villas and second-home complexes that have sprung up along here have managed to spoil **Zapallar**, the most architecturally graceful of the resorts, or Papudo, a small town dramatically hemmed in by steep, green hills. Two more resorts lie further north: **Los Vilos** and **Pichidangui**.

Valparaíso

Valparaíso es un montón, un racimo de casas locas (Valparaíso is a heap, a bunch of crazy houses)
Pablo Neruda

Spread over an amphitheatre of hills encircling a wide bay, **Valparaíso** is the most intriguing and distinctive city in Chile. Its most striking feature is the array of houses – a mad, colourful tangle of them tumbling down the hills to a narrow shelf of land below. Few roads make it up these gradients and most people get up and down on the city's *ascensores* (lifts), ancient-looking funiculars that slowly haul you up to incredible viewpoints.

When to visit the central coast p.101
Valparaíso's antiquated lifts p.107
Tours of Valparaíso and other
  activities p.109

Pablo Neruda p.112
Casablanca Valley wine route p.113
Viña del Mar orientation p.114

CASA MUSEO ISLA NEGRA

Highlights

❶ Valparaíso Chile's most remarkable city sits precariously on a series of undulating hills above a huge bay, with a quirky set of antique elevators that haul you up to panoramic lookouts. **See pp98–111**

❷ Casa Museo Isla Negra Pablo Neruda set up home in the village of Isla Negra and wrote many of his Nobel Prize-winning poems while gazing out at his favourite beach. His house has since been turned into an enchanting museum. **See p.111**

❸ Viña del Mar Away from the touristy gloss, Viña del Mar has a collection of beautiful

palaces, verdant parks and gardens, and interesting museums. **See pp113–119**

❹ Zapallar Soothingly empty beaches, opulent holiday homes and excellent seafood make this eternally fashionable coastal resort one the region's gems. **See p.120**

❺ Casablanca Valley The vineyards in this area are famed for their production of quality white wines, and can be visited on a variety of tours; independently by car, or by bus. **See p.113**

HIGHLIGHTS ARE MARKED ON THE MAP ON P.100

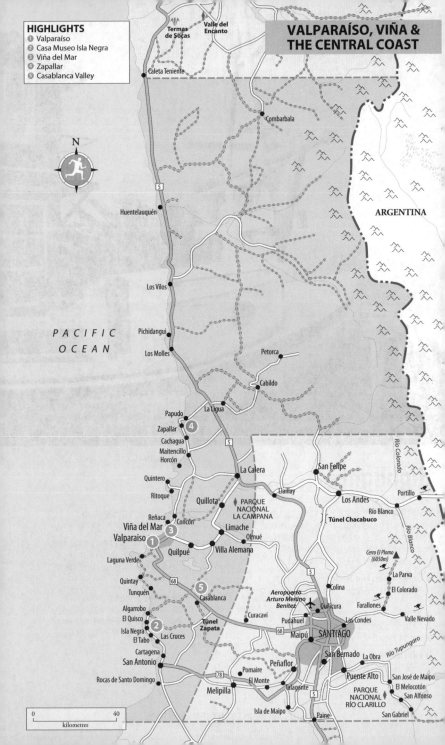

The eastern end of town near the bus station is of limited interest; instead head west to the **old town** which stretches along a narrow strip of land between Plaza Victoria and Plaza Wheelwright (also known as Plaza Aduana), at the city's historic core. The port district, with its British-style banks, atmospheric bars and old-fashioned shops, is the most idiosyncratic part of the city and should not be missed. Unfortunately you'll also have to contend with a certain amount of noise, general shabbiness and crime. However, just go up two or three **ascensores**, check out the enchanting **cerros Alegre** and **Concepción,** and sample the views by night, when the city's flickering lights are reflected in the ocean – and you're sure to fall under Valparaíso's spell.

2

Brief history

The bay was chosen as the site of the new colony's port as early as 1542, when Pedro de Valdivia decided it would "serve the trade of these lands and of Santiago". Growth was slow, however, owing to trading restrictions, but when Latin American trade was liberalized in the 1820s, after independence, Valparaíso started to come into its own. On the shipping route from Europe to America's Pacific Coast, it became the main port of call and resupply centre for ships after they crossed the Straits of Magellan. As Chile's own foreign trade expanded with the silver and copper booms of the 1830s, the port became ever more active, but it was the government's innovative creation of public warehouses where merchants could store goods at low prices that really launched Valparaíso into its economic ascent.

Progress and setbacks

Foreign businessmen, particularly British ones, flocked to the city where they ran trading empires built on copper, silver and nitrate. By the late nineteenth century they had turned Valparaíso into Chile's foremost financial and commercial centre. Even as it prospered, however, Valparaíso continued to be dogged by the kind of violent setbacks that had always punctuated its history, from looting pirates and buccaneers to earthquakes and fires. On March 31, 1866, following Chile's entanglement in a dispute between Spain and Peru, the Spanish admiralty bombarded Valparaíso, wreaking devastation. It took a long time to rebuild the city, but worse was to come. On August 16, 1906, a colossal **earthquake** practically razed the city to the ground, killing over two thousand people. The disaster took a heavy toll on Valparaíso's fortunes, which never really recovered. Eight years later, the opening of the Panama Canal signalled the city's inexorable decline.

Modern Valpo

Today, Valparaíso wears a rundown, moth-eaten air. Crime and poverty are worse than elsewhere in Chile, the sex trade is still rampant, and at night parts of the town are dangerous. That said, it's still a vital **working port**, moving thousands of containers

---

WHEN TO VISIT THE CENTRAL COAST

Most Chileans take their annual holiday in February, when all the resort towns are unbearably crowded. They also get busy on December and January weekends, but outside these times are remarkably quiet. November and March are probably the **best months** to visit, as the weather is usually agreeable and the beaches virtually deserted, especially midweek. Even in summer, however, the coast is prone to **fog** or cloudy weather, and temperatures in Valpo can be considerably lower than in Santiago.

From April to October **accommodation rates** in Viña are sometimes half of those listed on p.117, and even in November, December and March you should be able to negotiate a midweek discount; rates in Valpo are pretty stable throughout the year, save at New Year when they double or triple. Some, but not all, beaches are safe for **swimming**, though you should definitely stay out of the water if a red flag is displayed; you might also be put off by the frigid **Humboldt current**, which leaves the water chilly even in the height of summer.

annually, and has been the seat of Congress since the return to democracy in 1990. The port underwent a mini-economic boom in the early years of the new millennium, though the city's inhabitants, known as Porteños, do not seem to have benefited enormously. As the capital of Region V, it also has its share of galleries and museums, but the city's chief attractions lie in its crumbling, romantic atmosphere and stunning setting.

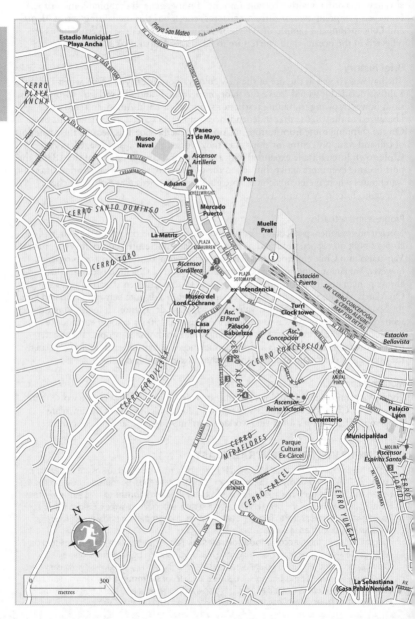

The Barrio Puerto

At the heart of Porteño history and identity, the **Barrio Puerto**, the port neighbourhood, is a good place to start exploring. However, you should keep a close eye on your belongings as pickpockets and thieves are rife during the day; at night the area is decidedly unsafe and should be avoided.

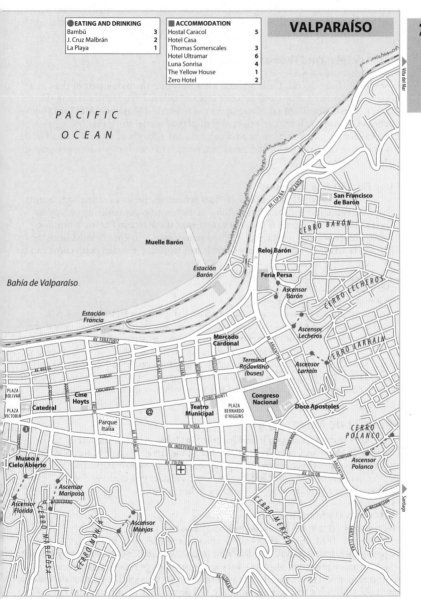

● EATING AND DRINKING	
Bambú	3
J. Cruz Malbrán	2
La Playa	1

■ ACCOMMODATION	
Hostal Caracol	5
Hotel Casa	
Thomas Somerscales	3
Hotel Ultramar	6
Luna Sonrisa	4
The Yellow House	1
Zero Hotel	2

VALPARAÍSO

2

Viña del Mar

Santiago

Plaza Sotomayor

The focal point of the Barrio Puerto is **Plaza Sotomayor**, a large public square dominated at one end by the imposing grey facade of the **ex-Intendencia de Valparaíso** (now occupied by the navy). At the other end is the triumphant **Monumento de los Héroes de Iquique**, where statues of Arturo Prat and other heroes of the War of the Pacific tower above a crypt housing their tombs (open to the public each May 21). Opposite the monument is the gateway to **Muelle Prat**, the only stretch of the port open to the public. Geared almost exclusively towards tourists, it's the embarkation point for half-hour **boat rides** around the bay (CH$2000).

Museo del Mar Lord Thomas Cochrane

Merlet 195 • Tues–Sat 10am–6pm • Free

From the ex-Intendencia, Calle Serrano leads west into the oldest part of the city, dotted with battered shops and dubious-looking sailors' bars. Halfway along the street, **Ascensor Cordillera** takes you up to the red-walled **Museo del Mar Lord Thomas Cochrane**, where you'll find an impressive display of model ships that belonged to Lord Cochrane, a British admiral who commanded a flotilla of ships on behalf of the rebels during the struggle for independence (see p.473), and stupendous **panoramic vistas** out to sea.

Plaza Echaurren and around

In the lower town, on Calle Serrano, is **Plaza Echaurren**, the city's oldest square and very picturesque save for the wine-swilling characters who permanently occupy its benches. Just off the square is the iron structure of the **Mercado Puerto**, a bustling market with numerous inexpensive seafood restaurants; it has been closed since the 2010 earthquake, but there are hopes that it will reopen. Note that petty crime can be a problem in this area.

Iglesia La Matriz and around

Santo Domingo s/n • No fixed opening times • Free

A couple of blocks east of the Mercado Puerto, the **Iglesia La Matriz** – a graceful, Neoclassical church with a seventeenth-century carving of Christ inside – sits at the foot of Cerro Santo Domingo surrounded by narrow, twisting streets full of colour, activity and a slightly menacing feel; this is a rough part of town, not to be explored alone or at night. If you continue along Serrano (which becomes Bustamante) you reach Plaza Wheelwright (also known as Plaza Aduana), flanked by the large, colonial-looking **Aduana** building, dating from 1854 and still a working customs house.

Paseo 21 de Mayo

A few steps from Aduana you'll find **Ascensor Artillería**, which takes you up to the **Paseo 21 de Mayo** on Cerro Playa Ancha. Of all the city's viewpoints, this one provides the most spectacular panorama, taking in the whole bay of Valparaíso and sweeping 20km north to the Punta de Concón; on very clear days you can even see the smokestacks at the oil refinery of Ventanas, 45km away.

Museo Naval y Marítimo

Paseo 21 de Mayo 45 • ☎ 32 243 7651, ⓦ museonaval.cl • Tues–Sun 10am–5.30pm • CH$700

The Paseo 21 de Mayo curves around the luxuriant gardens of a former naval school, an impressive whitewashed building that now houses the excellent **Museo Naval y Marítimo**. The beautifully presented displays – including paintings, photographs, weapons, uniforms, nautical instruments and personal objects – bring to life some of the central figures in Chile's history, such as Ambrosio O'Higgins, Lord Cochrane and Arturo Prat. The museum also has a display on the rescue of the 33 San José miners (see p.159).

Plaza Sotomayor and around

Valparaíso's **city centre** is formed by a narrow strip stretching from Plaza Sotomayor in the west to Plaza Victoria in the east. Almost completely devastated by the 1906 earthquake, it has evolved into a mixture of ugly, modern blocks and elegant buildings (many former banks or financial institutions) left over from the early twentieth century.

Calle Prat, which runs east from Plaza Sotomayor, has some good examples – take a look inside the **Banco Santander** opposite the Turri clock tower, originally the Banco de Londres and dripping with bronze and marble brought over from England. Next door, **Ascensor Concepción** (or Ascensor Turri) provides access to Cerro Concepción, a lovely residential area once the preserve of English businessmen. Further east, **Plaza Aníbal Pinto** is a pretty cobbled square overlooked by a couple of the city's oldest restaurants, including *El Cinzano* (see p.111).

Cerro Cárcel

From Plaza Aníbal Pinto, you can climb up Calle Cumming to **Cerro Cárcel**, where you'll find a collection of **cemeteries**; the names on the graves – Clampitt, Laussen, Van Buren, Matthews, Rivera – provide a fascinating glimpse at the diversity of the city's founders.

Parque Cultural Ex-Cárcel

Castro s/n • ⓦ excarcel.cl

Midway up Cerro Cárcel is **Parque Cultural Ex-Cárcel**, a former prison that has been transformed into a vibrant cultural hub. As well as hosting artist workshops, the complex stages a wide range of cultural events including exhibitions, concerts and theatrical performances.

Palacio Lyon

Condell 1550

Southeast from Plaza Aníbal Pinto, the main drag runs along Calle Condell, where you'll find the **Palacio Lyon**, a splendid mansion dating from 1881 (one of the few to survive the 1906 earthquake) and now housing the **Museo de Historia Natural**, which is currently closed for restoration. The **Galería Municipal de Arte**, in the cellars of the building, occasionally stages temporary art exhibitions.

Iglesia Catedral de Valparaíso

Plaza Victoria; administrative office on Chacabuco at the north side of the building • Mon–Fri 10am–1pm & 4–6.30pm; to visit, ask at the administrative office

Calle Condell ends at **Plaza Victoria**, a large tree-filled square where most of Valparaíso seems to come to chat and sit in the sunshine. It's flanked, on its eastern side, by the gothic-looking **Iglesia Catedral de Valparaíso**, whose simply decorated interior includes a delicate ivory carving of Christ and, most intriguingly, a marble urn (in the crypt) containing the heart of the famous Chilean statesman Diego Portales.

Museo a Cielo Abierto

From Plaza Victoria, calles Molina and Edwards lead up to the **Museo a Cielo Abierto**, a circuit of narrow streets and passageways painted with seventeen colourful, bold, abstract murals by students and leading local artists, the most memorable being the enormous paintings by Roberto Matta. The increased graffiti destruction of the murals is the most obvious sign, however, that it's worth keeping your wits about you.

La Sebastiana – Neruda's house

Av Ferrari 692 • Tues–Sun: March–Dec 10 10am–6pm; Jan & Feb 10.30am–6.50pm • CH$2500, including audio tour Bus "O" (officially the #612) from Av Argentina or, if you're on cerros Alegre or Concepción and don't fancy the 25min walk, Plaza San Luis at the top of Templeman; if you stay on the bus for the whole of the route you get a tour of the city.

Of the three Pablo Neruda homes open to the public – the others being La Chascona (see p.74) and Isla Negra (see p.111) – **La Sebastiana** offers the most informal look at the poet, who moved here in 1961 with Matilde Urrutia, his third wife. Perched high on the aptly named Bellavista hill, giving dramatic views over the bay, it was his *casa en el aire* (house in the air), and although he spent less time here than in his other homes, he imprinted his style and enthusiasms on every corner of the house. After the 1973 coup it was repeatedly vandalized by the military but has been meticulously restored by the Fundación Neruda, which opened it as a museum in 1992. Its narrow, sinuous passages and bright colours seem to mirror the spirit of Valparaíso, and the countless bizarre objects brought here by the poet are simply astonishing, from the embalmed Venezuelan Coro-Coro bird hanging from the ceiling of the dining room to the wooden horse in the living room, taken from a merry-go-round in Paris.

Cerros Alegre and Concepción

The hilltop residential quarter spread over **cerros Alegre** and **Concepción** is a rambling maze of steep streets and small alleys lined with elegant, brightly painted houses and aristocratic mansions clinging precipitously to the hillside. It grew up as the enclave of Valparaíso's immigrant businessmen, particularly the English, who left street names like Leighton, Templeman and Atkinson, and the Germans, whose influence can be seen in the many half-timbered, shuttered houses.

There are two points of access from the lower town; **Ascensor Concepción** (see box below), near the Turri clock tower on Calle Prat, takes you up to **Paseo Gervasoni** on

---

VALPARAÍSO'S ANTIQUATED LIFTS

Most of Valparaíso's fifteen **ascensores**, or funicular "lifts", were built between 1883 and 1916 to provide a link between the lower town and the new residential quarters spreading up the hillsides. Today only a handful of them are still operating, and appearances would suggest that they've scarcely been modernized. However, despite their rickety frames and alarming noises they've so far proved safe and reliable. What's more, nearly all drop off passengers at a panoramic viewpoint. The *ascensores* generally operate every few minutes from 7am to 11pm, and cost around CH$300 one-way. Here are a few of the best, from east to west:

Ascensor Polanco The most picturesque *ascensor*, and the only one that's totally vertical, Polanco is on Calle Simpson, off Avenida Argentina (opposite Independencia). It's approached through a cavernous, underground tunnel and rises 80m through a yellow wooden tower to a balcony that gives some of the best views in the city. A narrow bridge connects the tower to Cerro Polanco, with its flaking, pastel houses in varying states of repair.

Ascensor Concepción (also known as Ascensor Turri) Hidden in a small passage opposite the Turri clock tower, at the corner of Prat and Almirante Carreño, this was the first *ascensor* to be built, in 1883, and was originally powered by steam. It takes you up to the beautiful residential area of Cerro Concepción, well worth a visit (see p.106).

Ascensor El Peral Next door to the Tribunales de Justicio, just off Plaza Sotomayor, this *ascensor* leads to one of the most romantic corners of the city: Paseo Yugoslavo, a little esplanade looking west onto some of Valparaíso's most beautiful houses, and backed by a flamboyant mansion housing the Museo de Bellas Artes. It's worth walking from here to Ascensor Concepción.

Ascensor Artillería Always busy with tourists, but highly recommended for the stunning vistas at the top, from the Paseo 21 de Mayo. It was built in 1893 to transport cadets to and from the naval school at the top of the hill, now the site of the Museo Naval y Marítimo (see p.104).

Cerro Concepción, while **Ascensor El Peral** (see p.106), next to the Tribunales de Justicia just off Plaza Sotomayor, ascends to Cerro Alegre's **Paseo Yugoslavo**, one of the most attractive and peaceful parts of the city. A good way to explore the area is to walk between the two *ascensores*: see the map on p.107 for a suggested **walking tour**, which takes you through some narrow alleys and hidden passageways.

Museo de Bellas Artes de Valparaíso

Paseo Yugoslavo • Tues–Sun 10am–6pm • Free

Arriving at Paseo Yugoslavo you'll see an extravagant, four-storey mansion behind the esplanade. This is **Palacio Baburizza**, built in 1916 for a nitrate baron and now the home of the **Museo de Bellas Artes de Valparaíso**, a scarcely visited museum with a collection of nineteenth- and twentieth-century Chilean and European art. It's worth a look for the evocative paintings of an earlier Valparaíso by artists such as Juan Mauricio Rugendas, Alfred Helsby, Thomas Somerscales and, most notably, Juan Francisco González. The building is currently undergoing a renovation.

Casa Mirador de Lukas

Paseo Gervasoni 448 • Tues–Sun 11am–2pm & 2.45–6pm • CH$1300

The **Casa Mirador de Lukas**, located just a few steps from the Ascensor Concepción, pays homage to *El Mercurio*'s great satirist and cartoonist, known simply as Lukas, who possessed a sharp talent for capturing the spirit of his country in the hilarious drawings he produced for the newspaper between 1958 and 1988. There's also an appealing café.

CERRO ALEGRE & CERRO CONCEPCIÓN

- - - - Walking Tour

■ ACCOMMODATION		●BARS		●CAFÉS		●RESTAURANTS			
Casa Higueras	4	El Bar Inglés	2	Amor Porteño	10	Allegretto	7	Pasta e Vino	6
Casa Latina	1	El Cinzano	4	Café con Letras	8	Café Bijoux	5	Vinilo	11
Hotel Da Vinci	2	La Piedra Feliz	1	Café Turri	3	Le Filou de			
Pata Pata Hostel	3					Montpellier	9		

Paseo Atkinson

As you're walking around Cerro Concepción, don't miss **Paseo Atkinson**, an esplanade affording great panoramas and lined with pretty houses whose tiny front gardens and window boxes recall their original English owners. From here you can see the tall tower of the **Lutheran church**, a distinctive, green-walled structure built in 1897; a block or so farther away you'll find the towerless **St Paul's Anglican Church** (built in 1858) whose solemn interior contains a huge organ donated by Queen Victoria in 1903.

The Congreso Nacional

If you arrive in Valparaíso by bus the first thing that hits you as you emerge from the station is the imposing **Congreso Nacional**, described by Collier and Sater in their *History of Chile* as "half neo-Babylonian, half post-modernist atrocity". It was one of Pinochet's projects, but the dictator relinquished power before it was completed. Its working life began on March 11, 1990, when Patricio Aylwin was sworn in as president and Congress resumed its activities after a sixteen-year absence – away from the capital for the first time.

Given the inconvenience of its distance from the capital, politicians have repeatedly discussed a plan to return Congress to Santiago and convert the building into a gigantic hotel, but so far no decision has been made.

Plaza Bernardo Higgins and around

One of Chile's best **antique/flea markets** is held every Saturday and Sunday at Plaza Bernardo O'Higgins, though prices are fairly high. A short walk south of the plaza takes you to **Ascensor Polanco** (see p.106), the most fascinating of the funiculars, reached by a long underground tunnel and taking you up to a fine look-out tower. It's located on Simpson, off the southern end of Argentina.

ARRIVAL AND DEPARTURE

BY TRAIN

The Metro or Merval (🌐 www.merval.cl) departs for Viña del Mar (every 5–20min) from the centrally located Puerto and Bellavista stations. You need to buy a plastic charge card (CH$1200) first, and then top it up with credit before travelling.

BY BUS

Buses from Santiago and other major cities pull in at the Terminal Rodoviario (📞 32 939646) on the eastern end of Pedro Montt, opposite the Congreso Nacional – it's about a 20min walk west to the old town centre. There

are buses up and down the coast from here, mainly with Sol de Pacifico (📞 32 228 1026), Pullman Bus (📞 32 225 3125, 🌐 pullman.cl) and Mirasol (📞 32 223 5985). To get to Viña del Mar, pick up one of the frequent *micros* on Pedro Montt; they take about 15 min, twice that time in bad traffic; the train is more convenient. Plenty of *micros* and *colectivos* also go into the centre from right outside the bus station.

Destinations Arica (hourly; 26hr); Isla Negra (every 15min; 1hr 30min); La Serena (hourly; 6hr); Puerto Montt (3–4 daily; 16hr); Santiago (every 15min; 1hr 30min–1hr 45min); Temuco (2–3 daily; 9hr 30min).

GETTING AROUND

By micro and colectivo Countless *micros* run east and west through the city: those displaying "Aduana" on the window take you west through the centre, past the port, while those marked "P. Montt" take you back to the bus station. Some bus routes take you to the upper town, and you can catch *colectivos*

at Plazuela Ecuador, at the bottom of Calle Ecuador.

On foot To climb to the upper town, it's easiest to use the *ascensores*.

By taxi Taxis are numerous; there are stands at the bottom of most of the *cerros*.

INFORMATION

Tourist information There are several tourist information kiosks (daily 10am–2pm & 3–6pm), including one on Calle Blanco, close to Plaza Aníbal Pinto, and one on Muelle Prat by the port. Note that (despite an old sign)

there is no official tourist office at the bus station, which is filled with accommodation touts offering partial (at best) information. Two useful Spanish-language websites are 🌐 valparaisochile.cl and 🌐 granvalparaiso.cl.

TOURS OF VALPARAÍSO AND OTHER ACTIVITIES

There are innumerable tours on offer in Valparaíso; two of the best operators are **Ruta Valparaíso** (📞 32 259 2520, 🌐 rutavalparaiso.cl) and **Santiago Adventures** (📞 32 244 2750, 🌐 santiagoadventures.com). Half-day city tours generally cost from CH$18,000 (full-day tours from CH$38,000). Both agencies also offer excursions throughout the region. Additionally, Chilean Cuisine (📞 09 6621 4626, 🌐 cookingclasseschile.cl) offers enjoyable cookery classes, while Wine Tours Valparaíso (🌐 winetoursvalparaiso.cl) organizes wine tasting trips in the Casablanca Valley (see p.113).

2

ACCOMMODATION

Valparaíso has a good range of accommodation to suit all budgets. There are hotels in the lower sections of town, but you won't get the full Valparaíso experience unless you head up to one of the *cerros*: Alegre and Concepción are by far the most popular, but Bellavista, Cárcel, Artillería and several others are also developing, and provide a less touristy experience. Many places will pick you up from the bus station if you call ahead. Rates for all include breakfast.

HOTELS AND B&BS

Casa Higueras Higuera 133, Cerro Alegre 📞 32 249 7900, 🌐 www.hotelcasahigueras.cl; map p.107. One of the best top-end hotels in the city, Casa Higueras has stately 1930s-style en suites, a pool and Jacuzzi with exquisite vistas, and the classy (and, considering the quality, reasonably priced) Montealegre restaurant. CH$147,000 (US$285)

Casa Latina Papudo 462 Cerro Concepción 📞 32 249 4622, 🌐 casalatina.cl; map p.107. This popular B&B is within walking distance of many attractions and features nineteenth-century architecture smartly mixed with contemporary furnishings. The rooms range in size and level of comfort, from cosy singles with shared bathrooms to smart en-suite doubles. CH$35,000

★ **Hotel Casa Thomas Somerscales** San Enrique 446, Cerro Alegre 📞 32 233 1006, 🌐 hotelsomerscales .cl; map pp.102–103. Each of the eight en suites at this beautifully restored home of renowned local painter Thomas Somerscales is fitted out with period furniture and artwork, as well as modern comforts. Stunning views, a roof terrace and a large stained-glass window make this one of the most memorable hotels in town. CH$88,000 (US$170)

Hotel Da Vinci Urriola 426, Cerro Alegre 📞 32 317 4494, 🌐 hoteldavincivalparaiso.cl; map p.107. A cross between an art gallery and a hotel: the en suites, some split-level, are set around a central atrium, bathed with light from a towering window, while carefully placed photos and paintings provide a mellow ambience. CH$50,000

Hotel Ultramar Tomás Pérez 173, Cerro Cárcel 📞 32 221 0000, 🌐 hotelultramar.cl; map pp.102–103. Striped, spotted and checked decor – though fortunately not all together – give this thoroughly modern hotel, a refurbished 1907 Italianate town house, a unique feel. Rooms with a view are worth paying a little extra for. CH$40,000

The Yellow House Capitán Muñoz Gamero 91, Cerro Artillería 📞 32 233 9435, 🌐 theyellowhouse.cl; map pp.102–103. Even by Valpo's high standards, the views from *The Yellow House*, located in a 200-year-old building, are spectacular. Most of the rooms at this welcoming B&B are en suite, and there's also a comfortable apartment with a kitchenette. Walking tours, excursions, treks, Spanish lessons and cookery classes are available. Double CH$24,000, apartment CH$40,000

Zero Hotel Tomás Lautaro Rosas 343, Cerro Cárcel 📞 32 211 3113, 🌐 zerohotel.cl; map pp.102–103. This lovely pale blue town house has been turned into an attractive boutique hotel with tasteful high-ceilinged en suites (some with sea views). There are terraces and a glass-enclosed "winter garden" to relax in, as well as nice touches such as an honesty bar. CH$118,000 (US$230)

HOSTELS

Hostal Caracol Hector Calvo 371, Cerro Bellavista 📞 32 239 5817, 🌐 hostalcaracol.cl; map pp.102–103. A clean, friendly and rightly popular hostel, located on an up-and-coming *cerro*, near the Museo a Cielo Abierto, offering both a seven-bed dorm and private rooms. The owners also run a nearby "apart-hotel" with self-contained apartments. Dorm CH$8000, double CH$28,000, apartment CH$40,000

Luna Sonrisa Templeman 833, Cerro Alegre 📞 32 273 4117, 🌐 lunasonrisa.cl; map pp.102–103. Minimalist but comfortable rooms, pristine facilities, fine breakfast (with bread from the excellent Pan de Magia at Almirante Montt 738) and a sociable atmosphere make this an excellent choice. Staff are very friendly and knowledgeable – the place is owned by a travel writer, so you would expect nothing less. There are also a couple of great self-contained apartments (🌐 elnidito.cl). Dorm CH$8500, double CH$22,000, apartment CH$51,500

Pata Pata Hostel Templeman 657, Cerro Alegre 📞 32 317 3153, 🌐 patapatahostel.cl; map p.107.

Super-friendly staff, a great location, good-value accommodation (in four- to eight-bed dorms or cute private rooms), ample communal spaces, and a great breakfast featuring banana and *dulce de leche* toasted sandwiches make this hostel a fine choice. Dorm **CH$8000**, double **CH$22,000**

EATING, DRINKING AND ENTERTAINMENT

Valparaíso has some of Chile's best and most inventive restaurants, and an excellent nightlife scene (especially on Thurs, Fri and Sat). The city's speciality is its old-fashioned, charming bar-restaurants serving *comida típica* to local families, who turn out in their dozens to join in the singing and dancing on weekends, when many places have live *bolero*, *tango* or *música folklórica*. There is also a range of younger, hipper bars, many with live music and dancing. Take care wherever you are after dark, especially anywhere near the port area.

CAFÉS AND CHEAP EATS

Amor Porteño Almirante Montt 418, Cerro Concepción ☎ 32 221 6253, ⓦ amorporteño.cl; map p.107. Excellent ice-cream parlour/coffee shop, with a tiny dining area decorated with flowery murals, vintage mirrors and a chalkboard with quotes from the *I Ching*. As well as real Argentine *helado* (from CH$1000), you can tuck into *churros* and *medialunas* (sweet, doughy croissant-like pastries). Daily 10am–9pm.

Bambú Independencia 1790 ☎ 32 223 4216, ⓦ bambuvegetariano.cl; map pp.102–103. Good-value vegetarian food such as soups, salads, omelettes, soya burgers and tofu concoctions in a city centre location. Set meals from CH$2100. Cookery, yoga, pilates and tai chi classes are also available. Mon 10.30am–6pm, Tues 10.30am–8pm, Wed–Fri 10.30am–6pm, Sat 10.30am–5pm.

Café con Letras Almirante Montt 316, Cerro Concepción ☎ 32 223 5480, ⓦ cafeconletras.cl; map p.107. Low-key, faintly melancholy café-cum-bookshop, where aged wooden posts prop up the ceiling and black-and-white photos adorn the walls. It's a good spot for a quiet meal, a coffee (CH$1100–3150) and an *alfajore* biscuit (CH$700). Mon–Sat 11am–10pm, Sun 4–10pm.

Café Turri Paseo Gervasoni, Cerro Concepción ☎ 32 225 2091, ⓦ www.turri.cl; map p.107. Come for a sundowner and a dessert – such as the toothsome meringue torte with *lúcuma*, an indigenous fruit with a vaguely toffee-like flavour (CH$2800) – rather than a full meal at this touristy spot. The real star, however, is the panoramic view from the terrace. Mon–Sat 10am–11pm, Sun 10am–10pm.

RESTAURANTS

Allegretto Pilcomayo 259, Cerro Concepción ☎ 32 296 8839, ⓦ allegretto.cl; map p.107. British–Chilean-run restaurant with colourful decor, black-and-white photos, local beer on tap and *taca taca* (table football). The menu features thin-crust pizzas (CH$6400–7800), risottos, and gnocchi, and there's a good weekday lunch special (CH$4900). The owners also run a B&B. Daily noon–4pm & 7–11pm.

Cafe Bijoux Abtao 561, Cerro Concepción ☎ 32 322 5306; map p.107. Attractive restaurant with a decorative old cash register, ship's steering wheel and open parasols dotted around. The menu features tapas-style dishes, fresh fish and pasta, plus Valpo's dark and fruity El Puerto beer. Mains CH$5000–8000. Mon–Fri & Sun noon–11pm, Sat noon–1am.

★ **J. Cruz Malbrán** Condell 1466, up side alley next to the Municipalidad; map pp.102–103. An extraordinary place, more like a museum than a restaurant, packed with china, old clocks, musical instruments, crucifixes and other kitsch trinkets. It also claims to have invented the *chorrillana* (a vast plate of steak strips, onions, eggs and French fries; CH$4400), which is not to be missed. Mon–Thurs noon–2am, Fri & Sat noon–4.30am, Sun 1pm–2am.

★ **Le Filou de Montpellier** Almirante Montt 382, Cerro Concepción ☎ 32 222 4663, ⓦ lefilou demontpellier.cl; map p.107. A delightful little piece of France in Valpo: postcards of Montpellier and paintings by local artists decorate the place, while the ever-changing set lunch (CH$4600–8900) may include quiche, boeuf bourguignon and tarte tatin. Tues–Thurs 1–4pm, Fri & Sat 1–4pm & 8–11.30pm, Sun 1–4pm.

Pasta e Vino Templeman 352, Cerro Concepción ☎ 32 249 6187, ⓦ pastaevinoristorante.cl; map p.107. One of Valpo's finest restaurants, *Pasta e Vino* provides an inventive and ambitious take on Italian cuisine – squid-ink ravioli filled with smoked salmon, for example. The only problem is getting a table, and reservations are vital at weekends. Mains CH$8000–12,500. Tues–Sat 1–3.30pm & 8pm–midnight.

Vinilo Almirante Montt 540, Cerro Concepción ☎ 32 223 0665, ⓦ cafevinilo.cl; map p.107. Intimate bistro with a select menu of contemporary Chilean dishes (CH$9000–11,000) such as rabbit in a red wine and strawberry sauce, a bizarre mix of abstract and children's artwork and a stack of vintage vinyl. Try *Vinilo's* own Cerro Alegre ale while you're here. Mon–Thurs 9am–1am, Fri & Sat 9am–2.30am, Sun 10am–10pm.

BARS AND PUBS

★ **El Bar Inglés** Cochrane 851 (rear entrance at Blanco 870) ☎ 32 221 4625; map p.107. This wonderfully atmospheric bar dates back to the early 1900s and is a great place for a beer. Check out the wall map with listings of incoming boats from all over the world, and – if you're feeling confident – take on the regulars at a game of dominos. Mon–Fri noon–11pm.

El Cinzano Plaza Aníbal Pinto 1182 ☎ 32 221 3043, ⓦ barcinzano.cl; map p.107. Hugely popular restaurant-bar (set lunch CH$3300) with a fantastic atmosphere, especially on Thurs, Fri and Sat nights when the place fills with locals and ageing crooners singing sentimental ballads. Mon–Wed 10am–1am, Thurs 10am–2am, Fri & Sat 10.30am–4.30am.

La Piedra Feliz Errázuriz 1054, near the junction with Blanco ☎ 32 225 6788, ⓦ lapiedrafeliz.cl; map p.107. Mellow place with creaky wooden floors, regular art exhibitions, salsa classes, poetry readings (in Spanish) and live music – including jazz, bolero, rock and disco – every night. Tues–Sat 9pm–late.

★ **La Playa** Serrano 567 ☎ 32 259 4262; map pp.102–103. Sociable spot with a long, mahogany bar, dark wood-panelled walls and posters of Jack Nicholson, James Dean and BB King. There's live evening music at the weekend, when a downstairs dance area is opened up and the crowds don't disperse until sunrise. Mon–Wed 10am–10.30pm, Thurs–Sat 10am–late.

ENTERTAINMENT

Valpo is *the place* to go in Chile to ring in the New Year, with huge parties and fireworks extravaganzas; be sure to arrive by midday on the 30th or you'll get stuck in horrible traffic.

FILM AND THEATRE

Cine Hoyts Pedro Montt 2111 ☎ 32 259 4709; map pp.102–103. Cinema screening mainstream films. You can also find art movies at various cultural centres about town; check the back of *El Mercurio de Valparaíso* for details.

Teatro Municipal On the corner of Pedro Montt and Plaza O'Higgins ☎ 32 225 7480; map pp.102–103. For an evening of culture, check out the programme at the city's main theatre, which plays host to regular plays, music and dance performances.

DIRECTORY

Banks and exchange The main financial street is Prat, where you'll find plenty of banks with ATMs and *cambios*. Banco de Santiago is generally the best bet for currency exchange.

Car rental Rosselot, Victoria 2675 (☎ 32 235 2367, ⓦ rosselot.cl).

Consulates UK, Blanco 1199, 5th floor ☎ 32 221 3063; Germany, Blanco 1215, office 1102 ☎ 32 225 6749.

Hospital Try public hospital Carlos Van Buren, Colón and San Ignacio (☎ 32 225 4074, ⓦ hcvb.cl), or private clinic Clinica Valparaíso, Avenida Brasil 2350 (☎ 600 411 2000, ⓦ clinicavalparaiso.cl).

Internet Most hotels offer internet/wi-fi access, and there are also numerous cyber cafés.

Post office Prat 856.

South of Valparaíso

The resorts **south of Valparaíso** are among the busiest and most developed in the region. Most – including Algarrobo, El Tabo and Cartagena – sit on overcrowded beaches, are overrun with ugly apartment blocks and are jam-packed with noisy vacationers. However, a few places in the area are well worth a visit: peaceful **Quintay**, the **vineyards** of the Casablanca Valley, and – most notably – the village of **Isla Negra**, site of Pablo Neruda's extraordinary house and now a museum.

Quintay

Secluded and relatively untouched by tourism, the village of **Quintay** makes an ideal day-trip from Valparaíso. It has a scenic cove and a series of small beaches, backed by pine and eucalyptus trees, cacti and wild flowers, perfect for an idle wander. A 45min walk to the north takes you to Playa Grande, a lovely stretch of golden sand, now sadly marred by building work. There are a few fish restaurants, a former whaling station and a lighthouse. Keep an eye out for sea otters in the harbour.

Casa Museo Isla Negra

☎ 35 461284, ⓦ fundacionneruda.org • Tues–Sun: March–Dec 10am–6pm, Jan & Feb 10am–8pm • Guided or audio tour CH$3500; advance reservations necessary

2

PABLO NERUDA

The tiny village of **Isla Negra** was put on the map when **Pablo Neruda** moved into a half-built house on the beach in 1939. Born **Neftalí Reyes** in 1904, this son of a local railwayman made his name in the world of poetry as a teenager under the pseudonym Pablo Neruda. He published his first collection, *Crepusculario*, in 1923 at his own expense, and success came quickly. The following year, he published a slim volume of sensual, tormented verses, *Veinte Poemas de Amor y una Canción Desesperada* (Twenty Love Poems and a Song of Despair), and suddenly found himself, aged 20, with one of the fastest-growing readerships on the continent.

RANGOON AND BEYOND

Despite this success, Neruda still needed to earn a living to fund his writing, and so, aged 24, he began his career as **Chilean consul** in Rangoon, the first of many posts. It seems ironic that this most "Chilean" of poets, whose verses are imprinted with the forests, rain, sea, lakes and volcanoes of southern Chile, should have spent so much of his adult life far from his native land. His years in Rangoon, Colombo, Jakarta and Singapore were often intensely lonely, but also coloured with vivid episodes and sexual adventures. The most dramatic of these was his love affair in Rangoon with **Josie Bliss**. Described by Neruda as his "Burmese panther… a love-smitten terrorist capable of anything", she was a jealous and possessive lover who would sometimes terrorize him with her silver dagger. When he was transferred to Ceylon (now Sri Lanka), he left without telling her, but she turned up on his doorstep several months later. Neruda's outright rejection of her was to haunt him for many years, and Bliss makes several appearances in his poems.

POLITICIZATION AND EXILE

During his time in Asia, Neruda's poetry was inward-looking, reflecting his experience of dislocation and solitude. His posts in Barcelona (1934) and Madrid (1935–36), however, marked a major turning-point in his life and work: with the outbreak of the **Spanish Civil War**, and the assassination of his friend, Federico García Lorca, Neruda became increasingly politicized. He threw himself into the task of providing Spanish refugees with a safe passage to Chile, and at the same time sought to give his poetry a meaningful "place in man's struggle", with *España en el Corazón*. On returning to Chile he joined the Communist Party, and was **elected as a senator**. His politics were to land him in serious trouble, however, when newly elected president González Videla, who had previously enlisted Neruda's help, switched sides from left to right, and outlawed communism. When Neruda publicly attacked him, the president issued a warrant for his arrest, and he was forced into hiding. In 1949 the poet was smuggled across the Andes on horseback, and spent the next three years in exile, mainly in Europe.

MATILDE URRUTIA

It was during his **exile** that Neruda met the woman who was to inspire some of his most beautiful poetry: Matilde Urrutia, whom he was later to marry. Neruda had been married twice before: first, briefly, to a Dutch woman he'd met as a young consul in Rangoon; and then for eighteen years to the Argentinian painter, Delia del Carril. The poet's writings scarcely mention his first wife, nor their daughter – his only child – who died when she was 8, but Delia is described as "sweetest of consorts, thread of steel and honey…my perfect mate for 18 years". It was so as not to hurt Delia that *Los Versos del Capitán* – a book of passionate love poems written for Matilde – was published anonymously.

THE RETURN HOME

Nonetheless, when the order for his arrest was revoked in 1955, three years after his return to Santiago, Neruda divorced Delia and moved into **La Chascona**, in Santiago, and then to **Isla Negra** with Matilde. Based in Chile from then on, Neruda devoted himself to politics and poetry almost in equal measure. In 1970, Salvador Allende, whose campaign Neruda had tirelessly participated in, was elected president at the head of the socialist Unidad Popular. The following year, Neruda was awarded the Nobel Prize for Literature. His happiness was to be short-lived, however. Diagnosed with cancer, and already bedridden, the poet was unable to withstand the shock brought on by the 1973 military coup, which left his dear friend Allende dead. Less than two weeks later, on September 23, Neruda died in Santiago.

CASABLANCA VALLEY WINE ROUTE

The Casablanca Valley, famed for its excellent white wines, is accessed via Ruta 68, which connects Valparaíso and Viña with Santiago. **Ruta del Vino Valle de Casablanca** (☎ 32 274 3933, ⓦ casablancavalley.cl), Portales 90, in Casablanca, organizes tours (CH$23,000–79,000) of the wineries. You can also visit the vineyards independently (a list of all those participating in the *ruta del vino* is available on the website); having your own car makes things a lot easier, but it is possible to visit some using the frequent Valparaíso/Viña–Santiago buses.

2

From 1939, poet **Pablo Neruda** spent forty years of his life, on and off, in the village of Isla Negra, enlarging his house and filling it with the strange and beautiful objects he ceaselessly gathered from far-flung corners of the world. The Fundación Neruda, acting on the wishes of the poet's widow, Matilde Urrutia, transferred Neruda's and Matilde's graves to its garden and operates the house as the **Casa Museo Isla Negra**. Inside this museum, the winding passages and odd-shaped rooms are crammed full of fascinating exotic objects like ships' figureheads, Hindu carvings, African and Japanese masks, ships in bottles, seashells, butterflies, coloured bottles, Victorian postcards and a good deal more.

There's little else to Isla Negra save a small, pretty beach, which makes a great picnic spot.

ARRIVAL AND DEPARTURE | SOUTH OF VALPARAÍSO

QUINTAY

Five daily buses (fewer at weekends; 1hr) depart from the corner of 12 de Febrero and Rawson in Valparaíso; there are also frequent *colectivos* from the rank on 12 de Febrero.

ISLA NEGRA

Pullman (ⓦ pullman.cl) and Tur Bus (ⓦ turbus.cl) both run buses from Santiago's Terminal Alameda to Isla Negra (every 30min; 2hr). There are also services (every 15min; 1hr 30min) from Valparaíso's bus station.

Viña del Mar

A 15min bus or train ride is all it takes to exchange the colourful *cerros* and chaotic alleys of Valparaíso for the tree-lined avenues and ostentatious high-rises of **VIÑA DEL MAR**. This is Chile's largest and best-known beach resort, drawing tens of thousands of mostly Chilean vacationers each summer. In many ways, it's indistinguishable from beach resorts elsewhere in the world, with oceanfront condos, bars, restaurants and a casino. But lurking in the older corners of town are extravagant palaces, elegant villas and sumptuous gardens. Many date from the late nineteenth century when Viña del Mar – then a large hacienda – was subdivided into plots that were sold or rented to the wealthy families of Valparaíso and Santiago who came to spend their summers by the sea. The city also has a pair of **beautiful botanical gardens** and a museum with an important collection of Easter Island art.

Plaza Vergara

Viña's centre is marked by the large, green **Plaza Vergara**, full of tall, stately trees and surrounded by some fine, early twentieth-century buildings including the Neoclassical **Teatro Municipal**, the stately **Hotel O'Higgins** and the Italian Renaissance-style **Club de Viña**, a gentlemen's dining club

Avenida Valparaíso

Avenida Valparaíso, Viña's main commercial street, borders the south side of Plaza Vergara. Much of the shopping activity occurs in the five blocks between the plaza and

---

VIÑA DEL MAR ORIENTATION

Viña del Mar falls into two separate sections, divided by the **Estero Marga Marga**, a dirty lagoon (largely reclaimed for parking) that cuts through the town to the ocean. South of the Marga Marga is the old part of town, Viña's lively commercial centre with **Plaza Vergara** (also known as **Plaza de Viña**) and **Avenida Valparaíso** at its core. North of the river are the main **beaches** – Viña boasts 3.5km of sandy coast – and most of the tourist **restaurants** and **bars**.

Calle Ecuador. There's also a good **feria artesanal** in Pasaje Cousiño, a narrow passage off the south side of the avenue, just west of Plaza Vergara.

Quinta Vergara

Daily: winter 7am–6pm; summer 7am–7pm • Free

The exceptionally beautiful **Quinta Vergara** park, filled with exotic, subtropical trees and surrounded by wooded hills, sits two blocks south of Plaza Vergara, across the railway tracks. The amphitheatre hosts regular concerts, including the hugely hyped, kitsch **Festival Internacional de la Canción** (International Music Festival) every February. During this time, the traffic and the crowds are out of hand, and booking accommodation ahead is essential.

Museo de Bellas Artes

Quinta Vergara • Previously Tues–Sun 10am–1.30pm & 3–5.30pm • CH$600

In the centre of Quinta Vergara sits **Palacio Vergara**, a dazzling, whitewashed Venetian-style palace built in 1906. The palace is now home to the **Museo de Bellas Artes**, which has a decent collection of Chilean and European paintings, including works by **Rubens**, **Poussin** and **Tintoretto**. The museum was closed for restoration at the time of research, but is scheduled to reopen.

Palacio Rioja

Quillota 214 • Tues–Sun 10am–1.30pm & 3–5.30pm • CH$600

The **Palacio Rioja**, built in the style of an eighteenth-century French chateau and surrounded by a sumptuous park, is all that remains of the once extensive vineyards that gave the town its name. Situated just north of the Marga Marga, it was built in 1906 for Don Fernando Rioja Medel, a Spanish millionaire who owned the Banco Español among other enterprises. His family lived here until 1956, when the building was acquired by the Municipalidad which now runs it as a reception centre and a **museum**. The entire ground floor is perfectly preserved and provides a fascinating close-up view of early twentieth-century luxury, with its *belle-époque* furniture and glittering ballroom. In the summer, the **Conservatorio de Música** in the basement gives concerts in the palace.

Palacio Carrasco

Libertad 250 • Mon–Fri 9.30am–1pm & 2–6.30pm, Sat 10am–1pm • Free

Near the Palacio Rioja is the **Palacio Carrasco**, an elegant, three-storey building designed in a French Neoclassical style. It now functions as the city's cultural centre, hosting regular exhibitions of work by both Chilean and international artists.

Museo Francisco Fonck

4 Norte 784 • Mon–Sat 10am–7pm, Sun 10am–2pm • CH$2000

The excellent **Museo Francisco Fonck** has one of Chile's most important **Easter Island**

2

collections, plus some fascinating pre-Hispanic exhibits. It is named after Prussian medic Franz Fonck (1830–1912), who studied botanical and archeological sites in central Chile and left his collections to the state. One of the museum's best pieces stands by the entrance in the garden: a giant stone *moai*, one of just six that exist outside Easter Island. Inside, the three ground-floor rooms dedicated to Easter Island include wooden and stone carvings of those long, stylized faces (some around five hundred years old), as well as jewellery, weapons, household and fishing utensils, and ceremonial objects.

Castillo Wulff

Av Marina 37 • Tues–Sat 10am–1.30pm & 3–5.30pm • Free

In a prime waterfront location, the neo-Gothic **Castillo Wulff** was built in 1906 for a local nitrate and coal baron. Formerly a museum, it is now an exhibition space, and is well worth a quick look around: check out the glass-floored passage through which you can gaze at the waves breaking below.

The beaches

Take any of the Reñaca or Concón buses from Puente Libertad (the bridge just north of Plaza Vergara), and get off at 10 or 12 Norte for Playas Acapulco and El Sol, or ask the driver to let you off on the coast road for the beaches further north.

Viña's most central beach, and the only one south of the Marga Marga, is the sheltered, sandy **Playa Caleta Abarca** at the eastern end of Calle Viana. Just off the beach, at the foot of Cerro Castillo, is the **Reloj de Flores**, a large clock composed of colourful plants and mechanical dials.

Just beyond Castillo Wulff is the **Estero Marga Marga** – follow it inland a couple of blocks to reach the bridge that crosses it. On the other side is the **Casino Municipal** and the coast road, **Avenida Perú**. A pedestrian promenade runs alongside the ocean but there's no sand here, just a stretch of rocks.

A few blocks north, Avenida Perú swerves inland to make way for the long unbroken strip of sand stretching for over 3km towards Reñaca (see p.119). Though effectively a single beach, the different sections each have their own name: just north of Avenida Perú is the 200m-long **Playa Acapulco**, which is very popular but a bit hemmed in by high-rises, followed by **Playa El Sol** and **Playa Los Marineros**, where it's often too rough for swimming. Finally there is **Playa Larga**, which has restaurants and showers – it's very crowded in the summer.

Jardín Botánico Nacional

Jardín Botánico Nacional April to early Oct 10am–6.30pm; early Oct to March 10am–7.30pm • Mon–Sat CH$1200, Sun CH$1500 • Ⓦ jardin-botanico.cl **Zipline** Dec–Feb daily 11am––7pm; March–Oct Sat, Sun & public holidays 11am–7pm • From CH$3000 • Ⓦ canopysuramerica.cl • Bus #20, eastbound, from Calle Bohn (10min)

Set in a sheltered valley 6km from central Viña and surrounded by sun-baked hills, the **Jardín Botánico Nacional** contains 3000 plant species from Latin American, Europe and Asia. The gardens are a great place to unwind, but if you fancy a bit of action, it is also possible to go ziplining here. There are five different routes, some suitable for children.

ARRIVAL AND DEPARTURE

VIÑA DEL MAR

BY TRAIN

The Metro or Merval (Ⓦ www.merval.cl) depart for Valparaíso (every 5–20min) from the centrally located Miramar and Viña del Mar stations. You need to buy a plastic charge card (CH$1200) first, and then top it up with credit before travelling.

BY BUS/MICRO

Buses from Santiago and elsewhere arrive at the bus terminal at the eastern end of Avenida Valparaíso. To go down the coast, your best bet is to catch a bus from Valparaíso (see p.108), reached by any *micro* (every 10min) marked "Puerto" or "Aduana" from Plaza Vergara or Arlegui; alternatively take the Metro (see below). Buses/*micros* up the coast don't stop at the bus terminal, but at Libertad (just north of Puente Libertad), with frequent services to Reñaca and Concón, and several daily to Horcón, Maitencillo, Zapallar and Papudo.

Destinations Cachagua (hourly; 1hr 30min); Concón (every 15min; 15min); Horcón (hourly; 1hr); La Ligua (hourly; 2hr); Maitencillo (hourly; 1hr 20min); Papudo (2–3 daily; 1hr 45min); Reñaca (every 15min; 25min); Santiago (every 15min from Terminal Alameda; 1hr 30min–1hr 45min); Zapallar (hourly; 1hr 30min).

BY CAR

Car rental is available at Hertz, Quillota 766 (☎ 32 238 1025, Ⓦ hertz.cl).

INFORMATION

Two useful websites are Ⓦ vinadelmar.cl and Ⓦ eyeonvina.com.

Tourist office Off the northeast corner of Plaza Vergara, next to *Hotel O'Higgins* (Mon–Fri 9am–2pm & 3–7pm, Sat & Sun 10am–2pm & 3–7pm; ☎ 800 800830, Ⓦ visitevinadelmar.cl).

Sernatur Valparaíso 507, on the third floor (office #305) of an office block set back from the main street, next to an amusement arcade (Mon–Thurs 8.30am–2pm & 3–5.30pm, Fri 8.30am–2pm & 3–4.30pm; ☎ 32 269 0082).

ACCOMMODATION

Viña offers all manner of places to stay, but most are overpriced. Only a few offer sea views, as the oceanfront is taken up by residential condominiums. If you are coming in high season or during national holidays, book well in advance; at other times prices drop. Rates for all those below include breakfast.

Casa del Sol Romero 375 ☎ 32 296 7243, Ⓦ bbcasadelsol.com. This friendly B&B in the Recreo neighbourhood has a collection of comfortable, clean and spacious en suites. There's a kitchen for guests, wi-fi, and a selection of board games, books and DVDs to keep you entertained. CH$46,000

Che Lagarto Diego Portales 131 ☎ 32 262 5759, Ⓦ chelagarto.com. This reliable, sociable hostel has colourful four- to 12-bed dorms (including a women-only one), plus a few overpriced private en suites, overlooking a tree-filled garden. There's a communal kitchen, TV lounge, and internet/wi-fi. Dorm CH$6800, double CH$36,500

★ **Hotel Agora** 5 1/2 Poniente 253 ☎ 32 269 4669, Ⓦ hotelagora.cl. Appealing Art Deco-style hotel that wouldn't look out of place in Miami. Located on a quiet side street, it has impeccable pastel-shaded en suites with fridges and flatscreen TVs, and a stylish yellow-and-white tiled lobby. CH$45,000

Hotel del Mar San Martin 199 ⓣ32 250 0700, ⓦenjoy.cl. Viña's flagship 5-star hotel, a cylindrical building right on the seafront, has a grand Romanesque feel. The exquisite en suites have balconies, and there's a casino and several restaurants, including the outstanding *Savinya*. CH$93,000

Hotel Monterilla 2 Norte 65 ⓣ32 297 6950, ⓦmonterilla.cl. The en suites at this intimate family-run boutique hotel have been decorated with considerable flair, while the service is personalized and the location convenient for Viña del Mar's bars and restaurants. CH$85,500

Reloj de Flores Los Baños 70 ⓣ32 296 7243, ⓦhostalrelojdefloresbb.com. Under the same management as *Casa del Sol*, *Reloj de Flores* is a slightly cheaper option, with a range of clean rooms with either private or shared bathrooms. Guests have use of a kitchen and wi-fi access. CH$28,000

2

EATING AND DRINKING

CHEAP EATS AND SNACKS

Entre Masas 5 Norte 235 ⓣ32 297 9919. Excellent little bakery, specializing in *empanadas* (around CH$1000 each): there are dozens of varieties including crab and cheese, spinach and ricotta, and chorizo and goat's cheese. There's another branch in Reñaca (Av Central 75). Daily 10am–10pm.

Jerusalem Quinta and Alvarez. Popular with students, this no frills Middle Eastern eatery serves a steady stream of inexpensive juices, falafel wraps and kebabs. There are plenty of options for vegetarians, and you can eat at the plastic tables outside or get a takeaway. Mains from CH$1200. Mon–Sat 11.30am–9.30pm.

Panzoni Paseo Cousino 12B ⓣ32 271 4134. This charming Italian joint has a handful of tables, great service and inexpensive pastas (CH$3300–4900) and salads. You may have to queue at lunchtime, but it's worth the wait. Mon–Sat noon–4pm & 8pm–midnight.

RESTAURANTS

Delicias del Mar San Martín 459 ⓣ32 290 1837, ⓦdeliciasdelmar.com. Smart Basque-influenced *marisquería* with a loyal clientele, relaxed atmosphere, and great wine to accompany the crab lasagne, paella or the "Corvina DiCaprio", which was created to honour the visit of the Hollywood star. Mains CH$8000–12,000. Daily noon–4pm & 7pm–midnight.

★ **Divino Pecado** San Martín 180 ⓣ32 297 5790. Classy Italian offering mouthwatering fish and seafood dishes (mains CH$8000–11,000) like tuna carpaccio and *scallops au gratin*. Reservations are necessary at the weekend. Mon–Thurs 12.30–3pm & 8–11pm, Fri & Sat 12.30–3pm & 8pm–midnight, Sun 12.30–3.30pm & 8–11pm.

Enjoy del Mar Peru 100 ⓣ32 250 0788. Owned by *Hotel del Mar* and occupying a prime location, *Enjoy del Mar's* outdoor terrace is a wonderful spot for a coffee, beer or ice cream, while crashing waves provide a calming soundtrack. Main meals (CH$6500–10,900) though, are a little overpriced. Daily 9am–1am.

La Kouzina 3 Norte 370 ⓣ32 317 8422, ⓦlakouzina.cl. A world away from the many flashy, touristy restaurants in town, La Kouzina offers friendly service, a homely atmosphere and simple Mediterranean-style food (three-course set lunches CH$3900 and CH$6400). Mon–Thurs 12.45–3.30/4pm, Fri & Sat 12.45–2.30/4pm & 7.45pm–late, Sun 12.45–4pm.

BARS

Café Journal Agua Santa and Alvarez ⓣ32 266 6654, ⓦcafejournal.cl. Proximity to Viña's university ensures a healthy crowd of student drinkers, with pitchers of beer setting them up for a night dancing and carousing. It's busy throughout the week (with Wed a big night). Mon–Thurs & Sun 10am–3am, Fri & Sat 10am–3am.

NIGHTLIFE AND ENTERTAINMENT

Nightlife tends to be seasonal, reaching a heady peak in January and February when everyone flocks to **Reñaca's bars and clubs**, a suburb further up the coast (see p.119). During the summer months, *micros* run to and from Reñaca right through the night. In winter, the partying dies out, and the focus shifts back to Viña.

CLUBS

Ovo Casino Municipal ⓣ32 284 6100, ⓦenjoy.cl. *The* place to be seen sipping a pisco sour and striking a pose; without a doubt, Viña del Mar's swishest nightclub, with a dress code to match. Sat 12.30am–4/5am.

Scratch Quillota 898 ⓣ32 238 1381, ⓦscratch.cl. For more than 20 years this club has been pulling in the crowds, and on weekends it is packed to capacity (1200 people) until sunrise. DJs play a mix of reggaeton, dance and pop. Thurs, Fri & Sat 10pm–5/6am.

FILM AND THEATRE

Cine Arte Plaza Vergara (through passage off west side of square) ⓣ32 288 2798. Excellent little arts cinema. Especially worth a visit during the Festival Internacional de Cine Viña del Mar (ⓦcinevina.cl), Nov/Dec.

Teatro Municipal Plaza Vergara ☎ 32 268 1739. The grand Neoclassical Teatro Municipal, which dates back to the 1920s, puts on theatrical performances, classical music concerts and dance shows.

DIRECTORY

Banks and exchange Most banks and *cambios* are on Arlegui and Libertad, and there are innumerable ATMs scattered about town.

Internet Babylonia Cyber Café, Ecuador 79, charges CH$600/hr.

Post office Between Plaza Vergara and Puente Libertad.

North of Viña

North of Viña, the coast road meanders to the small fishing village of **Papudo**, about 75km away, and beyond to the farming town of **La Ligua** from where you can reach the family resort of **Los Vilos**. Hugging the oceanside in some stretches, darting inland in others, the northern coast road is far quieter than its southern counterpart, and very beautiful in parts. **Cachagua** and **Zapallar** are the most exclusive resorts along this coast. Countless local buses head to **Reñaca** and neighbouring **Concón**, but services to the other resorts further north are less frequent; most can also be reached from Valparaíso and Santiago. Unless you have your own vehicle, the best option is to pick one or two places and head for these, rather than resort-hopping on public transport.

Reñaca

Lively, developed **REÑACA**, 6km north of central Viña, is a 1.5km stretch of coast swamped by bars, restaurants and apartment blocks. The beaches here are among the cleanest in the country, and the resort is particularly popular with Chile and Argentina's beautiful young things. Reñaca's **clubs** are also pretty pricey but remain resolutely popular throughout the summer season. Every summer a host of new clubs appears, and others disappear, so ask around for the latest. Accommodation is generally overpriced in Reñaca, and you're better off staying in Viña.

Concón

CONCÓN, 10km north of Reñaca, is a strange sort of place: part concrete terraced apartment blocks, part elegant villas with flower-filled gardens, and part rundown, working-class fishing village, with six beaches spread out along the bay. When the wind is blowing south, nasty fumes drift over from the nearby oil refinery.

The most interesting bit of town is **La Boca**, the ramshackle commercial centre at the mouth of the Río Aconcagua. The *caleta* here was used to export the produce of the haciendas of the Aconcagua valley in the nineteenth century and is now a bustling fish quay, lined with modest **marisquerías**.

The most popular beaches are the rapidly developing **Playa Amarilla** and **Playa Negra**, south of La Boca, both good for bodyboarding. More attractive, and quieter, is **Playa Ritoque**, a long stretch of sand a few kilometres north of town.

Horcón

The charming and picturesque – if slightly tatty – fishing village of **HORCÓN**, about 30km north of Concón, is a chaotic tumble of houses straggling down the hill to a rocky bay. (En route, you'll pass Quintero, a scruffy, forbidding town with filthy beaches, to be avoided at all costs.) In the summer, Horcón is taken over by artisans on the beach selling jewellery made from seashells and unfeasible numbers of young Chileans who come to chill out for the weekend; this is the hippy alternative to Reñaca.

The **beach** in front of the village is crowded and uninviting, but a short walk up the main street and then along Avenida Cau-Cau takes you down a steep, rickety staircase to the remote **Playa Cau-Cau**, a pleasantly sheltered beach surrounded by wooded hills, though a hideous condo mars the beauty of the area. An hour's walk along the beach north towards Maitencillo takes you to Playa Luna, a nudist beach.

Maitencillo

Stretching 4km along one main street, **MAITENCILLO** is little more than a long, narrow strip of holiday homes, *cabañas* and hotels along the shoreline. The chief reason for coming here is **Playa Aguas Blancas**, a superb white-sand beach sweeping 5km south of the village, backed by steep sandstone cliffs.

Cachagua

CACHAGUA, a short way north of Maitencillo, has a stunning beach, with a wide expanse of pale sand curling round the bay, backed by gentle hills, and is synonymous with Chile's upper crust. It is blessed by a relative lack of holiday homes on the land off the beach, which instead is home to a golf course. Ask for directions to the long staircase from Avenida del Mar down to **Playa Las Cujas**, a tiny, spectacular and often empty beach. Just off the coast, the Isla de los Pingüinos is a **penguin sanctuary** to which local fishermen sometimes offer boat rides – accept at your peril, for the smell of hundreds of Humboldt penguins can be nauseating.

Zapallar

The classiest and most attractive of all the Litoral's resorts, **ZAPALLAR** is a sheltered, horseshoe bay backed by lushly wooded hills where luxurious holiday homes and handsome old mansions nestle between the pine trees. Apart from the beach, you can also stroll along the coastal path around the bay, or walk up Avenida Zapallar, admiring the early twentieth-century mansions. More strenuous possibilities include hiring a sea-kayak or climbing the 692m **Cerro Higuera**.

Papudo

The development in **PAPUDO**, just 10km around the headland, hasn't been as graceful as in Zapallar, and several ugly buildings mar the seafront. However, the steep hills looming dramatically behind the town are undeniably beautiful, and the place has a friendly, local atmosphere. The best beach is **Playa Grande**.

La Ligua

The chief appeal of **LA LIGUA**, a bustling agricultural town, is its setting, enfolded by undulating hills that take on a rich honey glow in the early evening sunlight. It is also known for its confectionery: *dulces de La Ligua* – sweet, sugary cakes famous throughout Chile. In town, there's a small museum, and an artisans' market in the main square.

Pichidangui

North of the Papudo–La Ligua crossroads, the Panamericana follows the coast for some 200km before dipping inland again, towards Ovalle (see pp.127–129). This stretch of highway takes you past a succession of gorgeous, white-sand **beaches** dotted with a few fishing villages and small resorts. Set 4km back from the Panamericana, 50km beyond the Papudo–La Ligua interchange, is **PICHIDANGUI**, with a lovely beach, up there with

Chile's finest: 7km of white, powdery sand fringed by eucalyptus trees, with little beachfront development to spoil the view.

Los Vilos

Local legend has it that **LOS VILOS**, 30km north of Pichidangui, takes its name from the Hispanic corruption of "Lord Willow", a British pirate who was shipwrecked on the coast and decided to stay. The town later became notorious for highway robberies. Today it is a great place to spend a couple of days by the sea without paying over the odds. However, it gets incredibly packed in January and February. The town's chief attraction is its long golden **beach**, but there's also a **fish market** and **Isla de los Lobos**, a seal colony 5km south of the bay.

2

ARRIVAL AND DEPARTURE

By bus Cachagua, Concón, Horcón, La Ligua, Maitencillo, Reñaca and Zapallar are all served by regular bus to and from Viña del Mar, while Papudo has a twice daily service. From Santiago there are also twice hourly buses to La Ligua and hourly buses (3hr 15min) to Los Vilos from the Terminal de Buses Santiago and the Terminal San Borja. Daily buses likewise head to Pichidangui from the capital's Terminal de Buses Santiago (Condor Bus; ☎ 2 779 3721) and also from Valparaíso (Buses La Porteña, which leave from the company's office at Molina 366; ☎ 32 216568); journeys take around 2hr 30min from either.

ACCOMMODATION

CONCÓN

Mantagua 3km north of town ☎ 32 215 5900, ⓦ mantagua.cl. Concón is an easy day-trip from Viña, but if you want to stay try Mantagua, a smart, modern and very pricey hotel with minimalist en suites and cosy cabins. There's a pool, good restaurant and plenty of activities on offer. Double **CH$162,000 (US$317)**, cabin **CH$134,000 (US$263)**

LOS VILOS

Hostel Lord Willow Calle Hostería 1444 ☎ 53 541037. Overlooking the beach, this whitewashed, palm-tree-shaded hotel has a range of clean if slightly cramped rooms with TVs and private bathrooms. There's a pool, restaurant and wi-fi access. Breakfast, however, costs extra. **CH$24,000**

MAITENCILLO

Cabañas Hermansen Avenida del Mar 0592 ☎ 32 277 1028, ⓦ hermansen.cl. A 5min drive north of Aguas Blancas, this lodge has great views of the beach, rustic cabins with cute wooden picnic tables, bike rental and switched-on staff. The attached *La Canasta* is the only decent bar in the area; it also serves good pizzas. **CH$59,000**

PAPUDO

Hotel Carande Chorrillos 89 ☎ 33 791105, ⓦ hotelcarande.cl. The best of Papudo's nondescript hotels, Carande has rather drab, but clean and cosy en-suite rooms; those at the top of the building have sea views. There's also a decent restaurant. **CH$40,000**

PICHIDANGUI

La Rosa Náutica El Dorado 120 ☎ 53 531133, ⓦ rosanautica.cl. There are a mixture of standard hotel rooms and more atmospheric wooden cabins at La Rosa Náutica; both types are simple but comfortable. There's also a pool and a good restaurant. Double **CH$42,600**, cabin **CH$63,300**

ZAPALLAR

★ **Hotel Isla Seca** At the northern end of the bay ☎ 33 741224, ⓦ hotelislaseca.cl. If you feel like splashing out, this swanky hotel offers classically styled rooms with balconies; note that those with sea views cost significantly more than those without. There's also an excellent restaurant. **CH$95,800 (US$188)**

EATING

PAPUDO

El Barco Rojo Av Irarrazaval 300 ☎ 33 791488. Owned by a hip Parisian who arranges nightly funky jazz and Latin concerts, this restaurant's famous seafood menu is high quality and generally inexpensive, and there's an excellent wine list. Mains from CH$4000. Fri–Sun 7pm–midnight.

ZAPALLAR

★ **El Chiringuito** At the southern tip of the bay ☎ 33 741024. Down by the *caleta*, this restaurant serves up legendary seafood (from CH$8000) – the scallops, in particular, are absolutely divine. Summer Mon–Thurs 12.30pm–6pm, Fri & Sat 12.30pm–midnight; autumn and winter often weekend only.

El Norte Chico

127 Ovalle

129 Around Ovalle

132 Andacollo and around

134 Coquimbo and the coast

136 La Serena

143 The Elqui Valley

151 Vallenar and around

154 Copiapó

158 Around Copiapó

164 Parque Nacional Pan de Azúcar

CERRO TOLOLO OBSERVATORY

El Norte Chico

A land of rolling, sun-baked hills streaked with sudden river valleys that cut across the earth in a flash of green, the Norte Chico, or "Little North", of Chile is what geographers call a "transitional zone". Its semi-arid scrubland and sparse vegetation mark the transformation from the country's fertile heartland to the barren deserts bordering Peru and Bolivia. Starting around the Río Aconcagua, just north of Santiago, it stretches all the way to Taltal, and the southernmost reaches of the Atacama, more than 800km further north.

A series of **rivers** – notably the Choapa, the Limarí, the Elqui, the Huasco and the Copiapó – flow through the Norte Chico region from the Andes to the coast, allowing the surrounding land to be irrigated and cultivated. The result is spectacular: lush, vibrant green terraces laden with olives, apricots and vines snake between the brown, parched walls of the valleys, forming a sensational visual contrast. The most famous product of these valleys is **pisco**, the pale, aromatic brandy distilled from sun-dried grapes and treasured by Chileans as their national drink (a claim vigorously contested by the Peruvians, who consider it their own).

The largest population centre – and one of the country's most fashionable seaside resorts – is **La Serena**, its pleasing, colonial-style architecture and lively atmosphere making it one of the few northern cities worth visiting for its own sake. It's also an ideal base for exploring the beautiful **Elqui Valley**, immortalized in the verses of the Nobel laureate Gabriela Mistral, and home to luxuriant vines and idyllic riverside hamlets. Just down the coast from La Serena lies the **Parque Nacional Fray Jorge**, with a microclimate that supports a small, damp cloudforest. Another botanical wonder is the famous *desierto florido* or **flowering desert**. Occasionally, after heavy winter rains, the normally dry earth sprouts vast expanses of vibrantly coloured flowers. This rare, unpredictable phenomenon, centred on **Vallenar**, occurs on average once every four to eight years.

Skies that are guaranteed cloudless almost year-round and very little air pollution have made the region the obvious choice for some of the world's major **astronomical observatories**. They range from the state-of-the-art facility at dazzling-white **Tololo** to the modest municipal installation at **Mamalluca**, near the picturesque village of **Vicuña**, where you don't have to be an expert reserving months in advance to look through the telescope.

The Norte Chico also boasts a string of superb **beaches**, some totally deserted and many of them tantalizingly visible from the Panamericana as you enter the region, just north of Santiago. **Bahía Inglesa** is famous throughout Chile for its turquoise waters, though increasingly prolific algae is turning the bay greener.

Copiapó, the northernmost major city in the region, serves as a useful springboard for excursions into the nearby **desert** or, further afield, up into the high cordillera. Here the **Parque Nacional Nevado de Tres Cruces**, the **Volcán Ojos del Salado** and **Laguna Verde** present some of Chile's most magnificent yet least-visited landscapes: snow-topped volcanoes, bleached-white salt flats and azure lakes. A couple of hours to the

La Serena's churches p.138
Obervatories around La Serena p.141
Gabriela Mistral p.150
Pisco p.151

The price of gold p.154
The flowering desert p.155
The rescue of Los 33 p.159
Climbing Volcán Ojos del Salado p.160

FERIA MODELO DE OVALLE

Highlights

❶ Feria Modelo de Ovalle Wander this food market and fill your bags with plump olives, giant pumpkins, ripe tomatoes and very smelly cheeses. **See p.127**

❷ La Serena Chile's second-oldest city offers long beaches, beautiful churches and a lively ambience. **See pp.138**

❸ Stargazing Observe the unbelievably limpid night skies at impressive observatories, from Del Pangue to Mamalluca. **See p.141, 146**

❹ Horseriding in the Elqui Valley Pretend you're in the Wild West as you trek through Chile's untrammelled northern plains. **See pp.143**

❺ Desierto florido If you're lucky to be in the right place at the right time, see the desert around Vallenar burst into bloom. **See p.151**

❻ Planta Capel Sample the fiery, fruity brandy that is Chile's national drink, straight from the barrel at the Elqui Valley's largest distillery. **See p.152**

❼ Nevado de Tres Cruces One of the country's least-known national parks, with emerald-green lakes, snowcapped volcanoes and plentiful wildlife. **See p.159**

HIGHLIGHTS ARE MARKED ON THE MAP ON P.126

HIGHLIGHTS
1. Feria Modelo de Ovalle
2. La Serena
3. Stargazing
4. Horseriding in the Elqui Valley
5. Desierto florido
6. Planta Capel
7. Nevado de Tres Cruces

N

PACIFIC
OCEAN

Taital

PARQUE NACIONAL
PAN DE AZÚCAR
Caleta Pan de Azúcar

El Salvador

Chañaral

Diego de
Almagro

Portrerillos

Paso de
San Francisco

Caldera

Bahía Inglesa

SALAR DE
MARICUNGA
Laguna
Santa Rosa

Laguna
Verde

Mina Marte

Volcán Copiapó
(6080m)

Tres
Cruces

Ojos del
Salado

Puerto Viejo

Copiapó

PARQUE NACIONAL
NEVADO DE TRES CRUCES

7

Nantoco

Bahía Salada

Laguna del
Negro
Francisco

Carrizal Bajo

Juntas

RESERVA NACIONAL
LLANOS DE CHALLE

5

Huasco

Vallenar

Alto del Carmen

El Tránsito

Isla Chañaral

Domeyko

San Félix

RESERVA
NACIONAL
PINGUINO DE
HUMBOLDT

Cerro las Campanas

Cerro la Silla

Pinto

Isla Choros

La Higuera

ARGENTINA

Mamalluca
Observatory

La Serena
Coquimbo

2

3

Guanaquero

Vicuña

6

Montegrande

Cerro
Tololo

Pisco Elqui

Del Pangue
Observatory

4

Tongoy

Andacollo

Pichasca

PARQUE
NACIONAL
FRAY JORGE

Ovalle

1

Monte Patria

Termas
de Socos

Valle del
Encanto

Caleta Teniente

EL NORTE CHICO

0   40
kilometres

north, near the towering cliffs and empty beaches of **Parque Nacional Pan de Azúcar**, a small island is home to colonies of seals, countless pelicans and thousands of penguins.

Bear in mind that, whereas the Norte Grande, Chile's northernmost region, can be visited year-round, the Norte Chico is at its best in the **summer months** (Oct–March) when the valleys are at their greenest, the coast is likelier to be free of fog and the ocean and sky are pure blue. On the downside, resorts like La Serena and Bahía Inglesa can be horribly overcrowded and overpriced in the high season, especially January.

Brief history

Mining has shaped the region's growth, giving birth to towns, ports, railways and roads, and drawing large numbers of settlers to seek their fortune here. **Gold** was mined first by the Incas for ritual offerings, and then intensively, to exhaustion, by the Spaniards until the end of the eighteenth century. Next came the great **silver** bonanza of the nineteenth century, when a series of dramatic silver strikes – some of them accidental – set a frenzy of mining and prospecting in motion, propelling the region into its heyday. Further riches and glory came when the discovery of huge **copper** deposits turned it into the world's largest copper producer from the 1840s to 1870s. Mining is still the most important industry here, its presence most visible up in the cordillera, where huge mining trucks hurtle around the mountain roads, enveloped in clouds of dust.

3

Ovalle

Almost 380km north of Santiago – some 140km beyond Los Vilos – a lone sign points to the little-visited market town of **OVALLE**. The town's main claim to fame is as the birthplace of one of the country's outstanding contemporary writers, Luis Sepúlveda. It's also a good base for exploring the dramatic **Hurtado Valley** or the deeply rural **Limarí Valley**, home to a few low-key attractions, including the Monumento Natural Pichasca, the Termas de Socos hot springs and the petroglyphs at the Valle del Encanto.

The Plaza de Armas

The **Plaza de Armas**, with expansive lawns, nineteenth-century Phoenix palms and rows of jacaranda, marks Ovalle's centre. Dominating the east side of the square is the white-and-mustard **Iglesia San Vicente Ferrer**, a large, colonial-style church dating to 1849, with thick adobe walls and a diminutive tower. From the plaza, a pedestrian mall leads three blocks east along Vicuña Mackena.

Museo del Limarí

Covarrubias and Antofagasta • Tues–Fri 10am–1pm & 3–6pm, Sat 10am–1pm, Sun 10am–2pm • CH$600, free Sun • ☎ 53 433680

Ovalle's excellent **Museo del Limarí** stands on the northeast edge of town in the grand old building that once housed the train station. The museum's collection of **Diaguita pottery** is beautifully restored and shown to great effect in modern cases. Famed for its exquisite geometric designs painted in black, white and red onto terracotta surfaces, the pottery was produced by the Diaguita people who inhabited this part of Chile from 1000 AD until the Inca invasions in the sixteenth century.

Feria Modelo de Ovalle

Av la Feria and Benavente • Mon, Wed, Fri & Sat 6am–7pm, Sun 6am–2.30pm

About ten blocks east of the plaza, you'll find a huge, ramshackle iron hangar that houses the colourful **Feria Modelo de Ovalle**, the largest fresh-produce market in the north of Chile and definitely worth a visit; you can pick up fantastic home-made cheeses (including some alarmingly pungent goat cheeses) as well as delicious dried figs and a range of fruit and vegetables.

ARRIVAL AND DEPARTURE OVALLE

By bus The bus terminal, known as Medialuna, is at Ariztía Oriente 769 (☎53 626612). Rural buses leave from the Feria Modelo and outside the Mercado Municipal at Victoria and Independencia.

Destinations Antofagasta (25 daily; 14hr); Arica (6 daily; 24hr); Calama (15 daily; 17hr); Chañaral (10 daily; 9hr); Copiapó (10 daily; 7hr); Iquique (7 daily; 19hr); La Serena (every 15min; 1hr 20min); Los Vilos (10 daily; 2.5hr); Santiago (18 daily; 6hr); Vallenar (20 daily; 4.5hr).

ACCOMMODATION

Gran Hotel Vicuña Mackenna 210 ☎53 621084, ⓦgranhotelovalle.cl. A good mid-range option, offering 25 serviceable doubles – some nicer and pricier than others – with unique artwork on the walls, as well as internet and breakfast. CH$31,000

Hotel Plaza Turismo Victoria 295 ☎53 662500, ⓦplazaturismo.cl. This spruce hotel in front of the Plaza de Armas offers spacious, well-kept rooms in a handsome old building with its own restaurant and parking. CH$64,000

Hotel Roxy Libertad 155 ☎53 620080, ⓔhotelroxy @hotmail.com. For an economical option, try this hotel with comfortable if dated rooms arranged around a large, brightly painted patio filled with flowers and chairs. CH$24,000

Jaime's Crazy House Tocopilla 92 ☎53 626761, ⓦjaimecrazyhouse.com. Offering essentially a couple of bunk beds out the back of a dingy computer repair store, Peruvian-born Caesar is nonetheless an amicable host and provides good local information and hearty breakfasts. Dorm CH$6000

EATING AND DRINKING

Ovalle's **restaurants** tend to limit themselves to the standard dishes you find everywhere else in Chile – which is frustrating, considering this is the fresh-produce capital of the North. However, you will find a few worthwhile spots.

Los Braseros Vicuña Mackenna 595 ☎53 624917. Serves delicious if unoriginal fare, including juicy *parrillas* (CH$13,900 for two) and river prawns (CH$8900) in pleasant surroundings marred only by the giant TV screen. Mon–Sat 10am–4pm & 7.30pm–midnight, Sun10am–4pm.

Café Pub Real Vicuña Mackenna 419. If you're in need of real coffee (a capuccino is CH$1500), head to this appropriately named café which morphs into a pub five nights a week. Café Mon–Sat 9am–8.30pm; Pub Tues–Sat 9pm–late.

Club Social de Ovalle Vicuña Mackenna 489 ☎53 630412. The fanciest restaurant in town has a traditional salon setting and serves decent fish and

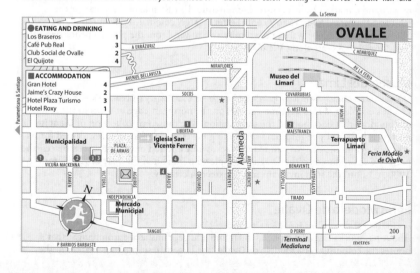

seafood dishes with a good selection of Limarí Valley wines. Mains CH$7000. Mon–Sat 10am–11pm.

El Quijote Arauco 294. An intimate, bohemian sort of bar and restaurant, with political graffiti and poetry on the walls, and an inexpensive menu featuring simple staples like *cazuela* and *lomo* (CH$1500). Mon–Sat 11am–5pm & 7pm–2am.

DIRECTORY

Banks You'll find several ATMs around the plaza.

Shopping Talabartería el Huasito, Libertad 126, ☎ 53 621199, ⓦ elhuasito.blogspot.com. A traditional leather shop selling finely crafted belts, wallets, bags and *huaso* (cowboy) gear.

Around Ovalle

If you have your own car, you can take the scenic road northeast of Ovalle – an alternative route to Vicuña and the Elqui Valley (see p.143–150) – which winds slowly up into the mountains, passing ancient petrified wood stumps at **Pichasca** and the delightful oasis village of **Hurtado**, the main settlement along the dramatic but seldom visited **Hurtado Valley**. If you head west, you'll find a concentration of rock carvings in the **Valle del Encanto**, a hot springs resort at the **Termas de Socos** and the impressive cloudforest reserve of **Parque Nacional Fray Jorge**.

Monumento Natural Pichasca

Daily 8.30am–5.30pm • CH$2500 • ☎ 53 620058

Northeast of Ovalle, a first-rate paved road climbs through the fertile Hurtado Valley, skirting – 12km out of town – the deep-blue expanse of water formed by the Recoleta Dam, one of three that irrigate the Limarí Valley. About 50km up the road, past a string of tiny villages, a side road to San Pedro Norte dips down across the river leading, just beyond the village, to the Conaf-run **Monumento Natural Pichasca**, the site of a seventy-million-year-old petrified wood. As you arrive at the parking area, two paths diverge: the right-hand path leads north to a hillside scattered with stumps of **fossilized tree trunks**, some of them imprinted with the shape of leaves; the left-hand, or southern, path leads down to an enormous **cave** formed by an 80m gash in the hillside topped by a massive overhanging rock. Archeological discoveries inside the cave point to human habitation some ten thousand years ago.

Hurtado

Just under 30km further northeast of Pichasca, set amid dramatic mountain scenery, is the traditional oasis village of **HURTADO**. Set at an altitude of around 1200m, with just four hundred inhabitants, the main draw, a few kilometres outside the village, is a Mexican-style ranch, the *Hacienda Los Andes* (see p.131).

Valle del Encanto

19km west of Ovalle • Daily 8am–4.30pm • CH$500

The dry, dusty **Valle del Encanto** boasts one of Chile's densest collections of **petroglyphs** – images engraved on the surface of rocks – carved mainly by people of the El Molle culture (see p.465) between 100 and 600 AD. Most of the images are geometric motifs or stylized human outlines, including faces with large, wide eyes and elaborate headdresses. A few of the images are very striking, while others are faint and difficult to make out; the best time to visit is between 2 and 3pm, when the outlines are at their sharpest, unobscured by shadows. Note that you're allowed to camp in the park for free, but the toilets are in poor condition.

3

3

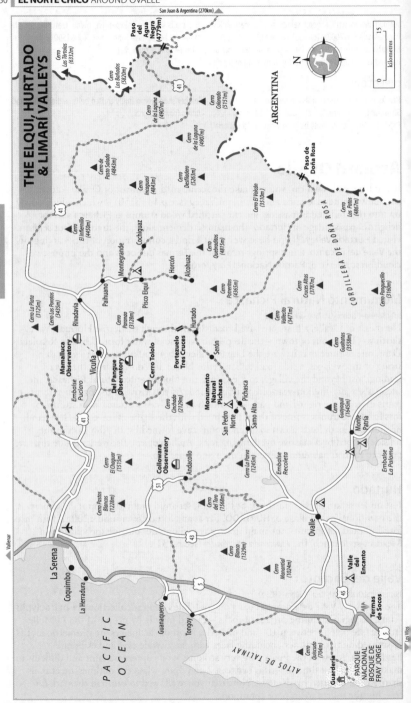

San Juan & Argentina (270km)

THE ELQUI, HURTADO & LIMARÍ VALLEYS

N

0 _____ 15
kilometres

ARGENTINA

Paso del
Agua
Negra
(4779m)

Cerro
Los Tórtolas
(6332m)

Cerro
Los Bañados
(5821m)

41

Cerro
Colorado
(5151m)

Cerro
de la Laguna
(4907m)

Cerro
de la Laguna
(4907m)

Paso de
Doña Rosa

Cerro
de Pasto Salado
(4843m)

Cerro
Incaguasi
(4843m)

Cerro
Deshadero
(5263m)

Cerro El Volcán
(3510m)

Cerro
Los Patos
(4867m)

41

Cerro
El Infiernillo
(4450m)

Cochiguaz

Cerro
Quebraditas
(4815m)

CORDILLERA DE DOÑA ROSA

Cerro Panguecillo
(3160m)

Montegrande

Cerro
Cruces Altas
(3787m)

Horcón

Cerro La Plata
(3125m)

Cerro Los Parotos
(3435m)

Rivadavia

Paihuano

Pisco Elqui

Alcohuaz

Cerro
Potrerillos
(4365m)

Cerro
Vallecito
(3471m)

Cerro
Paranoa
(3128m)

Hurtado

Cerro
Guaitatos
(3558m)

Mamalluca
Observatory

Vicuña

Cerro Tololo

Portezuelo
Tres Cruces

Serón

Embalse
Puclaro

Del Pangue
Observatory

Cerro
Cinchado
(2129m)

Monumento
Natural
Pichasca

Pichasca

Cerro
Guayaquil
(1645m)

Samo Alto

Monte
Patria

41

San Pedro
Norte

Embalse
La Paloma

Collowara
Observatory

Cerro
El Chaquar
(1515m)

Andacollo

Cerro La Parva
(1245m)

Embalse
Recoleta

51

Cerro Pastos
Blancos
(1228m)

Cerro
del Toro
(1568m)

Vallenar

43

Ovalle

La Serena

Coquimbo

La Herradura

Cerro
Blanco
(1329m)

Cerro
Monumental
(1024m)

Valle
del
Encanto

5

45

Guanaqueros

Tongoy

Termas
de Socos

5

PACIFIC
OCEAN

ALTOS DE TALINAY

Cerro
Quiscudo
(704m)

Los Vilos

Guardería

PARQUE
NACIONAL
BOSQUE DE
FRAY JORGE

Termas de Socos

Panamerican Norte km 370, 35km southwest of Ovalle • Baths CH$3900 (or free for guests of the hotel); pool reserved for guests of the hotel (see p.132) • ☎ 53 198 2505, Santiago ☎ 2 236 3336, ⓦ termasocos.cl

The thermal baths complex of **Termas de Socos** lies 2km down a track just south of the turn-off to Ovalle. It is notable for its 22°C (72°F) outdoor pool, surrounded by palm and eucalyptus trees, wicker armchairs and huge potted ferns, as well as the cubicles containing private bathtubs where you can soak in warm spring water, supposedly rich in medicinal properties.

Parque Nacional Fray Jorge

Panamericano Ruta CH 5, Autopista del Elqui • Daily 9am–4.30pm • CH$2500 • ☎ 53 620058

A UNESCO world biosphere reserve since 1977, **Parque Nacional Fray Jorge** sits on the Altos de Talinay, a range of steep coastal hills plunging into the Pacific some 80km west of Ovalle and 110km south of La Serena. It extends over 100 square kilometres, but its focal point, and what visitors come to see, is the small **cloudforest** perched on the highest part of the sierra, about 600m above sea level.

The extraordinary thing about this forest is how sharply it contrasts with its surroundings, indeed with everywhere else in the area. Its existence is the result of **camanchaca**, the thick coastal fog that rises from the ocean and condenses as it meets the land, supporting a cover of dense vegetation – fern, bracken and myrtle trees – normally found only in the south of Chile. Close to the parking area, a 1km path dotted with information panels guides you through a poorly labelled range of plants and trees, and leads to the **forest** proper, where a slippery, wooden boardwalk takes you through tall trees dripping with moisture. The whole trail takes less than half an hour to walk. Three kilometres beyond the Conaf control there's a **picnic** area, but note that camping is no longer allowed anywhere in the park.

3

ARRIVAL AND DEPARTURE   AROUND OVALLE

MONUMENTO NATURAL PICHASCA
By bus On market days (Mon, Wed, Fri, Sat & Sun) it's possible to get to the turn-off to San Pedro de Pichasca on a rickety bus from Ovalle's Feria Modelo (see p.127), but this involves walking 3km from the main road to the site entrance, and then a further 2km to the cave and fossil remains.

HURTADO
By bus Buses leave from Ovalle's Feria Modelo for Hurtado (3–4 daily; 3hr).

VALLE DEL ENCANTO
By bus Though there is no direct bus service to the park, you can take any westbound bus and asked to be dropped off at the highway turn-off and then walk the final 5km.
By car From Ovalle, head 19km southwest to a heavily potholed dirt road that leads 5km south of Ruta 45 into the ravine.

TERMAS DE SOCOS
By bus There are twice daily services from Ovalle (30min) and La Serena (1.5hr).

PARQUE NACIONAL FRAY JORGE
By taxi There's no public transport to the park, so unless you've got a rental car, your best bet is to arrange a trip by taxi (try Tacso in Ovalle ☎ 53 630989, or El Faro in La Serena ☎ 51 225060) or take a tour from La Serena (see p.178).
By car If you're driving here, allow about 1.5hr from Ovalle, and 2hr from La Serena. The park is reached by a dirt road that branches west from the Panamericana 14km north of the junction with Ruta 45 to Ovalle. From the turn-off, it's 27km to the park entrance, where you pay your fee and register your visit.

ACCOMMODATION

HURTADO
Hacienda Los Andes Casilla 98, Río Hurtado ☎ 53 691822, ⓦ haciendalosandes.com. A Mexican-style ranch run by German expats, with spacious rooms enjoying mesmerizing views across the verdant valley.

Excellent meals are served and they have their own private observatory. The main focus here is equestrian, and they also offer multi-day horseback adventures (from US$770 per person), with all meals and transfers to and from Vicuña or Ovalle included. C̲H̲$̲6̲0̲,̲0̲0̲0̲

TERMAS DE SOCOS
Camping Socos ☎ 53 631 490, **ⓦ** campingtermassocos
.cl. Right next to the hotel and thermal baths is this campsite with its own outdoor pool and a handful of cabins that sleep up to four people. Open Nov–March. Camping CH$4500 per person, cabin $13000

Socos Panamerican Norte km 370, 35km southwest of Ovalle **☎** 53 198 2505, Santiago **☎** 2 236 3336, **ⓦ** termasocos.cl. This studiously rustic hotel offers excellent package deals including access to the baths and three meals in the restaurant. CH$36,000

Andacollo and around

Enfolded by rolling, sun-bleached hills midway between Ovalle and La Serena, **ANDACOLLO** is a tidy little town of small adobe houses grouped around a long main street. It lies along a side road which branches northeast from the Ruta 43, the most direct, scenic route between Ovalle and La Serena. Andacollo has been an important gold- and copper-mining centre ever since the Inca mined its hills in the sixteenth century, but is best known as the home of the **Virgen de Andacollo**, a small wooden carving that draws over one hundred thousand pilgrims to the town each year between December 23 and 26 for the Fiesta Grande de la Virgen, four days of music and riotous dancing performed by costumed groups from all over Chile. The town is also home to one of the country's newest observatories, open to the public for evening stargazing.

The Basílica

Plaza Pedro Nolasco Videla • Daily 9am–6.30pm • Donation expected

Andacolla is home to two temples erected in honour of the Virgin. Larger and grander is the **Basílica**, which towers over Plaza Pedro Nolasco Videla, the main square, in breathtaking contrast to the small, simple scale of the rest of the town. Built from 1873 to 1893, almost entirely of wood in a Roman–Byzantine style, its pale, cream-coloured walls are topped by two colossal 50m towers and a stunning 45m dome. Inside, sunlight floods through the dome, falling onto huge wooden pillars painted to look like marble.

Templo Antiguo

Plaza Pedro Nolasco Videla **Templo** Daily 9am–9pm • Free **Museo del Pelegrino** Daily 9am–6.30pm • Donation expected • **ⓦ** santuarioandacollo.cl

On the other side of the square stands the smaller, stone-built **Templo Antiguo**, dating from 1789. This is where the image of the Virgin stands for most of the year, perched on the main altar, awaiting the great festival when it's transported to the Basílica to receive the petitions and prayers of the pilgrims. Devotees of the Virgin de Andacollo have left an astonishing quantity of gifts here over the years, all displayed in the crypt of the Templo Antiguo as part of the **Museo del Pelegrino**.

Collowara Observatory

Ticket office Urmeneta 599 • Daily 9am–1pm & 2.30–8pm; tours Oct–April 9pm, 10.30pm & midnight; June–Sep 7pm, 8.30pm & 10pm • CH$3500 • **☎** 51 432 964, **ⓦ** collowara.cl • There is no organized transport to the observatory, but a return taxi costs around CH$8,000; ask the driver to pick you up when the tour ends

For a celestial experience, the **Collowara Observatory** (named after the Aymara term for "land of the stars") lies some 15km northeast of Andacollo, atop the 1300-metre Cerro Churqui. Built specifically for public use, like that run by the Municipalidad of Vicuña (see pp.144–146), this observatory also features a top-quality Smith-Cassegrain telescope. The two-hour **evening tours** start with a high-tech audiovisual talk (in Spanish and

English) about the galaxy and other astronomical matters, followed by the opportunity to observe the heavens through one of the telescopes – unless, of course, you're unlucky enough to be here on a cloudy night. It's best to make a reservation in advance.

ARRIVAL AND INFORMATION

ANDACOLLO

By bus/colectivo You can reach Andacollo by bus (every 2hr) or *colectivo* from La Serena (1hr) or Coquimbo (1hr 20min).

Tourist information Urmeneta 599 (Mon–Fri 9am–1.30pm & 2.30–5.30pm; ☎51 546 494, ⓦ andacollochile.cl).

ACCOMMODATION AND EATING

Hostal Arcón de Oro Alfonso 652 ☎51 431720, ⓦhostalarcondeoro.cl. This family-run hotel has neat rooms, with a special deal for wedding night guests, should the urge strike to tie the knot. CH$32,000

Sol de Andacollo Chepiquilla 90 ☎09 8815 8723. Come here to feast on typical Chilean dishes cooked in solar-powered ovens (mains around CH$3,600). Worth the 10min walk out of town. Daily noon–5pm.

Coquimbo and the coast

West of Ovalle, the Panamericana turns towards the ocean and skirts a string of small resorts that provide a calmer and more attractive beach setting than the built-up coast at La Serena. Spread over a rocky peninsula studded with colourful houses, the busy port of **COQUIMBO** was established during colonial times to serve neighbouring La Serena and became Chile's main copper exporter during the nineteenth century. Despite its impressive setting, the town has a slightly rough-edged, down-at-heel air, but is useful as an inexpensive base from which to enjoy La Serena's beaches, or for taking public transport to the nearby resorts of Guanaqueros – a fishing village 37km south with a sweeping beach – and Tongoy, 13km further south. A couple of blocks north of Coquimbo's main street, Avenida Costanera runs along the shore, past the large **port**, the **terminal pesquero**, and along to the lively **fish market**. This area makes for a pleasant stroll along the ocean, provided you don't mind the strong whiff of fish.

Cruz del Tercer Milenio

Juan Pablo II s/n • Daily 9.30am–6pm • ☎51 320125 • CH$1500 • ⓦ www.cruzdeltercermilenio.cl

From Coquimbo's main street, Aldunate, several stairways lead up to lookout points with sweeping views down to the port and across the bay; if you can't face the climb, take any *micro* marked "**Parte Alta**". The peak is crowned with a hideous, concrete 93-metre-high Cruz del Tercer Milenio ("Third Millennium Cross"), ablaze at night, and claims to be the only major spiritual monument in the world built at the turn of the millennium (which is just as well if they all looked like this one). The only conceivably redeeming feature is that you can enjoy superb panoramic views of the coast from up here. There is a religious museum here and an elevator which whisks visitors up to the arms of the cross.

Mezquito Centro Mohammed VI

Los Granados 500, Cerro Dominante • April–Nov Mon–Fri 9am–12.30pm & 2.30–5pm; Dec–March daily 9am–12.30pm & 2.30–6.30pm • ☎51 310440

A gift from the king of Morocco, this hilltop mosque provides a curious religious counterbalance, competing for attention (and panoramic vistas) with the Cruz del Tercer Milenio. It's a replica of the Mezquita Kutubia in Marrakech and construction was completed in 2007. As well as a mosque, it also functions as a cultural centre and library. Visitors can marvel at the ornate tile work inside.

Barrio Inglés

North of the central **Plaza de Armas**, and mostly on Aldunate, you'll find the **Barrio Inglés**, a district with the city's finest houses, many of them carved in wood by English craftsmen during the prosperous mining era. The restored buildings are beautifully lit at night and often double as bars, restaurants or music venues. Halfway along Aldunate is the pretty **Plaza Gabriela Mistral**, with its colourful artisan markets (Mon–Fri 11am–8pm).

Domo Cultural Animas

Plaza Gabriela Mistral • Mon–Fri 9am–5pm • ☎ 51 317006 • Free

In the middle of the plaza is the **Domo Culturas Animas**, a small archaeological museum exhibiting a pre-Columbian sacrificial graveyard dating from between 900 and 1100AD, with the skeletal remains of humans and llamas.

Guayacán

The southern shore of the peninsula, known as **Guayacán**, has a sandy beach, dominated at one end by a huge mechanized port used for exporting iron. While you're here, take a look at the tall steeple of the nearby **Iglesia de Guayacán**, a prefabricated steel church designed and built in 1888 by Alexandre-Gustave Eiffel, of the tower fame, and the **British cemetery**, built in 1860 at the behest of the British Admiralty and full of the graves of young sailors etched with heart-rending inscriptions like "died falling from aloft" (if the cemetery gates are locked, ask in the caretaker's house).

La Herradura

Guayacán's beach curves south to that of **La Herradura**, which although long, golden and sandy is marred by its proximity to the Panamericana. That said, the night-time views across the bay to the tip of Coquimbo are superb, and if you want to spend a night or two at the seaside, La Herradura makes a convenient, cheaper alternative to La Serena's Avenida del Mar.

Tongoy

Some 30km south of Coquimbo and 5km west of the Panamericana along a toll-paying side road lies **TONGOY**, a popular family resort spread over a hilly peninsula. It has two attractive sandy **beaches**, the Playa Socos, north of the peninsula, and the enormous Playa Grande, stretching 14km south. While there are plenty of hotels, *cabañas* and restaurants, development has been low-key, and the place remains pretty and relatively unspoiled.

ARRIVAL AND DEPARTURE   COQUIMBO AND AROUND

COQUIMBO

By bus Coquimbo's busy bus terminal is on the main road into town, at Varela and Garriga. Nearly all the main north–south inter-city buses stop here, as do local buses to coastal resorts like Tongoy (every 30min; 40min) and Guanaqueros (every 30min; 30min). Buses to La Serena (every 10min; 25min) can be picked up from the corner of Melgarejo and Alcalde.

By colectivo You can also get to the resorts, and to

Guayacán and La Herradura, by *colectivo* – they pick up behind the bus terminal and throughout the centre of town.

TONGOY

By bus Various bus companies from Coquimbo offer frequent services to Tongoy (every hour; 30min). From La Serena, Buses Serenamar (☎ 51 239144) and Sol de Elqui (☎ 51 215946) service Tongoy (every hour; 1hr).

ACCOMMODATION

COQUIMBO

Hostal Nomade Regimiento Coquimbo 5 ☎ 51 315665, ✉ hostalnomade.cl. There's a haunted mansion feel to this rambling old HI hostel in the former

French Consulate building. Spacious, if austere dorms, are complemented by superb views over the bay, a vegetable garden, kitchen and large common area. Dorm CH$15,000, double CH$25,000

Hotel Iberia Lastra 400 ☎51 312141, ⓦhoteliberia.cl. Located just off Aldunate in Barrio Inglés, Iberia offers spacious rooms, with and without bath, in an attractive old building. **CH$20,000**

Hotel Lig Aldunate 1577 ☎51 311171, ⓔhotellig @gmail.com. A satisfactory option just two blocks from the bus terminal with 24 bright, comfortable rooms with cable TV, wi-fi and private parking. Breakfast is an additional $2500. **CH$23,500**

LA HERRADURA

Cabañas Bucanero Av La Marina 201 ☎51 265153, ⓦbucanero.cl. There are terrific views of the bay from these 11 fully equipped *cabañas* set around an inviting pool. Each cabin has two bathrooms, a kitchen, cable TV and wi-fi. **CH$40,000**

Hotel La Herradura Av La Marina 200 ☎51 261647. Just off the beach, this family-friendly hotel offers decent rooms at reasonable prices. Breakfast, cable TV and wi-fi included. No credit cards. **CH$27,000**

TONGOY

Cabañas Tongoy Urmeneta Norte 237 ☎51 391902, ⓦcabanastongoy.cl. Rustic A-framed huts with small gardens, play areas for children and private parking, located close to the water's edge. No credit cards accepted. **CH$50,000**

Camping Ripipal Av Playa Grande ☎51 391192. On the beach 2km from the centre of town, this quiet, year-round **campsite** has good amenities, a children's play area and wi-fi. **CH$7000** per person

Hotel Panorámico Av Mirador 745 ☎51 391944, ⓦhotelpanoramico.cl. Set right on the water, this 15-room hotel is crammed with 1950s items including a great TV set and a stand-up hairdryer. Marine spa treatments offered. **CH$40,000**

EATING, DRINKING AND ENTERTAINMENT

COQUIMBO

For simple, cheap seafood lunches, go to the little *marisquerías* by the fish market; some have lovely water views. There are a number of lively bars clustered around Barrio Inglés.

Las Delicias Bilbao 54, local 11. Office workers and locals in the know come here for their daily fish fix and to watch *telenovelas* on the small TV. Service is no-nonsense, but the CH$1800 lunch menu is a steal. Daily 9am–6pm.

Dolce Helado Aldunate 862. If the ice-cream stand out front doesn't tempt you in, then live music wafting from the terrace will. Filling and reasonably priced Italian fare includes seafood lasagne (CH$2800). Mon–Fri 10am–11pm, Sat 1–11pm, Sun 1–8pm.

Pub Aduana Argandoña 360 ☎09 789 3469, ⓦpubaduana.cl. Pisco cocktails (CH$2500) and people-watching are the orders of the night at this popular bar with street-side tables and live music. Thurs–Sat 10pm–5am.

LA HERRADURA

Bucanero Av La Marina 201 ☎51 265153, ⓦbucanero.cl. Perched on a jetty projecting into the ocean, this is La Herradura's plushest restaurant, offering good but overpriced seafood (mains around CH$7000) and great views across to Coquimbo (best at night). Daily midday–7pm.

Club de Yates Av Costanera ☎51 564698. This sea-facing restaurant does decent steak as well as seafood and pasta mains (around CH$6000) and a popular Sunday buffet lunch ($8500). Tues–Thurs noon–8pm, Fri & Sat noon–midnight, Sun 1–5pm.

TONGOY

On the beachfront near the *caleta*, you'll find a row of excellent little **restaurants** serving delicious seafood.

Negro Cerro Av Playa Grande ☎51 391566. Diners flock to this seaside restaurant for the exquisite *pastel de jaiba* (crab pie) and CH$3500 lunch specials. Daily 10am–midnight.

La Picá del Veguita Av Playa Grande ☎51 391475. A seaside restaurant with amicable service, a well-positioned terrace and giant portions of simple yet honest fare. Grilled fish and chips are CH$6000. Daily 9am–10pm.

La Serena

Sitting by the mouth of the Río Elqui, 11km north of Coquimbo and 88km north of Ovalle, **LA SERENA** is for many visitors their first taste of northern Chile, after whizzing straight up from Santiago by road or air. Situated 2km inland from the northern sweep of the Bahía de Coquimbo, the **city centre** is an attractive mix of pale colonial-style houses, carefully restored churches and bustling crowds. Aside from the noteworthy **Museo Arqueológico**, the city's main appeal lies in just strolling the streets and squares, admiring the grand old houses, browsing through the numerous craft markets, wandering in and out of its many stone churches and hanging out in the leafy, central Plaza de Armas.

In the warmer months, hordes of Chilean tourists head for the six-kilometre **beach**, just 3km away along the Avenida del Mar – a rather charmless esplanade lined with oceanfront aparthotels and *cabañas* that are gloomily empty out of season. La Serena is also surrounded by some rewarding places to visit. Close at hand, and with good bus and *colectivo* connections, are the fine beaches at Tongoy (see p.135) and, above all, the glorious **Elqui Valley** (see p.143–150), one of the must-sees of the region.

Brief history

La Serena is Chile's second-oldest city, with a history chequered by violence and drama. Founded by Pedro de Valdivia in 1544 as a staging post on the way to Peru, it got off to an unpromising start when it was completely destroyed in an **Indian attack** four years later. Undeterred, Valdivia refounded the city in a new location the following year, but La Serena continued to lead a precarious existence, subjected to frequent and often violent raids by pirates, many of them British.

The nineteenth century

Happier times arrived in the nineteenth century, when the discovery of large silver deposits at Arqueros, just north of La Serena, marked the beginning of the region's great

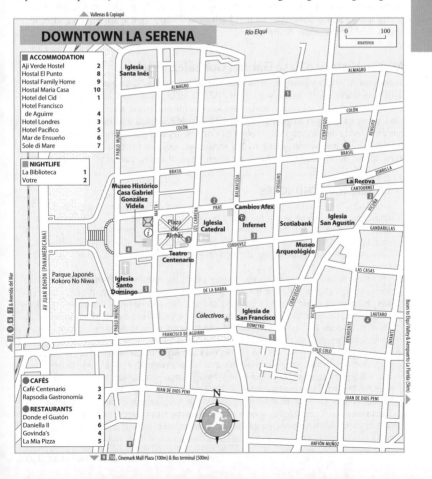

DOWNTOWN LA SERENA

Vallenas & Copiapó

Río Elqui

0   100
metres

ACCOMMODATION
Aji Verde Hostel	2
Hostal El Punto	8
Hostal Family Home	9
Hostal Maria Casa	10
Hotel del Cid	1
Hotel Francisco de Aguirre	4
Hotel Londres	3
Hotel Pacifico	5
Mar de Ensueño	6
Sole di Mare	7

NIGHTLIFE
La Biblioteca	1
Votre	2

CAFÉS
Café Centenario	3
Rapsodia Gastronomía	2

RESTAURANTS
Donde el Guatón	1
Daniella II	6
Govinda's	4
La Mia Pizza	5

Cinemark Mall Plaza (100m) & Bus terminal (500m)

silver boom. These heady days saw the erection of some of the city's finest mansions and churches, as the mining magnates competed in their efforts to dazzle with their wealth.

The twentieth century
In the 1940s, **Gabriel González Videla,** president of Chile and a local Serenense, instituted his **"Plan Serena",** through which the city developed its signature architectural style. One of the key elements of Videla's urban remodelling scheme was the vigorous promotion of the Spanish colonial style, with facades restored or rebuilt on existing structures and strict stylistic controls imposed on new ones. Unimaginative and inflexible though some claimed these measures to be, the results are undeniably pleasing, and La Serena boasts an architectural harmony and beauty noticeably lacking in most Chilean cities.

Iglesia Catedral
East side of the Plaza de Armas • Mon–Fri 9.30am–1pm & 3.30–7pm • Free

Grand and dominating, the pale walls of the **Iglesia Catedral** date from 1844, when the previous church on the site was finally pulled down because of the damage wrought by the 1796 earthquake. Inside, among its more curious features are the wooden pillars, disguised to look like stone. Just off the opposite side of the square, on Cordovez, the pretty **Iglesia Santo Domingo** was first built in 1673 and then again in 1755, after it was sacked by the pirate Sharp.

Museo Histórico Casa Gabriel González Videla
Southwest corner of the Plaza de Armas • Mon–Fri 10am–6pm, Sat 10am–1pm • ☎ 51 206797, ⓦ museohistoricolaserena.cl • CH$600

This two-storey adobe house was, from 1927 to 1977, home to Chile's erstwhile president, Gabriel González Videla, best known for outlawing the Communist party after using its support to gain power in 1946. Inside, a small and rather dull **museum** has an eclectic display of photos, objects, documents and paintings relating to the president's life and works, along with a section on regional history; the temporary art exhibitions, occasionally held here, are often better than the permanent display.

LA SERENA'S CHURCHES

Including Iglesia Catedral and Iglesia Santo Domingo on the Plaza de Armas, a remarkable 29 **churches** dot La Serena, lending an almost fairy-tale look to the city. This proliferation of places of worship dates from the earliest days of the city, when all the religious orders established bases to provide shelter for their clergy's frequent journeys between Santiago and Lima (the viceregal capital). Nearly all the churches are built of stone, which is unusual for Chile, and all are in mint condition.

Standing at the corner of Balmaceda and de la Barra, the **Iglesia San Francisco** is one of La Serena's oldest churches, though the date of its construction is unknown, as the city archives were burnt in the pirate Sharp's raid of 1680. Its huge walls are one metre thick, covered in a stone facade carved in fanciful Baroque designs. Inside, the **Museo de Arte Religioso** (Tues & Thurs 10am–1pm & 4–7pm; ☎ 51 224477; donation welcome) contains a small but impressive collection of religious sculpture and paintings from the colonial period.

Beautiful for its very plainness, the 1755 **Iglesia San Agustín,** on the corner of Cienfuegos and Cantournet, was originally the Jesuit church but was taken over by the Augustinians after the Jesuits were expelled from Chile in 1767. Its honey-toned stone walls were badly damaged in the 1975 earthquake, but have been skilfully restored. On the northern edge of town, overlooking the banks of the Río Elqui, the recently restored seventeenth-century **Iglesia Santa Inés** was constructed on the site of a rudimentary chapel erected by the first colonists and its thick white adobe walls recall the Andean churches of the northern *altiplano*.

Museo Arqueológico

Corner of Cordovez and Cienfuegos • Tues–Fri 9.30am–5.50pm, Sat 10am–1pm & 4–7pm, Sun 10am–1pm • ☎ 51 224492, ⓦ www.dibam.cl/sdm_m_laserena • CH$600, Sun free

Entered through an imposing nineteenth-century portico, La Serena's **Museo Arqueológico** boasts two outstanding treasures, though most of the displays could do with improving. The first of these is its large collection of **Diaguita pottery**, considered by many to be among the most beautiful pre-Columbian ceramics in South America. The terracotta pieces, dating from around 1000 to 1500 AD, are covered in intricate geometric designs painted in black and white and, in the later phases, red. Starting with simple bowls and dishes made for domestic use, the Diaguita went on to produce elaborately shaped ceremonial pots and jars, often in the form of humans or animals, or sometimes both, such as the famous *jarros patos*, or "duck jars", moulded in the form of a duck's body with a human head.

The moai

The museum's other gem is the giant stone statue, or **moai**, from Easter Island, "donated" to La Serena at the behest of President González Videla in 1952. Until the mid 1990s, it stood in a park on Avenida Colo Colo, covered in graffiti and urinated on by drunks. Then, as part of an exhibition of Easter Island art in 1996, it travelled to Barcelona, where it was accidentally decapitated. Tragedy turned to good fortune, however, when the insurance money from the accident paid for a brand-new *sala* to be built for the statue in the archeological museum. This is where you'll find it today, standing on a raised platform against a flattering azure backdrop, the joins at the neck hardly showing.

La Recova

Corner of Cienfuegos and Cantournet • Daily 10am–7pm

Of La Serena's numerous **craft markets**, the biggest and best is the bustling **La Recova**, occupying two large patios inside an arcaded building opposite the Iglesia San Agustín. The quality of the merchandise is generally high, and goods include finely worked objects in *combabalita* (a locally mined marble), lapis lazuli jewellery, alpaca sweaters and candied papaya.

Parque Japonés Kokoro No Niwa

Pedro Pablo Muñoz and Eduardo de la Barra • Tues–Sun 10am–6pm • CH$1000

Backing onto the Panamericana, two blocks west of the Plaza de Armas, the **Parque Japonés Kokoro No Niwa**, whose Japanese name means "Garden of the Heart", is an oasis of perfectly manicured lawns, ponds awash with water lilies, ice-white geese and little Japanese bridges and pagodas. Unfortunately, the sense of peace and tranquillity it creates is undermined by the din of the highway.

Avenida del Mar

There's no bus or *colectivo* service along Av del Mar; take a micro headed for Coquimbo from almost any street corner (if in doubt, go to Av Francisco de Aguirre) and get off on the Panamericana at Cuatro Esquinas or Peñuelas (6km from the city), both a short walk from the beach

Stretching 6km round the rim of a wide, horseshoe bay 2km west of the city, the **Avenida del Mar** is a staid collection of glitzy hotels, tourist complexes and *cabañas* that bulge with visitors for two months of the year and are otherwise empty. In January and February hundreds of cars inch their way up and down the avenue, bumper to bumper, and mostly Chilean tourists pile onto the sandy beaches, which are clean but spoiled by the horrific high-rise backdrop.

OBSERVATORIES AROUND LA SERENA

Thanks to the exceptional transparency of its skies, northern Chile is home to the largest concentration of astronomical **observatories** in the world. The region around La Serena, in particular, has been chosen by a number of international astronomical research institutions as the site of their telescopes, housed in white, futuristic domes that loom over the valleys from their hilltop locations. Among the research organizations that own the observatories are North American and European groups that need a base in the southern hemisphere (about a third of the sky seen here is never visible in the northern hemisphere).

Some of the observatories offer guided tours, including the impressive **Cerro Tololo Inter-American Observatory**, whose 4m telescope was the strongest in the southern hemisphere until it was overtaken by Cerro Paranal's Very Large Telescope, the most powerful in the world, located near Antofagasta (see p.175). All the tours listed below take place during the day and are free of charge but are strictly no-touching; a more hands-on night-time experience is provided by the small but user-friendly observatory on **Cerro Mamalluca** (see p.146), 9km north of Vicuña, as well as by the newer Del Pangue observatory 17km south of Vicuña (see p.146) and the **Collowara** observatory outside Andacollo (see p.132).

Las Campanas 155km northeast of La Serena ☎51 207301, ⊚lco.cl. The Carnegie Institute's observatory contains four telescopes, with two 6.5-metre telescopes under construction as part of its Magellan Project. Contact the observatory's offices in La Serena to make reservations; they're located next to Cerro Tololo's offices on Colina El Pino. Sat 2.30–5.30pm.

Cerro Tololo 88km east of La Serena, reached by a side road branching south of the Elqui Valley road ☎51 205200, ⊚www.ctio.noao.edu. Tours need to be booked several days in advance; you'll need to collect your visitor's permit from the observatory's offices in La Serena (up the hill behind the university, at Colina El Pino) the day before the tour. Sat 9.15am–noon & 1.15–4pm.

La Silla 150km northeast of La Serena, reached by a side road branching east from the Panamericana ☎2 4644100 in Santiago, ☎51 272601 in La Serena, ⊚eso.org. The site of the European Southern Observatory's fourteen telescopes, including two 3.6m optical reflectors. Book tours in advance through the observatory's Santiago offices or the La Serena office near the airport at Panorámica 4461. Aug–May Sat 2–4pm.

ARRIVAL AND DEPARTURE
LA SERENA

By plane The Aeropuerto La Florida (☎51 270191) is 5km east of the city and served by taxis and transfers plus *micros* on the main road (ranging from CH$400–4000).

Airlines LAN (Balmaceda 406 ☎51 229069 or ☎600 526 2000); Sky Airline (Eduardo de la Barra 495, ☎51 218372). Destinations Antofagasta (2 daily; 1hr 15min); Santiago (8 daily; 1hr).

By bus Inter-city buses operate from La Serena's large bus terminal on El Santo, a 15min walk southwest of the central plaza. There's no direct bus from the terminal into town, but there are plenty of taxis, charging about CH$2500. Buses for the Elqui Valley depart from the main terminal every 30min, but also stop southeast of the centre at the Plaza de Abastos, on Calle Esmeralda (just south of Colo Colo). To get to Tongoy, take a Serenamar bus (☎51 323422) from the terminal. Destinations Andacollo (every 2hr; 1hr); Antofagasta (20 daily; 12hr); Arica (5 daily; 24hr); Calama (11 daily; 15hr); Chañaral (11 daily; 7hr); Copiapó (32 daily; 5hr); Horcón (3

daily; 2hr 45min); Iquique (8 daily; 18hr); Montegrande (every 30min; 1hr 50min); Ovalle (every 15min; 1hr 20min); Pisco Elqui (every 30min; 2hr); Santiago (every 30min; 7hr); Vallenar (15 daily; 2hr 45min); Valparaíso (6 daily; 5hr); Vicuña (every 30min; 1hr).

By micro The coastal resorts of Tongoy and La Herradura are more easily reached from Coquimbo – to get there, take a *micro* (marked "Coquimbo Directo 1") from Av Francisco de Aguirre or Calles Brasil, Infante or Matta. Alternatively, you can flag down a *micro* from the Panamericana, a 5min walk west.

By colectivo Two *colectivo* services (look for the yellow taxis) from La Serena operate from Calle Domeyko one block south of Iglesia San Franciso: Anserco, at no. 530 (☎51 217567), goes to Andacollo, Vicuña and Ovalle; Tasco, at no. 575 (☎51 224517), goes to Vicuña, Montegrande and Pisco Elqui. The service is slightly more expensive than the bus.

INFORMATION

Tourist information There is a helpful and friendly Sernatur office on the west side of the Plaza de Armas at Matta 461 (Jan

& Feb daily 9am–9pm; March–Dec Mon–Fri 9am–6pm; Sat 10am–2pm; ☎51 225199, ⊚turismoregiondecoquimbo.cl).

Conaf Regimiento Arica 901, Pañuelas, Coquimbo (Mon–Fri 9am–5pm; ☎51 244306). Provides information on Parque Nacional Fray Jorge, Monumento Natural Pichasca and Parque Nacional Pinguino de Humboldt.

TOURS

The two most popular day tours from La Serena are to the **Elqui Valley** (also easily reached on public transport) and to the cloudforest reserve at **Parque Nacional Fray Jorge** (see p.131), about 2hr south of the city and not served by public transport. Other favourite destinations include night tours to the Cerro Mamalluca observatory near Vicuña; the ancient petroglyph site of the **Valle del Encanto**, near Ovalle (see p.129); **Monumento Natural Pichasca**, where you'll find the remains of a "fossilized wood" (see p.129); and the **Reserva Nacional Pinguino de Humboldt**, a penguin and dolphin sanctuary 120km north of La Serena that is not served by public transport. Most tours cost from CH$15,000 to CH$30,000 per person and a selection of reliable operators is given in the listings below.

TOUR OPERATORS
Eco Turismo Andres Bello 937 ☎51 218970, ⓦeco-turismo.cl.
Talinay Chile Av Francisco de Aguirre ☎51 218658,

ⓦwww.talinaychile.com. This agency also offers mountaineering trips in the Andes.
Nomade Experience Matta 510 ☎51 217925, ⓦnomade-experience.cl.

ACCOMMODATION

You'll find a large choice of budget accommodation and mid- to upscale options in the centre, while Avenida del Mar, 3km from town, is lined with overpriced beachside *cabañas* and hotels.

HOTELS
Hostal Family Home Av El Santo 1056 ☎51 212099, ⓦwww.familyhome.cl. Delightful house that lives up to its name and is conveniently located between the bus terminal and the central plaza, with single, double and triple rooms (some en suite), plus use of a kitchen. CH$25,000
Hostal Maria Casa Las Rojas 18 ☎51 229282, ⓦhostalmariacasa.cl. Friendly, family-run option situated a block from the bus terminal with rooms off a lovely garden. Includes free internet, shared bathrooms and a communal kitchen. CH$16,000.
Hotel del Cid O'Higgins 138 ☎51 212692, ⓦhoteldelcid.cl. Great hotel run by a Scottish–Chilean couple, with 28 spotless and comfortable rooms around a flower-filled terrace. Secure parking is offered. CH$45,000
Hotel Francisco de Aguirre Cordovez 210 ☎51 222991, ⓦdahoteles.com. One of La Serena's plushest hotels, with stylish rooms in a handsome old three-storey building and a glamorous poolside restaurant with food that is toothsome and well presented. CH$87,500 (US$175)
Hotel Londres Cordovez 550 ☎51 219066, ⓦhotellondres.cl. Centrally located, with clean and tidy rooms, some with private bath and others with just a washbasin. All rooms have cable TV and wi-fi. CH$36,000
Hotel Pacífico Av de la Barra 252 ☎51 225674, ⓔreservas@hotelpacifico.cl. Ancient, rambling hotel just three blocks from the Plaza de Armas with clean, basic rooms (some with bath, some without) and friendly staff. CH$28,000.

Mar de Ensueño Av del Mar 900 ☎51 222381, ⓦhotelmarensueno.com. If you're in La Serena in summer with the kids in tow, this beachside complex with ocean-facing rooms and fully equipped cabins is a good bet. Includes buffet breakfast, swimming pool, gym, bicycles for guest use and a games room. CH$86,000 (US$172)

HOSTELS
Aji Verde Hostel Vicuña 415 ☎51 489016, ⓦajiverdehostel.cl. A fun atmosphere pervades this central hostel with young staff, a roof terrace, kitchen and plenty of common areas for connecting with fellow travellers. Dorm CH$7500, double CH$18,000
★ **Hostal El Punto** Andres Bello 979 ☎51 228474, ⓦhostalelpunto.cl. Charming, German-run hostel with spacious, impeccably clean rooms, some with private bath, and one dorm. Mosaic-tiled courtyards, a restaurant and big breakfasts with home-made jam and goat's cheese ensure this place books up fast. There's also parking, kitchen and internet. Dorm CH$7500, double CH$16,000

CAMPSITES
Sole di Mare Parcela 66, Peñuelas ☎51 312531; buses between La Serena and Coquimbo stop nearby. Lovely, grassy campsite down at the quieter end of the beach, halfway between La Serena and Coquimbo. Good facilities and lots of shade. CH$3000 per person

EATING AND DRINKING

The restaurants on Avenida del Mar are overpriced but have fine sea views, while those downtown are better value yet unexceptional. The La Recova **market** has dozens of good-value *marisquerías* (seafood restaurants) on the upper gallery of the handicrafts market, making it a perfect place for lunch. For the freshest seafood around, head to the Sector de Pescadores at Playa Peñuelas, 6km along the coast between La Serena and Coquimbo.

CAFÉS

Café Centenario Cordovez 391 ⓦteatrocentenario .blogspot.com. Lavazza coffee, regional wines and local beer are served in this chic corner spot on the south-east corner of Plaza de Armas. Try the house speciality, *café camanchaca* – a mix of pisco, espresso and milk (CH$2550). Mon–Fri 8am–8pm.

Rapsodia Gastronomía Prat 470 ⓣ51 212695. La Serena's best bet for a good coffee, with tables dotting a little patio under a huge palm. The Mediterranean salad with salmon carpaccio is CH$4500. Mon–Wed 9am–9pm, Thurs & Fri (& Sat Jan & Feb) 9am–11pm.

RESTAURANTS

Daniella II Av Francisco de Aguirre 335 ⓣ51 227537. Typical Chilean restaurant with friendly service and a traditional menu of local fish and meat dishes like *pastel*

de jaiba (a crab and corn pie) and *lomo a lo pobre* (steak with chips, onions and fried egg). Set lunches are CH$2000. Mon–Fri & Sun 10am–9pm, Sat 10am–6pm.

Donde el Guatón Brasil 750 ⓣ51 211519. Lively, friendly and intimate, this colonial-style restaurant serves the best *parrilladas* in La Serena (main course CH$5000). Daily 12.30–4pm & 7.30pm–1am.

Govinda's Lautaro 841 ⓣ51 224289. A lunchtime vegetarian spot run by Hare Krishnas, serving wholegrain bread, fresh and healthy Italian and Indian-inspired fare as well as fragrant teas. Set lunches CH$2000. Mon–Fri 1–3pm.

La Mia Pizza Av del Mar 2100 ⓣ51 212232. Locals pile into this beachside restaurant for its crisp, thin-crust pizzas loaded with fresh toppings (CH$5000). The pastas, steaks and fish dishes are also recommendable. Mon–Sat 12.30pm–midnight, Sun 12.30–4.30pm.

NIGHTLIFE AND ENTERTAINMENT

Nightlife is concentrated on O'Higgins between Av Francisco de Aguirre and de la Barra, where there are many student bars. The pubs and discos by the beach are more seasonal, reaching their heady zenith in Jan and Feb.

La Biblioteca O'Higgins and Av Francisco de Aguirre. Chain-smoking students congregate around small wooden tables, feeding the dukebox while downing *terremoto* cocktails (sweet white wine, pineapple ice-cream and Amaretto). Daily 2pm–4.30am.

Cinemark Mall Plaza Av Albert Solari 1400 ⓣ51 470310, ⓦcinemark.cl. This six-screen cinema near the bus terminal shows blockbuster films and also hosts themed festivals. Admission CH$3800.

Teatro Centenario Cordoves 391 ⓣ51 212659, ⓦteatrocentenario.blogspot.com. One of the best jazz

venues in Chile, located in a recently remodelled theatre in the city's old cinema. Local and international acts perform to a head-nodding, wine-sipping crowd. Tickets CH$5000–15,000. March–Nov every second Sat 8pm–late; Dec–Feb every Sat 8pm–late.

Votre Av del Mar 5685 ⓣ09 6316 4676, ⓦclubvotre.cl. If you're looking for some nocturnal action, this three-level beachside disco, bar and sushi lounge pulls in all ages – all year round. Entrance CH$6000. March–Nov Wed–Sat 11.30pm–5am; Dec–Feb Mon–Thurs & Sun 11pm–4am, Fri & Sat 11.30pm–5am.

DIRECTORY

Banks and exchange There are plenty of ATMs on or near the Plaza de Armas and at Cordovez and Cienfuegos. For currency exchange, try Cambios Afex, Balmaceda 413.

Car rental In addition to the airport, there are many outlets on Av Francisco de Aguirre, including Avis at no. 063 (ⓣ51 545300, ⓦavis.cl); Budget at no. 015 (ⓣ51 218272); Econorent at no. 0135 (ⓣ51 220113, ⓦeconorent.cl); Hertz at no. 0225 (ⓣ51 226171,

ⓦhertz.cl); and Santiago rent a car at no. 0660-B (ⓣ51 211951, ⓦsantiagorentacar.com).

Internet Infernet at Prat and Balmadeda.

Post office On the west side of Plaza de Armas, on the corner of Prat and Matta.

Taxis 24hr radio taxis ⓣ51 212122.

Surfing Surfboard and wetsuit hire for CH$5000 from Poisson, Av del Mar 1001; surfing lessons are CH$12,000.

The Elqui Valley

Quiet, rural and extremely beautiful, the **ELQUI VALLEY** unfolds east from La Serena and into the Andes. Irrigated by canals fed by the Puclara and La Laguna dams, the valley floor is given over entirely to cultivation – of papayas, custard apples (*chirimoyas*), oranges, avocados and, most famously, the vast expanses of grape vines grown to produce **pisco**. It's the fluorescent green of these vines that makes the valley so stunning, forming a spectacular contrast with the charred, brown hills that rise on either side.

Some 60km east of La Serena, appealing little **Vicuña** is the main town and transport hub of the Elqui Valley. Moving east from here, the valley gets higher and narrower and is dotted with tiny villages like **Montegrande** and the odd pisco distillery. **Pisco Elqui**, 105km east of La Serena, is a very pretty village that makes a great place to unwind for a couple of days. If you really want to get away from it all, head for one of the rustic *cabañas* dotted along the banks of the **Río Cochiguaz**, which forks east of the main valley at Montegrande, or delve beyond Pisco Elqui into the farthest reaches of the Elqui Valley itself. Buses and a paved road will get you all the way to Horcón but not to the farthest village of all, **Alcohuaz**.

GETTING AROUND   THE ELQUI VALLEY

By bus Many tour companies in La Serena offer day trips to the Elqui Valley, but it's hardly worth taking a tour, as public transport up and down the valley is so frequent and cheap. If you're here in Jan or Feb, it might be worth investing in a day pass, which costs CH$5500 and is valid for 24hr, so that you can hop on and off any bus plying the valley as many times as you choose. The two main bus companies are Sol de Elqui (☎ 51 215946) and Via Elqui (☎ 51 211707).

Vicuña

An hour by bus inland from La Serena, **VICUÑA** is a neat and tidy agricultural town ringed by mountains and laid out around a large, luxuriantly landscaped square. It's a pleasant, easy-going place with a few low-key attractions, a good choice of places to stay and eat, a couple of pisco distilleries just out of town and two visitor-friendly observatories on its doorstep. If you're looking to stretch your legs, there are panoramic views of the town and entire Elqui Valley from the top of Cerro de la Virgen, north-east of the centre.

Plaza de Armas

Life revolves firmly around the central **Plaza de Armas**, which has at its centre a huge stone replica of the **death mask** of Nobel Prize-winning poet **Gabriela Mistral**, the Elqui

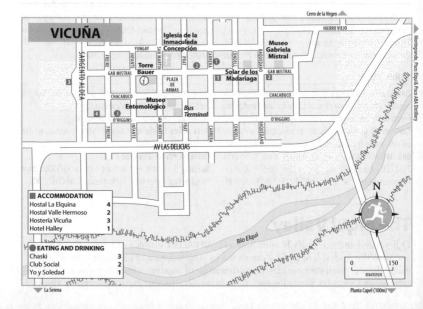

Valley's most famous daughter. On the square's northwest corner stands the **Iglesia de la Inmaculada Concepción**, topped by an impressive wooden tower built in 1909 – take a look inside at its vaulted polychrome ceiling, painted with delicate religious images and supported by immense wooden columns. Right next door, the eccentric **Torre Bauer** is a bright-red, mock-medieval tower prefabricated in Germany in 1905 and brought to Vicuña on the instructions of the town's German-born mayor, Adolfo Bauer; the adobe building supporting it houses the Municipalidad.

Museo Entomológico

Chacabuco 334, on the south side of the Plaza de Armas • Jan–March daily 10am–8pm; April–Dec Mon–Fri 10.30am–1.30pm & 3.30–7pm, Sat & Sun 10.30am–7pm • CH$600

The **Museo Entomológico** hoards a fascinating collection of horror-movie creepy-crawlies hailing from Chile, the Amazon, Africa and Asia, including hairy spiders and vicious-looking millipedes, plus exotic butterflies and shells. Hopefully this is the closest you'll get to two of Chile's deadliest critters: the *araña del rincon* (recluse spider) and the blood-sucking *vinchuca*, which spreads Chagas disease.

Museo Gabriela Mistral

Calle Gabriela Mistral 759 • Jan & Feb Mon–Sat 10am–7pm, Sun 10am–6pm; March–Dec Mon–Fri 10am–5.45pm, Sat 10.30am–6pm, Sun 10am–1pm • CH$600 • ☎ 51 411233, ⊛ mgmistral.cl

Four blocks east of the square, the **Museo Gabriela Mistral** displays photos, prizes, articles and personal objects bequeathed to the city by the poet, along with panels giving an account of her life and works. The museum itself is a striking building, taking its inspiration from the natural elements of Mistral's beloved Elqui Valley – stone, light, water and mountains. Also on the grounds is a new children's library (Mon–Fri) housing a four-thousand-strong collection of books. Next door is the modest house where Mistral was born in 1889.

El Solar de los Madariaga

Calle Gabriela Mistral 683 • Daily 10am–7pm • CH$500 • ☎ 51 411220

A few doors down from the Museo Gabriela Mistral is the **Solar de los Madariaga**, an old, colonial-style house preserved as a museum, displaying a modest collection of nineteenth-century furniture and clothes.

Pisco Capel distillery

Camino Peralillo, 2km southeast of Vicuña • Daily 10am–12.30pm & 2.30–6pm • Tours CH$1000; museum CH$500 • ☎ 51 554337, ⊛ piscocapel.cl

Just out of town, across the bridge by the filling station, you'll find the **Planta Capel**, the largest pisco distillery in the Elqui Valley. It has a small museum outlining the history of pisco and also offers slick guided tours in English and Spanish every half-hour, with tastings and the chance to buy bottles and souvenirs at the end.

Pisco ABA distillery

Ruta 41 Km 63, 8km east of Vicuña • Mon–Sat 9am–6pm; Sun 10am–6pm • Tours free • ☎ 51 411039, ⊛ piscoaba.cl

ABA is a family-owned boutique distillery in the village of El Arenal. It produces around sixty thousand bottles a year, including the ABA and Fuegos piscos as well as a creamy mango sour cocktail. Tours includes tastings, a glimpse of its bucolic 148-acre farm where Muscat grapes are hand-picked, and a visit to its production facilities, where distillation takes place in huge copper stills. Call ahead for a tour in English.

ARRIVAL AND INFORMATION **VICUÑA**

By bus Buses drop passengers off at the terminal on the corner of O'Higgins and Prat, one block south of the Plaza de Armas. Santiago services are operated by Expreso Norte (☎ 51 411348) and Pullman Buses (☎ 51 411466).

Destinations La Serena (every 30min; 1hr); Montegrande (every 30min; 50min), Pisco Elqui (every 30min; 1hr); Santiago (4 daily; 7hr).

Colectivos Taxi *colectivos* leave from the bus terminal for La Serena and while their set fares are marginally more than the bus, the journey takes less time. They also service the immediate area, and for local journeys you'll need to negotiate a price with the driver.

Tourist office Northwest corner of the plaza, beneath the Torre Bauer (Mon–Fri 8.30am–6pm, Sat 9am–6pm, Sun 9am–2pm; ☎ 51 209125).

ACCOMMODATION

Hostal La Elquina O'Higgins 65 ☎ 51 411317. Dowdy rooms with and without private bathrooms are set around a flower-filled patio; the garden is perfect for camping (CH$3000). Kitchen, wi-fi and breakfast included. **CH$16,000**

★ **Hostal Valle Hermoso** Gabriela Mistral 706 ☎ 51 411206, ⓦ www.hostalvallehermoso.com. Motherly Lucia presides over this restored century-old abode house with a bright central patio. Minimalist but sweet rooms have comfortable beds and private bath with piping-hot showers. Some English spoken. **CH$24,000**

Hostería Vicuña Sargento Aldea 101 ☎ 51 411301, ⓦ hosteriavicuna.cl. Vicuña's top hotel is overpriced but has a fabulous pool and one of the town's better restaurants, with unadventurous but good-quality meat and fish dishes. **CH$54,000**

Hotel Halley Gabriela Mistral 542 ☎ 51 412070, ⓦ turismohalley.cl. This central hotel comes recommended, with large albeit dark, impeccably decorated rooms in a colonial-style building, and access to a pool. **CH$34,000**

EATING AND DRINKING

Chaski O'Higgins 159 ☎ 51 412273 ⓔ chaskigastronomia@gmail.com. This restaurant's rustic outdoor setting belies its sophisticated cuisine: think salmon curry, beef with chutney and quinoa, and steaming cups of chai tea (mains CH$7500). The owners also offer cycling and horseriding tours. Mon & Wed–Sat 10am–4pm & 6–9.30pm, Sun midday–6pm.

Club Social Gabriel Mistral 445. The atmosphere is always convivial inside this grand, sprawling colonial building which is popular for its typical Chilean dishes, seafood pancakes (CH$6800) and button-popping *parrilladas* (CH$20,000 for two, with wine). Daily 10am–midnight.

Yo y Soledad Carrera 320. If you're returning from an observatory tour and have the late-night munchies, you'll find this lively restaurant and bar at your service. Set lunches (CH$2500) are also good. Mon–Thurs 11am–1am, Fri–Sun 11am–3am.

Cerro Mamalluca observatory

Office Gabriela Mistral 260, Vicuña • Office Mon–Fri 8.30am–8.30pm, Sat & Sun 10am–2pm & 4–8pm; tours Oct–April 8.30pm, 10.30pm & 12.30am; May–Sept 6.30pm & 8.30pm • CH$3500 • ☎ 51 411352, ⓦ mamalluca.org • Assemble 30min before your slot at the administrative office in Vicuña, from where transport is provided (CH$1500 return); reservations essential. If you have your own transport you must still report to the office, to confirm and pay, and to follow the minibus in a convoy.

Nine kilometres northeast of Vicuña, the **Cerro Mamalluca observatory**, built specifically for public use, is run by the Municipalidad de Vicuña and features a 30cm Smith-Cassegrain telescope donated by the Cerro Tololo team. The two-hour **evening tours** start with a high-tech audiovisual talk on the history of the universe, and end with the chance to look through the telescope. If you're lucky, you might see a dazzling display of stars, planets, galaxies, nebulas and clusters, including Jupiter, Saturn's rings, the Orion nebula, the Andromeda galaxy and Sirius. These tours are aimed at complete beginners, but serious astronomers can arrange in-depth, small-group sessions with at least a few weeks' notice.

Del Pangue Observatory

Office San Martin 233, Vicuña • Office daily 10am–7pm; tours Jan & Feb 9pm & 11pm; June–Aug 6pm; rest of year 8pm; no tours five days around the full moon; tour times often change depending on planet positions • CH$15,000 • ☎ 51 412584, ⓦ observatoriodelpangue .blogspot.com • Assemble 30min before the tour at the Vicuña office, from where you must take the transport provided (free); private vehicles are not allowed.

With a spectacular mountaintop setting 17km south of Vicuña and not far from the Tololo scientific observatory, **Del Pangue** offers an intimate and personalized star-gazing experience specifically designed for amateur astronomers. Two-hour tours are conducted by bona fide astronomers, and Del Pangue's new, state-of-the-art 63cm Obsession telescope is light years ahead of other public observatories. Two telescopes and a variety of adjustable eyepieces ensure you get up close and personal with the moon's craters, distant galaxies and blazing stars.

English, Spanish and French-speaking astronomers deliver sophisticated yet down-to-earth celestial commentary and can also answer questions on life, the universe and everything in between. Group tours are limited to ten people. Wear warm clothes as it gets cold on the mountain.

Montegrande

The picturesque village of **MONTEGRANDE**, 34km east of Vicuña (if you're driving, take the right turn for Paihuano at Rivadavia), features a pretty church whose late-nineteenth-century wooden belfry looms over a surprisingly large square. The childhood home of Gabriela Mistral, Montegrande assiduously devotes itself to preserving her memory: her profile has been outlined in white stones on the valley wall opposite the plaza, and the school where she lived with, and was taught by, her sister, has been turned into a **museum** (Tues–Sun 10am–1pm & 3–6pm; CH$300), displaying some of her furniture and belongings. Just south of the village, her **tomb** rests on a hillside, opposite the turn-off for Cochiguaz.

Close by is the wacky **Galería de Arte Zen**, where you can admire esoteric art and have a tarot card reading. One kilometre before the village is the Cavas del Valle organic winery, run by a retired couple who offer free tours and tastings (☎51 451352, ⓦcavasdelvalle.cl; daily 10am–8.30pm).

ARRIVAL AND DEPARTURE   **MONTEGRANDE**

By bus Buses stop in the village and pass by half-hourly. Three buses weekly (Mon, Wed & Fri) go along the Río Cochiguaz.

Destinations Pisco Elqui (every 30min; 10min); Vicuña (every 30min; 50min).

ACCOMMODATION AND EATING

El Galpón La Jarilla ☎51 1982587, ⓦelgalpon-elqui .cl. Halfway between Montegrande and Pisco Elqui, in a wonderful quiet location with mountain views, is one of the area's best places to stay. Stylishly built, it is owned by a friendly Chilean who lived for many years in the US. Each of the rooms has a huge bathroom, TV and a minibar; two- and five-person cabins are also available. The well-kept grounds have an eye-catching swimming pool. Double CH$60,000, cabin CH$75,000

El Mesón del Fraile ☎51 451232. Beckoning opposite the museum, this restaurant has tables on a wide, breezy balcony and serves delectable stone-oven pizzas and the regional goat speciality, *cabrito al jugo* (CH$6500). Tues–Sun midday–9pm.

Las Pléyades ☎51 451107. The only hotel in Montegrande itself. Its five rustic, chic rooms have artistic touches and come with private bathroom, swimming pool and access to a river beach. CH$40,000

Pisco Elqui and around

PISCO ELQUI was known as La Unión until 1939, when Gabriel González Videla – later President of Chile – cunningly renamed it to thwart Peru's efforts to gain exclusive rights to the name "Pisco". An idyllic village with fewer than nine hundred inhabitants, it boasts a beautiful square filled with lush palm trees and flowers, overlooked by a colourful church with a tall, wooden tower. Locals sell home-made jam and jewellery in the square, and its abundant shade provides a welcome relief from the sun.

Pisco Mistral

O'Higgins s/n • Guided tours daily Jan & Feb 11.30am–9pm; rest of year Tues–Sun 10am–6pm • CH$6000 • ☎51 451358, ⓦpiscomistral.cl
On the south side of the Plaza de Armas, the **Pisco Mistral** is Chile's oldest pisco

distillery, which today (and now considerably modernized) produces the famous Tres Erres brand. There are **guided tours** around the old part of the plant, with tastings and a pisco sour at the end. You can also visit the 144-year-old private distillery at **Los Nichos**, 4km on from Pisco Elqui (daily April–Nov 10am–6pm; Dec–March 11am–7pm; ☎51 451085, ✆fundolosnichos.cl; tour CH$1000).

Pueblo Artesanal de Horcón

Horcón • Tues–Sun noon–6.30pm

Beyond Pisco Elqui, the narrow road leads through increasingly unspoiled countryside and ever deeper into the valley. After 8km you'll pass by a large craft market known as the *Pueblo Artesanal de Horcón*, which lies just before the sleepy village of the same name (the end of the road for two buses daily from La Serena). Here you can browse among the many stalls for all sorts of local arts, crafts and foods, or just enjoy a fresh juice and a massage by the river.

3

ARRIVAL AND INFORMATION

PISCO ELQUI AND AROUND

By bus Buses stop in by the plaza and also go up into the village. Three buses weekly (Mon, Wed & Fri) go along the Río Cochiguaz.

Destinations Montegrande (every 30min; 10min); Vicuña (every 30min; 50min).

By jeep Jeep Tours La Serena (☎09 9454 6000, ✉info @jeeptour-laserena.cl) offers day-long tours and transfers

(Nov–April; CH$95,000 per person) to San Juan in Argentina.

Tours Elqui Expediciones (☎09 742 10488, ✆elquiexpediciones.cl) and Turismo Migrantes (☎51 451917, ✆turismomigrantes.cl), both on O'Higgins, offer horseriding, trekking, cycling and observatory excursions, as well as day-trips to remote thermal springs near the Argentinian border.

CROSSING THE ARGENTINE BORDER

Via Ruta 41 After Rivadavia – where the right fork leads to Pisco Elqui – Ruta 41 from La Serena follows first the Río Turbio and then the Río de la Laguna all the way to the Paso del Agua Negra (4779m) and the Argentine border, nearly 170km away. Only partly tarmacked, often narrow and hemmed in by imposing mountains, many of them over 4000m high, this road (open Oct/Nov–April only) is one of the most dramatic linking the two countries. Seventy-five kilometres on from Rivadavia you'll come to the Complejo Aduanero

Junta del Toro, the Chilean customs post (Nov–April daily 8am–6pm; ☎51 651184). The Argentine border lies some 95km from the customs post. On the other side of the frontier, the RN 150 winds down to the easygoing market town of Rodeo and hits the adobe-built town of Jachal, from where the RN 40 strikes south to the laid-back provincial capital of San Juan, nearly 270km on from the border post. For more details on these places consult the *Rough Guide to Argentina*.

ACCOMMODATION

Elquimista Aurora de Chile s/n ☎51 451185, ✆elquimista.cl. Enjoy the silence and dazzling views from your own *cabaña* perched on a hillside about 1km from town. *Cabañas* are kitted out with antique Asian furniture and quality mattresses. English spoken. **CH$55,000**

Hostal Triskel Baquedano ☎09 9419 8680, ✆hostaltriskel.cl. Genial owner Yayo is a wealth of local information and offers simple yet cosy rooms with shared bathrooms in a stylishly rustic setting with a peaceful, labyrinthine garden. Dorm **CH$8000**, double **CH$20,000**

★ **Misterios de Elqui** Prat s/n ☎51 451126, ✆misteriosdeelqui.cl. For a real treat, stay 800m out of town on the road to Alcohuaz. Designer-magazine *cabañas* with fabulous views are spaced comfortably apart among

landscaped gardens leading down to a stunning swimming pool. **CH$65,000**

Refugio del Angel El Condor s/n ☎51 451292, ✉refugiodelangel@gmail.com. Less than 1km southeast of the plaza, this pretty riverside campground feels a world away from the village. Rustic wooden bridges lead to shady camping spots, with picnic tables and hot showers. **CH$5000** per person

★ **El Tesoro de Elqui** Prat s/n ☎51 451069, ✆tesoro-elqui.cl. The friendly German owners offer attractive, spotless abode-style *cabañas* with hammocks slung on the verandas, amid fragrant gardens, vine-covered terraces and a gorgeous pool. There is one dorm and the restaurant is one of the best in town. Dorm **CH$9500**, cabin **CH$27,000**

EATING

El Durmiente Elquino Las Carreras s/n. ☎09 8906 2754. Pebble floors, local artwork and mellow music set the scene for dining on Chilean staples as well as chicken and corn pancakes (CH$4700) and virtuous quinoa salads (CH$4000). Local wines and pisco cocktails fuel the late-night revelry. Daily midday–1am.

✱ **Miraflores** Road to Horcón ☎51 285901. Not to be missed, this wonderful restaurant is a family-run place a couple of kilometres along the road that goes out of town towards Alcohuaz. Here you can feast on excellent roast meats like suckling pig and *bife de chorizo* cooked up on the *parrillada* (CH$7800) while savouring mesmerizing views down the valley. Tues–Sun 1–5pm.

Misterios de Elqui Prat s/n ☎51 451126, ⓦmisteriosdeelqui.cl. This tastefully decorated restaurant offers the most romantic setting in town: a wide wooden balcony with sweeping views down the valley. A gourmet chef prepares delicious food, such as prawn crêpes (CH$6200). Wed–Sun 1–3pm & 8–10pm.

El Tesoro de Elqui Prat s/n ☎51 451069. An eclectic menu mixes international and Chilean influences, ranging from goulash and grilled fish to home-made muesli, waffles, real coffee and to-die-for papaya ice cream. Lunch menu CH$7000. Daily 9–11am & 1.30–10pm.

Alcohuaz

Some 15km beyond Pisco Elqui is the tiny community of **ALCOHUAZ**. Apart from a handsome terracotta-hued church (in sharp contrast to Horcón's, which is sky blue), this remote settlement has little to offer in the way of standard attractions.

Colmenares Alcohuaz

☎09 9003 5297, ⓔnelsoncorreacl@yahoo.com

Alcohuaz is home to a popular curiosity, the **bee-cure centre** known as Colmenares Alcohuaz, or "Alcohuaz Hives". People come from throughout the country to treat all kinds of ills by means of apitherapy (bee stings) – after being tested for allergies, of course. You can also buy a variety of excellent bee products such as honey, royal jelly, propolis and creams to treat skin ailments.

ARRIVAL AND DEPARTURE   ALCOHUAZ

By bus Though there are two buses daily to Horcón, 8km beyond Pisco Elqui, there is no public transport along the final 7km rough stretch to Alcohuaz. Hitchhiking is common or tour companies in Pisco Elqui offer half-day bicycle excursions, dropping you off in Alcohuaz by minibus and letting you ride back.

ACCOMMODATION AND EATING

La Casona Distante ☎09 9226 5440, ⓦcasonadistante.cl. Literally "the secluded ranch", this seventy-year-old abode house on verdant acres has stunning valley views from the charming rooms, and a swimming pool. Meals, massage, bike hire and horseriding trips can be arranged. CH$50,000

Refugios La Frontera ☎09 9279 8109, ⓦrefugioslafrontera.cl. These seven cabins boast a magical setting by the river willows. There's a swimming pool and a restaurant, *El Cielo*, where you can sample the region's river prawns ($6000) and stare into space at their new observatory. CH$50,000

Along the Río Cochiguaz

Back in Montegrande, a rough, unpaved road branches off the main route, dips down the valley and follows the northern bank of the **RÍO COCHIGUAZ**, a tributary of the Elqui. Rustic *cabañas* dot the riverbank; many offer holistic therapies and meditation classes. The small community of **Cochiguaz**, 11km along the valley, was founded in the 1960s by a group of hippies in the belief that the Age of Aquarius had shifted the earth's magnetic centre from the Himalayas to the Elqui Valley. But don't let this put you off – the multicoloured highland scenery is fabulous and the remoteness and tranquillity of the valley irresistible.

3

GABRIELA MISTRAL

Possibly even more than its pisco, the Elqui Valley's greatest source of pride is **Gabriela Mistral**, born in Vicuña in 1889 and, in 1945, the first Latin American to be awarded the **Nobel Prize for Literature**. A schoolmistress, a confirmed spinster and a deeply religious woman, Mistral's poetry reveals an aching sensitivity and passion, and her much romanticized life was punctuated with tragedy and grief.

Lucila Godoy de Alcayaga, as she was christened, was just 3 years old when her father abandoned the family, the first of several experiences of loss in her life. It was left to her older sister, Emiliana, to support her and her mother, and for the next eight years the three of them lived in the schoolhouse in the village of **Montegrande**, where Emiliana worked as a teacher. At the age of 14, she started work herself as an assistant schoolteacher, in a village close to La Serena. It was here, also, that she took her first steps into the world of literature, publishing several pieces in the local newspaper under the pseudonyms "Alguien" ("Someone"), "Soledad" ("Solitude") and "Alma" ("Soul"). When she was 20 years old, a railway worker, Romelio Ureta, who for three years had been asking her to marry him, committed suicide; in his pocket, a card was found bearing her name.

Although it would seem that his love for her was unrequited, the intense grief caused by Ureta's suicide was to inform much of Mistral's intensely morbid poetry, to which she devoted her time with increasing dedication while supporting herself with a series of teaching posts. In 1914 she won first prize in an important national poetry competition with *Los Sonetos de la Muerte* (Sonnets of Death), and in 1922 her first collection of verse was published under the title *Desolación* (Desolation), followed a couple of years later by a second collection, *Ternura* (Tenderness). Her work received international acclaim, and in recognition the Chilean Government offered Gabriela Mistral a position in the consular service, allowing her to concentrate almost exclusively on her poetry; here the parallel with Pablo Neruda is at its strongest. As consul, she spent many years abroad, particularly in the US, but her poems continued to look back to Chile, particularly her beloved **Elqui Valley**, which she described as "a cry of nature rising amidst the opaque mountains and intense blue sky". Her most frequently recurring themes, however, were her love of children and her perceived sorrow at her childlessness.

Gabriela Mistral did however serve as a surrogate mother for her adored nephew, **Juan Miguel** or "Yin Yin", who had been placed in her care when he was just 9 months old. Once again, though, tragedy struck: at the age of 17, Yin Yin committed suicide in Brazil, where she was serving as consul. It was a loss from which she never recovered, and for which her Nobel Prize, awarded two years later, could do little to console her. Gabriela Mistral outlived her nephew by twelve years, and in 1957, at the age of 67, she died in New York of cancer of the pancreas, leaving the proceeds of all her works published in South America to the children of Montegrande.

Cancana

CH$6000 per person • ☎ 09 904 73859, ⊛ cancana.cl

In keeping with the valley's reputation for UFO sightings and celestial activity, the new Cancana observatory at Cochiguaz offers nightly star-gazing through two 35cm Meade telescopes; most people visit on a tour from Pisco Elqui.

ARRIVAL AND DEPARTURE

By bus Public transport between Montegrande and Cochiguaz is limited to three weekly bus services (Mon, Wed & Fri), leaving Pisco Elqui early in the morning, before

ALONG THE RÍO COCHIGUAZ

following the Río Cochiguaz and then turning back and heading on to La Serena. Hitchhiking is also very common along this route.

ACCOMMODATION AND EATING

El Alma Zen 11km from Montegrande ☎ 09 9047 3861. Spa therapies and river swimming meet poolside posing at this hotel across from the Cancana observatory. The two-storey cabins by the pool are nice but uninspiring; for something more back-to-nature, try the riverside domes with shared bathroom. Dome **CH$25,000**, cabin **CH$45,000**

Camping Cochiguaz 17km from Montegrande ☎ 51 451154. At the end of the road from Montegrande, this riverside campground is as far as you can get from civilization without forfeiting hot showers or picnic tables. Horseriding tours arranged. **CH$5000** per person

Camping Parque Ecológico Río Mágico Cochiguaz, 11km from Montegrande. A great option for campers, offering seclusion by the river and hot showers. Night-time revelry revolves around a central campfire and a lively bar. CH$5500 per person

Spa Cochiguaz Parcela 8B, El Pangue, 11.5km from Montegrande ☎51 481160, ⓦcochiguaz.com. This wellness complex offers rudimentary rooms as well as much nicer cabins with indigenous wallhangings. If you're not into meditation or spa therapies, there's a fine pool to splash about in. The vegetarian restaurant is open to the public and serves three top-notch meals a day (set lunch CH$6000). CH$45,000

Vallenar and around

North of La Serena, the Panamericana turns inland and heads via a couple of winding passes (Cuesta Buenos Aires and Cuesta Pajonales) towards the busy but somewhat run-down little town of **VALLENAR**, 190km up the road. The town, which acts as a service centre for local mining and agricultural industries, was founded in 1789 by Governor Ambrosio O'Higgins, who named the city after his native Ballinagh in Ireland. It makes a convenient base for an excursion east into the fertile **upper Huasco Valley**, laced with green vines and small pisco plants, or northwest towards the coast and, in the spring, the wild flowers of the **Parque Nacional Llanos de Challe**.

The self-appointed "*capital del desierto florido*" (and vigorously promoted as such by the tourist authorities), Vallenar is indeed the best base for forays into the **flowering desert** (see box, p.151), if you're here at the right time. The **Museo del Huasco** at Ramírez 1001 (Mon–Fri 9am–1pm & 3–6pm; ☎51 610635; CH$600) has some moderately diverting displays on indigenous cultures and photos of the nearby flowering desert.

ARRIVAL AND INFORMATION   VALLENAR

By bus Vallenar's main bus terminal is on the corner of Prat and Av Guillermo Matta, some six blocks west of the main square.

Destinations Antofagasta (10 daily; 9hr); Calama (10 daily; 11hr); Caldera (10 daily; 3hr); Chañaral (10 daily; 4hr); Copiapó (10 daily; 2hr); Iquique (2 daily; 14hr); La Serena

---

PISCO

Pisco has been enjoyed by Chileans for more than four centuries, but it wasn't until the 1930s that it was organized into an effective commercial industry, starting with the official creation of a pisco *denominación de origen*. Shortly afterwards, a large number of growers, who'd always been at the mercy of the private distilleries for the price they got for their grapes, joined together to form cooperatives to produce their own pisco. The largest were the tongue-twisting *Sociedad Cooperativa Control Pisquero de Elqui y Vitivinículo de Norte Ltda* (known as "Pisco Control") and the *Cooperativa Agrícola y Pisquera del Elqui Ltda* (known as "Pisco Capel"), today the two most important producers in Chile, accounting for over ninety percent of all pisco to hit the shops.

The basic **distillation technique** is the same one that's been used since colonial times: in short, the fermented wine is boiled in copper stills at 90°C, releasing vapours that are condensed, then kept in oak vats for three to six months. The alcohol – of 55° to 65° – is then diluted with water, according to the type of pisco it's being sold as: 30° or 32° for *Selección*; 35° for *Reservado*; 40° for *Especial*; and 43°, 46° and 50° for *Gran Pisco*. It's most commonly consumed as a tangy, refreshing aperitif known as **Pisco Sour**, an ice-cold mix of pisco, lemon juice and sugar – sometimes with whisked egg-white for a frothy head and angostura bitters for an extra zing.

Note that the Peruvians also produce pisco and consider their own to be the only authentic sort, maintaining that the Chilean stuff is nothing short of counterfeit. The Chileans, of course, pass this off as jealousy, insisting that their pisco is far superior (it is certainly grapier) and proudly claiming that pisco is a Chilean, not Peruvian, drink. Whoever produced it first, there's no denying that the pisco lovingly distilled in the Elqui Valley is absolutely delicious, drunk neat or in a cocktail. A visit to one of the distilleries in the region is not to be missed – if only for the free tasting at the end.

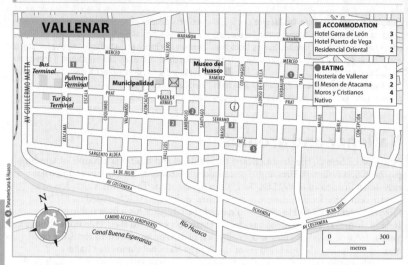

(15 daily; 2hr 45min); Ovalle (20 daily; 4.5hr); Santiago (26 daily; 9hr 30min).

Tourist office Vallenar has a small tourist office on the 2nd floor of the building on the corner of Calles Colchagua and Prat (Mon–Fri 8.30am–6pm; ☎51 611501, ✉ turimovallenar@gmail.com). Staff can advise on tour guides and car rentals.

ACCOMMODATION

Hotel Garra de León Serrano 1052 ☎51 613753, ✉ reservas@hotelgarradeleon.cl. This hotel offers smart, spacious rooms with air conditioning, cable TV and pristine bathrooms, plus its own car park. **CH$57,000**

Hotel Puerto de Vega Ramírez 201 ☎51 613870, ⓦ puertodevega.cl. A boutique hotel near the bus terminal, with beautifully decorated rooms and suites,

covered parking, a small swimming pool in a tidy garden, afternoon tea and huge, delicious breakfasts. **CH$64,200**

Residencial Oriental Serrano 720 ☎51 613889, Elaoriental_chang@hotmail.com. Shabby, budget rooms, some with private bathroom, set around a quiet patio. The hot water is erratic and breakfast is an extra $2,000. **CH$15,800**

EATING

Hostería de Vallenar Alonso de Ercilla 848 ☎51 614379, ⓦ hotelesatacama.cl. This surprisingly good restaurant attached to a *hostería* offers well-cooked Chilean cuisine with imaginative sauces. Seafood mains are CH$6500. Daily 12.30–3pm & 7.30–11pm.

El Meson de Atacama Serrano 802 ☎09 746 61706. A second-storey restaurant where, as well as Chilean meat and fish staples, you'll also find more adventurous offerings like soy and vodka salmon, stuffed eggplants, and paella (mains around CH$5000). Mon–Sat 12.30–4pm & 8pm–late; Sun 12.30–4pm.

Moros y Cristianos Cruce Carretera 5 Norte ☎51 614040.

The best of Vallenar's restaurants is this stylish place out on the Panamericana by the Huasco turn-off, run by a Lebanese–Chilean and serving slightly more interesting meat and fish dishes than the norm. The lunch menu is CH$8,500. Daily noon–5pm.

Nativo Ramirez 1387 ☎51 618308, ⓦ nativoatacama.cl. With its loud music and rock art-inspired walls, this is a good spot to sink a beer over a plate of picadillos. Pizzas, seafood ceviche and fish mains are all made to be shared – and portions are generous. If you're feeling virtuous, there are also plenty of salad options (CH$3000). Mon–Sat 1pm–3am.

Reserva Nacional Pinguino de Humboldt

129km north-west of La Serena and 126km south-west of Vallenar • CH$2500 • ☎09 95443052

Bottle-nosed dolphins, colonies of Humboldt penguins, sea lions and otters frolic in the two-thousand-acre-plus **Reserva Nacional Pinguino de Humboldt**. The reserve comprises three main islands: Choros, Damas and Chañaral, the first two best visited from La Serena. Travelling 87km north of La Serena, a dirt road heads 42km west to Punta de Choros, from where you can sail along the east coast of Isla Choros and go ashore on Isla Damas, the only island where it's possible to disembark. A rough 22km coastal road links Punta de Choros with Caleta Chañaral, the jumping off point for the furthest and most wildlife-rich island, Isla Chañaral. It's more common, however, to visit Isla Chañaral from Vallenar: 50km south of town is a turn-off opposite Domeyko and the 76km dirt track leads to Caleta Chañaral. Plenty of tour operators in La Serena and Vallenar offer day-trips to the reserve.

ARRIVAL AND DEPARTURE · RESERVA NACIONAL PINGUINO DE HUMBOLDT

ISLA CHOROS AND ISLA DAMAS
By boat Boats can be hired (CH$7,000 per person) at Punta de Chorros.

ISLA CHAÑARAL
By bus From Vallenar, buses leave for Caleta Chañaral every Friday at 3pm (also Wed Jan–March) and return Sundays at 5pm with Buses Alvarez (☎09 7618 4389).

By boat From Caleta Chañaral you can take boat trips (CH$60,000 per boat; Aurora Campusano is a reliable local guide ☎09 9349 3192) that circumnavigate the island.

ACCOMMODATION

There is a basic campsite at Caleta Chañaral with cold showers (☎09 9165 8455; CH$8,000 per site) and Aurora Campusano also rents out rooms in her house (double CH$18,000). Note that camping is not permitted on Isla Damas.

The upper Huasco Valley

From Vallenar, a paved road follows the Río Huasco through a deep, attractive valley that climbs towards the mountains. The road weaves back and forth across the river, taking you through dry, mauve-coloured hills and green orchards and vineyards. About 20km from Vallenar, you pass the enormous **Santa Juana dam**, which after a season of heavy rainfall overflows into a magnificent waterfall that can be viewed close-up from an observation deck.

Alto del Carmen

Thirty-eight kilometres from Vallenar, the valley forks at the confluence of the El Carmen and El Tránsito rivers. The right-hand road takes you up the **El Carmen Valley** where, just beyond the fork, you'll find **Alto del Carmen**, a pretty village that produces one of the best-known brands of pisco in Chile; you can visit the Planta Pisquera Alto del Carmen for a free tour and tastings (Mon–Fri 9am–noon & 2–6pm, Sat 9am–noon; ☎51 616035).

San Félix

A further 26km up the road, **San Félix** has a beautiful setting and a hundred-year-old **pisco plant** that produces high-quality, traditionally made pisco called Horcón Quemado. You can try – and buy – the pisco in their shop (daily 8am–5pm; ☎51 610985).

ARRIVAL AND DEPARTURE · UPPER HUASCO VALLEY

By bus Buses Pallauta (☎51 612117) leave from the corner of Marañon and Alonso de Ercilla in Vallenar. Destinations Alto del Carmen (5 daily; 1hr); San Félix (5 daily; 1.5hr).

ACCOMMODATION

Complejo Turístico y Deportivo Portezuelo Sector La Falda s/n, Alto del Carmen, ☎09 9548 3571. A relaxed and leafy spot by the river, with 50 camping sites, 20 cabins, natural swimming pools and horseriding activities arranged. Camping CH$3,000 per person, cabin CH$20,000

> ## THE PRICE OF GOLD
> A massive threat currently hangs over the Upper Huasco valley: locals fear water shortages and contamination of the pristine Río Huasco from a massive **gold-mining project** by Canadian giant Barrick Gold. The company is currently exploring the Pascua Lama deposits straddling the Argentinian border, believed to be the world's largest untapped gold deposit, and environmental groups claim the company's activities have already had a detrimental effect on glaciers.

Hospedaje y Restaurante El Churcal Hijuela 75 ☎ 09 7684 4222, ⓦ elchurcal.cl. Just 1km outside San Félix, you'll find rooms for a range of budgets at this eco-minded place with solar-powered showers and plenty of fruit trees. The restaurant offers a CH$3000 lunch menu. **CH$15,000**

Parque Nacional Llanos de Challe

Jan & Feb 8.30am–8pm; March–Dec 8.30am–5.30pm • CH$4000 • ☎ 52 611555

If you have the good luck to be around while the desert's in bloom, head for the **PARQUE NACIONAL LLANOS DE CHALLE**, northwest of Vallenar, for the full impact. This 450-square-kilometre swath of coastal plain has been singled out for national park status because of the abundance of **garra de león** – an exquisite, deep-red flower in danger of extinction – that grows here during the years of the *desierto florido*. The park is crossed by an 82km dirt road branching west from the Panamericana, 17km north of Vallenar, and terminating at **Carrizal Bajo**, a once-important mining port now home to a tiny fishing community.

ARRIVAL AND INFORMATION

By bus Three buses a week leave from Vallenar's bus terminal for Carrizal Bajo with Buses Carmelita (☎ 51 613037).

By 4WD If you have a 4WD, a tent and a taste for wilderness, follow the very rough track north of Carrizal Bajo up to Puerto Viejo, near Caldera and Copiapó. The deserted beaches along this stretch, particularly the

PARK NACIONAL LLANOS DE CHALLE

northern half, are breathtaking, with white sands and clear, turquoise waters.

Conaf The Conaf information office is 11km north of Carrizal Bajo at the pretty, white-sand Playa Blanca (Jan & Feb 8.30am–8pm; March–Dec 8.30am–5.30pm; ☎ 52 611555).

ACCOMMODATION

Camping Playa Blanca There is a beachside campsite near the Conaf office with solar-powered hot showers (CH$800 extra), barbecues, picnic tables and drinking water. **CH$4,000** per person

Copiapó

Overlooked by arid, rippling mountains, the prosperous city of **COPIAPÓ** sits in the flat basin of the **Río Copiapó**, some 60km from the coast and 145km north of Vallenar. To the east is the most northerly of Chile's "transverse valleys" and beyond it the transformation from semi-desert to serious desert is complete, and the bare, barren Atacama stretches a staggering 1000km north towards the Peruvian border. Just to the north of the city, Arabian-style dunes await exploration. There isn't a great deal to do here, however, and Copiapó's main use to travellers is as a springboard for excursions into the surrounding region (see pp.158-160).

Brief history

When Diego de Almagro made his long trek south from Cuzco in 1536, following the Inca Royal Road down the spine of the Andes, it was into this valley that he descended, recuperating from the gruelling journey at the *tambo*, or resting place, where Copiapó now stands. The valley had been occupied and cultivated by the Diaguita people starting

THE FLOWERING DESERT

For most of the year, as you travel up the Panamericana between Vallenar and Copiapó you'll cross a seemingly endless, semi-desert plain, stretching for nearly 100km, sparsely covered with low shrubs and *copao* cacti. But take the same journey in spring, and in place of the parched, brown earth, you'll find green grass dotted with beautiful flowers. If you're really lucky and you know where to go after a particularly wet winter, you'll happen upon fluorescent carpets of multicoloured flowers, stretching into the horizon.

This extraordinarily dramatic transformation is known as the **desierto florido**, or "flowering desert"; it occurs when unusually heavy rainfall (normally very light in this region) causes dormant bulbs and seeds, hidden beneath the earth, to sprout into sudden bloom, mostly from early September to late October. In the central strip, crossed by the highway, the flowers tend to appear in huge single blocks of colour (*praderas*), formed chiefly by the purple *pata de guanaco* ("guanaco's hoof"), the yellow *corona de fraile* ("monk's halo") and the blue *suspiro de campo* ("field's sigh"). The tiny forget-me-not-like *azulillo* also creates delicate blankets of baby blue.

On the banks of the *quebradas*, or ravines, that snake across the land from the cordillera to the ocean, many different varieties of flowers are mixed together, producing a kaleidoscope of contrasting colours known as *jardines*. These may include the yellow or orange lily-like *añañuca* and the speckled white, pink, red or yellow *alstroemeria*, a popular plant with florists also known as the "Peruvian lily". West, towards the coast, you'll also find large crimson swaths of the endangered *garra de león* ("lion's claw"), particularly in the Parque Nacional Llanos de Challe (see p.154), near Carrizal Bajo, created especially to protect them. Of course, removing any plant, whole or in part, is strictly forbidden by law.

There's no predicting the *desierto florido*, which is relatively rare – the frequency and intensity varies enormously, but the general phenomenon seems to occur every four to five years, although this has been more frequent in recent years. The best **guide** in Vallenar, and a veritable gold-mine of information about the dozens of flower varieties, is Roberto Alegría (☎ 51 613908, ✉ desiertoflorido2010@hotmail.cl).

around 1000 AD and was then inhabited, beginning around 1470, by the Inca, who mined gold and copper here. Although Spanish *encomenderos* (see p.468) occupied the valley from the beginning of the conquest, it wasn't until 1744 that the city of Copiapó was founded, initially as "San Francisco de la Selva". A series of random silver strikes in the nineteenth century, most notably at Chañarcillo, threw the region into a frenzied boom.

Copiapó today

Following a period of decline at the beginning of the twentieth century, Copiapó is once more at the centre of a rich mining industry, revolving around copper, iron and gold. The city shot to international notoriety in October 2010, when 33 workers from the nearby San José mine were rescued after 69 days trapped underground (see box, p.159).

Plaza Prat

A lively, busy city of some 127,000 inhabitants, Copiapó has a fairly compact downtown composed of typical adobe houses, some churches and the odd mansion, with the large, tree-filled **Plaza Prat** at its centre. The square is lined with 84 towering old pepper trees planted in 1880. On its southwest corner stands the mid-nineteenth-century **Iglesia Catedral**, designed by the English architect William Rogers, sporting a Neoclassical three-door portico and topped by an unusual, tiered wooden steeple.

Museo Mineralógico

Corner of Colipí and Rodriguez • Mon–Fri 10am–1pm & 3.30–7pm, Sat 10am–1pm • CH$600

Just off the northeast corner of Plaza Prat, the University of Atacama's **Museo Mineralógico** displays a glittering collection of over two thousand mineral samples from around the world, including huge chunks of malachite, amethyst, quartz, marble and onyx; it's a pity that the museum is so poorly presented, with virtually no explanations or guides of any kind.

Museo Regional de Atacama

Corner of Atacama and Rancagua • Mon 2–5.45pm, Tues–Fri 9am–5.45pm, Sat 10am–1pm & 3–5.45pm, Sun 11am–1.45pm • ☎ 52 212313, ⓦ www.museodeatacama.cl • CH$600; free Sun

The **Museo Regional** repays a visit, not least for its new display on the trapped miners of the San José mine (see p.159), including one of the rescue capsules used to winch the 33 buried miners to safety and their fateful hand-written note: "We are fine in the shelter – the 33." The handsome mansion that houses the museum, the **Casa Matta**, was built in the 1840s for one of Copiapó's wealthy mining barons. The other well-presented displays cover the exploration of the desert, the development of mining, the War of the Pacific, pre-Columbian peoples of the region and the Inca road system.

Plazoleta Juan Godoy

Towering over a tiny square that is the site of a busy Friday market selling fresh produce and household items, the imposing, red-walled 1872 **Iglesia San Francisco** sits one block south and west of the museum. The square's centre is marked by a statue of a rough-clad miner, tools in hand – none other than **Juan Godoy**, the goatherd who accidentally discovered the enormous silver deposits of nearby Chañarcillo in 1832, now honoured in Copiapó as a local legend.

ARRIVAL AND DEPARTURE   **COPIAPÓ**

BY PLANE

The Desierto de Atacama international airport (☎ 52 525104) is just over 50km north-west of the city, at Chamomate, not far from Caldera. Both the Manuel Flores Salinas minibus and Casther bus meet arriving planes and both will take you into town for CH$6000; a taxi costs CH$18,000.

Airlines LAN, Colipí and Los Carrera (☎ 52 213512); Sky Airlines Colipí 526 (☎ 52 214640); PAL Colipí 484, Local F in

EATING AND DRINKING
Bavaria	3
Don Elías	2
Flor de la Canela	1
Il Giardino	5
Kactus	6
Legado	4

ACCOMMODATION
Hotel La Casona	5
Hotel Chagall	4
Hotel Montecatini I	2
Hotel Palace	6
Residencial Ben Bow	3
Residencial Casagrande	1

NIGHTLIFE
Orum Discoteque	1

COPIAPÓ

the Mall Plaza Real off the main square (☎52 524603).
Destinations Note that some of these routes require stopovers; the travel times listed include stopovers. Antofagasta (1 daily; 40min); Arica (2 weekly; 2hr 35min); Calama (2 daily; 40min); Iquique (2 daily; 1hr 15min); Santiago (8 daily; 1hr 15min).

BY BUS

Copiapó's main bus terminal is at Chañarcillo 655, two blocks south of Plaza Prat. Across the road, also on Chañarcillo, is the Tur Bus terminal, while one block south, at Freire and Colipí, sits the Pullman Bus terminal. Inter-city services are offered by all the main companies, including Flota Barrios

(☎52 213645), Pullman Bus (☎52 212977), Expreso Norte (☎52 231176) and Tur Bus (☎52 238612). For Caldera and Bahía Inglesa, Casther (☎52 218889), Expreso Caldera (☎09 6155 8048) and Trans Puma (☎52 235841) run a frequent service from the corner of Esperanza and Chacabuco, opposite the Líder Hypermarket. Alternately you can catch one of the yellow *colectivos* (CH$2,500) that wait on the same corner opposite Líder.

Destinations Antofagasta (15 daily; 7hr); Arica (11 daily; 17hr); Calama (15 daily; 10hr); Caldera (every 30min; 1hr); Chañaral (10 daily; 2hr); Iquique (12 daily; 13hr); La Serena (20 daily; 4hr 45min); Ovalle (6 daily; 7hr); Santiago (22 daily; 12hr); Vallenar (10 daily; 2hr); Valparaíso (6 daily; 12hr).

INFORMATION AND TOURS

Tourist information Los Carrera 691 (Mon–Fri 8.30am–7pm, ☎52 212838, ✉infoatacama @sernatur.cl). There is a well-organized, helpful Sernatur office on the north side of Plaza Prat.

Conaf Juan Martínez 56 (Mon–Thurs 8.30am–5.30pm & Fri 8.30am-4pm; ☎52 213404). Provides information on protected areas in the region, including Pan de Azúcar and Nevado de Tres Cruces national parks; it's also a good source of information on road conditions in the *altiplano*.

TOUR OPERATORS

A handful of companies and individuals offer tours out of Copiapó. The main full-day destinations are located east into the cordillera, taking in Parque Nacional Nevado de Tres Cruces and sometimes Laguna Verde and Ojos del Salado (see p.159, 160); and north to Parque Nacional Pan de Azúcar (see p.164). Half-day trips go north into

the Atacama dunes, west to the beaches around Bahía Inglesa (see p.163), or east up the Copiapó River Valley (see p.158). Ask at Sernatur in Copiapó for a list of guides.
Aventurismo Vallejos 577 ☎52 316395, ⓦaventurismo.cl. Maximiliano Martínez has been taking tourists up to Ojos del Salado, Laguna Verde and around for longer than anyone else in the business; trips to Laguna Verde and Laguna Santa Rosa cost CH$400,000 for four people.

Mapandino Outdoor Carrera 755, Office 203 ☎09 9681 4242, ⓦwww.mapandino.cl. This outfit has bilingual guides who specialize in multi-day trips, including guided climbs up Ojos del Salado as well as three-day camping excursions to Parque Nacional Nevado de Tres Cruces, Pan de Azúcar and Llanos de Challe (CH$200,000 per person). They also offer half-day tours to the now-closed San José mine, 32km north-east of the city (CH$30,000 per person).

GETTING AROUND

By Car Rodaggio, Colipí 127 (☎52 212153, ⓦrodaggio .cl), rents out good-value 4x4 jeeps. Most other firms are situated on Ramón Freire, including Carmona at no. 268 (☎52 216030, ✉carmonarentacar@entelchile.net),

Europcar at no. 50 (☎52 216272, ⓦwww.europcar.cl) and Salfa Rent at no. 330 (☎52 200400, ⓦsalfa.cl.) Hertz is on the opposite side of the highway at Copayapú 173 (☎52 213522, ⓦhertz.cl).

ACCOMMODATION

★ **Hotel La Casona** O'Higgins 150 ☎52 217277, ⓦlacasonahotel.cl. This small, charming and impeccably decorated hotel has an English-speaking owner and serves excellent breakfasts, included in the price. CH$49,000
Hotel Chagall O'Higgins 760 ☎52 213775, ⓦchagall .cl. Modern hotel with an attractive lobby and bar, spacious, new-looking rooms, smart baths, a good restaurant and private parking. CH$74,550
Hotel Montecatini I Infante 766 ☎52 211363. Bright, spacious rooms falling into two classes: smart, newer *ejecutivo* and older but cheaper *turista*, both with private bath. There's also parking. CH$30,000

Hotel Palace Atacama 741 ☎52 212852. Reasonable but overpriced rooms with private bath and TV around an attractive patio; try bargaining the rate down. Breakfast is an extra CH$1200. CH$28,900
Residencial Ben Bow Rodriguez 541 ☎52 217634. Cramped but perfectly fine little rooms, some with private bath. If you're in need of some morning fuel, breakfast costs an extra CH$1500. CH$14,000
Residencial Casagrande Infante 525 ☎52 244450. Spacious yet dingy rooms off a shabby central courtyard that are among the cheapest in town. The two rooms off the back patio are the nicest. Breakfast is an additional CH$800. CH$14,000

3

EATING AND DRINKING

Bavaria Chacabuco 497 ☎52 213422, ⊕www .bavaria.cl. Located on the west side of Plaza Prat, this branch of the ubiquitous chain serves sandwiches, snacks and meat dishes (mains CH$8,500). Mon–Sat 1–4pm & 8–11.30pm, Sun 1–4pm & 8.30–10.30pm.

Don Elías Los Carrera 421 ☎52 364146 For a cheap and cheerful meal, the least insalubrious option in town is this great value diner with bargain set lunches (CH$2,800) and fish and meat dishes that keep the locals piling in. Mon–Sat 10am–10.30pm, Sun 10am–5.30pm.

Flor de la Canela Chacabuco 710 ☎52 219570, ⊕flordelacanelarestaurant.com. If you don't mind eating to a soundtrack of boisterous *cumbia*, this Peruvian restaurant offers first-rate service and cuisine. Ceviche (CH$16,000) and *lomo saltado* (CH$7,300) are both tasty and well presented, while the passionfruit cheesecake CH$3,900 is the sweetest of endings. Mon–Fri 12.30– 4.30pm & 7pm–12.30am, Sat 12.30–5pm &

7pm–1.30am, Sun 12.40–6pm.

Il Giardino Rancagua 341 ☎52 232246, ⊕ilgiardino.cl. Pretty, colourful restaurant with a romantic ambience, sun-dappled courtyard and a young chef who prepares tasty fish, salads and pastas. Mains around CH$7,000. Tues–Sat 1–3.30pm & 8pm–midnight, Sun 1–4.30pm.

Kactus Atacama 260 ☎52 237357, ⊕kactusrestaurant.cl. Colourful murals and 14 ways with tequila set the scene for this Mexican restaurant in a restored 1920s house. Spicy enchiladas (CH$7,000) and *quesadillas* (CH$4,500) line the stomach before the party gets started with the aforementioned tequila. Mon–Sat 6pm–1am.

Legado O'Higgins 12 ☎52 523895, ⊕www .legadocopiapo.cl. Intimate and friendly, this restaurant offers pricy yet good-quality meat and fish dinners. The star dish, 400 grams of Wagyu beef, will set you back CH$17,000. Mon–Sat 7.30pm–midnight.

NIGHTLIFE AND ENTERTAINMENT

Orum Discoteque Los Carrera 2440 ☎52 234100, ⊕antaycasinohotel.cl. This sleek club inside the Antay Casino & Hotel is the hottest place in town to let your hair

down. Weekends are all about retro and pop standards, while week nights mix things up with salsa and karaoke. Entrance CH$800. Wed & Thurs 9pm–2am, Fri & Sat 9pm–late.

DIRECTORY

Banks and exchange There are several ATMs on the main square. Intercambios Limitada is the only *casa de cambio* in town, located on the first floor of the Mall Plaza Real off the main square at Colipí 484.

Camping gear *Bencina blanca* (white gas) and butane gas are available at Ferretería El Herrerito, Atacama 699.

Dolomiti, 469 Atacama, has a range of Camping Gaz appliances and other outdoor stuff.

Internet Meg@net at Los Carrera 599 has a good connection for CH$600 per hour.

Post office North side of Plaza Prat at Los Carrera 691.

Around Copiapó

The region around Copiapó features some of the most striking and varied landscapes in Chile. To the east, the **Río Copiapó Valley** offers the extraordinary spectacle of emerald-green vines growing in desert-dry hills, while high up in the Andes, you'll ascend a world of salt flats, volcanoes and lakes, encompassed by the **Parque Nacional Nevado de Tres Cruces**, the **Volcán Ojos del Salado** and the blue-green **Laguna Verde**. To the west, **Bahía Inglesa**, near the port of **Caldera**, could be a little chunk of the Mediterranean, with its pristine sands and odd-shaped rocks rising out of the sea. Further south, reached only in a 4WD, the coast is lined with wild, deserted **beaches** lapped by turquoise waters.

Río Copiapó Valley

Despite an acute shortage of rainfall, the **RÍO COPIAPÓ VALLEY** is one of the most important grape-growing areas of Chile. This is thanks mainly to new irrigation techniques that have been developed over the past fifteen years, tapping into the valley's abundance of underground flowing water. While the Copiapó Valley is not quite as pastoral or picturesque as the Elqui Valley, its cultivated areas provide, more than anywhere else in the north, the most stunning contrast between deep-green

THE RESCUE OF LOS 33

On August 5, 2010, a boulder collapsed inside the San José copper and gold mine, 32km north-east of Copiapó, trapping 33 workers some 700m below the desert. That may well have been the end of the story – the miners consigned to statistics in Chile's notoriously dangerous mining industry – but for a fortuitous combination of determined families, a captivated media and a president in dire need of a ratings boost. In the aftermath of the accident, relatives of the trapped miners set up camp outside the pithead and refused to budge, urging the company to continue their search effort.

LIMELIGHT IN THE DARKNESS

The families kept up the pressure via the national media, compelling the then new right-wing president Sebastián Piñera – perceived to be out of touch with the working class and reeling from a ratings blow following his handling of February's earthquake and tsunami – to get involved. On day 17 of the search operation, just as hope was fading, rescue workers struck media gold – a handwritten note attached to their drillhead which read: "We are fine in the shelter – the 33." The miners' relatives were euphoric, the president triumphant and the international media dispatched to "Camp Hope" to cover the miracle (and soap opera) unfolding in the Chilean desert.

Food, medicine, pornography and video cameras were sent down a narrow communications shaft to the desperate men. What happened next was beamed around the world: one miner proposed a church marriage to his partner; a two-timer was exposed when his wife *and* mistress turned up at Camp Hope to lend support; a musical miner kept his colleagues entertained with Elvis impersonations; and another lay in the hot, dark tunnel while above ground his wife give birth to his daughter, named, appropriately, "Esperanza" (hope).

SAVED

Just after midnight on October 13, 69 days after the miners were buried alive (the longest underground entrapment in history), state-of-the-art rescue capsules hauled the first of "Los 33" to freedom, to an estimated global TV audience of 1.5 billion people. In the aftermath of the rescue, the miners enjoyed a flurry of media attention and were flown around the world and paraded as heroes. Most, however, chose to remain tight-lipped about what really went on in that subterranean hell, and as well as struggling with post-traumatic stress, the majority now live quiet, unassuming lives in Copiapó.

produce and parched, dry earth – from September to May, in particular, it really is a sight to behold.

Museo Minero

Mon–Fri 9am–4pm • Free • ☎ 6649 3785, ⊕ museominerodetierraamarilla.cl

Aside from the Río Copiapó Valley's scenery, you'll find the excellent new Museo Minero in the town of Tierra Amarilla, 16km south-east of Copiapó; it is set inside a restored nineteenth-century house and provides an overview of mining in the Atacama region.

ARRIVAL AND DEPARTURE	**RIO COPIAPÓ VALLEY**
By bus From Copiapó, Casther, Expreso Caldera and Trans Puma have several daily services up the Copiapó River	Valley. Buses go as far as Manflas, 150km south-east (the last 12km of the journey is along an unpaved road).

Parque Nacional Nevado de Tres Cruces

8.30am–6pm • CH$4000 • ☎ 52 213404

East of Copiapó, the Andes divide into two separate ranges – the Cordillera de Domeyko and the Cordillera de Claudio Gay – joined by a high basin, or plateau, that stretches all the way north to Bolivia. The waters trapped in this basin form vast salt flats and lakes towered over by enormous, snowcapped volcanoes, and wild vicuña and guanaco roam the sparsely vegetated hills. This is a truly awe-inspiring landscape, conveying an acute sense of wilderness and space. It's easier to fully appreciate it here than around San Pedro de Atacama, for instance, thanks to the general absence of tourists. The number of visitors has started to increase, however, following the creation in 1994 of the **PARQUE NACIONAL NEVADO DE TRES CRUCES**, which takes in a dazzling white salt flat, the **Salar de Maricunga**; two beautiful lakes, the **Laguna Santa Rosa** and **Laguna del Negro Francisco**; and the 6753m volcano **Tres Cruces**.

The bumpy road up to Parque Nacional Nevado de Tres Cruces takes you through a brief stretch of desert before twisting up narrow canyons flanked by mineral-stained rocks. As you climb higher, the colours of the scoured, bare mountains become increasingly vibrant, ranging from oranges and golds to greens and violets. Some 165km from Copiapó, at an altitude of around 3700m, the road (following the signs to Mina Marta) reaches the first sector of the park, skirting the pale-blue **Laguna Santa Rosa**, home to dozens of pink flamingos.

Immediately adjacent, the gleaming white **Salar de Maricunga** is Chile's most southerly salt flat, covering an area of over 80 square kilometres. A two- to three-hour drive south from here, past Mina Marta, the park's second sector is based around the large, deep-blue **Laguna del Negro Francisco**, some 4200m above sea level and home to abundant birdlife, including wild ducks and flamingos. Towering over the lake, the 6080-metre **Volcán Copiapó** was the site of an Inca sacrificial altar.

Laguna Verde

Close to but not part of the park, by the border with Argentina, the stunning, blue-green **Laguna Verde** lies at the foot of the highest active volcano in the world, the 6893m **Volcán Ojos del Salado**. The first, sudden sight of **Laguna Verde** is stupendous. The intense colour of its waters – green or turquoise, depending on the time of day – almost leaps out at you from the muted browns and ochres of the surrounding landscape. The lake lies at an altitude of 4500m, about 250km from Copiapó on the international road to Argentina (follow the signs to Paso San Francisco or Tinogasta). At the western end of the lake, a small shack contains a fabulous **hot-spring bath**, where you can soak and take blissful refuge from the biting wind outdoors. The best place to camp is just outside the bath, where a stone wall offers some protection from the wind, and hot streams provide useful washing-up water. At the lake's eastern end there's a *carabineros* checkpoint, where you should make yourself known if you plan to camp.

Volcán Ojos del Salado

Laguna Verde is surrounded by huge volcanoes: Mulas Muertas, Incahuasi and the monumental **Ojos del Salado**. At 6893m, this is the highest peak in Chile and the highest active volcano in the world; its last two eruptions were in 1937 and 1956. A popular climb (Oct–March), it takes up to twelve days and is not technically difficult, apart from the last 50m that border the crater. The base of the volcano is a 12km walk from the abandoned *carabineros* checkpoint on the main road, and there are two *refugios* on the way up, one at 5100m (four beds, with latrines) and another at 5750m (twelve beds with kitchen and lounge). Temperatures are low at all times of year, so take plenty of warm gear.

CLIMBING VOLCÁN OJOS DEL SALADO

To climb the mountain you need to pay a CH$70,000 fee to Aventurismo (see p.157), which acts as a caretaker; this can be paid at the office in Copiapó or at one of the *refugios* (see p.161). As the volcano sits on the border with Argentina, climbers need to present written permission from the Dirección de Fronteras y Límites plus a *permiso regional*, obtained from the tourist office, to the *carabineros* before climbing up. If you need to arrange transport to the base, or a guide for the ascent, contact Aventurismo, Mapandino Outdoor or Sernatur in Copiapó (see p.157).

ARRIVAL AND INFORMATION

By car From Copiapó, it's about a 3hr drive to Laguna Santa Rosa, and a 6hr drive to Laguna Verde. There is no public transport to this area – for information on tours here see p.157.

Conaf In summer (Dec–March), Conaf has its two park headquarters at Laguna Santa Rosa and about 4km from Laguna del Negro Francisco (both 8.30am–6pm;

PARQUE NACIONAL NEVADO DE TRES CRUCES

☎ 52 213404); the *guardaparques* are very friendly and take visitors on educational excursions to the lake and around, but if you want to stay over check with Conaf in Copiapó first. Park fees are not enforced through the rest of the year but there are *guardaparques* at the Chilean immigration post at Complejo Fronterizo Maricunga, 100km west of the Argentinian border.

ACCOMMODATION

Refugio Laguna del Negro Francisco 4km from the lake ☎ 52 213404. This large, comfortable *refugio* sleeps up to 15 people and has bunk beds, electricity, hot showers and a kitchen. It is necessary to bring your own food and drinking water. **CH$10,000** per person

Refugio Laguna Santa Rosa Western shore of the lake ☎ 52 213404. A tiny wooden *refugio* maintained by Conaf, this is a basic but convenient place to sleep (no bunk beds, floor space only), with great views of the lake backed by the snowcapped Volcán Tres Cruces. Note that there is no water here. **Free**

3

Caldera

Just over 70km north-west of Copiapó, **CALDERA** is a small, easygoing seaside town with a smattering of nineteenth-century buildings, a beach, a pier and a few good fish restaurants. Chosen as the terminus of Chile's first railway by mining and railway pioneer William Wheelwright, it became the country's second-largest port in the last decades of the nineteenth century, when it exported all the silver extracted in the region's dramatic silver boom.

Caldera's two ports are still busy – one exporting table grapes, the other exporting copper – but they don't totally dominate the bay, which remains fairly attractive. The town's principal landmarks are the Gothic-towered **Iglesia de San Vicente** on the main square, built by English carpenters in 1862, and the former **train station** at the pier, dating from 1850.

Centro Cultural Estación

Wheelwright s/n • Museo Paleontológico Tues–Sun 10am–2pm & 4–7pm • CH$600 • ☎ 52 316891, ⓦ estacioncaldera.cl

The former train station has been converted into the Centro Cultural Estación Caldera, which hosts community events and houses the fascinating little Museo Paleontológico, with its collection of fossils, rocks and locally unearthed artefacts.

The pier and beaches

The **pier**, down by the beach, makes for a pleasant stroll and is the starting point for **boat rides** around the bay in summer. Caldera's main **beach** is the sheltered, mid-sized and rather dirty Copiapina, while to the west of the pier, the large, windswept Playa Brava stretches towards the desert sands of the Norte Grande.

The cemetery

Av Diego de Almeyda s/n • Daily 8am–7pm

The cemetery 1km east of town is also worth a wander; dating from 1876, it was the first non-denominational cemetery in Chile, and harbours the weathered graves and mausoleums of English, Welsh, German and Chinese immigrants.

ARRIVAL AND INFORMATION

By plane Caldera lies 20km north-west of the Desierto de Atacama international airport (☎ 52 525104). Minibus services Anakena and Casther offer transfers to town for CH$5000; taxis cost CH$12,000.

CALDERA

By bus Buses to Copiapó leave from a small terminal at the corner of Cifuentes and Ossa Varas. Long-distance services to Chañaral and further north are provided by Pullman Bus and Tur-Bus, from Caldera's main terminal at Gallo and Vallejos.

Destinations Chañaral (12 daily; 1hr); Copiapó (every 30min; 1hr).

By micro and colectivo Micros for Bahía Inglesa leave from the Plaza de Armas every 15min in Jan and Feb. The rest of the year, black taxi *colectivos* leave from the plaza.

Tourist office Plaza de Armas (Jan & Feb daily 10am–1am; March–Dec daily 9am–2pm & 4–7pm; ☎ 52 316076).

ACCOMMODATION

Costa Fosil Gallo 560 ☎ 52 316451, ⊕ www.jandy.cl. Three levels of bright and spotless rooms, some with ocean glimpses, sit around a tranquil, flower-filled patio. An information board, a massive map of the region and friendly staff ensure guests feel right at home. <u>CH36.500</u>

Puerta del Sol Wheelwright 750 ☎ 52 315 205, ⊕ hosteriapuertadelsol.com. Caldera's best hotel is right on the bay and features a mix of smart rooms and A-frame cabins, some with water views. There's an attractive outdoor restaurant, bar and pool area, and an enormous kitchen for guests to use. Double <u>CH$45,000</u>, cabin <u>CH$48,000</u>

Residencial Millaray Cousiño 331 ☎ 52 315528, ⊕ rubenhmarre@yahoo.es. On the plaza, this is the nicest budget choice in town, with simple, airy rooms (some without bath) looking onto a leafy patio. The price doesn't include breakfast. <u>CH$16,000</u>

EATING AND DRINKING

Fresh seafood is sold at Caldera's *muelle pesquera* (fishing jetty) where a handful of outdoor restaurants hustle up fish dishes, paella and piping hot octopus *empanadas* (Mon–Fri 11am–7pm, Sat & Sun 11am–9pm).

Il Pirón de Oro Cousiño 218 ☎ 52 315790. In a town that prides itself on its fish and shellfish, this no-frills restaurant with lime-green tablecloths is arguably the best, serving imaginatively prepared dishes, including exquisite crab pie (CH$6000). Daily 11am–4pm & 7–10pm.

Nuevo Miramar Gana 090 ☎ 52 315381. The location of this seafood restaurant couldn't be better, right on the beach, with wonderful views of the bay. For a romantic evening, order a plate of oysters (CH$6000) and watch the lights flicker on the water. Daily noon–4pm & 7pm–midnight.

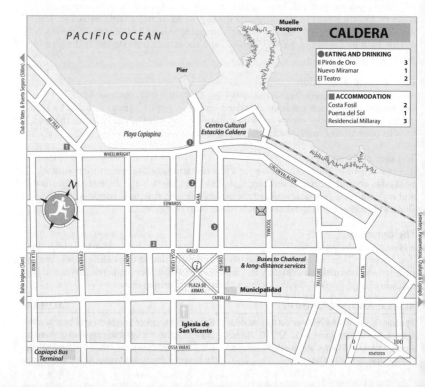

PACIFIC OCEAN

Muelle Pesquero

CALDERA

● EATING AND DRINKING
Il Pirón de Oro	3
Nuevo Miramar	1
El Teatro	2

▮ ACCOMMODATION
Costa Fosil	2
Puerta del Sol	1
Residencial Millaray	3

Pier

Playa Copiapina

Centro Cultural Estación Caldera

WHEELWRIGHT

CIRCUNVALACIÓN

EDWARDS

GANA

TOCOMAL

GALLO

OSSA CERDA

COUSIÑO

Buses to Chañaral & long-distance services

VALLEJOS

MATTA

MONTT

CIFUENTES

XONTLYTSI

PLAZA DE ARMAS

(i)

CARVALLO

Municipalidad

Iglesia de San Vicente

OSSA VARAS

Copiapó Bus Terminal

Club de Yates & Puerto Seguro (500m)

AV PRAT

Bahía Inglesa (5km)

Cemetery, Panamericana, Chañaral & Copiapó

0   100
metres

El Teatro Gana 12 ☎ 52 316768, ⓦ cafeelteatro.com. A café, restaurant and bar, with a pool table that adds to the lively atmosphere. The grilled *reineta* with creamy

papas a la Francesa (CH$10,000) is large enough for two. Mon–Sat 1–4pm & 8pm–midnight, Sun 1–5pm.

Bahía Inglesa and around

The **beaches** of **Bahía Inglesa** are probably the most photographed in Chile, adorning wall calendars up and down the country. More than their white, powdery sands – which, after all, you can find the length of Chile's coast – it's the exquisite clarity of the turquoise sea and the curious rock formations that rise out of it which set these beaches apart.

Northern beaches

Several beaches are strung along the bay to the north of Caldera, separated by rocky outcrops: the long Playa Machas is the southernmost beach, followed by Playa La Piscina, then by Playa El Chuncho and finally Playa Blanca. Surprisingly, this resort area has not been swamped by the kind of ugly, large-scale construction that mars Viña del Mar and La Serena, and Bahía Inglesa remains a fairly compact collection of *cabañas* and a few hotels. While the place gets hideously crowded in the height of summer, at most other times it's peaceful and relaxing.

Southern beaches

South of Bahía Inglesa, beyond the little fishing village of Puerto Viejo that marks the end of the paved road, the coast is studded with a string of **superb beaches** lapped with crystal-clear water and backed by immense sand dunes. The scenery is particularly striking around **Bahía Salada**, a deserted bay indented with tiny coves some 130km south of Bahía Inglesa. You might be able to find a tour operator that arranges excursions to these beaches, but if you really want to appreciate the solitude and wilderness of this stretch of coast, you're better off renting a jeep and doing it yourself.

ARRIVAL AND DEPARTURE   BAHÍA INGLESA

By colectivo You can visit Bahía Inglesa for the day from Caldera, just 6km away; plenty of taxi *colectivos* leaving from Caldera's plaza connect the two resorts, and also

Copiapó. The best place to catch a *colectivo* back to Caldera is on the corner by *Rocas de Bahia*.

ACCOMMODATION

The problem with staying here is that **accommodation** tends to be ridiculously overpriced, but you should be able to bargain the rates down outside summer.

Cabañas Villa Alegre El Morro 578 ☎ 52 315074; ✉ jorge-22-23@hotmail.com. These five humble but well-equipped cabins enjoy ocean views and come with cable TV; all but one has kitchen facilities. **CH$30,000**

Camping Bahía Inglesa Playa Las Machas ☎ 52 315424. A large, expensive campsite just off Playa Las Machas and overlooking *Bahía Inglesa*, with hot showers, picnic tables and a swimming pool. There are also cabins which sleep up to four people, the cheapest with shared bathroom. Camping **CH$26,000** per site, cabin **CH$30,000**

★ **Domo Bahía Inglesa** El Morro 610 ☎ 09 8162 8642, ⓦ domobahiainglesa.com. At the end of the promenade, these three futuristic mini-dome *cabañas*,

with huge beds and private bathrooms, are quite the novelty. Staff can also arrange tours to remote beaches as well as the Parque Nacional Pan de Azúcar. **CH$42,000**

Hotel Rocas de Bahía El Morro 888 ☎ 52 316005, ⓦ rocasdebahia.cl. All 36 rooms in this whitewashed, five-storey apartment block enjoy ocean views from their private balconies. There's a pleasant pool and a good seafood restaurant open Dec–March. **CH$64,900**

Los Jardines de Bahía Inglesa Copiapó 100 ☎ 52 315359, ⓦ jardinesbahia.cl. A few blocks back from the beachfront, these smart *cabañas* sleep up to 11 people. There's a good-sized pool, a table tennis table and a decent Italian restaurant. **CH$57,000**

EATING AND DRINKING

El Domo El Morro 610 **☏**09 816 28642, **ⓦ**domobahiainglesa.com. Sitting in front of its namesake hotel (see p.163) this tent-like cupola is the place to try satiating dishes like mixed seafood ceviche (CH$8,900). It's also a great spot to just linger over a real coffee or nurse a drink while taking in the ocean vistas. Tues–Sun 12.30–11.30pm.

El Plateado El Morro 756 **☏**09 9826 0007, **ⓦ**elplateao.cl. The most sophisticated restaurant in town with deck chairs on a terrace opposite the seafront. Serves international cuisine including flavoursome Thai and Indian curries (CH$8500). Daily 1–5pm & 5pm–midnight.

Chañaral

Sitting by a wide, white bay and the Panamericana, **CHAÑARAL**, 167km north of Copiapó, is a rather sorry-looking town of houses staggered up a hillside, with more than its fair share of stray dogs. Originally a small *caleta* used for shipping out the produce of an inland desert oasis, it still serves chiefly as an export centre, these days for the giant El Salvador copper mine, 130km east in the cordillera. Despite efforts to clean it up, Chañaral's huge beach remains contaminated by the toxic wastes deposited by the mine. You can visit the **Parque Nacional Pan de Azúcar** from Chañaral, which sits 30km up the coast, although it is preferable to visit as a day-trip from Copiapó.

ARRIVAL AND DEPARTURE | CHAÑARAL

By bus Many north–south buses make a stop in the town; those that don't will drop you off if you ask.
Destinations Antofagasta (11 daily; 5hr); Arica (6 daily; 15hr); Calama (11 daily; 8hr); Copiapó (12 daily; 1hr); Iquique (9 daily; 11hr); La Serena (12 daily; 7hr); Mejillones (4 daily; 6hr); Ovalle (11 daily; 9hr); Santiago (11 daily; 14hr); Taltal (2 daily; 2hr 30min); Tocopilla (7 daily; 8hr); Vallenar (12 daily; 4hr).

ACCOMMODATION

Hostería Chañaral Müller 268 **☏**52 480050, **ⓦ**hosteriachañaral.cl. In a town with limited accommodation options, this is by far the nicest place to stay. The well-maintained rooms sit off a pleasant, plant-filled garden with private bathrooms and plenty of hot water. There's also wi-fi, a games room and one of the town's better restaurants serving good seafood (mains CH$8000). **CH$37,000**
Hotel Aqualuna Merino Jarpa 521 **☏**52 523868, **ⓦ**www.aqualunahotel.cl. For a central option, this simple, 10-room hotel pulls out all the stops: comfy mattresses, cable TV, wi-fi, breakfast and parking. **CH$28,000**
Hotel Jiménez Merino Jarpa 551 **☏**52 480328, **ⓦ**hoteljimenez.cl. A budget choice with a prime position on the main street close to the Pullman Bus stop, with basic but clean and bright rooms, some with private bath, and all with wi-fi and cable TV. **CH$16,000**

EATING

Alicanto Panamericana Norte 49 **☏**52 481168. Take in ocean views as you make your way through fresh seafood hauled in by local fisherman at the adjacent cove. Mains CH$4,000. Daily 9.30am–5pm.

El Rincón Porteño Merino Jarpa 567 **☏**52 480071. This restaurant does a steady trade in basic Chilean staples like fried fish and *lomo con papas* (steak and chips) for CH$5100. Set lunches are CH$3000. Mon–Sat 10am–10pm.

Parque Nacional Pan de Azúcar

8.30am–12.30pm & 2–6pm • CH$4000 • **☏**52 213404

Home to two dozen varieties of cactus, guanacos and foxes, and countless birds, **PARQUE NACIONAL PAN DE AZÚCAR** is a 40km strip of desert containing the most stunning coastal scenery in the north of Chile. Steep hills and cliffs rise abruptly from the shore, which is lined with a series of pristine white-sand beaches. Though bare and stark, these hills make an unforgettable sight as they catch the late afternoon sun, when the whole coastline is bathed in rich shades of gold, pink and yellow. The only inhabited part of the park is **Caleta Pan de Azúcar**, 30km north of Chañaral, where you'll find a cluster of twenty or so fishermen's shacks as well as the Conaf information centre and a campsite (see p.165).

Isla Pan de Azúcar

Opposite the village, 2km off the shore, the **Isla Pan de Azúcar** is a small island sheltering a huge collection of marine wildlife, including seals, sea otters, plovers, cormorants, pelicans and more than three thousand Humboldt penguins; you can (and should – it's well worth it) take a boat trip out to get a close look at the wildlife. The island's distinctive conical silhouette gives the park its name "sugarloaf".

Mirador Pan de Azúcar

For fabulous panoramic views up and down the coast, head to **Mirador Pan de Azúcar**, a well-signposted lookout point 10km north of the village; the different varieties of cactus are fascinating and you may have the place all to yourself – unless you're joined by a curious grey fox or guanaco.

Las Lomitas

More difficult to reach, and less rewarding, **Las Lomitas** is a 700m-high clifftop about 30km north of the village; it's almost permanently shrouded in mist and is the site of a large black net, or "fog catcher", that condenses fog into water and collects it below.

ARRIVAL AND DEPARTURE
PARQUE NACIONAL PAN DE AZÚCAR

By bus There is no public transport to the park, but Chango Turismo (☎ 52 481107, ✉ pepecat02@hotmail.com) runs a bus to Caleta Pan de Azúcar from Chañaral (CH$10,000); it leaves at 9am and 3pm opposite the Pullman Bus terminal and returns from the park at 8am and 8pm (phone to confirm times).

By car There are two access roads to the park, both branching off the Panamericana: approaching from the south, the turn-off is at the north end of Chañaral, just past the cemetery; approaching from the north, take the turn-off at Las Bombas, 45km north of Chañaral. Both roads are bumpy but passable in a car.

By taxi You could get a taxi (around CH$20,000 each way from Chañaral; worth it if there are four in your group).

GETTING AROUND

By boat Boat trips to the Isla Pan de Azúcar depart from the *caleta* and cost CH$5,000 per person (minimum 15 people). It takes about 90min to do the circuit; the best times are around 7–8am and 6pm, when the penguins come out to eat. Ask in the village for Segundo Lizana, Manuel Carasco or Alex Guerra who all offer the same trip at the standard price.

INFORMATION AND TOURS

Conaf Near the village (daily 8.30am–12.30pm & 2–6pm). Offers maps, leaflets and souvenirs. This is where you pay your park fee.

Chango Turismo Panamericana Norte, Salida Sur, Chañaral ☎ 52 481107, ✉ pepecat02@hotmail.com.

As well as offering daily transport to and from the park (see p.164), these friendly tour operators run guided jeep tours around the park from CH$35,000 per person. Alternatively, you can come on a day tour from Copiapó (see p.157).

ACCOMMODATION AND EATING

Rough camping is not allowed in the park, but there are a number of authorized **camping** areas. In Caleta Pan de Azúcar, a handful of restaurants on the water's edge serve fried fish, rice and *empanadas*.

Camping Los Pingüinos Just north of the Caleta Pan de Azúcar ☎ 52 481209. A campsite with bathrooms, drinking water, picnic tables, rubbish collection and first-aid supplies. CH$5000 per person

Pan de Azúcar Camping y Cabañas Playa Piqueros, south of Caleta Pan de Azúcar ☎ 52 219271, 🌐 pandeazucarlodge.cl. Has the park's best camping facilities, with barbecues and picnic tables, as well as a handful of fully equipped solar-powered *cabañas*. Camping CH$5000 per person, cabin CH$30,000

El Norte Grande

171 Antofagasta

174 Around Antofagasta

176 Calama

178 Chuquicamata

178 San Pedro de Atacama

183 Around San Pedro

187 Iquique

193 Inland from Iquique

197 Parque Nacional Volcán Isluga

201 Pisagua

201 Hacienda de Tiliviche

202 Arica

209 The Azapa Valley

210 Putre

211 Parque Nacional Lauca

213 Reserva Nacional las Vicuñas

214 Salar de Surire

VOLCÁN PARINACOTA, PARQUE NACIONAL LAUCA

El Norte Grande

"El Norte Grande" occupies almost a quarter of Chile's mainland territory but contains barely five percent of its population. Its most outstanding feature is the Atacama Desert; the driest desert in the world, it contains areas where no rainfall has been recorded – ever. Its landscape is typically made up of rock and gravel spread over a wide plain, alleviated only by crinkly mountains. To the west, the plain is lined by a range of coastal hills that drop abruptly to a shelf of land where most of the region's towns and cities are scattered. To the east, the desert climbs towards the altiplano: a high, windswept plateau composed of lakes and salt flats ringed with snowcapped volcanoes.

Formidable and desolate as it is, the region contains a wealth of superb attractions, and, for many visitors, constitutes the highlight of a trip to Chile – particularly for European travellers, who will find nothing remotely like it back home. The Pacific seaboard is lined by vast tracts of stunning **coastal scenery**, while inland the **desert pampa** itself impresses not only with its otherworldly geography, but also with fascinating testimonies left by man. One of these is the trail of decaying nitrate **ghost towns**, including **Humberstone** and **Santa Laura**, easily reached from Iquique. Another is the immense images known as **geoglyphs** left by indigenous peoples on the hillsides and ravines of the desert – you'll find impressive examples at **Cerro Pintados**, south of Iquique, **Cerro Unitas**, east of Huara, and **Tiliviche**, between Huara and Arica.

As you journey towards and up into the cordillera, you'll come across attractive **oasis villages**, some – such as **Pica** and **Mamiña** – with **hot springs**. Up in the Andes, the altiplano is undoubtedly one of the country's highlights, with its dazzling **lakes**, **salt flats and volcanoes**, its abundance of **wildlife** and its tiny, whitewashed villages inhabited by native Aymara. The main altiplano touring base – and, indeed, one of the most popular destinations in the whole country, for Chileans and foreigners alike – is **San Pedro de Atacama**, a pleasant oasis 315km northeast of Antofagasta, where numerous operators offer excursions to the famous **El Tatio geysers** and the haunting moonscapes of the **Valle de la Luna**.

Further north, the stretch of altiplano within reach of Iquique and Arica boasts wild vicuña and spectacular scenery, preserved in **Parque Nacional Lauca** and several adjoining parks and reserves. Some towns and cities of the Far North, mainly Antofagasta and Calama, tend to be dreary and uninviting, but serve as unavoidable departure points for excursions into the hinterland. Bear in mind also, the **Bolivian Winter**, when sporadic heavy rains between December and February in the altiplano can wash roads away and seriously disrupt communications and access.

ALMA Observatory p.175
San Pedro de Atacama orientation p.178
Tours from San Pedro p.181
Paragliding paradise p.189
Tours from Iquique p.191
The nitrate boom p.195
The legend of La Tirana p.198
Crossing the Altiplano p.210

The Aymara of Chile p.202
Tours from Arica p.207
Chinchorro mummies p.210
Parinacota's wandering table p.213
Walks and climbs in Parque Nacional Lauca p.214
Conaf refugios in El Norte Grande p.215

VALLE DE LA LUNA

Highlights

❶ Valle de la Luna Watch the setting sun heighten the textures and deepen the colours of the valley's sweeping dunes and undulating rock formations. **See p.185**

❷ The Salar de Atacama Explore the vast salt flats of the Atacama Desert, the driest place on Earth – parts of it never, ever see rain. **See p.185**

❸ El Tatio At 4300m, pools of boiling water send clouds of steam into the air at the crack of dawn. **See p.186**

❹ Iquique's beaches and mountains The city has made a name for itself as a surfers' haven and is also one of the best places to paraglide in the world. **See p.187**

❺ The Pintados geoglyphs Discover these mysterious, indigenous images, the largest collection of geoglyphs in South America. See p.194

❻ Lauca and Isluga parks Trek through a landscape of mineral baths, cobalt lakes, sparkling salt flats and spongy bogs at dizzying altitudes. **See p.211 & p.197**

❼ Altiplano wildlife Thousands of llamas and alpacas, vicuñas and vizcachas, flamingoes and condors – a photographer's dream. See p.211

HIGHLIGHTS ARE MARKED ON THE MAP ON P.170

EL NORTE GRANDE

HIGHLIGHTS
1. Valle de la Luna
2. Salar de Atacama
3. El Tatio
4. Iquique's beaches and mountains
5. The Pintados geoglyphs
6. Lauca and Isluga parks
7. Altiplano wildlife

PERU

BOLIVIA

ARGENTINA

PACIFIC
OCEAN

N

Tacna

Visviri
⑦
PARQUE
NACIONAL
LAUCA
⑥
Putre   Parinacota
Socoroma   Tambo Quemado
Arica
San Miguel
de Azapa
RESERVA
NATURAL
LAS VICUÑAS
SALAR DE
SURIRE
Enquelga   Colchane
Islunga   SALAR DE
PARQUE   COLPASA
NACIONAL
VOLCAN ISLUGA
⑥
Pisagua   Tiliviche   Chusmisa
Huara   Cerro Unitas   Mamiña
SALAR DE UYUNI
Iquique   ④
Humberstone   Pozo Almonte   La Tirana
Pica
⑤   Matilla
Cerro   RESERVA
Pintados   NACIONAL
PAMPA DEL
TAMARUGAL

Ollagüe

Tocopilla
Chug Chug
Geoglyphs
Chiu   RESERVA
Chiu   NACIONAL
Maria Elena   Caspana   EDUARDO
Gatico   Chuquicamata   Ayquina   AVAROA
Pedro de   Calama   El Tatio   ③
Cobija   Valdivia
San Pedro
de Atacama
Chacabuco   Valle de la Luna
Mejillones   ①   Toconao
SALAR DE   Camar
Baquedano   ATACAMA   Socaire
②   Peine
Antofagasta

Cerro Paranal

Taltal

0   80
kilometres

Brief history

It seems almost inconceivable that such a hostile land can support life, but for thousands of years El Norte Grande has been home to indigenous peoples who've wrested a living either from the sea or from the fertile oases that nestle in the Andean foothills. The excessive dryness of the climate has left countless relics of these people almost perfectly intact – most remarkably the **Chinchorro mummies** (see box, p.210), buried on the desert coast near Arica some seven thousand years ago. It wasn't until the nineteenth century that Chile's more recent inhabitants – along with British and German businesses – turned their attention to the Atacama, when it became apparent that the desert was rich in **nitrates** that could be exported at great commercial value. So lucrative was this burgeoning industry that Chile was prepared to go to war over it, for most of the region at that time in fact belonged to Bolivia and Peru. The **War of the Pacific**, waged against Bolivia and Peru between 1878 and 1883, acquired for Chile the desired prize, and the desert pampas went on to yield enormous revenues for the next three decades.

The twentieth century and beyond

With the German invention of synthetic nitrates at the end of World War I, Chile's industry entered a rapid decline, but a financial crisis was averted when new mining techniques enabled low-grade **copper**, of which there are huge quantities in the region, to be profitably extracted. Today, this mineral continues to play the most important role in the country's economy, making Chile the world's leading copper supplier.

GETTING AROUND	EL NORTE GRANDE	**4**

Many of the region's attractions can be reached by public transport, though in order to explore the region in depth you'll need to book some tours or, better still, rent a 4WD vehicle. Whatever your mode of transport, don't underestimate the distances involved in getting to most points of interest, particularly in the altiplano. It makes sense to isolate a few chosen highlights rather than try to see everything, which would be interminably time-consuming.

Antofagasta

A Bolivian town until 1879, when it was annexed by Chile in the War of the Pacific, Antofagasta is Chile's fifth largest and most rapidly growing city. Many tourists bypass this decidedly lacklustre desert city altogether, and with good reason. Overpriced and unattractive, the regional capital holds little of cultural or aesthetic interest, but is a major transport hub and one of Chile's most prosperous cities, serving as an export centre for the region's great mines, most notably Chuquicamata (see p.178). Sitting on a flat shelf between the ocean and the hills, Antofagasta has a compact downtown core, made up of dingy, traffic-choked streets that sport a few handsome but run-down old public buildings, and a modern stretch along the coastal avenue. The area around Latorre and Condell, between Bolivar and Riquelme streets, is best avoided after 9.30pm – Antofagasta has a prostitution problem.

A couple of blocks northeast of the central square, along Bolívar, you'll find the magnificently restored nineteenth-century **offices and railway terminus** of the former Antofagasta and Bolivia Railway Company, complete with polished wooden verandas and dark-green stucco walls (albeit with no public access). Further north still, and an easy stop-off if you're heading out to the airport, is **La Portada**, an iconic natural arch of rock looming out of the sea.

South of the city centre the busy coastal avenue runs past a couple of tiny, coarse-sand **beaches**, first at the Balneario Municipal, then, much further south, at the Playa Huascar, the latter only suitable for sunbathing – take *micro* #103 from Washington, near the square. In this direction lies one of the city's most curious sights, the **Ruinas de Huanchaca**, vestiges of a disused silver refinery.

Plaza Colón

In Antofagasta's centre sprawls the large, green **Plaza Colón**, dominated by a tall clock tower whose face is supposedly a replica of London's Big Ben – one of many tangible signs of the role played by the British in Antofagasta's commercial development. The city's administrative and public buildings, including the Neo-Gothic Iglesia Catedral, built between 1906 and 1917, surround the square.

El Museo Regional

Bolívar 188 • Tues–Fri 9am–5pm, Sat & Sun 11am–2pm • CH$600 • ⓦ dibam.cl

The 1866 customs house (or Ex-aduana as it is now called) is the oldest building in the city, and within it sits the Museo Regional. The museum houses an impressive mineral display downstairs and, upstairs, a collection of clothes, furniture, toys and general paraphernalia dating from the nitrate era.

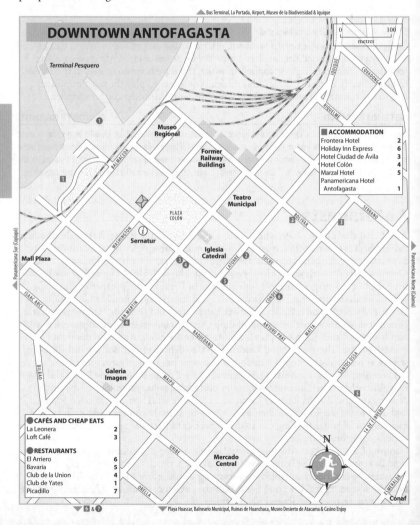

DOWNTOWN ANTOFAGASTA

Bus Terminal, La Portada, Airport, Museo de la Biodiversidad & Iquique

0   100
metres

Terminal Pesquero

Museo Regional

Former Railway Buildings

Teatro Municipal

PLAZA COLÓN

Sernatur

Iglesia Catedral

Mall Plaza

Galeria Imagen

ACCOMMODATION

Frontera Hotel	2
Holiday Inn Express	6
Hotel Ciudad de Ávila	3
Hotel Colón	4
Marzal Hotel	5
Panamericana Hotel Antofagasta	1

Panamericana Sur (Copiapó)

Panamericana Norte (Calama)

CAFÉS AND CHEAP EATS

La Leonera	2
Loft Café	3

RESTAURANTS

El Arriero	6
Bavaria	5
Club de la Union	4
Club de Yates	1
Picadillo	7

Mercado Central

N

6 & 7

Playa Huascar, Balneario Municipal, Ruinas de Huanchaca, Museo Desierto de Atacama & Casino Enjoy

Conaf

Ruinas de Huanchaca

Micro #2, #3, #4 or #10 from the Terminal Pesquero (or Fish Market; summer months only), or a Mejillones-bound micro from Latorre 2748.

These remains of an old Bolivian silver refinery sit on a hilltop a short distance inland, 3km south of the city centre by the Universidad del Norte. The **Ruinas de Huanchaca** were built to process the silver brought down from the Potosí mine (at that time the most important silver mine in South America), before being shipped out of Antofagasta. Looking at the square and circular walls of the complex from below, you'd be forgiven for thinking they were ruins of a pre-Columbian fortress.

ARRIVAL AND DEPARTURE ANTOFAGASTA

By air Coming in by air, you'll arrive at the Aeropuerto Cerro Moreno, 25km north of the city, right on the Tropic of Capricorn. From here, regular *colectivos* and infrequent *micros* head to the centre or you can take a minibus directly to your accommodation (they await every arrival).

Airlines LAN, Prat 445 ☎ 55 265151; Sky Airlines, Washington 2548 ☎ 55 459090.

Destinations Arica (3 daily; 1hr 30min); Calama (3 daily; 35min); Iquique (4 daily; 45min); La Serena (3 daily; 2hr); Santiago (17 daily; 2hr).

By bus The main Terminal Carlos Oviedo Cavada is located

on Pedro A. Cerda 5750, about a 15min drive from the centre – a cab will set you back approximately CH$5000. A much cheaper option is to take *colectivo* (shared taxi) #111 – also from right outside the terminal – which will drop you off in the centre for CH$600.

Destinations Arica (4 daily; 10hr); Calama (hourly; 3hr); Caldera (hourly; 6hr); Chañaral (16 daily; 5hr); Chuquicamata (5 daily; 3hr); Copiapó (hourly; 7hr); La Serena (16 daily; 11hr); María Elena (2 daily; 3hr); Mejillones (every 30min; 40min); Santiago (hourly; 20hr); Tocopilla (6 daily; 2hr 40min).

INFORMATION AND TOURS

Conaf office Av Argentina 2510 (Mon–Fri 9am–1pm & 2.30–5.30pm; ☎ 55 383320). This is the place to come for details on the protected areas around San Pedro de Atacama, which lies within this region.

Sernatur tourist office Prat 384 (Mon–Thurs 8.30am–5.30pm, Fri 8.30am–4.30pm; ☎&☎ 55 4518 1820, ✉ infoantofagasta@sernatur.cl). For tourist

information on the city of Antofagasta, head to the ground floor of the Intendencia at the corner of the central plaza.

Travel agencies You'll find many travel agencies downtown, including Nortour, Baquedano 474 ☎ 55 227171, ✉ nortour@nortour.tie.cl; Viajes Palanisa, San Martín 2457 ☎ 55 561120, ✉ patricia.alanis @entelchile.net.

ACCOMMODATION

You'll find an abundance of **accommodation** in Antofagasta, but the range tends to jump from cheap and basic to expensive (and not necessarily good quality), with very few mid-priced options in between. Most places are in the downtown core, with the mostly expensive hotels, catering primarily to business travellers, on the coastal avenue.

Frontera Hotel Bolívar 558 ☎ 55 281219. Probably the best budget choice in the city, offering simple but spotless, modern rooms, some with private bathrooms, wi-fi and cable TV. No breakfast served. CH$15,000

Holiday Inn Express Av Grecia 1490, ☎ 800 808080 or 55 228888, ⊛ holidayinn.cl. Modern, super-clean American chain hotel, with pool and parking – a good place to pamper yourself if the desert is getting to you. It's connected to the centre by plenty of *micros*. CH$82,000 (US$164)

Hotel Ciudad de Ávila Condell 2840 ☎ 55 221040. Though the central location isn't the safest at nights, this no-frills, bargain-rate accommodation fills up quickly; most rooms have private bath and external windows. Booking in advance is advisable. CH$14,000

Hotel Colón San Martín 2434 ☎ 55 261851. Decent

option with clean, fairly comfortable and light rooms with private bath, cable TV and wi-fi. Those facing the road can be rather noisy though. There's a restaurant next door owned by the same people serving good value home-cooked meals. CH$30,000

Marzal Hotel Prat 867 ☎ 55 268063. Modern yet slightly kitsch hotel six blocks from the central square, offering spacious rooms with private bath as well as parking. CH$42,000.

Panamericana Hotel Antofagasta Balmaceda 2575 ☎ 55 228811, ⊛ panamericanahoteles.cl/antofagasta .html. Large, venerable chain hotel overlooking the ocean, with well-furnished but overpriced rooms. The restaurant's outdoor terrace is one of the most pleasant lunch spots in the city. CH$42,500

EATING, DRINKING AND NIGHTLIFE

Antofagasta's **restaurants** tend to be busy and lively, with a couple of classy establishments standing out among the grill houses and pizzerias. On the coast just west of the town centre is the **Mall Plaza**, Balmaceda 2355, home to several newer eating establishments. Among these are the usual American fast-food outlets, but also a few more sophisticated options. At the corner of Ossa and Maipú, the huge, pink-and-cream Mercado Central sells fresh food and *artesanía*. The nightlife scene, thanks mainly to the number of university students around town, is surprisingly vibrant, with a few decent **bars** to choose from outside the city centre and a choice of **dance spots** all located down at Playa Huascar, way south of town (take a taxi).

CAFÉS AND CHEAP EATS

La Leonera Latorre 2670 ☎ 55 251436. Perhaps the best cheap eat in town, no-frills *La Leonera* has been a local's favourite for years, offering brisk service and a good-value lunch menu (CH$3000). Expect the likes of fried fish, *empanadas* and stews. Mon–Sat 9am–1am.

Loft Café Prat 470. Just metres from Plaza Colon, *Loft Cafe* serves up salads, baguettes and coffee to businessmen and students alike. Multicoloured lamps and modern paintings make this café stand out among the other dreary central options. Mon–Sat 8.30am–9.30pm.

RESTAURANTS

★ **El Arriero** Condell 2644. Two brothers play old jazz tunes on the piano every night at this inviting, Spanish-inn-style spot, complete with hanging hams. Try the excellent, moderately priced *parrilladas*. Mon–Sat 11.30am–4pm & 7.30pm–midnight, Sun 11.30am–4pm.

Bavaria Latorre 2624 ☎ 55 283821. The same pine decor, the same grilled meat, the same indifferent service you find in every other branch of the *Bavaria* chain in the

country. At least you know what you're getting – and the German-style food's not bad, after all, nor is it expensive. Mon–Fri 8am–midnight, Sat & Sun 10am–midnight.

Club de la Unión Prat 474, ☎ 55 268371. This attractive restaurant, housed in a 1904 building, offers old school charm, efficient service and international fare. The ground floor is for members only, while the first floor is open to the public. There's a daily lunch menu (CH$4600) and à la carte in the evenings. Mon–Sat 1–4pm & 8–11pm, Sun 1–4pm.

Club de Yates Balmaceda 2701 at Sucre. This elegant restaurant on the waterfront has lovely ocean views and an expensive but good seafood-based menu, more imaginative than most. Mon–Sat 1–4pm & 8–11pm, Sun 1–4pm.

★ **Picadillo** Av Grecia 1000 ☎ 55 247503. Popular restaurant offering the likes of beef carpaccio marinated in ginger for starters and delicious, unusual sushi, plus inventive desserts; both music and service are faultless. Reservations recommended at weekends. Mon–Fri 12.30pm–3.30pm & 7.30pm–1am, Sat 8pm–2am.

DIRECTORY

Banks and exchange There are several ATMs on the central square and the main commercial streets, including Prat, Washington and San Martín. You can change the major foreign currencies at Ancla, Baquedano 524.

Camping gas White gas (*bencina blanca*) and butane gas available at Andesgear on the ground floor of the Mall Plaza.

Car rental Avis, Baquedano 364 ☎ 55 563140, ✉ antofagasta@avischile.cl; Budget, Aeropuerto ☎ 55 563143, ✉ antofagasta@budget.cl; Econorent, Pedro Aguirre Cerda 6100 ☎ 55 594177, ✉ antofagasta@econorent.cl.

Internet There are lots of internet outlets with good prices and connections along Latorre, close to the plaza.

Post office On the central square, at Washington 2613.

Around Antofagasta

If you have time to kill or if deserted nitrate era ghost towns and different types of rock formations are your thing, you may want to dedicate a day or afternoon to exploring the area surrounding the city of Antofagasta. Highlights include an old Bolivian silver refinery, the cliff formations of La Portada (a natural arch, now a symbol of the region) and a couple of natural history museums.

Museo Desierto de Atacama

Av Angamos 01606 • Tues–Sun 10am–1pm & 2.30–7pm • CH$2000 • Bus #303 from Plaza Colón

A must for aspiring geographers and geologers, this attractive new museum, set in a modern building located in front of the Casino Enjoy complex, is divided into several parts. These include a "rock garden", exhibiting rocks and minerals indigenous to northern Chile; rooms named "the creation of space" dedicated to explaining how the desert and altiplano were formed; an exhibition on "the miner", looking at the history of mining in this part of Chile; and a room financed by the European Southern Observatory (ESO)exploring astrology in the Atacama desert. There's also a space dedicated to temporary exhibitions.

La Portada

Micro #15 from the Terminal Pesquero; if you're driving, follow the coast road north and take the turn-off to Juan López, from where La Portada is well signed

A huge eroded arch looming out of the ocean, **La Portada** sits 16km north of Antofagasta along the coast road. Declared a national monument in 1990, the arch has become something of a regional symbol, and its picture graces postcards and wall calendars all over Chile. Makeshift signs quite rightly warn you not to approach the crumbling cliffs or descend the rickety steps to the unsafe beach, while the nearby bar-restaurant and shops are often closed, even in high season, lending the place a sadly abandoned air. Upkeep of La Portada has improved, however, since the opening of the new **museo de la biodiversidad** (Tues–Sun 10am–6pm; free) located on the site and dedicated to the flora and fauna of northern Chile's coastal region.

The Cerro Paranal Observatory

Tours Jan–Nov last two weekends of the month, Sat & Sun 2pm; you'll need to book months in advance by phone or online • Free • ☎ 55 435000, Ⓦ eso.org

A little under two hours south of Antofagasta, perched on **Cerro Paranal** at 2644m above sea level, is the **CERRO PARANAL OBSERVATORY,** run by the ESO. While you have to be a recognized researcher to stand any chance of looking through its **Very Large Telescope** (VLT), one of the world's strongest, on certain weekends you can visit the dazzling site, set among suitably lunar, and even Mars-like, landscapes of reddish rock. In fact, NASA tested the Mars Pathfinder rover in the nearby Atacama Desert (a more glamorous claim to fame is that parts of the James Bond movie *Quantum of Solace* were filmed here).

The VLT – strictly speaking a set of four 8.2m telescopes, each weighing 430 tonnes, whose combined might enables observers to see objects as small as humans on the Moon – has been fully operational since 2001. It's housed in a futuristic-looking set of four trapezoidal cylinders dramatically located on the barren Cerro Paranal, which averages 330 clear nights a year. A luxurious 120-room residence (for scientists only), complete with a cafeteria and an indoor garden (both open to the public), stands nearby. To get here, head south from Antofagasta on the Panamericana (Ruta 5); the unpaved turn-off

---

ALMA OBSERVATORY

The **Atacama Large Millimeter Array** (ALMA; Ⓦ almaobservatory.org), a joint North American, East Asian, European and Chilean venture, started scientific observations in 2011 and is the largest, most powerful astronomical project in existence. Positioned at a staggering 5000m above sea level at a site east of San Pedro de Atacama called the Chajnantor plateau, this is the highest astronomical observatory of its kind on the planet. The ALMA uses state of the art technology, initially comprising 66 giant high-precision antennae working together at millimetre and submillimetre wavelengths. These can be moved up to 16km across the desert, but act as a single giant telescope. ALMA's slogan – "in search of our cosmic origins" – gives an exciting sense of what this project is really about.

For the first time in history, astrologers will be able to study new stars being born, watch planetary systems and galaxies with unprecedented clarity, and, with time, be able to answer big questions about the origins of life itself.

24km south of the Mina Escondida crossroads leads due south over a mountain pass to the observatory. Remember to take warm clothing, as it is very cold inside the observatory. If you do not have your own transport, you can join an organized tour from Antofagasta with Desertica Expediciones (Ⓔ desertica.expediciones@gmail.com, Ⓣ09 9792 6791).

The nitrate pampa

Northeast of Antofagasta, the vast *pampa salitrera*, or **NITRATE PAMPA**, pans across the desert towards the cordillera – it's not the prettiest landscape in the world, a mass of scruffy plains that look as though they have been ploughed, fertilized and then left for fallow. Between 1890 and 1925 there were over 80 *oficinas* here, extracting the nitrate ore and sending it down to the ports by railroad. Some of them are still standing, abandoned and in ruins, including Chacabuco, crumbling in the desert heat.

Two highways cross the pampa: the Panamericana, heading due north to Iquique, and Ruta 25, branching off northeast to the mining city of Calama. The former skirts **María Elena**, home to the last remaining nitrate *oficina* (or plant), and a place that can be reached on public transport. Although you can find basic accommodation if you look hard enough (there are two hotels), you may as well forge on if you can; it's a desperately soulless place to spend the night.

The Chug Chug geoglyphs

The Panamericana is crossed by a lateral road, Ruta 24, 107km north of the Carmen Alto junction. This is connected to Tocopilla, 60km west, and Chuquicamata, 66km east. Just short of 50km along the road for Chuquicamata, a sign points north to the **CHUG CHUG GEOGLYPHS**, reached by a 13km dirt road that's just about passable in a car. These consist of some three hundred images spread over several hills, many of them clearly visible from below, including circles, zoomorphic figures, human faces and geometric designs. It's an impressive site, and certainly deserves a visit if you're driving in the area.

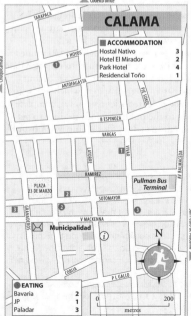

CALAMA

■ **ACCOMMODATION**
Hostal Nativo	3
Hotel El Mirador	2
Park Hotel	4
Residencial Toño	1

● **EATING**
Bavaria	2
JP	1
Paladar	3

Calama

Sitting on the banks of the Río Loa, at an altitude of 2250m, **CALAMA** is an ugly, bland town, whose chief role is as a service centre and residential base for **Chuquicamata**, the massive copper mine 16km north (see p.178). It's best avoided if possible, but many visitors end up spending a night here on their way to or from San Pedro de Atacama, the famous oasis village and tourist centre 100km east.

▶ **Brief history**

Calama began life as a *tambo*, or resting place, at the intersection of two Inca roads – one running down the Andes, the other connecting the altiplano with the Pacific – and both Diego de Almagro and Pedro de

Valdivia visited on their journeys into Chile. It was never heavily populated by pre-Hispanic peoples, who preferred nearby Chiu Chiu, with its less saline water supply. The town took on a new prominence, however, as an important stop on the Oruro–Antofagasta railway in the late nineteenth century, and its future was sealed with the creation of the Chuquicamata copper mine in 1911. Today its busy streets are built around a surprisingly small and laid-back central core.

Parque El Loa

Avenida O'Higgins s/n • Daily 10am–8pm • Free

About 2km from the centre of town is the Parque El Loa, a good spot for a picnic. One of the park's star attractions – the archeological museum, which holds displays on pre-Colombian history – has been closed since the 2007 earthquake. The other famous landmark, a mini reconstruction of the famous Chiu Chiu church, is still there.

ARRIVAL AND DEPARTURE   CALAMA

BY PLANE

If you're flying to Calama you'll land at the Aeropuerto El Loa, 5km south of the centre – the only way into town from here is by taxi (CH$5000).

Destinations Antofagasta (3 daily; 35min); Arica (2 daily; 35min); Iquique (2 daily; 30min); La Serena (2 daily; 3hr); Santiago (5 daily; 2hr direct, 3hr via Antofagasta).

BY BUS

Arriving by bus you'll be dropped at your bus company's office, generally near the city centre; there's no single

terminal. Pullman Bus and Tur Bus both have terminals of their own, the latter inconveniently situated more than 1km north of town. Hail down *colectivo* (shared taxi) #5 or #11 right outside the Tur Bus terminal to get to the centre (CH$600).

Destinations Antofagasta (6 daily; 3hr); Arica (6 daily; 10hr); Chañaral (10 daily; 8hr); Chuquicamata (every 30min; 30min); Copiapó (14 daily; 9hr 30min); Iquique (4 daily; 7hr); La Serena (14 daily; 12hr 30min); San Pedro de Atacama (1 hourly; 1hr 30min); Santiago (14 daily; 22hr 30min); Toconao (1 daily; 2hr 30min).

INFORMATION

Tourist office Opposite the Municipalidad, Latorre 1689, on the corner of Vicuña Mackenna (Mon–Fri 8am–1pm & 2–6pm; ☎ 55 531707). Offers maps and other basic information, but not much else.

ACCOMMODATION

Calama has a wide range of **accommodation**, but many places are overpriced owing to the mining clientele, and many can get fully booked during the San Pedro tourist seasons. Beware of overbooking and always call or send an email to confirm if possible.

Hostal Nativo Sotomayor 2215 ☎ 55 310377. This centrally located, family-run hotel offers friendly service and plain, immaculately clean rooms with wi-fi and cable TV. CH$16,000

Hotel El Mirador Sotomayor 2064 ☎ 55 340329, ⓦ www.hotelmirador.cl. A lovely, small hotel with spacious rooms – including one with a Victorian cast-iron bath – and attractive furnishings, set in a colonial-style house that dates from the 19th century. CH$48,000

Park Hotel Camino al Aeropuerto 1392 ☎ 55 715800, ⓦ www.parkplaza.cl. At the top end of the scale, *Park Hotel*, popular with business guests, boasts elegant decor, a good restaurant and an attractive swimming pool – a godsend in the sweltering summer months. CH$50,000

Residencial Toño Vivar 1970 ☎ 55 341185. Good, quiet budget choice which has been going for years, offering very simple rooms, some with private bathrooms. CH$16,000

EATING AND DRINKING

Bavaria Sotomayor 2093 ☎ 55 341496. *Bavaria*, on the plaza, is part of a well-known nationwide chain offering decent if very predictable mid-price meat dishes and sandwiches from its downstairs café and upstairs restaurant. Daily noon–4.30pm & 7.30pm–midnight.

JP Felix Hoyos 2127. Another good choice is the friendly

and unpretentious *JP* – just a short walk from the plaza – that serves tasty, if pricey, fish and seafood dishes such as *sopa de mariscos* and *pescado frito*. Tues–Sat noon–3.30pm & 8–11.30pm, Sun noon–3.30pm.

Paladar Vivar 1797 ☎ 55 926554, ⓦ www .paladarrestaurant.cl. The swish *Paladar* has an imaginative menu compared with other Calama eating options, comprising sharing platters and international

cuisine with a French twist, plus a great Chilean wine list. Daily noon–1.30am.

DIRECTORY

Banks and exchange You'll find plenty of ATMs on Sotomayor, as well as a *cambio* around the corner at Vivar 1818.

Car rental Avis, Aeropuerto (☎ 55 793968); Europcar, Balmaceda 2634 (☎ 55 346742); and Hertz, Aeropuerto (☎ 55 315762).

Chuquicamata

Official guided tours (by minibus, departing Mon–Fri 1.30pm; tours also leave at 3.30pm Jan & Feb; 1hr 30min) must be booked in advance from Codelco's Calama office on Av. Granadero and Av. Central (☎ 55 322122, ✉ visitas@codelco.cl), or through Calama's tourist information office (see p.177) • Free, but donations to a children's charity supported by the mine are welcomed

One of the world's largest open-pit copper mines, **CHUQUICAMATA** (16km north of Calama) produces six hundred thousand tonnes per year – outstripped only by Mina Escondida, 200km southeast of Antofagasta, whose capacity exceeds eignt hundred thousand tonnes. Carved out of the ground like a giant, sunken amphitheatre, the massive mine dwarfs everything within it, making the huge trucks carrying the ore up from the crater floor – whose wheels alone are an incredible 4m high – look like tiny, crawling ants. Its size is the result of some ninety years of excavation, and its reserves are predicted to last at least until the middle of the twenty-first century. Along with all of Chile's large-scale copper mines, or "*grandes minerías*" as they're called, Chuquicamata belongs to Codelco, the government-owned copper corporation. Codelco also used to maintain an adjacent company town, complete with its own school, hospital, cinema and football stadium, but the nine thousand workers and their families who lived there have now been moved to Calama, making way for further excavation.

Tours

The tours take place almost entirely on a bus, though you're allowed to get out at the viewpoint looking down to the pit – wear sensible shoes and clothing that covers most of your body. The rest of the tour takes you round the machinery yards and buildings of the plant, which you see from the outside only.

San Pedro de Atacama

The little oasis village of **SAN PEDRO DE ATACAMA** (100km southeast of Calama), with its narrow dirt streets and attractive adobe houses, has transformed itself, since the 1990s, into *the* tourism centre of Chile. Sitting at an altitude of 2400m between the desert and the altiplano, or *puna* (the high basin connecting the two branches of the cordillera), this has been an important settlement since pre-Hispanic times, originally as a major stop on the trading route connecting the llama herders of these highlands with the fishing communities of the Pacific. Later, during the nitrate era, it was the

---

SAN PEDRO DE ATACAMA ORIENTATION

San Pedro's main street is **Caracoles**, which is where you'll find the biggest concentration of accommodation, eating places and services. Early in the new millennium, Calle Antofagasta was renamed Gustavo Le Paige and all houses in the village were given a number, but, with some establishments, you might find that the changes have still not quite sunk in. Fortunately, as San Pedro is a very small place, you should always be able to find your destination without difficulty.

main rest stop on the cattle trail from Salta in Argentina to the nitrate *oficinas*, where the cattle were driven to supply the workers with fresh meat.

The large numbers of Chilean tourists and hordes of gringos here can come as quite a shock if you have just arrived from more remote parts of northern Chile. San Pedro has recently begun to lose some of its charm and is lined with overpriced, trendy-looking hotels with poor service. Luckily, you will find exceptions (see p.181).

Iglesia de San Pedro

Free

The focus of San Pedro is the little **plaza** at its centre, dotted with pepper trees and wooden benches. On its western side stands the squat white **Iglesia de San Pedro**, one of the largest Andean churches in the region. It's actually San Pedro's second church, built in 1744, just over one hundred years after the original church was erected near the present site of the archeological museum. The bell tower was added towards the end of the nineteenth century, and the thick adobe walls surrounding the church rebuilt in 1978.

The interior

Inside, religious icons look down from the brightly painted altar, among them a stern-looking Saint Peter, the village's patron saint. Overhead, the sloping roof is made of rough-hewn planks of cactus wood and gnarled rafters of reddish algarrobo timber, bound together with leather straps.

4

SAN PEDRO DE ATACAMA

ACCOMMODATION	
Awasi	11
Camping Los Perales	10
Casa de Don Tomás	12
Hostal Katarpe	6
Hostal Sonchek	4
Hostal Takha-Takha	7
Hostal Vilacoyo	2
Hostería San Pedro	9
Hotel Altiplánico	1
Hotel Kimal	8
Hotel Kunza	13
Hotel Terrantai	5
Residencial Chiloé	3

● RESTAURANTS	
Adobe	11
Blanco	10
Café Etnico	4
La Casona	9
Las Delicias de Carmen	1
La Estaka	12
Paacha	8
Pizzeria El Charrúa	3

● BARS	
Café Export	7
Chela Cabur	6
Grado 6	2
● CAFÉS	
Babalu	5
Tierra Todo Natural	13

0 _____ 100
metres

Casa Incaica

Opposite the Iglesia de San Pedro, on the other side of the square at Toconao 421b, sits San Pedro's oldest building, the lopsided **Casa Incaica**, now a souvenir store. The house dates from the earliest days of the colony (a plaque outside claims it is the former home of Spanish conquistador Pedro de Valdivia), though its roof seems to be in imminent danger of collapse. A narrow alley full of **artesanía** stalls, where you can buy alpaca knitwear and other souvenirs, links the square to the main bus stops to the north.

Museo Arqueológico Gustavo Le Paige

Gustavo Le Paige 380 • Mon–Fri 9am–6pm, Sat & Sun 10am–6pm; guided tours in various languages nine times daily Tues–Sun; with 24 hr notice, you can organize a private tour on Mon • CH$2500; tours CH$1800 extra

Don't miss the excellent **Museo Arqueológico Gustavo Le Paige**, just off the northeast corner of the square. Named after the Belgian missionary-cum-archeologist who founded it in 1957, the museum houses more than 380,000 artefacts gathered from the region around San Pedro, of which the best examples are displayed in eight "naves" arranged around a central hall. Charting the development, step by step, of local pre-Columbian peoples, the displays range from Neolithic tools to sophisticated ceramics, taking in delicately carved wooden tablets and tubes used for inhaling hallucinogenic substances, and a number of gold cups with engraved faces used by village elders during religious ceremonies.

ARRIVAL AND DEPARTURE SAN PEDRO DE ATACAMA

By bus Several bus companies have regular services from Calama to San Pedro; they all have different drop-off points, all of which sit a couple of blocks off the main square, mostly along Licancabur. You have to change at

Calama (often with a delay) for major destinations, including Iquique, Arica and Santiago.
Destinations Antofagasta (3 daily; 6hr), Calama (hourly; 1.5 hr).

GETTING AROUND

By bike There are many places that rent bikes in San Pedro. H2O on Caracoles charges CH$4000 per half-day or CH$6000 per day and give out a handy map and emergency bike-repair kit.

By car For car rental try Europcar, Calama 479 ☎ 569 7388 9848, ⓦ europcar.es.
By taxi The taxi situation in San Pedro is complicated – you must call ahead so ask your hotel to arrange this for you.

INFORMATION AND TOURS

TOURIST INFORMATION

Tourist office Toconao, corner of Gustavo Le Paige (Mon, Tues, Thurs & Fri 9.15am–8.15pm, Wed 9.15am–6pm, Sat & Sun 10am–8.15pm; ☎ 55 851420, ⓔ sanpedrodeatacama@gmail.com, ⓦ sernatur.cl). The helpful tourist office on the main plaza hands out regional maps and lists of tour companies. Check ⓦ sanpedroatacama.com for more information and links.

TOUR OPERATORS

Atacama Connection Corner of Caracoles and Toconao ☎ 55 851421, ⓦ atacamaconnection.com. Long-running operator with very good reputation offering standard regional tours from the centre of San Pedro including popular excursions to the Tatio Geysers and Valle de la Luna.
★ **Cosmo Andino** Caracoles s/n ☎ 55 851069, ⓦ cosmoandino.cl. Well-established and respected company offering interesting variations on the most

popular tours, as well as off-the-beaten track expeditions. Choose to explore the countryside on foot, or go on a 4x4 tour across the mountains. Both day and overnight tours are highly recommended.
Desert Adventure Caracoles, esq. Tocopilla ☎ 55 851067, ⓦ desertadventure.cl. Professional and reliable outfit which has been going strong since 1990, offering tours around San Pedro with enthusiastic and well-informed guides who speak English, French, German, Italian and Portuguese, as well as Spanish.
Estrella del Sur Caracoles 238 ☎ 55 852109. Reliable, family-run company offering trips across the border into Bolivia to see the fabulous Salar de Uyuni (covered in the *Rough Guide to Bolivia*).
Rancho Cactus Toconao 568 ☎ 55 851506, ⓦ rancho-cactus.cl. For an alternative San Pedro experience, try the horse treks run by Rancho Cactus. Treks last from a few hours to three days and are led by guides passionate about both the region and the horses. English and French spoken.

★ **Space Obs** Caracoles 166 ☎ 55 851935, ⊛ spaceobs .com. Excellent, highly memorable tours (in English, French, Spanish and German) of Northern Chile's night sky led by enthusiastic and personable astronomers. Book in advance.

Vulcano Expediciones Caracoles 317 ☎ 55 851023, ⊛ vulcanochile.com. This the best operator for mountain and volcano ascents, trekking, sandboarding and bike tours. They also offer fun horseriding tours around San Pedro and even adventurous 4-day treks into Bolivia.

ACCOMMODATION

There are loads of places offering **rooms** in San Pedro, including a number of comfortable *residenciales* plus some classy, upmarket places for those on a far more generous budget. Recently, more of the latter have sprung up, often with a now hackneyed pseudo-native architectural style – lots of adobe, stone walls and thatched roofs – but mercifully, there have been no high-rises (it's against the law to construct anything higher than two storeys). A wonderful alternative for those on a smaller budget is provided by a scheme of *albergues turísticos*, rural guesthouses in the nearby villages of Peine and Socaire. For details and bookings contact the tourist office. You'll also find a few **campsites** within easy reach of the village centre; the best is listed below. If you're travelling alone and at a busy time, many *residenciales* may ask you to share with another traveller.

HOTELS

★ **Awasi** Tocopilla 4 ☎ 55 851460, ⊛ awasi.cl. This special place is exclusive, without being stuffy. Eight rooms each come with a guide and vehicle for guests to tailor the shape of their stay. The staff are young and friendly, the food outstanding and comfort paramount. Relax and be spoiled. 2-night fullboard CH$645,880 (US$1340) per person

Casa de Don Tomás Tocopilla s/n ☎ 55 851055, ⊛ dontomas.cl. Located away from the buzz of central San Pedro, 300m south of the crossroads with Caracoles, this rustic, well-established hotel has spacious rooms, a pool, good breakfasts, a friendly welcome, and subsequent to all the above, consistently good reviews. CH$67,000

Hostal Katarpe Domingo Atienza 441 ☎ 55 851033, ⊛ katarpe.cl. Pleasant place with good-value,

comfortable rooms, all with private bath and fluffy towels. Wi-fi in all rooms too. CH$36,000

Hostal Sonchek Gustavo Le Paige 198 ☎ 55 851112, ✉ soncheksp@hotmail.com. Great-value hotel run by a personable and eco-conscious Slovenian–Chilean couple (recycling system and solar panel in place) and their cats. Rooms are cosy (those with private bathrooms are particularly attractive) and there's a small communal kitchen and garden. Wi-fi available. CH$16,000

Hostal Takha-Takha Caracoles 101a ☎ 55 851038. Small but tidy and quiet rooms giving onto a pleasant garden. There's a lovely new (but small) pool and you can also camp here. A good bet for singles. Camping CH$10,000 per person, double CH$72,000

Hostería San Pedro Solcor ☎ 55 851011, ⊛ dahoteles .com. Well-maintained, very comfortable accommodation

---

TOURS FROM SAN PEDRO

San Pedro has a high concentration of **tour operators** (see p.180) offering excursions into the surrounding altiplano, all broadly similar and all at pretty much the same price. This can, of course, be a curse as well as a blessing, for it increases tourist traffic in the region to the point where it can be difficult to visit the awe-inspiring landscape of the *puna* in the kind of silence and isolation in which it really ought to be experienced. Some of the tours are responsibly managed but many are not; the astounding environmental damage of late has finally, if belatedly, forced local communities (but not the national authorities) to take action; they now charge entrance fees to each site and do their best to clean up after visits. The **tourist office** keeps volumes of complaints registered by tourists (usually concerning reliability of vehicles or lack of professionalism) and they are worth consulting to find out which operators to avoid.

Tours usually take place in minibuses, though smaller groups may travel in jeeps. Competition keeps prices relatively low – you can expect to pay from around CH$8000 to visit the Valle de la Luna, CH$21,000 for a tour to the Tatio geysers, and around CH$30,000 for a full-day tour of the local lakes and oases. Don't necessarily choose the cheapest tour, as some companies cram passengers in and offer below-par services, so it may be worth paying a couple of thousand pesos more. Do visit several companies – or their websites, where available – to get a feel for how they operate and to work out which one you prefer. If you don't speak Spanish, check that they can offer guides who speak your language (French, German and English are most common languages on offer).

– mostly in pretty little bungalows – along with a fantastic swimming pool and good restaurant. CH$110075 (US$188)

Hotel Altiplánico Domingo Atienza 282 ☎ 55 851212, ⊚ altiplanico.cl. Located in a calm spot 250m from the centre, on the way to the Pukará de Quitor, this gorgeous hotel complex is built in typical San Pedro adobe style, with fantastic views, tasteful decor, comfortable en-suite rooms, a swimming pool (albeit odd-looking), internet access, a café-bar and bicycle rental. CH$110,000 (US$200).

Hotel Kimal Domingo Atienza ☎ 55 851030, ⊚ kimal.cl. Spacious, light and very attractive rooms, combining contemporary, spartan architecture with plants and warm rugs. A better deal is to be had in the new section of the hotel directly opposite, called *Poblado Kimal*, where you can stay in lovely private *cabañas* for slightly less. Both sections have pools. *Hotel Kimal* CH$110,500 *Poblado Kimal* CH$95,000

★ **Hotel Kunza** Avenida las Chilcas s/n, ☎ 55 852136, ⊚ hotelkunza.cl. Located outside the village, this mega stylish boutique hotel is decorated in gorgeous Atacama chic. Panoramic views of the snowcapped Andes from each private adobe-style hut are a highlight, as is the spa and wonderful restaurant. The staff are exceptionally professional and friendly, and the hotel organizes regional excursions. CH$211,000/US$410

Hotel Terrantai Tocopilla 411 ☎ 55 851045, ⊚ terrantai.com. Modern, stylish but slightly snobbish B&B with bare stone walls and minimalist wooden furniture, conveniently located near the plaza. There's a little orchard out back and a small pool with sun-loungers. CH$105,000

Residencial Chiloé Domingo Atienza 404 ☎ 55 851017. Simple but rather uninspiring rooms kept very clean by the friendly owner. They also have a restaurant serving a good-value *menú del día*. CH$22,000

HOSTELS

Vilacoyo Residencial Tocopilla 387 ☎ 55 851006, ⊕ vilacoyo@sanpedroatacama.com. Very friendly, homely hostel with private and shared rooms set around a relaxing hammock-strewn courtyard. Kitchen and shared bathrooms are spotless. 12 hours of hot water per day. Dorm CH$8000 per person, double CH$16,000

CAMPSITES

Camping Los Perales Tocopilla 481 ☎ 55 851114. The best campsite in San Pedro, located a short distance south of the plaza, with lots of trees, hot water, a climbing wall and an outdoor kitchen. CH$4000 per person.

EATING AND DRINKING

Thanks to the steady flow of young travellers passing through town, San Pedro boasts a lively **restaurant scene**. Just about every restaurant offers a fixed-price evening meal, usually including a vegetarian option; despite fierce competition, though, prices are notably higher than in other parts of the country. For cheaper, filling set meals, try one of the handful of restaurants by the taxi rank at the top end of Licancabur. As with the accommodation, you'll see a definite "San Pedro look" among local restaurants, with a predilection for "native-style" adobe walls, wooden tables with benches, faux rock-paintings and other wacky decorations, and trendy staff who, more often than not, are working migrants from cities in the south. While most restaurants double up as bars, party animals should note that **nightlife** in San Pedro is very tame: bar-restaurants close at 1 or 2am and there are no nightclubs to speak of.

CAFES

Babalu Caracoles 160. Tiny *heladería* offering home-made ice creams that quench the thirst. Daily-changing flavours include pisco sour, chirimoya and lip-smackingly good fruits of the forest. Daily 10am–8pm.

Tierra Todo Natural Caracoles 271 ☎ 55 851585. Friendly resto-café specializing in wholesome home-made food, including wholemeal bread, pizzas, *empanadas*, fish, fantastic salads and pancakes – a good choice for vegetarians. There are also delicious but expensive fruit juices. Daily 8.30am–12.30am.

RESTAURANTS

Adobe Caracoles 211 ☎ 55 851132. Bustling outdoor restaurant with a roaring fire lit every night, serving the usual Chilean fare. Try the *carne a lo pobre* (beef with chips, fried egg and fried onion). Uncomfortable benches and perhaps not the best value in town but a warm

atmosphere and wi-fi nevertheless. Fixed menu at lunch only. Mon–Thurs & Sun 11.30am–1am, Fri & Sat 11.30am–2am.

★ **Blanco** Caracoles s/n ☎ 55 851164. Conceived in white minimalist-chic adobe, this stylish joint certainly stands out from the crowd and is arguably the best restaurant in town. The select, sophisticated menu – try the *lomo con salsa de vainilla* (tenderloin with vanilla sauce) – and great wines will not disappoint. Daily 6pm–12.30am.

Café Etnico Tocopilla 423 ☎ 774 15534. Argentine-run restaurant and bar with great-value lunches and dinners, and a funky ambience. The friendly, helpful owner is full of information on things to do in the area and beyond. You can rent bikes and sandboards here too. Mon, Tues & Thurs–Sun 10am–1am.

La Casona Caracoles 195a ☎ 55 851337. Busy, informal restaurant with an elegant dining room inside a large, colonial-style house. The fire-lit bar out the back, complete with a mini Virgin Mary shrine, is a great spot for after-dinner drinks. Daily 9am–12am.

★ **Las Delicias de Carmen** Calama 370b ☎ 908 95673. Popular spot dishing up enormous portions of hearty, home-cooked food, served by the charismatic owner Carmen. Try the freshly baked *empanadas* and sweeter treats such as the lemon meringue pie. Grab a spot on the lovely patio behind the main building if you can. Daily 8am–10.30pm.

La Estaka Caracoles 259 ☎ 55 851286. Rustic restaurant-bar with young waiters and waitresses, and attractive paintings by local artist on display and for sale. Very popular, though hardly a budget option. Mon–Thurs & Sun noon–1am, Fri & Sat noon–2am.

Paacha Domingo Atienza s/n, in *Hotel Kimal* ☎ 55 851030. Small, moderately priced restaurant with an attractive interior, serving *nueva andina* cuisine (international–Andean fusion, basically). There's a lunch and dinner set menu for CH$13,000. Daily 7.15am–10.30pm.

Pizzeria El Charrúa Tocopilla 442 ☎ 55 851443. The wonderful aroma wafting out of this intimate pizzeria entices hungry punters inside. It may only have 4 tables but it serves the best thin crust pizza in town, plus exciting salads. Note that there's no alcohol on sale – opt for a fresh fruit juice instead. Daily 11am–11pm.

BARS

Café Export Caracoles and Tocanao. Service is sometimes a bit on the slow side, but there's a fun atmosphere at this small resto-bar, probably aided by the excellent happy hour. The striking decor includes Valle de la Luna-inspired tables, hand-crafted using adobe. Daily 6pm–1am.

Chela Cabur Caracoles 211 ☎ 55 851576. The name says it all: *Chela Cabur* translates as "mountain of beer" in Kunza-Chilean. Owned by a Finnish beer aficionado, this laid-back place – kitted out with wooden benches and music posters on the walls – only serves *cerveza* and is extremely popular with the local youth. Mon–Thurs & Sun noon–1am, Fri & Sat 12pm–2am.

Grado 6 Le Paige 456. This pocket-sized, low-ceilinged cave-like bar does very good cocktails. An imaginative lunch and dinner set menu for CH$5000 also pulls in the punters. Tues–Sun noon–3pm & 7pm–1.30am.

DIRECTORY

Banks and exchange BCI bank on Caracoles and four ATMS dotted around the small centre. Several *casas de cambio*, on Toconao and Caracoles.

Festivals The village celebrates its saint's day on June 29 with exuberant dancing and feasting.

Internet There are plenty of cyber cafés around the village, with two Apacheta cafés on the main plaza, which charge CH$800 per hour. There's also free wi-fi on the plaza itself.

Post office Just off the main plaza on Toconao s/n, opposite the archeological museum.

Swimming pool There's a swimming pool (permanently open) at Pozo Tres, a 3km walk east of the archeological museum along the Paso de Jama.

Around San Pedro

The spectacular landscape around San Pedro includes vast, desolate plains cradling numerous **volcanoes** of the most delicate colours imaginable, and beautiful **lakes** speckled pink with flamingoes. You'll also find the largest **salt flat** in Chile, the **Salar de Atacama**, a whole field full of fuming **geysers** at El Tatio, a scattering of fertile **oasis villages**, and several fascinating **pre-Columbian ruins**.

The otherworldliness of this region is reflected in the poetic names of its geographical features – Valle de la Luna (Valley of the Moon), Llano de la Paciencia (Plain of Patience), Garganta del Diablo (Devil's Throat) and Valle de la Muerte (Valley of the Dead), to mention but a few. You might prefer to explore these marvels by yourself (there's no public transport, so you'd have to rent a 4WD), but several companies in San Pedro trip over themselves to take you on guided tours, often a more convenient option (see p.180). There is a fee to pay at each of the park entrances, ranging from CH$2000 to CH$11,000. With the exception of the Puritama thermal baths that are controversially owned by the luxury *Hotel Explora*, the entrance fees go straight back to the local community and help maintain the parks.

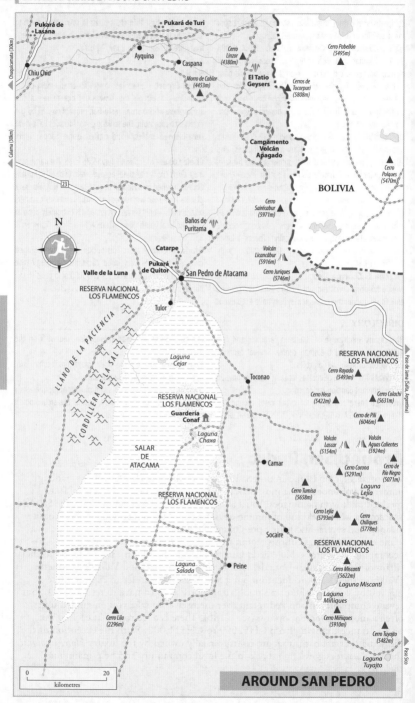

4

AROUND SAN PEDRO

Pukará de Quitor

3km north of San Pedro • Daily 9am–6pm • CH$2000

Just 3km north of San Pedro (head up Calle Tocopilla then follow the river), the **PUKARÁ DE QUITOR** is a ruined twelfth-century fortress built into a steep hillside on the west bank of the Río San Pedro. It has been partially restored and you can make out the defence wall encircling a group of stone buildings huddled inside. According to Spanish chronicles, this *pukará* was stormed and taken by Francisco de Aguirre and thirty men as part of Pedro de Valdivia's conquest in 1540. Another 4km up the road you'll find the ruins of what used to be an Inca administrative centre at **Catarpe**, but there's little to see in comparison with the ruins of Quitor.

Valle de la luna

16km west of San Pedro on the old road to Calama • Summer 8.30am–7.30pm; winter 8.30am–5.30pm • CH$2000

The **VALLE DE LA LUNA**, or Valley of the Moon, really lives up to its name, presenting a dramatic lunar landscape of wind-eroded hills surrounding a crust-like valley floor, once the bottom of a lake. An immense sand dune sweeps across the valley, easy enough to climb and a great place to sit and survey the scenery.

The valley is at its best at sunset, when it's transformed into a spellbinding palette of golds and reds, but you'll have to share this view with a multitude of fellow visitors, as all San Pedro tour operators offer daily sunset trips here. A more memorable (but more demanding) experience would be to get up before day breaks and cycle to the valley, arriving at sunrise (see p.180 for bike rental info). Note that the valley is part of the Conaf-run Reserva Nacional Los Flamencos, and camping is not permitted.

4

Tulor

9km southwest of San Pedro • Summer 8.30am–7.30pm; winter 8.30am–5.30pm • CH$3000

The site of the earliest example of settled habitation in the region, **TULOR** dates from around 800 BC. It was discovered only in the mid-twentieth century by Padre Le Paige, founder of the Museo Arqueológico in San Pedro. Today, the uppermost parts of the walls are exposed, protruding from the earth, while the rest remains buried under the sand. Two reconstructions of these igloo-like houses stand alongside the site.

Salar de Atacama

Summer 9am–7pm; winter: 8am–6pm • CH$2000

The northern edge of this 3000-square-kilometre basin covered by a vast crust of saline minerals lies some 10km south of San Pedro. The largest salt flat in Chile, **SALAR DE ATACAMA** is formed by waters flowing down from the Andes which, unable to escape from the basin, are forced to evaporate, leaving salt deposits on the earth. It's not a dazzling white like the Salar de Surire (see p.214), or Bolivia's Salar de Uyuni, but it's fascinating all the same – especially when you get out and take a close look at the crust, which looks like coffee-coloured coral reef, or ice shards, and clanks when you walk on it. The *salar* contains several small lakes, including **Laguna Chaxa**, home to dozens of flamingoes, and the beautiful **Laguna Salada**, whose waters are covered with floating plates of salt.

Many tour companies also take you for a float in the saline waters of **Laguna Cejar**, 19km from San Pedro. This emerald green lagoon contains even more salt than the Dead Sea. Your guide will warn you to wear shoes when walking on the banks, as very sharp salt crests can cut your feet. Remember to bring bottles of water to wash the salt off afterwards.

The southern oases

Heading south from San Pedro, on the eastern side of the Salar de Atacama, you enter a region of beautiful lakes and tiny oasis villages. The first oasis, 38km south, is **Toconao**, whose softwater stream enters the village through the **Quebrada de Jérez** (CH$2000), a steep, narrow gorge with figs and quinces growing on its southern banks. Though not as pretty as some of the other villages, Toconao does possess a handsome whitewashed bell tower dating to 1750 and set apart from the main church.

Some 35km further south you reach **Camar**, a tiny hamlet with just sixty inhabitants, set amid lush green terraces. **Socaire**, 15km beyond, is less picturesque, save for its little church set by a field of sunflowers. **Peine**, off a track branching west from the "main road" between Camar and Socaire, has a mid-eighteenth-century church and a large swimming pool, invariably full of squealing children. It is possible **to stay** in Peine and Socaire under the rural guesthouse scheme run from San Pedro, for details of which consult the San Pedro tourist office (see p.180).

The lakes

One of the most stunning lakes in the region, **Laguna Miscanti** (near Socaire, 4350m above sea level; CH$2500), boasts brilliant blue waters. Adjacent lies the much smaller **Laguna Miñeques**, whose waters are a deep, dark blue; both lakes are protected areas, part of the Reserva Nacional Los Flamencos. Further south, pastel-coloured **Laguna Tuyajto** is home to dozens of flamingoes and is set against a fabulous backdrop of mineral-streaked mountains, while **Laguna Lejía**, further north, is filled with emerald-green waters tinged white with salt deposits floating on the surface; it, too, is home to large numbers of flamingoes.

The Tatio geysers

95km north of San Pedro • CH$5000

A trip to the **TATIO GEYSERS** is quite an ordeal: first, you drag yourself out of bed in the dead of night with no electric lights to see by; then you stand shivering in the street while you wait for your tour company to come and pick you up at around 4am; and finally, you embark on a three-hour journey on a rough, bumpy road. Added to this is the somewhat surreal experience of finding yourself in a pre-dawn rush hour, part of a caravan of minibuses following each other's lights across the desert.

But hardly anyone who makes the trip regrets it. At 4300m above sea level, these geysers form the highest **geothermal** field in the world. It's essentially a large, flat field containing countless blowholes full of bubbling water that, between around 6am and 8am, send billowing clouds of steam high into the air (strictly speaking, though, geysers spurt water, not steam). At the same time, the spray forms pools of water on the ground, streaked with silver reflections as they catch the first rays of the sun. It's a magnificent spectacle. Take great care, however, when walking around the field; the crust of earth is very thin in some parts, and serious accidents can happen.

You should also remember that it will be freezing cold when you arrive, though once the sun's out the place warms up quite quickly. There's also a swimming pool near the geysers, visited by most tour companies, so remember to take your swimming gear. It's worth noting, however, that tour guides will refuse to take you if you're visibly hungover when they come to pick you up at 4am, so it's best to have a quiet one the evening before.

Baños de Puritama

CH$11,000

On the way back from trips to the Tatio geysers, some tour companies also pay a visit to the **Baños de Puritama**, a rocky pool filled with warm thermal water, 60km south of the geysers and run by a local community but owned and maintained by San Pedro's *Hotel Explora*.

Iquique

Dramatically situated at the foot of the 800m coastal cordillera, with an enormous sand dune looming precariously above one of its barrios, **IQUIQUE**, 390km north of Calama, is a sprawling, busy and surprisingly cosmopolitan city. The town is also fast gaining a reputation as one of the world's finest spots for paragliding (see p.190). Predictably cloudless skies and winds that come in off the Pacific and rise up the dunes create near-perfect conditions; you'll see many enthusiasts swooping down to the beaches, silhouetted by dawn or dusky sunsets. Iquique rivals Arica as the best place to base yourself for a tour of the extreme northern tip of the country. From here, you can easily arrange excursions into the interior, whose attractions include the famous nitrate ghost towns of **Humberstone** and **Santa Laura** (both UNESCO World Heritage sites) , the beautiful hot-spring oases of **Pica** and **Matilla**, and the stunning altiplano scenery of **Parque Nacional Volcán Isluga**.

Iquique falls into two quite distinct areas: **downtown**, lined with shops, services and old historic buildings, and the modern stretch along the **oceanfront**, given over almost entirely to tourism. The **Zofri** duty-free zone is just north of the centre, in an industrial area.

Brief history

Iquique started out as a small settlement of indigenous fishing communities, and during the colonial period became a base for extracting guano deposits from the coast. It continued to grow with the opening of a nearby silver mine in 1730, but it wasn't until the great nineteenth-century nitrate boom that it really took off as a city.

Following its transferral to Chilean hands during the War of the Pacific (1878–83), Iquique became the **nitrate capital** of Chile – where the largest quantities of ore were shipped from, and where the wealthy nitrate barons based themselves, building opulent mansions all over the rapidly expanding city. By the end of the nineteenth century, Iquique was the wealthiest and most hedonistic city in Chile – it was said that more champagne was consumed here, per head, than in any other city in the world.

The twentieth century

With the abrupt end of the nitrate era after World War I, Iquique's boom was over, and the grand mansions were left to fade and crumble as the industrialists headed back to Santiago. Fishing stepped in to fill the economic gap and over the years Iquique transformed itself into the world's leading exporter of fishmeal, though copper subsequently took over as the city's main industry.

Iquique today

Iquique's central square and main avenue conserve some splendid buildings from the **nitrate era**, which, along with the city's beaches, are for many people a good enough reason to visit. Seizing upon this, the authorities have invested in an ambitious restoration scheme aimed at enhancing the beauty of this historic part of the city. Still more people, mainly Chileans, head here for the duty-free shopping at Iquique's **Zona Franca**, or "Zofri".

Plaza Prat

Teatro Municipal Mon–Fri 10am–6pm, Sat 10am–2pm • CH$1500

The focus of town is the large, partly pedestrianized **Plaza Prat**, dominated by the gleaming white **Teatro Municipal**, whose magnificent facade features Corinthian columns and statues representing the four seasons – spoiled at night by criminally hideous fairy lights. It was built in 1889 as an opera house and showcased some of the most distinguished divas of its time. Productions have been temporarily suspended

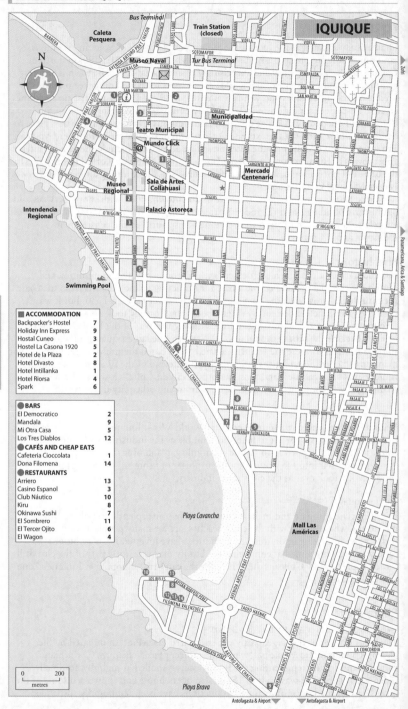

IQUIQUE

Bus Terminal
Caleta Pesquera
Train Station (closed)
Tur Bus Terminal
Museo Naval
Municipalidad
Teatro Municipal
Mundo Click
Sala de Artes Collahuasi
Museo Regional
Mercado Centenario
Palacio Astoreca
Intendencia Regional
Swimming Pool
Playa Cavancha
Mall Las Américas
Playa Brava

Antofagasta & Airport   Antofagasta & Airport

ACCOMMODATION	
Backpacker's Hostel	7
Holiday Inn Express	9
Hostal Cuneo	3
Hostel La Casona 1920	5
Hotel de la Plaza	2
Hotel Divasto	8
Hotel Intillanka	1
Hotel Riorsa	4
Spark	6

● BARS	
El Democratico	2
Mandala	9
Mi Otra Casa	5
Los Tres Diablos	12

● CAFÉS AND CHEAP EATS	
Cafeteria Cioccolata	1
Dona Filomena	14

● RESTAURANTS	
Arriero	13
Casino Espanol	3
Club Náutico	10
Kiru	8
Okinawa Sushi	7
El Sombrero	11
El Tercer Ojito	6
El Wagon	4

0   200
metres

4

while restoration works are carried out, but you can still take a look inside to admire the lavish, if slightly faded, furnishings and the grand proportions of the auditorium.

Opposite the theatre, in the centre of the square, the **Torre Reloj** is a tall white clock tower with Moorish arches, adopted by Iquique as the city's symbol. On the northeast corner of the square, the **Casino Español** – formerly a gentlemen's club, now a restaurant – features an extravagant interior with oil paintings depicting scenes from *Don Quijote*; it's definitely worth a visit.

Calle Baquedano

Leading south, **Calle Baquedano** is lined with an extraordinary collection of late nineteenth-century timber houses, all with porches and balconies and fine wooden balustrades, and many undergoing loving restoration. This is the showcase of Iquique's nitrate architecture and has been designated a national monument. The street is pedestrianized from the plaza all the way down to the seafront, using noble materials such as fine stone for the paving and polished timber for the sidewalks.

Three buildings are open to the public: the **Sala de Artes Collahuasi** at no. 930 (Mon–Fri 10am–2pm & 3.30–7pm, Sat 10am–2pm; free), an impeccably restored building used for temporary art exhibitions, usually of outstanding quality; the **Museo Regional** at no. 951 (Tues–Sat 9am–5.30pm; CH$1500), which houses an eclectic collection of pre-Columbian and natural history artefacts, including deformed skulls and a pickled two-headed shark; and the **Palacio Astoreca** (Mon–Fri 10am–1pm & 4–7pm, Sat 11am–2pm; free; entrance on O'Higgins), a glorious, though deteriorating, mansion featuring a massive wood-panelled entrance hall with a painted glass Art Nouveau ceiling.

The harbour

A short walk north from Plaza Prat is the **Museo Naval** (Mon & Sat 10am–1pm, Tues–Fri 10am–1pm & 4–7pm; free), which displays letters, maps and photos relating to Arturo Prat, hero of the War of the Pacific (see p.474), and, just behind, the **Caleta Pesquera**, or fishermen's wharfs, where the huge, yawning pelicans strutting around the pier make compelling viewing. You can take hour-long **boat tours** around the harbour which leave from Muelle Pasajero (CH$3000; daily 11am), worth it for the views onto the steep desert mountains, rising like huge slabs of chocolate cake behind the city.

The beaches

Two beaches lie within striking distance of the city centre: **Playa Cavancha**, the nearest,

---

PARAGLIDING PARADISE

Iquique has fast gained a reputation for being one of the best places on Earth to **paraglide**, thanks to the unique geography of the city; the mountain range and air current that comes all the way from the Antarctic create the perfect conditions for flying. Plus, you'll regularly hear paragliding instructors proudly boast about the fact you can fly 365 days a year in Iquique – it hardly ever rains and temperatures hover between 16 and 25 degree celsius all year round. Tandem flights lasting approximately 45 minutes usually leave from Alto Hospicio and land on either Playa Cavancha or Playa Brava (equipment, pick-up and drop-off are included). If you've time to spare and you're really serious about flying, you might consider enrolling on a two week course, at the end of which you'll receive a licence, which allows you to brave the Iquique skies on your own, without an instructor. Be sure to book in advance.

The pros at **Pura Vuelo** (☎57 311127, ⓦpuravuelo.cl) come highly recommended. A tandem flight will set you back CH$35,000 and includes a set of photos of you flying, which you can download from their website afterwards.

most popular, and more sheltered; and **Playa Brava**, larger, less crowded and more windswept, which is only suitable for sunbathing due to a strong current and crashing waves rendering it dangerous for swimming (although you do see adrenalin junkies surfing at either end of the beach). You can walk to Playa Cavancha, which begins at the southern end of Amunategui, but it's very cheap to take one of the numerous taxis constantly travelling between the plaza and the beach; many continue to Playa Brava, as well, for a slightly higher fare. Further south, between Playa Brava and the airport, there's a series of attractive sandy beaches including **Playa Blanca**, 13km south of the centre, **Playa Lobito**, at Km 22, and the fishing cove of **Los Verdes**, at Km 24. You can get to these on the airport bus or *colectivo* (see p.190).

The Zofri

Mon–Sat 11am–9pm

About 3km north of the centre, located in a large industrial compound, the duty-free shopping complex known as the **Zofri** is widely touted as one of the great attractions of the north. Thousands of Chileans flock here from up and down the country to spend their money at what turns out, at close quarters, to be a big, ugly mall crammed full of small shops selling mainly electronic items like cameras, watches and domestic gadgets, but also perfumes and food. There's a curious mixture of the upmarket and the tacky, with the latter tending to dominate. The building itself is shabby and old-fashioned, and the bargains aren't really good enough to deserve a special trip. If you do want to check it out, take any *colectivo* marked "Zofri" heading north out of town – the east side of the Plaza or Calle Amunategui are both good bets for catching one.

ARRIVAL AND DEPARTURE

IQUIQUE

BY PLANE

If you're arriving by air, you'll land at Diego Aracena airport, a whacking 40km south of the city. From here, you can get to the centre by bus (Transfer ☎57 310800; CH$4500), *colectivo* (CH$1500) or regular taxi (CH$6000 shared, or CH$12,000 private).

Airlines Comet, San Martín 385 ☎57 420230; LAN, Tarapacá 465 ☎57 427600; Sky Airlines, Tarapacá 530 ☎57 415013 or 57 424139 at airport; TAM, Serrano 430 ☎57 390600.

Destinations Antofagasta (7 daily; 45min); Arica (3 daily; 35min); Calama (4 weekly; 30min); Santiago (11 daily; 2hr 20min).

BY BUS

Iquique's main bus terminal is in a rather run-down quarter at the northern end of Patricio Lynch, several blocks from

the centre – best take a taxi to the centre, or wait for a *colectivo*. Tur Bus, however, has its own terminal (also known as Terminal Esmeralda) in a beautifully converted town house, proudly sporting a dazzling 1917 vintage black Ford, in a more agreeable neighbourhood at the corner of Ramírez and Esmeralda. To save yourself from trekking to the terminals to buy a ticket in advance, you can purchase (and compare prices) at the bus company stands opposite the Mercado Centenario on Barros Arana.

Destinations Antofagasta (17 daily; 7hr); Arica (every 30min; 4hr 30min); Calama (3 daily; 7hr); Caldera (12 daily; 12hr); Chañaral (12 daily; 11hr); Chuquicamata (3 daily; 6hr 30min); Copiapó (12 daily; 13hr); La Serena (hourly; 16hr); La Tirana (7 daily; 1hr 40min); Mamiña (2 daily; 2hr 30min); María Elena (3 daily; 5hr); Mejillones (3 daily; 5hr); Pica (7 daily; 2hr); Santiago (hourly; 25hr); Tocopilla (12 daily; 3hr).

GETTING AROUND

By car Best value car rental may well be at Stop, Bulnes 168 ☎57 575316, ✉rentacarstop@importadorastop.cl. You could also try Autos Procar, Serrano 796 ☎57 470668; Budget, Bulnes 542 ☎57 416095, ⊛budget.cl; Hertz, Aníbal Pinto 1303 ☎57 510432, ⊛autorentas.cl; JR Rent a Car, Arturo Fernández 1591 ☎57 429019, ✉jrpropuestas@yahoo.es.

By taxi Except for fares from the bus terminal and airport,

nearly all Iquique's taxis function like *colectivos*, with fixed, low prices but flexible routes. This is very handy for shuttling to and from the beach, or even going from your hotel to a restaurant. Find out from Sernatur or your hotel what the going rate is, and confirm this with the taxi driver before you get in. Recommended companies include Taxi Aeropuerto Plaza Prat (☎57 413368) and Playa Brava radio Taxi (☎57 443460).

TOURS FROM IQUIQUE

A number of Iquique tour companies (see p.191) offer one-day circular tours – from around CH$20,000 per person – taking in the nitrate ghost towns of **Humberstone** and **Santa Laura** (see p.193–194); the geoglyphs of Pintados (see p.194); the oases villages of **Matilla** and **Pica**, with a plunge in Pica's hot springs (see p.194); and the basilica and nitrate museum of **La Tirana** (see p.196). Another standard tour offered by some companies is the highly memorable route up into the cordillera, continuing north across the altiplano and descending in Arica; these excursions take in **Parque Nacional Volcán Isluga** (see p.197–200), the **Salar de Surire** (see p.214) and **Parque Nacional Lauca** (see p.211–213). The tour entails three overnight stays, with prices starting around CH$200,000 per person (see box, p.207). To learn to surf or body board, try Escuela de Body Board y Surf (☎62 942638, ✉jhoncastrosilva@gmail .com) or Pablo Riveros at Iquique Xtremo (w iquiquextremo.cl). There are also numerous travel agents in town including Iquitour, Patricio Lynch 563, ☎57 428772, ✉iquitour@gmail.com.

INFORMATION AND TOURS

TOURIST INFORMATION
Sernatur office Aníbal Pinto 436 (Mon–Fri 9am–5pm; summer daily till 8pm; ☎57 419241, ✉infoiquique @sernatur.cl).

TOUR OPERATORS
Avitours Baquedano 997 ☎57 413334, w avitours.cl.
Coki Orden y Patria 2824 ☎57 321289, ✉cokitouriqq @hotmail.com.

Iquique Biking Baquedano 1440 w iquiquebiking.cl. For biking tours of the city and the altiplano.
Surire Tours Baquedano 170 ☎09 886 5364, w www.suriretours.com.cl.
Turismo Lirima Gorostiaga 301 (corner of Baquedano) ☎57 391384, ✉turismolirima@hotmail.com. Longest on the scene.

ACCOMMODATION

Iquique is a popular holiday resort and offers an abundance of **accommodation**. Both in the centre and by the beaches, always ask what the "best price" is, as many places will give discounts when pushed. One thing to bear in mind is that, owing to the region's severe water shortage, water supplies are occasionally cut in the busy summer months, sometimes without warning.

DOWNTOWN IQUIQUE
Hostal Cuneo Baquedano 1175 ☎57 428654, ✉hostalcuneo@hotmail.com. With a good location in an old timber building on the historic stretch of Calle Baquedano, this hospitable, homely and good-value *hostal* has small and neat if slightly dark rooms off a leafy patio. **CH$18,000**
★ **Hostel La Casona 1920** Barros Arana 1585 ☎57 413000, w casonahostel.com. Once the family residence of the very personable owner Isabel, *La Casona 1920* is an original nitrate-era building. A home away from home, this hostel has a lovely outdoor patio (films shown on projector every Sunday), an attractive, well-equipped kitchen and, best of all, a very pleasant, friendly atmosphere. Ask Isabel to take you salsa dancing – she's a pro. French, English and, Portuguese spoken. Dorm **CH$6000**, double **CH$20,000**
Hotel Intillanka Obispo Labbé 825 ☎57 311105. Friendly and efficiently run hotel offering 30 spacious, light rooms with fans rather than air con, and private bathroom. The decor's dreary and the place hasn't had a revamp for years, but it's very clean. **CH$29,900**
Hotel de la Plaza Paseo Baquedano 1025 ☎57 417172. An airy and light Georgian building on the main

stretch with pictures of old Iquique adorning the walls. A leafy staircase leads up to pleasant, clean rooms, and a restaurant and bar is due to open soon. **CH$30,000**
Hotel Riorsa Vivar 1542 ☎57 423823. Located on the southern edge of town, an easy walk from the beach, and offering good-quality, tidy rooms with private bathroom and cable TV. The very helpful owner is also a plus. **CH$32,130**

THE BEACHES
★ **Backpacker's Hostel** Amunategui 2075 ☎57 320223, w hosteliquique.cl. Excellent HI-affiliated hostel (discount for HI members) offering weekly barbecues, surfboard and wetsuit rental, and clean rooms and facilities. The huge kitchen is a big plus point, as is the leafy outdoor space and location right next to the beach. Dorm **CH$65,000**, double **CH$8000**
Holiday Inn Express 11 de Septiembre 1690 ☎57 433300. You know what you're getting at this impersonal but immaculate US chain hotel, with a pool, a/c and spacious rooms with ocean views (at the front). Special discounts Fri–Sun. **CH$69,000**

Hotel Divasto Los Rieles 738 ☎ 57 372525, ⊛ hoteldivasto.cl. Grand nitrate-era house on the tip of Playa Cavancha, with lots of character and beautifully furnished rooms with verandas. A modern annexe out the back has plainer, less expensive rooms. **CH$65,450**

Spark Hotel Amunategui 2034 ☎ 57 410 000. This new, super-slick hotel has a rather formal feel to it, and is popular with business guests and couples on a romantic break. There's a lovely outdoor pool on the ground floor as well as what is probably the best sushi restaurant in town. Top floor rooms have amazing views of the beach and city. **CH$70,000 (US$158)**

EATING, DRINKING AND NIGHTLIFE

While there's a reasonable choice of **restaurants** in the centre, it's worth coming out to have at least one evening meal by the beach, to see the ocean lit up with coloured lights projected from the promenade. As for entertainment, you'll find several **nightclubs** that get very crowded in summer and maintain a gentle buzz during low season. They are nearly all down on the Costanera Sur. Iquique's main **cinema** is at Mall Las Américas on Avenida Héroes de la Concepción (see "Iquique and its Beaches" map). For a quick, cheap eat, the lively **Mercado Centenario** on Barros Arana between Latorre and Sargento Aldea is popular for fish lunch specials, though hygiene standards are dubious.

CAFÉS AND CHEAP EATS

Cafeteria Cioccolata Av Anibal Pinto 487 ☎ 57 532290. This very sweet, old-fashioned tearoom opposite the tourist office serves up obscenely huge slices of cake, waffles and pancakes. The lemon yellow interior is filled with business men and ladies who lunch. There are other branches on Arturo Prat and the Zofri. Mon–Fri 8.45am–10pm, Sat 11am–10pm.

Dona Filomena Filomena Valenzuela 298 ☎ 57 311 235. Very reliable *empanada*, beer and pizza joint, popular with a young-ish crowd. Simple wooden decor and attractive outside seating. Also does delivery. Mon–Thurs & Sun 11am–midnight, Fri & Sat 11am–1.30am.

RESTAURANTS

Iquique has an impressive choice of **restaurants**, with sushi being an increasingly popular choice. Almost all of them serve a good value *menu del día* at lunchtime.

DOWNTOWN IQUIQUE

Casino Español Plaza Prat 584 ☎ 57 333911. Huge, fabulous dining room decorated like a mock Moorish palace, complete with beautiful tiles and suits of armour. The Spanish food is unexceptional, and a little overpriced, but this is a must-visit. Mon, Sat & Sun noon–3.30pm, Tues–Fri noon–3.30pm & 8–10.30pm.

★ **El Tercer Ojito** Patricio Lynch 1420a ☎ 57 426517, ⊛ eltercerojito.cl. This peaceful garden oasis is the mellowest place to spend a shady afternoon or candle-lit evening. A healthy menu of seafood, salads, sushi, pasta, cocktails, juices and lassis showcases the best ingredients the region has to offer, with the odd Asian or Peruvian twist. Service is impeccable. Be sure to leave room for pudding; the home-made kulfi is superb. Tues–Sat 12.30–5pm & 7.30pm–1am, Sun 12.30–5pm.

El Wagon Thompson 85 ☎ 57 341428. Nitrate-era paraphernalia lines the walls of this warm and friendly restaurant. Take your pick from an extensive menu of imaginative fish and seafood dishes – the spicy *pescado a la Huara-Huara* is particularly good. There's also a great choice of wines and live music at weekends. Mon–Sat 1–4pm & 8pm–2am, Sun 1–4pm.

THE BEACHES

Arriero Filomena Valenzuela 270 ☎ 57 431508. This classic Chilean restaurant is kitted out in traditional country decor, and, miraculously, doesn't look kitsch. The delicious and authentic Chilean dishes include *parrillada*, *pastel de choclo* and *risotto de quinoa*. Tues–Sun 11.30am–3.30pm & 8pm–1am.

Club Náutico Los Rieles 110 ☎ 57 432951. First-rate, reasonably priced restaurant that's been going strong for years, with great views from its outdoor terrace, especially at night. Daily noon–3pm & 7pm–midnight.

★ **Kiru** Amunategui 1912, ☎ 57 760795, ⊛ kiru.cl. Peruvian restaurant that feels sophisticated and exclusive – there's no sign at the door; just follow the palm-fringed corridor and chill-out music. The chef rustles up fantastic fusion dishes and memorable ceviche, and there are plenty of wines and cocktails at the trendy, well-stocked bar. Mon–Sat 1–3.30pm & 8pm–1am, Sun 1–3.30pm.

Okinawa Sushi Arturo Prat 580 ☎ 57 376033. This open air sushi bar-cum-surf shop overlooking the beach has, unsurprisingly, a cool surfer vibe. On the menu is sushi with a Peruvian touch. No alcohol served but you can bring your own (with receipt). Mon–Sat 1.30–4pm & 7–10.30pm.

El Sombrero Los Rieles 704 ☎ 57 363900. Part of the *Hotel Terrado Suites*, this rather formal, expensive restaurant specializes in seafood – invariably served in rich, roux-based sauces. It's right by the sea, with floor-to-ceiling windows giving great views. Daily 1–3.30pm & 8–11.30pm.

BARS

Most bars in Iquique double up as restaurants, so it's perfectly fine to go to a restaurant just for drinks, and vice versa. Much of Iquique's nightlife is concentrated around Playa Brava.

El Democratico Obispo Labbe 466. If it's the true essence of Chile you're after, this scruffy 80-year-old local, with huge dried fish hanging from the walls, fits the bill. On weekdays it's filled with drunk fishermen, but come the weekend, young locals and live bands join the party. Don't come to eat, unless it's a boiled egg you're after, but do try the Chilean beers and, if you're brave, an old-school Chilean cocktail, "El Terremoto", made from pineapple ice cream, sweet white wine, whisky and grenadine. Don't dress up! Daily 11.30am till late.

Mandala Hernan Fuenzalida 1028 ☎ 57 412449. This stylish hangout has benefitted from the creative flair of its architect-cum-artist-cum-chef and owner, Rodrigo. Attractive recycled lampshades and other bits and bobs adorn the place, and there's an airy patio with sofas – perfect on a balmy summer's night. There's also great cocktails and a sushi bar on the roof terrace. DJs on weekends. Mon–Thurs noon–4pm & 7pm–1am, Fri & Sat noon–4pm & 7pm–3am.

Mi Otra Casa Baquedano 1334 ☎ 87339167. Lovely "bar cultural" set in an attractive building that dates back to the 1700s, when Iquique was a Peruvian city. This artist hang-out holds poetry and gallery nights and serves an Argentine inspired menu and unusual cocktails such as "palmito sour" (palm hearts, pisco, lemon and sugar). Reggae music adds to the chilled-out vibe and there are a handful of tables outside. Mon–Thurs 12.30–4pm & 7pm–2am, Fri & Sat 12.30–4pm & 8pm–4am.

Los Tres Diablos Filomena Valenzuela 784 ☎ 57 480530. A new kid on a trendy block, this smart resto-bar is Iquique's place to be seen. Come here for a pisco cocktail and snack on fusion food with a Mexican slant. The ceviche is to die for, as is the Chinese red decor and terrace, complete with night lanterns, hibiscus and pool (the latter just for show). Mon–Wed 1–4pm & 8pm–1am, Thurs–Sat 1–4pm & 8pm–2am.

DIRECTORY

Banks and exchange Iquique has numerous ATMs, including those at Banco Santander, Plaza Prat; BCI, Tarapacá 404; Corp-Banca, Serrano 343; Scotiabank, Uribe 530. There are a few *casas de cambio* on Patricio Lynch.

Internet There are several places both in the centre and near the beach. Mundo Click at Latorre 370 charges CH$400 per hour.

Post office The main office is at Bolívar 485, a few blocks northeast of Plaza Prat.

Inland from Iquique

Iquique lies within easy reach of many inland sights. Just half an hour away, **Humberstone** and **Santa Laura** are perhaps the most haunting of all the nitrate ghost towns. South of here, close to the Panamericana, **Cerro Pintados** features a dense collection of geoglyphs, among the most impressive in Chile. East of Pintados sits the pretty oasis village of **Pica**, with a lovely thermal pool, while **Mamiña**, further north, is the Norte Grande's hot-springs town *par excellence*. You can also visit **La Tirana**, an important pilgrimage centre, famous for its colourful festival in July. Public transport around this area is sporadic but manageable.

Humberstone

45km inland from Iquique • Daily 9am–6pm • CH$2000

The best-preserved ghost town in Chile, **HUMBERSTONE** is a nitrate *oficina* that was abandoned in 1960 and today appeals especially to lovers of industrial architecture. It sits some 45km inland from Iquique, by Ruta 16 just before it meets the Panamericana. The town began life in 1862 as Oficina La Palma, but was renamed in 1925 in honour of its British manager, James "Santiago" Humberstone, an important nitrate entrepreneur famous for introducing the "Shanks" ore-refining system to the industry. In its time it was one of the busiest *oficinas* on the pampas; today it is an eerie, empty ghost town, slowly crumbling beneath the desert sun.

What sets Humberstone apart from the other ghost towns is that just about all of it is still standing – from the white, terraced workers' houses (now in total disrepair) and the plaza with its bandstand, to the theatre, church and company store. The **theatre**, in particular, is highly evocative, with its rows of dusty seats staring at the stage. You should also seek out the **hotel**, and walk through to the back where you'll find a huge, empty **swimming pool** with a diving board – curiously the pool is made from the sections of a ship's iron hull. Located a short distance from the town are the sheds and workshops, with old tools and bits of machinery lying around, and invoices and order forms littering the floors.

Santa Laura

At **SANTA LAURA**, about 2km down the road and clearly visible from Humberstone, you'll see only a couple of remaining houses, but the processing plant is amazing, seeming to loom into the air like a rusty old dinosaur. As you walk around the site, listening to the endless clanging of machinery banging in the wind, the sense of abandonment is nigh-on overwhelming.

Reserva Nacional Pampa del Tamarugal

About 20km south of the junction between Ruta 16 and the Panamericana, the latter passes through the **RESERVA NACIONAL PAMPA DEL TAMARUGAL**, an extensive plantation of wispy, bush-like *tamarugo* trees. These are native to the region and are especially adapted to saline soils, with roots that are long enough to tap underground water supplies. There's a Conaf-run **campsite** here, exactly 24km south of Pozo Almonte, on the west side of the Panamericana. While the *tamarugos* aren't really interesting enough to merit a special trip, you can take a look at them on your way to the far more impressive **Cerro Pintados**, with the largest collection of **geoglyphs** in South America, situated within the reserve's boundaries.

Cerro Pintados geoglyphs
45km south of Pozo Almonte • Daily 9.30am–6.30pm • CH$1000

Extending 4km along a hillside, the **Cerro Pintados** site features approximately four hundred images (not all of them visible from the ground) of animals, birds, humans and geometric patterns, etched on the surface or formed by a mosaic of little stones around the year 1000 AD. The felines, birds, snakes and flocks of llamas and vicuñas scratched into the rock are thought to have been indicators for livestock farmers. The circles, squares, dotted lines and human figures are more enigmatic, however, and may have had something to do with rituals, perhaps even sacrifices.

ARRIVAL AND DEPARTURE   **CERRO PINTADOS**

By car Cerro Pintados begins 5km west of the Panamericana, reached by a gravel road that branches off the highway 45km south of Pozo Almonte, almost opposite the turn-off to Pica. There's a Conaf control point 2km along the road, where you pay your entrance fee.

By colectivo If you haven't got your own transport, you should be able to arrange a lift there and back with a *colectivo* from the stand outside Iquique's Mercado Centenario – it's probably not a good idea to hitch and then try walking to the site from the Panamericana, owing to the relentless heat and lack of shade.

Pica

As you cross the vast, desert pampa, the neighbouring oases of Pica and Matilla first appear as an improbable green smudge on the hazy horizon. As you get nearer, it becomes apparent that this is not a mirage and you are, indeed, approaching cultivated fields and trees. It's a remarkable sight, and anyone who has not seen a desert oasis should make a special effort to visit. By far the larger of the two oases, **PICA** is a sleepy little town overflowing with lemon and lime trees, bougainvilleas and jasmine.

It's the largest supplier of fruits to Iquique – *limas de Pica* are famous throughout the country – and one of the treats of visiting is drinking the delicious *jugos naturales* – orange, mango, pear, guava and grapefruit juices – freshly squeezed in front of you in

THE NITRATE BOOM

Looking around the desert pampa, it's hard to believe that this scorched, lifeless wasteland was once so highly prized that a war was fought over it – and still more difficult to imagine it alive with smoking chimneys, grinding machinery, offices, houses and a massive workforce. But less than a century ago, the Far North of Chile was the scene of a thriving industry built on its vast **nitrate deposits**, heavily in demand in Europe and North America as a fertilizer. Nitrates were first exploited in the Atacama Desert in the 1860s, when the region belonged to Bolivia (around Antofagasta) and Peru (around Iquique and Arica). From the early stages, however, the Chilean presence was very strong, both in terms of capital and labour.

THE WAR OF THE PACIFIC

When in 1878 the Bolivian government violated an official agreement by raising export taxes on nitrate (hitting Chilean shareholders, including several prominent politicians), Chile protested by sending troops into Antofagasta. Two weeks later, Chile and Bolivia were at war, with Peru joining in (on the Bolivian side) within a couple of months. **The War of the Pacific** (see p.474) went on for five years, and resulted in Chile taking over all of the nitrate grounds.

THE BOOM YEARS

With the return of political stability after the war, the nitrate industry began to boom in earnest, bringing in enormous export revenues for Chile, and a trail of processing plants, known as **oficinas**, sprang up all over the pampa. Each *oficina* sat in the centre of its prescribed land, from where the raw nitrate ore was blasted using gunpowder. The chunks of ore, known as *caliche*, were then boiled in large copper vats, releasing a nitrate solution which was crystallized in the sun before being sent down to the ports to be shipped abroad. The plants themselves were grimy, noisy places. It was a hard life for the labourers, who worked long hours in dangerous conditions, and were housed in squalid shacks, often without running water and sewerage. The (mostly British) managers, meanwhile, lived in grand residences, dined on imported delicacies and enjoyed a whirl of elegant social activities. Nitrate provided more than half of the Chilean government's revenues until 1920, by which time the boom was over and the industry in decline.

THE BEGINNING OF THE END

It was **World War I** that dealt the first serious blow to the nitrate companies, when the suspension of sales to Germany – Chile's major European buyer – forced almost half of the *oficinas* to close down. The final death knell was sounded when Germany, forced to seek alternative fertilizers, developed cheap synthetic nitrates which quickly displaced Chile's natural nitrates from their dominant role in the world market. Most of what was left of the industry was killed off by the **World Depression** in the 1930s, and today just one *oficina* – **María Elena** – remains in operation.

---

the little streetside kiosks. The tidy plaza, by the entrance to town, is overlooked by a beautiful, pale-coloured **church** dedicated to St Andrew. It has a grand Neoclassical facade and was built in 1880.

Cocha Resbaladero

General Ibáñez s/n • Daily 9am–9pm • CH$1000

Pica's real selling point is the **Cocha Resbaladero**, a gorgeous **hot-springs pool** carved into a rocky hollow with two caves at one end. It's quite a walk from the main part of town, but there are several places to stay up here if you want to be close to the waters. To enjoy the waters in peace, arrive early before the buses of day-trippers start arriving at midday.

ARRIVAL AND INFORMATION   PICA

By bus Seven daily buses depart Iquique for Pica (2hr).
Tourist office Balmaceda 299 (Mon–Fri 8.30am–1.30pm & 3–6pm, Sat & Sun 10.30am–1.30pm & 3–6.30pm;

57 741310). The town's friendly Oficina de Turismo sits opposite the Municipalidad building just past the main square on the way to the hot springs.

ACCOMMODATION

Camping Sombre Verde ☎ 09 8403 2348. A 10min walk from the centre, signposted off Balmaceda, is this excellent campsite, offering great facilities and plenty of trees for shade. CH$1500 per person

Hotel Los Emilios Lord Cochrane 213 ☎ 57 741126. The nicest place to stay in the centre, *Hotel Los Emilios* offers comfortable rooms with private bath in a handsome old house with a plunge pool in the back garden. CH$16,000

Residencial El Tambo Ibañez 68 ☎ 57 741041. This is located up by the hot springs, and offers basic but clean rooms with shared bathrooms and hot water, plus a patio and a few attractive wooden *cabañas* (for four) overlooking the pool. Double CH$9000 , cabin CH$25,000

EATING AND DRINKING

The best fruit-juice stalls are on Ibañez, towards the hot springs, and there's a wonderful shop selling home-made jams and conserves a little further along from the campsite.

El Bandio Balmaceda 319. Good, standard meat-based Chilean dishes are served in the creaky rooms of this eccentric old purple building in the centre of town. Mon–Sat noon–11.30pm.

Los Naranjos Barbosa 200. For something a bit different, this homely little place has a hearty menu of tasty Andean specialities like llama stew with quinoa. Mon–Sat 12.30–3pm & 8.30–11pm, Sun 12.30–3pm.

Matilla

The tiny, pretty village of **MATILLA**, about 5km southwest of Pica, has a beautiful church, albeit more humble than Pica's. You'll also see an eighteenth-century wine press, just off the plaza, originally used by the Spaniards; the roots of grapevines were brought over by the conquistadors. While you're here, try the wonderful *jugos* in the café opposite the church.

Santuario de la Tirana

All buses between Iquique and Pica make a stop in La Tirana

Driving back to the Panamericana from Pica, if you take the right-hand (northbound) road, rather than the left-hand one, you'll pass through the little town of La Tirana, 10km before you get back to the highway. It's a rather cheerless place, made up of dusty streets and neglected adobe houses, which makes it all the more surprising when you come upon the immense, paved square stretching out before the imposing **SANTUARIO DE LA TIRANA**. This curious church, at once grand and shabby, is made of wood covered in cream-coloured corrugated iron. It's the home of the Virgen del Carmen, a polychrome carving that is the object of a fervent cult of devotion.

The fiesta

Every year, from July 12 to 18, up to eighty thousand pilgrims come to honour the Virgin and take part in the riotous fiesta in which dozens of masked, costumed dancers perform *bailes religiosos*. These dances have their roots in pre-Spanish, pre-Christian times, with an exuberant, carnival feel wholly out of keeping with traditional Catholic celebrations. If you're not around to see them in action, you should at least visit the small museum in a wing of the church where many of the costumes and masks are displayed ((no fixed hours; try asking the caretaker to let you in if it's shut).

Mamiña

A paved road branches east from the Panamericana at Pozo Almonte and climbs gently through the desert to **MAMIÑA**, 125km – a two-and-a-half-hour drive – northeast of Iquique. First impressions are not encouraging; huddled on a hillside overlooking a valley, its narrow streets and crumbling stone houses seem to belong to a forgotten town, left to the mercy of the heat and dust. Continue down the valley, however, and its charms become more apparent as you come upon the fertile terraces emerald with alfalfa, and the little stream running through the gorge (*quebrada*).

The hot springs

The real lure of Mamiña, though, is the **hot springs** for which the town is famous throughout Chile; the delicious bottled mineral water from here is on sale in the region only, as production is small. Unlike Pica, Mamiña doesn't have just one hot spring, but many, and their waters are piped to every house in the village.

Furthermore, these waters are not merely hot, but are reputed to cure all manner of afflictions, from eczema and psoriasis to respiratory problems and anxiety. Indeed, the town is named in honour of an Incan princess whose blindness was reputedly cured here. Whatever their medicinal value, there's no doubt that the waters are supremely relaxing to bathe in. This you can do in any of the village's hotels or *residenciales*, usually in your own private *tina*, or bathtub.

Baños Ipla

Daily 8am–1.30pm & 3–9pm • CH$1500

There are also a number of public springs, including the **Baños Ipla**, down in the valley, whose four unattractive *tinas* are filled with hot sulphurous water (45°C/115°F) bubbling up from underground. Nearby, the **Vertiente del Radium** is a little fountain whose radioactive waters are supposed to cure eye infections and, according to legend, once restored the sight of an Inca princess.

Barros Chino

Daily 9am–4pm • CH$1500

A short walk from the Vertiente del Radium, behind the water-bottling plant, you'll find the mud baths of **Barros Chino** where you can plaster yourself in mud (don't let the caretaker do it for you), lie on a wooden rack while it dries, then wash it off in a small thermal pool.

ARRIVAL AND DEPARTURE   MAMIÑA

By bus Buses leave from outside the market in Iquique   twice daily (2hr 30min).

ACCOMMODATION

Accommodation is centred in two quite separate areas, one on the ridge overlooking the valley, and the other down in the valley, by the Baños Ipla. Many are run on a **full-board basis**. You can **camp** for free by the pool on the track out to Cerro del Inca, about a 30min walk from the Ipla baths.

Hotel Kusitambu Sulumpa s/n ☎ 57 574644, ⓦ www .hotelkusitambu.cl. Meaning place of rest in Aymara, the recently refurbished *Hotel Kusitambu* has basic rooms, all with private bathroom, and two *cabañas* with thermal water in the bathrooms, but sadly no pool. Breakfast is an extra CH$2000. Popular with miners. **CH$36,000**

Hotel Termas la Coruña Santa Rosa 687 ☎ 57 573664, ⓦ www.termaslacoruña.cl. With unbeatable views of the Mamiña valley, and just 100m from the plaza, this strategically located hotel has an outdoor hot spring pool, tennis court and games room. Rooms are simple but clean. **CH$40,000**

Parque Nacional Volcán Isluga

At the one-horse town of **Huara**, 33km up the Panamericana from the turn-off to Iquique, a good road branches east into the desert, then climbs high into the mountains, continuing all the way to Oruro in Bolivia. It's paved as far as **Colchane**, on the Chilean side of the border, but the main appeal lies in getting off the tarmac once you're up into the cordillera and heading for the deserted wilderness in and around **Parque Nacional Volcán Isluga.** Here you'll find a remote, isolated landscape of wide

THE LEGEND OF LA TIRANA

La Tirana is named after an Inca princess whose story is vividly recorded in twelve large panels inside the town's church. It all began in 1535 when **Diego de Almagro** marched south from Cuzco to conquer Chile. He took with him some five hundred Spaniards and ten thousand locals, including Huillac Huma, high priest of the cult of the Sun God, who was accompanied by his beautiful 23-year-old daughter, **la ñusta** (the princess). Unknown to Almagro, the party also included a number of **Wilkas**, or high-ranking warriors from the Inca Royal Army. When the party reached Atacama la Grande, the high priest slipped away from the group and fled to Charcas, where he planned to stir up rebellion against the Spaniards.

Later, the princess followed her father's lead and she too escaped – with a hundred Wilkas and followers – and fled to the *tamarugo* forests of the pampa. She organized her followers into a fierce army that, for the next four years, waged a relentless war against their oppressors. Her mission was clear: death to all Spaniards, and to all Indians who had been baptized by them. Before long, this indomitable woman became known far and wide as La Tirana del Tamarugal – the **Tyrant of the Tamarugal**.

STAR CROSSED LOVERS

One day, in 1544, La Tirana's army returned to their leader with a prisoner – a certain **Don Vasco de Almeyda**, one of the Portuguese miners established in Huantajaya. According to the legend, "*Mirarle y enamorarse fue una sola cosa*", simply to look at him was to fall in love with him. La Tirana, hitherto immovable, fell passionately in love with the foreigner. But according to everything she stood and fought for, he must be sentenced to death. In desperation, she consulted the stars and her tribe's gods, and claimed that they had ordered her to keep him alive until four moons had passed.

For the next four months, a tender love grew between La Tirana and her prisoner. The princess neglected her people and her duties, arousing the suspicion of the Wilkas. As the fourth month was coming to an end, La Tirana asked her loved one if they would be reunited for eternity in heaven if she too were a Christian. On his affirmative reply, she begged him to baptize her. Almeyda began to do so, but before he could finish, the couple were showered with arrows from the bows of the betrayed Wilkas. As she lay dying in the wood, the princess cried, "I am dying happy, sure as I am that my immortal soul will ascend to God's throne. All I ask is that after my death, you will bury me next to my lover and place a cross over our grave."

A TOWN IS BORN

Ten years later, when Padre Antonio Rondon arrived in these parts to evangelize the Indians, it was with astonishment and joy that he discovered a simple cross in a clearing of the wood. The priest erected a humble chapel on the site, later replaced by a larger building that became, in time, the centre of worship in a town that took its name from the beautiful princess who had died there.

plains, dramatic, snowcapped volcanoes (one of which is the park's namesake) and semi-abandoned villages, home to indigenous Aymara herding communities that have been a part of this windswept land for thousands of years.

Unlike Parque Nacional Lauca, further north, this region hasn't yet been "discovered", and it's unlikely you'll come across many other tourists. There are a number of attractions on the way up, as well, in particular the weird desert geoglyph known as the **Gigante de Atacama**, in the pampa, and the frozen geysers of **Puchuldiza**, on the lower slopes of the Andes.

Enquelga

Parque Nacional Volcán Isluga's administrative centre is in **Enquelga**, a dusty, tumbledown hamlet – 3850m above sea level – home to a small Aymara community. Many of its inhabitants, particularly the women, still dress in traditional, brightly coloured clothes, and live from tending llamas and cultivating potatoes and barley.

Aguas Calientes

Two kilometres on from Enquelga, **Aguas Calientes** is a long, spring-fed pool containing warm (but not hot) waters, set in an idyllic location with terrific views of Volcán Isluga. The pool is surrounded by pea-green *bofedal* – a spongy grass, typical of the altiplano – and drains into a little stream, crossed every morning and evening by herds of llamas driven to and from the sierra by Aymara shepherdesses. There's a stone changing-hut next to it, and a few **camping** spaces and picnic areas, protected from the evening wind by thick stone walls.

Isluga

Six kilometres east of Enquelga, still within the park's boundaries, **Isluga** is composed of a hundred or so stone and adobe houses huddled around one of the most beautiful churches on the altiplano. Built in the seventeenth century (it's not known when, exactly), it's a humble little construction of thick, whitewashed adobe that flashes like snow in the constant glare of the sun. The main building, containing a single nave, is enclosed by a low wall trimmed with delicate arches; just outside the wall sits the

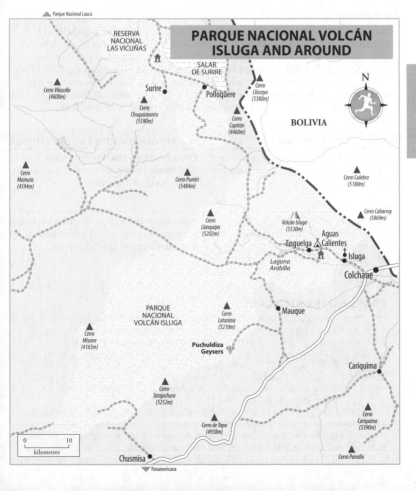

PARQUE NACIONAL VOLCÁN ISLUGA AND AROUND

two-tier bell tower with steps leading up to the top, where you can sit and survey the scenery or watch the hummingbirds that fly in and out.

The church, along with the entire village, remains locked up and abandoned for most of the year – Isluga is a "**ceremonial village**", whose inhabitants come back only for festivals, important religious ceremonies and funerals; the principal fiestas are held on February 2 and 3, March 10, Easter week, and December 8, 12 and 21 to 25.

Colchane

Ten kilometres from Isluga, at the end of the paved road from Huara, at 3730 metres above sea level, **COLCHANE** is a small, grim border town of grid-laid streets and truckers' canteens. Most days, the only reason you might want to come here is for **accommodation** or to cross over into **Bolivia** (see p.200). Twice a month, however, on alternate Saturdays, Colchane takes on a bit of life and colour as the neighbouring altiplano villagers bring their fresh produce, weavings and knitwear to sell at the **market**.

Cariquima

Charming **CARIQUIMA**, just 17km south of Colchane, has picturesque, cleanly swept streets and an old altiplano-style church with a painted interior. Seek out the **crafts cooperative**, housed in a beautifully decorated building along one of the village's few streets, and where you'll find high-quality woollens for sale. Cariquima sits in the lee of the dramatic Nevado Cariquima, while, 5km to the north is the minute hamlet of **Ancovinto**. There you'll see a forest of giant cacti that sway in the breeze and enjoy fantastic views across the altiplano to Bolivia and the Salar de Coipasa.

ARRIVAL AND DEPARTURE	**PARQUE NACIONAL VOLCÁN ISLUGA**

By organized tour There's no public transport around this region, so you must take an organized tour from Iquique (see p.191) or rent a 4WD.

CROSSING THE BOLIVIAN BORDER
Via Colchane Note that border control (daily 8am–7pm) is sometimes closed at lunch time.

ACCOMMODATION

Camino del Inca Teniente Gonzalez s/n, Colchane. This family-run hotel has very basic but clean rooms with shared bathrooms and hot water. CH$12,000
Conaf refugio Enquelga. Conaf *refugio* with accommodation for five people; it's supposed to be open year-round, but sometimes isn't. Call Arica's Conaf office to reserve a bed (see p.207). CH$5500 per person

---

CROSSING THE ALTIPLANO

With the proposed **Ruta Altiplánica de Integración** – a paved highway stretching 1500km across the altiplano, from San Pedro de Atacama in Chile to Cusco, Peru – still not having come to fruition, crossing the altiplano's pothole-riddled dirt tracks by jeep remains the road adventure of a lifetime and should be enjoyed to the full before the arrival of tarmac and increased traffic. Probably the best starting point is Iquique (the ascent in altitude is more gradual in this direction), heading into the cordillera as far as Parque Nacional Volcán Isluga, continuing north across the altiplano to Parque Nacional Lauca, and finally descending in Arica. It's a **700km journey**, and takes about four days at an easy pace.

If you do the trip, remember that there's no petrol station once you're off the Panamericana, which means taking it all with you in jerry cans (*bidones*, available in most ironmongers). Always take far, far more than you think you need. Another essential precaution is to take two spare tyres, not just one. There's more on 4WD driving in Basics (see p.28).

Pisagua

Most people whizz up the Panamericana between Iquique and Arica in about four hours without stopping, but some 80km north of the turn-off to Iquique, a poorly paved side road (no public transport) leads 52km west down to **Pisagua** – a crumbling, evocative nitrate port that makes an interesting option for a night's stopover. The final stretch down to the port is very steep, giving dramatic views down to the little toy town cowering by the ocean, the only sign of life on this barren desert coast.

Pisagua is a funny sort of place, part scruffy, ramshackle fishing town, part fascinating relic of the past. It was one of the busiest and wealthiest ports of the nitrate era, and is still dotted with many grand nineteenth-century buildings, some of them restored and repainted, others decaying at the same slow pace as the rest of the town (which has only about 150 inhabitants today). Most striking of all is the handsome, white-and-blue timber **clock tower**, built in 1887 and still standing watch from the hillside.

The old theatre

In front of the main square

This fine wooden building erected in 1892, with a typical nineteenth-century facade featuring tall wooden pillars, a balcony and a balustrade, is Pisagua's main monument to the nitrate era. You can borrow the key from the *carabineros* station at the far end of town, and wander inside to take a look at the large, empty stage, the rows of polished wooden seats, and the high ceiling, lavishly painted with cherubs dancing on clouds. The ghostliness of the place is made all the more intense by the monotonous sound of the waves crashing against the building's rear wall, which plunges directly down to the sea.

ACCOMMODATION	PISAGUA
Hostal La Roca Manuel Rodriguez 20 ☎ 57 731502. Lovely modern-rustic, family-run hotel with big clean rooms, all boasting private bathrooms with hot water. Ask for a room with sea view. Friendly owner Sra Catherine will	make you feel at home. **CH$24,000** **Campsite** Playa Seis. Situated on the beach, this municipal campsite is free but lacks shade.

Hacienda de Tiliviche

Ten kilometres north of the turn-off for Pisagua, just before the bridge across the Quebrada de Tiliviche, a short track branches left (west) to the **HACIENDA DE TILIVICHE**. At the end of the track you'll find the old *casa patronal*, a charmingly dilapidated house overlooking a yard full of clucking chickens and lethargic dogs. It was built in 1855 for a British nitrate family and remained in British hands until very recently; the current owners have plans to renovate it and turn it into a hotel.

The British Cemetery

Set within the grounds of Hacienda de Tiliviche, on the other side of the stream, stands a nostalgic testimony to the nitrate era: the old **British Cemetery**, enclosed by tall iron railings and a huge, rusty gate – you can borrow the key from the hacienda caretaker. Inside, about a hundred lonely graves stand in the shade of a few *tamarugo* trees at the foot of the desolate mountain that rises over the *quebrada*. This stark desert setting is strikingly at odds with the very English inscriptions on the tombstones ("Thy will be done" and the like). The graves read like a who's who of the erstwhile British business community, including people like Herbert Harrison, the manager of the Tarapacá Waterworks Company and, most famously, **James Humberstone**, the manager of several nitrate *oficinas*.

The geoglyphs

The southern wall of Tiliviche's *quebrada* also features some of the most impressive **geoglyphs** in Chile. They're best viewed from the lay-by just off the Panamericana, a few hundred metres up from the bridge on the northern side of the *quebrada*. From this vantage point, you can see the images in all their splendour – a large crowd of llamas covering the hillside. All of the llamas are moving in the same direction, towards the sea, and it's thought that the drawings were designed to guide caravans descending from the mountains on their journey towards the coast.

Arica

ARICA likes to call itself "*la ciudad de la eterna primavera*" – "city of everlasting spring". Chile's northernmost city, only 19km south of the Peruvian border, is certainly blessed with a mild climate, which, along with its sandy beaches, makes it a popular holiday resort for Chileans and Bolivians. Although a lingering sea fog can dampen spirits, in the winter especially, just head a few kilometres inland and you'll usually find blue skies.

The city's compact, tidy centre sits proudly at the foot of the Morro cliff, the site of a major Chilean victory in the War of the Pacific (and cherished as a symbol of national glory).

THE AYMARA OF CHILE

The **Aymara** people are the second-largest indigenous linguistic group of South America (after the Quechua). The culture flourished around **Lake Titicaca** and spread throughout the high-plain region, known as the altiplano, of what is now Bolivia, Peru and Chile. Today there are around three million Aymara scattered through these three countries, with the Chilean Aymara forming the smallest group, totalling some forty thousand people. Following the big migrations from the highlands to the coast that took place in the 1960s, most of the Aymara people of Chile now live and work in the coastal cities of **Arica** and **Iquique**. At least thirteen thousand Aymara, however, remain in the altiplano of northern Chile, where their lifestyle is still firmly rooted in the traditions of the past thousand years. The main economic activities are llama and sheep herding and the cultivation of crops such as potatoes and barley.

Traditionally, the Aymara live in **small communities**, called *ayllu*, based on extended family kinship. Their houses are made of stone and mud with rough thatched roofs, and most villages have a square and a small whitewashed church with a separate bell tower – often dating from the seventeenth century when **Spanish missionaries** evangelized the region.

RELIGIOUS BELIEFS

Nowadays many of the smaller villages, such as Isluga (see p.199), are left abandoned for most of the year, the houses securely locked up while their owners make their living down in the city or in the larger cordillera towns like **Putre**. Known as "ceremonial villages" they're shaken from their slumber and burst into life when people return for important religious festivals or funerals. Andean **fiestas** are based on a fascinating blend of Catholic and indigenous rites. At the centre of Aymara culture is respect for the life-giving **Mother Earth**, known as *pachamama*, and traditional ceremonies – involving singing and dancing – are still carried out in some communities at sowing and harvest time.

The Aymara also believe that the tallest mountains looming over their villages contain spirits, or *mallku*, that guard over them, protecting their animals and crops. Once a year, on **May 3** – Cruz de Mayo – the most traditional communities climb up the sacred mountains, where a village elder speaks to the *mallku*, which appears in the form of a condor. Today's young Aymara go to local state schools and speak Spanish as their main language, and while traditional lifestyles continue in the altiplano, it's with increasingly closer links with mainstream Chilean life.

It was this war that delivered Arica, formerly Peruvian, into Chilean hands, in 1883, and while the city is emphatically Chilean today, there's no denying the strong presence of *mestizo* and Quechua-speaking Peruvians on the streets, trading their fresh produce and *artesanía*. This, added to its role as Bolivia's main export centre, makes Arica more colourful, ethnically diverse and vibrant than most northern Chilean cities, even if parts of it look somewhat impoverished.

The liveliest streets are pedestrianized Calles 21 de Mayo and Bolognesi, the latter clogged with **artesanía stalls**, while by the port you'll see the smelly but colourful **terminal pesquero**, where inquisitive pelicans wander around the fish stalls. Though far

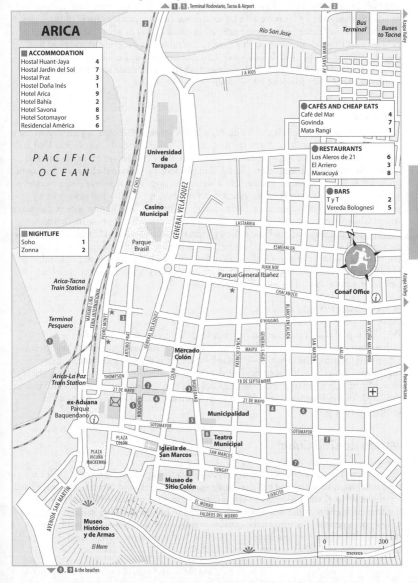

ARICA

ACCOMMODATION
Hostal Huant-Jaya	4
Hostal Jardín del Sol	7
Hostal Prat	3
Hostel Doña Inés	1
Hotel Arica	9
Hotel Bahía	2
Hotel Savona	8
Hotel Sotomayor	5
Residencial América	6

CAFÉS AND CHEAP EATS
Café del Mar	4
Govinda	7
Mata Rangi	1

RESTAURANTS
Los Aleros de 21	6
El Arriero	3
Maracuyá	8

BARS
T y T	2
Vereda Bolognesi	5

NIGHTLIFE
Soho	1
Zonna	2

PACIFIC OCEAN

Terminal Rodoviario, Tacna & Airport

Bus Terminal

Buses to Tacna

Río San José

AV SANTA MARIA

J A RIOS

Azapa Valley

Universidad de Tarapacá

GENERAL VELASQUEZ

AV CHILE

Casino Municipal

Parque Brasil

LASTARRIA

ESMERALDA

Arica-Tacna Train Station

MAXIMO LIRA
FERIA INTERNATIONAL

PEDRO MONTT

ARTURO PRAT

GENERAL VELASQUEZ

Parque General Ibañez

JUAN NOE

CHACABUCO

Conaf Office

BLANCO ENCALADA

O'HIGGINS

GENERAL LAGOS

SAN MARTIN

GALLO

AV VICUÑA MACKENNA

Terminal Pesquero

Arica-La Paz Train Station

THOMPSON

21 DE MAYO

COLÓN

Mercado Colón

PATRICIO LYNCH

MAIPU

18 DE SEPTIEMBRE

21 DE MAYO

ex-Aduana
Parque Baquedano

BOLOGNESI

BAQUEDANO

SOTOMAYOR

Municipalidad

SOTOMAYOR

PLAZA COLÓN

PLAZA VICUÑA MACKENNA

Iglesia de San Marcos

Teatro Municipal

SAN MARCOS

YUNGAY

Museo de Sitio Colón

AVENIDA SAN MARTIN

Museo Histórico y de Armas

El Morro

EL MORRO

FALDEOS DEL MORRO

EJERCITO

Azapa Valley

Panamericana

0   200
metres

& the beaches

from beautiful, Arica does boast a couple of fine pieces of nineteenth-century architecture, pretty squares filled with flowers and palm trees, and a young, lively atmosphere. It's a pleasant enough place to spend a couple of days – or longer, if you feel like kicking back on the beach.

Iglesia de San Marcos

Plaza Colón • Daily 9am–2pm & 6–8pm • Free

In the centre you'll find the small, tree-filled **Plaza Colón**, dominated by the **Iglesia de San Marcos**, a pretty white church with a high, Gothic spire and many tall, arched windows. Designed by Gustave Eiffel, this curious church, made entirely of iron, was prefabricated in France before being erected in Arica in 1876, when the city still belonged to Bolivia. The riveting key used to assemble the structure was kept in a display case inside the church, but when Chilean troops attacked, it was thrown into the sea to prevent the invaders from dismantling the church and stealing it as a war trophy (instead, they took the whole city).

El Morro

Arica's most visible feature is the 110m-high cliff known as **El Morro**, which signals the end of the coastal cordillera. Steps starting at the southern end of Calle Colón lead you to the top, where sweeping, panoramic views (especially impressive at night) and the **Museo Histórico y de Armas** await. This 130m cappuccino-coloured cliff is *the* source of pride for Arica's citizens, heightened by a big sign saying "*Arica siempre Arica, mayor es mi lealtad*" (roughly translated as "Arica, forever Arica, my loyalty will always be to you"). It's also an important national landmark, to its historical significance as the place where Chile won a crucial 1880 battle against Peru during the War of the Pacific.

At the top is a very nationalistic military museum and a statue of Christ with his arms outstretched – a symbol of peace between the two once-enemy nations. It's a pleasant ten to fifteen minute hike up Calle Colón, but you can get a taxi to take you and wait for you while you explore and admire the wonderful view of the city and beaches, before dropping you off in town afterwards.

Museo Histórico y de Armas

El Morro • Mon–Fri 8am–6pm, Sat & Sun 8am–8pm • CH\$800

Built on top of a former Peruvian fortification, this museum is owned by the army, rather than the government, and has clearly had more money spent on it than most Chilean museums. The exhibits – primarily nineteenth-century guns and military uniforms – are very well displayed, but the theme is rather chauvinistic in tone, the main thrust being the superiority of the Chileans and the inferiority of the Peruvians in the Battle of the Morro, when Chilean forces stormed and took possession of the hilltop defence post.

Museo de sitio Colón

Colón 10 • Tues–Sun 10am–6pm • CH\$2000

This museum has a rather curious history: while carrying out construction work for a new hotel back in 2004, the builders came across some very old human remains. Plans for the new hotel stopped and the University of Tarapacá was called in and it soon became apparent that the site was a four thousand-year-old funerary space for the Chinchorro people. Because of the extremely fragile nature of these age-old human remains, transportation was out of the question and a museum on the site was opened to exhibit the 48 Chinchorro mummies found.

FROM TOP TATIO GEYSERS (P.186); VICUÑAS ON THE ALTIPLANO (P.213)

The Ex-aduana

Parque Baquedano • Mon–Fri 8.30am–8pm • Free

The 1874 **Ex-aduana** (customs house) is another Eiffel-designed building with an attractive stone facade of pink and white horizontal stripes. These days it's used as a cultural centre (it's also known as the "*casa de la cultura*") and puts on regular photographic and art exhibitions. Its pleasant location on a little square full of palm trees and shady benches, flanked to the south by the coastal avenue, adds to its charm.

The beaches

Arica is a major destination for serious surfers, who travel far and wide to test out the famous waves. The city holds a couple of important international surfing competitions every year, though sunbathers and swimmers will also appreciate Arica's beaches; although not as attractive as Iquique's sandy shores, the water is noticeably warmer. The closest beach to the centre is the popular **Playa El Laucho**, a curved, sandy cove about a twenty-minute walk down Avenida San Martín, south of El Morro. You can also get *micros* down the avenue, which continue to several other beaches, including **Playa La Lisera** and **Playa Brava**, both attractive, and the usually deserted **Playa Arenillas Negras**, a wide expanse of dark sand backed by low sand dunes, with a fish-processing factory at its southern end.

Northern beaches

Two kilometres north of the centre, **Playa Chinchorro** is a large, clean beach where you can rent jet skis in high season (Dec–March; CH$12,000 for 30min). To get there, take bus #12 or #14; both will drop you off one block from the beach. Further north, **Playa Las Machas** is quieter but more exposed to the wind, and popular with surfers. The only beaches suitable for swimmers are Playa Lisera, Playa Laucho and Playa Chinchorro – these all have lifeguards during the summer months.

ARRIVAL AND DEPARTURE

ARICA

BY PLANE

Arica's Chacalluta airport lies 18km north of the city and is connected to the centre by reasonably priced airport taxis (CH$5000) or minibus transfers (CH$2000).

Airlines LAN, Arturo Prat 391 ☎ 58 252650; Sky Airlines, 21 de Mayo 356 ☎ 58 251816 or 290768 at airport.

Destinations Antofagasta (1 daily; 45min); Calama (1 weekly; 1hr 20min); Copiapó (1 daily; 1hr 45min); Iquique (4 daily; 20min); Santiago (4 daily; 3hr).

BY BUS

Coming in by bus, you'll arrive at Arica's Terminal Rodoviario, which uniquely charges a CH$200 platform fee for all departures; make sure to pay this fee at your bus company desk, even if you already have a bus ticket. The terminal is quite a distance from town on Avenida Diego Portales, but you can easily catch a *colectivo* or *micro* into the centre.

Destinations Antofagasta (17 daily; 10hr); Calama (5 daily; 10hr); Chañaral (7 daily; 15hr); Copiapó (13 daily; 16hr); Iquique (every 30min; 4hr 30min); La Serena (13 daily; 18hr); Putre (1 daily; 3hr); San Pedro de Atacama (1 daily; 10hr); Santiago (10 daily; 29hr); Vallenar (10 daily; 20hr).

GETTING AROUND

By colectivos The easiest way to get around is to use the taxi *colectivo* system (unlike other South American countries, a "*colectivo*" here refers to shared taxis rather than buses). The average cost for a journey in a shared taxi is CH$500, or CH$550 by night. The colour and number on top of the taxi *colectivo* denotes which direction it´s heading. To avoid confusion, it´s best to take a private taxi from the bus station when you first arrive, until you figure out the number system.

Private taxis Radiotaxi Chacalluta, Patricio Lynch 371 ☎ 58 254812; Radio Taxi ☎ 58 257000.

By car For car rental try Europcar, Colón 996 ☎ 58 258911; Cactus, General Lagos 666 ☎ 58 258353. Hertz, Baquedano 999 ☎ 58 231487; Klasse, Velásquez 760 ☎ 58 254498.

INFORMATION AND TOURS

TOURIST INFORMATION

Sernatur office San Marcos 101 (Jan & Feb Mon–Fri 9am–9pm; March–Dec Mon–Thurs 9am–6pm, Fri 9am–5pm; ☎ 58 254506 or 252054, ⓦ sernatur.cl).

TOURS FROM ARICA

Three or four companies in Arica regularly offer **tours** up to **Parque Nacional Lauca** (see p.211–213). The problem is that the most commonly available tour takes place in a single day, which means rushing from sea level to up to 4500m and down again in a short space of time – really not a good idea, and very likely to cause some ill effects, ranging from tiredness and mild headaches to acute dizziness and nausea. In very rare cases the effects can be more serious, and you should always check that the company carries a supply of oxygen and has a staff member trained to deal with emergencies.

Altitude aside, the amount of time you spend inside a minibus is very tiring, which can spoil your experience of what is one of the most beautiful parts of Chile. Therefore it's really worth paying extra and taking a tour that includes at least one overnight stop in Putre; better still is one continuing south to the Salar de Surire (see p.214) and Parque Nacional Isluga (see p.197–200). However, it's worth noting that the availability of these longer tours can be frustratingly scarce during the quieter low season months. One-day trips usually cost around CH\$20,000 per person while you can expect to pay around CH\$45–100,000 for a one- or two-night tour, overnighting in Putre, and around CH\$180,000 for a three-night tour, sleeping in Putre and Colchane. See p.207 for a list of tour operators.

Conaf office Vicuña Mackenna 820 (Mon–Fri 8.30am–5.30pm; ☎58 201200). The regional Conaf office has basic maps and information on Parque Nacional Lauca and adjoining protected areas. You can also reserve beds at the Conaf *refugíos* in these areas, if you know exactly when you'll be arriving (see box, p.215).

TOUR OPERATORS

Geotours Bolognesi 421 ☎58 253927, ✉geotur @entelchile.net. Slick, professional but fairly impersonal company offering mostly one-day tours around Arica, as well as trips further afield to Lauca, Matilla and Pica. There are two other branches in San Pedro de Atacama and Iquique.

★ **Latinorizons** Colón 7 ☎58 250007, ⓦwww .latinorizons.com. Friendly and extremely reliable Belgian-run company offering a wide range of altiplano tours, including overnight, with a more adventurous feel than most of the others on offer. French and English spoken. Charlie, the very knowledgeable owner, also offers nice, clean rooms to rent in his home near El Morro.

Parinacota Expediciones Heroes del Morro 632 ☎58 233305, ⓦparinacotaexpediciones.cl. Well-established company offering several options for visiting Parque Nacional Lauca and around, including the usual day-trip, an overnight stop in Putre and a two-night tour taking in the Salar de Surire.

Tierra Expediciones ⓦtierraexpediciones.com. Highly recommended newcomer offering specialized tours such as trekking and photo-safaris, throughout northern Chile, lasting from a couple of days to one month. Run by a very enthusiastic and well-informed Chilean–Swiss couple. English, German and Italian spoken.

ACCOMMODATION

Unlike Iquique, Arica has very little seafront accommodation and most places to stay are situated in and around the town's centre. Here, there's no shortage of *residenciales*, ranging from the dirt-cheap to the polished and comfortable. Typically for these parts, however, there's a lack of decent mid-range accommodation.

HOTELS

Hostal Huanta-Jaya 21 de Mayo 660 ☎&☎58 314605. Very clean and pleasant sky-lit rooms off a leafy corridor, all with private baths. Centrally located, yet quiet. No air con but fans on request. CH\$20,000

Hostal Jardín del Sol Sotomayor 848 ☎58 232795, ✉info@hostaljardindelsol.cl. Small, tidy rooms with private bathrooms off a flower-filled courtyard with tables, chairs and loungers. Good value for money and very friendly, too, a great place to mix with like-minded travellers. All in, the best budget option in town. CH\$22,000

Hostal Prat Arturo Prat 555 ☎58 251292. Spartan but spotless little rooms with white walls, tiled floors and clean baths in the centre of Arica – be sure not to confuse with the *residencial* of the same name. CH\$15,000

Hotel Arica Av San Martín 599 ☎58 254540, ✉reservas@hotelarica.cl. Upmarket but rather dated and overpriced hotel overlooking the ocean, with pleasant rooms and a pool. Mediocre food is served at its expensive restaurant *Península*. CH\$77,350

Hotel Bahía Ave Luis Beretta Porcel 2031 ☎58 260676, ✉info@bahiahotel.cl, ⓦbahiahotel.cl. A 15min walk from the centre, this place has direct access to Chinchorro beach. Inexpensive, basic rooms are all glass-fronted with superb ocean views. **CH$26,000**

Hotel Savona Yungay 380 ☎ 58 231000, ✉ reservas @hotelsavona.cl. Low-rise, 1970s style hotel built around a bright patio garden with a swimming pool. Rather tasteless yet comfortable rooms have small private bathrooms. Bikes are available for hire. **CH$34,000**

Hotel Sotomayor Sotomayor 367 ☎ 58 585761, ✉ reservas@hotelsotomayor.cl. Formerly the *Hotel San Marcos*, this terracotta coloured building features clean, airy yet somewhat dated rooms (disappointing after the beautiful old Spanish tiles in the lobby) with private bath and parking. **CH$35,000**

Residencial América Sotomayor 430 ☎ 58 254148. Hotel in the heart of the city opposite the town hall, offering good-value budget rooms with an encouraging odour of furniture polish. Some rooms have private bathrooms. **CH$15,000**

HOSTELS

Hostel Doña Inés Manuel Rojas 2864 ☎ 56 5824 8108. Situated a 15min drive outside the centre (but easily accessible by *colectivo*) this HI hostel, owned by the very hyper, very sociable Roberto, is the place to come if you want to mix with other travellers and are up for a party. Do stay for one of Roberto's weekly *asados*. Dorm **CH$7800**, double **CH$16,500**

EATING AND DRINKING

You'll find the biggest concentration of **restaurants**, **cafés** and **bars** on the pedestrianized section of 21 de Mayo, the city's main thoroughfare. Arica seems to be the national capital of the **roasted-chicken-on-a-spit** industry – low-cost places serving it dot Maipú, between Baquedano and Colón. For good value sandwiches and exotic fruit juices, head to the colourful juice bars popular with the locals on Baquedano (between Maipu and 18 de Septiembre).

CAFES AND CHEAP EATS

Café del Mar 21 de Mayo 260 ☎ 58 231936. This new café on the main pedestrian strip is popular with Arica's residents, both young and old, thanks to its colourful decor, outside seating and tasty menu, which includes big salads, sandwiches, pizzas and, best of all, delicious crêpes. There are more sophisticated dishes served in the evenings. Mon–Sat 9.30am–midnight.

Govinda Blanco Encalada 200. Zen-like place a short walk from the centre, with tasty, vegetarian set menu lunches that include soup, salad and a main dish. Great for healthy lunches on small budgets. Mon–Fri 12.30–3.30pm.

Mata Rangi Terminal pesquero. Tucked inside the fishermen's harbour, a rustic inexpensive place serving unfussy fish and seafood lunches – sit by the window and watch the pelicans eat theirs as you eat yours. Picnic trips to a nearby penguin colony on the owner's boat can also be arranged (🖰 turismomarino.com). Daily noon–3.30pm.

RESTAURANTS

Los Aleros de 21 21 de Mayo 736 ☎ 58 254641. Traditional Chilean restaurant serving pricey yet excellent steaks, seafood and other meat dishes. Great quality and service – it's a favourite among locals, and deservedly so. Mon–Sat noon–

4pm & 8pm–midnight, Sun noon–4pm.

El Arriero 21 de Mayo 385 ☎ 58 232636. Mid-price grill house serving tasty fillet steaks and other meat dishes; often has live folk music at the weekends. Book ahead as it gets busy. Mon–Sat noon–4pm & 7–11pm.

★ **Maracuyá** Av San Martín 0321, Playa La Lisera ☎ 58 227600. Dramatically sited as it is, right over the ocean's edge, this smart restaurant (one of Arica's best) offers boldly prepared fish and seafood amid a spectacle of breaking waves. Daily noon–4pm & 8.30pm–midnight.

BARS

T y T 21 de Mayo 233. With a terrace strategically located on the main drag and a bright, stylish decor, this godsend of a café-bar serves real coffee; excellent breakfasts; a range of sandwiches, snacks and crisp salads; some hot dishes; and delicious cakes (such as raspberry cheesecake) and cookies. It offers a good selection of beers, wines and cocktails, too. Mon–Sat 11am–11pm.

Vereda Bolognesi Bolognesi 340 🖰 veredabolognesi .cl. By night, from about 8pm, this smart little shopping gallery in town turns into a buzzing patio bar zone – several resto-bars compete with their happy hours so it´s easy to get a good, fruity cocktail at a decent price. Mon–Sat 9am–12am.

NIGHTLIFE

The **disco** scene can get quite lively in high season, and even in low season there are a few locales where you'll always find a crowd on a Friday and Saturday night.

Soho Buenos Aires 209, Playa Chinchorro 🖰 discosoho .com. A stone's throw from Chinchorro beach, this nightclub is attached to *Pub Capitán Drake* and often has live music acts and several DJs. Entry is often free before 1.30am. Daily midnight till late.

Zonna Av Argentina 2787, ☎ 58 221509, 🖰 zonna.cl. This, the biggest, best-known and most popular nightclub in Arica has multiple rooms each playing different types of music ranging from salsa to 1980s hits. Ask about the weekly drink promotion. Thurs–Sun midnight till late.

DIRECTORY

Banks and exchange Arica has many ATMs – mostly on 21 de Mayo – and *casas de cambio* on Calle Colón.

Internet Cyber Technicomp, Sotomayor 199, charges CH$400 an hour.

Post office Arturo Prat 305.

The Azapa Valley

Avenida Diego Portales extends out of Arica's city centre into the green **AZAPA VALLEY**. The far western end of the valley is, to all intents and purposes, a suburb of Arica, crammed as it is with condos and villas, some of which have been converted into trendy discos, along with a couple of good restaurants. The highlight of a trip to the Azapa Valley is the Museo Archeológico, which houses a collection of the world's most ancient mummies. This museum is among Chile's best and is definitely worth the trip out here. If you're booked on a multi-day tour of the Altiplano, it's very likely this will be a stopoff.

Poblado Artesanal

On your way out towards the Azapa Valley, on Calle Hualles, just south of the river, the **Poblado Artesanal** is a replica of an altiplano village, where twelve white houses serve as workshops for artisans selling handicrafts ranging from ceramics and glass to knitwear and leather items; its hours of operation are erratic.

Museo Arqueológico

Km12, Azapa Valley • Daily: Jan & Feb 10am–7pm; March–Dec 10am–6pm • CH$2000

Twelve kilometres along the road from the Poblado Artesanal, the outstanding **Museo Arqueológico**, part of the University of Tarapacá, houses an excellent collection of regional pre-Columbian artefacts, including a collection of extraordinary Chinchorro mummies (see box, p.210) buried over four thousand years ago. Other exhibits include finely decorated Tiwanaku ceramics, ancient Andean musical instruments and snuff trays, and many beautifully embroidered tapestries – look out for the one in Case 11, decorated with images of smiling women – and displays on contemporary Aymara culture. All the pieces are extremely well presented, and there are unusually explanatory leaflets available in several languages, including English, French and German.

San Miguel de Azapa

In the nearby village of **San Miguel de Azapa**, the only place of interest is the fabulously multicoloured desert **cemetery**, which climbs like a mini-Valparaíso for the deceased towards a dune-like cliff. The colour comes from the artificial flowers laid on the graves. By the entrance sits the morbidly named **restaurant** *La Picá del Muertito* (the "Little Dead Man's Snack-Bar"), famous for miles around for its first-rate *pastel de choclo*, a sugar-glazed corn-bake containing meat, egg and olives.

Alto Ramírez

The Azapa Valley is also the site of several **geoglyphs**. The most impressive example is **Alto Ramírez**, a large, stylized human figure surrounded by geometric shapes; you can see it, at a distance, from the main road on the way to the museum (ask your *colectivo* driver to point it out to you) or take a detour to get a closer look.

4

By Colectivo *Colectivos* for the Azapa Valley, including the Museo Arqueológico and the nearby geoglyphs, leave from the corner of Lynch and Chacabuco in Arica's centre.

Putre

The busy little mountain town of **PUTRE**, surrounded by a patchwork of green fields and Inca terraces, lies 150km on from Arica at a height of 3500m. It's a popular overnight stop en route to the higher altitudes of **Parque Nacional Lauca** – climbers, in particular, like to spend a few days walking in the hills here before attempting the volcanoes in the park. Putre's rustic houses are clustered around a large, green square, overlooked by the Municipalidad.

The church

Off the northeast corner of the square you'll find the **church**, built in 1670 after an earthquake destroyed the original one, which, according to old Spanish chronicles, was clad in gold and silver. The current building, heavily restored in 1871, is considerably more modest, consisting of a small stone chapel and a whitewashed, straw-roofed bell

CHINCHORRO MUMMIES

In 1983, while laying a new pipeline near the foot of El Morro, the Arica water company came across a hoard of withered corpses buried a couple of metres beneath the sand. Work immediately ceased and archeologists from the University of Tarapacá were rushed in to assess the scene, which turned out to be a seven-thousand-year-old burial site containing 96 bodies – the largest and best-preserved find, to date, of **Chinchorro mummies**.

The ancient practice of mummification in this region – the oldest known in the world – was first identified in 1917 when a series of highly unusual human remains were discovered. Further excavations revealed similar findings spread along the coast, concentrated between Arica and Camerones, 65km south, and it became apparent that they were relics of an ancient society that archeologists have named the Chinchorro culture. Modern radiocarbon dating has established that the practice was well under way by 5000 BC – more than two millennia before the Egyptians began practising mummification.

ORIGINS OF THE CHINCHORRO

No one knows exactly where the Chinchorro people came from; some archeologists speculate that they moved down from the north, others that they came from the Andean highlands. What's clear, however, is that by 7000 BC scattered groups of people – possibly extended families – were spread along the coast of Chile's Far North, where they lived on the abundant crabs, clams, mussels, seaweed, pelicans, sea lions and other marine life of the region, supplementing their diet with guanaco and wild berries.

THE MUMMIFICATION PROCESS

The great simplicity of their hunter-gatherer lifestyle makes the sophisticated techniques they developed to **preserve the dead** all the more extraordinary. The practice involved removing the brain through a hole at the base of the skull, and removing all internal organs, which were probably discarded. After this, the cavities were dried with hot stones or fire and then refilled with straw and ashes. The bones of the arms and legs were replaced with sticks bound into place with reeds, and the skeleton was given extra padding before the body was stitched up. The face was then coated in paste, which dried into a hard mask with a sculpted nose and incisions marking the eyes and mouth. The finishing touch was provided by a wig made of human hair, which was attached to the skull.

The Chinchorro culture performed this elaborate process for over three thousand years until, for unknown reasons, the practice died out around 1500 BC, and the era of the oldest known form of artificial mummification came to an end.

tower. The village observes the Feast of the Assumption, August 15, with a week-long celebration that features much singing and dancing; accommodation is hard to find during this time.

ARRIVAL AND INFORMATION

By bus Buses La Paloma, Germán Riesco 2071 (☎58 222710; CH$3500), runs regular buses to Putre from Arica.
Tourist information Arturo Prat s/n (Mon-Fri 9am-6pm; ☎58 252803).

TOUR OPERATORS AND GUIDES

Alto Andino Nature Tours Baquedano ☎58 300013, ⓦbirdingaltoandino.com, ⓔaltoandino@yahoo.com. Run by an Alaskan naturalist who offers wildlife-viewing excursions, specializing in ornithology and marine mammals, in Parque Nacional Lauca and coastal areas; consult the website for more details. She also has a few simple, cheap rooms to rent.

Alvaro Mamani ⓔamamaniguia@gmail.com. For informative trips into the altiplano, Alvaro Mamani is a very personable Aymara guide.
Valentina Alave Local Valentina Alave offers walks to interesting cave paintings 7km from the village – ask at the Municipalidad for more information.

ACCOMMODATION

Hostal Pachamama Lord Cochrane s/n ☎58 585814, ⓦhostalpachamama.cl. This is one of the most relaxed places to stay with simple rooms grouped around a shady courtyard, shared bathrooms, a kitchen and free internet. It's a bargain. CH$20,000
Hotel Kukuli Baquedano 301 ☎099 161 4709. Run by the very friendly Libertad, this hotel has decent, comfortable en-suite rooms in a modern-ish building. Good-sized breakfasts and parking are a plus. CH$30,000

Hotel Q'antati Hijuela 208 ☎58 328763. On the western edges of town, about a 10min walk from the plaza, *Q'antati* is the smartest, and most expensive, place to stay in Putre, offering modern heated bedrooms with views out to the valley. CH$35,000
Residencial Cali Baquedano 399 ☎098 5361242, ⓔhostal_cali@hotmail.com. This simple, hospitable place on the main street into town has small and tidy rooms off a sunny backyard. It's a popular choice so book ahead in high season. CH$18,000

EATING AND DRINKING

★ **Kuchu Marka** Baquedano s/n. At this cosy place, you can get alpaca stew and other hearty mountain dishes like *picante de conejo* (a sort of rabbit curry) along with an excellent vegetarian option. Mon–Sat noon–11.30pm.

Rosamel Cochrane s/n. Simple restaurant on the square serving good set menus made up of local dishes such as stews and spicy meat dishes at affordable prices. Mon–Sat noon–3pm & 8–11pm, Sun noon–3pm.

Parque Nacional Lauca

A few hours east of Putre, up in the cordillera, **Parque Nacional Lauca** has become one of the most popular attractions in the north of Chile. A few of Arica's tour operators (see p.207) will get you there if you don't relish the idea of driving yourself.

Las Cuevas

A 4400-metre-high mountain pass signals the boundary of Parque Nacional Lauca. Up here the air is thin and cold, and the road is flanked by light-green *bofedal* (highland pasture) where herds of wild vicuña come to feed in the mornings. Ten kilometres into the park, you reach the Conaf hut (erratic opening hours) at **Las Cuevas**, a good place to stop to check on weather and road conditions and observe the comical antics of vizcachas, cuddly chinchilla-like rodents with curly tails and a spring-like leap.

Parinacota

From Las Cuevas the road continues through a wide, green plain filled with grazing llamas and alpacas. Some 19km on from the Conaf hut, it passes the turn-off for

PARINACOTA (the name means "flamingo lake" in Aymara), site of the park's headquarters and an idyllic *pueblo altiplánico* in its own right, composed of fifty or so crumbling, whitewashed houses huddled around a beautiful little **church**. Opposite the church, in the plaza, local women sell alpaca knitwear and other **artesanía**. Many of the village houses are under lock and key for much of the year, their owners returning only for important fiestas and funerals.

The church

Built in 1789, this is one of Chile's most assiduously maintained Andean churches, sporting brilliant white walls and a bright-blue wooden door, trimmed with yellow and green. Like most churches of the altiplano, it has thick stone and adobe walls and a sloping straw roof, and is enclosed within a little white wall incorporating the bell tower into one of its corners. It's usually open in the morning (if not, you can borrow the key from the caretaker – ask at the *artesanía* stalls). Inside, you'll find a series of faded, centuries-old friezes depicting the Stations of the Cross and vivid scenes of sinners suffering in hell. There's also an unusual collection of skulls belonging to former priests.

Lagunas de Cotacotani

A collection of small, interconnected lakes lying in a dark lava field, filled with exquisite jade-green water, the **LAGUNAS DE COTACOTANI** lie about 8km east of Parinacota, clearly

PARQUE NACIONAL LAUCA AND AROUND

PARINACOTA'S WANDERING TABLE

Among the oddities of Parinacota's venerable church is a **magical "walking" table** that's kept chained to the wall, for fear it will wander off in the night. According to local legend, the table can predict death and, if left unchained, stops outside the home of the next villager to die.

---

visible from the paved highway to Bolivia. The lakes were formed by volcanic eruptions and are surrounded by fine dust and cinder cones, further adding to their lunar appearance. The waters are filtered down from Lago Chungará and then continue to the *bofedal de Parinacota*, which is the source of the Río Lauca. On closer inspection the lakes aren't as lifeless as they first appear; many wild Andean geese flock here, while plentiful herds of alpaca graze the soggy marshland. This area is definitely worth exploring as a day hike from Parinacota, but if you are pressed for time take a good look from the *mirador* on the highway, marked by a giant multicoloured *zampoña* (Andean panpipes).

Lago Chungará

Eighteen kilometres on from Parinacota, at an altitude of 4515m, you'll see **LAGO CHUNGARÁ**, a wide blue lake spectacularly positioned at the foot of a snowcapped volcano that rises over its rim like a giant Christmas pudding covered in cream. This is 6330m-high **Volcán Parinacota**, one of the highest peaks in Chile and the park's most challenging climb (see box, p.214). When the lake is mill-pond calm, in other words when there is no wind, the reflection of the volcano is the most memorable view in the entire region. On the southern shore, right by the highway, you'll find a small stone **Conaf refugio** (see p.213). This is unquestionably the best place to stay in the park, allowing you to observe the changing colours of the lake and volcano at different times of day, from the transparent pinks of early morning to the deep blues and gleaming whites of the afternoon.

ARRIVAL AND INFORMATION

By bus You can reach Parinacota, where the park's headquarters are located, by bus from Arica with Buses La Paloma, Germán Riesco 2071 (Tues & Fri 11.30am; 3hr; ☎58 222710).
By car Take the CH-11 motorway from Arica for approximately 145km.

PARQUE NACIONAL LAUCA

Park information The Conaf administration centre, housed in a large, chalet-style building at Parinacota, makes a valiant attempt at informing the public about the park and its wildlife, though opening times are erratic.

ACCOMMODATION AND EATING

The **Conaf** administration centre sometimes offers **camping** space out the back. Alternatively, some villagers offer very basic rooms (without hot water); ask around.

Conaf refugio On the southern shore of Lago Chungará, right by the highway, ☎58 201200. A small stone *refugio* with four beds, a kitchen and unbeatable views. CH$5000 per person
Hostal y Restorant Uta Kala de Don Leo Parinacota

s/n ☎58 261526, ✉leonel_parinacota@hotmail.com. This is the first and only hostel in Parinacota – and thankfully it's a good one, with several comfy beds, hot water, heating, meals and splendid views onto fields of grazing llama. Breakfast and dinner included. CH$10,000 per person

Reserva Nacional las Vicuñas

Directly south of Parque Nacional Lauca, the **RESERVA NACIONAL LAS VICUÑAS** stretches over 100km south across spectacular altiplano wilderness filled with wild vicuña, green *bofedales*, abandoned Aymara villages, groves of *queñoa* – spindly,

4

WALKS AND CLIMBS IN PARQUE NACIONAL LAUCA

Parque Nacional Lauca doesn't offer a great many hiking possibilities, and most people are content to just admire the scenery and the wildlife. There are, however, at least three half-day or day **walks** you can do, and many more possibilities for **climbing**. Remember to respect the altitude, and to allow yourself more time to cover distances that you could walk quite easily at lower elevations. You must get authorization from DIFROL (governmental borders organization) if you are planning on climbing any or the mountains or volcanoes in the region. Fill in the authorization form on their website (🌐difrol.cl) at least two days before climbing, or else ask Putre's municipalidad to do it for you.

Cerro Choquelimpie No technical experience or equipment is necessary to climb this 5288m peak, reached in about four hours from the refugio at Lago Chungará. From the top, you get views down to the gold mine behind the mountain, and on to Lago Chungará and Volcán Parinacota.

Cerro Guane Guane A slow but straightforward climb up this 5096m peak is rewarded with panoramic views over the park. It's suitable for any fit person used to hill-climbing and takes around four hours to the top from the Conaf centre at Parinacota, and two to three hours back down.

Lago Chungará to Parinacota (or reverse) This 18km walk from the refugio at Lago Chungará to Parinacota takes about six hours. Follow the paved highway as far as the *mirador de Lagunas Cotacotani*, then climb down to the lakes, from where a jeep track continues to Parinacota.

Parinacota to Lagunas de Cotacotani A rewarding, not-too-difficult walk, taking

about three hours (one way) from Parinacota; ask the Conaf *guardaparque* to point you in the direction of the jeep track you need to follow.

Sendero de excursión de Parinacota An easy, 6km circular walk, marked by blue stones starting behind the Conaf centre, taking you past the *bofedal de Parinacota*, where you can observe numerous grazing alpaca. Good views onto surrounding mountains. Allow two to three hours.

Volcán Parinacota Suitable only for experienced climbers carrying crampons and ropes (though it's not always necessary to use them). Allow two days to get up and down from the base camp (a day's hike from Parinacota), including one night camping on the volcano. Avoid this climb between mid-December and February, because of the weather conditions. Volcan Parincota's brother volcano, Pomerape, is just across the border and makes an equally interesting climb.

rickety-looking trees belonging to a species that miraculously defies the treeline – and sweeping vistas of volcanoes. The reserve's administrative centre is about a ninety-minute drive from Putre, in **Guallatire** (4428m altitude), a pretty hamlet with a traditional seventeenth-century Andean church. There's also an obligatory *carabineros* checkpoint here, and a Conaf *refugio* that is seldom in service. Looming over the village, snowcapped **Volcán Guallatire** puffs wispy plumes of smoke from its 6060m peak, while a grassy-banked stream snakes at its foot.

ARRIVAL AND DEPARTURE   RESERVA NACIONAL LAS VICUÑAS

By organized tour and 4WD There's no public transport, you need to hire a high-clearance 4WD vehicle or take an organized tour. Note that the drive into the reserve involves

fording several streams, which are usually very low but can swell dangerously with heavy summer rains – check with Conaf in Arica before setting out.

Salar de Surire

Following the road south of Guallatire, you'll be rewarded, about 40km on, with sudden, dramatic views of the **SALAR DE SURIRE**, a dazzling white salt flat containing several lakes with nesting colonies of three species of flamingo. Originally part of

CONAF REFUGIOS

If you are travelling under your own steam but do not fancy camping in the open wilds of the cold, high altiplano, the various **Conaf refugios** (ⓦ conaf.cl) dotted around the Parque Nacional Lauca, Parque Nacional Isluga and in between make for excellent places to stay. They have proper beds, some have decent facilities, and they are nearly all located in amazing spots, with views to linger over. The only problem is that in recent years their upkeep has been shoddy and they are sometimes left in a pitiful state by previous visitors. Worst of all, even if you book ahead through the Conaf offices in Arica (see p.191) or Iquique, reservations are not always respected and you might turn up to find it shut or no room at the inn.

Parque Nacional Lauca, its status was changed to that of national monument in 1983 to allow borax to be mined from its surface. The mining is still going on today, and you can see the mine's enormous trucks driving over the *salar*, dwarfed by its massive dimensions but a nuisance nonetheless.

Polloquere

Sixteen kilometres further on from the Salar de Surire, skirting the southern edge of the salt flat, **Polloquere** (also known as Aguas Calientes) is the site of several pale-blue pools filled with hot thermal water and with a muddy bottom reminiscent of the Dead Sea, an absolutely stunning place to take a bath, despite the lack of facilities – though be sure to get here in the morning, before the bone-chilling afternoon wind picks up. There are a couple of picnic areas and **camping** spaces here, too, but it's a treacherously exposed site.

ARRIVAL AND DEPARTURE   SALAR DE SURIRE

By 4WD There is no public transport, and although it is sometimes possible to get a ride from the trucks that carry minerals to and fro, it's best to hire your own 4WD vehicle.

ACCOMMODATION

Conaf refugio On the west shore of the Salar, ⓣ 58 201200. In a wonderful location with terrific views onto the salt flat, this *refugio* has four beds, hot water and a kitchen, though is often closed and bookings are not always respected so do not rely on staying here. **CH$5500** per person

The Central Valley

221 Rancagua

223 The Rapel Valley

225 The Colchagua Valley

231 The Mataquito Valley

235 Talca

237 The Maule Valley

242 Chillán and around

244 The Itata Valley

247 The Bío Bío Valley

SALTO DEL LAJA

5

The Central Valley

Extending south from Santiago as far as the Río Bío Bío, Chile's **CENTRAL VALLEY** is a long, narrow plain hemmed in by the Andes to the east and the coastal range to the west, with lateral river valleys running between the two. This is the most fertile land in Chile, and the immense orchards, vineyards and pastures that cover the valley floor form a dazzling patchwork of greenery. Even in urban zones, country ways hold sway, and the Central Valley is perhaps the only part of Chile where it is not uncommon to see horse-drawn carts plodding down the Panamericana Highway.

While the main artery of the Panamericana runs all the way south from Santiago, through Rancagua to Los Angeles and beyond, the kernel of the Central Valley lies between the capital and the city of **Chillán**, some 400km south – a region where, during the colonial era, the vast private estates known as **estancias**, or haciendas, were established. The people have held on to many of their rural traditions and the cult of the *huaso*, or cowboy, is as strong as ever, as can be witnessed at the frequent **rodeos** held in stadiums known as *medialunas*.

Further south again, the busy city of **Concepción** guards the mouth of the **Bío Bío**, the mighty river that for over three hundred years was the boundary between conquered, colonial Chile and unconquered **Mapuche territory**, whose occupants withstood domination until 1883. Traces of the frontier still linger, visible in the ruins of colonial Spanish forts, the proliferation of Mapuche place names and the tin-roof pioneer architecture. Beyond the Bío Bío, towards the Lake District, the gently sloping plains giving way to verdant native forests and remote Andean lakes.

Many visitors bypass the Central Valley altogether, whizzing south towards the more dramatic landscapes of the Lake District and beyond. Certainly the agricultural towns dotted along the highway – **Rancagua**, **San Fernando**, **Curicó**, **Talca** and **Los Angeles** – are, on the whole, rather dull, but stray a few kilometres off the Panamericana and you'll catch a glimpse of an older Chile abounding with pastoral charms. Chief among these are the region's small, **colonial villages**, with their colourful adobe houses topped by overhanging clay-tiled roofs, many of which were, unfortunately, damaged in the 2010 earthquake (see p.225) and are now in various states of repair. Among the prettiest examples are **Vichuquén**, west of Curicó, and **Villa Alegre**, south of Talca in the Maule Valley, where you can also visit a trail of lush, emerald **vineyards**.

Away from the valley floor, you'll find attractions of a very different nature. To the west, up in the coastal hills, a couple of lakes offer great **watersports** facilities, notably **Lago Rapel**, while further west a number of inviting **beaches** and cheerful seaside towns are scattered down the coast, among them the popular surfer hangout of **Pichilemu**. East of the valley, the dry, dusty slopes of the Andes offer excellent **horseriding** and **hiking** opportunities, particularly along the trails of protected areas such as **Reserva Nacional Altos del Lircay**, near Talca. After a strenuous day in the mountains, relax in one of the many **hot springs** in the area, including the **Nevados de Chillán** at the base of a booming ski and adventure resort.

Rodeos p.223
Aftershocks p.225
La Ruta del Vino del Valle de
  Colchagua p.229

Surfing in Pichilemu p.230
Wine tours around Curicó p.232
Ruta del Vino Valle del Maule p.238
Treks in Parque Nacional Nahuelbuta p.258

VIÑA CLOS APALTA, RUTAL DEL VINO

Highlights

❶ Santa Cruz Visit the exceptional museum in this pretty wine valley town, then taste your way through some of the world's best red wines on the "Ruta del Vino". **See p.228**

❷ Pichilemu and the beaches Relax at this haven for surfing and other watersports, which also doubles as an inexpensive launch pad for visiting the area's deserted beaches and lakes. **See p.230**

❸ Parque Nacional Radal Siete Tazas This stunning park features lush forests, abundant waterfalls and natural swimming pools. **See p.234**

❹ Altos del Lircay Hiking trails, spectacular views and relatively easy access make one of Chile's few Andean parks perfect for camping trips. **See p.237**

❺ Nevados de Chillán Legendary hot springs on the side of a volcano; in the winter, the skiing is excellent, while the rest of the year you can hike, bike and embark on horse treks. **See p.244**

❻ Salto del Laja Marvel at these thundering waterfalls. **See p.254**

HIGHLIGHTS ARE MARKED ON THE MAP ON P.220

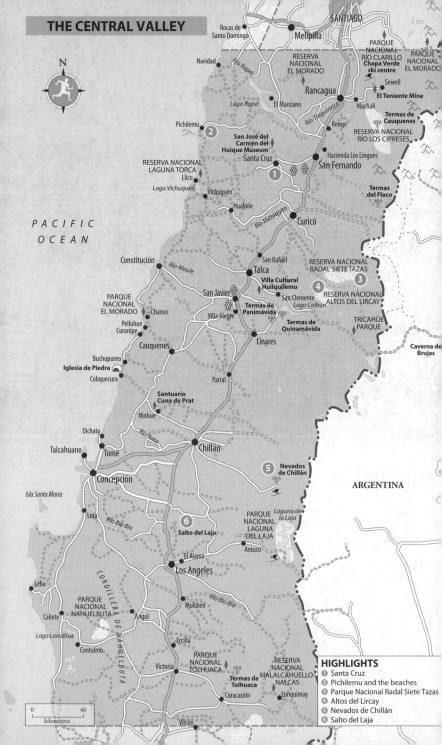

THE CENTRAL VALLEY

N

PACIFIC OCEAN

ARGENTINA

SANTIAGO

Rocas de Santo Domingo
Melipilla
Navidad
Río Rapel
RESERVA NACIONAL EL MORADO
PARQUE NACIONAL RÍO CLARILLO
Chapa Verde ski centre
PARQUE NACIONAL EL MORADO
Rancagua
Sewell
El Teniente Mine
Lago Rapel
El Manzano
Machalí
Termas de Cauquenes
Río Tinguiririca
Rengo
RESERVA NACIONAL RÍO LOS CIPRESES
Pichilemu ②
San José del Carmen del Huique Museum
Santa Cruz
Hacienda Los Lingues
RESERVA NACIONAL LAGUNA TORCA
Llico
① San Fernando
Vichuquén
Lago Vichuquén
Termas del Flaco
Hualañe
Río Mataquito
Curicó
Constitución
Río Maule
San Rafael
Talca
RESERVA NACIONAL RADAL SIETE TAZAS ③
Villa Cultural Huilquilemu
San Javier
④
San Clemente
Lago Colbún
RESERVA NACIONAL ALTOS DEL LIRCAY
PARQUE NACIONAL EL MORADO
Chanco
Termas de Panimávida
Villa Alegre
Termas de Quinamávida
TRICAHUE PARQUE
Pelluhue
Curanipe
Linares
Caverna de Brujas
Cauquenes
Buchupureo
Iglesia de Piedra
Cobquecura
Parral
Santuario Cuna de Prat
Ninhue
Río Ñuble
Dichato
Río Ñata
Talcahuano
Tomé
Chillán
Concepción
⑤ Nevados de Chillán
Isla Santa María
Lota
Río Bío Bío
PARQUE NACIONAL LAGUNA DEL LAJA
Laguna de la Laja
⑥ Salto del Laja
Antuco
El Álamo
Lebú
Los Ángeles
CORDILLERA DE NAHUELBUTA
PARQUE NACIONAL NAHUELBUTA
Cañete
Angol
Mulchén
Río Bío Bío
Lago Lanalhue
Contulmo
Ercilla
Victoria
PARQUE NACIONAL TOLHUACA
RESERVA NACIONAL MALALCÁHUELLO NALCAS
Termas de Tolhuaca
Lonquimay
Curacautín
Vilcún

0   40
kilómetres

HIGHLIGHTS

① Santa Cruz
② Pichilemu and the beaches
③ Parque Nacional Radal Siete Tazas
④ Altos del Lircay
⑤ Nevados de Chillán
⑥ Salto del Laja

The amount of annual **rainfall** picks up steadily as you head south; by the time you reach the Bío Bío there is a significant amount of rain every month. While winter is never too cold, most visitors come here between October and March.

GETTING AROUND   THE CENTRAL VALLEY

By bus Getting down the Central Valley by public transport is easy, with hundreds of buses ploughing down the Panamericana. Branching off into the cordillera and to the coast normally requires catching a "rural bus" from one of the cities dotted down the highway, though some of the more remote places can only be reached with your own transport.

By train A more leisurely and scenic option is the train from Santiago, stopping at Rancagua, San Fernando, Curicó, Talca and Chillán

Rancagua

Zipping down the Panamericana from Santiago, you can reach the unremarkable agricultural town of **RANCAGUA**, 87km south, in about an hour. With a little more time and your own transport, however, the old road from Santiago (signed Alto Jahuel, running east along the highway) makes a far more appealing route, winding its way past estates of vines, fruit trees and old haciendas, half-hidden behind their great adobe walls.

Rancagua presents a picture that is to repeat itself in most of the Central Valley towns – large, well-tended central plaza; single-storey adobe houses; a few colonial buildings, which were damaged in the 2010 earthquake but are being restored; sprawling, faceless outskirts. Once in town, you'll find little to hold your interest for more than a few hours – unless your arrival coincides with a **rodeo** (see box, p.223) – but Rancagua makes a useful jumping-off point for attractions in the adjacent Rapel Valley.

Plaza de los Héroes and around

Unusually, Rancagua's square is known not as the Plaza de Armas, but as the **Plaza de los Héroes**. The name honours the patriot soldiers, headed by Bernardo O'Higgins, who defended the city against Royalist forces in 1814, only to be crushed in what has gone down in Chilean history as the "Disaster of Rancagua". In the centre of the square, a rearing equestrian statue celebrates O'Higgins' triumphant return to the city, four years after he had left it in ruins, to present it with a coat of arms depicting a phoenix rising from the ashes. The square's other major monument is the towering, yellow-walled **Iglesia Catedral**. One block north of the square, at the corner of Cuevas and Estado, the **Iglesia de la Merced** was used as O'Higgins' headquarters; it suffered major structural damage in the 2010 earthquake and only its exterior can currently be viewed.

Museo Regional de Rancagua and around

Estado 685 • Tues–Fri 10am–6pm • Free • ☎ 72 221524, Ⓦ museorancagua.cl

The eighteenth-century house occupied by the **Museo Regional de Rancagua** was severely damaged in the 2010 earthquake and at the time of writing only its gardens could be visited. Opposite, at Estado 682, the 1812 **Casa del Pilar de Esquina** is a splendid two-storey late-colonial house; its rooms are also closed for restoration, although you can still wander around its patio.

Casa de Cultura

Cachapoal and Millán • Mon–Fri 8am–9pm • ☎ 72 224621

One block south of the Museo Regional, the **Casa de Cultura** is being restored following earthquake damage, but you can still appreciate its rural colonial architecture, including thick foundations made of river boulders mortared with mud.

5

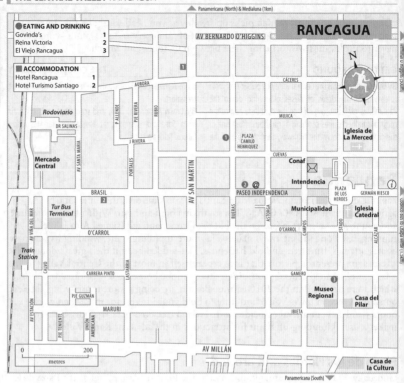

ARRIVAL AND DEPARTURE

By bus The main terminal for long-distance services, known as Terminal O'Higgins, is at O'Higgins 0480 (☏72 225425). The regional bus terminal, called Rodoviario, is at Salinas 1165 (☏72 236938).

Destinations Chillán (8 daily; 4hr); Concepción (16 daily; 5hr); Curicó (every 30min; 1hr 45min); Lago Rapel-El Manzano (every 20min; 2hr); Los Angeles (5 daily; 5hr); Pichilemu (every 30min: 3hr 30min); Puerto Montt (8 daily;

11hr); San Fernando (every 15min; 50min); Santa Cruz (every 15min; 2hr); Santiago (every 10min; 1hr–1hr 30min); Talca (every 30min; 2hr); Temuco (10 daily; 7hr).

By train The train station is at the corner of Estación and Carrera Pinto (☏72 238530).

Destinations Chillán (3 daily; 3hr 40min); Curicó (5 daily; 1hr 5min); San Fernando (5 daily; 30min); Santiago (5 daily; 1hr); Talca (5 daily; 1hr 50min).

INFORMATION AND TOURS

Tourist information Sernatur, Germán Riesco 277 (Mon–Thurs 8.30am–5.30pm, Fri 8.30am–4.30pm; ☏72 230413, ✉inforancagua@sernatur.cl).

Conaf Cuevas 480 (Mon–Thurs 8.30am–5.30pm &

8.30am–4.30pm; ☏72 204612, ✉rancagua.oirs@conaf.cl).

Turismo Dakota Mujica 605 ☏72 228166, ⊛turismodakota.cl. Can arrange local tours, treks and horseriding.

ACCOMMODATION

Hotel Rancagua Av San Martín 85 ☏72 232663, ✉contacto@hotelrancagua.cl. One of the nicer place to stay in town; there are 20 rooms in total, but aim to get one of the more modern en suites in the extension out the back. **CH$49,800**

Hotel Turismo Santiago Brasil 1036 ☏72 230860, ⊛www.hotelsantiago.cl. Squarely aimed at the business traveller with comfortable but antiseptic en suites, this 64-room hotel nevertheless boasts an outdoor pool and a restaurant. **CH$50,000**

RODEOS

The Central Valley is the birthplace and heartland of Chilean **rodeo**, whose season kicks off on Independence Day, September 18. Over the following six months, regional competitions eliminate all but the finest horses and *huasos* in the country, who go on to take part in the national championships in Rancagua (Chile's rodeo capital) on the first weekend in April. Rodeos are performed in *medialunas* ("half moons"), circular arenas divided by a curved wall, forming a crescent-shaped stadium and a smaller oval pen called an *apiñadero*. In Rancagua it is on the northern edge of town (on the corner of Av España and Germán Ibarra). The participants are **huasos** – cowboys, or horsemen – who cut a dashing figure with their bright, finely woven ponchos, broad-rimmed hats, carved wooden stirrups and shining silver spurs. The mounts they ride in the rodeo are specially bred and trained *corraleros* that are far too valuable for day-to-day work.

A rodeo begins with an inspection of the horses and their riders by judges, who award points for appearance. This is followed by individual displays of horsemanship that make ordinary dressage look tame. In the main part of a rodeo, pairs of *huasos* have to drive a young cow, or *novillo*, around the edge of the arena and pin it up against a padded section of the wall. Rodeos are as much about eating and drinking as anything else, and the canteen and foodstalls by a *medialuna* are a good place to sample **regional food**, gourmet wine and the sweet fruity alcohol known as *chicha*. Rodeo events are spread over the course of a weekend and end with music and dancing. This is where you can see the **cueca** (see p.38) being danced at its flirtatious best. For the dates of official rodeos, contact the **Federación del Rodeo Chileno** in Santiago (☎ 2 481 0990) or visit ⊛ federaciondelrodeochileno.cl.

EATING

Govinda's Bueras 283 ☎ 72 222978. Bucking the town's cowboy trend, this Hare Krishna vegetarian restaurant sees a lunchtime rush for its satiating portions of lasagne, lentil stew and *empanadas*. Lunch menu CH$3600. Mon–Fri 1–5pm.

Reina Victoria Paseo Independencia 667 ☎ 72 239867. For something sweet, join the steady stream of shoppers and schoolchildren at this bustling café for coffee, cakes, biscuits and huge tubs of ice cream. Savoury offerings include the ubiquitous *completo* (hot dog; CH$1000). Daily 7.30am–10pm.

El Viejo Rancagua Estado 607 ☎ 72 227715. Crammed with historic photos and memorabilia, this ramshackle restaurant does a cheap lunch menu (CH$1500) and on Fri and Sat nights transforms into an atmospheric bar, with live tango, bolero and folkloric music. Mon–Thurs lunch, Fri lunch & 8pm–4am, Sat 8pm–4am.

DIRECTORY

Airlines LAN Astorga 233-B ☎ 72 235573.
Banks and exchange Paseo Independencia has numerous banks with ATMs. For a *casa de cambio*, there's AFEX at Cuevas 483 in the Mall Vivo.
Car rental Car rental is available from Arriendo Comercial

Oriente, El Cobre 590 (☎ 72 211571).
Internet Surf the web at Internet del Centro, Independencia 657 (CH$400 per hr).
Post office Campos 322 (Mon–Fri 9am–6pm, Sat 10am–1pm).

The Rapel Valley

Rancagua makes a good base for exploring several attractions in the adjacent **RAPEL VALLEY**, including the 40km-long **Lago Rapel**, the largest artificial lake in Chile. In the opposite direction, a paved highway known as the Carretera del Cobre heads 60km east into the cordillera to the copper mine of **El Teniente** and the **Chapa Verde ski centre**, while a southern fork takes you to the **Reserva Nacional Río los Cipreses**.

El Teniente copper mine and Sewell

60km east of Rancagua • Tours with VTS Sat & Sun leaving from Rancagua or Santiago • From CH$23,000 per person • ☎ 72 952692, ⊛ vts.cl or ⊛ sewell.cl

El Teniente is the largest underground mine in the world, with more than 1500km of tunnels. Local legend has it that its name – "the lieutenant" – refers to a disgraced

5

Spanish officer who, while heading to Argentina to escape his creditors, discovered enormous copper deposits, thus making a fortune and saving himself from bankruptcy. Today the mine belongs to Codelco, the government-owned copper corporation, which also owns the famous Chuquicamata mine in northern Chile.

You aren't allowed to just turn up and visit, but tour agency VTS offer group excursions that can be arranged in advance. Their tours include a visit to the abandoned company town of **Sewell**, staggered in dramatic tiers up the mountainside. After that, you don protective gear and go down the shafts to the gloomy underground tunnels.

Chapa Verde ski centre

Ticket office Miguel Ramírez 655, Rancagua • Lift tickets CH$23,000 adult, CH$14,000 children; full ski and snowboard equipment rental from CH$19,000 • ☏ 72 217651, ⓦ chapaverde.cl

A few kilometres north of El Teniente mine, and ranging from 2300m to 3100m, is the Codelco-owned **Chapa Verde ski centre**, initially built for the company's miners but now open to the public between July and September. There are no hotels or other accommodation, but check with ski area administration for information on private homes for rent.

Reserva Nacional Río de Los Cipreses

Daily 8.30am–5pm • CH$2000, camping CH$5000 • ☏ 72 297505

A couple of kilometres on from the turn-off to El Teniente, you'll come to a southern fork that branches towards **RESERVA NACIONAL RÍO DE LOS CIPRESES**, 20km beyond. A little-visited gem, the reserve encompasses 36 square kilometres of protected land stretched along the narrow canyon of the Río de los Cipreses, with altitudes ranging from 900m to 4900m. It's a great spot for multi-day **hiking** or **horseriding**, and you may spot rare burrowing parrots, foxes, eagles and condors.

Sector El Ranchillo

At the entrance, a Conaf office provides maps and a diorama of the park. Ask about the trails that offer a look at the parakeets nesting in the cliffs. From the office, a jeep track leads 6km to **Sector El Ranchillo**, a camping and picnic area with a swimming pool. This is the end of the track, and vehicles must be parked.

Sector Maitenes

From the camping and picnic area, take the left fork just before El Ranchillo, continue past a second gate (locked) and after another 6km you'll reach **Sector Maitenes**, with a few camping spots and running water. Beyond, a trail follows the river along the canyon, passing through forests and with occasional views of high Andean peaks like Cerro El Indio and Cerro El Cotón. Lateral ravines regularly branch out from the river, leading to waterfalls, lakes and "hanging" valleys carved out of the hills by glaciers. These aren't signed, however, so unless you're with an *arriero* (horseman), stick to the main path.

Sector Urriola

Twenty kilometres on from Sector Maitenes, you reach **Sector Urriola**, where there's a rustic *refugio* (1500m) and a few camping areas; count on taking around six or seven hours to get here on foot from Maitenes, and about four or five on horseback. Beyond Urriola, the path continues for a further ten or so kilometres, giving great views onto the 4900m-high Volcán Palomo. To hire a horse (CH$12,000 a day), ask around at the community of Chacayes at the park's entrance.

Lago Rapel

5

The forty-kilometre-long artificial **LAGO RAPEL** nestles in the low coastal hills southwest of Rancagua. Most of the action is centred around the main town of El Manzano, on the lake's eastern shore. The lake's main attractions are its excellent **watersports facilities**, with speed boats, windsurfers and jet skis available for rent from several hotels and campsites.

ARRIVAL AND DEPARTURE   THE RAPEL VALLEY

CHAPA VERDE SKI CENTRE

By bus Codelco's own bus service, Buses El Teniente, runs from Av Miguel Ramírez 665, Rancagua, next to the Lider Vecino supermarket (departures June–Sept weekdays 9am, weekends 8.30am & 9.30am, return trip daily 4.30pm; CH$10,000; times are prone to change so it is worth confirming with the ski centre).

By car You can drive up in your own vehicle (4WD is advisable) as long as you call for a permit beforehand.

RESERVA NACIONAL RÍO DE LOS CIPRESES

By bus and taxi There's no direct public transport to the park, but you can take a bus from Rancagua to Coya (1hr) from where taxis can drive you the 12km to the park entrance (CH$5000).

LAGO RAPEL

By bus Gal Bus (☎72 240579) runs buses to El Manzano from Rancagua's regional terminal (every 20min; 2hr 30min) as does Sextur (☎72 231342; 4 daily; 2hr 30min).

ACCOMMODATION AND EATING

LAGO RAPEL

Camping Náutico Rapel ☎2 862 6300, ⓦ campingnauticorapel.cl. Campers have access to a pool and volleyball court as well as a wharf that's ideal for a spot of lake fishing. Camping ‾CH$20,000‾ per site

Club Alemán Along the lakeshore 8km west of El Manzano ☎09 883 3397, ⓦ cabanasrapel.cl. Fully equipped cabins sleep up to eight people, and camping is

also offered. Facilities include a swimming pool and children's playground. Camping ‾CH$4000‾ per person, cabin ‾CH$25,000‾

Jardín del Lago 10km north of El Manzano ☎09 743 4420, ⓦ jardindellago.cl. Smart, self-contained, apartment-style cabin accommodation sleeping up to nine people. There are also jet skis, canoes and row boats for hire. ‾CH$44,000‾

The Colchagua Valley

The 120-kilometre-long valley of the Río Tinguiririca is known locally as the **Colchagua Valley** after the province through which it runs. This is serious fruit-production territory, as signalled by the numerous fruit stalls and large Del Monte factories lining the highway on the approach to San Fernando. Forty-one kilometres west is **Santa Cruz**, a starting point for visiting various vineyards. Still further east, high in the cordillera, the **Termas del Flaco** is an inexpensive option for soaking in hot springs. Around San Fernando, the **Ruta del Vino del Valle de Colchagua** takes in a trail of local vineyards as well as the world-class **Museo de Colchagua**, with historical regional and

---

AFTERSHOCKS

Central Chile was devastated by one of the most powerful **earthquakes** in recorded history when an 8.8-magnitude quake struck off its coast on February 27, 2010, triggering a powerful Pacific-wide **tsunami**. The earthquake cost 521 lives, injured 12,000 and left more than 800,000 people homeless. Concepción, 115km southeast of the epicentre, was hardest hit, with looting and violence bringing further chaos to the city. The cities of Curicó, Talca and Chillán also suffered severe damage, while the tsunami washed away parts of the coastal towns of Constitución, Talcahuano, Pichilemu and Iloca. The cities of Valparaíso and Santiago sustained some, albeit comparatively small, damage.

Roads and bridges were repaired soon after the earthquake, and in the ensuing months and years the region has picked itself up and rebuilt with heroic determination. Note however that many of the region's century-old adobe homes and haciendas, particularly those in the Colchagua Valley, are lost forever or have expensive and lengthy renovations ahead of them.

5

international artefacts, while if you continue to the coast, you'll get to the hip, budget seaside town of **Pichilemu**, popular with surfers.

San Fernando

Surrounded by low, rippling hills washed golden in the sunlight, **SAN FERNANDO**, some 55km south of Rancagua, is a busy little agricultural town that makes for a pleasant amble along its streets. The main commercial artery is Manuel Rodríguez, which, on the corner with Valdivia, has the huge nineteenth-century **Iglesia de San Francisco**, a Neo-Gothic church with a 32m-high tower, which took quite a blow in the 2010 earthquake and is in urgent need of repair. There is a similar monument, the **Capilla San Juan de Dios**, eight blocks north, on the corner of Negrete and Manso de Velasco. The verdant Plaza de Armas is surrounded by handsome colonial buildings, with the cavernous nineteenth-century **Parroquia San Fernando Rey** church on its southeastern corner.

Museo Casa Patronal de Lircunlauta

Manso de Velasco and Jiménez • Tues–Fri 9am–1pm & 3–7pm, Sat & Sun 10am–1pm & 4–6pm • CH$1000

The **Museo Casa Patronal de Lircunlauta** is the oldest building in San Fernando. It was originally the *casa patronal* of the eighteenth-century Hacienda Lircunlauta, whose owner donated 450 "blocks" of land to San Fernando when the town was founded in 1742. One of its more interesting exhibits is on the Uruguayan rugby team whose plane crashed into the high Andes, some 55km east of San Fernando, in October 1972. Their plight was made famous by the book and film *Alive*. Sixteen of the forty-five players on board survived the crash and endured 72 days in the mountains, eating the corpses of their teammates, until they were eventually rescued. The exhibit includes photos of the survivors and the local huaso who helped rescue them.

ARRIVAL AND DEPARTURE

SAN FERNANDO

By bus The main bus terminal (☎72 713912) is on Av Manso de Velasco and Rancagua.

Destinations Angol (1 daily; 7hr); Chillán (6 daily; 3hr); Concepción (4 daily; 4hr 30min); Curicó (every 30min; 50min); Los Angeles (9 daily; 4hr 30min); Pichilemu (every 30min; 2hr 50min); Puerto Montt (5 daily; 12hr); Rancagua (every 15min; 50min); Santa Cruz (every 15min; 50min); Santiago (every 15min; 2hr); Talca (9 daily; 1hr 30min);

Temuco (11 daily; 7hr) Termas del Flaco (Nov–Easter 3 daily; 2hr 30min); Valdivia (4 daily; 9hr).

By train The train station is three blocks south of the bus terminal at Quechereguas s/n (☎600 585 5000).

Destinations Chillán (3 daily; 3hr 10min); Curicó (5 daily; 30min); Rancagua (5 daily; 30min); Santiago (5 daily; 1hr 30min); Talca (5 daily; 1hr 20min).

INFORMATION AND TOURS

Tourist information Manuel Rodríguez 742 (Mon–Thurs 10am–7pm, Fri 9am–2pm, Sat 10am–1pm; ☎72 957215, ⓦcapitaldecolchagua.cl). Staff speak English.

Andes Adventures ☎09 9630 1152,

ⓦandesadventures.cl. Offers fishing, trekking and horseriding trips in the Colchagua Valley as well as overnight excursions into the high Andes.

ACCOMMODATION

While hotels options are uninspiring in San Fernando itself, for those with their own transport, the Colchagua Valley's verdant charms can be soaked up at one of the rural guesthouses that lie right on its doorstep.

Hotel Marcano Manuel Rodríguez 968 ☎72 714759, ⓦhotelmarcano.cl. Popular with business travellers and just two blocks from the bus terminal, en-suite rooms are brightly coloured and have big TVs and pictures of Chilean rural scenes. <u>CH$25,700</u>

★ **Mapuyampay Hostal Gastronómico** Parcela 2, Huemul, 45km southeast of San Fernando ☎09 9327

2589, ⓦmapuyampay.cl. The rural retreat and cooking school of Ruth Van Waerebeek, the Belgian-born executive chef of Concha y Toro winery, is a real foodie find. Spacious guest rooms are set within landscaped gardens and tastefully accented with tribal furnishings. Gourmet meals are prepared by Ruth and her husband Vicente, using ingredients plucked straight from the garden. Meals and

cooking classes extra. Open Oct–April. CH$48,000
Posada Curali Curali 130 ☎ 72 713445, ☜ posada
curali.cl. A decent budget option, whose eight musty,
canary-yellow rooms have immense en suites and are set
around a pretty, vine-covered patio. Staff are warm and
welcoming. CH$28,000

★ **Tumunan Lodge** Las Peñas, 27km southeast of
San Fernando ☎ 09 9630 1152, ☜ tumunanlodge.com.

A destination in itself, this British–Chilean run lodge in the
foothills of the Andes is surrounded by dazzling scenery,
with a series of trails leading into the mountains. There are
just four luxurious en-suite rooms, and guests socialize
wine-in-hand by the cosy fireplace. Attentive service, an
inviting pool, wood-fired hot tub, sumptuous home-
cooked meals and guided fly-fishing, horseriding and
hiking offered. CH$59,000

EATING AND DRINKING

Arenpastycaf Chillán 557 ☎ 72 715314,
☜ arenpastycaf.cl. An international menu and good
buffet lunches (CH$3000) keep punters pouring into this
bright and breezy café-bar-restaurant. One glimpse of the
drinks menu, and you'll want to make a night of it. Mon–
Sat 10am–11.30pm.
Café Roma Manuel Rodríguez 815 ☎ 72 749100. With
its welcoming red-brick interior and a TV tuned to
telenovelas, this café is a good spot for a light meal,
sandwich, cake and freshly squeezed juice or coffee.
Lunches (CH$3400 set menu) are more substantial, with
meat, fish and pasta dishes. Daily 8am–10.30pm.

★ **Casa Silva** Hijuela 3, Casa Lotel A Angostura, 7km

north of San Fernando ☎ 09 6847 5786, ☜ casasilva.cl.
This winery restaurant is one of the Central Valley's top
dining experiences: feast on imaginative tapas, top-quality
beef (mains around CH$8000) or a five-course degustation
with matching wines (CH$50,000) while overlooking lush
vineyards and manicured polo fields. For those without
wheels, taxi pick-up from San Fernando is CH$9000 return.
Mon–Sat 12.30–3.30pm & 7.30–11.30pm.
Luciano Toscani Av O'Higgins 651B ☎ 72 584810. An
appealing trattoria decked out with photos and sketches of
vintage motorbikes. Tasty pizzas and pastas and a
reasonably priced set lunch (CH$3900) are on offer.
Mon–Sat 10am–2am; Sun 11am–7pm.

DIRECTORY

Banks There is a cluster of banks with ATMs on Manuel
Rodríguez and Av O'Higgins.
Car rental You can rent a car with Rental Autos at
O'Higgins 854 (☎ 72 716925).

Internet Access is available (along with a strong cup of
coffee) at *Cyber-Café Rigoletto*, Manuel Rodríguez 751
(CH$600 per hr).
Post office Av O'Higgins 545.

Termas del Flaco

Nov–Easter 6am–11pm • CH$2000 • Buses Amistad (☎ 72 513085) provides transport to the *termas*, with one daily departure from
Rancagua, three daily from San Fernando and one daily from Santiago. Buses Termatur and Cordillera also run services from San Fernando.
Note that all buses leave San Fernando between 3.30 and 4.30pm

Some 107km east of San Fernando, sitting high in the cordillera 1700m above sea
level, the **TERMAS DEL FLACO** are among the cheapest and consequently most-visited
thermal baths in the Central Valley. They're reached by a serpentine dirt road that
follows the Río Tinguiririca through a beautiful gorge, so narrow in parts that
carabineros allow traffic to go in only one direction at a time.

Bizarrely, traffic is only allowed up late in the day, between 4pm and midnight
(Mon–Sat), while traffic can start the trip down between 6am and 2pm (Mon–Sat);
Sunday is variable, so ask the *carabineros* in San Fernando (☎ 72 972319). Given the
awkwardness of these hours, you'll need to stay at the baths overnight if you visit
during the week.

The baths

The wild beauty of the cordillera and the feeling of remoteness and solitude are, upon
arriving, suddenly interrupted with the appearance of numerous shack-like, tin-roofed
houses – almost all of them *residenciales*, with little to distinguish one place from the
next, and most operating on a full-board basis – crowded around the thermal baths.
Nor are the actual baths themselves particularly attractive, consisting of several
rectangular concrete, open-air pools. The waters, however – which reach up to 57°C
(135°F) in some pools – are bliss. If you manage to get here midweek, when there are

5

no crowds (except during high season, Jan & Feb), you can lie back, close your eyes and just relax, without another soul around.

Around the termas

You'll find several short treks around the *termas*, including one that leads to a set of dinosaur footprints preserved in the rock. Many local guides offer horseriding trips, including Eugenio Mancilla (☏09 8987 4453).

ACCOMMODATION	TERMAS DEL FLACO
Hotel Cabaña Las Vegas Office at Cillero 34, Rancagua ☏72 222478, ⓦvegasdelflaco.cl. Guests at these comfortable and roomy wooden *cabañas* have access to a large dining room with floor-to-ceiling windows looking down to the valley and the hotel's own small thermal pool. The price includes all meals; minibus transfer from	Santiago or Rancagua is CH$15,000. **CH$110,000** **Posada Amistad** Next to the bus stop ☏72 817227, ⓔbuses_amistad@hotmail.com. Roll straight off the bus and into these small, basic rooms set around a garden patio. The *posada* ejoys a prime position overlooking the baths. Open Dec–Feb. **CH$40,000**

Santa Cruz and around

Forty-one kilometres west of San Fernando, the paved road running through the Colchagua Valley to the coast takes you past a trail of **wineries** (see box, opposite). The small, well-preserved town of **SANTA CRUZ**, 40km from San Fernando, sits in the heart of this renowned wine-making district and boasts the **Museo de Colchagua**, one of the best museums in the country.

Museo de Colchagua

Errázuriz 145 • Sept–Feb Tues–Sun 10am–7pm; March–Aug Tues–Sun 10am–6pm • CH$5000 • ☏72 821050, ⓦmuseocolchagua.cl

The private **Museo de Colchagua** is housed in a splendid, plum-coloured colonial hacienda. Owned by international arms dealer Carlos Cardoen (the so-called "king of cluster bombs"), it has a well-designed, extensive and eclectic collection, including fossils, a huge amount of amber, pre-Columbian pottery and jewellery, relics from the War of the Pacific and memorabilia from the Chilean Independence movement. Among the most evocative exhibits are the beautiful old saddles, carved wooden stirrups and silver spurs in the *huaso* display, as well as the multimedia exhibit on the 2010 rescue of "Los 33" (see p.159), complete with a reconstruction of their "refugio".

▲ ❶ & Hacienda El Huique (28km)

SANTA CRUZ

0 ___ 250
metres

● EATING AND DRINKING
La Casita de Barreales	1
Club Unión Social	2
Prape's	3

■ ACCOMMODATION
D'Vid	2
Hostal Casa Familia	1
Hotel Santa Cruz	3

Estadio Municipal

Museo Histórico de Colchagua

ⓘ Ruta del Vino Office

Bus Terminal

Mercado

San José del Carmen del Huique Museum

Closed for repairs until 2013 • ☏72 933083, 2 693 0171, ⓦwww.museoelhuique.cl

Twenty-four kilometres beyond Santa Cruz, along the road towards the coast, and 6km past the Los Errázuriz bridge, sits the superb **San José del Carmen del Huique Museum**. One of the Central Valley's loveliest haciendas, its history dates from the seventeenth century, in the colonial period, but the current *casa patronal* was built in the early years of independence, in 1829. Standing alongside, and entered through a huge doorway, is the **chapel**, sporting a 23m-high bell tower.

ARRIVAL AND INFORMATION

By bus The bus terminal is at Casanova 478 (☎ 72 822191). Destinations Pichilemu (every 30min; 1hr 50min); Rancagua (every 15min; 2hr); San Fernando (every 15min; 50min); Santiago (every 15min; 3hr).

By colectivo Yellow taxi *colectivos* depart from in front of the terminal for the 30min journey to San José del Carmen

SANTA CRUZ AND AROUND

del Huique Museum (CH$600).

Tourist office In the municipal building at Plaza de Armas 242 (Mon–Thurs 8.30am–6pm, Fri 8.30am–5pm; ☎ 72 821042, ⓦ municipalidadsantacruz.cl). In summer an information booth (daily 9am–9pm) operates out of the mini clock-tower at the Plaza de Armas.

ACCOMMODATION

★ **D'Vid** Alberto Edwards 205 ☎ 72 821269, ⓦ dvid.cl. This excellent nine-room B&B is one of the best places to stay in the area – and a relative bargain. The chic modern rooms, most of which are en suite, have incredibly comfy beds; there's also a small pool. **CH$25,000**

Hostal Casa Familia Los Pidenes 421 ☎ 72 825766, ⓦ hostalcasafamilia.cl. On a quiet residential street northeast of the plaza with neat but unremarkable rooms equipped with wi-fi and cable TV. The friendly owners serve a good breakfast with fruit and eggs. **CH$35,000**

LA RUTA DEL VINO DEL VALLE DE COLCHAGUA

The Valle de Colchagua lies in the heart of one of Chile's finest wine-making districts. Seven wineries in the area have formed an itinerary called **La Ruta del Vino del Valle de Colchagua**. Tours (half-day from CH$22,000, full-day with lunch from CH$47,000) run daily and include visits to two to three wineries with multilingual guides and the chance to sample wines at each. Lunch is taken in some of the best restaurants in the valley. Reservations must be made at least 24 hours in advance at the office at Plaza de Armas 298 in Santa Cruz (May–Aug Mon–Fri 9am–6pm, Sat 10am–2pm; Sept–April 9am–6pm, Sat & Sun 10am–6pm; ☎ 72 823199, ⓦ rutadelvino.cl). Tours can also include a visit to the Museo de Colchagua (see p.228). The best time to take the tour is in late March, when the wineries organize their own Fiesta de la Vendimia (grape-harvest festival). The following are some of the best wineries to visit independently:

Viña Casa Silva Hijuela 3, Casa Lotel A Angostura, 7km north of San Fernando ☎ 72 913117, ⓦ casasilva.cl. Founded in 1892, this picturesque vineyard has classic wine-tasting facilities, an exclusive hotel in a beautifully restored colonial building (CH$163,000), a polo pitch and a top-notch restaurant. Hour-long tours are offered five times daily (CH$16,000–22,000).

Viña Clos Apalta Ruta I-50 Camino San Fernando to Pichilemu Km36, Cunaquito ☎ 72 953350, ⓦ lapostolle.com. The titular tipple produced at Lapostolle's gravity-fed winery is organic and biodynamic. Standard one-hour tasting tours of the 445-acre estate are offered (CH$20,000) as well as visits with horseriding (CH$50,000) or lunch (CH$60,000). Four enchanting, luxurious cabins are nestled into the forested hillside above the vineyards in case you want to stay the night. **CH$250,000**

Viña Laura Hartwig Camino Barreales s/n ☎ 72 823179, ⓦ www.laurahartwig.cl. On the outskirts of Santa Cruz, this compact winery has 198 acres of vines dating from 1979. As well as tasting tours (CH$10,000–15,000), there's the option of sleeping among the grapevines at the *Hotel Terra Viña* or dining on first-rate Italian fare at the adjacent restaurant *Vino Bello*. **CH$89,000**

Viña Montes Parcela 15, Millahue de Apalta, Santa Cruz ☎ 72 817815, ⓦ monteswines.com. A tractor ride through the picturesque 23-year-old vineyard is included in the tours of Monte's Apalta estate 43km northeast of Santa Cruz. As well as standard 1hr tours (CH$12,000–30,000), they offer guided nature hikes and a lunch option (CH$27,000).

Viña MontGras Camino Isla de Yáquil s/n, Palmilla, ☎ 72 822845, ⓦ www.montgras.cl. This 494-acre bodega 12km west of Santa Cruz produces, among others, the rare Carmenère wine. It is well set up for visits, with vineyard tours (CH$6000–15,000), blind tastings, a harvest experience and a make-your-own-wine activity all on offer.

Viña Santa Helena Angostura s/n Km133 Sur ☎ 72 913081, ⓦ santahelena.cl. Set on 222 acres of vineyards 5km north of San Fernando. Daily tours are offered of their century-old cabernet sauvignon vineyard and cellar (CH$5000–25,000).

Viña Viu Manent Carretera del Vino Km37, Santa Cruz, ☎ 72 858751, ⓦ viumanent.cl. Just 7km east of Santa Cruz, a visit to this third-generation, family-owned winery includes a vintage carriage ride through the 370-acre estate (CH$14,000). Wine-making, and wine and food pairing workshops are also offered, and there is a gourmet restaurant if you're inspired to lunch among the grapes.

5

Hotel Santa Cruz Plaza de Armas 286 ☎72 209600, ⓦhotelsantacruzplaza.cl. On the edge of the Plaza de Armas sits this impressive hotel owned by Carlos Cardoen (see p.228) with a large and somewhat incongruous casino attached to it. There are two swimming pools, a spa with wine-based treatments and the top-class restaurant *Las Varietales*. **CH$165,000 (US$330)**

EATING AND DRINKING

La Casita de Barreales Camino Barreales s/n ☎72 824468, ⓦlacasitadebarreales.cl. If you're looking for spice in your life, head to this popular Peruvian restaurant on the edge of town. Seafood-centric dishes like *ceviche mixto* (CH$5800) are balanced by carb-and-carne classics like *lomo saltado* (beef strips with fries, rice and vegetables) for CH$6900. Tues–Sat 1–3.30pm & 8–11.30pm, Sun 1–3.30pm.

Club Unión Social Plaza de Armas 178 ☎72 822529, ⓦclubsocialsantacruz.cl. Chilean staples (CH$6000–7000) and more adventurous dishes like eel omelette (CH$6000) are served beneath a relaxing vine-covered terrace. Mon–Sat noon–11pm, Sun noon–9pm.

Prape's Errázuriz 319 ☎72 821158, ⓦsushiprapes.cl. This Japanese restaurant has pretty authentic food, including California rolls (from CH$3000), teriyaki salmon (CH$5500) and tempura ice cream (CH$2500). It's also a fine spot for an evening cocktail. Mon–Sat noon–3pm & 6pm–midnight.

Pichilemu

The bustling surfer town of **PICHILEMU** lies 87km west of Santa Cruz. Built around a wide, sandy bay at the foot of a steep hill, the town dates from the second half of the nineteenth century, when Agustín Ross Edwards set out to create a European-style seaside resort. Today Pichilemu wears the charming, melancholy air of a faded Victorian seaside town. From the seafront, a broad flight of steps sweeps up the hillside to the splendid **Parque Ross**, planted with century-old Phoenix palms and extravagant topiary.

On the edge of the park, jutting out over the hillside, the grand old **casino** – Chile's first but now functioning as a cultural centre – is perhaps the most evocative of Ross's legacies. In contrast, Pichilemu's central streets are crammed with snack bars and *schoperías* catering to the crowds of young surfers who come to ride the waves – among the best in all of Chile.

ARRIVAL AND INFORMATION PICHILEMU

By bus Arriving in town by bus, you'll be dropped a couple of blocks north of the main street, Ortúzar, or at the terminal at the corner of Millaco and Los Alerces. Services are provided by Pullman del Sur (☎72 843008) and Buses Nilahue (☎72 841456).
Destinations Rancagua (every 30min: 3hr 30min); San Fernando (every 30min; 2hr 50min); Santiago (12 daily;

3hr 30min).
Tourist information There are two tourist information booths in town: one at Angel Gaete 365 and another at the end of the street on the Costanera (daily: March–Oct 9am–1pm & 2–5.30pm; Nov–Feb 8am–8pm; ☎72 841017, ⓦpichilemu.cl), but staff are often absent.

SURFING IN PICHILEMU

The most challenging surf is at Punta de Lobos, 6km south, where the **national surfing championships** are held. Look out for the sea lions in the beach's peculiar escarpments. Closer to town, surfers wade into the chilly sea (the ocean temperature rarely rises above 14°C) at La Puntilla, which juts out at the western end of the calmer main beach, Playa Las Terrazas. Just south of here lies Playa Infiernillo, with a faster wave for more experienced surfers. Pichilemu took a battering in the 2010 **tsunami** and earthquake, but bounced back faster than a surfer after a wipeout.

SURF SCHOOLS

Surf schools abound in Pichilemu, including Lobos del Pacífico (Av Costanera 720 ☎09 8930 7696, ⓦlobosdelpacifico.cl), which has two-hour classes for CH$12,000 and full-day surfboard and wetsuit hire for CH$8000. Viejos Lobos (Punta del Lobos ⓦsurfinchile.com) has similar rates and also offers day trips to beaches down the coast.

ACCOMMODATION

HOSTELS

Pichilemu Surf Hostal Eugenia Diaz Lira 167 ☎ 09 270 9555, ⓦ surfhostal.cl. Stylish private rooms with ocean views and heaters? Check. Chic restaurant right on the beach? You bet. Communal kitchen? Sure thing. Free bike rental? They've got it. Surf school? Of course. Beachfront hot tubs? Absolutely. What this Dutch-owned boutique hostel doesn't have is not worth mentioning. Dorm CH$9000, double CH$32,000

Surf Hostal Backpackers La Puntilla ☎ 09 7492 6848, ⓦ surfhostalbackpackers.cl. Just a few steps from one of the town's best surfing spots, backpackers chill out at this boat-shaped hostel (the town's former tea house), taking in 360 degree sea views from the kitchen, lounge and top-floor dormitory. Dorm CH$9000–$11,000

BEACH RESORTS AND CAMPING

Cabañas Buena Vista Cerro La Cruz ☎ 72 842488, ⓦ cabanasbuenavista.com. This eco-friendly resort has fully equipped cabins and the English-speaking staff can help organize Spanish, surf and kayak classes. CH$25,000

Camping La Caletilla Doctor Eugenio Suárez 905 ☎ 72 841010, ⓦ campingpichilemu.cl. The delightful *dueña* lavishes campers with every modern comfort: electricity, hot showers, barbecues and bike rental. And wait till you see the ocean views. CH$4000 per person

DunaMar Comercio s/n ☎ 72 841676, ⓦ dunamar.cl. Located 3km south of town, this modern beach resort boasts rooms with kitsch seaside paintings and balconies with great views. The breakfasts are fit for a surfer's appetite. CH$35,000

EATING AND DRINKING

La Casa de la Empanada Anibal Pinto 268. Even the street dogs drooling out front know *empanadas* don't come better than this: huge, deep-fried and prepared while you wait (choose from 36 varieties). CH$1200 each. Daily 11am–11pm.

Costa Luna Costanera 870, Infiernillo ☎ 72 842905. A swish setting for a sunset cocktail, this oceanfront restaurant has live music most nights and decor worthy of an interior-design magazine. Seafood mains (CH$8200) are

satisfying, but the main draw here is the view. March–Nov Fri & Sat lunch & dinner, Sun lunch; Dec–Feb daily lunch & dinner.

La Gloria JJ Prieto 980 ☎ 72 841052. Located ten blocks south of the seafront, this popular restaurant is worth the walk for its excellent and inexpensive seafood, including tasty *machas a la parmesana* (CH$6000) and dressed crab. Daily 10am–10pm.

NIGHTLIFE AND ENTERTAINMENT

Waitara Av Costanera 1039 ☎ 72 843004. The party starts late at this massive beachside club, where reggaeton and drum'n'bass dominate the dance floor. The

terrace, meanwhile, is a breezy place to sink a beer. Entry CH$3000 (women free before 12.30am). Fri & Sat 10pm–5am.

The Mataquito Valley

The Teno and Lontué rivers converge to form the broad Río Mataquito, which meanders west through Chilean wine country towards the Pacific. The town of **CURICÓ** (54km south of San Fernando) sits in the Mataquito Valley and makes a convenient place to break your journey. **Curicó** aside, the main attractions of the Mataquito Valley are the wineries (see box, p.232), the Lago Vichuquén, near the coast, and the Siete Tazas waterfalls, southeast towards the mountains.

Curicó

Bustling little Curicó, founded in 1743, is the only town of any significance in the Mataquito Valley. An agro-industrial centre servicing the surrounding vineyards, it suffered badly in the 2010 earthquake but a construction boom is currently under way. While Curicó has little to hold your interest for more than a few hours, it is the gateway for excursions to both nearby wineries and Parque Nacional Radal Siete Tazas.

Plaza de Armas

Curicó is built around one of the most beautiful central **plazas** in Chile, luxuriantly planted with sixty giant Canary Island palms. Standing in their shade, on the northern

5

Tourist information

■ ACCOMMODATION		● EATING	
Hotel Comercio	1	La Casa de la Esquina	2
Hotel Prat	3	Whay Hau	1
Hotel Raices	2		

side of the square, is a highly ornate, dark-green wrought-iron **bandstand**, constructed in a New Orleans style in 1904, while close by an elaborate fountain features a cast-iron replica of *The Three Graces*. In contrast to these rather fanciful civic commissions, the memorial to **Toqui Lautaro** – the Mapuche chief at whose hands Spanish conquistador Pedro de Valdivia came to a grisly end – is a raw and powerful work, carved out of an ancient tree trunk.

Standing on the northwest corner of the square, the **Iglesia La Matriz** makes for a curious sight, its grand Neoclassical facade giving way to a spacious and modern brick interior.

Cerro Carlos Condell

You can also climb **Cerro Carlos Condell**, the little hill on the eastern edge of town, and survey the scene from its 99m-high summit or take a dip in its public swimming pool (Dec–Feb daily 10am–8pm; CH$2000).

ARRIVAL AND DEPARTURE
CURICÓ

By bus Curicó's main bus terminal (☎75 558118) is at Maipú and Prat, about four blocks west and one block north of the Plaza de Armas. Tur Bus (☎75 312115) has long-distance services and is inconveniently located a good 20min walk southeast of the Plaza at Manso de Velasco and Castellon, while Linea Azul (☎75 227017) is half a block north of Tur Bus on Manso de Velasco.

Destinations Chillán (16 daily; 2hr 50min); Puerto Montt

(2 daily; 11hr 30min); San Fernando (every 30min; 50min); Santiago (every 30min; 2hr 30min); Talca (every 15min; 1hr 15min); Vichuquén (2 daily; 2hr 30min).

By train The station (☎600 585 5000) is at Maipú 697, opposite the bus terminal.

Destinations Chillán (3 daily; 2hr 35min); Rancagua (5 daily; 1hr 5min); San Fernando (5 daily; 30min); Santiago (5 daily; 2hr); Talca (5 daily; 50min).

INFORMATION AND TOURS

Tourist information Level 2, Manso de Velasco 744 (☎75 543026, ✉turismo@curico.cl). The under-resourced tourist office is at the base of Cerro Carlos Condell in the Corporación Cultural building.

Vive Maule Office 1, Carmen 747, ☎75 316078, 🌐vivemaule.cl. Offers fly-fishing, rafting, cycling, trekking and horseriding excursions in the Mataquito Valley, with experienced bilingual guides.

WINE TOURS AROUND CURICÓ

While you're in Curicó, it's worth making the easy excursion 5km south to the **winery** of Miguel Torres (daily Nov–April 9am–7pm; May–Oct 10am–5pm; ☎75 564121, 🌐www.migueltorres.cl; 45min tours CH$3000 without tasting, CH$8000 with tastings), the innovative Spanish vintner who revolutionized Chile's wine industry in the 1980s. The superb *Restaurant Viña Torres* (Mon–Thurs, Sat & Sun 12.30–3.30pm, Fri 12.30–3.30pm & 8.30–11pm) serves four-course lunch menus for CH$14,000 or CH$21,900 with wine, and there is a guesthouse with a pool overlooking the vineyards (CH$60,000). To get here, take a bus heading to Molina (every 10min) and ask to be let off outside the *bodega*, which is right next to the Panamericana.

Other wine tours are arranged by **Ruta del Vino Valles de Curicó**, which has an office (Mon–Fri 9am–2pm & 3.30–7pm; ☎75 328972, 🌐rutadelvinocurico.cl) in *Hotel Raices* (see p.233). Prices start from CH$63,500, including lunch and transport and a visit to two wineries. Over the third weekend in March, a **wine festival** takes place in **Curicó's Plaza de Armas**, and is a celebration of the grape harvest, complete with dances and beauty pageants.

ACCOMMODATION

Hosteria Los Queñes Camino Los Queñes s/n, 40km east of Curicó ☎09 6240 5164, ⓦhosterialosquenes.cl; direct buses from Curicó (5–8 daily; 1hr) leave from the bus station with Buses San Cristobal (☎75 321512). When the urge hits to flee town, this American–Chilean -run lodge offers a comfortable way to experience the great outdoors, with a restaurant, bar, pool and hot tub. Rafting, kayaking and other outdoor activities organized. **CH$36,000**

Hotel Comercio Yungay 730 ☎75 201600,

ⓦhotelcomercio.cl. The heated indoor pool and attractive "superior class" rooms with flat-screen TVs overlooking it are the main draws, although the standard en suites are also decent. **CH$52,000**

Hotel Raices Carmen 727 ☎75 543440, ⓦhotelraices.cl. The best place to stay and eat in town is this slick modern hotel with cream and white en suites, as well as a large lounge area complete with palm-fringed garden, giant fireplace, bar, café and restaurant. The gourmet set lunches are not to be missed (CH$5900). **CH$64,000**

EATING

La Casa de la Esquina Isabel la Católica 392 ☎75 310767. Spanish bullfighting posters adorn the walls, but the menu is a journey through the entire Mediterranean, from Greek salad to pasta to seafood paella (mains CH$5000–6000). Mon–Sat 11.30am–3.30pm &

7.30pm–midnight.

Whay Hau Yungay 853 ☎75 326526. This restaurant serves reliable Cantonese fare – fried rice, noodles and stir fries (CH$3000) – in a formal dining room with mini chandeliers. Daily noon–midnight.

DIRECTORY

Banks and exchange There are several ATMs on Estado, near the Plaza.

Car rental For car rental, try Rent a Car Curicó, Manso de Velasco 520 (☎75 312297).

Internet Centro de Llamadstets Camilo, Henrique 414 (CH$400 per hr).

Post office Carmen 556 (Mon–Fri 9am–6pm, Sat 9am–12.30pm).

Vichuquén and around

West of Curicó, a scenic road follows the northern bank of the Río Mataquito through the fertile river valley. Eighty-five kilometres along the road, just beyond Hualañé village, take the right fork and follow the signs for a further 25km along a dirt road to tiny **VICHUQUÉN**, one of the best-preserved villages in the Central Valley. Most of the brightly painted adobe houses date from the mid-nineteenth century, but Vichuquén's history goes back much further: there was a settlement here long before the arrival of the Spaniards, and it was chosen by the Inca as a site for one of their *mitimaes* – agricultural colonies populated by Quechua farmers brought down from Peru. You'll find relics of the Inca occupation – and a three-thousand-year-old mummy – in the **Museo Colonial**, on Calle Rodríguez (daily 10.30am–1.30pm & 4–6pm; CH$550).

Llico

Just beyond Hualañé village, a left fork in the road's junction leads to nearby **LLICO**, a rugged little seaside town perched on the edge of an exposed sandy beach whose turbulent waves attract many surfers – during January and February numerous surf tournaments bring a buzz to this usually quiet beach.

Lago Vichuquén

Four kilometres beyond Vichuquén you'll reach the southern tip of **Lago Vichuquén**, a long, narrow lake enclosed by deep-green, pine-covered hills. Considerably more upmarket than Lago Rapel, this is a popular holiday destination with Santiago's upper crust, whose beautiful villas line the lakeshore.

Laguna Torca

April–Nov 8.30am–6pm; Dec–March 8.30am–8pm • CH$3500 • ☎75 400269

Beyond the northern tip of Lago Vichuquen, the road comes to a junction. The right fork takes you across the rickety Puente de Llico to **RESERVA NACIONAL LAGUNA**

5

TORCA, a marshy man-made lake a couple of kilometres away, preserved as a breeding sanctuary for 106 species of birds, including hundreds of black-necked swans.

ARRIVAL AND INFORMATION
VICHUQUÉN AND AROUND

By bus There are two buses daily to Vichuquén from Curicó (2hr 30min), and four daily to Llico (2hr 30min), with Buses Diaz (☎75 311905) and Buses Bravo (☎75 312193); the Llico services pass by the Conaf office at Laguna Torca.

Tourist information There's a Conaf office just beyond the Puente de Llico bridge, hiding behind the large house with the veranda.

ACCOMMODATION AND EATING

LLICO

Residencial Miramar Carrera Pinto 48 ☎09 9595 2279, ✉hosteria.miramar@gmail.com. The en-suite rooms are a bit cramped, but they have balconies and sea views; there's also a good seafood restaurant here (mains CH$4500). CH$24,000

LAGO VICHUQUÉN

Camping Vichuquén Just beyond Aquelarre ☎09 9991 8039, ⊚campingvichuquen.cl. This family-friendly campground rents out boats and kayaks and also organizes biking and hiking excursions, and night-time activities. It has a laundry, bakery and mini-market. CH$5000 per person

Marina Vichuquén On the southern shore of Lago Vichuquén, in the village of Aquelarre ☎75 400265, ⊚marinavichuquen.cl. You'll find good food and accommodation at this hotel, with smart, spacious rooms with lots of natural light, as well as excellent watersports facilities and horseriding (all available for non-guests, too). CH$59,500

LAGUNA TORCA

Camping Laguna Torca Turn right immediately after the Puente de Llico, then first left ☎75 310231. Nestled in a eucalyptus grove, this camping area has drinking water, hot showers and electricity. CH$10,000 per site

Parque Nacional Radal Siete Tazas

April–Nov 8.30am–5.30pm; Dec–March 8.30am–8pm • CH$4000 • ☎75 310231

Of all the natural phenomena in Chile, the **Siete Tazas**, 71km southeast of Curicó, must be one of the most extraordinary. In the depths of the native forest, a crystal-clear mountain river drops down a series of seven waterfalls, each of which has carved a sparkling *taza* ("teacup") out of the rock. The falls are inside **PARQUE NACIONAL RADAL SIETE TAZAS**, reached by a poor dirt road from the village of Molina, 18km south of Curicó – be sure to fill up with petrol there. Though busy on summer weekends, this park is practically empty the rest of the year. Also within the reserve are forests, several hiking trails and the **Velo de Novia** ("Bride's Veil"), a 50m waterfall spilling out of a narrow gorge. For keen hikers, it's also possible to trek from Siete Tazas to Reserva Nacional Altos del Lircay (see p.237), but you'll need to hire a local guide.

ARRIVAL AND INFORMATION
PARQUE NACIONAL RADAL SIETE TAZAS

By bus In Jan and Feb you can get to the Siete Tazas on public transport from Molina, 18km south of Curicó, with Buses Hernández and Buses Radal (12 daily; 2hr 30min).
Tourist information Conaf has a small hut on the road

towards the Siete Tazas, but for more information you need to go to the administrative office at the Parque Inglés sector of the park, 9km further east (daily: Dec–Feb 8.30am–8pm; March–Nov 8.30am–5.30pm).

ACCOMMODATION

Camping Los Robles and Camping Rocas Basálticas Parque Inglés ☎71 228029. Conaf operates two popular campsites, both without electricity, although Los Robles campers can enjoy a hot shower. Los Robles CH$8000 per site, Rocas Basálticas CH$1500 per person
Hostería Flor de Canela Parque Inglés ☎75 491613. This guesthouse near the administrative office offers adequate but small and draughty rooms with either private

or shared facilities. A restaurant serves simple meals (mains CH$3000) and breakfast for CH$2,000. CH$25,000
Valle de Las Catas Halfway between Parque Inglés and the Siete Tazas, close to the Puente de Frutillar ☎09 9168 7820, ⊚www.sietetazas.cl. For swimming, horse rides and accommodation ranging from camping to cabins, try this private ranch inside the park. Camping CH$10,000 per site, cabin CH$40,000

Talca

TALCA is mainly used as a jumping-off point for several rewarding excursions spread along the valley of the **Río Maule** (see p.235). The city boasts its fair share of services and commercial activity, mostly centred on the main shopping street, **1 Sur**, with a pedestrianized section between 3 Oriente and 6 Oriente. Away from the frantic bustle of this thoroughfare, however, the rest of Talca seems to move at a snail's pace, not least the tranquil **Plaza de Armas**, shaded by graceful bougainvilleas, jacarandas and magnolias. Half-hidden beneath their foliage is a handsome 1904 iron bandstand.

The Cathedral

Northwest corner of Plaza de Armas • 10am–12.30pm & 5–7pm

The Neo-Gothic **Cathedral**, built in 1954, and restored in 2011 following earthquake damage, is pale grey with a long, thin spire and series of turrets running along each side. It's worth popping inside to look at the delicately coloured stained-glass Belgian windows and the sombre main altar.

Museo O'Higginiano

1 Norte and 2 Oriente • Closed for repairs at time of writing

One block east of the cathedral, the **Museo O'Higginiano** occupies a handsome colonial house that hosted some of the most important developments of the independence movement. It was here that Bernardo O'Higgins, future "Liberator" of Chile, lived as a child; where the Carrera brothers established the first Junta de Gobierno in 1813; and where in 1818, O'Higgins signed Chile's declaration of independence.

ARRIVAL AND DEPARTURE   TALCA

By bus Most buses pull in at the terminal (☎ 71 203992) on 2 Sur and 12 Oriente, ten blocks east of the Plaza de Armas; Tur Bus uses its own terminal a couple of blocks to the south. To get into the centre, take any *colectivo* or *micro* along 2 Sur (and to get back to the terminals, along 1 Norte).
Destinations Chanco (3 daily; 3hr); Chillán (8 daily; 2hr 30min); Concepción (every hour; 3hr 30min); Constitución (summer every 30min; winter 7 daily; 2hr 20min); Curanipe (summer 8 daily; winter 4 daily; 2hr 45min); Los Angeles (10 daily; 3hr 45min); Pelluhue (summer 8 daily; winter 4 daily; 2hr 30min); Puerto Montt (8 daily; 8hr 30min); Rancagua (every 30min; 2hr); San Fernando (every 30min; 1hr 30min); San Javier (every 20min; 30min); Santiago (every 20min; 3hr 30min); Temuco (12 daily; 5hr 30min); Vilches Alto (summer: 9 daily; winter 4 daily; 2hr); Villa Alegre (every 30min; 1hr).

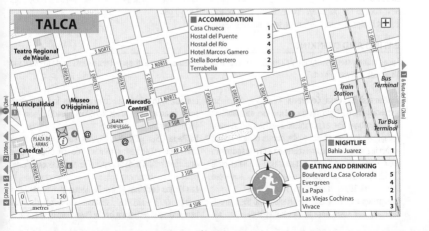

TALCA

■ ACCOMMODATION	
Casa Chueca	1
Hostal del Puente	5
Hostal del Río	4
Hotel Marcos Gamero	6
Stella Bordestero	2
Terrabella	3

■ NIGHTLIFE	
Bahia Juarez	1

● EATING AND DRINKING	
Boulevard La Casa Colorada	5
Evergreen	4
La Papa	2
Las Viejas Cochinas	1
Vivace	3

5

By train The train station (☎600 585 5000) is at 11 Oriente 1150.
Destinations Chillán (3 daily; 1hr 45min); Constitución (2 daily; 3hr 30min); Curicó (5 daily; 45min); Rancagua (5 daily; 1hr 50min); San Fernando (5 daily; 1hr 20min); Santiago (7 daily; 2hr 45min).

INFORMATION AND TOURS

TOURIST INFORMATION
Sernatur 1 Oriente 1150 (Mon–Thurs 8.30am–5.30pm, Fri 8.30am–4.30pm; Dec–Feb Sat 10am–1pm; ☎71 233669, ✉infomaule@sernatur.cl). The extremely helpful Sernatur office is on the Plaza.
Conaf 2 Poniente and 3 Sur (☎71 228029).

TOUR OPERATORS
Turismo El Caminante ☎71 197 0097, ⓦtrekkingchile .com. A great general adventure tour operator.

Maule Sorprendente ☎09 666 88640, ⓦmaulesorprendente.cl. Offers day trips to the coast, including the Sahara-like Dunas de Putú sand dunes.
Costa y Cumbre Tours ☎09 9943 5766, ⓦcostaycumbretours.cl. Offers both coastal and mountain tours with a trilingual guide, including multi-day trekking trips and day excursions to the little-visited Arco Iris waterfalls.

ACCOMMODATION

★ **Casa Chueca** 4km down the road to Las Rastras ☎71 197 0096 or 09 9419 0625, ⓦtrekkingchile.com. This German–Austrian guesthouse/hostel is well worth the detour. Surrounded by banana and palm trees, the "Crooked House" offers an abundance of services, amenities and tours, including a pool, intensive Spanish lessons and a climbing wall. It's closed June–Aug. To get here, phone ahead and then catch the Taxutal "A" bus on 13 Oriente to the *El Toro Bayo* restaurant, an old colonial building at the end of the route, where you'll be picked up. The knowledgeable owners, who also run the tour company Turismo El Caminante (see p.236), also have a refuge (**CH$9000** per person) in the beautiful Melado Valley. Dorm **CH$9,000**, double **CH$19,000**
Hostal del Puente 1 Sur 407 ☎71 220930, ⓦhostaldelpuente.cl. In a quiet spot next to the river, this welcoming place has en-suite rooms set around a patio and attractive gardens. Bike rental available. **CH$28,000**
Hostal del Río 1 Sur 411 ☎71 510218, ⓦhostaldelrio.cl. Next door to the *Hostal del Puente*, this is a reasonable budget choice. The small rooms are set around a large car park and have modern private baths and cable TV. **CH$24,000**
Hotel Marcos Gamero 1 Oriente 1070 ☎71 223388, ⓦmarcosgamero.cl. While the en suites are fairly standard for this price range, the eclectic collection of aged record players, etchings and old irons strewn about the place give it a certain charm. **CH$54,000**
Stella Bordestero 4 Poniente 1183 ☎71 236545, ⓦturismostella.cl. A tranquil complex with eight timber cabins set in landscaped gardens with a jellybean-shaped pool. For those on a tight budget, there are also five rooms with shared bath, kitchen and a lounge area with computer. Excellent value. **CH$25,000**
Terrabella 1 Sur 641 ☎71 226555, ✉terrabella @hotel.tie.cl. Just half a block from the plaza, the best hotel in town has 21 newly refurbished rooms, most of which overlook a serene leafy garden with a sparkling swimming pool. There's also a restaurant (no charge for room service), computers for guest use and friendly staff. **CH$50,000**

EATING AND DRINKING

Talca's culinary scene is surprisingly varied. The cheapest lunchtime menus are at the small restaurants inside the Mercado Municipal (enter via 1 Norte).

Boulevard La Casa Colorada Av 2 Sur 1014. Six restaurants walked into a patio: a Japanese, an Arabic, an Italian, an Argentine, a Chilean and a seafood. Talca's latest culinary hit may sound like a joke, but it's genius: friends gather in the informal central courtyard and mix and match their orders from different restaurants. The falafel plate (CH$2990) is particularly authentic. Mon–Wed 9.30am–11.30pm, Thurs–Sat 9.30am–3am.
Evergreen 2 Oriente 1135. Vegetarians and the vitamin-deficient seek sustenance at this buffet-style meat-free canteen, with a wide selection of dishes including chop suey, lasagne and salads (CH$1500 lunch). Mon–Fri 10am–4pm.
La Papa 1 Sur 1271 ☎71 613784. Ladies who *once* (do afternoon tea) and a few men who do too, catch up over cinnamon rolls (CH$550) and coffee at this popular café. Daily 10am–7pm.
Las Viejas Cochinas Rivera Poniente, 2km west of the plaza ☎71 221749, ⓦlasviejascochinas.cl. This barnyard-sized restaurant by the River Claro has become a

Talca institution on the strength of one dish: *pollo mariscal* (chicken in a seafood and brandy sauce). At CH$11,000, it feeds four. Be prepared for long waits at weekends. Mon–Sat noon–midnight.
Vivace 2 Sur 1659 ☎71 232350, ⓦ restaurantvivace.cl.

Delicious home-made pastas (CH$5000–7000) and grilled meats go down a treat with something off the classy, Maule Valley-centric wine list. Mon–Sat 11.30am–3.30pm & 7pm–midnight, Sun 11.30am–3.30pm.

NIGHTLIFE AND ENTERTAINMENT

Bahia Juarez 1 Poniente 1240 ☎71 686373, ⓦ bahiajuarez.cl. You'll find plenty of nocturnal action at this restaurant, pub, karaoke bar, nightclub and lounge complex. There's food and drink discounts before 10pm (go for the fajitas and tequila cocktails). After midnight, the CH$5000 entrance fee is redeemable against the bar or

restaurant. Mon–Fri 5pm–late, Sat 8pm–5am.
Teatro Regional de Maule 1 Oriente 1484 ☎71 340591, ⓦ teatroregional.cl. A meeting point for Talquino culture vultures, this modern theatre boasts a steady and varied programme of live music, theatre, dance and children's shows.

DIRECTORY

Airlines LAN 3 Oriente 1179 (☎71 226748).
Banks and exchange You can change money at Casa de Cambio Marcelo Cancino at 1 Sur 898, Oficina 15, and several ATMs on 1 Sur, just east of the plaza.
Car rental You can rent a car from Rent a Car Rosselot at San Miguel and Varoli (☎71 247979, ⓦ rosselot.cl).

Internet For internet access head to Zona Express Internet, 1 Sur 1064 (CH$500 per hr), or Cibertel, 2 Oriente 1112 (CH$550 per hr).
Post office 1 Oriente 1150 (Mon–Fri 9am–6pm, Sat 9am–noon).

The Maule Valley

The **Río Maule** flows into the sea almost 75km west of Talca at the industrial port of **Constitución**, south of which a coast road leads to the seaside villages of **Chanco**, **Pelluhue**, **Curanipe** and **Buchupureo**. To the east of Talca, the river has been dammed, resulting in Lago Colbún. Just east of Talca, the **Villa Cultural Huilquilemu** is a handsome nineteenth-century hacienda, now a museum, closed at the time of writing following earthquake damage, while further east, high in the cordillera, the **Reserva Nacional Altos del Lircay** provides trails through dramatic mountain scenery. Further south, you'll find the neighbouring hot springs resorts of Panimávida and Quinamávida and, down on the valley floor, a proliferation of **vineyards**, many of them conveniently located between the town of **Villa Alegre** and village of **San Javier** on a route served by plenty of local buses from Talca.

Villa Cultural Huilquilemu

Camino San Clemente Km 7 • Closed for repairs until 2013 • ☎71 413641 • 15min bus ride from Talca on any *micro* heading to San Clemente

Ten kilometres along the San Clemente Highway, on the paved road that heads east out of Talca towards the Argentinian border, is **VILLA CULTURAL HUILQUILEMU**. A beautifully restored *casa patronal* built in 1850, it now functions as a museum but is currently closed for restoration following earthquake damage. Inside, three long rooms off a series of colonnaded courtyards are devoted to religious art, housing paintings, statues, cassocks, furniture and two vivid, life-sized tableaux carved out of wood depicting the Last Supper and the appearance of the Angel Gabriel to the Virgin Mary.

Reserva Nacional Altos del Lircay

Daily: March–Nov 8.30am–5pm; Dec–Feb 8.30am–7pm • CH$4000

As you continue east along the road to the Argentinian border, a left fork onto a poor dirt road some 30km on from Villa Huilquilemu leads 27km to the mountain village

5

RUTA DEL VINO VALLE DEL MAULE

The **Ruta del Vino Valle del Maule** includes four wineries which are open to the public, and visits can be arranged independently or through the Ruta del Vino Valle del Maule office at the *Hotel Casino* in Talca at Av Circunvalación Oriente 1055 (Mon–Fri 9am–6.30pm, Sat & Sun noon–7pm; ☎09 8157 9951, ⓦ valledelmaule.cl). While the office doesn't provide package tours or transport to the vineyards, staff can refer you to private Talca-based operators, who charge from CH$70,000 for full-day transport.

GETTING TO THE WINERIES

All these wineries are easy to visit on day-trips from Talca, either by taxi or on public transport down the Panamericana, into Villa Alegre, up to San Javier and back to Talca. Unless otherwise specified, all these wineries should be contacted in advance.

Viña Balduzzi Balmaceda 1189 in San Javier ☎73 322138, ⓦ balduzzi.cl. One of the best wineries to visit on your own, as you can drop in without a reservation for a 45min guided tour (CH$5000) of its *bodegas*. With 200 acres of vineyards and beautiful grounds featuring an old *casa patronal*, a chapel and a *parque centenario* full of 100-year-old trees, this is a very picturesque example of a Central Valley winery.

Viña Coral Victoria Camino San Clemente Km 11 ☎71 621404, ⓦ corralvictoria.cl. On the road east from Talca to San Clemente, this boutique winery has a small but perfectly formed 27 acres of vineyards and also offers horseriding. The meat-centric restaurant (daily 1–4pm) is good value.

Viña Gillmore Camino Constitución Km 20 in San Javier ☎73 197 5539, wtabonko.cl. This family-run winery is one of the oldest vineyards in Chile. Also known as Tabontinaja or Tabonko, it has a good set-up for tourists, with tours examining the ecology of its vineyards. There's also a guesthouse – rooms have Jacuzzis – and spa where you can indulge in a wine bath. Guesthouse CH$93,000

Viña Vía Wines Fundo La Esperanza s/n in San Rafael ☎08 429 1158, ⓦ www.viawines.com. North of Talca, covering 1300 acres, this is the flagship vineyard for the brand best known for its Oveja Negra (Black Sheep) variety. Two-hour tours start from CH$8500 and multi-course lunches are CH$13,000.

of **Vilches Alto** and from here to the entrance of the **RESERVA NACIONAL ALTOS DEL LIRCAY**, 2km beyond. This is an extremely beautiful part of the central cordillera, with a covering of ancient native forests and fantastic views onto surrounding mountain peaks and volcanoes streaked with snow. The road is difficult to pass in winter months, so the best time to visit is between October and May. The **hiking trails** here are among the best in the region. Close to the entrance, an **information centre** has displays on the park's flora and fauna and the area's indigenous inhabitants, whose traces survive in the **piedras tacitas** (bowls used for grinding corn) carved out of a flat rock face a few hundred metres away along a signed path.

The trail to Enladrillado

Of the various **trails** inside the reserve, the most popular is to a hilltop platform at 2300m known as **Enladrillado**, which New Agers and even some locals believe is a UFO landing pad. From the reserve entrance (get more detailed directions from the *guardaparque*), follow the steep track up the hillside for about 2.5km, then follow the signed turn-off, from where it's a stiff uphill walk of about five hours; count on an eight-hour round-trip. The views from the top are exhilarating, down to the canopy of native *coigües* and *lenga* forests covering the valley beneath, and across to the towering **Volcán Descabezado** and surrounding peaks. Up here you'll also find areas of exposed volcanic rock resembling giant crazy paving, giving the spot its name, which translates roughly as "brick paving".

The trail to Laguna del Alto

The hike from *Camping Antahuara* (see p.239) to **Laguna del Alto**, a lagoon inside a volcanic crater, is an eight hour round-trip, with great lookout spots along the way. If you want to explore further, try it on **horseback**: in Vilches Alto, contact don Eladio (☎09 9341 8064).

ARRIVAL AND INFORMATION

By bus Buses Vilches (☎71 243366) runs four daily buses up to Vilches Alto in winter (April–Dec) and nine in summer (Jan–March).

Tourist information The staff at *Refugio Don Galo*

RERSERVA NACIONAL ALTOS DEL LIRCAY

(see p.239) can help organize trips, including overnight stays, and have lots of information on hikes and excursions. Hiking maps for the park can be purchased in Talca (see pp.235–237) at Exploring Outdoor in the Mall Plaza Maule.

ACCOMMODATION AND EATING

There is one official campsite in the park, and a primitive spot with no facilities about 4km from the entrance. Because of wildfire dangers, no campfires are permitted. In Vilches Alto, 2km west of the park, you will find several places to stay and eat.

Camping Antahuara 500m from Conaf office inside the park ☎71 228029. Hot showers, well-maintained toilets and electricity ensure campers live it up at this Conaf-run campsite in the forest. There is a primitive campsite one hour further east in the park. **CH$2500** per person

Hostería de Vilches Camino Vilches Alto Km 22 ☎09 9826 7046. The eight delightful fully equipped cabins are

ringed by native forest; there's also a small movie theatre and restaurant and staff can arrange horseriding and fishing excursions. **CH$35,000**

Refugio Galo Hijuela R, Vilches Alto ☎2 196 0619. Here you'll find basic but decent digs, a restaurant with set lunches (CH$9500) and owners who are a good source of local information. They can organize guided horseriding, trekking and rappelling excursions. **CH$30,000**

Lago Colbún and around

Chile's largest artificial reservoir, **LAGO COLBÚN**, was created between 1980 and 1985 when the Río Maule was dammed as part of a huge hydroelectricity project, and it wasn't long before its shores, framed by undulating hills, were dotted with holiday chalets, wooden cabins and mini-markets. The town of Colbún is not actually on the lake, but just west of it. The lake's southern shore, where there are several campsites, can be a pain to get to – though two bridges span the lake, access to them is often barred by the hydroelectricity company, which means going back to the Panamericana and driving instead along the southern bank of the Río Maule. This route provides access to Colbún Alto, a small village on the southwest shore of the lake.

Termas de Panamávida

Day visit CH$10,000–15,000; accommodation 140,000 (US$289) · ☎73 211743, ⓦ termasdepanimavida.cl · Buses Villa Prat (☎2 376 1758) runs one service daily from Santiago (via Talca) to Termas de Panimávida

The Río Maule road also leads to a couple of neighbouring hot-springs resorts, 5km south of the town of Colbún. The first one you reach is the **TERMAS DE PANIMÁVIDA**, a nineteenth-century hacienda-style building built around numerous courtyards and patios. The gardens are immaculate but the rambling old building has rather gone to seed. It is, however, full of character, especially the distinctly Victorian-looking wing housing the long row of cubicles where guests soak in the thermal waters (not especially hot at 33°C/91°F), mud baths and steam rooms. Non-guests are free to visit for the day.

Termas de Quinamávida

Day visit CH$10,000–20,000; accommodation CH$137, 000 (US$283) · ☎73 627100, ⓦ quinamavida.cl

Five kilometres south of Termas de Panamávida, the **Termas de Quinamávida** is another labyrinthine hotel, this one attracting an elderly clientele and featuring a huge indoor thermal pool in addition to the usual *tinas*, mud baths, massage and Turkish baths. Non-guests are free to visit for the day.

Tricahue Parque

Around 25km east of Lago Colbún, at the confluence of the Maule and Armerillo rivers, is the village of Armerillo, close to the little-visited and remote **Tricahue Parque**,

5

filled with tree-covered mountains, lakes and the 2000m Picudo Peak. A great way to explore the area is by staying at *Refugio Tricahue* (see below).

ARRIVAL AND DEPARTURE
LAGO COLBÚN AND AROUND

LAGO COLBÚN

By car There are various approaches to Lago Colbún, stretching 40km from east to west. From Talca, drive east and carefully follow signs to stay on Ruta 115, a scenic mountain road to the northern shore of the lake.

By bus From Talca there are services with Interbus (☎71 613140) from the main terminal (10 daily; 1hr 10min).

TRICAHUE PARQUE

By bus Interbus runs six daily buses from Talca (1hr 30min).

ACCOMMODATION

LAGO COLBÚN

Cabañas Lago Colbún Ribera Norte ☎09 9895 6401, ⓦcabanaslagocolbun.cl. Set on the lake with head-on views of the Andes, these sheltered, fully equipped cabins in the woods sleep up to six people. There's a swimming pool and kayaks for rent. **CH$45,000**

Chez L'Habitant Camino Colbún Alto Km 10.5 ☎09 9132 4064, ⓦecoturismolagocolbun.cl. There are stunning lake views from the cabins and rooms at this eco-friendly lodge. The owner whips up home-cooked meals, and horseriding, kayaking and trekking excursions are offered should you want to work them off. Or simply chill out at the private beach or star-gaze while melting in the wood-fired hot tub. **CH$65,000**

Complejo Turístico Valshi Paso Pehuenche Km 58 ☎09 9221 8793, ⓦvalshi.cl. A relaxing complex with swimming pool, ping-pong tables and cabins that sleep up to 10 people. Reiki and reflexology treatments offered. Campers are also accommodated. Camping **CH$3000** per person, cabins **CH$20,000**

TRICAHUE PARQUE

Refugio Tricahue ⓦrefugio-tricahue.cl. This peaceful 12-bed hostel has a Finnish sauna and pool, and the welcoming owner organizes fishing trips, walks, bike tours, swimming in thermal pools and, in the winter, snowshoe hikes. The best room in the house has a private bathroom and a glass roof. Dorm **CH$6000**, double **CH$14,000**

San Javier and Villa Alegre

Twenty kilometres south of Talca is a massive iron bridge over the Río Maule, followed by the turn-off to **SAN JAVIER**, a bustling little town sitting in the heart of the Maule Valley's wine country. Its main interest lies in its proximity to two dozen local **vineyards** (see box, p.238) spread between and around San Javier and the nearby village of **Villa Alegre**, all of which are marked on a map distributed by Sernatur in Talca.

Nine kilometres further south South from San Javier, you approach **VILLA ALEGRE** through a stunning avenue of trees whose branches meet overhead to form a dense green canopy. A stroll down the village's main street, lined with fragrant orange trees, takes you past grand *casas patronales* in luxuriant grounds.

ACCOMMODATION
SAN JAVIER AND VILLA ALEGRE

Residencial Narvaez Cancha De Carreras 2365, San Javier ☎73 321203, ⓔcontacto@residencialnarvaez.cl. A good budget option in San Javier, this central hotel includes parking, cable TV, wi-fi and a restaurant. The cheapest rooms have shared bathroom. **CH$12,000**

Hotel Colonial Maule Cancha de Carreras s/n, Villa Alegre ☎73 381214, ⓦhotelcolonialmaule.com. For a peaceful place to stay in Villa Alegre, try this attractive old house with landscaped gardens, a swimming pool and restaurant. **CH$36,290**

Constitución and the coastal road

At the mouth of the Río Maule is the busy port of **CONSTITUCIÓN**. While it's now a popular holiday resort, the occasional foul stench of the local cellulose plant makes it unlikely you'll want to stay too long. Apart from the weird rock formations on the town's grey sand beaches, the main reason you might want to come here is to move on to the 60km stretch of quiet beaches and small fishing towns to the south.

Chanco

From Constitución, a paved road follows the coast to the little seaside resort of **Curanipe**, 80km south. You pass extensive pine plantations bordered by grey, empty beaches and sand dunes before reaching **CHANCO**, a tiny village populated by ageing farmers who transport their wheat, beans and potatoes to market on creaky, ox-drawn carts. Much of the village's colonial architecture was destroyed in the 2010 earthquake.

Reserva Nacional Federico Albert

March–Dec 8.30am–5.30pm; Jan & Feb 8.30am–7.30pm • CH$3500 • ☎ 73 551004

On the northern edge of Chanco, the **RESERVA NACIONAL FEDERICO ALBERT** is a dense pine and eucalyptus forest planted in the late nineteenth century in an attempt to hold back the advance of the coastal sand dunes – which by then had already usurped much valuable farmland. A 3km **path** skirts the edge of the reserve, leading to an enormous sandy **beach** with small kiosks, picnic tables and running water.

Pelluhue and Curanipe

The summer seaside resort and popular surfing destination of **PELLUHUE** (11km south of Chanco) is an undisciplined collection of houses strung around a long, curving black-sand beach. Though it's popular with backpackers and has cheaper accommodation, the town has an untidy, slightly ramshackle feel to it that doesn't encourage you to stay long; unless you're here to surf, you'd be better off 7km south in the prettier village of **CURANIPE**. With a backdrop of rolling hills, wheat fields and meadows, Curanipe's dark-sand **beach**, with colourful wooden fishing boats, is a lovely place to hang out, though that's just about all there is do here. Bring enough cash with you as there are no ATMs in these parts. A further 35km south of Curanipe, the mostly paved road arrives at the isolated surfer hangout of Buchupureo (see p.246).

ARRIVAL AND DEPARTURE
CONSTITUCIÓN AND THE COAST ROAD

CONSTITUCIÓN

By bus From Talca, Constitución is served by several buses daily with Buses Contimar and Pullman Bus. Buses pull in opposite the train station on the riverside, a few blocks northeast of the plaza.

By train Two daily trains run here from Talca (going to Talca, the right side of the train has the best views).

RERSERVA NACIONAL FEDERICO ALBERT

By bus Pullman del Sur goes to Chanco from Talca (3 daily;

3hr); Buses Amigo runs here from Constitución (6 daily; 1hr 30min).

PELLUHUE AND CURANIPE

By bus Interbus (☎71 613140) runs regular services from Talca to Pelluhue and Curanipe. Pullman del Sur has four daily services from Santiago to Curanipe via Talca. If you're coming from Constitución, change buses in Chanco.

ACCOMMODATION

CONSTITUCIÓN

Alonso de Ercilla Colo Colo 334 ☎41 222 7984, ⓦ www.hotelalonsodeercilla.cl. This modern hotel with warm wooden touches and friendly staff is a good mid-range choice. It's just one block from the main plaza. **CH$55,800**

Hostería Constitución Echeverría 460 ☎71 671450. A fairly smart place perched on the banks of the Maule; rooms have private baths, good river views and a decent restaurant with CH$5000 set lunches. **CH$25,000**

RERSERVA NACIONAL FEDERICO ALBERT

Camping Reserva Nacional Federico Albert 300 metres from park entrance ☎73 551004. This attractive camping area inside the wooded reserve has hot showers, drinking water and electricity. **CH$10,000** per site

Hostal Mohor Av Fuentealba 135 ☎09 9782 6956, ⓔ hostal.mohor@gmail.com. A rudimentary but clean hotel; all rooms have cable TV but only some have private bathroom. Breakfast included. **CH$20,000**

5

PELLUHUE AND CURANIPE

Cabañas Campomar Camino Pelluhue, Curanipe Km3 ☎73 541000, ⓦwww.cabanascampomar.cl. About 3km south of Curanipe, near the top of a steep hill, these log cabins sleep up to six and have great ocean views. Includes a pool, children's playground and parking. **CH$36,000**

Hostal de Piedra Condell 1606, Pelluhue ☎73 541115, ⓦhostaldepiedra.cl. Set on the seafront between Pelluhue and Curanipe, this eighteenth-century stone house has comfortable rooms, a salt-water pool and a restaurant. **CH$25,000**

Suhaila Spa & Resort Ruta MN 80 Km 22.5, 10km south of Curanipe ⓦluzdeluna-suhaila.cl. Three fully equipped cabins come decorated with Indian touches, with access to a wood-fired hot tub and private beach. In high season, massage and other therapies are offered and the German owners sometimes cook for guests. **CH$40,000**

Chillán and around

Lively Chillán is famous as the birthplace of Bernardo O'Higgins, the founding father of the republic, and is worth visiting for its vast **handicrafts market** and fascinating **Mexican murals**. Thanks to periodic earthquakes and regular Mapuche attacks, Chillán has repeatedly been rebuilt since being founded in 1550. Most of Chillán's present architecture dates from just after the 1939 earthquake.

Plaza Bernardo O'Higgins

The main square is **Plaza Bernardo O'Higgins**, dominated by a giant, 36m concrete cross commemorating the thirty thousand inhabitants who died in the 1939 earthquake, and the futuristic, earthquake-resistant **cathedral**, built between 1941 and 1961 in the form of nine tall arches.

Escuela México

O'Higgins 250 • Mon–Fri 10am–1pm & 3–6.30pm • Donation

A few blocks northwest of the Plaza, the **Escuela México**, a school built with money donated by the Mexican government following the 1939 disaster, looks out over leafy **Plaza de los Héroes de Iquique**. On Pablo Neruda's initiative, two renowned Mexican artists, David Alfaro Siqueiros and Xavier Guerrero, decorated the school's main staircase and library with fabulous murals depicting pivotal figures in Mexican and Chilean history. The Mexican images, entitled *Muerte al Invasor*, feature lots of barely clothed native heroes and evil-looking, heavily armed Europeans engaged in various acts of cruelty. The Chilean tableau is even more gruesome, dominated by the lacerated, bleeding body of the Mapuche *toqui*, Galvarino, and his bloodthirsty Spanish captors. The school allows visitors access to the murals in return for a small donation.

Feria de Chillán

Maipón and 5 de Abril • Mon–Sat 8am–8pm, Sun 8am–2pm

Five blocks south, filling Plaza de la Merced, the **Feria de Chillán** is an exuberant open-air market selling a vast range of fresh produce and *artesanía*, ranging from knitwear and leather items to jewellery, paintings and second-hand books. A souvenir-hunter's paradise, the market is especially lively on Saturdays, when it bulges out of the square and spreads into the surrounding streets.

Parque Monumental Bernardo O'Higgins

The **Parque Monumental Bernardo O'Higgins**, a short bus ride south along Avenida O'Higgins, is a handsomely landscaped park featuring a 60m wall covered with a badly faded mosaic depicting the life of the city's most famous son. In a small chapel nearby,

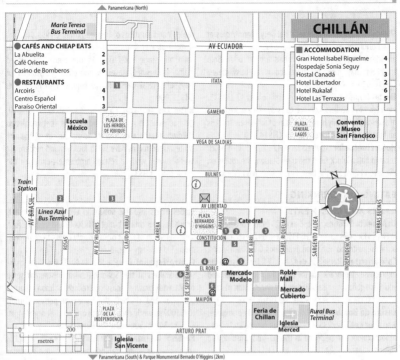

Panamericana (North)

CHILLÁN

CAFÉS AND CHEAP EATS
La Abuelita — 2
Café Oriente — 5
Casino de Bomberos — 6

RESTAURANTS
Arcoiris — 4
Centro Español — 1
Paraíso Oriental — 3

ACCOMMODATION
Gran Hotel Isabel Riquelme — 4
Hospedaje Sonia Seguy — 1
Hostal Canadá — 3
Hotel Libertador — 2
Hotel Rukalaf — 6
Hotel Las Terrazas — 5

Panamericana (South) & Parque Monumental Bernado O'Higgins (2km)

O'Higgins' mother, Isabel Riquelme, and his sister, Rosita, are both buried, not far from the site where Bernardo was born.

ARRIVAL AND DEPARTURE

CHILLÁN

By bus Most long-distance buses use the Terminal María Teresa at O'Higgins 010 (☎42 272149), on the northern edge of town. Línea Azul has its own terminal at Constitución 01, four blocks west of Plaza Bernardo O'Higgins (☎42 423835). Local and regional buses operate out of the Terminal Rural, Maipón 890, a few blocks southeast of the Plaza (☎42 423814).

Destinations Concepción (every 30min; 1hr 30min); Curicó (8 daily; 2hr 30min); Los Angeles (every half hour; 1hr

30min); Puerto Montt (8 daily; 9hr); Rancagua (8 daily; 4hr); San Fernando (5 daily; 3hr); Santiago (every 30min; 5hr); Talca (every hour; 2hr); Temuco (13 daily; 4hr).

By train The station is at Av Brasil and Av Libertad (☎600 585 5000), five blocks west of the Plaza.

Destinations Curicó (3 daily; 2hr 30min); Rancagua (3 daily; 3hr 35min); San Fernando (3 daily; 3hr); Santiago (3 daily; 4hr 30min); Talca (3 daily; 1hr 45min).

INFORMATION AND TOURS

TOURIST INFORMATION

Oficina de Turismo In the Municipalidad opposite the Plaza at 18 de Septiembre 590 (April–Dec Mon–Fri 8am–6pm; 18 de Septiembre Jan–March daily 8am–8pm; ☎42 433494).

Sernatur 8 de Septiembre 455 (Mon–Fri 8.30am–5.30pm; ☎42 223272, ✉infochillan@sernatur.cl).

TOUR OPERATORS

Albaour Constitución 691, 2nd floor (☎42 227392).

ACCOMMODATION

Gran Hotel Isabel Riquelme Constitución 576 ☎42 434400, ⊚www.hotelisabelriquelme.cl. This salmon-coloured hotel gazes proudly over the Plaza. While it is undoubtedly the grandest place in town, the en suites are a

little unexciting and overpriced. Its excellent restaurant serves innovative Chilean fare and is a popular local haunt. CH$69,000

Hospedaje Sonia Seguy Itata 288 ☎42 214879.

5

Slightly ramshackle and chaotic but very friendly digs at rock-bottom prices. Most rooms have TVs, shared facilities are clean and home-cooked meals are on offer. Solo travellers may have to share rooms at busy times. CH$10,000

Hostal Canadá Libertad 269, second floor ☎ 42 234515. Ideal for solo travellers, here you can stay in the spare rooms of a welcoming family home. The shared facilities are spotless and there's a roof terrace to relax on. CH$14,000

Hotel Libertador Libertad 85 ☎ 42 223255, ⊛ hlbo.cl. Located half a block from the train station, the rooms on the second floor are the best, but all have big bathrooms,

cable TV and paintings of European cities. CH$33,000

Hotel Rukalaf Arauco 740 ☎ 42 233366, ⊛ rukalaf.cl. Solid mid-range hotel right in the centre, frequented mainly by business travellers, and offering discounts for stays of several days. Has parking and room service. CH$32,900

Hotel Las Terrazas Constitución 664 ☎ 42 437000, ⊛ lasterrazas.cl. Excellent hotel split between two buildings that face each other across the street. The airy whitewashed rooms have swish facilities and modern art on the walls, while a relaxed ambience permeates the whole place. CH$32,000

EATING AND DRINKING

CAFÉS AND CHEAP EATS

La Abuelita Constitución 635 ☎ 42 231450. The best place in Chillán for cakes (around CH$1350) and coffee, served in an attractive *pastelería* with wood furnishings. Daily 9am–9pm.

Café Oriente El Roble 655 ☎ 42 430124. Look beyond the unprepossessing location on the edge of a shopping mall and you'll find good coffee, sandwiches and sweet Arabic pastries (CH$1000). Mon–Fri 9am–9pm, Sat 10am–3pm.

Casino de Bomberos El Roble and 18 de Septiembre, 2nd floor ☎ 42 222233. Cheap Chilean cuisine and plenty of local colour can be found at this no-frills, bustling fire station canteen. Set lunches are CH$1500. Mon–Fri 9am–midnight.

RESTAURANTS

Arcoíris El Roble 525 ☎ 42 227549. A rainbow sign

guides diners into this bohemian vegetarian restaurant, which has a lunchtime buffet (CH$3000) and fresh juices. A small selection of meat dishes kindly caters to carnivores. Mon–Sat 8.30am–4pm.

Centro Español Arauco 555 ☎ 42 321061. Penguin-suited waiters at this Spanish–Chilean restaurant serve paella with prawns, mussels, scallops, salmon, chorizo, pork ribs and chicken; the huge one-person portion (CH$5000) is easily enough for two. Mon–Sat noon–4pm & 7–11.30pm, Sun noon–3.30pm.

Paraíso Oriental Constitucion 715 ☎ 42 212296. Cough-medicine-pink tablecloths aside, this popular Chinese spot is good for generous portions of fried rice and noodles (CH$3500–8000), either eat in or take away. Daily 11.30am–midnight.

DIRECTORY

Banks and exchange There are several ATMs on Arauco and Constitución. To change travellers' cheques or cash, try Schüler Cambios at Constitución 550, office 15.

Car rental Larrañaga, 18 de Septiembre 870 (☎ 42 210112, ✉ contacto@larranaga.cl).

Hospital Herminda Martín Argentina and Francisco

Ramírez (☎ 42 212345).

Internet Planet, Arauco 683, 2nd floor (CH$600 per hr); Hi-Net Cyber Café, Arauco 760 (CH$500 per hr).

Post office The main *correo* is at Libertad 505 (Mon–Fri 8.30am–6.30pm, Sat 9am–12.45pm).

The Itata Valley

Lush and very beautiful, the broad **Itata Valley** is home to a string of tranquil coastal towns, including the idyllic surfing village of Buchupureo, 120km northwest of Chillán. En route, 50km northwest of Chillán, is the **naval museum** in the village of Ninhue. Meanwhile, the ski centre and hot-springs resort of **Nevados de Chillán** sits 80km east, high in the cordillera.

Nevados de Chillán

Ski season runs June–Oct • Ski pass CH$30,000 per day

The most famous and developed mountain resort south of Santiago is the **Nevados de Chillán**, an all-season tourist complex which includes one of the largest ski resorts in

Chile, 80km east of Chillán, nestled at the foot of the 3122m **Volcán Chillán**. Formerly known as the Termas de Chillán, it possesses three year-round open-air **thermal pool complexes** surrounded by glorious alpine scenery. The resort's **skiing** facilities include eight lifts and 25 runs, one of which is almost 13km, the longest in South America. Summer activities also abound, from hiking and horseriding to mountain biking and rock climbing. One ski lift also remains open in the summer for access to the Nevados Bike Park (⟡nevadosbikepark.cl; CH$10,000).

Valle de Aguas Calientes

An ideal one-day hike or horseriding trip from Nevados de Chillán is to the Valle de Aguas Calientes, where natural hot springs flow at the confluence of three rivers. The resort lies 8km uphill from the sprawling village of Valle Las Trancas.

Parque de Aguas Nevados de Chillán and around

Parque de Aguas Nevados de Chillán pools CH$6000; Valle Hermoso pools CH$4500; Hotel Nevados de Chillán pools CH$17,000

At the base of the Nevados de Chillán ski resort is the rustic Parque de Aguas Nevados de Chillán, with four hot sulphur pools; 2km downhill at the Valle Hermoso thermal complex, there are three outdoor pools. The two hot sulphur pools at the Hotel Nevados de Chillán (see p.245) are also open to the public.

ARRIVAL AND INFORMATION

NEVADOS DE CHILLÁN

By Bus Buses Nilahue has a service from Santiago to Valle Las Trancas (1 daily; 7hr). From Chillán's Terminal Rural, Rem Bus (☎42 229377) goes to Valle Las Trancas (7 daily; 1hr 50min). Note that the final 8km stretch from Valle Las Trancas up to the ski resort is a gravel road with only one public bus daily during winter and none outside the ski season. Private transfers along the 8km stretch cost from CH$14,000 one-way; hitchhiking is also common and easy in the winter. In the summer, Valle Las Trancas is a 15min drive from the ski slopes; in the winter after a lot of snow, those times can double.

By car If you're driving, note that a 4WD is necessary in winter.

Touristă information Camino Termas de Chillán Km 85 (☎42 206100, ⟡nevadosdechillan.com). Tourist info is available at the Nevados de Chillán ski centre.

ACCOMMODATION AND EATING

The most expensive accommodation can be found in the Nevados de Chillán resort itself, close to the slopes. Prices drop substantially as you move downhill towards the village of Valle Las Trancas, where most people stay and a glut of cabins, lodges, hostels and restaurants lines the road between kilometre 68 and 75. Rates vary dramatically throughout the year, with July the most expensive month.

LODGES, CABINS AND HOTELS

Cabañas Los Andes Camino Termas de Chillán Km 70.4 ☎42 1970071, ⟡cabanaslosandes.com. British–Brazilian-run cabins set in undulating, forested surrounds. In winter, the large café and bar is a good après ski hangout and in summer, the owners offer guided hiking excursions. **CH$50,000**

★ **Ecobox Andino** Camino Shangri-La Km 0.2, Valle Las Trancas ☎42 423134, ⟡ecoboxandino.cl. Four impeccably styled cabins made from recycled shipping containers are linked by raised wooden platforms and set within a magical ñirres forest. Plenty of natural light streams through the picture windows, which look onto snowcapped mountains, and the pool and hot tub are pure Zen. **CH$80,000 (US$160)**

Gran Hotel Termas de Chillán Nevados de Chillán resort ☎2 233 1313 in Santiago, ☎42 434200 in Chillan, ⟡termaschillan.cl. This imposing, five-star hotel is the plushest around, with spacious en suites in soothing colours, heated pools, restaurant, bar and casino. The state-of-the-art spa centre offers hot mud baths, facials, hydro-massages and a range of other treatments. **US$2600** per person for seven nights half board

★ **M.I. Lodge** Camino a Shangri-La s/n ☎09 932 17997, ⟡milodge.com. With its own observatory, climbing wall, skate ramp, swimming pool, hot tubs and exquisite French restaurant, the "Mission Impossible" lodge brings everything but the mountain right to your doorstep. Comfortable rooms with head-on volcano views, first-rate service and outings to the lodge's zip-line canopy adventure park arranged. Rates include dinner and breakfast. **CH$45,000**

Nevados de Chillán Nevados de Chillán resort ☎42 206105, ⟡nevadosdechillan.com. Owned by the same company that controls the ski centre, rates here include breakfast and dinner, ski passes and use of the hotel's thermal pools. Downstairs rooms are seriously dated, but those upstairs are newer with king-sized beds

5

and fine views. Also has a spa, restaurant and bar. CH$140 (US$280) per person per day with half board

HOSTELS

Chil'In Hostal & Restaurant Camino Termas de Chillán Km 72.5 ☎ 42 247075, ⊛ chilin.cl. A large French-run hostel with clean dorms and doubles, all with shared bathrooms. A crackling fireplace warms up the living room and the restaurant does the best pizzas

in the valley (CH$4000). Sound insulation is poor, however, and earplugs essential. Dorm CH$16,000, double CH$31,500

Riding Chile Camino Termas de Chillán Km 73 ☎ 09 7779 1973, ⊛ ridingchile.com. A cozy little hostel run by an affable young Argentine–Chilean couple with a handful of rooms, two lounge areas and a restaurant with delicious fajitas (CH$3500) and chocolate fondue (CH$8000). Dorm CH$14,000, double CH$25,000

EATING AND DRINKING

Parador, Jamón, Pan y Vino Camino Termas de Chillán Km 74 ☎ 42 432100, ⊛ paradorjamonpanyvino.cl. The longest-running restaurant in the valley serves typical fare in a setting that oozes old-world charm. Quell the hunger with the *Olla Parador* (CH$14,000), a hearty, meaty stew which feeds two. Daily 12.30–9.30pm.

Snow Pub Camino Termas de Chillán Km 71.5 ☎ 42 213910, ⊛ snowpub.cl. For après ski action, look no further than this popular pub where the music is loud, the beer is cheap (CH$1000), and by 2am, the dance floor is packed. Jan & Feb Mon–Wed & Sun 11.30am–11.30pm, Thurs–Sat 11.30am–4.30am; June–Oct daily 11.30am–late.

Santuario Cuna de Prat

Closed for repairs until 2013 • Previously Tues–Sun 10am–6pm • CH$1000

Naval enthusiasts will not be let down by the colonial **Hacienda San Agustín de Puñal** just outside the village of **Ninhue**, 50km northwest of Chillán. Arturo Prat was born here in 1848, and the area is now a shrine to the naval hero, who died in 1879 in the Battle of Iquique while trying to capture the Peruvian ironclad gunship, Huáscar (see p.476), armed only with a sword.

Inside the hacienda is a museum devoted to the hero, the **SANTUARIO CUNA DE PRAT**. While the national obsession with the young officer – a thousand Chilean plazas and streets are named after him – continues to mystify outsiders, the museum's collection of polished, lovingly cared-for naval memorabilia and colonial furniture are worth a visit in their own right, and the building they're housed in, with its large interior patio and elegant verandas, is a beautiful example of colonial rural architecture.

Buchupureo

The pristine surfer's paradise of Buchupureo lies 120km northwest of Chillán and 132km north of Concepción. This sleepy farming village is essentially a few houses scattered around the sweeping, dark-sand Playa La Boca, with a verdant backdrop of thick pine forests and a stable microclimate ideal for growing papaya. At dawn and dusk, crab fishermen use oxen to haul in their colourful boats, while surfers hit the left point break to ride long, fast, tubular waves that reach up to six metres.

While only hardy types in wetsuits brave the chilly waters around these parts, a slow-flowing fresh-water river runs parallel to Buchupureo's Playa La Boca, with temperatures that, in summer, are ideal for splashing about in. Horseriding is also popular along the beach, and hotels in the area can arrange excursions with local guides. Note that a mostly (and soon to be entirely) paved road links Buchupureo with Curanipe (see p.241), 35km north.

Around Buchupureo

When surf's not up in Buchupureo, there's always the string of beaches up and down the coast, including 16km south at Playa Rinconada. Some 10km south of Buchupureo is the livelier, but far less pretty town of Cobquecura, home to an offshore colony of sea lions. Five kilometres north of Cobquecura is the awe-inspiring Iglesia de Piedra, a series of lofty caves with passages leading down to the ocean.

By bus From Chillán, Buses Petoch leaves from the Terminal Rural (7 daily; 2hr 45min). From Concepción, Magabus (☎41 221 5147) leaves from Serrano and Las Heras (4 daily; 3hr 30min). In summer, at least one bus daily plies the coastal route south of Curanipe to Buchupureo and Cobquecura.

ACCOMMODATION AND EATING

★ **La Joya del Mar** Playa La Boca ☎42 197 1733, ⓦlajoyadelmar.com. Luxurious villas perched on the hillside have wide picture windows, immense bathtubs and balconies with breathtaking ocean views. There's also an infinity pool, Jacuzzi and top-notch restaurant run by the Californian owners (mains around $8000). Surfing lessons, mountain biking and fly-fishing outings arranged. $\overline{\text{CH\$87,000 (US\$174)}}$

Los Maquis Camino Buchupureo Km 9.7 ☎42 197 0703, ⓦlosmaquishotel.com. A stylish, luminous bed and breakfast with riverside hot tubs, run by a friendly Chilean–Australian couple. Breakfast is served in bed, guests can use the kitchen and transfers from Concepción airport are offered. $\overline{\text{CH\$35,000}}$

El Puerto Playa La Boca ☎52 197 1608, ⓦelpuertobuchupureo.cl. Check the surf without leaving bed at these excellent-value timber cabins, some with kitchenettes. The owner and his two friendly dogs take good care of guests, and the restaurant, which serves flavourful, simple seafood dishes (mains CH\$2500–4800) is a popular local haunt. $\overline{\text{CH\$20,000}}$

The Bío Bío Valley

South of Chillán and the Itata Valley, Chile is intersected by the great **Río Bío Bío**, generally considered the southern limit of the Central Valley. One of Chile's longest rivers, it cuts a 380km diagonal slash across the country, emptying into the ocean by the coastal city of Concepción, over 200km north of its source in the Andean mountains. For more than three hundred years the Bío Bío was simply "La Frontera", forming the border beyond which Spanish colonization was unable to spread, fiercely repulsed by the native **Mapuche** population.

Today, the Bío Bío Valley, which stretches 400km southwest from the mouth of the Río Bío Bío, still feels like a border zone between the gentle pastures and meadows of central Chile, and the lakes and volcanoes of the south. While the valley floor is still covered in the characteristic blanket of cultivation, dotted with typical Central Valley towns such as **Los Angeles** and **Angol**, the landscape on either side is clearly different. To the west, the **coastal range** – little more than gentle hills further north – takes on the abrupt outlines of real mountains, densely covered with the commercial pine forests' neat rows of trees and, further south, there are hints of the dramatic scenery to come in the Lake District, with native araucaria trees in their hundreds within **Parque Nacional Nahuelbuta**.

Cut off by these mountains, the towns strung down the coast road south of Concepción – such as **Lota**, **Arauco**, **Lebu** and **Cañete** – feel like isolated outposts. To the east, the Andes take on a different appearance, too: wetter and greener, with several outstandingly beautiful wilderness areas like **Parque Nacional Laguna del Laja** and **Parque Nacional Tolhuaca**.

Concepción

The sprawling, fast-paced metropolis of **CONCEPCIÓN** is the region's administrative capital and economic powerhouse, and Chile's second-largest city, sitting at the mouth of the Bío Bío, 96km southwest of Chillán. Surrounded by some of Chile's ugliest industrial suburbs, Concepción's centre is a spread of dreary, anonymous buildings. This lack of civic splendour reflects the long series of catastrophes that have punctuated Concepción's growth – from the incessant Mapuche raids during the city's days as a Spanish garrison, guarding La Frontera, to the devastating earthquakes that have razed it to the ground dozens of times since its founding in 1551. It does, however, have the energy and buzz of a thriving commercial centre, and the large

5

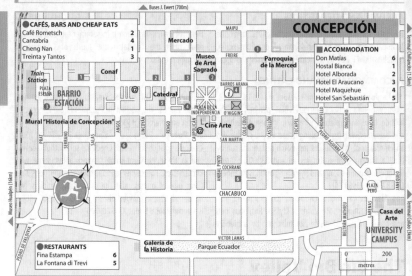

CONCEPCIÓN

CAFÉS, BARS AND CHEAP EATS
Café Rometsch 2
Cantabria 4
Cheng Nan 1
Treinta y Tantos 3

ACCOMMODATION
Don Matías 6
Hostal Bianca 1
Hotel Alborada 2
Hotel El Araucano 3
Hotel Maquehue 4
Hotel San Sebastián 5

RESTAURANTS
Fina Estampa 6
La Fontana di Trevi 5

number of students here at the Universidad Austral de Chile gives the place a young, lively feel and excellent nightlife.

Plaza de la Independencia

Concepción's focal point is the busy **Plaza de la Independencia**, where Bernardo O'Higgins read the Chilean declaration of independence in January 1818. In the centre, a classical column rises above the main fountain, atop which stands a gold-painted statue symbolizing the region's agricultural wealth. On the western side of the plaza rises the Romanesque–Byzantine **Catedral de la Santísima Concepción**, built between 1940 and 1950 and adorned with faded mosaics by Alejandro Rubio Dalmati.

Adjacent to the cathedral at Caupolicán 441 is the **Museo de Arte Sagrado** (Mon–Fri 9am–1pm & 2–6pm, Sat 10am–2pm; free), featuring colonial artwork, marble statues, gold-embroidered vestments and religious artefacts.

Galería de la Historia

Parque Ecuador • Mon 3–6.30pm, Tues–Fri 10am–1.30pm & 3–6.30pm, Sat & Sun 10am–2pm & 3–7pm • Free • ☎ 41 285 3756

For an in-depth introduction to Concepción, the **Galería de la Historia** at the southern end of Lincoyán has a series of impressive dioramas, some depicting the rather unsavoury crushing of the Mapuche by the conquistadores. Still, the sound and light effects are well done.

Casa del Arte

Larenas and Chacabuco • Tues–Fri 10am–6pm, Sat 10am–5pm, Sun 11am–2pm • Free • ☎ 41 220 3835

The **Universidad Austral de Chile**, set in splendid, landscaped gardens surrounded by thickly wooded hills, is Chile's third-largest university and houses one of Chile's largest national art collections in the **Casa del Arte**. The bulk of the collection consists of nineteenth-century landscapes and portraits by Chilean artists, but the showpiece is the magnificent mural in the entrance hall, *Presencia de América Latina*, by the Mexican artist Jorge González Camarena in 1964. Dominating the mural is the giant visage of an *indígena*, representing all the indigenous peoples of the continent, while the many faces of different nationalities superimposed on it indicate the intrusion of outside cultures and fusion of races that characterize Latin America.

Historia de Concepción

5

Arturo Prat 450

In addition to the mural in the Casa del Arte, you'll find another one, though not in the same league, next to the **railway station** in the Edificio Gobierno Regional: over 6m long and 4m tall, the massive *Historia de Concepción*, painted by Chilean artist Gregorio de la Fuente, was installed in 1964.

Museo Hualpén

Western end of the Bío Bío estuary • Tues–Sun 10m–6.30pm • CH$2000 for parking • ☎ 41 242 6399

A fifteen-minute taxi ride from Concepción's centre, a large park with several kilometres of footpaths and an extensive collection of native and exotic trees surrounds the **Museo Hualpén**. A traditional single-storey hacienda houses an eclectic collection of souvenirs from every corner of the globe, picked up by the millionaire industrialist Pedro del Río over three world trips in the nineteenth century.

Huáscar

Talcahuano, 16km northeast of Concepción • Tues–Sun 9.30am–noon & 2–5.30pm • CH$1000 • ☎ 41 274 5715 • White buses marked "Base Naval" go from along O'Higgins right to the entrance of the base

The industrial city and naval base of Talcahuano is where the historic ironclad gunship **Huáscar** is moored. You need to ask the guard for permission to visit the ship at the entrance of the base. The *Huáscar* was built for the Peruvian navy at Birkenhead in 1866 and controlled the naval engagements during the War of the Pacific until 1879, when it was trapped off Cape Angamos, near Antofagasta, and forced to surrender. Kept in an immaculate state of preservation, the *Huáscar* is one of only two vessels of its type still afloat today.

ARRIVAL AND DEPARTURE

CONCEPCIÓN

By plane Aeropuerto Carriel Sur (☎ 41 273 2000, ⓦ carrielsur.cl) is 5km northwest of the city. Several minibus companies offer inexpensive door-to-door transfers to the airport, including Airport Service (☎ 41 224 8776).

Airlines LAN, O'Higgins 648 (☎ 600 526 2000); Sky Airlines, O'Higgins 537 (☎ 600 600 2828).

Destinations Puerto Montt (2 daily; 1hr 10min); Santiago (14 daily; 1hr); Temuco (3 weekly; 35min).

By bus Most buses arrive at Terminal Collao, northeast of the centre at Tegualda 860, just off the Autopista General Bonilla (☎ 41 274 9000); plenty of mini-buses and taxis will take you into town. If you arrive with Tur Bus or Linea Azul, you may be dropped at the smaller Terminal Chillancito, also called Terminal Henríquez, at Henríquez 2565. There are direct buses to most towns and cities between Santiago and

Puerto Montt, most leaving from Terminal Collao. A notable exception is Tur Bus, whose downtown office is Tucapel 530 (☎ 41 231 5555), and which leaves from both Terminal Collao and Terminal Chillancito. If you're heading up the coast to Tomé, take a taxi *colectivo* from Chacabuco. The coastal route south of Concepción to Cañete, Arauco, Lebu and Contulmo is served by Buses J. Ewert and leaves from their office at Lincoyán 1425 (☎ 41 285 5587).

Destinations Cañete (hourly; 3hr); Chillán (every 30min; 1hr 30min); Contulmo (4 daily; 4hr); Lebu (hourly; 3hr); Los Angeles (every 30min; 2hr); Puerto Montt (20 daily; 10hr); Santiago (every 30min; 6hr); Talca (hourly; 3hr 30min); Temuco (hourly; 4hr); Tomé (every 15min; 40min); Valdivia (11 daily; 6hr 40min).

GETTING AROUND

Bicycle repairs Martínez, Maipu 297.

Car rental For car rental head to Avis, Salas 29

(☎ 41 288 7420), or Budget, Chacabuco 175 (☎ 41 221 2438).

INFORMATION AND TOURS

TOURIST INFORMATION

Conaf Barros Arana 215 (Mon–Thurs 8.30am–5.30pm, Fri 8.30am–4.30pm; ☎ 41 262 4000).

Sernatur Aníbal Pinto 460 (Mon–Fri 9am–6pm; ☎ 41 274 1337, ✉ infobiobio@sernatur.cl).

TOUR OPERATORS

Turismo Cocha, Chacabuco 839 (☎ 41 291 0175); Gestur, Rengo 484 (☎ 41 222 5975).

5

ACCOMMODATION

Don Matías Colo Colo 155 ☎41 255 6846, ⓦaparthoteldonmatias.cl. The cramped rooms could do with sprucing up, but they have flat-screen TVs, windows with double-glazing and some with private, modern bathrooms. The adjacent restaurant serves Chilean staples. **CH$38,000**

Hostal Bianca Salas 643-C ☎41 225 2103, ⓦhostalbianca.cl. While service can be dour, this is a solid budget option, with small but bright rooms and a common area where you can make use of the wi-fi or prepare your own food. **CH$25,000**

Hotel Alborada Barros Arana 457 ☎41 291 1121, ⓦhotelalborada.cl. The reflective glass exterior, modern lobby, plant-filled walkway and classical music offer no warning that the en suites will be shockingly pink. You'll either love it or hate it. **CH$50,000**

Hotel El Araucano Caupolicán 521 ☎41 274 0606, ⓦwww.otelaraucano.cl. A stellar – and reasonably priced – hotel boasting en suites with flat-screen TVs and tubs. There's an indoor pool, sauna and good restaurant with a terrace overlooking the plaza. **CH$40,000**

Hotel Maquehue Barros Arana 786 ☎41 221 0261, ⓦhotelmaquehue.cl. This 7th-floor hotel offers very good value – bathrooms have bidets and lizard-skin-style decor. Some rooms command fine city views. There's a computer for guest use. **CH$25,000**

Hotel San Sebastián Rengo 463 ☎41 295 6719, ⓦhotelsansebastian.cl. Rooms at this small, amiable hotel are a little old-fashioned if spotless and have cable TV and private bathrooms. Parking offered. **CH$25,000**

EATING AND DRINKING

Concepción has a good range of **restaurants** and boasts the liveliest nightlife in the Central Valley, fuelled by the large student population. The Barrio Estación is buzzing at night, particularly on Calle Prat and Plaza España, revolving mainly around a string of small restaurants that double up as bars on the weekend evenings. You can also enjoy inexpensive meals at one of the dozens of little *picadas* in the Mercado Central, on the corner of Freire and Caupolicán.

CAFÉS, BARS AND CHEAP EATS

Café Rometsch Barros Arana 685 ☎41 274 7040, ⓦportalrometsch.cl. Cavity-inducing ice-cream sundaes, cakes and crêpes (CH$2900–4250) are available at this long-standing café, which is decorated with city sketches. Mon–Fri 8.30am–8.30pm, Sat 9am–7pm.

Cantabria Caupolicán 415 ☎41 252 2693, ⓦcafecantabria.cl. Prices are a little steep here on account of the prime people-watching location, but the good coffee and decadent cakes (CH$2000) make it eminently worthwhile. Mon–Sat 8am–10pm.

Cheng Nan Freire 877 ☎41 252 0202. An inexpensive self-service vegetarian joint with wholesome, mainly Chinese, dishes, a few pastas and salads (lunch menu CH$2000). The food is much fresher at lunchtime. Mon–Sat 9.30am–6pm.

Treinta y Tantos Prat 404. A long-standing student haunt serving more than 30 varieties of inexpensive *empanadas* (around CH$1000) in a cosy setting with mellow music. Mon–Sat evenings only.

RESTAURANTS

Fina Estampa Angol 298 ☎41 222 1708. Waiters in red shirts and large white kerchiefs around their necks serve delicious Peruvian food (CH$6000–9000) like ceviche and *lomo saltado* (steak strips with tomato, onion, chips and rice). Mon–Sat 1–4pm & 8pm–midnight, Sun 1–4pm.

La Fontana di Trevi Colo-Colo 336 ☎41 279 0300, ⓦfontanaditrevi.cl. Chequered tablecloths and a display of dozens of wine bottles form the backdrop for tasty but standard Italian pizzas and pastas (CH$3700–9000). Mon–Sat noon–4pm & 6.30–10.30pm, Sun 12.30–4.30pm.

DIRECTORY

Banks and exchange There are many banks with ATMs, mainly on O'Higgins, by the central plaza. To change money, try Cambio Fides and AFEX at Barros Arana 565.
Cinema Cine Arte, O´Higgins 650 (☎42 222 7193).
Consulates Argentina, Ongolmo 532, 2nd floor (☎41 223 0257); Canada, Caupolicán 245 (☎41 236 7553); Italy,

Barros Arana 243 (☎41 222 9506).
Hospital San Martín and Lautaro ☎41 272 2500.
Internet Matrix, Caupolicán 346 for CH$600 per hour; Cyberprint, Barros Arana 374 for CH$500 per hr.
Post office O'Higgins and Colo-Colo (Mon–Fri 8.30am–7pm, Sat 8.30am–1pm).

The northern beaches

North of Concepción, a series of small towns and golden, sandy bays stretches up the coastline as far as the mouth of the Río Itata, 60km beyond. Heading up the road, 12km out of the city centre, you pass through the suburb of **Penco**, where the remains of a Spanish fort, **Fuerte La Planchada**, recall the area's turbulent history.

A couple of gentle hills separate Penco from **Lirquén**, a small industrial harbour used for exporting timber. Its beach is nothing special, but the nearby tangle of narrow streets known as the **Barrio Chino** is full of first-class, excellent-value seafood restaurants, famous throughout the region for their clam dishes and *paila marina*. Beyond Lirquén, the road runs inland for 30km, and the only access to the ocean along here is controlled by *Punta de Parra* (see p.251).

Tomé and around

Some 28km out of Concepción, the thriving timber centre, textile town and port of **Tomé** is squeezed into a small flat-bottomed valley, its suburbs pushed up the slopes of surrounding hills. Hidden from the drab town by a rocky point is the long, white-sand **Playa El Morro**. The beach, while very attractive, gets dreadfully crowded on summer weekends; a quieter alternative is **Playa Cocholgue**, a fine white beach studded with rocky outcrops, reached by taking the 4km side road off the main coast road as you head out of Tomé.

Dichato and around

Eight kilometres north of Tomé, **Dichato** is the most popular beach resort along this part of the coast, with a handful of **accommodation** options spread along the crescent-shaped, coastal avenue, Pedro Aguirre Cerda. About 4km north, the road turns to dirt and passes through dense forests with tracks leading off to a series of isolated, yellow-sand **beaches**, pounded by strong waves. Among the most beautiful of these are **Playa Purda**, 8km north of Dichato, and tiny **Playa Merquiche**, a further 2km north.

ARRIVAL AND DEPARTURE   THE NORTHERN BEACHES

By bus North of Concepción, the first 50km, up to Pingueral, is paved and served by regular buses and *colectivos* from Concepción.

ACCOMMODATION

TOMÉ

Cabañas Broadway Av Werner 1210, Playa El Morro ☎ 41 265 8475. For your own private beach pad, you could do worse than move into one of these ten fully equipped cabins, which sleep up to four. **CH$25,000**

Hotel Althome Sotomayor 669, Playa El Morro ☎ 41 265 0807, ✉ althome.hotel@gmail.com. This serviceable hotel has no-frills rooms, some with ocean views, and all with private bathrooms. Parking included. **CH$25,000**

Punta de Parra Camino a Tomé Km 19 ☎ 09 7669 1019. Situated between Lirquén and Tomé, the company

controlling this stretch of coast offers cabins and charges CH$2000 per non-guest for admittance to the powdery white sands. There's a restaurant and a beautiful coastal walk along the old rail tracks to several even more secluded beaches. **CH$35,000**

DICHATO

El Encanto 4km north of Dichato, towards the Río Itata ☎ 41 265 0462. This restful campsite with electricity and hot showers also has a handful of cabins with kitchens that sleep up to six people. Camping **CH$10,000** per site, cabins **CH$45,000**

The southern coast road and beyond

South of Concepción, a road skirts the ocean, passing through the towns of Coronel, **Lota** and Arauco. This area was deserted until the mid-nineteenth century, when the enormous submarine coal seam – the **Costa del Carbón** – was discovered running off the coast. About 150km south of Concepción, **Lebu** has great beaches, while nearby **Cañete**'s Mapuche museum is worth a visit en route to pretty **Lago Lanalhue**, 51km from Lebu. Rural areas along the coast all the way to Temuco are hotly contested battlegrounds. Intentional forest fires set by Mapuche groups asserting ancestral land claims were once frequent, and travellers were warned to avoid conflict areas where land seizures were taking place, as bloody confrontations with police occurred frequently. The issue remains unresolved, but there have been no recently confirmed fires or seizures.

5

Lota

Squeezed into a small valley on the edge of the sea, the soot-streaked town of **LOTA** was the site of Chile's first and largest coal mine, opened by industrialist Matías Cousiño in 1849. Production finally ceased in 1997, and today the ex-colliery is turning its attention to tourism, with hotels, swimming pools and a casino. The town centre, in the lower part of town known as Lota Bajo, does not inspire enthusiasm. Spread up the hillside west of the centre is Lota Alto, containing the former miners' residences, as well as the impressive **Iglesia San Matías**, where the coal baron lies buried.

The coal mine

Tues–Sun 10am–5pm • CH$4000 • ☎ 41 287 0682, ⓦ lotasorprendente.cl

You can visit the **coal mine** on **tours** guided by ex-miners, which takes you down the 820m shaft of the **Chiflón del Diablo** and also takes in the Pueblito Minero, a re-creation of miners' houses that were constructed for the film set of the Chilean movie *Sub Terra*.

Parque Isidora Cousiño

Tues–Sun 10am–6pm • Park CH$1600, museum CH$600, free for park visitors • ☎ 41 287 0682, ⓦ lotasorprendente.cl

On a headland to the west of town lies **PARQUE ISIDORA COUSIÑO**, a formal garden laid out by an English landscape gardener in 1862 under the direction of Cousiño's wife, *doña* Isidora Goyenechea. The park also has colonial homes, a museum containing a motley collection of photographs and colonial possessions, and actors who dress and speak like characters from the nineteenth century.

Isla Santa María

From Lota's pier you can take a two-hour boat ride to **ISLA SANTA MARÍA**, a small, lush island with steep cliffs, rolling hills and a population of about three thousand farmers and fishermen. The island's mild climate and fertile soil have supported small Mapuche communities for hundreds of years. There are secluded bays scattered around the island, with good beaches, sea lion colonies and excellent fishing opportunities.

Lebu

Seventy-six kilometres south of Lota, a 31km side road shoots off the highway to the small coastal town of **LEBU**, one of the few places still mining coal in this region. It has huge, unspoiled **beaches**, including **Playa Millaneco**, 3km north, where you'll find several massive caves overgrown with ferns and lichen. Lebu's only other attraction is its pair of bronze cannon on display in the plaza, which were cast in Lima in 1778 and bear the Spanish coat of arms.

Cañete

Back on the highway, 16km south of the turn-off for Lebu, **CAÑETE** is a busy agricultural town perched on a small rise above a bend in the Río Tucapel. Just off the northern end of the main street, commanding fine views over the river valley, the historic **Fort Tucapel** was founded by Spanish conquistador Pedro de Valdivia in 1552 and is the site of his gruesome death at the hands of the Mapuche chief Lautaro two years later.

Mapuche Museum

Camino Contulmo s/n • Jan & Feb Mon–Fri 9.30am–7pm, Sat & Sun 11am–7pm; March–Dec Tues–Fri 9.30am–5.30pm, Sat 11am–5.30pm, Sun 1–5.30pm • CH$600 • ☎ 41 261 1093, ⓦ www.dibam.cl

Just south of town, 1km down the highway, the **Mapuche Museum** houses a fine collection of indigenous artefacts, including textiles, silver jewellery, musical instruments and weapons. Perhaps the most striking exhibit is the *ruca* in the museum's garden – a traditional Mapuche dwelling made of wood and straw.

Lago Lanalhue

Ten kilometres out of Cañete, the road reaches the northern shore of **LAGO LANALHUE**, nestled among dense pine forests on the western slopes of the coastal range. Its waters are crystal clear and warmer than the Pacific, and its heavily indented shores form numerous peninsulas and bays, some of them containing fine white sand. You can buy basic provisions in the village of **Contulmo**, about 5km along the highway; while you're there, carry on a couple of kilometres around the south shore of the lake to visit the **Molino Grollmus** (officially Jan–April Mon–Sat 10–11am & 6–7pm, but in reality more sporadic; CH$500), an early twentieth-century wooden mill whose gardens contain an impressive collection of *copihues* (Chile's national flower). Some 44km east of Contulmo, the highway forks, with one branch heading to the town of Angol (see p.256), and the other continuing south to the Panamericana.

5

ARRIVAL AND DEPARTURE

CAÑETE

By bus Buses J. Ewert operates numerous services from Concepción to Cañete (hourly; 3hr).

By car From Cañete, a dirt road climbs 46km to Parque Nacional Nahuelbuta (see p.256), while the highway curves south through a lower pass in the Cordillera de Nahuelbuta.

ISLA SANTA MARÍA

By plane El Club Aéreo Concepción (☎41 248 0022, ⓦ clubaereoconcepcion.cl) offers charter flights to the island for around CH$100,000 for three people.

By boat Boats depart Sun at noon and Tues, Wed and Fri at 11am (CH$5000 return; ☎41 288 9175, ⓦnavierasm.cl). Given that boats return to Lota on Mon and Thurs at 8am and Tues and Fri at 3pm, you're better off – at least if you

THE SOUTHERN COAST ROAD

want to spend any time here – staying on the island overnight, unless you opt to take the more expensive option and fly back and forth.

LAGO LANALHUE

By bus Buses J. Ewert has services to Contulmo (4 daily; 4hr).

LEBU

By bus Regular services with Buses J. Ewert and Linea Azul go from Concepción to Lebu (hourly; 3hr).

LOTA

By bus Buses J. Ewert, Expresos Del Carbón, Los Alces and Ruta 160 go from Concepción to Lota (every 15min; 1.5hr). Ask to be let off in Lota Alto.

ACCOMMODATION AND EATING

CAÑETE

Club Social de Cañete Condel 283 ☎41 261 1653. The best place to eat in town is this plaza-side restaurant in an unprepossessing building. It specializes in well-cooked meat and fish dishes, including wild boar and sea bass (mains CH$5000–8000) and desserts include the exotic potato and hazelnut ice cream. Mon–Sat noon–1am, Sun noon–6pm.

Nahuelbuta Villagrán 644 ☎41 261 1593, ⓦ hotelnahuelbuta.cl. The pleasant rooms have cable TV and private bath while the adjacent café offers a wide selection of meals from sandwiches to lasagne. Café open until 11.30pm. **CH$26,000**

LAGO LANALHUE

Cabañas Playa Dorada 12km from Cañete ☎09 9879 9014. On the north tip of the lake, these modern cabins come with heating, TV, mini kitchens and ample living space. **CH$65,000**

Terrazas del Lanalhue Camino Cañete Km9.5 ☎09 9499 5330, ⓦterrazasdelanalhue.cl. On the northern side of the lake, 2km from Peleco, this range of cosy, fully equipped cabins have TV, space for up to five people and direct wharf access. **CH$50,000**

LEBU

Plaza Saavedra 691 ☎41 251 2227. A well-maintained hotel on the plaza with ten comfortable rooms with private bath and cable TV. The hotel's restaurant often serves the local speciality – king crab. **CH$30,000**

LOTA

Angel de Peredo Carlos Cousiño 147 ☎41 287 6824, ⓔ hotelangeldeperedo@yahoo.es. Simple lodging is available at this 44-room hotel with its own bowling alley dating from the 1930s, and a restaurant which specializes in seafood dishes (CH$3500 mains). **CH$18,000**

5

The Salto del Laja

From Concepción, the southern coastal route makes an appealing diversion but if you're in a hurry, take the direct 85km trunk road back to the Panamericana. Some 50km south from there, the first major town you reach is Los Angeles; halfway along this route, the Panamericana crosses the Río Laja. Until recently the highway passed directly by the **Salto del Laja**, which ranks among the most impressive waterfalls in Chile, cascading almost 50m from two crescent-shaped cliffs down to a rocky canyon.

ARRIVAL AND DEPARTURE · SALTO DEL LAJA

By bus If you're relying on public transport, your best bet is to visit the falls on a short trip from Los Angeles – take one of the frequent Jota Be services – they run in both directions (hourly; 30min).

By car The Salto del Laja makes a good break spot on the long drive from Santiago, but beware of old maps that show the highway cruising by the falls. To actually get to the Salto del Laja, you'll need to follow the turn-off signs for the "Salto", which lead to the old highway. From there you will see the falls. There are parking spaces around the bridge, and a short path passes through the cabins and campground of *Los Manantiales* (see p.254) to a closer viewpoint.

ACCOMMODATION

Los Manantiales Panamericana Sur Km 480 ☎ 43 314275, ⓦ losmanantiales.saltosdellaja.com. This large 1970s-style complex includes hotel rooms, fully serviced cabins and a campground. There are three natural pools and the restaurant (CH$3800 set lunch) has views over the waterfalls. Camping CH$12,000 per site, double CH$30,000, cabin CH$50,000

El Rincón Panamericana Sur Km 494, El Olivo ☎ 09 441 5019, ⓦ elrinconchile.cl. This German-run guesthouse

has average doubles (some with private bathrooms) and an attractive log cabin in lovely surroundings. It also offers home-cooked meals and hearty breakfasts with muesli, fruit and yoghurt. Double CH$27,000, cabin CH$37,000

Salto del Laja Panamericana Sur Km 485 ☎ 43 321706, ⓦ saltodellaja.cl. A hotel with swish suites, waterfall views and a restaurant located on an island with sixty acres of parkland and delightful swimming holes. CH$45,000

Los Angeles

LOS ANGELES is an easy-going agricultural town, pleasant enough but without any great attractions. At the north end of Colón, eight blocks from the orderly Plaza de Armas, is the colonial **Parroquia Perpetuo Socorro**, a church whose handsome colonnaded cloisters enclose a flower-filled garden. Otherwise, the town is really just a jumping-off point for the **Parque Nacional Laguna del Laja** (see below).

ARRIVAL AND DEPARTURE · LOS ANGELES

By bus The long-distance bus terminal is on Av Sor Vicenta 2051 (☎ 43 363035), on the outskirts of town. Tur Bus has its own terminal next door at Av Sor Vicenta 2061. The Terminal Rural is at Villagrán 501 (☎ 43 315128).

Destinations Angol (every 30min; 1hr); Chillán (every 30min; 1hr 30min); Concepción (every 30min; 2hr); El Abanico (every 30 min; 1hr 30min); Puerto Montt (23 daily; 8hr); Rancagua (5 daily; 6hr 15min); Talca (6 daily; 3hr 45 min); Temuco (every 45 min; 2hr 30min).

INFORMATION AND TOURS

TOURIST INFORMATION

Tourist office Almagro 250, level 8, office 811 (Mon–Thurs 8.30am–1.30pm & 3–6pm, Fri 8.30am–5.30pm; ☎ 43 317107).

Conaf Manso de Velasco 275 (Mon–Fri 8.30am–2.30pm; ☎ 43 322126).

TOUR OPERATORS

Harold Wicki ☎ 09 9720 4393, ⓦ www.kumbre.cl. Offers guided tours to Parque Nacional Laguna del Laja. English spoken.

ACCOMMODATION

Gran Hotel Muso Valdivia 222 ☎ 43 313183, ⓦ www .hotelalmuso.cl. Even if you're not a fan of 1980s architecture, then you'll at least appreciate the plaza-side

location of this five-storey hotel. Rooms are bright and clean but try to get one with plaza views. CH$40,000

Hotel Oceano Colo Colo 327 ☎ 43 342412,

@ hoteloceano327@gmail.com. A good central budget option, with helpful staff and 11 neat, sunny rooms with air conditioning and clean private bathrooms. Breakfast and parking included. CH$32,000

Residencial Central Almagro 377 ☎ 43 323381. If you are on a really tight budget, this family-run residencial has austere yet passable, recently renovated rooms, some with private bathrooms. No breakfast served. CH$16,000

EATING

Club de la Unión Colón 285 ☎ 43 322218. A classy restaurant, with appetizing Chilean fare and a tasty set lunch menu (CH$4500). Dishes like asparagus salad and *ossobuco* are served to a predominantly suit-wearing clientele. Mon–Sat 11am–11pm.

Tucafé Colo Colo 378 ☎ 43 327513. This low-key restaurant feels a little like dining in someone's living room and has a good selection of breakfast items, sandwiches and ice creams; the set lunches include big, healthy salads and lasagne (CH$3900). Mon–Fri 8am–9pm, Sat 9am–8.30pm.

DIRECTORY

Banks and exchange There are numerous ATMs on Colon.

Internet Cyber 3W at Caupolican 312, charges CH$450 per hour.

Parque Nacional Laguna del Laja

Daily: May–Nov 8.30am–6.30pm; Dec–April 8.30am–8pm • CH$1200 • ☎ 43 321086

Set in an otherworldly volcanic landscape of lava flows and honeycombed rock, the **Parque Nacional Laguna del Laja** takes its name from the great green lake formed by the 1752 eruption of **Volcán Antuco** (2985m). The road from Los Angeles, 93km away, is paved for the first 66km to **Antuco**; after that, the road surface is gravel but in decent condition for the 30km to the park entrance. The park boundary is 4km east of the village of **EL ABANICO**, but the Conaf hut, where you pay your entrance fee, is a further 4km east, and the administrative and environmental **Centro de Informaciones**, at Chacay, lies another kilometre beyond the hut.

Salto Las Chilcas and Salto del Torbellino

From the Conaf hut, an easy path leads a couple of kilometres to a pair of large, thundering waterfalls, **Salto Las Chilcas** and **Salto del Torbellino**, fed by underground channels from the lake, which emerge here to form the source of the Río Laja. Hikes to the summit are not particularly difficult, but allow four to five hours for the trip up and three hours for the hike down. Wear strong boots as the volcanic rocks will shred light footwear.

The road east

The road through the park continues east from the information centre towards the lake, passing the small **ski centre**, **Centro de Esquí Volcán Antuco** (5km along the road, ☎ 42 322651, ⌘ skiantuco.cl; July–September; CH$19,000), which has a small restaurant and simple refuge. At this point, the road deteriorates into a terrible dirt track that skirts the southern shore of the lake for 22km, continuing to the Paso Pichachén. Few vehicles make it along here, so the road serves as an excellent walking trail through the sterile landscape, with changing views of the lake and of the mountains of **Sierra Velluda** in the southwest, which are studded with hanging glaciers.

ARRIVAL AND DEPARTURE   PARQUE NACIONAL LAGUNA DEL LAJA

By bus From Los Angeles' Terminal Rural, Buses Elper (☎ 43 362785) and Expreso Volcán (☎ 09 997 40360) run

services to El Abanico (every 30min; 1hr 30min).

ACCOMMODATION AND EATING

Cabañas y Camping Lagunillas 2km from park entrance ☎ 43 321 086. A secluded camping area and four spacious cabins by the banks of the Río Laja. There is

also a restaurant. Open year-round. Camping CH$10,000 per site, cabin CH$30,000

5

Angol

Sixty-four kilometres southwest of Los Angeles, **ANGOL** is the final major town before Temuco, the gateway to the Lake District, and serves as a useful base for visiting the nearby **Parque Nacional Nahuelbuta**. In the centre of the town's attractive Plaza de Armas a large, rectangular pool is guarded by four finely carved – and comically stereotypical – marble statues of women representing the continents of Asia, Africa, Europe and America.

Museo Dillman Bullock

Camino Angol Km 5 • Mon–Fri 9am–1pm & 2.30–6pm, Sat & Sun 9am–1pm, 3–6pm • CH$450 • ☎ 45 711142 • Regular *colectivos* from the Plaza de Armas

Located within an agricultural college in the suburbs, 5km south down Avenida Bernardo O'Higgins, **Museo Dillman Bullock** has beautifully landscaped gardens and a strange assortment of archaeology including pre-Columbian funeral urns, a moth-eaten mummy, Mapuche artefacts and malformed foetuses.

ARRIVAL AND INFORMATION   ANGOL

By bus Angol's long-distance bus terminal is at Oscar Bonilla 428, seven blocks from the Plaza; rural services operate from Lautaro and Ilabaca (☎ 45 712021), two blocks from the Plaza.

Tourist information Plaza de Armas (Jan & Feb Mon–Fri 8.30am–8pm, Sat & Sun 10am–1pm & 4–8pm; rest of year Mon–Fri 8.30am–5.30pm; ☎ 45 990840, ⊚ angol.cl).
Conaf Prat 191 (☎ 45 712191).

ACCOMMODATION AND EATING

Club Social Caupolicán 498 ☎ 45 718082, ⊖ hotelclubsa@hotmail.com. A centrally located hotel with light, airy rooms, an outdoor pool, aged billiard tables and a decent restaurant serving meat and fish dishes. CH$41,000

Duhatao Prat 420 ☎ 45 714320, ⊚ hotelduhatao.cl. This sleek boutique hotel has stylish rooms decorated with ethnic and recycled furnishings, and a restaurant and bar which serves international cuisine (mains around CH$5000). CH$43,500

Parque Nacional Nahuelbuta

Daily: 8.30am–6pm • CH$4000 • ☎ 2 196 0245

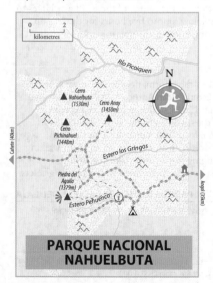

PARQUE NACIONAL NAHUELBUTA

From Angol, a dirt road (difficult to pass after rain) climbs 35km west to the entrance of **PARQUE NACIONAL NAHUELBUTA**, spread over the highest part of the Cordillera de Nahuelbuta. The park was created in 1939 to protect the last remaining **araucaria** (monkey puzzle) trees in the coastal mountains, after the surrounding native forest had been wiped out and replaced with thousands of radiata pines for the pulp and paper industry. Today it's a 68-square-kilometre enclave of mixed evergreen and deciduous forest, providing the coastal cordillera's only major refuge for wildlife such as foxes, pumas and *pudús* (pygmy deer).

You're unlikely to catch sight of any of these shy animals, though if you look up among the tree trunks you may well see large black woodpeckers hammering away. Of the park's trees, star billing

OPPOSITE PARQUE NACIONAL NAHUELBUTA, P.256

5

TREKS IN PARQUE NACIONAL NAHUELBUTA

From the Centro de Informaciones there are two treks: an interesting, 700m interpretative loop through the forest and an easy one-hour, 4km hike (look out for the giant araucaria about a 5min walk along the path, estimated to be 1800 years old) up to the **Piedra del Aguila**. This craggy rock, 1450m above sea level, offers superb views that on clear days take in the whole width of Chile, from the Andes to the Pacific. At a slightly lower, flatter rock a few metres west, you can enjoy even better views onto the smoking volcanoes of the northern Lake District.

To get here by car, take the road through the park to the signed car park, from where it's a twenty-minute walk up to the viewpoint past a series of information panels on the trees. There's another rewarding trek up the gentle slopes of **Cerro Anay**, 4km north of the information centre, reached by a jeep track followed by a short path. Its 1400m peak is the best place to take in the whole of the park.

goes to the towering araucarias, with their thick umbrellas of curved, overlapping branches covered in stiff pine needles. Some of these trees are over 40m high, and the most mature ones in the park are more than a thousand years old.

ARRIVAL AND INFORMATION   PARQUE NACIONAL NAHUELBUTA

By bus In the summer Buses Angol and Buses Nahuelbuta come from Angol's rural terminal and stop at El Cruce, a 1hr walk from the entrance. The park is open all year but expect snow and 4WD conditions in winter (June–Sept).

Tourist information Centro de Informaciones, 5km west along the road from the entrance (daily: 8.30am–6pm; ☏ 2 196 0245). Here you can find out more about the park's flora and fauna.

ACCOMMODATION AND EATING

Camping ☏ 2 196 0245. There are two camping areas: *Camping Pehuenco* is 5km from the entrance on the Angol side, beside the information centre and park headquarters,

and has 11 sites with picnic tables and cold showers. Some 5km north of here, *Camping Coimallín* is smaller and more rustic. CH$12,000 per site.

Parque Nacional Tolhuaca

Daily: 8.30am–6pm • CH$3000

Back on the Panamericana, 40km south of the turn-off to Angol, a detour into the Andean foothills will take you to another area of protected native forest, **PARQUE NACIONAL TOLHUACA**, a pristine landscape offering some of the finest hiking in the region. The park covers a long and relatively narrow strip of land stretching through the valley of the Río Malleco, hemmed in by steep, thickly wooded hills. Dominating the bottom of the valley is the wide and shallow **Laguna Malleco**, bordered by tall reeds rich in birdlife, while other attractions include waterfalls, small lakes and hundreds of araucaria trees.

The best **approach** to the park is along the 57km dirt road (via the village of Inspector Fernández) branching east from the Panamericana, a couple of kilometres north of **Victoria**. This leads directly to the Conaf administration on the southeastern shore of Laguna Malleco, where you'll also find **camping** (CH$12,000 per site) and picnic areas. From here, a footpath follows the northern shore of the lake for about 3km, through lush evergreen forest to the **Salto Malleco**, where the lake's waters spill down into the Río Malleco, forming a spectacular 50m waterfall.

Sendero Prados de Mesacura and Sendero Lagunillas

About halfway along the lake path, another trail branches north, climbing steeply up the hillside before forking in two. The left fork follows the 12km **Sendero Prados de Mesacura** across a gentle plain before climbing steeply again through dense forest. The right fork follows the **Sendero Lagunillas** (also 12km), climbing moderately to a group

PARQUE NACIONAL TOLHUACA

of small lakes near the summit of Cerro Amarillo, from where you get fabulous panoramic views onto the surrounding peaks, including the 2800m Volcán Tolhuaca. Both of these are full-day hikes, requiring an early start.

Sendero Laguna Verde

Following the flat path along the northern bank of the Río Malleco eastwards, after about 5km you'll reach the trailhead of the 8km **Sendero Laguna Verde**, which climbs up and around a steep hill to the small, emerald-green Laguna Verde, 1300m above sea level and surrounded by soaring peaks. This makes a good camping spot.

Termas de Tolhuaca

Daily 9am–6pm • CH$8000 • ☎ 45 881211, ⓦ termasdetolhuaca.cl

From the Conaf office, a bouncy 9km dirt road leads to the **TERMAS DE TOLHUACA**, just outside the park's boundaries. The source of the *termas* is at the bottom of a narrow, rocky canyon, inside a large cave, where bubbling, sulphurous water seeps out of the rocks, and steam vents fill the cave with fumaroles, forming a kind of stone-age sauna. The small pools around the cave are too hot to paddle in, but a little further down the canyon, where the thermal water has mixed with cold stream water, there's a gorgeous natural pool that you can bathe in.

The administration operates two **hotels** (see below), and you can also visit the *termas* for the day. It can get very busy in January and February, especially at weekends, but outside these months the place is blissfully quiet.

ACCOMMODATION	PARQUE NACIONAL TOLHUACA
Araucaria Termas de Tolhuaca ☎45 881211, ⓦ termasdetolhuaca.cl. The higher of the two Termas de Tolhuaca hotels is also larger, with 64 beds, and is near a large swimming pool filled with thermal water. The pleasant rooms have private bathrooms and central heating generated by the thermal water. __CH$50,000__	**El Notro** Termas de Tolhuaca ☎45 881211, ⓦ termasdetolhuaca.cl. Lower down in the canyon, this is the smaller of the two hotels. Rooms here are very simple for the price, but the location is stunning. It's close to the restaurant which has a hearty lunch menu (CH$10,000). __CH$50,000__

The road to Lonquimay

At **Victoria**, a paved road branches east from the Panamericana to the small agricultural town of **Lonquimay**, 115km away, passing the entrance to the **Reserva Nacional Malalcahuello-Nalcas** en route. There's nothing especially appealing about Lonquimay itself, but the road there – running through a narrow valley overlooked by towering volcanoes – is spectacular, particularly the stretch across the **Cuesta de las Raíces**.

5

Curacautín and around

Fifty-six kilometres out of Victoria, the road passes through the logging town of **Curacautín**, from where a 40km dirt road branches south to Lago Conguillío, in **Parque Nacional Conguillío** (see pp.269–271). As the northern gateway to the park, Curacautín has its fair share of hotels, but there's more dramatic scenery further along the road, including the 60m waterfall, **Salto del Indio**, just off the road, 14km out of Curacautín, and, 7km beyond, the 50m **Saltos de la Princesa**.

Reserva Nacional Malalcahuello-Nalcas

Daily: 8.30am–1pm & 2–6pm · CH$3000 · malalcahuello@conaf.cl

Some 30km west of Curacautín, you'll pass the entrance to the **RESERVA NACIONAL MALALCAHUELLO-NALCAS**, with the administrative office just a few hundred metres from the road. The Conaf staff are extremely helpful and friendly. The attractions here are hiking, fly fishing, horse treks and, from June to October, skiing at the Corralco ski resort (lift ticket CH$23,000, equipment rental CH$16,000; ☎2 202 9325, ⓦcorralco .com), which has 28.5km of pistes on the side of the Lonquimay Volcano.

Hiking in the reserve

Hiking trips on the Lonquimay Volcano take about four hours up, one down, and an ice axe and crampons are required. Ask for information at Conaf or the hostel *La Suizandina* (see p.261). Another popular walk is the 7km **Sendero Piedra Santa**, a trail through different types of vegetation that illustrate the techniques used by Conaf to protect and manage native forest. The trail passes through quite separate areas of evergreen *tepa*, *raulí*, *coigüe*, *lenga* and the famous araucaria. Parts of the path give excellent views onto 3125m **Volcán Llaima** and 2890m **Volcán Lonquimay**. Count on around five hours to complete the trail.

Cuesta de Las Raíces

A couple of kilometres further along the main road from the administration of the Reserva Nacional Malalcahuello-Nalcas, a gravel road (signed Volcán Lonquimay) branches north, and then forks in two. The right fork leads 26km to the village of Lonquimay, across the **CUESTA DE LAS RAÍCES**, part of the volcanic chain that forms the highest peaks in this section of the Andes. This is a beautiful drive, through lush araucaria forests, with birds of prey, such as buzzards, swooping around the tree branches.

From the pass at the top, you get an extraordinary view down over the araucarias, spread out below like a vast green carpet. The left fork leads 4km to the small **Los Arenales ski centre** (July–Oct; lift pass CH$5000, equipment rental CH$10,000; ☎45 891111). From here, the track continues up to a lookout point over **Cráter Navidad**, the gaping hole produced when the volcano last erupted, on Christmas Day 1988.

Túnel de Las Raíces

Open 24hrs · CH$400 each way

An alternative route to Lonquimay is through the **Túnel de Las Raíces**. Built in 1930 as a railway tunnel, in an abortive attempt to connect the Pacific and Atlantic by railroad, this 4.5km tunnel was once the longest in South America, but is only wide enough for traffic to pass through in one direction at a time; be prepared to wait up to an hour for the traffic direction to reverse.

Lonquimay

After the excitement of driving through the tunnel or crossing the Cuesta de Las Raíces, the rather sedate little town of **LONQUIMAY**, sitting at the end of the paved road, is something of a let-down. A quiet collection of wooden houses and corner shops, the town boasts only one interesting feature – a bizarre street plan. It's laid out in the shape of a rugby ball, with an elliptical Plaza de Armas. Lonquimay is, however, beautifully located on a flat, fertile plain, to the east of the Andes. The only part of the country to cross the cordillera, it was claimed by Chile because the Bío Bío rises here, fed by numerous meandering rivers that flow through a 100km stretch of pampa.

ARRIVAL AND DEPARTURE

CURACAUTÍN

By bus Curacautín is serviced by buses from Chillán (1 daily; 4hr); Concepción (2 daily; 5hr); Los Angeles (2 daily; 3hr); and Temuco (every 10min; 2hr). Buses Bío Bío has a direct service from Angol to Curacautín (2 daily; 2hr).

LONQUIMAY

By bus To get to Lonquimay from Angol, take Buses Bío Bío

THE ROAD TO LONQUIMAY

to Victoria (every hour; 1hr 30min) and change for another Buses Bío Bío service to Lonquimay (2 daily; 1hr 45min).

RESERVA NACIONAL MALALCAHUELLO-NALCAS

By bus Buses Bío Bío and Erbuc run between Lonquimay and Curacautín (20 daily; 45min) passing via the Reserva Nacional Malalcahuello-Nalcas.

ACCOMMODATION AND EATING

LONQUIMAY

Hostal Follil Pewenche Carrera Pinto 110 ☎ 45 891110, ⓦ pewenche.cl. A large blue timber house, with friendly service, en-suite rooms and a restaurant (mains CH$3000). **CH$18,000**

Hotel Turismo Caupolicán 925 ☎ 45 891087, ✉ hotel.turismo@gmail.com. Eleven neat, sunlit rooms with flowery curtains, cable TV and wi-fi; four also have private bathrooms. **CH$20,000**

RESERVA NACIONAL MALALCAHUELLO-NALCAS AND AROUND

A large hotel is being constructed at the Corralco ski resort (see p.260) at the base of the Lonquimay Volanco. While there's no official camping in the reserve, Conaf staff often let

people camp for free in the gardens by the warden's house.

Suizandina Lodge Camino Internacional Km 83 ☎ 45 197 3725, ⓦ suizaandina.com. This very popular hostel lies 30km east of Curacautín and offers a range of rooms with wi-fi, as well as camping. The staff can provide hiking information, horse and bike riding, snowshoeing tours and there's also a Swiss restaurant. Dorm **CH$13,000**, double **CH$41,000**, camping **CH$6000** per person

Termas de Manzanar Camino Internacional Km 18 ☎ 45 881200, ⓦ termasdemanzanar.cl. This smartly furnished hotel is 3km past the Salta del Indio, 18km east of Curacautín and 23km from the reserve. The more expensive en suites come with Jacuzzis and there's also a restaurant and 39°C thermal pools (non-guests pay CH$8000). **CH$51,000**

The Lake District

264 Temuco

269 Parque Nacional Conguillío

271 Lago Villarrica and around

283 The Siete Lagos

288 Valdivia and around

293 Osorno

295 Parque Nacional Puyehue and around

298 Lago Llanquihue and around

305 Parque Nacional Vicente Pérez Rosales and around

308 Estuario de Reloncaví

309 Puerto Montt

CLIMBING VOLCÁN VILLARICA

The Lake District

The Lake District, which stretches 339km from Temuco in the north to Puerto Montt in the south, is a region of lush farmland, dense forest, snowcapped volcanoes and deep, clear lakes, hidden for the most part in the mountains. Until the 1880s, when small farm settlements arrived, the entire region was blanketed in thick forests: to the north, the high, spindly araucaría; on the coast, dense *selva valdiviana*; and to the very south, two-thousand-year-old alerces - "Chile's Yosemite". These forests were inhabited by the Mapuche (literally "people of the land"), who fought off the Inca and resisted Spanish attempts at colonization for 350 years before finally falling to the Chilean Army in the 1880s.

In the century since the subjugation of the Mapuche, German, Austrian and Swiss settlers have transformed this region into some of the finest **dairy farmland** in Chile, and the extent of German influence is evident in architectural and culinary form, particularly in Valdivia, Osorno, Puerto Varas and Frutillar. Native culture survives as well: the Mapuche heritage is a badge of honour in today's Chile, and at least half a million of the region's population claim this ancestry, many of whom reside on the extensive indigenous *reducciones* (reservations) throughout the Lake District.

The efforts of the European settlers also opened the area up to travellers, and visitors have been coming here for over a hundred years. Yet while much of the Lake District's population lives in the main cities of Temuco, Osorno, Valdivia and Puerto Montt, with the exception of Valdivia these are mainly transportation hubs, with less to offer than the roads less trodden. The real action lies in the region's many national parks and around the adventure sports capitals of **Pucón** and **Puerto Varas**, where the options abound for hiking, volcano-climbing, rafting, kayaking, canyoning, horseriding and soaking in the many thermal springs. In the winter, skiing down volcanoes draws an adventurous crowd.

Temuco

Once a Mapuche stronghold, **TEMUCO**, 677km south of Santiago, is the largest city in southern Chile. Most visitors use it solely as a transport hub or as a base for exploring nearby Parque Nacional Conguillío. But the city itself has a rich **Mapuche heritage**, particularly evident in and around the colourful **markets**, which are among the best places in the country to hear Mapudungun (the Mapuche language) spoken, and there are still occasional clashes between the Mapuche and the police, particularly over land rights.

Temuco was founded in 1881, and it was only when the railway from Santiago arrived in 1893 that the city began to prosper. An influx of seven thousand European

Skiing and hiking in Parque Nacional Conguillío p.270
Musher for a day p.273
Hot springs around Pucón p.278
Exploring Parque Nacional Huerquehue p.279
Villarrica's demonic peaks p.280

Climbing Volcán Villarrica p.282
The Villarrica traverse p.283
Crossing the Río Valdivia p.293
Hot springs in Puyehue p.297
The land-and-lake crossing into Argentina p.301
Ferries from Puerto Montt p.311

PARQUE NACIONAL CONGUILLIO

Highlights

❶ Parque Nacional Conguillío Hiking is spectacular in this Andean park, where fresh volcano fields mix with ancient araucaría forests. **See p.269**

❷ Villarrica Become a musher for a day with Chile's only husky dog operator, or join a weeklong dog-sledding expedition across the Andes. **See p.272**

❸ Pucón At the capital of adventure tourism in the Lake District, you can climb smoking Volcán Villarrica, raft the rapids of the Trancura or hike in the neabry nature reserves. **See p.273**

❹ Valdivia Find a surprising mix of European history at this lively coastal city, where a German brewery and old Spanish forts are surrounded by rivers and bays. **See p.288**

❺ Lago Llanquihue Spectacular waterfall, one of the region's more challenging volcano climbs, whitewater rafting and some of the best food in the region, all within easy reach of one of the Lake District's most beautiful bodies of water. **See p.298**

❻ Estuario de Reloncaví A top spot for hiking, kayaking or horse-trekking into the oldest forests of the Americas, including the Cochamó Valley, known as "Chile's Yosemite". **See p.308**

HIGHLIGHTS ARE MARKED ON THE MAP ON P.266

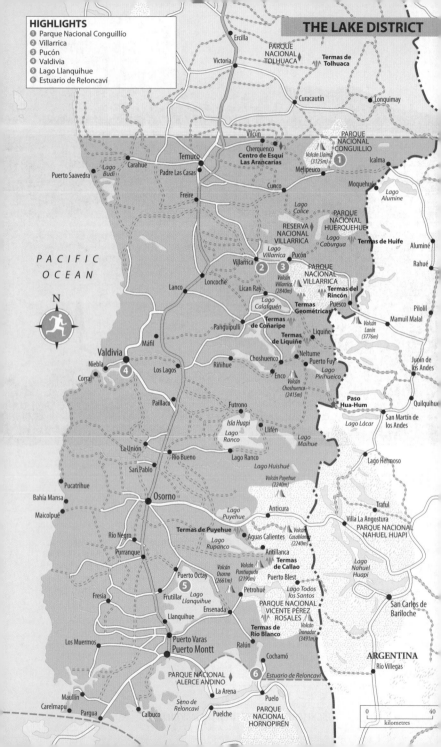

immigrants from seven different countries formed the farming and commercial nucleus that soon transformed the forested valleys and plains.

The diagonal **Avenida Caupolicán** separates the city's quiet and exclusive residential districts to the west and the unattractive maze of shops and offices to the east. Temuco's centre is the relaxing **Plaza Aníbal Pinto**, luxuriant with fine native and imported trees, set off by a large monument depicting the struggle between the Spanish and the Mapuche Indians, while a few blocks north lies the **Monumento Natural Cerro Ñielol**, a densely forested hill with some enjoyable walking trails and home to the *copihue* (Lapageria rosea), Chile's national flower.

Museo Regional de la Araucanía

Av Alemania 84 • Mon–Fri 9am–5pm, Sat 11am–5pm, Sun 11am–2pm • CH$1000, Sun free • Bus #1 or *colectivo* #11 from Manuel Montt

Temuco's biggest attraction is the **Museo Regional de la Araucanía**, which sits ten blocks west of the centre. Housed in a fine 1920s-vintage building, it showcases beautifully presented exhibits which chart the history and migration of the Araucanían people and the Spanish conquest and subsequent European settlement of the Lake District. While spotlights in the large basement subtly illuminate displays of Mapuche weaponry, pottery and an enormous canoe, the star of the show is the **Mapuche jewellery**; the Mapuche learned silverwork from the Spanish and fine examples of the craft, including heavy silver *collares*, passed on from mother to daughter, are on display here.

The markets

Mercado Municipal Portales between Bulnes and Aldunate • Summer Mon–Sat 8am–8pm & Sun 8am–3pm; winter Mon–Sat 8am–5pm **Feria Libre** Two blocks of Av Pinto between Barros Arana and Av Balmaceda • Daily: summer 8.30am–6pm; winter 8.30am–5pm

A few blocks northeast of the Plaza lies sprawling **Mercado Municipal**. The heart of the market consists of countless craft stalls selling silver Mapuche jewellery, baskets, musical instruments, woven ponchos and more. Near the little-used railway station is Chile's liveliest and most colourful fruit and vegetable market, the **Feria Libre**, pungent with fish, tobacco smoke and spices from the *merkén* (smoked chilli powder) stalls. This is a good place to savour typical local dishes, such as *cazuela* in one of the numerous hole-in-the-wall eateries, and one of the few places you'll see *piñones* (araucaria tree nuts traditionally boiled and eaten by the Mapuche) for sale.

ARRIVAL AND DEPARTURE
TEMUCO

BY PLANE
Temuco's airport, Maquehue (☎45 554801), lies 6km southwest of town. Transfer Araucanía (☎45 339900) can arrange transfers for CH$4500 if you call in advance, and there are plenty of cabs outside.
Airlines LAN, Bulnes 687 (☎600 526 2000, ⊚lan.com); Sky Airlines, Bulnes 655, Oficina 4 (☎45 747300, ⊚skyairline.cl).
Destinations Puerto Montt (1–2 daily; 45min); Santiago via Concepción (6 daily; 2hr).

BY BUS
If you're coming from a nearby town by bus, it's best to use Buses JAC, as you'll be dropped off at their own central terminal at Aldunate and Balmaceda (☎45 231340). Most long-haul buses have ticket offices in the centre but depart from the main long-distance bus terminal, Terminal Rodoviario Araucaria (☎45 225005), inconveniently

located out of the centre at Vicente Pérez Rosales 1609, and served by *colectivos* and bus #7 from the city centre. The Terminal de Buses Rurales on Pinto and Balmaceda (☎45 210494) runs services to more local destinations.
Companies Buses JAC has frequent departures to all major destinations in the Lake District; Igi Llaima and Nar Bus, Miraflores 1535 (☎45 407777), serve Argentine destinations; Tur Bus, General Lagos 576 (☎45 270458), and Pullman, Claro Solar 561 (☎45 212137), serve Santiago and all major destinations north of the Lake District; Cruz del Sur, Lagos at Claro Solar (☎45 730320), covers the Lake District and Chiloé.
Destinations Concepción (4 daily; 5 hr); Melipueco (6 daily; 2hr 30min); Osorno (every 30min; 4hr); Pucón (every 30min; 2hr); Puerto Varas (every hour; 5hr); San Martín de Los Andes, Argentina (1 daily; 7hr); Santiago (every 30min; 9hr); Valdivia (every 30min; 2hr 30min); Villarrica (every 30min; 1hr 30min).

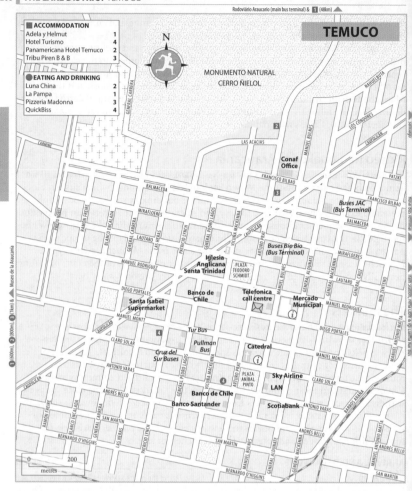

INFORMATION AND TOURS

Conaf Bilbao 931, second floor (Mon–Fri 8.30am–2pm; ☏45 298100). Offers information about the region's national parks, including Parque Nacional Conguillío.

Tourist information Sernatur office on the northeast corner of Plaza Aníbal Pinto at Claro Solar 899 (Jan & Feb Mon–Sat 9am–8pm, Sun 10am–2pm; March–Dec Mon–Thurs 9.30am–1pm & 3–5.30pm, Fri 9am–1pm & 3–4.30pm; ☏45 211969, ✉infoaraucania@sernatur.cl).

TOUR OPERATORS

Turismo Multi Tour ☏09 9818 1358, ⌨chile-travel .com/multitour. Long-standing and highly recommended family run outfit offering multi-day tours of the area around Temuco; these include visits to Parque Nacional Conguillío and to Mapuche communities.

ACCOMMODATION

Adela y Helmut Km 5 N ☏45 582230, ⌨www .adelayhelmut.cl. This small German–Chilean-run farm 48km out of town comes warmly recommended by travellers. Stay either in a dorm or a fully equipped mini-aprtment inside a large *cabaña*, feast on home-cooked *asado*, smoked trout or the ample breakfast which includes eggs and honey from the property, or take part in one of the many tours of the Lake District organized by the helpful owners. Dorm CH$9000, apartment CH$23,000

Hotel Turismo Lynch 563 ☎45 951090, ⓦwww .hotelturismotemuco.cl. This central, three-storey, 30-room business hotel has gracious English-speaking staff and boasts large, spic-and-span rooms with modern amenities. The café is a good place for a light meal. **CH$40,000**

Panamericana Hotel Temuco Prat 220 ☎45 233830, ⓦwww.panamericanahoteles.cl. This may be a chain hotel, but its central location at the foot of Cerro Ñielol, its

comfortable cream-and-brown rooms and a plethora of amenities (including a large outdoor pool) makes this a good upper end choice. Wi-fi doesn't extend to all rooms. **CH$69,000**

Tribu Piren B&B Prat 69 ☎45 985711, ⓦwww .tribupiren.cl. The helpful English-speaking owner at this attractive, centrally located B&B helps to organize tours of the area, and the compact rooms are equipped with cable TV. Popular with international travellers. **CH$24,000**

EATING AND DRINKING

Luna China Av Alemania 304 ☎45 273177. A couple of blocks from the Museo Regional de la Araucanía, this popular restaurant serves enormous portions of prawns in garlic sauce, Peking duck and other Chinese-inspired dishes. And if you order a prawn dish, it will actually consist of prawns and not 75 per cent water chestnuts. Mon–Sat 12.30–3.30pm & 7–11pm, Sun 12.30–3.30pm.

La Pampa Caupolicán 155 ☎45 212525. Steak is not the only thing on the menu at this bustling Argentine restaurant, though it's certainly the star attraction, as well as the weekend special of *asado criollo* (slow-cooked ribs), washed down with one of the excellent reds from the extensive wine menu. The less carnivorous can't go wrong with the trout dishes or the fresh salads. Mon–Sat noon–

4pm & 7pm–midnight, Sun noon–4pm.

Pizzeria Madonna Av Alemania 660 ☎45 329393. This Italian *trattoria* with chequered tablecloths really delivers when it comes to excellent pizza and imaginative pasta dishes. Portions are big enough to share, though you may not want to do so with the divine tiramisu. Daily noon– 3.30pm & 7–11.30pm.

QuickBiss Antonio Varas 755 ☎45 211219. This downtown cafeteria, with its combination of loud zebra stripes and soft natural woods, is justifiably popular with locals (and vegetarians) thanks to its large selection of soups, *empanadas*, sandwiches and salads. Self-service at lunchtime and a simple *menú* in the evenings. Daily 11am–11pm.

DIRECTORY

Banks and exchange There are numerous banks with ATMs around Plaza Aníbal Pinto. For a decent exchange rate, try Cambio Global, Bulnes 655, Local 1.

Car rental Avis, San Martín 755 ☎45 465280; Hertz, Andrés Bello 792 ☎45 318585.

Hospital Clínica Alemana, Senador Estébanez 645 ☎45 244244.

Internet access All accommodation options reviewed offer free wi-fi.

Post office Portales 839.

Parque Nacional Conguillío

Oct–March • CH$5000 • ⓦ parquenacionalconguillio.cl

The grey peak of Volcán Llaima (3125m) looms over the horizon about 80km east of Temuco. Wrapped around its neck is **PARQUE NACIONAL CONGUILLÍO**, a park the volcano has been doing its best to destroy with belch after belch of black lava. The northern sector is lush, high forest, with steep cliffs covered in spindly armed araucaría trees often draped in furry lime-green moss. In the south, however, the volcano has wreaked havoc. The road from Temuco passes over a wide lava flow, consisting of either rolling plains of thin dust or walls of spiked, recently congealed rock.

Volcán Llaima is actually one of the three most active volcanoes on the continent; its last serious eruption was in 1957, though as recently as 1994 a lake, Laguna Arco Iris, was formed by a fresh lava flow that blocked a river.

The northern route into the park is through the village of **Curacautín** (97km from Temuco), entering the park at sector Laguna Captrén, while the southern road from **Melipeuco** enters at sector Truful-Truful, and from the west, a little-used dirt road runs from the village of Cherquenco past the Centro de Esquí Las Araucarías.

SKIING AND HIKING IN PARQUE NACIONAL CONGUILLÍO

The park splits neatly into two main sectors, formed by the volcano's western and eastern slopes. The **western slopes** (Sector Los Paraguas) come into their own in winter, boasting a small ski centre, the Centro de Esquí Las Araucarias (☎45 239999), with breathtaking views, two drag lifts, three runs and a refuge near the tree line. In summer the focus shifts to the **eastern slopes**, which form the bulk of the park.

DAY HIKES

Those with sufficient experience, an ice axe and crampons can make the difficult seven-hour **ascent of Volcán Llaima**, but you need permission from Conaf. Be prepared to deal with crevasses and fumaroles, and beware of sulphur fumes at the summit. The park also offers a good selection of hikes for all abilities. For incredible views of the Sierra Nevada range through araucaría forest, take the 7km (2.5hr) trail from Playa Linda, at the east end of Lago Conguillío, to the base of the Sierra Nevada. The challenging **Travesía Río Blanco** (5km; 5hr), which crosses a small glacier before continuing into the Sierra Nevada proper, is recommended for very experienced trekkers only.

From the western shores of Laguna Verde, the 11km (5hr) **Sendero Pastos Blancos** runs to the Laguna Captrén, traversing spectacular scenery and rewarding you with panoramic views of Sierra Nevada, Lago Conguillío and the Truful-Truful valley. From the Truful-Truful Conaf ranger station, you can take the **Sendero Subtramo Arpehue**, part of the Sendero de Chile, to Laguna Captrén, passing the Andrés Huenupi Mapuche community along the way.

SHORT TRAILS

The Truful-Truful ranger station is also the starting point for two **short nature trails**: the Cañadón Truful-Truful (900m; 30min) passes by colourful strata, exposed by the Río Truful-Truful's flow, while the Las Vertientes trail (800m; 45min) is characterized by the subterranean springs that rush out of the ground. The Laguna Captrén ranger station is the starting point for the **Sendero Los Carpinteros**, also part of the Sendero de Chile, a fairly easy 8km, five-hour round-trip that starts from Lago Captrén, and loops around the lagoon before continuing to the administration centre and joining the El Contrabandista trail. This trail which was formerly used by the Pehuenche hunters and cattle rustlers going to and from Argentina. The highlight is an araucaría that's estimated to be 1500 years old.

ARRIVAL AND INFORMATION

PARQUE NACIONAL CONGUILLÍO

By bus Nar Bus (☎45 257074) runs eight buses a day from Temuco (four on Sun) to Melipeuco – the southern gateway to the eastern section of the park, 91km east of Temuco and 30km south of the park administration; from here, you'll have to take a taxi. There are frequent Buses Flota Erbuc (☎45 233958) services daily from Temuco to Curacautín, the northern gateway to the park, 75km from Temuco and 30km from the administration. From Curacautín there are two shuttles to the park's Laguna Captrén (Mon and Fri only); otherwise you can get a taxi. In winter, buses go the 106km from Temuco to the western ski slopes, but off-season, rural buses stop 18km short at the village of Cherquenco, from where you must walk or hitchhike.

By car The rutted roads within the park are suitable for 4WDs only.

Information Conaf's excellent Centro de Información Ambiental (Oct–March daily 9am–1pm & 3–6.30pm) sits at the heart of the park, near the wide Lago Conguillío, with displays on the park's geology, fauna and flora, good trail maps for sale and a number of short excursions on offer.

ACCOMMODATION

Camping in the park is expensive. There are five campsites (Nov–April only), mainly along the south shore of Lago Conguillío and Lago Captrén, all run by concessionaires and charging CH$5000 per person. Wild camping is not allowed.

La Baita Conguillío Conguillío ☎45 581073, ⓦlabaitaconguillio.cl. A complex consisting of an attractive lodge and six fully equipped, 4–6 person *cabañas* at Laguna Verde, on the edge of a dense wood. It's also an activity centre, coordinating trekking and eco-tourism in the summer, and skiing and snow-walking in the winter. Double CH$55,000, cabin CH$55,000

Centro de Ski Las Araucarías ☎45 239999, ⓦskiaraucarias.cl. This ski centre has two comparably priced *refugios*: Las Paraguas and Pehuén, the former offering dorms (bring own sleeping bag), while the latter also has several doubles, some en suite and some with shared bath. There are also fully-equipped 4–6 person apartments in two separate buildings. Dorm $\overline{\text{CH\$10,000}}$, double $\overline{\text{CH\$26,000}}$, apartment $\overline{\text{CH\$60,000}}$

Domos In the La Caseta sector, on the banks of Lago

Conguillío, reserve online via the park website. This glamping site is brand new; each dome comes with a double and a single bed, as well as a small gas cooker. $\overline{\text{CH\$50,000}}$ per dome

Lago Villarrica and around

6

LAGO VILLARRICA, tucked in the mountains some 86km to the southeast of Temuco, is Chile's most visited lake. The reason for its popularity is **Pucón**, a prime outdoor adventure centre. At the other end of the lake from Pucón is **Villarrica**, its more sedate counterpart.

The area around Lago Villarrica was first settled by the Spanish in the late sixteenth century, but they didn't have much time to enjoy their new territory: their towns were sacked by the Mapuche in 1602. Recolonization didn't take place until the Mapuche were subjugated 250 years later. With the arrival of the railroad from Santiago in 1933, the area became one of Chile's prime holiday destinations.

Villarrica

Sitting on the southwestern edge of the lake with a beautiful view of the volcano, **VILLARRICA** is one of Chile's oldest towns, although it may not feel like it – it has been destroyed several times by volcanic eruptions and skirmishes with the Mapuche. Now that Villarica's waterfront has been transformed with an attractive promenade, replacing the rather dirty beaches, the place has once again been attracting its fair share of visitors, who find it to be a more low-key, authentic destination than the ultra-touristy Pucón. Plans are afoot to beautify Villarica even more with brand new sand beaches, a yacht harbour and an urban park with theatre.

Museo Histórico y Arqueológico

Pedro de Valdivia 1050 • Closed for renovation at the time of writing

Villarrica's main attraction is the municipal **Museo Histórico y Arqueológico**, located on the main drag. It features some good displays of silver jewellery and musical instruments, and an exclusive collection of unusual Mapuche masks, while in the garden sits a traditional thatched *ruca*.

Feria Artesanal

Next to the museum is the **Feria Artesanal**, a year-round Mapuche crafts market where you can also try Mapuche cooking and pick up traditional medicines made from local plants. You can learn even more about the Mapuche culture during the annual Muestra Cultural Mapuche – the **festival** (late Jan to early Feb), which features traditional crafts, food, music and dance.

ARRIVAL AND INFORMATION
VILLARRICA

By bus Long-distance buses, connecting to all major destinations in the Lake District and beyond, each have their own terminal: Buses JAC, Bilbao 610 (@ 45 411447); Tur-Bus, Muñoz 657 (@ 45 411534); and Pullman, across the street from Tur-Bus. There is a central Terminal de Buses at Valdivia 621 for the smaller bus companies; Buses San Martín (@ 45 411584) and Igi Llaima (@ 45 412733) serve Argentine destinations such as Bariloche and Junín de los Andes. Rural buses to Licán Ray and Coñaripe, meanwhile, stop across the street from the Buses JAC terminal; from

here, small shuttle buses connect the town with Pucón, leaving several times an hour.

Destinations Pucón (every 20min; 45min); Puerto Montt (hourly; 6hr); San Martín de los Andes, Argentina (4 weekly at 10am; 4hr); Santiago (4 daily; 9hr); Temuco (every 30min; 1hr); Valdivia (7 daily; 2hr 15min).

Tourist information Pedro de Valdivia 1070 (mid-March to mid-Dec Mon–Sat 9am–1pm & 2.30–6pm; mid-Dec to mid-March daily 9am–9pm; @ 45 206619).

6

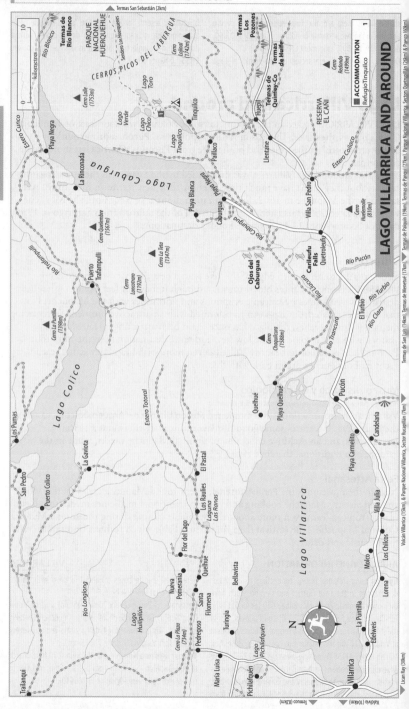

ACCOMMODATION 1

Refugio Tinquilco

Termas San Sebastián (2km)

Termas de Río Blanco

Río Blanco

PARQUE NACIONAL HUERQUEHUE

CERROS PICOS DEL CABURGUA

Sendero Los Huerquenes

Termas Los Pozones

Cerro Lojinal (1742m)

Termas de Huife

Cerro Lolle (1753m)

Lago Toro

Lago Verde

Lago Chico

Termas de Quimey-Co

Tinquilco

Huepil

Lago Tinquilco

Paillaco

Llentane

Cerro Redondo (1499m)

RESERVA EL CAÑI

Playa Negra

Estero Cunco

La Rinconada

Lago Caburgua

Playa Blanca

Poza Negra

Villa San Pedro

Estero Coilaco

Cerro Quelembre (1567m)

Caburgua

Río Caburgua

Cerro Huelemolle (810m)

Cerro La Teta (1347m)

Puerto Trafampulli

Cerro Loncotraro (1192m)

Ojos del Caburgua

Cariileufu Falls

Quetroleufu

Río Tradampulli

Río Pucón

Cerro La Puntilla (1398m)

Cerro Chaquilcura (1508m)

Río Liucura

El Turbio

Río Turbio

Lago Colico

Estero Totoral

Río Claro

Los Pumas

La Gaviota

Quelhué

Playa Quelhué

Río Trancura

Pucón

San Pedro

Puerto Colico

El Postal

Playa Carmelito

Candelaria

Flor del Lago

Los Raulíes

Laguna Las Ranas

Villa Julia

Nueva Pomerania

Quelhue

Bellavista

Lago Villarrica

Los Chilcos

Molco

Santa Filomena

Río Longlong

Lago Huilipilún

Turingia

Lorena

Cerro La Plaza (734m)

Pedregoso

Lago Pichilafquén

La Puntilla

N

Edelweis

Trailanqui

María Luisa

Pichilafquén

Villarrica

Volcán Villarrica (15km), & Parque Nacional Villarrica, Sector Rucapillán (7km)

Termas de Palguín (19km), Termas de Panqui (27km), Parque Nacional Villarrica, Sectors Quetrupillán (25km) & Puesco (60km)

Termas de San Luis (14km), Termas de Menetue (17km)

Valdivia (104km)

Temuco (82km)

Licán Ray (30km)

10

kilometres

0

ACCOMMODATION

Hostal Don Juan General Körner 770 ☎ 65 411833, ⓦ hostaldonjuan.cl. This one's a favourite with budget travellers during to its enthusiastic owners, splendid lake views from some of its rooms, and a plethora of little extras such as table tennis and table football for rainy days. The wood-panelled rooms are spartan but squeaky clean and there are several rustic but comfortable cabins holding 2–7 people. Double CH$17,500, cabin CH$26,000

Hostería de la Colina Las Colinas 115 ☎ 45 411503, ⓦ hosteriadelacolina.com. This fabulous hilltop inn and restaurant comes with a beautiful lake view and is run by two accommodating American teachers who know the area

inside out and provide guests with excellent hand-drawn hiking maps. There are no TVs in the homey, wood-panelled rooms and detached garden suites to detract from the peace and tranquility, but there is a book exchange, library and relaxing outdoor hot tub. CH$46,000

Hotel El Ciervo General Körner 241 ☎ 45 411215, ⓦ hotelelciervo.cl. Surrounded by well-tended gardens and facing the waterfront, this family-run lodge is owned by descendants of early German immigrants. Homespun rooms have fireplaces, fussy wallpaper and cable TV, and rates include use of swimming pool and German-style buffet breakfast. CH$84,000

EATING

La Cava de Roble Letelier 658 ☎ 65 416446. One of the better places in town for the carnivorously inclined, with game dishes on the menu competing with plain old steak for popularity. The venison and the wild boar are expertly done and the wine list is extensive. Daily 12.30–4pm & 7.30pm–midnight.

Hostería de la Colina Las Colinas 115 ☎ 65 411503. Guest and non-guests alike can enjoy imaginative takes on Chilean and international dishes, such as grilled fish and

Aztec soup, while looking over the lodge's beautiful garden and the lake below. Don't miss out on the fantastic home-made ice cream (the ginger variety is particularly good). Daily 12.30–3pm & 7–10.30pm.

Travellers Pub Letelier 753 ☎ 65 532769. This aptly named watering hole indeed attracts global wanderers with its diverse range of surprisingly good dishes, including vegetarian options, which draw inspiration from India, China and Southeast Asia. Daily 9.30am–midnight.

Pucón

On a clear day, you will be greeted by the awe-inspiring sight of **Volcán Villarrica** smouldering in the distance long before the bus pulls into **PUCÓN**, 25km from Villarrica. This small mountain town has firmly established itself as a top backpacker destination in the last decade. Each November–April season brings scores of hikers, climbers, whitewater enthusiasts and mountain bikers looking to climb Volcán Villarrica, brave the Río Trancura rapids or hike in the remote forested corners of the nearby Parque Nacional Huerquehue.

A day outdoors is usually followed by eating, drinking and partying in the town's restaurants and bars, or by a soak in the many surrounding thermal springs. The place gets particularly busy in January and February when Chilean students join forces with international backpackers.

MUSHER FOR A DAY

No longer must you travel to Siberia or endure minus 35 degree temperatures in the frozen Arctic wastes to take part in dog sledding expeditions. **Aurora Austral Patagonia Husky** (ⓦ www.novena-region.com), based near Villarica, is home to a mix of Siberian and Alaskan huskies. While there are some husky sledding opportunities near Ushuaia, Argentina (see p.435), Konrad is the only operator in the whole of South America who leads **multi-day husky sledding expeditions** that allow you to drive your own sled. You can choose either a day trip in the vicinity of Volcán Villarica or one of the multi-day expeditions – either to the Termas Geométricas hot springs 'or across the mountains into Argentina.

The sledding season runs from May to October, September being an excellent time to visit. Summer visitors (Dec–March) can test the half-tricycle, half-chariot contraptions (CH$30,000 per person, 2 person minimum). Konrad and his family also rent out three beautiful 2–6 person cottages with skylights (CH$30,000–50,000) on their peaceful piece of property, complete with wandering pet sheep, cats and dogs.

6

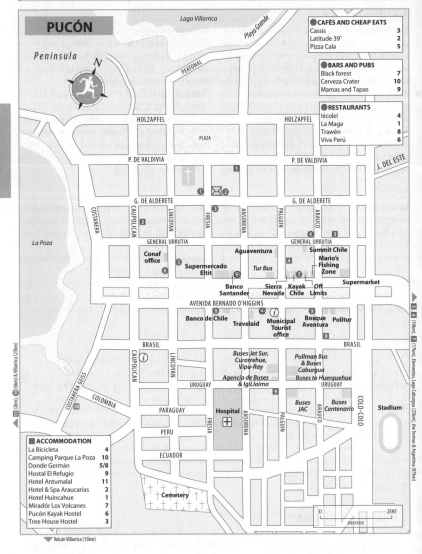

Pucón's wide, tree-lined streets are arranged in a compact grid, with most tour companies, supermarkets, banks and bars located along bustling **Avenida O'Higgins**, which bisects the town, with restaurants and guesthouses scattered nearby. O'Higgins ends by La Poza, a black-sand beach on the dazzling blue **Lago Villarrica**, while at the northern end of Calle Lincoyán you'll find Playa Grande, with a multitude of *pedalos*, jet skis and rowing boats for rent.

ARRIVAL AND DEPARTURE

PUCÓN

BY PLANE

There are summer-only flights to Pucón's tiny aerodrome from Santiago with LAN and Sky Airline, though the

majority of visitors fly into Temuco's considerably larger airport and arrange transfers from there.

BY BUS

Pucón doesn't have a main bus terminal. Instead, Buses JAC, Tur-Bus and Pullman each have their own purpose-built terminals. Buses JAC serve destinations along the Panamericana, such as Puerto Montt, Puerto Varas, Valdivia, Villarrica and Temuco. Tur-Bus has overnight departures to Santiago via Temuco. Buses Caburgua leave for Parque Nacional Huerquehue from their own little terminal opposite Buses JAC and Buses Curarrehue run to Curarrehue from the side of the Pullman bus station. At Palguín and Uruguay, the Agencia de Buses sells advance tickets for Igi Llaima and Intersur departures to Argentina's

Junín de los Andes and San Martín de los Andes; buses stop in front of the ticket office.

Companies Igi Llaima, Palguín 595 (❼45 443762); JAC, Palguin 605 (❼45 443963); Pullman, Palguín 555 (❼45 443331); Tur-Bus, O'Higgins 910 (❼45 443963).
Destinations Curarrehue (hourly; 45min); Parque Nacional Huerquehue (4–5 daily; 45min); Puerto Montt (every hour; 7hr); Puerto Varas (every hour; 6hr 30min); San Martín de Los Andes, Argentina (4 weekly 9.20am; 5hr); Santiago (2 daily; 10hr); Temuco (every 30min; 1hr 45min); Valdivia (7 daily; 3hr); Villarica (every 30min; 45min).

GETTING AROUND

Bicycle rental Sierra Nevada, O'Higgins at Palguin (❼45 444210) rents out decent mountain bikes for around CH$12,000 per day. *La Bicicleta* hostel (see p.276) is another

good choice for similarly priced bike rental.
Car rental Hertz, Fresia 220 ❼45 441664; Pucón Rent A Car, Colo Colo 340 ❼45 443052.

INFORMATION AND TOURS

TOURIST INFORMATION

Tourist office O'Higgins 447 (March–Nov daily 8.30am–6pm; Dec–Feb daily 8.30am–10pm; ❼45 449508, ⓦinformacionespucon.com). The helpful staff at the Oficina Municipal de Turismo speak some English. Here you can pick up a good free topographic map of Parque Nacional Villarica.
Conaf Lincoyán 336 (Mon–Fri 8.30am–noon & 2–5pm; ❼45 443781). Rangers can advise as regards national park trail conditions.
Travelaid Ansorena 425, Local 4 (❼45 444040, ⓦtravelaid.cl). Come here to book onwards travel anywhere in Chile (commission-free), to pick up detailed trekking and road maps of different parts of Chile, and to rent GPS systems for trekking around Pucón. English and German spoken.

TOURS

There are a multitude of **tour companies** in Pucón, mostly offering the same trips for similar prices. Most companies run **tours of the area**, which take in the Ojos de Caburgua waterfalls and any of the thermal springs at Huife, Palguín, Menetué and Pozones (CH$15,000–20,000), as well as night-time visits to Termas Los Pozones and rather touristy excursions involving a visit to one of the nearby Mapuche *reducciones*, where you can watch traditional crafts being made; lunch is often included (CH$20,000). We've picked out a selection of the more established operators, and arranged them according to the activity at which they are best.

Canopy Ziplining tours, involving sliding from treetop platform to platform while attached to a metal cord with a harness, are offered by most companies, but the most reliable operator is Bosque Aventura, Arauca at O'Higgins (❼45 444030, ⓦcanopypucon.cl). Outings typically cost CH$15,000–18,000.

Dog sledding Though Aurora Austral Patagonia Husky (ⓦwww.novena-region.com) is based out of Villarica (see box, p.273), Pucón is close enough for you to easily partake in the snow-and-husky adventures.
Fishing Both fly fishing and boat fishing trips can be arranged in the lakes and rivers surrounding the town. Prices for a half-day/full-day fishing on the Río Liucura are around CH$70,000/120,000, but substantial reductions are available for large groups. The better companies include Mario's Fishing Zone, O'Higgins 590 (❼09 760 7280, ⓦflyfishingpucon.com) and Off Limits, O'Higgins 560 (❼09 9949 2481, ⓦofflimits.cl).
Horseback riding You can go for a full-day or half-day ride in the mountain wilderness of the Parque Nacional Villarrica, or even on a multi-day horseback expedition across the Andes into Argentina. Prices start at about CH$30,000 for a half day, CH$50,000 for a full day. Antilco (15km east of Pucón, ❼09 9713 9758, ⓦantilco.com) is an experienced and highly recommended operator organizing anything from half-day trips to a nine-day glacier and hot springs ride. English and German spoken. Rancho de Caballos (❼08 346 1764, ⓦrancho-de-caballos.com) is another German-owned ranch 32km east of Pucón offering a range of horse treks from three hours to ten days, complete with barbecue and stays in rustic huts.
Mountaineering/rock climbing New, highly recommended outfit, Summit Chile Tours at General Urrutia 585 (❼45 443259, ⓦsummitchile.org) is headed by bilingual, highly qualified mountain guide Claudio, who leads small group (six maximum) treks in Villarica National Park – from the standard ascent of Volcán Villarica (CH$45,000) to the more technical two-day ascent of Volcán Lanín (CH$180,000) on the border with Argentina. Also on offer are half-/full-day (CH$24,000/30,000) rock climbing ventures in the area, suitable both for beginners and

6

6

advanced climbers. The building in which the tour company is housed is especially designed to accommodate climbers and mountaineering equipment is available for rent.

Rafting The nearby Río Trancura offers a popular class II–III run on the lower part of the river, with the more challenging class VI, upper Trancura, run made up almost entirely of drop pools. Both of these trips are half-day excursions; some operators allow you to combine the two. It's worth mentioning that when a surprise inspection of equipment was held in 2011, only the rafts of Aguaventura at Palguín 336 (T 45 444246, W aguaventura.com) passed the test. Prices for two to three hours rafting range from CH$25,000 for the lower Trancura to CH$30,000 for the upper Trancura.

Skydiving Aguaventura (see p.276) charges CH$150,000 for a 1hr tandem jump.

Volcán Villarrica This is a full-day excursion, usually leaving at around 7am, and prices are around CH$45,000–50,000. Climbing is not possible when the weather is bad, though some operators will still take customers up when it's cloudy, only to turn back halfway. There are several companies authorized by Conaf to climb the volcano, the best of which are: Paredón Andes Expeditions (T 45 444663, W paredonexpeditions.com), which takes groups no larger than eight people, and Elementos at Pasaje Las Rosas 640 (T 45 441750, W elementos-chile.com). In winter, companies such as Aguaventura, Palguín 336 (T 45 444246, W aguaventura.com), rents out skis and snowboards.

Water sports The exciting sport of hydrospeeding involves bodyboarding down the Río Liucura rapids (no greater than class III); the half-day excursion, including an hour in the river, costs CH$25,000 with Aguaventura (see p.276). Beginners and advanced kayakers alike should seek out Kayak Chile at O'Higgins 524 (T 45 441584, W kayakchile.net), an established American-run outfit specializing in kayaking trips on the Río Liucura. Learn the Eskimo roll in Lago Villarica (CH$38,000 half day/CH$60,000 full day), take to the Class III rapids in a double kayak with a guide (CH$45,000) or run the river in a ducky (CH$20,000).

ACCOMMODATION

HOTELS

Donde Germán Las Rosas 590 T 45 442444, W dondegerman.cl. Run by a knowledgeable local rafting guide, this charming wooden chalet has a spacious garden and terrace, and offers use of its kitchen, laundry service and free internet to its guests, as well as holding barbecues, renting bikes and arranging tours. The second branch at Brasil 640 has been completely rebuilt and boasts a swimming pool. Cheaper rooms share facilities. **CH$16,000**

★ **Hotel Antumalal** 2km outside Pucón T 45 441011, W antumalal.com. Built into the slope behind it, this architectural gem was designed by a student of Frank Lloyd Wright and is the most atmospheric hotel in town (as testified to by Queen Elizabeth, who once stayed here). The warm decor and large panoramic windows add to the comfort of the rooms, while the newly rebuilt spa features waterfalls and the organic cuisine at the on-site restaurant is superb, as is the service. **CH$160,000 (US$335)**

Hotel & Spa Araucarias Caupolicán 243 T 45 441284, W www.araucarias.cl. Located near the lakefront, this central hotel has an excellent private museum of Mapuche artefacts. Considering that room and *cabaña* rates include pool and sauna access as well as wi-fi and cable TV, it's an absolute bargain. **CH$70,500**

Hotel Huincahue Valdivia 375 T 45 443540, W hotelhuincahue.com. The 16 rooms of this opulent boutique hotel on the main square are flooded with natural light and come with marble bathrooms and wrought iron and wood furniture (for the best views of the volcano, grab room 202). An outdoor swimming pool is open in summer. **CH$110,000 (US$230)**

Miradór Los Volcanes 17km from Pucón towards Caburgua T 09 8189 8801, W miradorlosvolcanes.com. This collection of fully equipped luxury cabins (each holding 2–3 people), scattered about the hillside and boasting great views of the Villarica volcano, has drawn great praise from travellers. The owners – Cristian and Graciela – are as helpful as can be and extra comforts include an outdoor whirlpool spa. **CH$99,000**

HOSTELS

La Bicicleta Palguín 361 T 45 444583, E labicicletapucon@gmail.com. As the name suggests, this is a cyclist-friendly hostel, run by a congenial family with their own fleet of mountain bikes for rent. Dorms and rooms are compact but very clean. Dorm **CH$13,000**, double **CH$26,000**

Hostal El Refugio Palguín 540 T 45 441596, W hostalelrefugio.cl. With a handy location opposite the JAC bus station, this feels more like the home of a friend than a hostel, with a hammock in the guest lounge and the house pet wandering among the international crowd of guests. Knowledgeable Dutch–Chilean owners can advise about trekking and other activities. Dorm **CH$8000**, double **CH$22,000**

Pucón Kayak Hostel Km 10, Camino a Caburgua T 09 9899 2766, W puconkayakhostel.com. Ideally located on the bank of Río Trancura, this is a particularly good spot for water lovers. Choose between sleeping in a comfortable room in the main house or a gypsy wagon, going glamping in a geodome or roughing it in a basic bunkhouse. Kayaks are available for rent, drying facilities are provided and meals are served in the *quincho* (thatched barbecue area), which encourages socializing. Dorm **CH$9000**, room, dome or gypsy wagon **CH$12,000** per person

Tree House Hostel Urrutia 660 ☎45 444679, ⓦtreehousechile.cl. Set in an attractive garden with hammocks, this hostel is run by young and energetic staff who do their best to organize your stay. There are two common rooms and a guest kitchen, and the majority of rooms come with their own bathroom. Dorm CH$8000, double CH$30,000

CAMPSITES

Camping Parque La Poza Costanera Geis 769 ☎45 444982, ⓦcampinglapoza.com. Large, shaded campsite near the lake with hot showers and cooking facilities, popular with overland expeditions, cycling tourists and shoestring backpackers. CH$4000 per person

EATING AND DRINKING

CAFÉS AND CHEAP EATS

Cassis Fresia at Urrutia ☎45 442025. Popular wi-fi-equipped café where travellers linger for hours over coffee, cake and fresh fruit juice. The huge multi-grain sandwiches are a meal in themselves. Daily 8am–10pm.

Latitude 39° Gerónimo de Alderete 324 ☎09 7430 0016. This little Californian outpost becomes a home away from home to many a traveller staying in Pucón for more than two days. Apart from the super-friendly service, the Baja fish tacos, mini hamburgers and fat breakfast burritos really hit the spot. Daily 9.30am–11.30pm; shorter hours outside peak season.

Pizza Cala Lincoyán 361 ☎45 442025. Pucón's best pizzeria serves excellent thin-crust pizza, baked in a brick oven in front of you. The place really fills up when American football or baseball is on TV. Mains from CH$4500. Daily 12.30pm–midnight.

RESTAURANTS

★ **¡école!** Urrutia 592 ☎45 442025. Tasty, inexpensive and imaginative vegetarian dishes served in peace and quiet in a vine-covered courtyard or an attractive dining room. The vegetable lasagne has long been superb, as has the vegetable yellow curry with chutney and the home-made bread. Mains from CH$4500. Daily 8am–11pm.

★ **La Maga** Gerónimo de Alderate 264 ☎45 444277. Sate all your carnivorous cravings at Pucón's best *parilla*. The meat arrives cooked to perfection; you can't go wrong with the thick slabs of *bife de chorizo* (sirloin steak), though the fish dishes are almost equally good. There's an extensive wine selection and if you have room for dessert,

try the flan. Steaks from CH$7500. Daily noon–4pm & 7.30pm–midnight.

Trawén Fresia at O'Higgins ☎45 442025. *The* place for some of the most imaginative cuisine in town, this restaurant dishes up such treats as Antarctic krill *empanadas*, excellent home-made pasta, large, tasty sandwiches and combinations of fresh fruit juices. Daily 8am–11.30pm.

Viva Perú Lincoyán 372 ☎45 442025. Peruvian restaurant popular with locals, offering classic dishes from the land of the Inca, such as ceviche and *ají de gallina*. The lunchtime specials are good value and you can join the debate as to whether the Peruvian pisco sour is better than the Chilean. Daily noon–1am.

BARS AND PUBS

Black Forest Av O'Higgins 526. Trendy, dimly lit watering hole with a large horseshoe-shaped bar, specializing in good (though not cheap) cocktails and surprisingly imaginative sushi. You'll either love or hate the smoking policy. Daily 7pm–2am.

Cerveza Crater Ruta Villarica-Pucón, Km 6.5 ☎45 450427. Though you have to travel a little out of town, a trip to this lively brewepub rewards you with the Porter and the Golden Ale, as well as some solid German dishes for the peckish. Daily noon–2am.

Mamas and Tapas O'Higgins 597 ☎45 442025. In a large, dimly lit, wooden-and-glass building, a young drinking crowd knocks back beers and seriously strong pisco sours late into the night. Cheap dinner specials at this established traveller favourite, too. Mon–Thurs & Sun noon–1am, Fri & Sat noon–2am.

DIRECTORY

Banks and money There are ATMs in banks along O'Higgins and inside the Eltit supermarket. The *casa de cambio* on O'Higgins 261, Local C, offers a good exchange rate.

Hospital San Francisco, Uruguay 325 ☎45 441177.

Internet All accommodation options reviewed offer free wi-fi, free internet, or both. Otherwise, try *Cyber Unid@d*, Ansorena at O'Higgins.

Post office Fresia 183.

Ojos de Caburgua

Tahe the international road to Argentina, then follow signposted road for 17km or take a Caburgua-bound bus and ask to be dropped off by the entrance • Oct–March • CH$2500 entry payable by motorists

If you want to escape the bustle of Pucón for a while, head for the waterfalls near the tranquil **LAGO CABURGUA**. Thousands of years ago, an eruption blocked this southern

6

HOT SPRINGS AROUND PUCÓN

Ample amounts of volcanic activity mean that there are more commercialized **hot springs** around Pucón than in any other town in Chile. The facilities on offer vary, but the alleged health-giving properties of the waters are just about the same: bathing in them can benefit arthritis, nervous ailments and mental fatigue. Getting to some of the *termas* without your own car is difficult, though various companies in Pucón run **tours** to several of the hot springs below. The *termas* are mainly divided into two river valleys, the Río Liucura and the Río Trancura. Here are three of the best, arranged in order of proximity to Pucón.

Termas Los Pozones 2km beyond Termas de Huife ☎ 45 197 2350, ⓦ termas.cl (click on the Pozones link). The most rustic and natural of the hot springs In the area, these are simple, shallow pools dug out beside the river and dammed up with stones, with basic wooden changing huts above them. These *termas* are extremely popular with backpackers, and most tours from Pucón come here at night. There is a 3hr limit on visits. CH$5500 before 6pm, CH$6500 after. Daily 11am–6am.
Termas de Menetúe 5km west of San Luis bridge in the Río Trancura Valley ☎ 45 419488, ⓦ menetue .com. Set in beautiful gardens near the river, with naturally heated rock pools, spa, sauna and Jacuzzi, a small restaurant and *cabañas* (CH$138,000; "full-board" CH$79,000 "per person, including transfer from Pucón)". The swimming pools are open Dec–April, while the *termas* operate year-round. To get here,

head out of Pucón towards Argentina on the international road for 27km then turn left across the Puente (bridge) San Luis and continue west for 5km. CH$12,000. Daily 9am–7pm.
Termas de Panqui 15km further east of Termas de San Luis ☎ 45 442040, ⓦ termas.cl (click on the Panqui link). A North American reinterpretation of the Andean forest, Panqui concentrates on the more mystical side of the hot springs and calls itself a "Healing Retreat Centre". There are two thermal pools, a swimming pool, a mud bath, a medicine wheel, and also massages, Reiki and aquatic Shiatsu. You can camp here (CH$7500 per person), or stay in tepees (CH$12,000 per person) or in the mini-hotel (CH$34,000). The vegetarian restaurant serves hearty, healthy meals and there's a chance to join in the full moon celebrations. CH$9000. Daily 9am–9pm.

---

end of the valley, drowning it, and the water from the lake now flows out through subterranean streams and porous rock until it reappears as the **Ojos de Caburgua** (Eyes of Caburgua): three extremely photogenic waterfalls in the forest plunging into a deep pool of crystal-clear water. In hot weather, the air around the Ojos is cool and refreshing. The best time to visit is in the morning, before the crowds gather.

Parque Nacional Huerquehue

30km from Pucón • Officially open Jan–March but accessible at other times of year • CH$5000 • ⓦ parquehuerquehue.cl

Rising up almost 2000m from the eastern shore of Lago Caburgua are the forest-clad hills and peaks that form the 125-square-kilometre **PARQUE NACIONAL HUERQUEHUE**. Crowned by araucaria forests, the horseshoe-shaped **Cerros Picos de Caburgua** (Caburgua Mountains) enclose a dozen breathtakingly beautiful lakes of which the largest four – Tinquilco, Chico, Toro and Verde – are the most visited. At lower altitudes there are mixed forests of *coigüe* (southern beech) and the conifer *mañío*. The park is also home to over eighty **bird** species, including the Magellanic woodpecker, the delightful white-crested *fío-fío* and the red-chested *chucao*, as well as the little Darwin's frog.

ARRIVAL AND DEPARTURE   PARQUE NACIONAL HUERQUEHUE

By bus Buses JAC runs five daily services to the park from Pucón to the Conaf *guardería* at the park entrance during peak season (8.30am–7pm), while Buses Caburgua ply the

same route with four buses daily (8.30am–5.05pm; fewer out of peak season).

ACCOMMODATION AND EATING

Cabañas San Sebastián Termas San Sebastián ☎ 45 341961, ⓦ termalsansebastian.cl. Comprising

both a campsite and rustic but fully equipped *cabañas* with geothermal showers, one for a couple, the others for five people each, located next to the hot springs and with free access to the geothermal pool and individual thermal baths. Camping CH$5000 per person, cabin CH$35,000 **Camping El Rincón** Lago Tinquilco ☎ 09 8594 8261, ✉ ito.castillo@yahoo.com.ar. Ten camping spots by the lakeshore with a jetty from which to dive in, and boats and

water bicycles for rent. CH$8000 per site **Refugio Tinquilco** Lago Tinquilco ☎ 09 9539 2728, ⓦ tinquilco.cl. An airy wooden hostel in a beautiful streamside location with a sauna, book exchange and board games to entertain the guests and home-cooked meals available. Dorm CH$10,000, double CH$25,900

Santuario El Cañi

Nov–March • CH$4000 • All buses from Pucón bound for Parque Huerquehue pass by the entrance

Twenty-one kilometres east of Pucón, this near 990-acre sanctuary, comprising mixed Araucaría forest, was created in 1991 when the small Fundación Lahuen, made up of concerned locals, fought off logging interests to preserve this beautiful piece of land. The main **hiking trail** (9km; allow 3hr one way) runs steeply up through the forest from the park entrance, ascending to the attractive Laguna Negra, from which you get an all-encompassing view of the surrounding volcanoes on a clear day. There are plans to clear a new trail to connect Santuario El Cañi with Parque Nacional Huerquehue as part of the Sendero de Chile (ⓦ senderodechile.cl); the new trail will have campsites and *refugios* along it.

Aldea Intercultural Trawupeyüm

Curarrehue, 40km east of Pucón • Daily 10am–8pm • CH$1200 • Buses Curarrehue runs from Pucón to Curarrehue every 30min

Those interested in Mapuche culture will want to stop by the **ALDEA INTERCULTURAL TRAWUPEYÜM**. This excellent museum is located in the frontier town of Curarrehue behind the bright green Municipalidad buildings on the Plaza and housed inside a traditional Mapuche **ruca**. An enthusiastic guide is on hand to talk you through the exhibits, which include traditional musical instruments and weavings, and if you're lucky, you may find Mapuche chef Anita Epulef in residence; she sometimes sells traditional Mapuche dishes from one of the kiosks outside the museum.

EXPLORING PARQUE NACIONAL HUERQUEHUE

From the park entrance, the short and pleasant Sendero Ñirrico leads down to Lago Tinquilco through dense bamboo groves before rejoining the main trail. From Lago Tinquilco, there is a worthwhile two-hour hike up **Cerro Quinchol**, rewarding you with excellent views of Lago Caburgua beyond. A steep and more challenging hike continues up Cerro San Sebastián where you'll find snow on the summit even in summer; allow five hours for the climb. The most popular hike is the Sendero Los Lagos (9km), which climbs to a height of 1300m through dense forest to the beautiful Chico, Toro and Verde lakes from the *Refugio Tinquilco*; allow three hours one-way, as the trail is steep in sections and can be muddy. About halfway up there's a pictureque detour to the thundering **Salto Nido del Aguila**, and several scenic viewpoints along the way.

Past Lago Chico, the trail splits, the left fork leading to Lago Verde and the right to Lago Toro; the two join up. If you wander off the main trail along the shores of Lago Verde or Lago Toro, you can often have the spot completely to yourself. You can take in the tiny Lago de los Patos and Lago Huerquehue (2hr) before rejoining the Los Lagos loop, or you can continue along the **Sendero Los Huerquenes** to **Termas de San Sebastián**, a hot spring outside the park's northeastern boundaries, via the stunning Renahue viewpoint overlooking the lakes below. It's possible to hike to the Termas in one day (23km from the park entrance; 8–9hr), since much of the Sendero Los Huerquenes is downhill, and you can either stay at the comfortable *Cabañas San Sebastián* (see p.278) before retracing your steps, or make advance arrangements for a ride out to the nearest town, also called Renahue, and from where you can catch a bus back to Pucón. You'll find the free Conaf map of the park useful; it's readily available at the Pucón tourist office and Conaf office.

> ## VILLARRICA'S DEMONIC PEAKS
>
> The area covered by **Parque Nacional Villarrica** was inhabited long before the arrival of the Spanish, and the names of the peaks reflect this: Volcán Villarrica's original Mapuche name, Rucapillán, means "house of the devil", because of its frequent eruptions, while Quetrupillán, the dormant volcano next door, means "mute devil". Another peak towards the border with Argentina is called Quinquili, or "devil's fang".

Parque Nacional Villarrica

Day entry CH$1000; volcano ascent CH$4000; Villarrica traverse CH$8000 • ☎ 45 443781

The centrepiece of the **PARQUE NACIONAL VILLARRICA** is, of course, **Volcán Villarrica**, in all its smoking, snowcapped glory. Located just 15km south of Pucón, the vast park divides into three sectors: **Rucapillán**, **Quetrupillán** and **Puesco**, and stretches 40km to the Argentine border (74km by road). It also contains two other volcanoes and is one of the few national parks in the Lake District in which you can camp wild and hike for long distances. If you plan on doing lengthy hikes, be sure to take plenty of water (the seasonal streams can't be relied on) as well as the useful *JLM Pucón Trekking Map* and the TrekkingChile (ⓦtrekkingchile.com) map of Pucón, both widely available in Pucón.

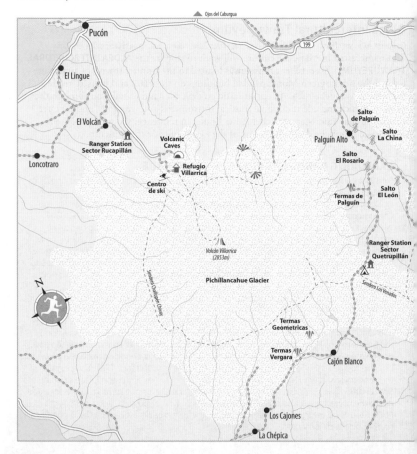

Sector Rucapillán

SECTOR RUCAPILLÁN, home to the magnificent **Volcán Villarrica** (2840m), presents a visual contradiction: below the tree line it's a lush forest; above, it's a black waste of lava, dotted with snow and encrusted with an icecap. The volcano forms the obvious focal point, standing sentinel over the park, and it's very active – there were sixteen recorded eruptions in the twentieth century, the most recent in 1984 (if you were wondering what the daily siren at noon means, one blast of the siren simply announces the time of day, whereas three blasts of the siren would signify a volcanic eruption).

6

The ski centre

12km from Pucón • Late June to mid-Oct 9am–5pm • Full-day lift ticket CH$24,000 in peak season • ⓦ www.skipucon.cl

A good road branches off the Pucón–Villarrica road, running up the northern slopes of the volcano. After 7km you reach the **park entrance**, and almost halfway up is the **ski centre**. Skiing here is an experience – how often do you get to ski on an active volcano? – though the snow quality is not as good as at the resorts around Santiago or in Valle Nevado. While on good days, the views are amazing, temperamental weather means that the seven ski lifts are affected whenever it's too windy; when smoke blows from the top of the crater, they shut down.

PARQUE NACIONAL VILLARRICA

6

CLIMBING VOLCÁN VILLARRICA

Pretty much as soon as you arrive in Pucón, you'll realize that that town's main attraction is the **Volcán Villarrica**, just begging to be climbed. The path leaves from the ski centre, and it's four hours up to a crater in which, if you're lucky and the gas clears, you'll see bubbling pits of molten rock. If it's not too windy, the chairlift (CH$5500) trims an hour off the climb. While it doesn't demand technical climbing skills, you do need a hard hat, ice-axe, sturdy boots, gaiters, waterproof overtrousers and crampons – all provided by the tour agency you go with. The view from the top on a clear day is stupendous (though you won't linger for long because of the noxious fumes), followed by a rollicking tobogganing down the side of a volcano along snow slides, using your ice-axe as a brake.

GUIDES AND PRICES

Conaf keeps a list of companies authorized to guide climbers up the volcano. A maximum of nine climbers are allowed with one guide. Though the tour agencies may tell you otherwise, there is nothing to stop you from tackling the mountain without a guide, as long as you have proper equipment, but unless you're an experienced mountaineer, it's not advisable. Competition keeps prices down to a reasonable CH$45,000 or so, which includes transport and all necessary equipment. Most agencies start off at around 6.30am, though a couple leave at 4.30am to beat the crowds. Do not be tempted to go for the cheapest trip – cost is commensurate with safety, and companies offering much cheaper deals can sometimes do so by using inferior equipment and hiring inexperienced guides. See p.276 for recommended operators.

The twenty runs are geared mostly towards beginners and intermediate skiers, though experienced boarders and skiers can have some fun off-piste. Boarders in particular can make use of the natural half-pipes created by the lava chutes. You can hire cheaper skis and snowboards from the agencies in Pucón; most agencies run transport to the slopes in season.

Cuevas Volcánicas
Daily: Jan & Feb 10am–8.30pm; March–Dec 10am–6pm • Bilingual tour CH$5000

Just under 1km after the park entrance, a signpost points you to the **Volcanic Caves**. A large lava tube, the main cave is dank and wet, but there's a dry path for 400m, and you can see the multicoloured minerals on the walls. Check out the museum exhibits on volcanology and seismology before embarking on the tour; hard hats are provided but you have to bring warm clothing, as the temperature inside the caves stays cool year-round.

Sector Quetrupillán
SECTOR QUETRUPILLÁN, the middle section of the park, is dominated by the rarely visited majesty of Volcán Quetrupillán (2009m). It's a remote area of wilderness, tucked between two volcanoes and accessible only on foot or down a 35km dirt road that turns south from the Camino International 18km out of Pucón, climbing through native coigüe and araucaría forest. Here you can find the contemporary hotel at **Termas de Palguín**, with its all-curing waters, and also four splendid **waterfalls** – Palguín, La China, El León and Turbina, a little way off the main track.

Sector Puesco
East of Quetrupillán, close by the border with Argentina, the third part of the park, **SECTOR PUESCO** is rather like the Canadian Rockies, with pine forests and craggy mountain sides. The Conaf station is at the Puesco frontier post. South of here, the tough **Sendero Momolluco** (22km; approx 8hr) leads southeast from the main road towards Volcán Lanín, before finishing at the remote Laguna Verde. From here, the **Sendero Lagos Andinos** (11km; 4.5hr) loops back to the main road via Lagunas

---

THE VILLARRICA TRAVERSE

The park's best long-distance hike, the **Villarrica traverse** (72km; 5 days), starts at the ski centre and consists of three trails joined together, the first half being the moderately difficult **Sendero Challupen-Chinay** (28.5km; 14hr), which skirts around the southern side of Volcán Villarrica and ends at the Quetrupillán Conaf ranger post and the basic Chinay campsite, connected to the main road by a very rough 10km-long dirt track. From the ranger post, this dirt road continues on to Coñaripe; you'll need a sturdy 4WD vehicle, even in the summer. For the Sendero Challupen-Chinay section, you'll need to carry all your water with you as there are no streams to be relied on.

    Sendero Los Venados heads southeast from the same ranger post, along the south side of Volcán Quetrupillán, passing the tranquil Laguna Azul – a haven for birds – before merging with the Sendero Las Avutardas (43.4km; 3 days), which finishes at the Argentina-bound road in the Puesco sector, around 2km south of the Conaf ranger post at Puesco. From here, you can hitch a lift to Curarrehue with the Chile-bound traffic. This section is crossed by numerous streams from which drinking water can be collected.

    Many hikers choose to do the Chinay-Puesco section only, as it's more picturesque. Before you start out, you must pay the park entry fee at the Conaf office in Pucón (see p.274) and inform them of your intended dates.

Huinfiuca, Plato and Escondida, ending at the Laguna Quilleihue, just across the main road.

ARRIVAL AND INFORMATION   PARQUE NACIONAL VILLARRICA

SECTOR RUCAPILLÁN
By organized tour There's no public transport to Sector Rucapillán, though there are dozens of tour buses. In the winter, most tour agencies will take you to the park for CH$7500 per person, leaving Pucón at 9.30am and returning at 4.30pm.

SECTORS QUETRUPILLÁN AND PUESCO
By bus For Sector Quetrupillán you can take a Curarrehue-bound bus from Pucón (every 30min) along

the international road, though the nearest you'll get will be the hamlet of Palguín Bajo, 10km away down a dirt track. For Sector Puesco, you need to get on an international bus heading to Junín de los Andes in Argentina (several weekly) and ask to be dropped off; you should be able to get off at the Puesco customs post and Conaf station.

Conaf Lincoyán 336, Pucón (Mon–Fri 8.30am–noon & 2–5pm; ☎45 443781). Rangers can advise on trail conditions and dish out trail maps.

ACCOMMODATION

Camping Wild camping is allowed, apart from in the zone east of the Puesco border post. There are also serviced campsites near the entrance to Rucapillán, but the only

campsite actually in the park is near the Quetrupillán Conaf station. Rucapillán site CH$6000 per site; Quetrupillán site CH$2500 per person

The Siete Lagos

Overshadowed by the popular resort of Pucón, the region known as **SIETE LAGOS** – Seven Lakes – is the next one south of Villarrica. Six of the lakes are in Chile, one (Lago Lácar) in Argentina, and all are linked by rivers in one hydrological system, with attractive villages along their shores.

    The busiest lakes are the largest ones, the relatively warm **Lago Calafquén**, 30km south of Villarrica along a tarred road, and **Lago Panguipulli**, 17km further on. The next valley down contains the slightly smaller **Lago Riñihue**, hardly visited and perfect for nature lovers and fishermen. To the east of Lagos Panguipulli and Riñihue, nestling deep in the pre-cordillera and surrounded by 2000m peaks, are the most remote of the Siete Lagos, **Lago Neltume** and **Lago Pirihueico**, neither of which was accessible by road until thirty years ago and today are rapidly making their way onto the map.

Lago Calafquén and around

The most developed of the seven lakes, **Lago Calafquén** features a paved road for the 30km along its northern shore between the settlements of **Lican Ray** and **Coñaripe**, and a mostly paved road around the rest. To the east is tiny **Lago Pellaifa**, created by a 1960 earthquake that altered the region's water flow. It's bordered by an international road to Argentina that passes a clutch of thermal springs around the mountain hamlet of **Liquiñe**.

Lican Ray

LICAN RAY, a small holiday town, lies 30km south of Villarrica, and boasts two pleasant black-sand **beaches**: Playa Chica, with a small forested promontory crisscrossed by several short hiking trails, and Playa Grande, a long strip of dark sand framed by the surrounding hills.

During the first weekend of January, the whole length of the main street, General Urrutia, is transformed into Chile's **largest outdoor barbecue** (*asado*) in which some three hundred lambs meet their spicy ends.

Coñaripe

Laid-back **COÑARIPE**, a 21km drive along the northern shore of Lago Calafquén, has just a couple of good black-sand beaches and a sleepy air. The small image of Christ on the lakeshore by the entrance to town is a memorial to two lava-engulfed victims and a testament to the uncertainty of living in this volcanically unstable area.

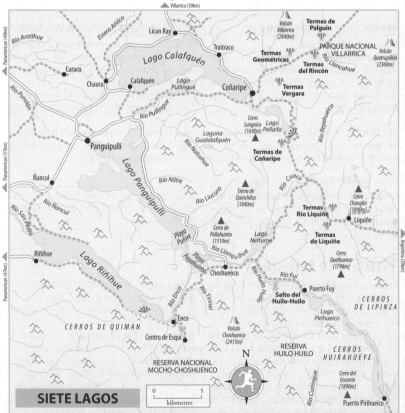

Termas Geométricas

12km northeast of Coñaripe • CH$16,000 • Late Dec to Feb daily 10am–9pm; rest of the year 11am–7pm • ☎ 2 214 1214 , ⓦ termasgeometricas.cl

Although the land around Coñaripe bubbles with numerous thermal springs, the most exclusive set of springs in the region is **Termas Geométricas**, with seventeen smart, slate-covered pools, linked by a series of wooden walkways strung along a half-mile of lush mountain stream. Grass-roofed shelters blend into the surroundings but there is no overnight accommodation here.

ARRIVAL AND INFORMATION

By bus In Lican Ray, buses leave from offices around the plaza. Buses JAC runs services to Villarrica (Mon–Fri every 15 min; Sat & Sun every 30min) and one bus daily goes to Panguipulli. Coñaripe is served by frequent buses from Villarrica, operated by Buses JAC, and Igi Llaima. There are also less-frequent buses from both Coñaripe (six in peak

LAGO CALAFQUÉN

season; three in off-season) and Liquiñe to Panguipulli, operated by Buses Pirehueico.

Tourist information Urrutia 310, Lican Ray (daily: Dec–Feb 9am–9pm; erratic hours rest of the year; ☎45 431516). The helpful and friendly Oficina de Turismo is on the plaza.

ACCOMMODATION AND EATING

Hotel Becker Manquel 105, Lican Ray ☎65 431553, ⓦ hotelbecker-lican.com. Lakefront hotel offering medium-sized rooms with an upstairs deck overlooking Playa Chica and a restaurant downstairs which does a decent *asado*, among other dishes. CH$30,000

Hotel Elizabeth Beck de Ramberga 496, Coñaripe ☎65 217279, ⓦ hotelelizabeth.cl. Coñaripe's only hotel has wood-panelled rooms with down comforters on the beds, satellite TV and the best restaurant in town, serving well-executed Chilean dishes. CH$22,300

Lago Panguipulli

Ten kilometres south of Lago Calafquén is the northern snout of long, thin **Lago Panguipulli**, a lake that stretches 26km southeast into the cordillera. On the lake's northwesternmost tip is the neat little town of **Panguipulli**, while a newly paved road skirts the eastern shore to the remote Lagos **Neltume** and **Pirehueico**.

Panguipulli

The attractive village of **PANGUIPULLI**, bright with colourful roses, dark copper beech trees and manicured lawns, was founded in 1885 as a trading post for Pehuenche and Mapuche Indians driven off the Argentine pampas. It grew beyond these humble origins in 1903 when a Capuchin mission was established here, and its church, the **Iglesía de San Sebastián,** is an impressive twin-towered latticed confection of yellow, red, brown and white. Paguipulli is best known today as the **town of roses**, with an estimated fourteen thousand closely pruned rose bushes lining the streets, and a crowd-pulling folk festival, **Semana de las Rosas**, during the last week of January, when the city hosts art exhibits and concerts.

ARRIVAL AND INFORMATION

By bus The bus terminal is at Gabriela Mistral 1000. Buses Pirehueico (☎63 311497) serves Valdivia and Puerto Montt several times daily, while Buses Lafit (☎63 311647) has services to Neltume and Puerto Fuy via Choshuenco four times daily (Mon–Sat 10am, 3pm, 4.30pm & 6.45pm) and

PANGUIPULLI

carries on to Puerto Pirihueico and San Martín de los Andes, Argentina.

Tourist information Near the church, on Plaza Arturo Prat (Jan & Feb daily 9am–8pm; March–Dec Mon–Sat 9am–5pm; ☎63 310435, ⓦ sietelagos.cl).

ACCOMMODATION & EATING

Gardylafquen Martínez de Rozas 722 ☎65 310921. Two storey restaurant, very popular with locals. Head to the vast upstairs dining area and order one of the excellent trout dishes. Daily noon–3pm & 7–11pm.

Hotel & Restaurant Le Francais Martínez de Rozas 880 ☎65 312496. While there's nothing particularly French about this place, the comfortable en-suite rooms have cable TV, and the restaurant serves hearty Chilean specials. CH$34,000

Lago Riñihue

LAGO RIÑIHUE, the beautiful flooded valley to the south of Lago Panguipulli and the last of the Siete Lagos, has been almost completely untouched by tourism. There is no apparent reason why: the tiny village of **Riñihue** on the western shore of the lake was the first to be connected to the railway in 1910 and there's a good tar road linking it with the Panamericana, 50km to the west. The area is well known by Chileans, at least, for producing famous Swiss- and German-style hard cheeses.

6

Lago Neltume and around

Five kilometres after the turnoff for Choshuenco, on what was Lago Panguipulli's shore road, pre-eruption, a gravel road branches left to smallish **LAGO NELTUME**, depositing you on its eastern shore, where much of the waterfront is private property and effectively closed to the public. The other side of the lake is a mountain: the densely forested side of the impressive Cerro Paillahuinte, which rises 1435m straight up from the water.

Salto del Huili-Huilo
CH$2000

Heading towards Argentina from Lago Neltume, you'll eventually reach the turnoff for the waterfall, **Salto del Huilo-Huilo**, a powerful torrent forced through a ten-metre-wide green cleft in the rock, cascading into the swirling aquamarine pool below to deafening effect.

Lago Pirehueico

Six kilometres on from Lago Neltume lies **LAGO PIREHUEICO**. Pirehueico means "worm of water" in the local Mapuche language, and there couldn't be a better name for this curving, twisting, snake-like lake, bordered by forest-clad mountains. It's crossed by a **ferry** from Puerto Fuy in the north to Puerto Pirehueico in the south. The crossing is beautiful and extremely worthwhile, not to mention far cheaper than the Puerto Varas-Bariloche crossing (see p.301).

ARRIVAL AND DEPARTURE
LAGO PIREHUEICO

By bus In summer there are seven daily buses running between Panguipulli and Puerto Fuy.
By ferry Ferry Hua-Hum (☎63 197 1585) crosses the lake from Puerto Fuy in the north to Puerto Pirehueico in the south (one crossing daily March–Dec at noon; Jan & Feb 3 daily at 8am, 1pm, and 6pm; 1hr 30min; CH$20,000 for cars, CH$3000 for bicycles, CH$1500 for passengers).

CROSSING THE ARGENTINE BORDER

Via Puerto Pirehueico From Puerto Pirehueico, it's 11km to the border, where there is a café and a customs post (8am–8pm year-round). In summer, there are four daily buses running across the border from Puerto Pirehueico to San Martín de los Andes.

ACCOMMODATION AND EATING

Marina del Fuy Puerto Fuy ☎63 197 2426, ⓦmarinadelfuy.com. Right on the lakeside by the dock, this cedar-shingled, tastefully decorated hotel is ideal for pre- and post-ferry travellers. The interior is suprisingly opulent, with interesting light fixtures, and the restaurant delivers with a good mix of international and Chilean dishes. **CH$136,000**
Montaña Magica Lodge Several kilometres from Puerto Fuy ☎63 197 2651, ⓦhuilohuilo.cl. This Tolkienesque creation, shaped like a grass-covered volcano with windows encases uniquely shaped wood-panelled rooms and an entry hall with a stream running through it; if you are tall, get a room on one of the lower floors. Wooden walkways connect the volcano to the giant tree-like *Hotel Baobab*, its pricier sister hotel. The restaurant serves wild boar, among other delicious offerings. **CH$146,200**

Valdivia and around

Fifty kilometres to the west of the Panamericana lies the attractive city of **VALDIVIA**, one of Chile's oldest settlements, founded by Pedro de Valdivia as a supply halt on the route to Lima, six days' sail from the Magellan Strait.

Brief history

Pedro de Valdivia chose the confluence of the rivers Calle Calle and Cruces as a suitable location for the city because it was defensible and had access to both the sea and the inland plains. Yet in 1599 it had to be abandoned after the Mapuche uprisings, and was almost immediately pounced on by the Dutch. To counter this threat, and that of pirates, the Viceroy in Peru ordered a string of forts to be built. These were strengthened when Britain threatened in 1770, and, by the time of the wars of Chilean independence, Valdivia was a formidable redoubt. Post-independence there was a great influx of German settlers who founded shipyards, breweries and mills, leaving a lasting legacy.

Valdivia today

Today Valdivia is a vibrant, cosmopolitan university town, a mixture of the colonial and the contemporary, even though many of its old buildings are gone – lost to earthquakes, fires and floods throughout the last century. On February 9 each year, the city celebrates the founding of Valdivia, and between the second and third Saturday in February all of Valdivia comes out to celebrate "Valdivia Week": the river lights up with a **parade of boats**, and a memorable fireworks show.

The waterfront

Unlike most Chilean towns, Valdivia's social centre is not its plaza but its **waterfront**, where the Río Calle Calle and the Río Cau Cau meet the Río Valdivia. Just to the south of the Mercado Fluvial, touts offer ferry tours (see p.290).

Mercado Fluvial

Valdivia's lively produce market, the **Mercado Fluvial**, sits on the riverfront, with fishermen expertly gutting the day's catch and throwing scraps to the clamouring seagulls and the family of sea lions who treat the market as their local takeaway. Opposite, on the other side of the path, vendors sell all types of fruit, vegetables, strings of smoked shellfish and smoked salmon. Across the road, the **Mercado Municipal** features crafts stalls – including some Mapuche artefacts – and inexpensive *marisquerías* (seafood restaurants).

Isla Teja

Opposite the town centre, across the Pedro de Valdivia bridge, sits **Isla Teja**. A haven of tranquillity, the island is home to a trio of good museums and has beautiful views back across the river to the Mercado Fluvial.

Museo Histórico y Antropológico Maurice van de Maele

Dec–Feb daily 10am–8pm; March–Nov Tues–Sun 10am–1pm & 2–6pm • CH$2000 or CH$3500 for combined ticket with Museo de la Exploración R.A. Philippi

Isla Teja's main attraction is the splendidly sited **Museo Histórico y Antropológico Maurice van de Maele**, in an old colonial house surrounded by a veranda. Once owned by Karl Anwandter, founder of Chile's first brewery, it's still furnished with the trappings of nineteenth-century European society, including a double piano, an ornate red-marble fireplace and a magic lantern. Also on display is a fascinating collection of old sepia prints of the first German settlers and the Anwandter family tree. The

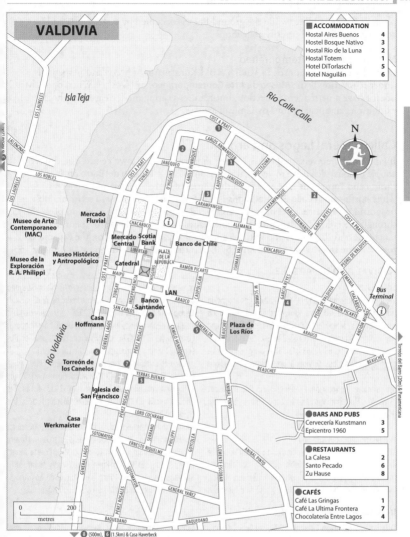

highlights are the collection of **Mapuche artefacts**, mainly splendid silverwork and cloth, and a room of memorabilia pertaining to British-born Lord Cochrane, who played a decisive role in securing independence for Chile.

Museo de la Exploración R.A. Philippi

Dec–Feb daily 10am–8pm; March–Nov Tues–Sun 10am–6pm • CH$2000 or CH$3500 for combined ticket with Museo Histórico y Antropológico Maurice Van de Maele

Next door to the Museo Histórico sits the **Museo de la Exploración R.A. Philippi**. Dedicated to the groundbreaking German-born naturalist, Rudolph Philippi, it's housed in a Jugendstil building that was originally dismantled and then put back together at its current location. Upstairs you'll find Philippi's study, complete with period furniture, numerous pickled denizens of the sea and a superb collection of photos of local wildlife, while the ground floor is occupied by larger fauna and colourful beetle and butterfly collections.

Museo de Arte Contemporaneo

Down by the water, housed in Valdivia's old Kunstmann brewery, and perpetually under renovation is the **Museo de Arte Contemporaneo**, or "MAC". When open, MAC doesn't have a permanent collection, but features visiting modern art and photography exhibitions and installations by Chilean artists.

Calle General Lagos and around

Inland from the rivers, to the east, lies the modern concrete town centre. You can see a couple of squat defensive towers that date from 1774 – **Torreón del Barro** on Avenida Picarte and **Torreón de los Canelos** on the corner of Yerbas Buenas and General Lagos, while north–south **Calle General Lagos** is filled with Valdivia's gems, a series of nobly proportioned nineteenth-century buildings. Take a stroll down the road and peek through the railings at the austere, double-staircased **Casa Werkmaister** (between Cochrane and Riquelme) and at the crinkly gabled **Casa Haverbeck** on the way out of town, or else stop by **Casa Hoffman** (1870), an attractive merchant house, at Yungay 733.

ARRIVAL AND DEPARTURE   VALDIVIA

BY PLANE
Valdivia's Aeródromo Pichoy (☎63 272295) lies around in front of Plaza de la República 30km northeast of town and is served by LAN, Maipú 271, (☎63 258844; ⓦlan.com) and Sky Airlines Schmidt 303 (☎63 226280; ⓦskyairline.cl). Transfer Valdivia (☎63 225533; CH$5000 per person) runs a door-to-door minibus service; a taxi should cost around CH$17,000.
Destinations Concepción (1 daily; 1hr); Puerto Montt (1 weekly; 1hr); Santiago (2 daily; 2hr); Temuco (2 weekly; 45min).

BY BUS
Most long-distance buses travelling north–south along the Panamericana service the highly efficient bus terminal (☎63 220498), on the corner of Anwandter and Muñoz, five blocks from the city centre; you'll also find most bus

comapany offices here. Coastal buses to Niebla and beyond operate from the city end of Puente Pedro de Valdivia.
Companies Buses JAC (☎63 212925, ⓦwww.jac.cl) has frequent departures to all major Lake District destinations; Pullman (☎63 278576, ⓦwww.pullman.cl) and Tur Bus (☎63 213840, ⓦturbus.cl) serve the Lake District and all major destinations in central and northern Chile, while Cruz del Sur (☎63 213840 ⓦwww.pullmansur.cl) heads to the island of Chiloé and Igi Llaima (☎63 213542) and Tas Choapa (☎63 213124, ⓦwww.taschoapa.cl) cross the border to Argentina.
Destinations Ancud (4 daily; 5hr); Bariloche, Argentina (1 daily at 8.45am; 7hr); Castro (4 daily; 7hr); Osorno (every 30min; 1hr 30min); Pucón (6 daily; 3hr); Puerto Montt (every 30min; 3hr 30min); Puerto Varas (every 30min; 3hr); Santiago (every hour; 11hr); San Martín de Los Andes, Argentina (3 weekly on Wed, Fri & Sun at 7.30am; 8hr).

INFORMATION AND TOURS

Tourist information Chacabuco 210, 3rd floor C (Mon–Thurs 8.30am–5.30pm, Fri 8.30am–4.30pm; ☎63 278748, ⓦvaldiviaturismo.cl). Sernatur office with a helpful map of the region. There's also an information kiosk at the bus station (☎63 212212; daily 8am–10pm).

TOUR OPERATORS
Catamarán Marqués de Mancera By the Mercado Fluvial ☎63 249191, ⓦmarquesdemancera.cl. This catamaran runs a large loop behind Isla del Rey, with 35min stops at the Corral and Mancera forts (5hr; bilingual guide, lunch and *onces* included); tours cost between CH$16,000 and CH$35,000, depending on your location on the boat, and depart at 1.30pm.

Embarcaciones Bahía By the Mercado Fluvial ☎63 378727. With its fleet of four boats, Bahía specializes in 3hr tours of the Santuario de la Naturaleza Carlos Anwandter (CH$12,000, including *onces* and a guide), as well as hour-long cruises along the river (CH$6000).
Orion III By the Mercado Fluvial ☎09 9842 5219. This 108-person boat is the only one to offer trips to the forts that include both Isla Huapi and the two forts (CH$20,000; 6hr; bilingual guide, lunch on Isla Huapi and *onces* included).
Valditur ☎63 213766 or ☎09 9645 7700, ⓦvalditur.cl. Experienced, multilingual operator Claus runs trips to the forts, trekking and canopy excurions to Parque Oncol and Valdivia city tours, among others. English, German and Portuguese spoken.

ACCOMMODATION

HOTELS AND B&B

Hostal Río de Luna Prat 695 ☎63 253333, ⓦhostalriodeluna.cl. A large, quiet and pleasant guesthouse with a blue colour scheme. The airy en-suite rooms overlook Río Calle Calle, breakfast includes ham, cheese and pie and the bus station's a 2min walk away. CH$42,000

Hostal Totem Carlos Anwandter 425 ☎63 292849, ⓦturismototem.cl. Quiet, welcoming guesthouse with squeaky wooden floors and spacious, en-suite rooms (some rather dark). Breakfast includes ham and home-made marmalade and the helpful management speaks English and French. CH$25,000

Hotel DiTorlaschi Yerbas Buenas 283 ☎63 224103, ⓦhotelditorlaschi.cl. Founded by a family from Antofagasta, this wood-panelled lodging option is primarily a business hotel and features all appropriate facilities (cable TV, wi-fi, laundry service) and polished wooden floors. The rooms have plush beds, disabled visitors are provided for and the self-catering apartments are arranged around an attractive garden. Double CH$47,000, apartment CH$46,000

Hotel Naguilán Gral Lagos 1927 ☎63 212851, ⓦhotelnaguilan.com. Though it's a brisk 20min walk to the centre, this hotel has a winning location right on the waterfront and river views from all its spacious rooms, themselves decorated in contemporary style. The suites have private terraces and the restaurant serves excellent fusion cuisine. CH$57,000 (US$120)

HOSTELS

Hostal Aires Buenos García Reyes 550 ☎63 222202, ⓦairesbuenos.cl. Central, well-run, HI-affiliated hostel, bustling with the local and international backpacking set. Dorms are cheery and secure (with lockers for valuables), there's a TV lounge for mingling and guest kitchen, and friendly staff are on hand to help and advise. Dorm CH$9000, double CH$25,000

Hostel Bosque Nativo Fresia 29 (off Janequeo) ☎63 433782, ⓦhostelnativo.cl. The best hostel in town, in a beautifully restored 1920s house with cosy wood-panelled rooms, kitchen, lounge and rooftop terrace. Profits go towards the preservation of native Chilean forest and foreigners get discounted room prices. The staff couldn't be lovelier. Dorm CH$9500, double CH$20,000

EATING AND DRINKING

CAFÉS

Café Las Gringas Prat 327 ☎63 433435. Tiny corner café/bar specializing in hard-to-find regional microbrews. There are *tablas* (mixed platters) to share and other light dishes to complement the beer, such as sandwiches and *crudos* (German-style carpaccio). Mon–Sat noon–3pm & 8pm–midnight.

Café La Ultima Frontera Pérez Rosales 787 ☎63 235363. The decor inside this bohemian café is as entertaining as the food, which includes real coffee, imaginative vegetarian dishes, great milkshakes, and hearty sandwiches – all brought to you by an easygoing, pierced and dreadlocked staff. Daily 11.30am–11pm.

Chocolatería Entre Lagos Pérez Rosales 622 ☎63 212039. A famous chocolate shop, known for its rich cakes, and connected to a *salón de té* that sells giant veggie sandwiches, a wide range of ice creams and fresh-squeezed natural fruit juices. Mon–Sat 9am–10pm, Sun 10am–10pm.

RESTAURANTS

★ **La Calesa** O'Higgins 160 ☎63 225467. The low-key location along a residential street hides one of Valdivia's culinary gems; this Peruvian restaurant serves authentic favourites such as *ají de gallina* (chicken stew) and *suspiro limeño* (meringue-topped vanilla custard) for dessert. Mon–Sat 7.30–11.30pm.

Santo Pecado Yungay 745 ☎63 239122. The eclectic dishes at this lounge-restaurant reflect its colourful decor, with such favourites as chicken curry and *tortilla Iberica* as well as Chilean standards. The pisco sour mousse is so good that its consumption must indeed be a sin. Mon–Sat noon–4pm & 8pm–midnight.

Zu Hause Bueras 219 ☎63 520707. The menu at this popular Swiss establishment is a cross between *raclette*, *fondue* and *machas a la parmesana*; by all accounts, it seems to be a happy one. The service is attentive and there are some unusual beers to complement the food, too. Mon–Fri 11.30am–11pm.

BARS AND PUBS

★ **Cervecería Kunstmann** On the road to Niebla ☎63 292969, ⓦwww.cerveza-kunstmann.cl. Come hungry, as this cheesy restaurant-brewery-museum serves monster portions of smoked meat, sauerkraut and potatoes to accompany its range of beer. Try the honey-tinted Miel or the darker Torobay, and finish off with beer in ice cream form. Mains from CH$5500. Daily noon–midnight.

Epicentro 1960 Esmeralda 675 ☎63 214129. The decor of the latest Valdivia hotspot is as subtle as the earthquake it commemorates, but it's a great spot for a beer and the occasional live local band, and a convivial atmosphere reigns throughout. Mon 8pm–2am, Tues–Sat 8pm–4am, Sun 1pm–4am.

DIRECTORY

Banks and exchange There are various banks with ATMs around the Plaza de la República, including Banco Santander. For *cambios*, try Cambio La Reconquista, Carampangue 325 or Cambio Arauco, Arauco 331, Local 24.
Car rental Assef y Méndez Rent a Car, General Lago 1335

(☎ 63 213205) or Hertz, Picarte 640 (☎ 63 218316); both have offices at the airport.
Hospital Clinica Alemana, Beaucheff 765 ☎ 63 246201.
Internet All accommodation options reviewed offer free wi-fi; most offer free internet access.

Fuerte de Niebla

March–Nov Tues–Sun 10am–5.30pm; Dec–Feb daily 10am–7pm • CH$1000, free on Wed; English-language tours available at extra cost •
Colectivos run regularly from Yungay near the Mercado Fluvial and cost CH$1000

At the mouth of the Río Valdivia, 18km from the city, in the village of Niebla, the **Fuerte de Niebla** (or Castillo de la Pura y Limpia Concepción de Montfort de Lemus) was originally built by the Spanish from 1667 to 1672 as part of an extensive line of defences of this key position in their empire. Today it's been restored and houses a small museum dedicated to the fortification of the Valdivia area, but the most interesting things are the old features: the powder room, double-walled and well below ground level, the crenellated curtain wall hacked out of the bare rock, and the twelve slightly rusting cannons.

Half the cannons are missing their cascabels (round metal knobs at the back); these are the original fort cannons which were defaced by the forces of Lord Thomas Cochrane (see p.473) when they overwhelmed the fort. Two of the original cannons now grace Santiago's Plaza de Armas.

Corral and around

Nov–March daily 9am–6pm; April–Oct Tues–Sun 10am–5.30pm • CH$1000 • Regular ferries from Niebla (see box, p.293)

On the other side of the estuary from Niebla lies the little village of **CORRAL**; it used to be a thriving port until it was flattened by the 1960 tidal wave. Another Spanish fort, the somewhat dilapidated **Castillo de San Sebastián de la Cruz**, with its 21 cannon – originally the most powerful of all the Spanish forts in the vicinity – was constructed in 1645 and is a short walk from the pier.

Castillo de San Pedro de Alcántara

Dec–Feb daily 10am–6pm; March–Nov Tues–Sun 10am–5pm • Fort CH$1000 • Regular boats from Niebla (ask to be dropped off and picked up again)

Between Niebla and Corral sits the pretty Isla Mancera, with the most intact of the forts, **Castillo de San Pedro de Alcántara**, visible a little way up its forested side. The fort was built in 1645 and reinforced first in 1680 and later in 1762; its grounds house the atmospheric ruins of the San Francisco Convent and you can also descend into the dungeons. When the boat from Niebla drops you off, don't forget to ask to be picked up again.

Parque Oncol

To drive here, cross Río Cruces and turn right at the first intersection, then follow the road for 28km; boat tours from Valdivia also available (see p.290)) • ⓦ parqueoncol.cl

Twenty-eight kilometres from Valdivia lie the 1863 acres of protected Valdivian rainforest that make up Parque Oncol, home to the rare Darwin's frog, the puma and the epudú (pygmy deer). Hikers can tackle the park's trails, which range in length and difficulty, the most rewarding being the hike to the peak of Cerro Oncol for exquisite views of Valdivia and its environs.

CROSSING THE RÍO VALDIVIA

The only way across the river from Niebla to Corral is by a 30min ferry ride (daily 9am–5.40pm; CH$1000). Frequent boats leave from the pier at the entrance to Niebla, some stopping at the small and pleasant **Isla Mancera**. Though the journey is often obscured with the *niebla* (rolling fog) that lends the village its name, quite often you'll catch sight of sea lions and black-necked swans along the way.

Santuario de la Naturaleza Carlos Anwandter

Boat tours from Valdivia (see p.290)

After the 1960 earthquake, the 50km of low-lying land around the Río Cruces north of Valdivia was flooded, forming an extensive delta which has been protected as the UNESCO-listed **Santuario de la Naturaleza Carlos Anwandter**. This marsh now forms an important breeding ground and resting place for 119 species of birds, including the black-necked swan, black skimmer and the white-faced ibis.

Osorno

Despite being founded in one of the best defensive positions of all the Spaniards' frontier forts, Osorno was regularly sacked by Mapuche Indians from 1553 until 1796, at which point Chile's governor, Ambrosio O'Higgins, ordered it to be resettled. From tentative beginnings, it has grown into a thriving agricultural city mainly as a result of the industry of European settlers who felled the forests and began to develop the great dairy herds that form the backbone of the local economy today. The German heritage is evident in the row of of **wooden houses** along Calle Mackenna, built between 1876 and 1923, and declared national monuments.

As the transport hub for the southern Lake District and starting point for the region's main road into Argentina, Osorno has an abundance of public **buses**, making surrounding attractions such as **Parque Nacional Puyehue**, one of Chile's most-visited national parks, much easier to visit.

Orsorno's churches

What strikes you first about Osorno are its controversial **churches**: the **Catedral San Mateo** on the Plaza de Armas, and **Iglesia San Francisco** on Prat, three blocks east. Their modern concrete exteriors are not to everyone's taste because of their block-like structures and lattice roofs, but the design is unquestionably unique in the whole of Chile.

Museo Histórico Municipal

Matta 809 at Bilbao • Jan & Feb Mon–Fri 9.30am–6pm, Sat & Sun 2–7pm; March–Dec Mon–Fri 9.30am–5pm, Sat 2–6pm • CH$1000

One block southwest of Juan Mackenna is the worthwhile **Museo Histórico Municipal**, with displays on the history of Osorno, both before and after European conquest, illustrated with old photographs of the city, a collection of daggers and swords from the colonial era and various Mapuche artefacts. The best natural history exhibits include the bones, teeth and tusks of a mastodon (a prehistoric giant herbivore), and a mummified body, thousands of years old, found near Arica in the north of Chile.

ARRIVAL AND DEPARTURE   **OSORNO**

BY PLANE

Seven kilometres from Osorno, Aeródromo Cañal Bajo (☎ 64 247555) is served by daily LAN flights from Santiago via Temuco. Taxis to town cost around CH$5000. The LAN office is at Ramírez 802 (☎ 64 314909).

Destinations Santiago (2 daily; 2hr); Temuco (1 daily; 30min).

6

CAFÉS AND CHEAP EATS
Hojas del Sur 3
Mercado Municipal 1
RESTAURANTS
La Parilla de Pepe 4
Restaurant Clube de Artesanos 2
El Rincón de Wufehr 5

ACCOMMODATION
Hostal Bilbao Express 2
Hostal Vermont 4
Hotel Rucaitue 1
Hotel Villa Eduviges 3

BY BUS

Buses from Osorno serve all major destinations along the Carretera Austral from the central Terminal de Buses at Errázuriz 1400 (☏64 234149), while the Terminal de Buses Rurales, a block away at Mercado Municipal, Errázuriz 1300 (☏64 232073), serves local destinations including Aguas Calientes, with Expreso Lago Puyehue. Bariloche, Argentina, is served by Igi Llaima and Cruz del Sur. There are also departures for Coyhaique (see pp.363–367) with Queilen Bus and Buses Transaustral via Argentina.

Companies Buses Pirehueico (☏64 233050); Cruz del Sur (☏64 232777, ⊛www.pullmansur.cl); Expreso Lago Puyehue (☏64 243919); Igi Llaima (☏64 234371); Tas Choapa (☏64 233933, ⊛www.taschoapa.cl); Tur Bus (☏64 234170, ⊛turbus.cl); Via Tur (☏64 230118).

Destinations Aguas Calientes, Puyehue (8 daily; 1hr); Bariloche, Argentina (6 daily; 5hr plus border formalities); Coyhaique (2 weekly; 20hr); Panguipulli (5 daily; 2hr 30min); Puerto Montt (every 30min; 1hr 30min); Puerto Octay (6 daily; 1hr); Puerto Varas (every 30min; 1hr); Santiago (every hour; 10hr); Temuco (every 30min; 3hr); Valdivia (every 30min; 1hr 30min).

INFORMATION

Tourist information O'Higgins 667 (Mon–Fri 8.30am–6pm; ☏64 237575). Sernatur's helpful information office in the Gobernación building on the west side of the Plaza de Armas has good city maps and accommodation lists. There are also a couple of information kiosks: one on the plaza in summer, and another in the long-distance bus terminal (both daily 9am–6pm).

Conaf Martínez de Rozas 430 (Mon–Thurs 9.30am–1pm & 2.30–4.30pm, Fri 9.30am–1pm & 2.30–4pm; ☏64 234393). Staff sometimes lack up to date information on national park trail conditions.

ACCOMMODATION

Hostal Bilbao Express Bilbao 1019 ☏64 262200, ⊛hotelbilbao.cl. Jolly, welcoming (if not particularly memorable) and well-equipped hotel with a restaurant, snug rooms and internet access, this is better value than its sister establishment, *Hotel Bilbao* at Mackenna 1205 (☎63 264444), though breakfast leaves something to be desired. **CH$26,000**

Hostal Vermont Toribio Medina 2020 ☎64 247030, ⓦhostalvermont.cl. Finally! A proper backpacker hostel, run by a bilingual Chilean – a former backpacker herself. The rooms are simple yet comfortable and you can chill out with the hostel's many pets – cats, rabbit and two ducks called Luke and Anakin Skywalker. Dorm CH$8000, double CH$22,000.

Hotel Rucaitue Freire 546 ☎64 239922, ⓦhotelrucaitue .cl. With its warm reds and polished wooden floors, crisp linens and breakfast brought to your room on a little tray, this is an excellent mid-range option. Its location, smack bang in the centre of town, is another plus. **CH$49,000**

Hotel Villa Eduviges Eduviges 856 ☎64 235023 ⓦhoteleduviges.cl. This a good option for couples and groups, providing friendly service, rooms decked out in soothing pastel shades, complete with cable TV, and breakfast in a cheerful dining room. **CH$30,000**

EATING AND DRINKING

CAFÉS AND CHEAP EATS

Hojas del Sur Centro Cultural Sofía Hott, MacKenna at Cochrane. This quiet literary café inside one of Osorno's most attractive German mansions is particularly good for hot chocolate and cake (try the apple strudel); steer clear of the instant coffee, though, and go for one of their 16 teas. Mon–Sat 11am–9.30pm.

Mercado Municipal Prat at Errázuruz. By far the best place to find a cheap and filling meal; the market's many *comedores* serve *empanadas* and large portions of fish and the likes of *chupe de mariscos* (shellfish soup). Daily 11am–5pm.

RESTAURANTS

La Parilla de Pepe Juan MacKenna at Freire ☎64 249653. This steakhouse, inside one of Osorno's historic German houses, is highly rated by locals, and

justifiably so: Pepe the chef grills your slabs of beef expertly and the prices don't break the bank. Mon–Sat 12.30–3.30pm & 7.30–11.30pm, Sun 12.30–3.30pm.

Restaurant Clube de Artesanos Mackenna 634 ☎64 230307. This former union house is popular with locals for its inexpensive Chilean food, particularly fish and seafood, served in a hassle-free setting, along with the locally produced beer, Märzen. Mon–Sat 12.30–3pm & 7–11pm, Sun 12.30–3pm.

El Rincón de Wufehr Rodríguez 1015 ☎64 226999. The black-and-white photos and period objects conjure up images of ye olde Osorno, the menu is meat-heavy with a German influence and the portions abundant. If you've never had *crudos* (German-style carpaccio) before, this is the place to try it. Mon–Fri 12.30–3.30pm & 6.30–11.30pm, Sat 6.30–11.30pm.

DIRECTORY

Banks and exchange There are banks and ATMs around the plaza. For a *cambio* with good rates, try Cambio Tur, Mackenna 1004.

Car rental Europcar at the airport ☎63 203855.

Hospital Hospital Base, Av Bühler 1765, off southbound Arturo Prat ☎64 336412.

Internet All accommodation options reviewed offer free wi-fi or internet or both.

Parque Nacional Puyehue and around

CH$2000 , though note that at the time of writing, the trails in the park were closed following the 2011 eruption of Volcán Puyehue, which resulted in heavy ashfall in the area • ☎64 234393 • ⓦ parquepuyehue.cl

PARQUE NACIONAL PUYEHUE, 81km east of Osorno, is one of Chile's busiest national parks, largely because of the traffic on the international road that runs through its centre. It's part of a massive, 15,000-square-kilometre area of protected wilderness, bordering the Parque Nacional Vicente Pérez Rosales to the south, and some Argentine parks that stretch all the way to Pucón's Parque Nacional Villarrica in the north. The land is high temperate rainforest spread over two volcanoes, Volcán Puyehue (2240m) to the north, and Volcán Casablanca (1990m), on the west slope of which is the Antillanca ski resort. The park's divided into three sectors: **Aguas Calientes** where the *termas* are, **Antillanca** and **Anticura**, straddling the international road near the Argentine border.

The 47km road that shoots east from Osorno to **LAGO PUYEHUE** passes through the nondescript village of Entre Lagos. Around 30km after Entre Lagos, the road forks: the left-hand road heads on to the Anticura section of the Parque Nacional Puyehue and the Argentine border, while the right-hand one leads to the Aguas Calientes section and the Antillanca skiing resort.

Aguas Calientes

At **AGUAS CALIENTES** you'll find a Conaf station and information centre (closed at the time of writing) where there's a large, detailed **map of the park**, along with basic park maps that you can take with you. **Walks** in the area consist mainly of short, self-guided **nature trails**, such as the Sendero Rápidos del Chanleufú, a 1250m track alongside the river rapids. There are also a couple of **longer trails**, currently closed (see p.296–297).

6 Antillanca

Ski season July & Aug • ☎ 64 612070, ⓦ skiantillanca.cl • Ski day-passes around CH$15,000

The **ski centre** at **ANTILLANCA** lies 18km from Aguas Calientes by road, at the foot of the Volcán Casablanca (also known as Antillanca). The centre has three T-bar lifts, one chairlift and ski slopes for all skill levels. In winter, the resort is extremely popular with locals, and it gets so busy that traffic on the last 8km up to the ski centre is subject to time restrictions (up 8am–noon & 2–5.30pm; down noon–2pm & after 5.30pm). In summer it offers mountain biking, canoeing, fishing and hikes up the volcano.

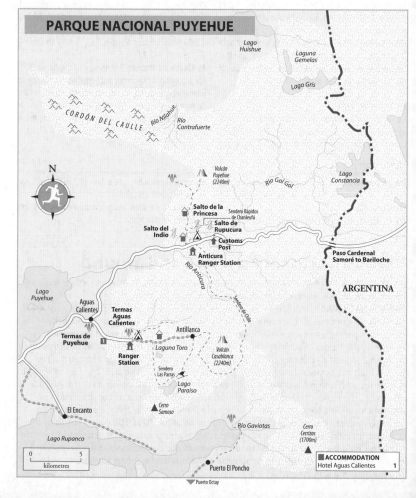

> ## HOT SPRINGS IN PUYEHUE
>
> Just as the Siete Lagos area is known for its abundance of hot springs, the Puyehue area also has its share of **healing waters**. While many of the hot springs lie in remote areas, visitors have two easily accessible options, the first being the thermal springs of one of Chile's most famous and fashionable hotels, the **Hotel Termas de Puyehue** (see p.298). Here both the indoor pools (Mon–Thurs & Sun 8am–8pm, Fri & Sat 8am–9pm) and outdoor pools (daily 11am–7pm) are open to non-guests; a day pass (CH$50,000 on weekdays, CH$55,000 on weekends) gives access to the pools, saunas and restaurants.
>
> The second, and cheaper, option is the resort at *Aguas Calientes* (see p.298), right at the entrance to the Parque Nacional Puyehue. It has *tinas* (personal bathtubs; CH$12,000), double *tinas* (so you can bathe with a friend), a hot outdoor pool (daily 9am–7pm; CH$18,000 on weekdays, CH$20,000 on weekends) and a very hot indoor pool (daily 9am–8pm; CH$20,500 on weekdays, CH$22,500 on weekends – price includes use of outdoor pool); use of the latter is included in the price of a *cabaña* in summer.

6

Trails from Antillanca

Part of the Sendero de Chile, two trails begin at Antillanca: the 25km Las Parras, which runs through native forest to Lago Paraíso, south of the main road, passing the indigenous community of Calfuco, and passing by the tiny Laguna Toro before finishing at the Aguas Calientes Conaf office; and the 50km trail that finishes at Anticura (see p.297). It is also possible to hike south to the eastern shores of Lago Rupanco, timing it so that your arrival coincides with a boat taxi to the southern shore, where you can catch a bus; *Zapato Amarillo* in Puerto Octay (see p.304) has detailed information on this trek.

Anticura

ANTICURA lies 22km from Aguas Calientes; to get here, head back to the junction by the *Hotel Termas de Puyehue* and then along the potholed international road to Argentina.

Short trails

You'll find a number of short **hikes** around the Conaf station; the prettiest is the 850m walk to El Salto del Indio (CH$1000), a half-hour loop through a forest of ancient coigüe to some thundering **waterfalls** amid dense greenery. From the Conaf side, a 1.3km track leads to the single gushing fall of Salto de Pudú, while from the other side of the office, an easy 1.5km ramble leads you to the Miradór del Puma, where you get a great view of Salto Anticura and the Volcán Puyehue beyond.

Sendero de Chile

More adventurous is the 50km trail that goes to Antillanca (see p.296) as part of the Sendero de Chile. The track is reasonably well maintained and signposted and runs through lush *ulmo, coigüe* and *lenga* forest, skirting the eastern flank of Volcán Casablanca and affording great views of the neighbouring volcanoes. Some parts of the trail are quite steep, though not technical, and shouldn't present any difficulties to reasonably fit hikers. Halfway along, on the Pampa Frutilla, the trail passes by two pretty little lagoons harbouring a wealth of waterfowl. The trail starts behind the Conaf office in Anticura and takes approximately two days to complete.

Volcán Puyehue trail

Another adventurous hike is the 22km return trail to Volcán Puyehue, which starts 2km west of Anticura, opposite a church, where there's a small Conaf office. The beginning of the path passes over some private property, where you'll have to pay CH$8000 to cross the land either on foot or you can arrange for a guide and horses (try El Caulle Expediciones, ☎09 641 2000, ✉elcaulle.com). The fee entitles you to use the basic refuge, which sleeps sixteen; it's a three-hour walk along the trail from the Conaf office.

Shortly past the refuge, the trail forks; the right-hand route goes up the volcano for 6km (2hr; no special equipment needed), and from the crater there are views over Lagos Puyehue and Rupanco. The left-hand path leads to a thermal spring next to an icy stream, half a day's walk from the refuge. You can mix the waters and bathe – an amazing experience at night, cooking yourself gently in the waters underneath the stars.

| ARRIVAL AND INFORMATION | PARQUE NACIONAL PUYEHUE |

By bus Expresos Lago Puyehue runs numerous daily buses from Osorno to Aguas Calientes between 7am and 7pm. In winter the Club Osorno Andino (☎ 64 232297) runs daily between Osorno and the Antillanca ski area.

By car Take Ruta 215 from the Panamericana towards the Argentinian border.
Information The Conaf office in the park was closed at the time of writing following the eruption; information can be obtained at the Conaf office in Osorno (see p.294).

ACCOMMODATION AND EATING

Note that wild camping is permitted in the national park.

Aguas Calientes Turismo & Cabañas Camino a Antillanca, Km 4 ☎65 236988, ⓦwww .termasaguascalientes.cl. At the popular hot springs site (see box, p.297), these cute chalet-style *cabañas* sleep four to ten people and are well equipped with fridges, cookers, *parrillas* on the balcony for barbecuing, terraces, but they are somewhat cramped and arranged in a military-style row that offers little privacy. Cabin CH$115,000
Antillanca Hotel and Tourism Centre Camino a Antillanca ☎65 612071, ⓦskiantillanca.cl. The only option for skiers, this hotel and *refugio* combo has a sauna, gym and shops; the rooms are rather basic and overpriced for what they are, though, making the *refugio* better value.

Hotel CH$60,000, refugio CH$35,000
Termas de Puyehue Ruta 215, Km76 ☎ 02 293 6000, www.puyehue.cl. With a view of Lago Puyehue, this vast five-star hotel features the region's best hot springs and refurbished spa (see box, p.297), open to non-guests also. The standard doubles are quite conventional, but the spacious suites are really worth the splurge and the two restaurants – one Italian, one French–Chilean fusion – provide sustenance in the form of fine international dishes. Excursions and full board included in the all-inclusive price; spa treatments included only in the exclusive all-inclusive suite price. Double CH$330,000, suite CH$570,000

Lago Llanquihue and around

Located just off the Panamericana, **LAGO LLANQUIHUE** is an immense inland sea of 870 square kilometres, a backdrop for one of the icons of the Lake District, the Mount Fuji-like **Volcán Osorno** (2661m), in all its stunning, symmetrical perfection, surrounded by gently rolling pastures. The little towns and villages around Lago Llanquihue have a shared German heritage, but differ greatly in character. **Puerto Varas**, at the lake's southernmost point, is a bustling adventure tourism centre to rival Pucón. **Frutillar**, on the lake's western shore, is a summer holiday resort beloved by Chileans, while **Puerto Octay**, to the north, is a neat little Bavarian-looking town. By the time you come to the village of **Ensenada**, on the far eastern shore of the lake, forest has overtaken dairy fields and the land begins to rise as you enter the foothills of the Andes. This forest extends to the border, and is protected by the **Parque Nacional Vicente Pérez Rosales**. The national park is a favourite scenic route into Argentina via the magical green waters of **Lago Todos Los Santos**.

South of Ensenada the road winds its way down through isolated country to the placid calm of Chile's northernmost fjord, a branch of the **Estuario de Reloncaví**. Here you can horse-trek into South America's oldest rainforest – the famous *alerce* groves found in the valleys above the village of **Cochamó**.

Puerto Varas

Arguably the most appealing base along the shore of Lago Llanquihue, **PUERTO VARAS** is a spruce little town with wide streets, grassy lawns and exquisite views of two volcanoes, Osorno and Calbuco, particularly at sunset. Like Pucón, the reason you come to Puerto Varas is because it's a prime location for all manner of outdoor activities, with volcanoes, rivers and forests throwing down a gauntlet that few outdoor enthusiasts can refuse.

The town's German colonial architecture gives it a European feel, and notable early twentieth century private residences include **Casa Kuschel**, on Klenner 299 (1910), Casona Alemana (1914) at Nuestra Señora del Carmen 788 and Casa Angulo (1910) at Miraflores 96.

ARRIVAL AND DEPARTURE
PUERTO VARAS

BY PLANE
The nearest airport is near Puerto Montt (see p.311). Most hotels can organize airport transfers.
Airlines LAN, Av Gramado 560 (☎600 526 2000, ⓦlan .com); Sky Airline, San Bernardo 430 (☎65 234252,

ⓦskyairline.cl).

BY BUS
Companies All of the main companies have offices in one of two terminals: Tur Bus, JAC and Cóndor share a terminal at

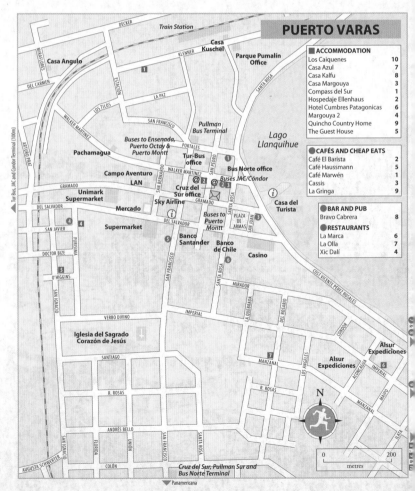

PUERTO VARAS

■ ACCOMMODATION

Los Caiquenes	10
Casa Azul	7
Casa Kalfu	8
Casa Margouya	3
Compass del Sur	1
Hospedaje Ellenhaus	2
Hotel Cumbres Patagonicas	6
Margouya 2	4
Quincho Country Home	9
The Guest House	5

■ CAFÉS AND CHEAP EATS

Café El Barista	2
Café Haussmann	5
Café Marwén	1
Cassis	3
La Gringa	9

● BAR AND PUB

Bravo Cabrera	8

● RESTAURANTS

La Marca	6
La Olla	7
Xic Dalí	4

THE LAND-AND-LAKE CROSSING INTO ARGENTINA

If you're Argentina-bound, **the land-and-lake crossing** between Puerto Varas and Bariloche allows you to experience the beauty of Chile's **Parque Nacional Vicente Perez Rosales**, and is an excellent alternative to a long bus journey. Starting out at 8.30am, you are first driven along the banks of Lago Llanquihue to **Petrohué**, before boarding the ferry that takes you across **Lago Todos Los Santos**, a spectacular expanse of clear blue-green. As you sail along the densely forested shores, skirting lovely Isla Margarita, the volcanoes Osorno (2660m) and Puntiagudo (2490m) loom to the north, with the majestic Tronador (3491m) to the east. After going through **Chilean customs** at Peulla, you then cross the Argentine border at **Paso Pérez Rosales**, and get stamped in at tiny Puerto Frías. At this point you'll board the ferry again for the short crossing of Laguna Frías, then transfer by bus to your final nautical leg of the journey – a car ferry across the vast **Lago Nahuel Huapi**, arriving at your destination around 9pm. At CH$117,990, crossing by lake is significantly pricier than a bus journey, but it's worth it. Book this popular trip in advance with **Turistour** (☎65 437127, ⊛www.turistour.cl).

6

Del Salvador 1093, while Cruz del Sur, Pullman Sur and Bus Norte share one at San Francisco 1317. Most companies also have offices in the centre of Puerto Varas where you can buy tickets. The one exception is Pullman, with its own central terminal and office at Portales 318. Tur Bus and Pullman serve all major destinations between Puerto Montt and Santiago, with connections to the north of Chile. Cruz del Sur has the most frequent departures to Chiloé. The efficient minibuses that connect Puerto Varas to Ensenada, Petrohué, Frutillar and Puerto Octay stop at a bus shelter at San Bernardo 240, while the Puerto Montt buses use a shelter in Del Salvador between San Pedro and Santa Rosa.

Bus company offices Buses JAC and Cóndor Bus, Walker Martínez 227-A (☎65 383204); Cruz del Sur, Pullman Sur and Bus Norte, Walker Martínez 239-B and San Francisco 1317 (☎65 236969, ⊛www.pullmansur.cl); Pullman Bus, Portales 318 (☎65 234612, ⊛www.pullman.cl); Tur-Bus, San Pedro 210 (☎65 234163, ⊛turbus.cl) and Del Salvador 1093 (☎65 233787).

Destinations Ancud (8 daily; 2hr 30min); Castro (8 daily; 4hr 30min); Ensenada (hourly; 1hr); Frutillar (4 daily; 40min); Puerto Montt (every 15min; 35min); Puerto Octay (3 daily; 1hr 15min); Santiago (6 daily; 18hr).

BY BOAT
By boat There are daily boat crossings to Bariloche, Argentina (see box p.301).

INFORMATION AND TOURS

TOURIST INFORMATION

Casa del Turista On the wharf, Piedraplén s/n, Muelle de Puerto Varas (Mon–Fri 9am–6.30pm, Sat & Sun 10am–6.30pm; ☎65 237956, ⊛puertovaras.org).

Municipal tourist office Del Salvador 320 (daily: Jan–March 9am–10pm; April–Dec Mon–Sat 9am–2pm & 3–8pm; ☎65 361194, ⊛puertovaras-chile.cl) offers info on tours and accommodation.

TOUR OPERATORS

The main tours offered by the many companies in Puerto Varas are rafting on the Río Petrohué (grade 3 and 4; from CH$25,000 for a half-day); canyoning (climbing down precipices and waterfalls; CH$35,000 for a half-day); climbing Volcán Osorno (from CH$115,000); hiking in the Parque Nacional Vicente Pérez Rosales (day trip around CH$20,000); and horseriding, generally on the slopes of Volcán Calbuco, through old coigüe forest (from CH$45,000 for a half-day).

Alsur Expediciones Aconcagua at Imperial ☎65 232300, ⊛alsurexpeditions.com. A good company – one of those authorized by Conaf as guides on Volcán Osorno and Volcán Calbuco. In addition to the standard

tours above, it offers sea-kayaking to the northern part of Parque Pumalín (CH$700,000 for a six-day trip; see p.352) and rafting trips on the Ríos Petrohué, Puelo and Futaleufú.

Campo Aventura San Bernardo 318 ☎65 232910, ⊛campoaventura.cl. Run by Lex Fautsch, who has developed a multilingual team, this is the place to go for horse-trekking, from one day to ten days into the foothills of Cochamó valley near the Estuario de Reloncaví (see p.308), as well as the multi-day, multi-activity Paddles, Saddles, Pedals tour. Customized options, like veggie meals, are available and canyoning and rafting are also among the activities on offer.

Ko'kayak Ruta 225, Km 40, Casilla 896, Ensenada ☎09 310 5272, ⊛kokayak.com. Excellent multilingual rafting and kayaking specialists who run half- to four-day rafting trips in the Lake District, as well as one- or three-day sea kayaking trips, with more challenging twelve-day expeditions to the southern fjords.

Pachamagua Walker Martínez 561 ☎65 542080, ⊛pachamagua.com. A reliable and professional canyoning specialist arranging all-day, adrenalin-filled excursions; *Casa Margouya* (see p.302) can help organize tours.

Yak Expediciones ☎08 332 0574 or 09 299 6487, ⓦwww.yakexpediciones.cl. Long-standing operator running multi-day sea-kayaking adventures to the northern part of Parque Pumalín (see p.352), Chepu valley in Chiloé, and the Reloncaví Fjord (see p.308), as well as multi-day trekking and horseriding in Río Puelo valley.

ACCOMMODATION

HOTELS, B&B AND LODGES

★ **Los Caiquenes** Ruta 225, Km 9.5 ☎08 159 0490, ⓦhotelloscaiquenes.cl. In a beautiful setting on the shores of Lago Llanquihue, this wood-shingled boutique hotel simply oozes tranquility. All centrally heated rooms are decked out in native woods, with king-size beds and Jacuzzis in the bathrooms, and as for the food, you suggest to the chefs what you'd like to eat and they use locally sourced ingredients to make it happen. CH$136,000 (US$285)

Casa Kalfu Tronador 1134 ☎65 751261, ⓦcasakalfu.cl. With a warm colour scheme and weavings on the walls, this rambling, blue-hued German mansion attracts a lively European, Argentine and Brazilian clientele. The bright, homely rooms are centrally heated and breakfast is included. CH$55,000

Hotel Cumbres Patagonicas Imperial 561 ☎65 222000, ⓦcumbrespatagonicas.cl. Besides offering a pool and rooftop spa, this central hotel combines great lake views with the comfort of its spacious rooms, all with king-size beds and crisp linens. The buffet breakfast is a cut above most, with granola and locally produced jam among the offerings. CH$95,000 (US$200)

Quincho Country Home Ruta 225, Km 7.5 ☎65 330737, ⓦquinchocountryhome.cl. The ultimate in luxurious seclusion, this lodge has ultra-plush rooms for eight guests only, a splendid common area with an enormous stone fireplaces and its own helicopter pad. Outings such as horseback riding, helicopter flights and sea kayaking are tailormade according to the guests' wishes, as are the gourmet dishes, prepared from seasonal ingredients. CH$285,000 (US$600)

The Guest House Santa Rosa 318 ☎65 232240, ⓦvicki-johnson.com. This is rather like staying in a friend's home – if your friend lived in a beautifully restored 1926 mansion, that is. There are eight big, sunny rooms, bathrooms with actual tubs, a living room with a wonderful collection of art books and extras including yoga classes and massage. Wi-fi is the only incongruity here. CH$93,000 (US$195)

HOSTELS

Casa Azul Manzanal 66 at Rosario ☎65 232904, ⓦcasaazul.net. Slightly uphill from the centre, this blue house has been hosting international travellers for years without waning in popularity. The buffet breakfast (CH$3000) includes home-made muesli, the garden with the bonzai trees is a lovely spot for relaxation and the owners organize tours to Parque Alerces, Volcán Osorno and the Saltos de Petrohué. Dorm CH$8000, double CH$20,000

Casa Margouya Santa Rosa 318 ☎65 237640, ⓦmargouya.com. Smack bang in the centre, this French-owned hostel has a chilled, hippyish vibe about it, thanks to the large, central communal area for guests to lounge around in and shared facilities. Guests get free use of the kitchen and the owners arrange all sorts of outdoor activities around the area. Dorm CH$9000, double CH$22,000

★ **Compass del Sur** Klenner 467 ☎65 232044, ⓦcompassdelsur.cl. This lovely three-storey hostel is popular with international travellers of all ages, who come to appreciate the creaky wooden floors, powerful showers and the communal vibe. The super-helpful staff or the friendly Chilean–Swedish owners can help you organize your stay. Camping CH$8000, dorm CH$10,000, double CH$28,000

Hospedaje Ellenhaus Walker Martínez 239 ☎65 233577, ⓦellenhaus.cl. There may be as much of a party atmosphere here as in heaven on a Sunday, and some of the management may be abrupt, bordering on rude, but this super-central labyrinthine hostel is one of the cleanest (and cheapest) sleeps in town. Breakfast CH$2000 extra. Dorm CH$5000, double CH$14,000

Margouya 2 Purisima 681 ☎65 237695, ⓦmargouya2.com. The sister hostel of the ever-popular *Margouya* (but quieter than the original) is housed in one of the town's restored historical mansions and doubles as a language school. Guests have use of the large garden and lounge with cinema-sized TV. Dorm CH$8000, double CH$19,000

EATING AND DRINKING

CAFÉS AND CHEAP EATS

Café El Barista Walker Martínez 211 ☎65 233130, ⓦelbarista.cl. A great spot for people-watching, this trendy café serves some of the best coffee for miles around, with large slices of tasty *kuchen* and a small but good selection of sandwiches as an accompaniment. Daily 9am–10.30pm.

Café Haussmann San Francisco 644 ☎65 237600. If you are hankering after *crudos* (Chilean–German special consisting of raw meat on toast with an accompaniment of

seasonings and sauces) and *kuchen* (cake), this Valdivian export does them best. Daily 10.30am–9pm.

Café Mawén Santa Rosa 218 ☎65 234020. This bright newcomer on the café scene successfully competes with other cafés for the laptop-toting clientele with its winning combination of inviting decor, extensive coffee and tea menu, and scrumptious cakes. Daily 8.15am–9pm.

Cassis Santa Rosa at Gramado ☎65 234020. Besides the winning lakeside location, this large, perpetually busy café has something to satisfy all tastes: sweet and savoury crêpes, chunky sandwiches, *tablas* to share, good coffee, and a delectable array of cakes and ice-cream flavours for those with a sweet tooth. Those missing their vegetables in Patagonia will be glad to see the salads, too. Daily 10am–10pm.

★ **La Gringa** Imperial at Tronador ☎7 801 0314. *La Gringa*'s expat owner hails from Seattle and does her all-American cookie-baking mom pround with sticky, gooey cinnamon rolls, melt-in-your-mouth brownies and delectable chocolate chip cookies. Her cheerful bakery, located inside the historic Casa Bechthold (1905), enjoys a loyal local following and the tasty *menú del día* (CH$5000) includes soup and a main. Daily 9am–6.30pm; summer till late.

RESTAURANTS

★ **La Marca** Santa Rosa 539 ☎65 232026, ⓦwww .lamarca.cl. With gaucho music on the stereo, cowboy paraphernalia on the wall and lamb grilling on a spit outside, this is one of the best steakhouses in the Lake District, as testified to by the nightly full house. The *bife de chorizo* is mouthwateringly juicy and there are a couple of token fish dishes for the steak-adverse. Though why would you be, in a place like this? Mon–Sat 7–11pm, Sun 1–4pm.

La Olla Vicente Perez Rosales 1071 ☎65 233540.

Particularly popular with local families and international tour groups, this upmarket fish and seafood restaurant, 5km west of town, dishes up hearty portions of well-executed dishes. The *corvina* dishes are excellent. Mains from CH$8000. Daily noon–11pm.

★ **Xic Dalí** Purísima 690 ☎65 234424. The most imaginative restaurant in town is run by three lovely Catalonian sisters who conjure up spectacular creations, such as calamari with meatballs and chocolate, and the classic *fideuá* (paella with vermicelli instead of rice) and *arrós negre* (seafood rice with squid ink) to share, just like in Spain. The decor is as quirky as the food, with Dalí miniatures on the walls and light fixtures resembling miniature solar systems. Reservations highly recommended. Mon–Sat 7.30pm–midnight.

BARS AND PUBS

Bravo Cabrera Vicente Pérez Rosales 1071 ☎65 233441. This is the"it" place at the moment and justifiably so: "BC" has an incomparable selection of around 50 beers, including many mircobrews from around Chile, as well as excellent wood-fired pizzas and *tablas* to share for the perpetually packed house. Occasional DJs liven up this already lively lakefront joint. Daily noon–3.30pm & 7.30–11pm.

DIRECTORY

Banks and exchange There are several banks with ATMs around the Plaza de Armas and along Del Salvador, including Banco de Chile, Del Salvador 210. For a *cambio*, try Inter, Del Salvador 257, Local 11 (in the Galería Real).

Hospital Clínica Alemana, Otto Bader 810 ☎65 582100.
Internet All accommodation options reviewed offer free wi-fi, free internet or both.
Post office San José 242 at San Pedro.

Frutillar

The Panamericana first approaches Lago Llanquihue at Frutillar Alto, 4km west of **Frutillar Bajo**, and collectively known as Frutillar. Up until the 1980s, apartheid divided Frutillar, with Frutillar Bajo reserved for the German–Chilean population and the mestizo population restricted to Frutillar Alto, forbidden to use the lower town's beaches. That has all changed now, and because it's so popular it gets very crowded here in summer, especially during the last week of January and the first week of February, when the town hosts a **classical music festival** (ⓦsemanasmusicales.cl).

Frutillar Bajo's two main streets, Vicente Pérez Rosales and Avenida Philippi, both run parallel to the coast; most services are located on Philippi.

Museo Colonial Alemán

Daily: summer 10am–7pm; winter Tues–Sun 10am–1.30pm & 3–5.30pm • CH$3500

At the bottom of the hill leading from Frutillar Alto, near the junction with Vicente Pérez Rosales, is a beautifully tended garden, an old water mill and several other traditional wooden buildings that make up the worthwhile **Museo Colonial Alemán**. The museum features a wide variety of household objects used by the earliest immigrants to Llanquihue, but most interesting is a circular barn *campanario*; inside, pairs of horses were once tethered to the central pillar and driven round in circles, threshing sheaves of corn with their hoofs. Further up the hill is the **Casa del Herrero**, the blacksmith's house, and higher up still is the reconstruction of a typical early farmhouse filled with period furniture and decorated with old family photos.

By bus You'll arrive in Frutillar Alto, not Frutillar Bajo, unless you've caught one of the summer minibuses that run directly here from Puerto Montt and Puerto Varas. From Frutillar Alto, catch one of the *colectivos* that operate shuttle services (CH$550) down to Frutillar Bajo (4km). Thaebus (San Pedro 255 ☎65 420120) operates departures from Frutillar Alto for both Puerto Montt (every 15min; 1hr 15min) and Puerto Octay (4–5 daily; 1hr 10min). Cruz del

Sur (☎65 421552), Alessandri and Portales, and Tur-Bus (☎65 421390), Diego Portales 150, serve long-distance destinations along the Panamericana.

Tourist information Avenida Philippi at O'Higginslo (Jan–March daily 8.30am–1pm & 2–9pm; ☎65 21080, ⊛frutillar.com). There's a small tourist information office on the lakefront.

ACCOMMODATION AND EATING

Hotel Am See Philippi 539 ☎65 421858, ⊛hotel amsee.cl. Wooden lakefront hotel with rooms of different sizes, half of which benefit from lake views, while the other half bask in the afternoon sun. The downstairs restaurant serves excellent *kuchen* (cake) as well as more substantial dishes, courtesy of the Argentine chef. CH$43,000

Hotel Aycara Philippi 1215 ☎65 421550, ⊛www .hotelaycara.cl. This beautifully renovated mansion dating back to 1910 has just eight bright wood-panelled rooms with antique furnishings and crisp linens. The restaurant,

specializing in dishes made from fresh local ingredients, comes highly recommended. CH$76,000 (US$160)

Se Cocina 2km from Frutillar ☎09 9757 7152, ⊛secocinachile.com. Two kilometres out of town, this wood-shingled restaurant is the best in Frutillar, with a menu that changes daily, relies on locally sourced produce and comprises expertly grilled meats and vegetarian options. There's also excellent beer produced on the premises. The weekday lunchtime *menú* is excellent value at CH$8500. Daily 12.30–4pm & 7.30–midnight.

Puerto Octay

Twenty-eight kilometres northeast of Frutillar, also on the shores of Lago Llanquihue, lies **PUERTO OCTAY**, the first German settlement on Lago Llanquihue. Dating to 1852, it's a friendly little place with a needle-steepled church and balconied houses with ornate eaves.

Museum "El Colono"
Independencia 591 • Tues–Sun 10.15am–1pm & 3–7pm • CH$1000

The small and well-organized Museum "El Colono" shares the 1920 Casa Niklitschek with the local library and its exhibits span the history of the area, from the earliest human settlement to the founding and growth of Puerto Octay. They comprise bilingual (Spanish/English) accounts, old photographs and period objects – from stone arrowheads to nineteenth-century household objects, agricultural machines and stills for making the sweet alcoholic *chicha* drink, a local speciality.

By bus There are hourly departures from Osorno to Puerto Octay on Buses Vía Octay, and also up to five buses daily from Frutillar and Puerto Montt.

Tourist information Next door to the Municipalidad on the Plaza de Armas (Dec–Feb daily 9am–9pm; ☎64 391491, ⊛puertooctay.cl).

ACCOMMODATION AND EATING

Hotel & Cabañas Centinela Península de Centinela, Km 5 ☎65 391326, ⊛hotelcentinela.cl. In a placid lakeside location at the tip of Península de Centinela, this stylish hotel boasts spacious, light, attractive rooms, decorated in its original 1913 "High Bavarian" style, as well as fully equipped *cabañas* (holding 4–6) with superb lake views. The acclaimed restaurant serves excellent steak and seafood dishes. Double CH$82,000, *cabaña* CH$95,000

Rancho Espantapájaros 6km from Puerto Octay towards Frutillar ☎65 330049. Local families and

travellers alike head to this family-run restaurant for the great all-you-can-eat barbecue buffet. The spit-roasted goat is excellent, as is the *jabalí* (wild boar). Mon–Sat 1–4pm & 7.30–11.30pm, Sun 1–4pm.

Zapato Amarillo On the road running north from the main square ☎65 210787, ⊛zapatoamarillo.cl. This well-signposted backpacker and cyclist favourite consists of a homely main lodge with grass roof and an eight-bed dorm, kitchen and communal area in a separate building. Canoe, bike, sailing boat and climbing gear rentals on offer, as well as free pick-up in town; the owners speak German and English and can organize a series of excursions to Vicente Pérez Rosales National Park, to Volcán Osorno or around Lake Rupanco. Dorm CH$10,000, double CH$29,000

Ensenada

The gravel road continues around Lago Llanquihue from Puerto Octay, passing the turnoff to Volcán Osorno (see p.306) shortly before you arrive in **ENSENADA**, a small village in a lovely lakeside location with a smattering of *hospedajes*, campsites and restaurants stretching pretty much all the way to Puerto Varas.

ARRIVAL AND DEPARTURE   ENSENADA

By bus There are frequent buses running to Ensenada from Puerto Varas and Puerto Montt, most continuing on to Petrohué; at least one hourly on weekdays; somewhat fewer on weekends.

ACCOMMODATION AND EATING

Casa Ko' Ruta 225, Km 37 ☏ 09 7703 6477, ⟳ casako .com. Owned by the good people of Ko'Kayak (see p.301), this shingled red house in a tranquil location makes a great base not just for water sports but also for horseback riding, trekking, canyoning and volcano ascents. An excellent breakfast is included in the price and the home-cooked three-course dinner is great value. Dorm CH$12,000, double CH$32,000

Hotel Ensenada Ensenada Ruta 225, Km 43.5 ☏ 65 212017, ⟳ www.hotelensenada.cl. This venerable hotel has been around for a hundred years and looks like the kind of stylish place that Bonnie and Clyde might have settled down at, with lots of colonial German antiques and large, well-appointed rooms, some with shared bathroom. The restaurant serves simple Chilean fare. CH$48,000

Yan Kee Way Lodge Ruta 225, Km 42 ☏ 65 212030, ⟳ yankeewaylodge.com. Hidden away in a beautiful lakeside location, this five-star lodge specializes in fly-fishing but also offers a variety of hiking, biking, canoeing and rafting excursions and more for non-fishing guests. The resort consists of exclusive, centrally heated chalets and bungalows, all with satellite TV and powerful wi-fi; there are saunas and wood-fired hot tubs for unwinding in in the evenings. Chalets CH$96,000 (US$200), bungalows CH$168,000 (US$350)

EATING AND DRINKING

Latitude 42 At the Yan Kee Way Lodge, Ruta 225, Km 42 ☏ 65 212030. This hotel restaurant – one of the best in the region (non-guests welcome) – offers perfectly executed dishes made from local and organic ingredients, such as in-house cognac-smoked salmon and outstandingly tender meats, all complemented by a comprehensive wine list. Daily 12.30–3.30pm & 7–11pm.

Restaurant Las Tranqueras Ruta 225, Km 41 ☏ 65 212056. This enormous lakeside banqueting hall specializes in traditional *asado* (Chilean barbeque) and more exotic meats. The wild boar in honey sauce with rustic mash is particularly good. Mon–Sat 12.30–11.30pm, Sun 12.30–4pm.

Parque Nacional Vicente Pérez Rosales and around

Daily: April–Nov 8am–6.30pm; Dec–March 8am–8pm • CH$1500 • ⟳ conaf.cl

PARQUE NACIONAL VICENTE PÉREZ ROSALES, Chile's first national park, was established in 1926, and covers an area of 2510 square kilometres. It is divided into three sectors: Sector Osorno, Sector Petrohué and Sector Peulla, and comprises some of the most sensational scenery in the Lake District: the emerald Lago Todos Los Santos, the thundering turquoise waters of the Saltos de Petrohué, and the imposing peaks of the area's main volcanoes: Osorno, Tronador and Puntiagudo. Coupled with the fact that this vast chunk of wilderness provides endless hiking opportunities, it's little wonder that this park is the most visited in the whole of Chile. If you are planning to do any extensive hiking here, you will find it useful to have a copy of the water-resistant *Llanquihue* map published by Trekking Chile (⟳ trekkingchile.com).

Volcán Osorno

Ski seaon mid-June to early Oct • Ski lift passes C$15,000/CH$18,000 for a half/full day

From the turnoff just short of Ensenada, a paved 14km road leads up **VOLCÁN OSORNO**. The higher you climb, the more capricious the weather becomes; take care when driving around the hairpin bends as there may be sudden gusts of ferocious wind. About halfway up the slope you'll come across the signposted Sendero El Solitario (6km; 2hr) leading east through dense forest before emerging on the road to Petrohué, about 1km away from the Saltos de Petrohué. The best view of the area is from the Conaf station at the top: to the west you can see across Lago Llanquihue, the central plain and across to the sea, and dominating the skyline to the south are the jagged peaks of Volcán Calbuco.

The *Centro de Ski & Montaña Volcán Osorno* has two chairlifts and seven runs open to skiers, though this isn't a skiing destination in the same vein as Portillo near Santiago, as the conditions can be very windy, but rather a novelty for those who'd like to ski

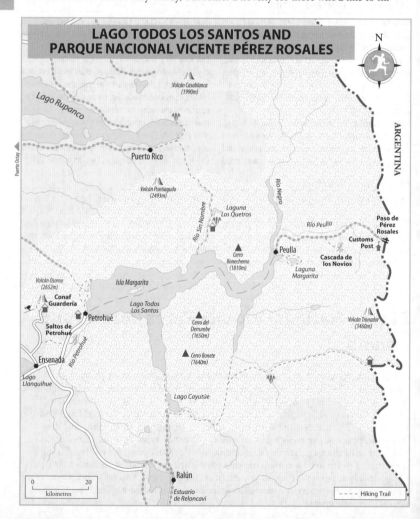

LAGO TODOS LOS SANTOS AND
PARQUE NACIONAL VICENTE PÉREZ ROSALES

down a volcano; equipment is available for rent. In January and February, the ski runs turn into a downhill bike park.

If climbing the volcano, it's about five hours to the summit (two to the snowline, three more to the top), and there are many crevasses, so ice equipment is needed and a guide mandatory. Conaf authorizes several companies to guide people up, including Al Sur (see Puerto Varas, p.301).

Lago Todos los Santos and around

6

The volcanic rock in the area was part of a tongue of lava sent this way by Volcán Osorno in 1850, an eruption that diverted the Petrohué River from its old course into Lago Llanquihue. At the end of the riverside road lies **LAGO TODOS LOS SANTOS**, deep green and stunningly clear, one of the most beautiful in the Lake District – it's also known as Lago Esmeralda (Emerald Lake) because of the intense colour of its water. Andina del Sud (❶ 2 484 8438, ⓦ andinadelsud.com) offers **tours** on the lake, which provide unsurpassed views of Volcán Osorno, the spiked peak of Volcán Puntiagudo, and, highest of all, the glacier-covered Monte Tronador.

Petrohué

Accessible by partially paved road from Ensenada, the sleepy hamlet of **PETROHUÉ** sits on the western shore of Lago Todos Los Santos. The settlement dates from the early twentieth century, when one Ricardo Roth began taking tourists across the lakes between Puerto Varas and Bariloche, a venture that led to the construction of two hotels – *Petrohué* and *Peulla* (see p.308*)* – and the foundation of the Andina del Sud tour company.

In Petrohué you will find an attractive black-sand beach, **Playa Larga** – the start of two good hiking trails. A pleasant 5km trail runs along the lakeshore, while **Sendero Los Alerzales** makes for a two-hour (6km) enjoyable hike through dense local forest, at one point crossing over the **Sendero Paso Desolación**, which climbs up the northeast side of Volcán Osorno to a height of 1100m and offers a fantastic view of Volcán Tronador and the lake below.

The Termas de Callao trail

To reach the trailhead, you'll need to rent a boat from the dock at Petrohué (CH\$55,000–65,000 for up to six people)

The 18km **Termas de Callao** trail (approximately 11hr) starts from the northern shores of Lago Todos Los Santos, by the Río Sin Nombre (No-Name River). Head up the river – the path is reasonably clear but be sure always to head upwards to the source – and after about three hours of climbing you reach the namesake hot springs (free and safe to bathe in) and a basic refuge. From here you can either go back down to Lago Todos Los Santos, having asked the boatman to pick you up again, or carry on up to the Laguna Los Quetros and over the pass – another two hours' hike – and then descend to Lago Rupanco, which takes another three hours. From the shores of Lago Rupanco, it's about another hour (west) to Puerto Rico, from where there are buses to Osorno. Check with Conaf regarding trail conditions before setting out and avoid wearing dark clothing when hiking, or else you risk attracting the local biting **horseflies** (*tábanos*) in summer.

Saltos de Petrohué

Daily: summer 8.30am–9pm; winter 9am–6pm • CH\$1200

The **Saltos de Petrohué**, a series of impressive waterfalls formed by an extremely hard layer of lava that has been eroded into small channels by the churning water, lie 10km northeast of Ensenada, off the gravel road that leads through dense forest towards Petrohué. The short Sendero Saltos leads you straight to the falls, where you can watch the incredible turquoise water roar and swirl below. The waterfalls are particularly

6

impressive on a fine day when Volcán Osorno rises directly above them. For a wetter experience, take an exhilarating *Katarata Outdoors* (☎09 9444 4339, ⊛katarataoutdoors.cl) speedboat ride through the iridescent spray to the foot of the falls (daily every 30min 9am–7.30pm). Though booking isn't necessary, out of peak season it's best to call ahead to make sure they're running.

Peulla

Day excursions to **PEULLA**, at the far end of the lake, leave at 10.30am (CH$35,000 per person, including transportation from Puerto Varas or Puerto Montt, or CH$27,000 from Petrohué). Those staying overnight have time to do the moderately difficult yet rewarding 8km climb to **Laguna Margarita** (4hr) or take a stroll to the beautiful **Cascada de Los Novios** waterfall nearby.

ARRIVAL AND INFORMATION   PARQUE NACIONAL VICENTE PÉREZ ROSALES

By bus Buses run from Puerto Montt via Puerto Varas to Petrohué and Lago Todos Los Santos, passing the Saltos de Petrohué along the way, at least once an hour in peak season, less frequently on weekends and twice daily the

rest of the year.
Information For information on the park, try the Conaf office in Puerto Montt (see p.312).

ACCOMMODATION AND EATING

PETROHUÉ
Camping Playa Petrohué ☎65 212036. Shaded Conaf-run campsite near the beach, with cold showers and firepits. CH$7000 per 5-person site
Hotel Petrohué Petrohué ☎65 212025, ⊛hotelpetrohue.com. Besides the priceless location, this stone-and-wood lodge features a tower, large fireplace in the guest lounge, skylights throughout and rooms with a romantic ambiance. Full board is available and includes a daily activity, such as rafting. Those of a more independent bent can opt for one of four cosy, fully equipped lakeside *cabañas* (sleeping 4–8). Double CH$145,000, cabin CH$135,000

PEULLA
Hotel Natura Peulla ☎65 560483, ⊛hotelnatura.cl. Under the same management as *Hotel Peulla*, and offering the same variety of tours, this hardwood-and-granite hotel is the newer and swankier option, with spacious rooms sporting flat screen TVs, king-size beds and patios. The

international dishes at the hotel's restaurant are complemented by the bay views out of the large windows and an extensive wine list. CH$78,900
Hotel Peulla Peulla ☎65 367094, ⊛hotelpeulla.cl. Loacted in the depths of dense forest, this refurbished 19th-century mountain lodge offers comfortable but dated wood-panelled rooms with hardwood floors and buffet breakfast. Excursions on offer include jet boat, fly-fishing, horseriding and (limited) trekking. CH$46,300

VOLCÁN OSORNO
Caféteria Mirador ☎65 233445. At the ski centre, there's a restaurant serving hearty Chilean dishes for lunch and sandwiches and coffee the rest of the day. Daily 10am–6pm.
Refugio Teski Ski Club ☎09 9700 0370. This spruced-up rustic lodge has compact dorms (bring own sleeping bag), a cosy little café with vibrant photographs of Volcán Osorno's deep-blue ice caves and the one touch of luxury – two outdoor hot tubs (CH$20,000). Dorm CH$13,600

Estuario de Reloncaví

On the way back to Ensenada from Parque Nacional Vicente Pérez Rosales, a southern fork, 1km before the town, will take you 33km along a good road, fringed with large bushes of wild fuchsia and giant rhubarb plants, to the tranquil **ESTUARIO DE RELONCAVÍ**. The fjord is a good place to escape and unwind or to horse-trek into the **Cochamó Valley**, home to the some of the oldest standing trees in South America. Your first view of the bay comes as you descend to the village of **Ralún**, from which an unpaved road leads you through wild, dramatic scenery deeper into pioneer country and the village of **Cochamó**.

ARRIVAL AND DEPARTURE

By bus Buses Fierro runs several services daily (8.15am–5pm) from Puerto Montt to Cochamó via Ralún.
By car The road is paved up to Ralún; beyond it's a gravel

ACCOMMODATION AND EATING

Campo Aventura Eco-Lodge Cochamó ☎ 65 216290, ⓦ campoaventura.cl. 5km south of the village, this well-established operator specializes in multi-day horse-trekking in the Cochamó Valley and more. Their accommodation consists of two rustic but comfortable lodges (campers also welcome) and their restaurant *La Mesa de los Sabores* cooks up excellent vegetarian and

ESTUARIO DE RELONCAVÍ

road, fairly rutted and narrow in places, but navigable in a car with high clearance.

fish dishes. Camping ⎯CH$4000⎯ per person, mandatory full board in Riverside Lodge ⎯CH$40,000⎯ per person; mandatory full board in Mountain Lodge combined with multi-day activity programmes, such as the popular 4-day/3-night Pioneer Trail Classic ⎯CH$303,000⎯ ⎯(US$635)⎯ per person

6

Puerto Montt

Seventeen kilometres south of Puerto Varas, the Panamericana approaches a large bay – the Seno de Reloncaví – with snowcapped Volcán Calbuco and Volcán Osorno towering beyond. On its edge lies the administrative and commercial capital of the Lake District – **PUERTO MONTT**, founded by the same influx of German colonizers that settled Lago Llanquihue to the north. The city is strung out along the bay, with the central part of town located on a narrow flat area along the main Avenida Diego Portales, and much of the city crowding the hills behind it.

Puerto Montt is an important transportation hub, with buses to many Chilean and Argentinian destinations. It's also a busy port, with a billion-dollar-a-year salmon farming industry, fishing and the embarkation point for long-distance ferry trips (see box, p.311). Though even some of the locals refer to it as "Muerto Montt" ("Dead Montt"), on a sunny day, this gritty town is quite attractive, with snow-tipped volcanoes visible across the bay from the seafront promenade.

Museo Juan Pablo II

Portales 991 • Mon–Fri 9am–6pm • CH$600
Next to the bus terminal is Puerto Montt's museum, **Museo Juan Pablo II**. Built to commemorate the pope's visit in 1987, this museum now also has archeology exhibits and dioramas of the oldest known human settlement of the Americas – **Monte Verde**, on the outskirts of Puerto Montt, where human tools found at the site date to 20,000 BC. This discovery in 1976 challenges the belief that human settlements started in the Bering Straits and migrated south.

Casa del Arte Diego Rivera

Quillota 116 • Mon–Fri 9am–8pm, Sat & Sun 11am–6pm • Free
Just off the Plaza de Armas, the Casa del Arte Diego Rivera is the product of a Chilean–Mexican collaboration, with works by local and international artists and photographers displayed inside the Sala Hardy Wistuba on the first floor. There's also a trendy café serving real coffee and good cake.

Angelmó

The fishing neighbourhood of **ANGELMÓ** sits at the western end of the bay, around 1km west of the bus terminal. Here the *costanera* (coastal road) features an excellent **feria artesanal**, its numerous stalls laden with wooden and copper souvenirs, woven

PUERTO MONTT

● BARS AND PUBS
Sherlock	4
Tablón de Ancla	5

● CAFÉS AND CHEAP EATS
Angelmó	3
Salón de Té Rhenania	6

● RESTAURANTS
Andén	1
Cotele	2

■ ACCOMMODATION
Casa Perla	3
Holiday Inn Express	5
Hospedaje Rocco	6
Hotel Puertosur	4
Hotel Seminario	2
Tren del Sur	1

Seno de Reloncaví

Isla Tenglo

Canal Tenglo

Carretera Austral

Mall Paseo del Mar

Museo Juan Pablo II

Bus Terminal

Santa Isabel Supermarket

Full Fresh Supermarket

Skorpios

Craft Market

Ferry Terminal

Navimag

Naviera Austral

Caleta Angelmó

Craft Market

Fish Market

Craft Stalls

Casa del Arte Diego Rivera

Mall Paseo del Mar

Aero Chaitén

BBVA

Lavatodo

LAN

Catedral

Sky Airline

Banco de Chile

Jesuit College

Jesuit Bell Tower

Argentine Consulate

Banco Santander

Banco Santander

Mall Paseo del Mar

AV DIEGO PORTALES

PETORCA

0   250   metres

FERRIES FROM PUERTO MONTT

One of the main reasons people travel to Puerto Montt is to catch a **ferry** south. From Puerto Montt you can sail to Chaitén and Puerto Chacabuco on the Carretera Austral, the Laguna San Rafael far in the southern fjords, Puerto Natales in Patagonia and Quellón in Chiloé. These ferry trips are almost always fully booked in summer, and you must **reserve ahead**. The quality of your experience will largely depend on the weather. The seas on these ferry rides are usually calm as most of the time the ferries are sailing through sheltered fjords, though it can still be windy. The exception is the trip to Puerto Natales, when the ship heads out to the Pacific across the often-turbulent Golfo de Penas.

6

PUERTO MONTT TO PUERTO NATALES

The Navimag trip from Puerto Montt to Puerto Natales is an incredible introduction to Patagonia. Lasting four days and three nights, the trip takes you through pristine and deserted waterways, past uninhabited islands and Chile's largest **glacier**, the Piu XI, with frequent sightings of marine life. It passes by **Puerto Edén**, the last remaining settlement of the **Kawéscar** people, before sailing into the cold and little-explored fjords of the south, and finally docking in Puerto Natales on the Seno Última Esperanza. If you're lucky with the weather, you'll not want to leave the deck for the duration of the trip, except to drink at the bar and to take part in a raucous game of bingo on the last night with a crowd of new friends.

The flipside is a cruise entirely shrouded in mist and fog, topped with a sleepless night as the ship navigates the turbulent waters of the open ocean, followed by the equally sickness-inducing waves of the **Golfo de Penas**, while you spend your trip stuck in the bar or the dining room, watching re-runs of films with people of whom, by trip's end, you may well have grown tired. In the off-season, you will also be sharing the boat (if not the main deck) with cattle. For ferry operators, see p.312.

---

baskets and furniture, woollen clothing, and lapis lazuli jewellery. On the opposite side of the road are stalls selling country cheeses, honey, bottles of powerful *licor de oro* and strings of smoked shellfish.

Beyond the *feria artesanal* lies a thriving **fish market**, a combination of many fish retailers and various eateries operated by ebullient mothers and daughters who crowd around the cauldrons, tempting punters by lifting the lids off steaming vats of *curanto* (see p.324).

ARRIVAL AND DEPARTURE   PUERTO MONTT

BY PLANE

El Tepual airport (☎65 294161) is 13km northwest of Puerto Montt and served by LAN, Sky Airlines, Aero Sur and Aero Chaitén. Flights are met by the ETM bus company, which will take you to the bus terminal for CH$1800.

Airlines LAN, O'Higgins 167 at Urmeneta (☎65 253002, ⓦ lan.com); Sky Airline, San Martín 189 at Benavente (☎65 437555, ⓦ skyairline.cl); Aero Sur, Urmeneta 149 (☎65 252523), Aero Chaitén, Quilllota 127 (☎65 253219).

Destinations Balmaceda/Coyhaique (2 daily; 1hr); Chaitén (1–2 daily; 40min); Concepción (1 daily; 1hr 45min); Punta Arenas (2 daily; 2hr 10min); Santiago (8 daily; 1hr 30min); Temuco (1 daily; 45min).

BY BUS

If you're arriving by bus, you'll pull in at the completely revamped terminal, which is on the seafront (Av Diego Portales s/n), six blocks west of the town centre. There's a

dining area, ATMs, tour operator offices and more. Frequent minibuses to regional destinations such as Puerto Varas, Frutillar and Ensenada depart from the eastern side of the terminal.

Companies All of the main companies have offices in the terminal (☎65 283000), including Tur Bus (☎65 253329, ⓦ turbus.cl) and Pullman (☎65 315561, ⓦ www.pullman .cl), serving all major destinations between Puerto Montt and Santiago, with connections to the north of Chile. Cruz del Sur (☎65 254731, ⓦ www.pullmansur.cl) has the most frequent departures to Chiloé; Queilén Bus (☎65 253468) also serves Chiloé and has weekly departures for Coyhaique via Argentina, while Tas Choapa (☎65 254828, ⓦ taschoapa.cl) and Igi Llaima (☎65 254519) head across the border to Argentina.

Destinations Ancud (every 30min; 2hr); Bariloche, Argentina (2 daily; 6hr); Castro (every 30min; 3hr 30min); Chaitén (1 daily; 12hr); Coyhaique via Osorno (4 weekly; 24hr); Frutillar (every 15min; 1hr); Futaleufú (2 weekly;

6

12hr); Hornopirén (1 daily; 6hr); Osorno (every 30min; 1hr 30min); Puerto Varas (every 15min; 30min); Ralún (2 daily; 2hr 30min); Santiago (every 30min; 14hr); Temuco (every hour; 5hr); Valdivia (every 30min; 3hr).

BY FERRY

The ferry terminal is 500m out of town, southwest towards the suburb of Angelmó. There are various different ferry companies (see p.312). You can take one of the many cabs or *colectivos* that run along the *costanera* both towards the Plaza and towards Angelmó.

Destinations Chaitén (1–2 weekly; 10hr); Laguna San Rafael (4 weekly, Dec–March; 5 days return); Puerto Chacabuco (4 weekly; 24hr); Puerto Natales (1–2 weekly; 4 days); Quellón (1–2 weekly; 6hr).

FERRY CRUISE OPERATORS

Naviera Austral Av Angelmó 2673 ☎65 270430, ⓦwww.navieraustral.cl. In peak season, there are departures to Chaitén (Mon, Thurs & Sat), and from Chaitén to Puerto Montt (Mon, Thurs & Fri). Check online schedule. Passengers CH\$16,000 one way, CH\$9500 per bike, CH\$88,000 per car.

Navimag Av Angelmó 1735 ☎65 432361 or ☎432362, ⓦwww.navimag.com. Services to Puerto Natales and Puerto Chacabuco and cruises to Laguna San Rafael. Accommodation ranges from Class C (a bunk with bedding, a locker for storage and a curtain for privacy; bring own towel) to Class AAA (own room with sea view, en-suite bathroom and private dining with the captain). Book your passage in advance during the peak months of Jan and Feb. Prices range from US\$420 for Class C to US\$1250 for Class AAA from Puerto Montt to Puerto Natales; Cabin AA to Puerto Chacabuco Is CH\$172,000 for a double; while a 5-day/4-night cruise to Laguna San Rafael is around CH\$524,000 (US\$1100) per person. Transporting a car costs CH\$160,000 to Puerto Chacabuco, CH\$280,000 to Puerto Natales.

Skorpios Av Angelmó 1660 ☎65 275646, ⓦskorpios .cl. Upmarket company running luxury cruises. The *Skorpios II* sails from Puerto Montt (every Sat) on a 7-day/6-night journey to the San Rafael Glacier. Single/double cabins per person US\$3150/2100. The *Skorpios III* sails to Puerto Natales (Tues and Fri) on a 4-day/3-night cruise through the fjords, taking in the Glacier Amalia, among others. Single/double cabins US\$2600/1750 per person.

BY CAR

For car rental, head to Budget, Antonio Varas 162 (☎65 286277), or Avis, Gallardo 450 (☎65 254888); rental booths available at the airport. If you wish to drive the Carretera Austral (see box p.351), some rental companies may insist that you rent a 4WD. Some companies will allow you to drop off their vehicles at another office, but this may cost you an additional CH\$300,000 or more.

INFORMATION

Tourist information Southeastern corner of the Plaza de Armas (April–Nov Mon–Fri 9am–1pm & 2.30–6.30pm, Sat 9am–1pm; Dec–March daily 9am–9pm; ☎65 261823; ⓦ puertomonttchile.cl).

Conaf Ochagavía 458 (Mon–Fri 9am–4pm ☎65 486102). Conaf's Patrimonio Silvestre office has some information on visiting the Alerce Andino, Hornopirén and Vincente Pérez Rosales national parks.

ACCOMMODATION

Casa Perla Trigal 312 ☎65 262104, ⓦcasaperla.com. Simple rooms in a Chilean home packed with antiques and decorations. It's a bit of a hike uphill from the main street, but pluses include a warm family atmosphere, an English- and German-speaking staff, and Spanish lessons. CH\$24,000
Holiday Inn Express Avenida Costanera s/n, next to Mall Paseo del Mar ☎65 566000, ⓦholidayinnexpress .cl. It's worth overcoming one's aversion to chain hotels, since this one has excellent views of the Seno de Reloncaví, a very central location and all the perks you'd expect, such as a fitness centre, sauna and excellent buffet breakfast. And did we mention that it's next to the city's best shopping mall? CH\$75,000
Hospedaje Rocco Pudeto 233 ☎65 272897, ⓦ hospedajerocco.cl. Backpackers enjoy a warm welcome from the Argentine hostess and her two lap poodles – Cookie and Shakira. The dorms and rooms are comfortable enough, the breakfast is excellent and kitchen use available at extra cost. Located just five blocks from the Navimag.

Dorm CH\$12,000, double CH\$25,000
Hotel Puertosur Huasco 143 ☎65 351212, ⓦhotelpuertosur.cl. Resembling a Piet Mondrian work from the outside, this smart four-star hotel is a great choice for its location and its comfortable rooms (the ones on the 4th floor come with terrace). You can also sample a good mix of Chilean and international cuisine while looking out to sea from *Restaurant Barlovento*. CH\$50,000
Hotel Seminario Av Seminario 490 ☎65 263946, ⓦhotelseminario.cl. A few blocks uphill from the coastal road, this non-smoking lodge features spacious rooms decked out in soothing creams and whites, with satellite TV and small desks. Price includes nice little extras, such as a buffet breakfast, use of a bike and an hour in the outdoor hot tub. CH\$46,800
Tren del Sur Santa Teresa 643 ☎65 343939, ⓦtrendelsur.cl. Uphill from the port you'll find this adorable, train-themed boutique hotel, where guests are referred to as "passengers" and where much of the furniture

is made from railway trestles. The 16 en-suite rooms are supremely comfortable (if a little dark) and centrally heated, making you wish you'd booked a return ticket. CH$36,900

EATING AND DRINKING

CAFÉS AND CHEAP EATS

Angelmó By the fish market. By far the best spot for an inexpensive seafood meal, this collection of no-frills eateries serves such goodies as *picorocos* (barnacles), *curanto* (see p.324), *almejas* (razor clams), *erizos* (sea urchins) and *chupe de locos* (abalone chowder). Daily noon–8pm.

Salón de Té Rhenania Antonio Varas 328 ☎ 65 282606. Bright and breezy, with cheerful chequered tablecloths, this Osorno export has rapidly won over the Puerto Montt clientele with its vast cake selection and excellent 3-course weekday lunch menu. It may well win you over, too. Mon–Fri 10am–11.30pm, Sat noon–9.30pm, Sun noon–8.30pm.

RESTAURANTS

Andén Santa Teresa 643 ☎ 65 343939, ⊛ trendelsur.cl. With its crisp white tablecloths and formally attired waiters, this could be an upper class dining car on the Orient Express. Except that it has a changing menu of Chilean dishes with international touches, with an emphasis on organic produce, innovative takes on ceviche, fish dishes and even gnocchi. Daily 7–11.30pm.

Cotele General Juan Soler Manfredini 1661, Pelluco ☎ 65 278000. You have to travel out of the centre for these exceptional steaks. Choose between the fillet, sirloin and the ultra-popular rib-eye, complemented by the extensive menu of Chilean reds, and observe the owner in action as he cooks your cut of meat to the desired degree. Mon–Sat 1–4pm & 7.30pm–midnight.

BARS AND PUBS

Sherlock Rancagua at Antonio Varas ☎ 65 288888. Whether or not you believe the myth that Sherlock Holmes once visited the city, this restobar is the place to investigate. Comfortable wooden furniture, a congenial atmosphere, inexpensive Chilean staples including *lomito* (steak sandwich) and *barros jarpa* (ham and melted cheese sandwich) and a wide range of beers, including the Kunstmann range, make it well worth your while. Daily 9am–2am.

Tablón del Ancla Antonio Varas and O'Higgins ☎ 65 263946. This informal bar-restaurant has intimate booths and serves enormous, cheap sandwiches, burgers and fish and meat dishes. You can also order a three-litre tower of Kunstmann beer that comes with its own tap. Daily noon–11.30pm.

DIRECTORY

Banks and exchange AFEX exchange, Av Diego Portales 516. There are many banks with ATMs along Guillermo Gallardo and Urmeneta.
Hospital Hospital Base, Seminario s/n ☎ 65 261100.

Internet All accommodation options reviewed offer free wi-fi; some offer free internet access also.
Laundry Lavatodo, O'Higgins 231.

6

Chiloé

319 Ancud

324 Around Ancud

327 Quemchi

327 Dalcahue

328 Around Dalcahue

330 Castro

334 Parque Nacional Chiloé

337 Chonchi

338 Isla Lemuy

339 Queilén and around

339 Quellón

340 Parque Tantauco

PALAFITOS, CASTRO

Chiloé

Located immediately to the south of the Lake District, the fascinating Chiloé archipelago – part of a mountain range that sank below the waves following the last Ice Age – is a haven of rural tranquillity. The main island, Isla Grande, is South America's second largest island. Sliced in half lengthways by the Panamericana, it connects the two main towns, Ancud and Castro, with the port of Quellón and is easily explored by bike, car or bus. The densely forested Parque Nacional Chiloé and Parque Tantauco offer great opportunities to explore unique Chilote wilderness, while coastal villages and islands off Isla Grande's east coast – the most accessible being **Isla Quinchao** and **Isla Lemuy** – provide glimpses into traditional Chilote life.

Chiloé was originally populated by the native Chonos and Huilliche (southern Mapuche), who eked out a living from fishing and farming before the Spanish took possession of the island in 1567. For over three hundred years, Chiloé was isolated from mainland Chile owing to the fierce resistance of the mainland Mapuche to European colonists. As a result, the slow pace of island life saw little change. Ancud, in fact, was the last stronghold of the Spanish empire during the wars of Independence, before the final defeat by pro-independence forces in 1826. In spite of being used as a stopover during the California Gold Rush, Chiloé remained relatively isolated until the end of the twentieth century, though now it draws scores of visitors with its unique blend of architecture, cuisine and famous myths and legends.

   More than 150 eighteenth- and nineteenth-century **wooden churches** and **chapels** dot the land. Chiloé is also one of the few places in the country where you can still see **palafitos**, precarious but picturesque timber houses on stilts, which were once the traditional dwellings of most of the fishermen of southern Chile. Much of the old culture has been preserved, assimilated into Hispanic tradition by a profound mixing of the Spanish and indigenous cultures that occurred here more than in other parts of South America, making today's Chiloé more "pagan Catholic" than Roman Catholic.

ARRIVAL AND DEPARTURE CHILOÉ

By ferry There are regular ferry services from Pargua, 59km southwest of Puerto Montt on the mainland (daily every 30min 6–1.20am; 35min; CH$600, cars CH$6900) to the village of Chacao on Isla Grande's northern shore; the ferry price is included in the price of the bus ticket to either Ancud or Castro. Scheduled ferry services also crisscross the gulf, linking Puerto Montt, Chaitén, Castro and Quellón.

Maquí – the wonder berry p.319
Chilote mythology p.321
Hot rocks: the culinary secrets of curanto p.324
Penguins in peril p.326
Chilote churches p.328

Castro: the indestructible city p.332
Festival costumbrista p.333
Hikes in and around Parque Nacional Chiloé p.337
Caleta Inío to Quellón by boat p.342

Highlights

❶ Curanto Dig into Chiloé's national dish, a savoury hotchpotch of meat, seafood and potato dumplings, cooked either in a pit in the ground or in a cast iron pot. **See p.324**

❷ Chepu Valley Stay at Chile's only self-sufficient eco-campsite and explore this tranquil valley's sunken forest in a kayak at dawn. **See p.325**

❸ Isla Quinchao A soothing spot to experience the slow pace of Chiloé's lesser isles and see one of the island's most celebrated wooden churches. **See p.329**

❹ Palafitos in Castro Slums or shrines? Insalubrious yet picturesque, Castro's traditional

fishermen's houses on stilts are the sole remaining examples in the country. **See p.331**

❺ Parque Nacional Chiloé Explore the remains of the region's once vast forests by hiking its interior trails. **See p.334**

❻ Whale watching Head out in search of the blue whale pod resident in Chiloé's waters, either with Austral Adventures **(see p.322)** or Darwin Adventure **(see p.340)**.

❼ Parque Tantauco A vast private nature reserve with a well-designed infrastructure offering access to pristine and remote corners of southern Chiloé. **See p.340**

HIGHLIGHTS ARE MARKED ON THE MAP ON P.318

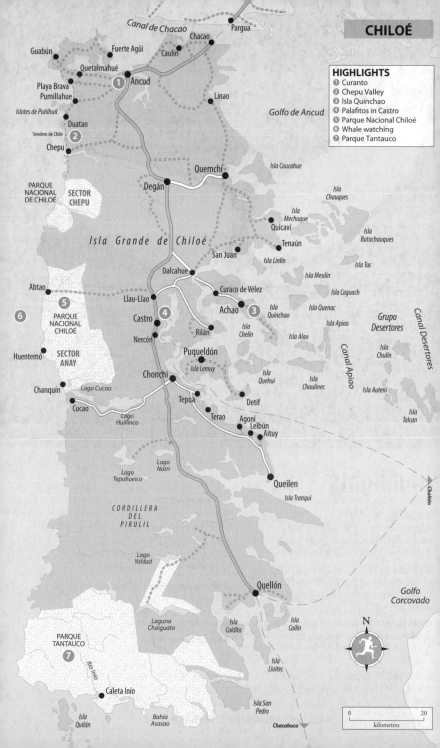

Ancud

ANCUD is a pretty little seaside town and a lively fishing port; numerous visitors find
themselves preferring the relaxed pace of life here to the hustle and bustle of grittier Castro.
Built on a small, square promontory jutting into the Canal de Chacao and the Golfo de
Quetalmahue, the town centres on the pretty **Plaza de Armas** (undergoing complete
renovation at the time of writing), which fills with craft stalls and street musicians in the
summer. The colourful **Mercado Municipal**, one block to the north, is the place to grab a
cheap meal or pick up fresh produce and some local crafts, though there's a more attractive
temporary produce and crafts market a few blocks east of the centre along Arturo Prat.

The town also makes a good base for exploration of the northern half of the island.
Among the attractions are a day-trip to the penguin colony at Puñihuil, a drive to the
nearby Península Lacuy (itself the start of the Chiloé section of the Sendero de Chile,
see p.10) or a rattle along the gravel roads that link the tiny villages along the east coast.

Brief history

Ancud was founded in 1769 as a Spanish stronghold and, after Peruvian independence
in 1824, became the crown's last desperate foothold in South America. Its forts resisted
one attempt at capture, but finally fell in January 1826 when the lonely and demoralized
Spanish garrison fled into the forest in the face of a small *criollo* attack. The remains of
these Spanish forts – **Fuerte San Antonio** in the town and **Fuerte Agüi** on a peninsula to
the northwest – can still be visited today.

Fuerte de San Antonio and around

Mon–Fri 8am–9pm, Sat & Sun 9am–8pm • Free

From the harbour, a crushed-shell promenade heads south past half a dozen intriguing
pieces of **sculpture**, while Calle Lord Cochrane follows the coast to the north to the
reconstructed walls of the Spanish **Fuerte de San Antonio**. The fort affords a sweeping
view over the Golfo de Quetalmahué and out to the Pacific Ocean, while its sixteen
cannon, combined with the fifteen in Fuerte Agüi (on the Península Lacuy across the
water), could sink any ship entering the Bahía de Ancud.

Calle Bellavista, parallel to Cochrane, leads further north to the **Playa Arena Gruesa**, a
popular swimming beach in summer, sheltered by high cliffs.

Museo Regional de Ancud

Libertad 370 • Jan & Feb Mon–Fri 10.30am–7.30pm, Sat & Sun 10am–7.30pm; March–Dec Tues–Fri 10am–5.30pm, Sat & Sun, holidays
10am–2pm • CH$600

The outside patio of the **Museo Regional** houses an exact replica of the *Goleta
Ancud*, a **schooner** with which the first Chilean settlers took possession of the
Magellan Strait in September 1843. It was the culmination of a great tradition of

---

MAQUÍ – THE WONDER BERRY

Stronger than a blueberry. More powerful than the açai berry. Able to battle ageing and
neurodegenerative diseases. Look! In the evergreen tree! It's Maquí the Wonder Berry! The **maquí
berry** (*Aristotelia chilensis*), also known as the Chilean wineberry, is native to Chile's Valdivian
rainforests and has been used by the Mapuche for centuries, both as a foodstuff and as a means
of preparing *chicha* (an alcoholic drink made from fermented berries). In recent years, scientific
studies have discovered that the maquí berry has far higher antioxidizing properties than its
nearest competing "superfoods" – blackberries, açai berries and blueberries. While studies are still
limited, it is believed that the consumption of antioxidants helps to prevent degenerative
diseases such as cancer and Alzheimer's. Maquí berry products can be found at ⓦ islanatura.com.

Chilote boat-building, which included boats made from rough planks lashed together with vines and caulked with alerce bark. Also outside is an entire skeleton of a blue whale.

Permanent collection

The indoor collection consists of partly interactive Spanish-language exhibits, covering various aspects of life in the archipelago, including traditional industries such as fishing, Chiloé's natural environment and wildlife, European conquest, archaeology and religious art, with striking photographs illustrating the impact of the 1960 earthquake which devastated much of the island.

Temporary exhibitions

Temporary exhibitions held in the basement have recently included a striking collection of photographs portraying daily life in different Mapuche communities in the Lake District.

7

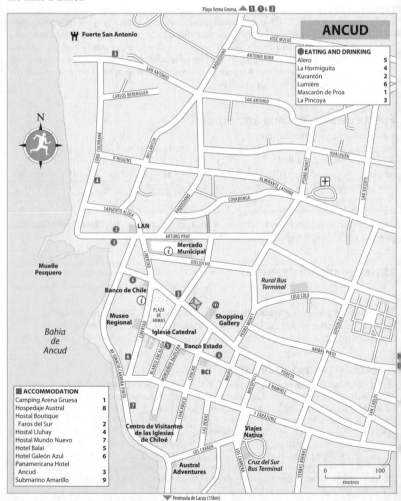

Playa Arena Gruesa, ▲ 1, 1 & 2

ANCUD

Fuerte San Antonio

JOSÉ MUCKE

BAQUEDANO

ANTONIO BURR

SAN ANTONIO

CARLOS BERENGUER

SAN ANTONIO

● **EATING AND DRINKING**

Alero	5
La Hormiguita	4
Kurantón	2
Lumière	6
Mascarón de Proa	1
La Pincoya	3

N

LORD COCHRANE

O'HIGGINS

BELLAVISTA

HUALHUÉN

ALMIRANTE LATORRE

PEDRO MONTT

SAN VICENTE

SARGENTO ALDEA

BAQUEDANO

COVADONGA

LAN

ARTURO PRAT

Mercado Municipal (i)

DIECIOCHO

LIBERTAD

Muelle Pesquero

Banco de Chile (i)

PLAZA DE ARMAS

@

Rural Bus Terminal

COLO COLO

Shopping Gallery

PEDRO MONTT

Museo Regional

Iglesia Catedral

LIBERTAD

Banco Estado

Bahía de Ancud

AV. IGNACIO CARRERA PINTO

BLANCO ENCALADA

MOCOPULLI

ANIBAL PINTO

PUDETO

MUÑOZ AGUILERA

CHACAO

BCI

MAIPÚ

GOTCOLCA

SAN CARLOS

E. RAMIREZ

CHACABUCO

F. ERRÁZURIZ

LAS HERAS

Centro de Visitantes de las Iglesias de Chiloé

Viajes Nativa

LOS CAVADA

LOS CARRERA

Austral Adventures

Cruz del Sur Bus Terminal

YERBAS BUENAS

■ **ACCOMMODATION**	
Camping Arena Gruesa	1
Hospedaje Austral	8
Hostal Boutique Faros del Sur	2
Hostal Lluhay	4
Hostal Mundo Nuevo	7
Hotel Balai	5
Hotel Galeón Azul	6
Panamericana Hotel Ancud	3
Submarino Amarillo	9

0 — 100 metres

▼ Peninsula de Lacuy (15km)

Centro de Visitantes de las Iglesias de Chiloé

Federico Errázuriz 227 • Daily 9.30am–7pm • ⓦ rutadelasiglesias.cl • Donations

If you are planning to visit Chiloé's spectacular **churches** (see pp.321, 328), this excellent museum/visitor centre makes an excellent starting point. Exhibits inside this church building include antique doors and other fragments, hung in the centre of the room and illuminated to great effect by the light from the stained-glass windows. Diagrams along the walls show each stage of construction of a typical Chilote church, but the biggest draw here are the incredibly detailed scale models of the island's most spectacular churches, giving you a taster of the real thing.

ARRIVAL AND DEPARTURE — ANCUD

By bus The majority of long-distance buses – Cruz del Sur and its affiliates – arrive at the Terminal de Buses on Los Carrera 850, a 10min walk from the Plaza de Armas. Try to avoid coming by Queilen Bus, which still uses the largely abandoned and inconveniently located old bus terminal 1.5km along Arturo Prat.

The rural bus terminal, serving numerous villages, is on Colo Colo, above the supermarket Full Fresh.

Destinations Castro (every 15min; 1hr 15min); Puerto Montt (every 30min; 1hr 30min–2hr); Quellón (16 daily; 4hr).

Destinations Caulín (1–4 daily except Sun; 30min); Chacao (every 15min; 30min); Chepu (1–2 daily except

7

CHILOTE MYTHOLOGY

The Chiloé islands have long been rife with myths and legends, especially in the remote rural regions, where tradition and superstition hold sway, with colourful supernatural creatures cropping up in stories throughout the archipelago.

Basilisco A snake with the head of a cockerel, the Basilisco turns people to stone with its gaze. At night, the Basilisco enters houses and sucks the breath from sleeping inhabitants, so that they waste away into shrivelled skeletons. The only way to be rid of it is to burn the house down.

Brujo This is the general term for a witch; in Chiloé, there are only male witches and their legendary cave is rumoured to be near the village of Quicaví. To become a witch, an individual must wash away baptism in a waterfall for forty days, assassinate a loved one, make a purse out of their skin in which to carry their book of spells and sign a pact with the devil in their own blood, stating when the evil one can claim their soul. Witches are capable of great mischief and can cause illness and death, even from afar.

Caleuche This ghostly ship glows in the fog, travels at great speeds both above and below the water, emitting beautiful music, carrying the witches to their next stop. Journeying through the archipelago, it's crewed by shipwrecked sailors and fishermen who have perished at sea.

Fiura An ugly, squat woman with halitosis, she lives in the woods, clothed in moss. The coquettish Fiura bathes in waterfalls, where she seduces young men before driving them insane.

Invunche Stolen at birth by witches, and raised on the flesh of the dead and cats'

milk, the Invunche was transformed into a deformed monster with one leg crooked behind his back. He feeds on goats' flesh and stands guard at the entrance to the legendary witches' cave, the Cueva de Quicaví, grunting or emitting bloodcurdling screams. If you're unlucky enough to spot him, you'll be frozen to that spot forever.

Pincoya A fertility goddess of extraordinary beauty, Pincoya personifies the spirit of the ocean and is responsible for the abundance or scarcity of fish in the sea. She dances half-naked, draped in kelp, on the beaches or tops of waves. If she's spotted facing the sea, the village will enjoy an ample supply of seafood. If she's looking towards the land, there will be a shortage.

Trauco A deformed and ugly troll who dwells in the forest, Trauco dresses in ragged clothes and a conical cap and carries a stone axe or wooden club, a *pahueldœn*. His breath makes him irresistible to women, and he is blamed for all unexplained pregnancies on the island.

Voladora The witches' messenger, the Voladora is a woman who transforms into a black bird by vomiting up her internal organs. The Voladora travels under the cover of night and can only be detected by her terrible cries, which bring bad luck. If the Voladora is unable to recover her innards at the end of the night, she is stuck in bird shape forever.

Sun; 1hr); Península Lacuy and Fuerte Agüi (1–3 daily except Sun; 45min); Puñihuil (2–3 daily; 1hr); Quemchi (up to 12 daily; 1hr); Quicaví (1–3 daily except Sun; 1hr 45min).

INFORMATION AND TOURS

Sernatur office Plaza de Armas at Libertad 665 (Jan & Feb daily 8.30am–7pm; March–Dec Mon–Thurs 8.30am–6pm, Fri 8.30am–5pm; ☏ 65 622800, ✉ infochiloe@sernatur.cl). Offers information on the entire archipelago. Very helpful staff.
Websites ⊛ chiloe.cl, ⊛ ancudmagico.cl, ⊛ interpatagonia.cl and ⊛ patagoniainsular.cl.

TOUR OPERATORS

Austral Adventures Av Costanera 904 ☏ 65 625977, ⊛ austral-adventures.com. Established American–Peruvian outfit catering to the more imaginative traveller, leading expertly guided trips not just to the standard attractions, such as the penguin colonies, but also on rugged hikes, and multi-day trips that allow immersion into Chilote culture. Also available are multi-day boat trips in their own *Cahuella* to the northern part of Parque Pumalín (gourmet meals included) as well as kayaking excursions and 3-day/2-night whale-watching packages.
Viajes Nativa Los Carrera 850, Office 3 ☏ 65 622303, ⊛ viajesnativa.cl. Reputable operator offering half-day and full-day trips to various points of interest on the island. These include a full day in Parque Nacional Chiloé and a day-long tour of Chiloé's most famous churches, as well as half-day excursions to the penguin colonies, and to Península Lacuy.

ACCOMMODATION

HOTELS

Hostal Boutique Faros del Sur Costanera Norte 320 ☏ 65 625799, ⊛ farosdelsur.cl. Superb clifftop views and a stunning lounge with enormous windows and tall ceilings characterize this boutique guesthouse, located a brisk 10min walk from the centre. The en-suite, wi-fi-enabled rooms are thoughtfully located in a wing separate from the lounge and the owner goes out of his way to make you feel welcome. CH$35,000

Hotel Balai Pudeto169 ☏ 65 622966, ⊛ hotelbalai.cl. "Quirky and whimsical" comes to mind when you make yourself at home among *Hotel Balai's* boat figureheads, wooden carvings and models of ships. The rooms are spacious and spotless, the location couldn't be more central and given the extras thrown in – breakfast, wi-fi – the prices are a steal. CH$24,000

Hotel Galeón Azul Libertad 751 ☏ 65 622567, ⊛ hotelgaleonazul.cl. In spite of the name, this hilltop hotel with splendid views across the Golfo de Quetalmahue is, in fact, yellow, but its high-ceilinged rooms, which rattle atmospherically in the wind, do put you in mind of a ship. CH$80,000

Panamericana Hotel Ancud San Antonio 30 ☏ 65 622340, ⊛ panamericanahoteles.cl. Built up on the peninsula just to the north, the priciest hotel in town has a luxurious log-cabin feel, carpeted rooms decorated in warm tones and large picture windows overlooking the sea. The restaurant serves a mixture of Chilote and international dishes. CH$72,000

HOSTELS

Hospedaje Austral Aníbal Pinto 1318 ☏ 65 624847, ⊛ ancudchiloechile.com; 15min walk from the centre of Ancud, or take Queilen bus to the terminal next door. Friendly and helpful Columbian–Chilean owners, king of the hill Lorenzo the dog and homely, wood-panelled rooms draw international travellers to this guesthouse. Dorm CH$6000, double CH$16,000

Hostal Lluhay Lord Cochrane 458 ☏ 65 622656, ⊛ hostal-lluhay.cl. Wonderfully plush en-suite rooms, a well-stocked bar, and breakfast included. Warm and welcoming owners offer home-made *empanadas*, and help to arrange tours. Dorm CH$10,000, double CH$25,000

★ **Hostal Mundo Nuevo** Costanera 748 ☏ 65 628383, ⊛ newworld.cl. Longtime favourite of international travellers, this friendly, spotless *hostal* has a sea view terrace, top-notch dorms and rooms with polished wooden floors and guest kitchen. A morning meal is included and they offer bike rental. Sit down to a good breakfast (which includes home-made bread) with an international crowd that's discovered the new world, ask helpful Swiss owner Martin for help with arranging excursions, or rent a car from him to explore the island solo. Dorm CH$10,000, double CH$36,000

Submarino Amarillo Las Américas 958 ☏ 65 620436, ⊛ subamarillo.net. Attractive, compact new hostel offering colourful dorms and doubles inside a traditional Chilote house rather than a yellow submarine. The friendly English- and German-speaking owners offer tours of Chiloé that are more off the beaten track. Dorm CH$9000, double CH$18,000

CAMPSITES

Camping Arena Gruesa Constanera Norte 292 ☏ 65 623428, ⊛ www.arenagruesa.cl. At this great cliff-top location, a few minute's walk from the Arena Gruesa beach, there are three choices of accommodation:

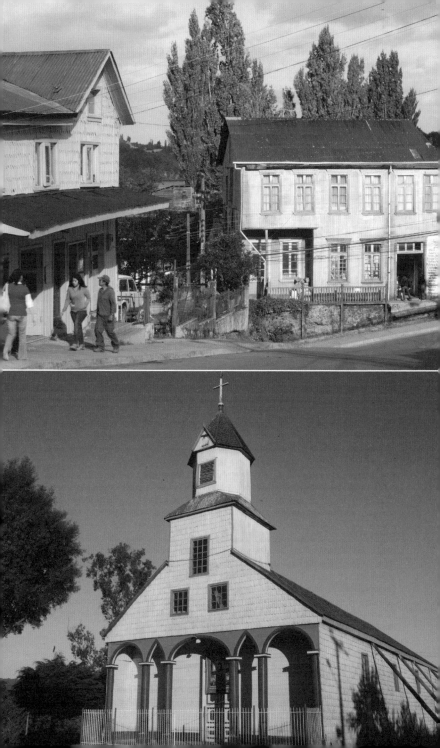

HOT ROCKS: THE CULINARY SECRETS OF CURANTO

Chiloé's signature dish, **curanto**, has been prepared for several centuries using cooking methods very similar to those used in Polynesia. First, extremely hot rocks are placed at the bottom of an earthen pit; then, a layer of shellfish is added, followed by chunks of smoked meat, chicken, *longanisa* (sausage), potatoes, *chapaleles* and *milcaos* (potato dumplings). The pit is then covered with *nalca* (Chilean wild rhubarb) leaves; as the shellfish cooks, the shells spring open, releasing their juices onto the hot rocks, steaming the rest of the ingredients.

Traditional *curanto* (*curanto en hoyo*) is slow-cooked in the ground for a day or two, but since traditional cooking methods are only used in the countryside, you will probably end up sampling *curanto en olla*, also known as *pulmay*, oven-baked in cast-iron pots. The dish comes with hot shellfish broth, known to the locals as "liquid Viagra", to be drunk during the meal. Other Chilote specialities include *cancato*, salmon steamed in tinfoil and stuffed with cheese, sausage and tomatoes, and *carapacho*, a filling crab stew with a crispy crust.

7

a large campsite with excellent sea views, hot water and individual shelters with lights for each site; several fully equipped cabins for 2/4/6/8 people; and well-kept rooms in the white-shingled hostel with access to wi-fi. Camping CH$4000 per person, double CH$22,000, cabin CH$33,000

EATING AND DRINKING

Alero Restaurant Ramirez at Blanco Encalada ☎65 622456. Tapas bar and restaurant serving food with a Mediterranean slant and featuring live music acts on weekends – from jazz to latino. Smokers are kept separate and there are poetry recitals some evenings. Daily 12.30pm–late.

La Hormiguita Pudeto 44 ☎65 626999. Cheerful little bakery specializing in cakes, enormous sandwiches and *empanadas* – both sweet and savoury. If you're looking for something more substantial, the 3-course lunch menu is hard to beat for value (CH$2500). Daily 12–3pm & 7–10.30pm.

★ **Kurantón** Prat 94 ☎65 623090. The legend reads: "Curanto: helping people to have good sex since 1826". When the bow-tied waiter places the dish in front of you, you'll be wondering whether those people had to wait to digest the mountain of shellfish, meat and potato dumplings first. Don't forget to drink your "liquid Viagra"

– the potent shellfish stock that comes with your dish. Curanto CH$7500. Daily 12.30–3pm & 7–11.30pm.

Lumière Ramirez 278 ☎65 621980. With a film projector above the door and black-and-white stills from classic films surrounding you, it's difficult to miss the cinematic theme of this bar, especially since the menu also includes popcorn. A great spot to linger over a cocktail or a beer. Daily noon–late.

Mascarón de Proa Baquedano s/n, on the premises of *Las Cabañas Las Golondrinas*. ☎65 621979. An unpretentious spot with a great sea view to the north of town, this restaurant cooks ample servings of extremely fresh fish. The hake is excellent. Mains from CH$6500. Daily 1–3pm & 7–11.30pm.

La Pincoya Prat 61 ☎65 622613. Overlooking the harbour, this family-run two-storey restaurant is a reliable bet for excellent fishy offerings, such as *curanto* and *ceviche* (Salmon *ceviche* CH$4500). Daily 1–3pm & 7–11pm.

DIRECTORY

Banks and exchange There are ATMs at Banco de Chile (621 Chorillos) on the Plaza, as well as BCI (Chacao at Ramírez).

Car rental Salfa Sur, Arturo Prat at Pedro Montt ⓦwww.salfasur.cl. The owner of *Hostal Mundo Nuevo* (see p.322) has a car to rent out to guests.

Hospital Almirante Latorre 301 ☎65 622356.

Internet All accommodation listings reviewed offer free wi-fi; some offer free internet as well. Otherwise, try the internet café inside the gallery at Pudeto 276 or at Montt at Ramírez.

Post office Pudeto at Blanco Encalada.

Telephone centres There's an Entel call centre at Pudeto 219.

Around Ancud

West of Ancud lies Península Lacuy, its clifftop **Fuerte Agüi** famous as Spain's last stronghold in Chile, while south of the town you find **Islotes de Puñihuil**, a thriving penguin colony that's home to both Magellanic and Humboldt penguins. Further south still, **Chepu Valley**, formed by the powerful tsunami after the earthquake of 1960, is a top destination for birders, its wetlands home to an abundant wealth of bird life. East of Ancud, a turn-off leads to **Caulín**, one of the best spots in Chile for oysters.

Caulín

Nine kilometres along the Panamericana on the way to Ancud from Chacao, a turn-off to the right leads to the hamlet of **Caulín** on the edge of a windswept, kilometre-wide sandy beach, where you can often see locals collecting and laying out a stinking grey seaweed to dry. Called *pelillo* ("fine hair") because it resembles human hair, this alga has a dual purpose: agar-agar, a gelatinous substance used in the food and cosmetics industries can be extracted from it, or the seaweed can be woven into a fibre. Caulín is famous for its specific type of small, sweet **oysters**, the likes of which are only otherwise found in New Zealand.

Península Lacuy

If you head west out of Ancud, you pass the turn-off towards Pumillahue at 14km, and shortly reach the edge of the **Península Lacuy**. Soon the road forks, with the left branch leading to the quiet white-sand beach of **Playa Guabún**, and **Faro Corona**, an isolated lighthouse on a remote promontory. The right fork deposits you, after 21km, below **Fuerte Agüi**, the last toehold of the Spanish Empire in South America. The rusting cannons are still in place, and from the ruins you get great views of the bay of Ancud and beyond.

Pingüineras de Puñihuil

Puñihuil • Aug–March Mon–Fri 10am–7.40pm • ☎ 09 8317 4302• Ⓦ pinguineraschiloe.cl• CH$6000

Reachable from Ancud along a partially paved 28km road or from the coastal village of Guabún via a 20km hike (see p.336) is the seaside village of Pumillahue. Just off the coast lies the rocky outcrop of the **Islotes de Puñihuil**, a **penguin colony** monitored by Ecoturismo Puñihuil, a local organization dedicated to the protection of the penguins. This thriving colony is unique to Chile in that it is visited by both Magellanic and Humboldt penguins in the breeding and rearing season, between December and March. The adults fish most of the day, so the optimum visiting time is early or late in the day.

Ecoturismo Puñihuil runs well-explained trips in zodiac dinghies to see the penguins and other marine fauna, including the delightful *chungungos* (sea otters). The excursions depart directly from the beach and last around forty minutes; there are limited spots available, so reservations are essential in peak season. While driving to Pumillahue is straightforward enough, it's easier to take a tour from Ancud with one of the reputable operators (see p.322). Additionally, Austral Adventures (see p.322) has teamed up with Ecoturismo Puñihuil to run **whale-watching excursions** since a pod of blue whales has been living off the west coast of Chiloé for several years now.

The Chepu Valley

From Pumillahue, it's a good six to eight-hour walk to the mouth of Río Chepu, one that can be rather muddy in parts, though you are rewarded with splendid views of the unspoiled coast. Alternatively, a new dirt road runs through some farmland straight to the **Chepu Valley**. You'll see plenty of gently undulating pastureland and, making up the scattered settlement of Chepu, a few farmhouses spread out along the gravel roads.

The sunken forest

The main attraction, however, is a large stretch of **wetlands**, created in 1960 when the tsunami caused by the most powerful earthquake ever recorded flooded a large section

7

PENGUINS IN PERIL

On an island just off the Chepu Valley coast lies the vulnerable **penguin colony of Ahuenco**; there have been reports of thoughtless travellers paying unscrupulous Chepu fishermen to ferry them across Río Lar along with dogs and even motorcycles and frightening the birds. Since authorities seem to be doing nothing to protect the penguins, it is vital that you go with a reputable guide, such as Chepu Adventures (see p.326); otherwise the colony may not survive for much longer.

of coastal forest. Today, the sunken forest provides a thriving habitat for over a hundred different bird species, as well as ample ground for **kayaking** and fishing. Chepu is also the entry point for the Sector Chepu of Parque Nacional Chiloé (see p.336) and is part of the Sendero de Chile.

ARRIVAL AND DEPARTURE
AROUND ANCUD

CAULÍN

By bus Buses Caulín (☎ 09 9222 8223) run to Caulín (1–4 daily) from Ancud's Terminal de Buses Rurales.

PENÍNSULA LACUY

By bus Minibuses Ahuí depart from Ancud's rural bus terminal for Fuerte Agüi (up to 3 daily except Sun) from 11.45am; last bus 6pm.

By car Take Av Costanera south out of Ancud and follow the signposted road.

PUMILLAHUE

By bus Buses Mar Brava (☎ 65 622312) runs two or three buses from Ancud (every day except Sun 6.45am–4pm).

By tour Austral Adventures and Viajes Nativa run trips to the penguin colony (see p.325).

By car Take Av Costanera south out of Ancud and follow the signposts.

CHEPU VALLEY

By bus Buses Peter runs from Ancud to Chepu (Mon–Fri 1 & 4pm, Sat 2pm).

By car Take the Panamericana from Ancud and then the dirt road to Chepu from Km25; there's an earlier turn-off towards Chepu at Km12, but this road is suitable only for 4WDs.

ACCOMMODATION AND EATING

CAULÍN

Hotel Caulín ☎ 09 9330 1220, ⓦ caulinlodge.cl. If you wish to linger in Caulín, this former German-owned sheep farm offers a seafront scattering of fully equipped *cabañas* with stoves, fridges and rustic fireplaces for up to six people. Horseriding excursions and guided walks can be organized. CH$38,500

THE CHEPU VALLEY

Agroturismo Chepu Cruce Las Huachas ☎ 09 8523 6960 or 09 9899 8914, ⓦ agroturismochepu.cl. Staying at this farmhouse, run by the welcoming Pérez family, is like visiting long-lost Chilean relatives who welcome you into their fold. You can take part in everyday agricultural activities or just enjoy Sonia's hearty home cooking. Only Spanish spoken. CH$10,000 per person

Chepu Adventures Camino a Chepu, Km13.2 ☎ 09 9379 2481 or 09 9227 4517, ⓦ chepuadventures.com; if you don't have your own transport, the owners will pick you up by pre-arrangement – get on any bus towards Castro and ask to be dropped off at the "Cruce de Chepu". This wonderful eco-campsite has become a destination in its own right through the effort of Fernando and Amory, a Santiago couple who gave up city life to devote themselves to the conservation of Chilote wildlife. Campers have access to hot showers and an indoor lounge/cooking area, while those wanting greater comforts stay in *dormis* (mini-cabins with bunk beds; bring own sleeping bag) or the en-suite 2-person cabins. The welcoming owners hold barbecues and organize nature outings, including the excellent self-guided "Kayaking at Dawn" in the sunken forest below (don't feel like paddling? rent a silent electric kayak instead). Wi-fi available. Camping CH$4000 per person, *dormi* CH$5000, cabin CH$30,000

EATING

CAULÍN

Ostras Caulín ☎ 09 9643 7005, ⓦ ostrascaulin.cl. Oysters come in many guises at this fine seafront restaurant: fried; in a cocktail; as a cream-of-oyster soup;

and, the most popular choice, as an oyster platter featuring one of three types of oysters on the half shell (from CH$7500). Daily during daylight hours.

PUÑIHUÍL
Restaurant El Rincón ☏ 09 9181 2240. Another good beachfront eatery with a similar menu to Bahía Puñihuil, but with tasty *empanadas de locos* as well. Avoid consuming *locos* (abalone) out of season as it is endangered. Daily noon–5.30pm.

Quemchi

East from the Panamericana, 41km south of Ancud, a picureque coastal road leads along the coast to **Quemchi**, an attractive little fishing town with narrow, irregular streets sloping down to the water's edge. On a sunny day, the sight of snow-tipped volcanoes beyond the village makes for an impressive sight. A couple of kilometres south, there's a tiny wooded island, **Isla Aucar**, only accessible by a 500m-long footbridge. Nestled on the island is a small wooden **church** with a duck-egg-blue roof and white walls.

ARRIVAL AND DEPARTURE   QUEMCHI

By bus Quemchi is served by up to 12 buses per day by 5 different bus companies from Ancud's Terminal de Buses Rurales. Buses Aucar runs services (6 daily 9am–7pm) from Ancud, and there's also a service (2 daily) by Expreso Quicaví. There are also buses (19 daily Mon–Fri 7am–7.45pm) from Castro.

ACCOMMODATION

El Chejo Diego Bahamonde 251 ☏ 65 691490. Wander into the kitchen at this wonderful family-run restaurant and peer into the pots to see what Elsa is cooking on any given day; the menu ranges from grilled fish to *casuela Chilote* (Chilote stew with *cochayuyo* seaweed). It is our informed opinion that Elsa's seafood *empanadas* are the best on the island. Daily 1–3.30pm & 7.30–10.30pm.

Hotel y Cabañas Costanera Diego Bahamonde 141 ☏ 65 691230, ✉ hospedaje_costanera@latinmail.com. "Hotel" might be stretching it a bit, as even something as basic as hot water is not reliable, but a few of the rooms (some with shared facilities) have sea views. CH$14,000

Dalcahue

The bustling, historical town of **DALCAHUE** lies 20km northeast of Castro via the turn-off at Llau-Llao. It is famous for its thriving traditional boat-building industry and the Sunday Feria Artesanal, when artisans come from nearby islands to sell woollen crafts, wood carvings and hand-woven baskets. Dalcahue also provides the only link with nearby **Isla Quinchao** (see p.329), the second largest in the Chiloé archipelago.
   Most of the action is centred around the attractive Plaza de Armas and the open-sided market building on the waterfront. On the plaza rises the imposing, UNESCO-listed Iglesia de Nuestra Señora De Los Dolores, which dates to 1893 and boasts a unique nine-arched portico.

ARRIVAL AND DEPARTURE   DALCAHUE

By bus Buses Dalcahue Expreso run daily (Mon–Sat every 15 min 7.15am–9.15pm; Sun every 30min) from Castro to Dalcahue.

ACCOMMODATION

The most attractive accommodation option near Dalcahue is the shingled lodge used by **Altué Expeditions** as their kayak centre (see p.333).

Hotel La Isla Av Mocopulli 113 ☏ 65 641246, ✉ hotellaisla@hotmail.com. Dalcahue's plushest digs feature large, comfortable rooms and possibly the most spacious showers in Chiloé inside a smart, shingled exterior. Good breakfast included. CH$35,000
Residencial La Playa Rodríguez 09 ☏ 65 641397. This cheapie with a lime green exterior is handily located a stone's throw from both the Plaza and the boat ramp, and though you can hear every word your neighbours say through the wall, the rooms with shared facilities are comfortable enough. CH$16,000

EATING

La Cocinera Next to the Feria Artesanal. This indoor collection of food stalls inside an establishment that resembles an upside-down boat is the best place to try inexpensive Chilote specialities. Shop around as local women dish up *curanto*, *empanadas*, *milcaos* (potato pancakes, some filled with meat) and sweets such as *calzones rotos* (lit: "torn underpants"). *Doña Lula*, Puesto 8, does fabulous *empanadas*; *Zenchita*, Puesto 2, is a favourite

for *curanto*, while *La Nenita*, Puesto 4, offers very fresh salmon ceviche. Daily 8am–9pm.

El Dalca Ramón Freire s/n ☎65 641222. Popular seafood restaurant above the boat ramp serves *curanto* on Sundays and wows locals and visitors alike with its *caldillo de mariscos* (shellfish stew) and fish dishes the rest of the time. Mon–Sat noon–3pm & 7–10.30pm, Sun noon–4pm.

Around Dalcahue

For those who wish to witness traditional Chilote life in settlements where time seems to stand still, there are few better places to do so than Chiloé's east coast. If you have your own vehicle, take the gravel roads to tiny, sleepy coastal villages, where on a grey and misty day you can almost imagine the characters from Chiloé's mythology (see p.321) coming to life. Those without their own wheels can cross over to the island of Quinchao, characterized by its rolling farmland, small towns with striking traditional churches and the busy market in Achao, attended by sellers from neighbouring islands.

Tenaún

From Dalcahue, an attractive gravel road heads northeast towards Quemchi, following the coast. Thirty-seven kilometres along, a small bumpy road with two forks (first take

---

CHILOTE CHURCHES

It is impossible to visit Chiloé and not be struck by the sight of the archipelago's incredible **wooden churches**. In the early nineteenth century these impressively large buildings would have been the heart of a Chilote village. Several of the churches have been declared national monuments, an honour crowned in 2001 when UNESCO accepted sixteen of them on its prestigious World Heritage list.

The churches generally face the sea and are built near a beach with an open area, plaza or *explanada* in front of them. The outside of the churches is almost always bare, and the only thing that expresses anything but functionality is the three-tiered, **hexagonal bell tower** that rises up directly above an open-fronted portico. The facades, doors and windows are often brightly painted, and the walls clad with *tejuelas* (wooden tiles or shingles). All the churches have three naves separated by columns, which in the larger buildings are highly decorated, supporting barrel-vaulted ceilings. The ceilings are often painted, too, with allegorical panels or sometimes with golden constellations of stars painted on an electric blue background.

HISTORY

Only the *pueblos* with a priest had a main church, or *iglesia parroquial*. If there was no church, the missionaries used to visit once a year, as part of their so-called *misión circular*. Using only native canoes, they carried everything required to hold a mass with them. When the priest arrived, one of the eldest Chilotes would lead a procession carrying an image of Jesus, and behind him two youths would follow with depictions of San Juan and the Virgin. They would be followed by married men carrying a statue of San Isidro and married women carrying one of Santa Neoburga.

If the *pueblo* was important enough there would be a small *capilla* (bell tower) with altars to receive the statues. The building where the missionaries stayed was known as a *residencia*, *villa*, *casa ermita* or *catecera*, and was looked after by a local trustee called a *fiscal*, whose function was somewhere between that of a verger and lay preacher. This honorary position still exists and, in Chiloé's remoter areas, the *fiscal* commands great respect in his community. For more information on Chiloé's churches, check out the informative ⓦ interpatagonia.com/iglesiaschiloe.

the left, then the right) heads down to the somnolent coastal village of **TENAÚN**. Smiling down at the attractive waterfront and quaint little fishermen's cottages is arguably Chiloé's most extraordinary **church**. Founded in 1734 but rebuilt in 1861, and recently spruced up, it's dazzling to look at: painted white with two huge pale blue stars daubed onto the wall above the entrance, and topped off by three vibrant blue and red towers.

Quicaví

Six kilometres beyond Tenaún on the main road, a turn to the east leads, after 7km, to the tiny seafront village of **QUICAVÍ**, whose sleepiness belies its importance in Chilote mythology. It's said that somewhere along the nearby coast lies the legendary **Cueva de Quicaví**, where a Spanish warlock left a powerful book of spells for the resident *brujos* after being defeated in a magic duel. The Spanish Inquisition, and many others besides, have searched for the cave in vain. Perhaps because of this wealth of superstition, the missionaries built a larger than usual **church** in Quicaví.

Isla Mechuque

Small launches depart from the jetties at Tenaún and Quicaví for the beautiful island of **ISLA MECHUQUE**, the largest and most easily accessible of the Chauques subgroup. Since a quorum of passengers is required, the surest way of making this magical trip past unspoiled island scenery is to go on an organized excursion from Castro in the summer (see p.333). The highlight of such trips to the tiny village of Mechuque with its shingled *palafitos* is a genuine *curanto en hoyo* prepared before your eyes in an outdoor pit (needs to be organized in advance).

Isla Quinchao

For some, **ISLA QUINCHAO** is the cultural heart of the whole of Chiloé. Rich in traditional wooden architecture, this island is a mere ten-minute ferry ride from Dalcahue. A paved road runs across Isla Quinchao through the only two towns of any size, **Curaco de Vélez** and **Achao**, both of which offer a taste of traditional Chilote life.

Curaco de Vélez

Twelve kilometres from the ferry terminal, **Curaco de Vélez** comprises a couple of streets of weather-beaten shingled houses set around a beautiful bay and bordered by gently rolling hills. The Plaza de Armas features an unusual sight – a decapitated **church steeple**, docked from the top of an old church, and a bust of locally born hero Almirante Riveros, who commanded the fleet that captured the Peruvian, ironclad *Huáscar* during the War of the Pacific (see p.474).

Achao

Fifteen kilometres southeast of Curaco lies the fishing village of **ACHAO** with its scattering of houses clad in colourful *tejuelas* (shingles), set against a backdrop of snowcapped volcano peaks across the gulf. It is famous both for the oldest church in the archipelago and a couple of simultaneous festivals in early February: *Encuentro Folklórico de las Islas del Archipiélago*, a folk festival that draws musical groups from all over Chiloé, and *Muestra Gastronómica y Artesanal*, which gives you a chance to both sample traditional Chilote cuisine and pick up the handiwork of the archipelago's artisans.

Iglesia Santa Maria de Loreto

Mon & Wed–Sun 11am–1pm & 2–4pm • Free

Achao is a living museum of Chiloé's *cultura de madera* (woodworking culture). Dominating the Plaza de Armas and dating back to 1764, **Iglesia Santa Maria de Loreto** is a prime example of a typical Chilote church and is thought to be the oldest one in the archipelago. The main framework is made from *ciprés de las Guaitecas* and *mañío*, a tree still common in southern Chile. The original *alerce* shingles which covered the exterior have mostly been replaced with *ciprés* boarding. Restoration work is a constant and expensive necessity – if you look around the *luma* wood floorboards, you can see the church's foundations, a rare glimpse into the way these old buildings were constructed. All the joints have been laboriously fixed into place with wooden plugs and dowels made from *canelo*, another type of Chilean wood.

ARRIVAL AND DEPARTURE

AROUND DALCAHUE

TENAÚN

By bus There are regular buses to Tenaún (7–11 daily) from Castro with Buses Ojeda (☎65 635477) and other minibuses between 8am and 7pm.

QUICAVÍ

By bus Buses Expreso Quicaví (☎09 248 4362) has services from Ancud (1–2 Mon–Sat), while Buses Rony Velásquez has one daily departure from Ancud (Mon–Fri 2.30pm).

ISLA QUINCHAO

By boat Ferry services (every 30min 7am–11pm; foot passengers free, cars Dec–Feb CH$4500 return, March–Nov CH$1500 return).

By bus Achao's Terminal de Buses (Miraflores at Zañartu), a couple of blocks east of the Plaza, has daily departures for Dalcahue (every 20min 7.15am–8.30pm). All buses to Achao call at Curaco de Vélez and some continue on to Castro.

ACCOMMODATION

ISLA QUINCHAO

Hospedaje Sol y Lluvia Ricardo Jara 9, Achao ☎65 661383. The nicest guesthouse in town, whose burnt-orange exterior hides spacious, comfortable rooms, some with shared bathrooms. The owners offer breakfast above and beyond the usual bread-and-instant-coffee combo. CH$38,000

Hostal Plaza Amunategui 20 ☎65 661283. It's difficult to say what's warmer: the atmosphere generated by the wonderful family who run this cheapie above the post office, or the large kitchen heated by the

traditional wooden stove. The cheaper rooms share facilities. CH$13,000

TENAÚN

Hospedaje Mirella Tenaún ☎09 647 6750, ✉mirellamontana@gmail.com. Part of the Agroturismo network, this friendly family-run guesthouse has room for seven guests and is run by the hospitable Mirella and the Soto family. *Curanto en hoyo* sometimes on offer; otherwise Mirella cooks up the catch of the day. CH$14000

EATING AND DRINKING

ISLA QUINCHAO

Hostería La Nave Arturo Prat s/n ☎65 661280. Located by the seafront, this local institution has been going strong for 30 years and shows no signs of quitting. Good for catch-of-the-day fish and shellfish dishes. Mon–Sat noon–10pm, Sun 12.30–3.30pm.

Mar y Velas Serrano 2, Achao ☎65 661375. Inexpensive fish and seafood dishes overlooking the sometimes busy boat ramp. Try the *cancato*, fish steamed with cheese, sausage and

shellfish. Mon–Sat 12.30–11pm, Sun 12.20–3.30pm.

Ostras Los Troncos Francisco Bohle s/n, Curaco de Vélez. Follow the road downhill from the Plaza de Armas to the coastal road and look out for the sign that'll direct you to the garden, festooned with fishing nets and lined with rough-hewn wooden tables and seats – a superb spot for slurping two dozen local oysters (CH$300–400 per oyster); bring your own wine. Daily in summer 11am–7pm.

Castro

Built on a small promontory at the head of a 20km fjord, lively **CASTRO** occupies an unusual position both physically and historically. Founded in 1567, it's the third-oldest city in Chile, but it never became strategically important because it's a terrible harbour for sailing ships, only flourishing because the Jesuits chose to base their mission here. Today, little remains of old Castro, though some buildings have miraculously survived, such as the groups of brightly coloured **palafitos** – shingled fishermen's houses on stilts – on the waterfront to the north and south of town.

Iglesia San Francisco

The centre of Castro is the **Plaza de Armas**. On the northeast corner sits Castro's church, the national monument of **Iglesia San Francisco**. Its iron-clad wooden structure is a mix of Classical and neo-Gothic styles and it was designed in 1906 by the Italian Eduardo Provasoli. The church's impressive interior is a harmonious blend of the island's native hardwoods, while the exterior is a less pleasing faded peach.

Palafitos

Though deemed unsanitary by some locals, Chiloé's famous **palafitos** are still found at several locations around Castro. Perched precariously on stilts above the water, these brightly painted, *alerce*-shingled, traditional wooden fishermen's dwellings are

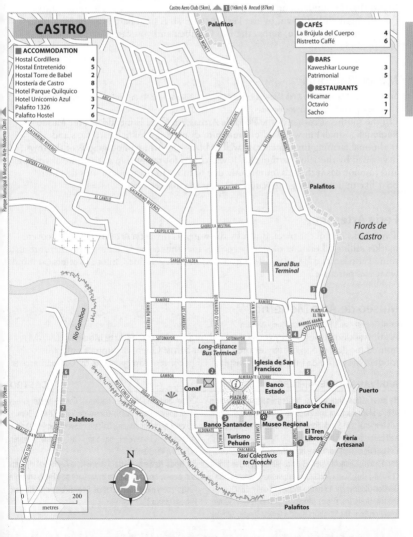

> ## CASTRO: THE INDESTRUCTIBLE CITY
>
> Castro has had its fair share of difficulties through the centuries. It was sacked by the Dutch both in 1600 and then in 1643, destroyed by earthquake in 1646, by fire in 1729, by earthquake again in 1739, by fire again in 1890, by fire once more in 1936, and most recently by earthquake and tidal wave in 1960. Anyone else would have given up and moved long ago, but the Chilotes keep hanging on.

an unforgettable sight. The idea was that you could moor your boat at your back door and walk out onto the street through the front one. The most impressive examples are found at the north end of town, off Pedro Montt, where they are perfectly reflected in the grubby mini-lake by the roadside. More **palafitos** are found slightly south along the same street, while others are used as restaurants at the southern end of town, by the Feria Artesanal. A final batch can be seen from the western end of Lillo, across the Río Gamboa and you can even stay in one (see pp.333, 334).

Museo Regional

Calle Esmeralda • Previously Jan & Feb Mon–Sat 9.30am–8pm, Sun 10.30am–1pm; March–Dec Mon–Sat 9.30am–1pm & 3–6.30pm • ☎ 65 635967 • Donations welcome

Off the southeast corner of the Plaza de Armas, on Calle Esmeralda, is the **Museo Regional**, a small but well-laid-out museum displaying Huilliche artefacts and traditional farming implements, as well as black-and-white photographs of the town, devastated by the 1960 earthquake. It was closed for renovation at the time of writing and rumour has it that it's imminently due to move to the modern, upside-down boat-like building along the waterfront near the market.

Feria Artesanal

Two blocks east of the plaza, down by the water, is the **Feria Artesanal**, a large covered market selling all manner of woolly goodies that the region is famous for. There are also some Peruvian and Bolivian offerings mixed in with genuine Chilote sweaters, so mind what you purchase.

Museo de Arte Moderno

Pasaje Diaz 181 • Jan & Feb daily 10am–6pm • Donation

A fair walk northwest of downtown, you'll find the **Museo de Arte Moderno** (MAM) housed inside a group of five restored wooden barns. Open in summer only, this modern art complex inside a park displays edgy contemporary works by Chilean artists.

ARRIVAL AND DEPARTURE   **CASTRO**

By bus Castro's long-distance bus terminal is at San Martín 486, a block north of the Plaza de Armas, while the rural bus terminal is at San Martín 667, down an alley two and a half blocks north of the Plaza.

Destinations (long distance bus terminal): Ancud (hourly; 1hr 15min); Chonchi (every 30min; 30min); Puerto Montt (11 daily; 3hr); Punta Arenas, via Argentina (2 weekly, 32hr); Quellón (hourly; 2hr 15min); Santiago (4 daily; 18hr).

Destinations (rural bus terminal): Achao (every 30min; fewer on Sun; 1hr 50min); Chonchi (every 30min; 30min);

Cucao and the Parque Nacional Chiloé, sector Anay (4–6 daily; 1hr 15min); Curaco de Vélez (every 30min, fewer on Sun; 1hr 30min); Dalcahue (every 30min; 30min); Puqueldón (3 daily, 1 on Sun; 1hr 15min); Queilén (12 daily; 1hr 30min).

By boat Naviera Austral (ⓦ www.navieraustral.cl) runs one weekly boat to Chaitén in January and February from Castro's new passenger terminal. Book tickets with Turismo Pehuén (see p.337).

FESTIVAL COSTUMBRISTA

At the northwest end of Castro lies the **Parque Municipal**. In mid-February the park hosts an enormous feast, the culmination of the **Festival Costumbrista**, a celebration of traditional Chilote life, when *curanto* is cooked in great cauldrons, *chicha* (cider) flows freely and balls of grated potato – *tropón* – are baked on hot embers. The inevitable burnt fingers and resultant hot-potato juggling that results from picking them up is known as *bailar el tropón* (dancing the *tropón*).

GETTING AROUND

Car rental Salfa Sur, Mistral 499 ☎65 630422 ⓦwww .salfasur.cl. If you're planning on exploring the seaside villages, it's best to rent a vehicle with high clearance to cope with the pitted gravel roads.

INFORMATION AND TOURS

Tourist information Plaza de Armas (daily 10am–8pm; ⊜turismo@municastro.cl). A large and well-stocked office (though the brochures are hidden behind the information desk and you need to know what to ask for) with several scale models of Chiloé churches.

Conaf office Gamboa 424 (Mon–Fri 10am–12.30pm & 2.30–4pm; ☎65 532503). Limited information about the Parque Nacional Chiloé (see pp.334–337).

offers multi-day trips around the Chiloé archipelago, as well as multi-activity trips in the Lake District and Patagonia; pick-up from Castro available.

Castro Aero Club Gamboa airfield ☎65 632264, ⊜clubaereocastro@telsur.cl. Scenic flights offered over the Chiloé archipelago in 4-seater planes. From US$60 per passenger.

Turismo Pehuén Esmeralda 198 ☎65 635254, ⓦturismopehuen.cl. An experienced outfit offering day trips which include tours of Chiloé's churches, trips to Isla Quinchao and excursions to the Parque Nacional Chiloé.

TOUR OPERATORS

Altué Expeditions Dalcahue ☎09 9419 6809, ⓦseakayakchile.com. Excellent outfit in Dalcahue that

ACCOMMODATION

HOTELS AND GUESTHOUSES

Hostal Entretenido Almirante Latorre 139 ☎65 531677, ⓦhostalentretenido.blogspot.com. Small, centrally located and friendly guesthouse with room for eight guests and a cat that rules the roost. Little perks include a games room with cable TV, mini pool table and a good view of Castro's bay from the patio. All rooms share facilities. CH$17,000

Hostería de Castro Chacabuco 202 ☎65 632301, ⓦhosteriadecastro.cl. An oversized chalet with spacious, modern, tastefully furnished rooms and suites and the excellent restaurant *Las Araucarías*, specialising in *curanto* and fish dishes, make this Castro's top end pick for visiting foreigners. The floor-to-ceiling windows in the suites offer good views of the bay, and the swimming pool and spa are a nice touch. CH$49,800

Hotel Parque Quilquico Quilquico ☎65 971100, ⓦhotelparquequilquico.cl. If you have your own vehicle, this brand new hotel, located in a large private park overlooking the Dalcahue channel, a 16km drive from Castro on the way to Rílan, is a great place to base yourself. You have a choice of plush rooms, decorated in earthy colours with plenty of natural light and wooden floors; highlights include fine Chilote cuisine in the on-site restaurant, an indoor pool and sauna and trails

ideal for short rambles within Parque Quilquico itself. CH$190,000

Hotel Unicornio Azul Av Pedro Montt 228 ☎65 632359, ⓦhotelunicornioazul.cl. The sister hotel of Ancud's *Galeón Azul*, this gaudy pink creation with turrets down by the port is probably as easy to miss as a blue unicorn. The centrally heated rooms with cable TV are comfortable, if a little worn and varying in size, and you get some great views from the top. CH$80,000

Palafito 1326 Riquelme 1326 ☎65 530053, ⓦpalafito1326.cl. The big brother of *Palafito Hostel*, this boutique hotel inside a *palafito* combines a traditional Chilote experience with great comfort. There's a lot of wood and a lot of light, sun terraces to relax on and great sea views from the best rooms. The owners arrange all manner of excursions. CH$119,000

HOSTELS

Hostal Cordillera Barros Arana 175 ☎65 532247, ⓦhostalcordillera.cl. While the owner of this slightly chaotic *hostal* speaks very little English, her warmth translates into any language. The *hostal* itself is akin to a family home with a large lounge, popular outdoor terrace and basic rooms but clean rooms (some with thin walls). Dorm CH$9000, double CH$18,000

Hostal Torre de Babel O'Higgins 965 ☎ 65 534569, ⓦ hostaltorredebabel.com. True to the name, the mañío-panelled walls of this place ring with the many languages of its international clientele. The owner throws in all-you-can-eat breakfast, provides wi-fi and organizes group trips into the countryside. Dorm CH$10,000, double CH$20,000

★ **Palafito Hostel** Riquelme 1210 ☎ 65 531008, ⓦ palafitohostel.com. Staying in this revamped palafito feels like being in a boat, what with the water lapping against the stilts during high tide, the curved walls of the well-furnished room and the little deck at the back of the dining area. Breakfast includes delicious home-made bread, the staff can help organize horseriding in Parque Nacional Chiloé and there's wi-fi throughout. The only downside is the hill you have to walk up to get into town. Dorm CH$13,000, double CH$32,000

EATING AND DRINKING

CAFÉS
La Brújula del Cuerpo O'Higgins 308 ☎ 65 633225. Travellers and locals alike gravitate to "The Body's Compass" – a busy café on the main square specializing in inexpensive Chilean takes on fajitas, burgers, salads, sandwiches, fresh fruit juices and real coffee. Daily 11am–midnight.

★ **Ristretto Caffé** Blanco 264 ☎ 65 532769. In a country where real coffee is as rare as hen's teeth, this dark wood café, with 57 different coffees on the menu, would be a breath of fresh air if it weren't for its smoking policy. Still, you can join the rest of the laptop-toting clientele for some great foccacias, fresh fruit juices and an extensive range of teas, including the likes of Italian Almond. Mon–Sat 8am–9pm.

RESTAURANTS
Hicamar Gamboa 413 ☎ 65 532655. Ambitious restaurant with good service specializing in well-prepared meat dishes; try the wild boar or the signature steak. Mains CH$7000. A couple of doors down, the budget *Hicamar Express* (same hours) serves large portions of fried chicken, burgers and hot dogs. Daily 1–3.30pm & 7–11.30pm.

★ **Octavio** Montt 261 ☎ 65 632855. With exemplary service, an excellent location in a *palafito* right over the water and a simple but expertly executed menu, this has been the best place in Castro for *curanto en olla* (CH$7500) for many years now. The other seafood dishes, such as the *mariscal* (seafood stew), are almost as good and the fish is always fresh. Daily 10am–midnight.

Sacho Thompson 213 ☎ 65 632079. The upstairs dining area of this local favourite offers excellent views across the fjord and the menu is all about the offerings of the sea. You cannot go wrong with anything clam-based, and while the choice of fish often seems to be limited to salmon and *congrio* (conger eel), all the dishes are well prepared. The *cancato* (salmon steamed with sausage and cheese) stands out. Mains from CH$6000. Daily noon–midnight.

BARS
Kaweshkar Lounge Blanco Encalada 31 ☎ 65 549545. This trendy lounge with retro furniture and indie music on the stereo has become a firm backpacker favourite. The menu features numerous vegetarian options, sweet and savoury crêpes and myriad cocktails. Live DJs some evenings in summer. Mon–Sat noon–4pm & 8pm–midnight.

Patrimonial Balmaceda 291 ☎ 65 534990. This second-floor watering hole overlooking the square draws a local crowd with its range of microbrews and unusual cocktails. Sandwiches and shared platters of meats available. Mon–Sat noon–1am.

DIRECTORY

Airlines LAN, O'Higgins 412 ☎ 600 526 2000; Sky Airlines, Blanco Encalada 388 ☎ 65 534643.
Banks and exchange There are ATMs around the Plaza de Armas, and a money exchange at Chacabuco 286.
Hospital Hospital Augusta Rifat, on Freire 852 (☎ 65 632445), has basic medical facilities.

Internet access All accommodation options reviewed offer free wi-fi; some also offer internet. Otherwise, try Via Entel, Esmeralda 579.
Post office Plaza de Armas, O'Higgins 388.

Parque Nacional Chiloé

Daily: Jan & Feb 9am–8pm; March–Dec 9am–1pm & 2–7pm • CH$2500 • ☎ 09 9644 2489, ⓔ vidasur@telsur.cl

On the island's western coast, the **PARQUE NACIONAL CHILOÉ** comprises over 420 square kilometres of native evergreen forest, covering the slopes and valleys of the **Cordillera de Piuchen**, largely unexplored by man and harbouring flora and fauna

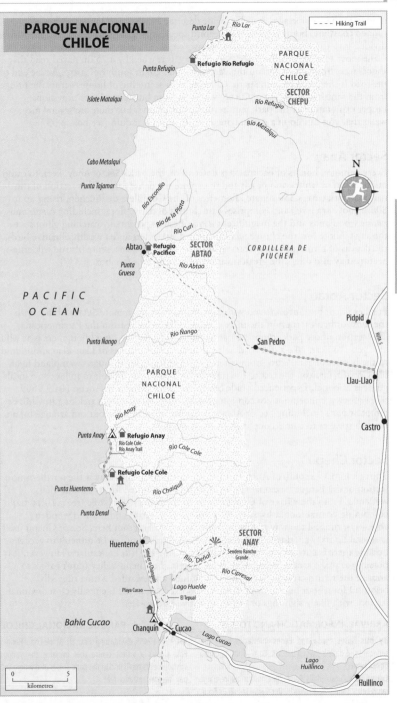

PARQUE NACIONAL CHILOÉ

- - - - Hiking Trail

Punta Lar — Río Lar

Refugio Río Refugio

Punta Refugio

PARQUE NACIONAL CHILOÉ SECTOR CHEPU

Islote Matalqui

Río Refugio

Río Metalqui

Cabo Metalqui

Punta Tajamar

N

Río Escondio

Río de la Plata

Río Curi

Abtao — Refugio Pacifico

SECTOR ABTAO

CORDILLERA DE PIUCHEN

Punta Gruesa

Río Abtao

PACIFIC OCEAN

Pidpid

Río Ñango

Punta Ñango

San Pedro

Llau-Llao

PARQUE NACIONAL CHILOÉ

Castro

Río Anay

Punta Anay — Refugio Anay

Rio Cole Cole-Rio Anay Trail

Río Cole Cole

Refugio Cole Cole

Punta Huentemo

Río Chaiquil

Punta Denal

SECTOR ANAY

Huentemó

Sendero Rancho Grande

Río. Denal

Río Cipresal

Sendero Chanquin

Playa Cucao

Lago Huelde

El Tepual

Bahía Cucao

Chanquín — Cucao

Lago Cucao

Lago Huillinco

Huillinco

0 — 5 kilometres

7

unique to the archipelago, as well as wide deserted beaches and long stretches of **rugged coastline**, home to dozens of seabird species, penguins and sea lions. The park is divided into three sectors, as detailed below.

The most accessible of the three, Sector Anay, is reached by a 25km paved road that shoots west from a junction on the Panamericana, 20km south of Castro. At the end of the road is the gateway to the park, Chanquín – a scattering of houses across the bridge from the ramshackle village of **Cucao**, where you can buy last-minute provisions. Proper exploration of the park requires at least four days, but there are several nice walks that you can do in a day, staying overnight in Chanquín (see box, p.337).

Sector Anay

Every summer, hordes of backpackers descend on the park's **Sector Anay**, keen to camp on its 20km of white-sand beach and to explore the dense forest. This section of the national park covers 350 square kilometres of the Cordillera de Piuchén, rising up to 800m above sea level, and comprises vast chunks of native flora, including *coigüe* and *mañío* woodlands and the magnificent *alerce*. Besides potentially catching glimpses of the shy Chilote fox, the elusive *pudú* (pygmy deer), otters and a wealth of native birds, the depths of primeval Chiloé forest allow you to experience a sense of true wilderness. Sector Anay also offers the greatest variety of hiking trails (see box, p.337).

Sector Abtao

Further north but unconnected with Sector Anay lies the remote **Sector Abtao**, with the most difficult terrain of the three though still reachable from the Panamericana. This section of the park comprises dense woodland and bogs, and hiking here is as wild as it gets. You can take a dirt road halfway between the villages of Llau-Llao and Pidpid to the hamlet of San Pedro, from where an 18km trail runs through swampland to an old Conaf *refugio* on the coast. The trail is overgrown and difficult to follow, so a local guide is essential. Experienced guide Sebastián "Bata" Kruger in Ancúd (☎09 9509 3741, ⓦwww.chiloeindomito.com; in Spanish only) specializes in trekking in Chiloé's remotest parts, including Sector Abtao; he speaks Spanish only, but can arrange for an English speaker to come along if given some warning.

Sector Chepu

Thirty kilometres **south** of Ancud and to the north of Sector Anay is the northernmost section of the Parque Nacional Chiloé, **sector Chepu**, noted for its birdlife-rich **wetlands**. From the village of Guabún, part of the Sendero de Chile (see p.10), a trail combining coastal footpaths, stretches of beach, rural road and marked wooden walkways, runs all the way to Chepu Valley (see p.325). From here, Sector Chepu itself is several hours' walk down the coast. The rugged trail here can be difficult to access, because there is currently no regular way of crossing the Río Lar estuary. However, it is possible to make arrangements with fishermen in the Chepu Valley (don't forget to arrange the return crossing!), and the determined are rewarded with a ruggedly beautiful four-hour hike along a densely wooded coast to the (generally closed) Conaf station, with likely sightings of *pudú* and native bird species.

ARRIVAL, INFORMATION AND TOURS   PARQUE NACIONAL CHILOÉ

By bus Buses Ojeda and Buses Interlagos both run services (4–6 daily between them 8.30am–6pm) to Cucao from Castro.

Conaf Near Cucao (daily 9am–7pm; visitor centre daily: Jan & Feb 9.30am–8pm; March–Dec 9am–1pm & 2–6pm;

☎09 9644 2489, ✉vidasur@telsur.cl). At the Conaf Ranger Post there's a visitor centre that explains the various environments you'll find in the park. This is also where you pay the park entrance fee.

HIKES IN AND AROUND PARQUE NACIONAL CHILOÉ

A couple of short **hikes** start from the visitor centre at the Conaf Ranger Post. The first is the circular, 770m "**El Tepual**", running through an area of *tepu* forest, a tree which thrives in this humid bogland; there are log walkways across the wetter sections of these enchanted-looking woods, with twisted moss-covered trunks intertwined with other native species. The second hike is the **Sendero La Playa**, which leads you through patches of *nalca* (native rhubarb) and tunnels of dense vegetation before emerging on the regenerating scrubland that takes you via sand dunes to the exposed Pacific coast. A little more taxing is the 3km (one-way) walk along the beach to Lago Huelde, where you pick up a 9km trail known as **Sendero Rancho Grande**, along the Río Deñal up to the edge of the tree line, revealing beautiful views below.

The park's longest hike is the beautiful 25km (6hr) **Sendero Chanquín**, which alternates between stretches of coastline, pounded by the fierce Pacific surf, and dense, native evergreen forest, before finishing up at the Conaf *refugio* at Cole Cole. There you'll find a rustic campsite overseen by the Huentemó community, and a Conaf ranger post that is only open in the summer. You can also continue another 8km north to the *Refugio Anay*, though the trail is rather difficult, as there is currently no shuttle across the Río Anay.

7

TOUR OPERATORS

Cahuelmapu ☎ 65 531008 or 09 9733 5094, ⓦ cahuelmapu.com. Reliable horseriding operator offering excursions in Parque Nacional Chiloé and elsewhere. Contact them directly or via *Palafito Hostel* in Castro (see p.334). Operators in Cucao also offer horse rides, but the quality of horses varies and not all are trained to carry beginners.

ACCOMMODATION AND EATING

All accommodation options below are situated in and around Chanquín. The *refugios* in the park are not in a great state of repair and are only open in peak season. They are not always staffed and you must bring own sleeping bags.

Camping Chanquín 200m past the Conaf Cucao visitors' centre on the banks of Lago Cucao ☎ 09 9644 2489. This campsite offers twenty camping spots with fire pits, showers and picnic tables provided. There are also four refurnished, fully equipped cabins for up to six guests each. Camping CH$4500 per person, cabin CH$35,000

El Fogón de Cucao ☎ 09 9946 5685. This pleasant, rustic bed and breakfast organizes horseriding and trekking expeditions and has a few spots for camping. There is a separate restaurant opposite with a fish-heavy set menu (peak season only). Camping CH$5000 per person, double CH$24,000

★ **Hostel Palafito Cucao** ☎ 65 971164 or 09 8903 4728. Under the same management as Castro's *Palafito Hostel* and *Palafito 1326* (see p.334), this new shingled guesthouse is ideally situated 200m from the park entrance. It boasts views of Lago Cucao from its centrally heated rooms and dorm, and the helpful staff are on hand to arrange excursions. There are no TVs to distract from your surroundings, though there is free wi-fi for those used to being wired. Dorm CH$15,000, double CH$45,000

Chonchi

Twenty-three kilometres south of Castro lies the attractive working town of **CHONCHI**. Founded in 1767, the town thrived on timber exports and was home to the wood baron Ciriaco Alvarez, who earned the name *El Rey de Ciprés* (The Cypress King) by stripping the archipelago of almost all of its native forest. The most sheltered harbour on the island is lined with beautiful old wooden buildings, structures that have hardly changed since the eighteenth century, though the Mercado Municipal, which juts over the bay, is a new addition.

Calle Centenario, Chonchi's steeply curving main street, leads down to a beach strewn with flotsam and jetsam, where you can see local women digging for razor clams at low tide. In February the town comes alive during the *Semana Verano Chonchi* – a folkloric festival featuring dancing, music, art and rodeo skills. Chonchi is also the home of the golden *licor de oro*, the potent concoction combining saffron, vanilla, milk, lemons, cloves, cinnamon and other ingredients to storm your palate.

Iglesia San Carlos de Borromeo

Centenario s/n • Free

The town's cheerfully painted **Iglesia San Carlos de Borromeo** (1900), with its attractive yellow exterior and blue tower, rewards a visit. Having survived the 1960 earthquake but lost its tower in 2008, it has recently been restored to its full glory, and the Neoclassical facade is one of the island's finest.

Museo de las Tradiciones Chonchinas

Centenario 116 • Previously Mon–Fri 9am–1pm & 2–6pm, Sat 9am–1pm • CH$600

A short way down the main street from the church is the informative **Museo de las Tradiciones Chonchinas**, a beautifully restored old traditional house filled with furniture, fittings and a large collection of photographs from the tree-felling heyday of *El Rey de Ciprés*. The museum was closed for renovation at the time of research.

ARRIVAL AND INFORMATION   CHONCHI

By bus There are frequent departures with operators such as Cruz del Sur, Transchiloé, Expresos Interlagos and Queilen Bus. Larger buses stop alongside the Plaza, while minibuses stop along the little triangular *plazuela* along Centenario.

Destinations Castro (14 daily; 30min); Quellón (14 daily; 1hr 45min).

Tourist office First floor of the Municipalidad building across the Plaza from the church (Jan–March daily 9am–7pm). A helpful little office.

ACCOMMODATION AND EATING

Esmeralda By The Sea Irrázaval 267 ☎ 65 671328, ✉ carlos@esmeraldabythesea.cl. A friendly beachside hostel with comfortable rooms of various sizes and a helpful English-speaking Canadian expat owner who organizes land and sea tours and has a wealth of local knowledge. It offers a book exchange, use of kitchen, internet, bike rental and evening meals. Dorm CH$7500, double CH$7500

Posada El Antiguo Chalet Irrázaval s/n ☎ 65 671221, ⓦ antiguochalet.galeon.com. You can lose yourself amid the antique furnishings and knick-knacks of this attractive property uphill from the pier. The cosy rooms are nicely furnished and the owners brew their own *licor de oro* and other concoctions. CH$28,000

El Trebol Irarrázaval 187 ☎ 65 671203. At the southern end of the waterfront above the local market, this is a local institution, serving primarily fish and seafood dishes to satisfied clientele. Mains from CH$3500. Daily noon–3pm & 7–11pm.

Isla Lemuy

On the coast, a 4km walk south of Chonchi at **Huicha**, a ferry heads to **ISLA LEMUY** – a tranquil spot seldom visited by tourists. It's dotted with traditional rural settlements, each boasting just a few houses and in some cases a fine old church. The most remote village of all is **Detif**, on an isolated, bleak headland at the far eastern end of the island, about 20km from Puqueldón, the island's main settlement. The drive to Detif is particularly picturesque with the ocean on both sides of the road as you navigate the narrow strip leading to the headland.

ARRIVAL AND DEPARTURE   ISLA LEMUY

By bus Buses Gallardo (☎ 65 643541) runs to Puqueldón from Castro (three daily Mon–Sat 7am–6.45pm, 9am departure Sun); the bus crosses to the island on the ferry.

By boat Ferry departs from a terminal 3km south of Chonchi (daily 8am–8pm; Mon–Sat every 30min, Sun every hour; 20min; free for passengers, CH$4000 per car; unless you're taking one of the Buses Gallardo, taxis are the only way to get to the terminal).

ACCOMMODATION AND EATING

El Castaño Aldachildo ☎09 7445 0886, ⓦautentichochiloe.com. Rural life needs no better introduction than a stay at this rustic Agroturismo guesthouse run by a friendly Italian–Chilean couple. There are just three doubles with neither TVs nor internet to distract you from your spectacular natural surroundings. Witness sheep-shearing, horseriding or cider making with Silvio or gorge yourself on Rosanna's delectable cakes and enjoy an *aperetivo italiano* with your hosts. CH$12,000 per person; half board (CH$16,000) and full board (CH$20,000) also available.

Parque Yayanes Av Pedro Montt 228 ☎09 8861 6462 or 09 7498 0655, ⓦparqueyayanes.cl. The best place to stay on the island consists of three adorable cabins (think polished wooden floors, wood-burning stoves and carved headboards). The two six-person cabins and the sole two-person cabin come fully equipped with kitchenettes and satellite TV. Jamie and Perla – the hospitable owners – bake pies and can cook meat, fish and vegetarian dishes to order (CH$5000 per meal), and sometimes hold impromptu barbecues. CH$25,000

Queilén and around

The paved road to Queilén runs above a string of pretty little villages down by the sea. **Tepua** in particular is worth a visit to see its graveyard filled with *mausoleos*, traditional shelters that protect mourners from the elements when they visit the graves of the dead, some of which are splendidly ornate. You'll either need a sturdy vehicle to tackle the steep dirt paths leading to the villages, or be prepared for a lot of walking.

Forty-six kilometres from Chonchi, the road pulls into **Queilén**, a sleepy little fishing town whose two main streets, Pedro Aguirre Cerda and Alessandri, bisect the neck of a long, sandy peninsula. The western end of town is very pretty, lined with fishermen's houses built on a long beach sheltered by the nearby **Isla Tranqui**. In February the town hosts a craft fair in which all types of local products are sold, from handicrafts and farming equipment to traditional medicines.

ARRIVAL AND DEPARTURE   QUEILÉN AND AROUND

By bus Queilén Bus (☎65 632173) runs services (12 daily 7.30am–8pm; fewer on Sundays; CH$2000) to Queilén from Castro.

ACCOMMODATION AND EATING

Espejo de Luna Ruta Chonchi a Queilén, Km 35 ☎09 7431 3090 or 09 7431 3091, ⓦespejodeluna.cl. Unmissable due to the distinctive shape of its restaurant, which resembles a boat on its side, this nature retreat combines thoughtful design (walkways and stairs covered in mesh to prevent slippage, lift down to the private beach for disabled guests) with great flair – spacious, light rooms in the lodge and private cabins (holding up to five people) hidden in the greenery. Non-guests can stop by for lunch or dinner; the dining room comes complete with wonderfully rustic touches such as the wood-burning stove and serves well-prepared meat and fish dishes with an emphasis on local ingredients. Double CH$175,000, cabin CH$198,000

Puerto Nativo ⓦwww.puertonativolodge.com (contact via email only). You don't need to be a fishing enthusiast to stay at this attractive lodge overlooking an isolated bay near Queilén, though hosts Marco and Carmen can certainly organize excursions to the nearby lakes and rivers (4 hours' fishing with guide US$200). The super-fresh home-cooked food and the warmth of the owners have been attracting rave reviews. Full board US$189 per person

Quellón

If you follow Route 5 south from the turn-off for Chonchi, after 70km you reach **QUELLÓN** – the end of the Panamerican Highway, which spans almost the entire length of two continents, and the end of Chiloé. Formerly a logging port, Quellón is now a scruffy commercial fishing port of growing importance, with fishermen in rubber boots loitering around the pier. It's based around three east–west streets that run parallel to the coast: the seafront *costanera* (Miramar and Pedro Montt); Ercilla, north of the *costanera*; and Ladrilleros, further north still. The main reason to come here is to catch a **ferry** across to Chaitén (see p.354) or down to Chacabuco (see p.386), or to organize transportation to Parque Tantauco (see pp.340–343).

ARRIVAL AND DEPARTURE

By bus Hourly Cruz del Sur and Transchiloé buses run to Castro (17 daily; 2hr) and Puerto Montt (13 daily; 6hr) via Chonchi (1hr 20min) from the terminal a block west of the Plaza on Pedro Aguirre Cerda.

By boat Ferries from Puerto Chacabuco and Chaitén – operated by Naviera Austral at Costanera Pedro Montt 457 (☎65 682207, ⓦwww.navieraustral.cl) – call at the harbour a block south. There are once-weekly, year-round

ferry departures to Chaitén on Thurs evenings (5hr; CH$18,000 per passenger; departure times vary) and for Puerto Chacabuco on Mon, Wed and Sat at 6, 11 and 10pm respectively (10–15hr; CH$37,000). Ferries may be subject to delays and cancellations, so check with the Naviera Austral office in advance. Outside peak season there are fewer services.

INFORMATION AND TOURS

Parque Tantauco office Av La Paz 68 (Mon–Fri 9am–1pm & 2–6pm; ☎65 773100, ⓦparquetantauco.cl). Extremely helpful office that can help arrange transport to Parque Tantauco, and also provide trail maps and general information.

TOUR OPERATORS

Darwin Adventure ⓦaventuradarwin.cl. Quellón-based operator Jorge Oyarse is an excellent source of info on the blue whale pod that resides in Chiloé's waters year-round. Whale-watching trips offered between mid-Dec and late March from Banderas Bay.

ACCOMMODATION

Hotel Chico Leo Montt 325 ☎65 681567. A decent waterfront choice, this hotel caters to budget travellers with its spic-and-span rooms, some with shared facilities. The restaurant's an excellent place for fish and seafood dishes. CH$20,000

Hotel Patagonia Insular Ladrilleros 1737 ☎65 681610, ⓦhotelpatagoniainsular.cl. Swish and airy, Chiloé's most modern hotel enjoys an enviable hilltop location just to the west of the centre. The large, comfortable rooms have porthole windows in the bathrooms and all the mod cons you'd expect from a

four-star hotel, and the restaurant serves fine Chilean and international dishes. CH$49,000

Hotel Tierra Del Fuego Montt 445 ☎65 682079, ⓔtierradelfuegoquellon@gmail.com. Behind a brown shingled exterior lies a cluster of compact, cosy rooms with cable TV and wi-fi. The two en-suite doubles on the top floor have sea views and are worth a splurge for the central heating alone; if you stay in the cheapies with shared facilities, you'll learn why this hotel is named after Chile's coldest province. CH$9,000

EATING AND DRINKING

Hostería Romeo Alfa Leo Montt 554 ☎65 680177. One of the best spots for all manner of gifts of the sea, served in a restaurant sitting right on the water. Dishes include ceviche, *chupe de locos* (abalone stew) and grilled fish with a variety of sauces. Mains from CH$6000. Daily 12.30–3.30pm & 7.30–11.30pm.

Isla Sandwich Ladrilleros 190 ☎65 680683. Trendy, popular café offering an almost baffling variety of

sandwiches (from CH$3000), as well as cakes, coffee and fresh fruit juices. Mon–Sat 11am–11pm.

El Madero Freire 430 ☎65 681330. A welcoming family-run restaurant with a roaring fireplace and whimsical decor, specializing in dishes featuring one of Quellón's biggest exports – salmon – as well as other fish, home-made pasta and meat. The generous sandwiches aren't bad either. Mains from CH$5000. Mon–Sat 10am–midnight.

Parque Tantauco

To the south of Isla Grande and to the west of Quellón lies **Parque Tantauco** (ⓦparquetantauco.cl), Chiloé's largest natural attraction with nearly 1200 square kilometres of unspoiled wilderness, making it at least double the size of Parque Nacional Chiloé. The park, funded by the Fundación Futuro, is the brainchild of

Sebastián Piñera, a Harvard-educated politician, self-made man and billionaire owner of LANChile, not to mention the current president of Chile.

After Douglas Tompkins unveiled Parque Pumalín (see pp.352–354), Piñera was inspired to start his own conservation project on Isla Grande. The project's goal is to "protect and conserve vulnerable ecosystems and species, and those at risk of extinction", as well as to restore a large chunk of the park's territory that was devastated by a forest fire in the 1940s, by replanting native species in the affected area. The park is located in one of the world's 25 "biodiversity hotspots", with unique ecosystems and wildlife habitats, and home to such species as the Chilote fox, the *pudú*, the *huillín* (otter) and the blue whale.

Consisting of Zona Sur and Zona Norte, Tantauco boasts 150km of well-signposted hiking trails of varying length and difficulty, encompassing both the coastal areas and Chilote rainfores. These trails are part of a well-designed infrastructure that also includes fully equipped campsites and unmanned basic *refugios*. Owing to the park's remoteness, moreover, it's not overrun by day-trippers in the summer.

Though it's possible to hike between Zona Norte and Zona Sur, the latter is otherwise only accessible by boat. You must allow four days to a week for the hike, bring all the necessary gear, including waterproof clothing, and inform the park authorities.

Zona Norte

It's possible to visit Zona Norte in a day, as there are a couple of nice short hikes, such as the **Sendero Siempreverde**, an interpretive walk leading through evergreen forest, or the **Circuito Muelle**, which goes from *Camping Chaiguata* along the banks of Lago Yaldad. Alternatively, the **Sendero Lagos Occidentales** is a 6km walk of moderate difficulty, leading you through evergreen forest from Lago Chaiguata to Lago Chaiguaco, where you can overnight at the *Refugio Chaiguaco* (bring own food and bedding).

From *Refugio Chaiguaco*, the trail continues through the forest to *Refugio Piramide* (15km; 5hr), next to a tiny lagoon. From there you can either head south towards Caleta Inío, or do a side trek to the coast along the river, stopping at the *Refugio Emerenciana* on the banks of the picturesque Laguna Emerenciana along the way (allow an extra three days for the detour).

A densely wooded trail heads south from *Refugio Piramide*, reaching *Refugio Huillín* after six hours (14km). From there it's a further six or seven hours (15km) to Río Inío, passing **Mirador Inío** on the way – a watchtower which gives you a great overview of the landscape. It's possible to organize a boat in advance to take you along Río Inío to the fishing village of Caleta Inío – the entry point to Zona Sur.

Zona Sur

Around Caleta Inío, you can explore the coastal caves where the indigenous Chonos once resided, as well as the pristine beaches and little islets off the coast. There is also a beautiful circuit around the Inío headland, which takes in stunning viewpoints and stretches of beach and forest; you can overnight at the *Refugio Quilanlar* (16km; 12hr). The extensive beaches near Inío are protected from the rough waters of the Gulf of

---

CALETA INÍO TO QUELLÓN BY BOAT

Taking a **boat** back to Quellón from Caleta Inío is an extremely rewarding experience, as you are likely to get glimpses of marine life such as sea lions and possibly even blue whales. There are three boats (☎65 680066, ⟨w⟩parquetantauco.cl; confirm reservation 24hr before departure) weekly between Quellón and Caleta Inío throughout Jan and Feb (Mon, Wed and Fri, departing Quellón at 9.30am and returning from Caleta Inío at noon on the same day; CH$28,000 one way). Boats are less frequent in March and Oct–Dec, and departures are always weather-dependent. Be prepared for a fairly bumpy ride in the Golfo Corcovado.

Corcovado by small offshore islands and the numerous coastal inlets are ideal for **kayaking**. Kayaks are available for rent in Caleta Inío (CH$1500 per hour).

ARRIVAL AND DEPARTURE
PARQUE TANTAUCO

By car Zona Norte can be accessed by vehicles with high clearance (preferably 4WD) along a dirt road branching off from the Panamericana, 14km north of Quellón, and labelled "Colonia Yungay". If you don't have a vehicle of your own, the park office in Quellón (see p.340) can help you rent a 4WD at a cost of CH$50,000–55,000 for three or four people. The 18km drive brings you to the park administration office by Lago Yaldad (see p.342), from where it's an additional 20km to Lago Chaiguata.

By bus In Jan and Feb, there are three buses weekly from Quellón to Zona Norte (Mon, Wed and Fri at 9.30am; CH$4000/8000 to Lago Yaldad and Lago Chaiguata, respectively); book through the Parque Tantauco office in Quellón (see p.340).

By foot If exploring the whole of the park, it's easier to hike from Zona Norte to Zona Sur and then catch a ride back to Quellón with one of the fishing boats if the regular boat is not running.

INFORMATION

Park administration office Lago Yaldad (Dec–March daily 9am–8pm). The office is permanently staffed only during the months indicated. Park entry costs CH$6000 per person and each visitor is given a detailed trail map on arrival. There's also a small visitor centre in Caleta Inío with information on trails and activities in the park. The park office in Quellón (see p.340) is particularly helpful.

ACCOMMODATION, EATING AND DRINKING

Camping in the park costs CH$3000 per person per night, with the exception of the fully equipped campsites at Lago Chaiguata area and Caleta Inío (see p.342). Smaller campsites along the trails consist of 4–6 camping spots each (also CH$3000 per person), while basic *refugios* (equipped with 8 bunk beds each; bring own bedding) cost CH$7000 per person. The only place to purchase limited food supplies, including fresh fish, is Caleta Inío; you must otherwise bring all supplies with you. All accommodation apart from the basic campsites and *refugios* has to be reserved via the park office in Quellón (☎ 65 773100).

LAGO CHAIGUATA

Camping Lago Chaiguata. Camping site with 15 spaces, complete with picnic tables, showers and a fully equipped indoor cooking area. Ranger station nearby. CH$3500 per person

Domo Chaiguata. Six geothermal domes with eight beds each for those who prefer glamping to camping. Facilities shared with the adjacent campsite. Bring own sleeping bag. CH$7000 per person or CH$50,000 per dome

CALETA INÍO

Camping Caleta Inío. Large campsite consisting of 24 spaces, complete with showers, fully equipped indoor cooking area, a large *fogón* for barbecue and even a *curanto* pit. CH$3500 per person

Casa de Huespedes. Attractive guesthouse offering six homely, wood-panelled rooms with down duvets: three en-suite twins, a standard double and two doubles with shared facilities. There's a guest kitchen and a large lounge for pre- and post-hike relaxation and breakfast is included in the room price. CH$35,000

Domo Inío. A cluster of geothermal domes with beds for those who prefer not to rough it completely. CH$7000 per person

7

Northern Patagonia

349 Parque Nacional Alerce Andino

350 Hornopirén and around

352 Parque Pumalín

355 The Futaleufú Valley

359 Parque Nacional Queulat and around

363 Coyhaique and around

367 West of Coyhaique

370 Around Lago General Carrera

374 South of Lago General Carrera

FLOWER MEADOW, CARRETERA AUSTRAL

Northern Patagonia

From Puerto Montt, the Carretera Austral, or "Southern Highway", stretches over 1000km south through the wettest, greenest, wildest and narrowest part of Chile, ending its mammoth journey at the tiny settlement of Villa O'Higgins. Carving its path through tracts of untouched wilderness, the route takes in soaring, snowcapped mountains, Ice Age glaciers, blue-green fjords, turquoise lakes and rivers, and one of the world's largest swaths of temperate rainforest. Most of it falls into Aysén, Chile's "last frontier", the final region to be opened up in the early twentieth century. A hundred years on, Aysén remains very sparsely populated, and still has the cut-off, marginal feel of a pioneer zone.

With the 2008 eruption of the Chaitén volcano (see p.354) now in the past, you can once again begin your exploration of the region from the north. Leaving Puerto Montt, you can travel through both **Parque Nacional Alerce Andino** and **Parque Nacional Hornopirén**, before taking the boat over to Caleta Gonzalo, where the Carretera cuts a passage through virgin temperate rainforest in the private nature reserve of **Parque Pumalín,** and finally emerging in the volcano-ravaged town of **Chaitén.**

South along the Carretera from Chaitén is the nondescript settlement of Villa Santa Lucía. From here, one branch of the road heads east, to the border village of Futaleufú, the pre-eminent centre for **whitewater rafting.** Continuing south, the Carretera emerges at the **Parque Nacional Queulat**, whose extraordinary hanging glacier and excellent trails make for one of the most rewarding places to get off the road. Don't miss the chance to luxuriate in the secluded hot pools of the luxurious **Termas de Puyuhuapi.**

The main town of **Coyhaique** marks the centre of the Carretera; to the west, **Puerto Chacabuco** is the principal starting point for boat excursions to the sensational **Laguna San Rafael glacier.** To the south, the road loops around South America's second largest lake, **Lago General Carrera**, while the final stretch of the Carretera connects the little town of **Cochrane** to the isolated hamlet of **Villa O'Higgins,** with a road branching off to the unusual settlement of **Caleta Tortel.**

Brief history

The original inhabitants of this rain-swept land were the nomadic, hunter-gatherer **Tehuelche** of the interior, and the canoe-faring **Alcalufe**, who fished the fjords and channels of the coast, though now only a handful of the latter remain. In 1903, the government initiated a colonization programme that ultimately handed over thousands

Alerce trees p.350
"Doing" the Carretera Austral p.351
Douglas Tompkins and the Pumalín project p.354
Chaitén Vive! p.353
Sendero de Chile: from Palena to Villa La Tapera p.356
Whitewater rafting on the Futa p.357

Damned if you do...Patagonia Sín Represas! p.358
Fly-fishing and lodges on the Carretera Austral p.362
Visiting the San Rafael Glacier p.369
Estancia Valle Chacabuco p.376
Death in the forest p.376
Argentina the hard way: the El Chaltén crossing p.379

8

Highlights

❶ The Carretera Austral Drive Chile's most spectacular – and still most challenging – road. **See p.351**

❷ Parque Pumalín Hike the trails and sail the fjords of Chile's largest private nature reserve. **See pp.352**

❸ Whitewater rafting at Futaleufú "Purgatory", "Hell" and "Terminator" are just three of the world-class rapids you can hurtle down on the "Fu". **See p.357**

❹ Ventisquero Colgante Gawk at the suspended glacier that seems to defy gravity in Parque Nacional Queulat. **See p.359**

❺ Termas de Puyuhuapi Soak your bones while gazing at the southern night skies in Chile's premier spa resort. **See p.361**

❻ Laguna San Rafael glacier Be dazzled by the icy beauty of this gigantic tongue of ice while you can – it may be gone by 2030. **See p.369**

❼ Crossing Lago General Carrera Take the thrilling ferry ride across the second-largest lake in South America. **See p.370**

❽ Villa O'Higgins border crossing Take up the challenge of crossing the border into Argentina both on foot and by boat through spectacular scenery. **See p.379**

HIGHLIGHTS ARE MARKED ON THE MAP ON P.348

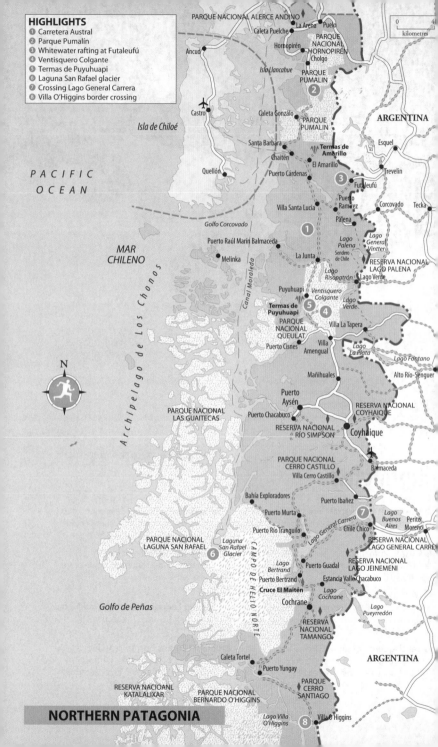

HIGHLIGHTS

1. Carretera Austral
2. Parque Pumalín
3. Whitewater rafting at Futaleufú
4. Ventisquero Colgante
5. Termas de Puyuhuapi
6. Laguna San Rafael glacier
7. Crossing Lago General Carrera
8. Villa O'Higgins border crossing

0   40
kilometres

PARQUE NACIONAL ALERCE ANDINO

La Arena   Puelo
Caleta Puelche
                    PARQUE
Hornopirén   NACIONAL
                    HORNOPIRÉN
Ancud   Cholgo

Isla Llancahue

                    Parque
Castro   Nacional
                    PUMALIN

ARGENTINA

Isla de Chiloé

Caleta González
                    PARQUE
                    PUMALIN

Esquel

Santa Barbara   Termas de
                    Amarillo
Chaitén
Quellón   El Amarillo
                    Futaleufú   Trevelin
               Puerto Cárdenas   ③
PACIFIC   Futaleufú
OCEAN   Puerto   Corcovado
                             Ramírez   Tecka
               Villa Santa Lucia
                             Palena
                    ①
Golfo Corcovado   Lago   Lago
                                  Palena General
Puerto Raúl Marín Balmaceda   Yintter
MAR   La Junta
CHILENO   Sendero   RESERVA NACIONAL
               Melinka   de Chile LAGO PALENA
                                        Lago Verde

                    Lago
                    Risopatrón
               Puyuhuapi   Ventisquero
                           Colgante Lago
                    ⑤   Verde
               Termas de   ④
               Puyuhuapi
                    PARQUE
                    NACIONAL   Villa La Tapera
                    QUEULAT
               Puerto Cisnes   Villa
                           Amengual
                                  Lago
                                  La Plata Lago Fontano
                    Mañihuales
                                        Alto Río Senguer
                    Puerto
                    Aysén
               Puerto Chacabuco RESERVA NACIONAL
                           COYHAIQUE
                    RESERVA NACIONAL
                    RÍO SIMPSON   Coyhaique
PARQUE NACIONAL
LAS GUAITECAS
                                        Balmaceda
                    PARQUE NACIONAL
                    CERRO CASTILLO
                    Villa Cerro Castillo

               Bahía Exploradores   Puerto Ibañez
                                        ⑦
               Puerto Murta   Lago   Perito
                                        Buenos Moreno
PARQUE NACIONAL   Laguna Puerto Río Tranquilo Aires
LAGUNA SAN RAFAEL San Rafael   Chile Chico
               ⑥   Glacier   RESERVA NACIONAL
                    Lago   LAGO GENERAL CARRE
                    Bertrand Puerto Guadal
                    Puerto Bertrand   RESERVA NACIONAL
                    Cruce El Maitén   LAGO JEINEMENI
                           Estancia Valle Chacabuco
                    Cochrane
                           Lago
                           Cochrane
                    RESERVA   Lago
                    NACIONAL   Pueyrredón
                    TAMANGO

Golfo de Peñas

                    Caleta Tortel   ARGENTINA
                    Puerto Yungay
RESERVA NACIOANL   PARQUE
KATALIXAR   PARQUE NACIONAL CERRO
             BERNARDO O'HIGGINS SANTIAGO

NORTHERN PATAGONIA

                    Lago Villa   ⑧ Villa O'Higgins
                    O'Higgins

of hectares of land to three large livestock companies. At the same time, a wave of individual pioneers – known as **colonos** – came down from the north to try their luck at logging and farming, resulting in massive deforestation and destruction of the natural environment.

Faced with Argentina's encroaching influence, the government set out to actively "Chileanize" this new zone. Over the years, the perceived need for state control of the region did not diminish, explaining the rationale behind the construction of the Carretera Austral, initiated by earlier governments but with the greatest progress achieved under **General Pinochet**. Building the road was a colossal and incredibly expensive undertaking: the first section was finished in 1983 and engineers completed the final 100km in 2000, from tiny Puerto Yungay to the frontier outpost of Villa O'Higgins, by the Argentine border.

Northern Patagonia today

In spite of the Carretera Austral, the settlements in Northern Patagonia still have a frontier feel to them and the people who live here reflect the area's intrepid settler spirit. Their resourcefulness allows them to overcome major natural disasters, such as volcanic eruptions, and every spring, they celebrate their *huaso* (cowboy) heritage in a series of rodeos, pitting their equestrian skills against one another.

Parque Nacional Alerce Andino

8

Dec–Feb daily 9am–7pm; shorter hours the rest of the year • CH$2000

Heading out of Puerto Montt, the Carretera Austral hugs the shore of the Reloncaví fjord, skirting wide mud flats and empty beaches. Some 40km down the road – just beyond the Puente de Lenca – a signed track branches left and leads 7km to the southern entrance of **PARQUE NACIONAL ALERCE ANDINO**, also known as "Chile's Yosemite", where you'll find a small **Conaf** hut, a ranger station and a **camping** area (see p.350). The park was created in 1982 to protect the region's ancient and rapidly depleting *alerce* forests, threatened with extinction by intense logging activity. Almost 200 square kilometres – half the park's land area – are covered by the massive, millenia-old *alerces*, mixed in with other native species like *coigüe* and *lenga*. This dense covering is spread over a landscape of steep hills and narrow glacial valleys dotted with dozens of lakes.

Hikes in Parque Nacional Alerce Andino

There's a good, long **day-hike** from the Conaf hut (at the southern entrance); the path follows the Río Chaica for 5km as far as the pretty **Laguna Chaiquenes**, surrounded by steep, forested hills. On the way, about an hour from the hut, you pass some impressive waterfalls and, twenty minutes later, a huge, 3000-year-old *alerce* tree. From Laguna Chaiquenes, the now deteriorating path heads north for a further 4km, as far as the long, thin **Laguna Triángulo**, where it peters out. Count on taking around three hours to get to Laguna Chaiquenes, and another three hours to get to Laguna Triángulo.

ARRIVAL AND DEPARTURE   **PARQUE NACIONAL ALERCE ANDINO**

By bus Hornopirén-bound Buses Fierro (☎65 289024) from Puerto Montt (up to three daily) can drop you off at Chaica, from where it's a 4km walk to the Chaica Conaf ranger station.

By car Take southbound Ruta 7 until Chaica (35km from Puerto Montt); the park entrance is to the left.

ACCOMMODATION

Alerce Mountain Lodge ☎65 286969, ⓦmountainlodge.cl. This sensitively designed timber lodge is built around the *alerces*, and accessed via a steep and extremely rough track which branches north from the access track to the national park. Set in a small depression by a lake, this is one of the most peaceful, beautiful and

ALERCE TREES

The famed **alerce** trees – accorded national monument status by the government in 1976 – are endemic to southern Chile and Argentina and grow in high, soggy soil, usually on mountainsides between 600m and 800m above sea level. Among the **largest and oldest trees in the world**, they can rise to a height of 45m, with a trunk diameter of up to 4m, and live for over three thousand years. After shooting up rapidly during their first hundred years, they slow down dramatically, their diameter increasing just 1mm every three years. As they grow, they lose their lower branches, keeping only their top crown of dark-green, broccoli-like leaves. The lighter, lower leaves belong to parasite trees, which often prove useful to the ancient *alerces*, supporting them when they topple and keeping them alive. The trees' grey, papery bark conceals a beautiful, reddish-brown and extremely **valuable wood**; a large tree is worth tens of thousands of dollars. In the late-nineteenth and early twentieth centuries, the trees were chopped down at random by early colonizers – sometimes to be used for telegraph poles or shingles, but often just to clear land which was later found to be useless for agriculture. Today, it's illegal to chop down an *alerce* owing to their protected status, but it's not forbidden to sell the wood of dead trees.

isolated places to stay in Chile. Excursions are led by friendly bilingual guides and include hikes and horseback treks. At the day's end, you can relax in a sauna and Jacuzzi. 3-night full board with double CH$370,000

Camping Near the Conaf hut there's a basic camping area with cold showers and fire pits. CH$3000 per person

Hornopirén and around

The sheltered, sandy cove of **La Arena** lies 13km south of the turn-off to Parque Nacional Alerce Andino; it's the departure point of a **ferry** (see below). After the thirty-minute crossing, the ferry lands at tiny **Caleta Puelche**, from where the road winds through 58km of thickly forested hills, before arriving at the village of **HORNOPIRÉN**. Here you catch a Naviera Austral ferry to Caleta Gonzalo, where the Carretera continues.

Perched on the northern shore of a wide fjord, at the foot of **Volcán Hornopirén**, the village enjoys a spectacular location and makes a good stop en route to the rest of the Carretera Austral.

ARRIVAL AND DEPARTURE
HORNOPIRÉN

By bus Buses Fierro (☎65 253022) runs to Puerto Montt up to three times daily (4hr). Kemel Bus (☎65 253022) also serves Puerto Montt three times daily. The two companies also make daily runs to Chaitén between themselves (6hr).
By ferry The La Arena–Caleta Puelche ferry is operated by Naviera Puelche (☎65 270761, ⊛ www.navierapuelche.cl) and runs every 45min (6.45am–12.30am; CH$9500 per car, passengers CH$600). Naviera Austral covers the two-stage

ferry crossing between Hornopirén and Caleta Gonzalo, with daily ferries from Hornopirén to Leptepú (departing 10.30am, returning 3.30pm), followed by the Fiordo Largo to Caleta Gonzalo crossing (departing 3.30pm, returning 2pm) from where the Carretera Austral continues to Chaitén via Parque Pumalín. Rates are CH$7500 for cars; book the Hornopirén–Caleta Gonzalo leg well in advance; outside the warmer months, service is sporadic.

ACCOMMODATION AND EATING

Hotel Termas del Llancahué Isla Llancahué ☎09 9642 4857 or 09 8529 9771, ⊛ termasdellancahue.cl. Located on Isla Llancaué, a 20min/1hr boat ride from Hornopirén depending on which boat you take, this simple resort features pools fed by water from the hot springs with fabulous ocean views. Day-trippers welcome (CH$14,000 for the hot springs; CH$7000 return for the boat); there are at

least two scheduled boats per day (3 & 8pm). CH$60,000
Residencial Austral Pasaje Pacifico Sur ☎65 217214, ✉ mariacovasich@hotmail.com. Attractive B&B with twelve wood-panelled en-suite rooms (some are somewhat cramped) with TVs and wi-fi, and a restaurant serving local specialities such as *curanto* (see p.324) and grilled salmon. CH$22,000

"DOING" THE CARRETERA AUSTRAL

"Doing" the Carretera Austral requires a certain amount of forward planning, and time should always be allowed for unexpected delays. In peak season, the villages are covered by a combination of minibuses, ferries and even local flights, but outside the summer months the services drop right off, barring the regular long-distance flights connecting Coyhaique to the rest of Chile. Cyclists will need to carry all necessary spare parts and supplies, because of the challenging road conditions and absence of bike shops (barring Coyhaique).

BY CAR

The words "Carretera Austral" or 'Southern Highway' conjure up images of a smooth, paved, multi-lane road, right? Wrong. The Carretera Austral is still very much a "triumph" of man over nature, and Chile's ultimate road trip to boot; though parts of the road have been "tamed", it is still a challenging – not to mention spectacularly scenic – drive. Those with their own vehicle may need to consider the entering it via Argentina and Futaleufú (make sure you have the correct paperwork) as the ferry services connecting the top end to Hornopirén are less frequent outside the summer months.

What type of car do I need?
Most car rental agencies will insist that you rent a 4WD for the journey, but while certain sections may be easier to drive in a 4WD, it's not mandatory. However, a vehicle with high clearance is.

What are the road conditions like?
The question you should be asking yourself is not "Will there be potholes?" It is: "Which of the following potholes should I hit to minimize the damage to my vehicle?" Some sections are more challenging than others; see below for a brief guide to the different stretches of road.

Will there be anywhere to buy petrol?
The vast majority of settlements along the Carretera Austral have petrol stations, so you needn't worry about running dry.

What essentials should I bring?
Make sure you have a spare tyre (*neumático*), and all equipment necessary to change said tyre, as you'll only be able to rely on yourself and passing motorists (all of whom should stop and help you should you need assistance). It's also a good idea to carry food, water and a sleeping bag.

What about crossing the border into Argentina?
You'll need to have the required paperwork from your car rental company as well as relevant insurance.

Any other precautions I should take?
Try to avoid driving at night, as not all curves in the road are marked with reflectors. Driving too close to other cars is a bad idea as the loose gravel flying out from under the wheels of the vehicle in front of you will crack your windscreen. Do not attempt to take corners at high speeds on the *ripio* (dirt and gravel) sections of the road, as you'll skid right off the side of the road. If travelling via Hornopirén and Caleta Gonzalo, book ferry tickets in advance (see p.350).

ROAD CONDITIONS BY SECTION

Chaitén to Villa Santa Lucia Partially paved, otherwise heavily potholed and prone to landslides in rainy conditions.
Villa Santa Lucía to Futaleufú Valley Somewhat potholed, mostly good gravel road.
Villa Santa Lucía to Puyuhuapi Somewhat potholed, at times narrow road.
Puyuhuapi to Puerto Cisnes crossroads The most challenging section is the Paso Queulat – narrow, steep, deeply rutted and with tight curves.
Parque Naciuonal Queulat to Puerto Cisnes Partially paved; the rest is a somewhat potholed dirt-and-gravel road.
Parque Naciuonal Queulat to the turn-off for Puerto Aysén Newly paved.
Coyhaique to Puerto Aisén Completely paved but with some blind turns.
Coyhaique to Cochrane Partially paved; otherwise mostly good gravel road with few potholes.
Cruce El Maitén to Chile Chico Mostly good gravel road, but narrow and with precipitous drop on one side.
Cochrane to Villa O'Higgins Mostly good gravel road, steep in parts; ferry crossing required at Puerto Yungay; some sections are very narrow with hairpin bends and sheer drop to one side.

8

Parque Nacional Volcán Hornopirén

To the east of Hornopirén unfold the 500 square kilometres of protected wilderness that make up **PARQUE NACIONAL VOLCÁN HORNOPIRÉN**. The park's namesake and centrepiece, 16km along a muddy track from the village, is the perfectly conical **Volcán Hornopirén**. Five kilometres further along the track lies the seldom-visited **Lago General Pinto Concha**, with excellent fishing and stunning views onto the 2111m **Volcán Yate** (1hr hike one-way). From Lago General Pinto Concha, another track leads to the base of Volcán Yate (2hr hike one-way).

Back towards the village, a turn-off from the track leads south around the end of the fjord to a modern bridge over the **Río Blanco**, with a short trail to your left leading up to the impressive Salto del Río Blanco waterfall. A well-defined 8km path follows the river upstream, passing through alternating patches of pastureland and grand stands of *alerce*, *coigüe*, *tepa* and *lenga*; above the tree line, you'll enter a landscape of ice-covered peaks and glaciers, making this a great **day-hike**.

Parque Pumalín

ⓦ www.parquepumalin.cl

South of Hornopirén, connected to it by two ferries, lies **PARQUE PUMALÍN**, the world's largest privately owned conservation area, covering 3200 square kilometres (790,400 acres) of land. The Pumalín Project, founded by North American millionaire Douglas Tompkins to protect one of the world's last strongholds of temperate rainforest, originally generated a considerable amount of controversy, yet few would deny that the park represents a magnificent environmental achievement. It's a place of overwhelming natural beauty, with hauntingly calm lakes reflecting stands of endangered *alerce* trees, ferocious waterfalls gushing through chasms of dark rock, and high, snowy-peaked mountains. Parque Pumalín falls into two sections, cut in half by a large chunk of land owned by ENDESA, the Spanish-owned energy corporation.

The northern section

The largely inaccessible **northern section** boasts the gloriously isolated **Termas de Cahuelmó**: a series of natural hot pools, carved out of the rock at the end of a steep, narrow fjord, reachable only by private boat from Hornopirén. Though there are several other remote hiking trails in the northern section, they are difficult and expensive to reach, so visitors to this less-explored part of the park do so by kayak or boat trip (see p.301, 322).

The southern section

The **southern section** has more infrastructure geared towards visitors. Near the ferry ramp at Caleta Gonzalo, the **Sendero Cascadas** climbs steeply through a canopy of overhanging foliage up to a 15m waterfall (3hr round-trip). Three other trails have been carved out of the forest, branching off from the Carretera Austral as it heads south through the park, passing the splendid Lago Blanco and other numerous natural highlights. Twelve kilometres down the road from Caleta Gonzalo and several kilometres south of Lago Blanco, **Sendero Laguna Tronador** is probably the most exciting, crossing a narrow gorge filled with a rushing, whitewater stream, climbing up to a look-out point with fabulous views onto Volcán Michinmahuida, and ending at a pristine lake with a camping area alongside (3hr round-trip).

One kilometre south, across the Río Blanco, **Sendero Los Alerces** is an enjoyable twenty-minute circular route, dotted with information panels, through a grove of ancient, colossal *alerces*. Another kilometre down the road, the **Sendero Cascadas**

DOUGLAS TOMPKINS AND THE PUMALÍN PROJECT

In 1995 it was publicly announced that a North American millionaire, **Douglas Tompkins**, had used intermediaries to buy a 3000-square-kilometre chunk of southern Chile – marking the beginning of a five-year national soap opera that transformed Tompkins into one of the most controversial public figures in the country. In 1991, the 49-year-old Californian, increasingly committed to environmental issues, sold his fifty percent share in the Esprit clothing empire, bought an abandoned ranch on the edge of the **Reñihué fjord**, 130km south of Puerto Montt, and moved there with his wife and kids. Inspired by the "deep ecology" movement pioneered by the Norwegian environmentalist **Arne Naess**, Tompkins set out to acquire more of the surrounding wilderness, with the aim of protecting it from the threat of commercial exploitation. As he did so, he was seized with the idea of creating a massive, privately funded national park, which would ensure permanent protection of the **ancient forest** while providing low-impact facilities for visitors.

THE MEDIA BACKLASH

Over the next four years Tompkins spent more than US$14 million buying up adjoining tracts of land, in most cases hiding his identity to prevent prices from shooting up. His initial secrecy was to have damaging repercussions, however, for once his land acquisitions became public knowledge, he was engulfed by a wave of suspicion and hostility, fuelled by several right-wing politicians and the press, with his motives questioned by everyone. The biggest cause for alarm, it seemed, was the fact that Tompkins' land stretched from the Argentine border to the Pacific Ocean, effectively "cutting Chile in two". Tompkins appeared on national television, explaining his intentions to create **Parque Pumalín**, a nature sanctuary with free access, slowly winning over some of the public.

SUCCESS WITH STRINGS

Eventually, the government agreed to support Tompkins' aims to establish the park – on the condition that for one year he would not buy more than 7000 contiguous hectares (17,250 acres) of land in the south of Chile. Tompkins was also prevented from purchasing Huinay, a 740,000-acre property owned by the Catholic University of Valparaíso, separating the two separate chunks of his land, which was instead sold to ENDESA, Chile's largest energy corporation.

Tompkins, determined to save a little more unspoiled terrain from development, purchased another chunk of land in 2001 near the Termas del Amarillo, south of Chaitén, while in 2005, Parque Pumalín, by this point managed by Chilean Fundación Pumalín (whose board includes Tompkins and his wife), was finally declared a **santuario de la naturaleza** (nature sanctuary), which gave it additional protection. Tompkins' wife Kristine is currently working on the conservation project of **Estancia Valle Chacabuco** near Cochrane (see p.376).

8

Escondidas is an easy walk through the forest to three high, slender waterfalls; you reach the first one after 25 minutes or so, and the other two, half an hour after that.

ARRIVAL AND DEPARTURE
PARQUE PUMALÍN

THE NORTHERN SECTION

By organized tour One option is to join a multi-day kayaking adventure trip with either Alsur Expediciones (☎65 232300, ⓦalsurexpeditions.com) or Yak Expediciones (☎09 9299 6487, ⓦyakexpediciones.cl), or take a multi-day boat trip with Austral Adventures (☎65 625977, ⓦaustral-adventures.com).

THE SOUTHERN SECTION

By bus Buses Fierro and Kemel Bus pass through the southern section en route from Puerto Montt to Chaitén (1 daily) and can drop you off along the way.

By car In peak season, there are daily car ferries from Hornopirén to Caleta Gonzalo (see p.350), the entry point to the park. Book well in advance.

By organized tour Chaitur (see p.354) runs tours to the park in summer months.

INFORMATION

Park information The Centro de Visitantes at Caleta Gonzalo (Dec–Feb Mon–Sat 9am–7pm, Sun 10am–4pm;

shorter hours the rest of the year; ⓦwww.parquepumalin .cl) has plenty of info on the park.

ACCOMMODATION AND EATING

Cabañas Río Gonzalo ☎ 65 232300. At Caleta Gonzalo, these seven *cabañas* (sleeping 2–5) are the epitome of rustic luxury, each individually designed, with comfy loft beds and ocean views. There are no kitchens; meals are to be had at the *Café Caleta Gonzalo*. There's also a good camping spot nearby. Camping CH$2000 per person, cabin CH$75,000

Café Caleta Gonzalo ☎ 65 232300. At Caleta Gonzalo, this appealing restaurant with massive fireplace serves Chilean dishes that use organic vegetables, and the delicious bread is home made. Large groups can book in advance for an *asado* (barbecue) and there are picnic boxes to take away. Summer daily 9am–10pm; shorter hours the rest of the year.

Camping Lago Blanco 36km north of Chaitén. This campsite has fantastic views of Lago Blanco from the covered sites, as well as hot showers and fire pits. CH$5500 per person

Camping Michinmahuida Located at the trailhead for the Sendero Laguna Tronador. This campsite is rather basic (no toilets) but drinking water is available and so are fire pits. CH$2500 per person

Chaitén

On May 2, 2008, **Volcán Chaitén**, at the foot of which nestles its namesake town, **erupted** for the first time in over nine thousand years, taking the local residents completely by surprise, as the volcano was thought to be dormant. The town, and much of the surrounding area, had to be evacuated as the 19-mile (30km) plume of ash and steam from the volcano affected the local water sources. Worse was to come when a mudslide caused floods which devastated the town. While the Bachelet government ordered the town to be abandoned, the Piñera administration subsequently reversed the decision and, with vital services now reinstated, Chaitén is once again connected to Puerto Montt and other destinations along the Carretera Austral by frequent boat and bus.

ARRIVAL AND DEPARTURE   CHAITÉN

By bus Chaitén is served by Buses Becker from Coyhaique via La Junta, as well as Buses Transaustral from Futaleufú and Palena, while Buses Fierro and Kemelbus run to Puerto Montt. Destinations Futaleufú (2 weekly; 3hr); Hornopirén (daily noon; 6hr); La Junta (2 weekly; 3hr); Palena (2 weekly; 3hr 15min); Puerto Montt (daily noon; 10hr).

By boat The Naviera Austral office at Av Corcovado (☎ 09 7976 0342, ⓦ www.navieraustral.cl) sells tickets for ferries to Quellón, Castro and Puerto Montt; double-check timetables as they're prone to change.

Destinations Castro (Jan & Feb Sat noon; 8hr); Puerto Montt (Fri & Sun; 10–12hr); Quellón (Mon 10am; 8hr).

By car From the north, you can either drive via Hornopirén, booking the Caleta Gonzalo ferry in advance (see p.350) or if you're coming via Chiloé, take the car ferry from Quellón.

By air Pewen Air Services (☎ 65 224000, ⓦ pewenchile .com), CieloMarAustral (☎ 65 264010, ⓔ cielomaraustral @surnet.cl) and Aerocord (☎ 65 262300, ⓦ aerocord.cl) have scheduled daily flights between Puerto Montt and Chaitén (CH$40,000 one way, CH$80,000 return).

INFORMATION AND TOURS

Chaitur O'Higgins 67 (☎ 65 731429 or 09/7468 5608, ⓦ chaitur.com). With the absence of a formal tourist office, the HQ of the indomitable Nicolas La Penna – a treasure trove of local information – is the place for organizing both onward travel and tours to Parque Pumalín and more. If Nicolas is not at the office, locals can point out his house so you can go and knock on his door.

CHAITÉN VIVE!

On May 12, 2008, a *lahar* (mudslide) caused by the eruption of **Volcán Chaitén** (see p.354) made the Río Blanco overflow, flooding and destroying a large part of the nearby town of **Chaitén**. The Chilean government declared the area unsafe and tried to relocate Chaitén's population, but in spite of government pressure, some hardy residents refused to move and reverted to a lifestyle without electricity or running water, which they had been used to for most of their lives. Since 2008, more people have returned; Chaitén's population now numbers around eight hundred people out of the former four thousand. Though signs of recent devastation are still very much evident in the form of wrecked houses half-buried in grey mud, a defiant piece of graffiti reads: "Chaitén vive!"

ACCOMMODATION AND EATING

Hospedaje Don Carlos Almirante Riveros s/n ☏ 09 9128 3328. Homely, family-run guesthouse a block from the waterfront, with compact rooms and good beds. En-suite rooms are more expensive. Breakfast included. CH$17,000
Hostería Llanos Corcovado 387 ☏ 09 8826 0448. Seafront residence run by a friendly elderly lady, with wood-panelled en-suite rooms and frilly bedspreads. Breakfast includes a hefty slice of cake. CH$18000

Hotel Schilling Corcovado 230 ☏ 09 8868 4922. The only hotel in town, *Schilling* has a cavernous, atmospheric guest lounge and some of its rooms offer sea views. CH$36,000
El Quijote O'Higgins s/n ☏ 09 8863 3752. Join the locals at this cheery, family-run restaurant for heaped portions of super-fresh grilled fish and simple side dishes. Daily noon–3.30pm & 7–10pm.

DIRECTORY

Banks and exchange A Banco Estado has just reopened, but it does not accept Visa cards; bring plenty of cash.

Internet A small internet café is due to open at the Chaitur office (see opposite).

The Futaleufú Valley

The 80km trip up the **FUTALEUFÚ VALLEY** is one of the most enjoyable diversions off the Carretera Austral. Heading east from the drab crossroads settlement of Villa Santa Lucía, south of Chaitén, you first skirt the southern shore of Lago Yelcho for 30km, before arriving at a fork in the road. The right turn goes to the quiet border village of **Palena**, while the left branch follows the turquoise **Río Futaleufú** for 17km through towering gorges, lush forests and snow-streaked mountain peaks to its namesake town.

8

Palena

Though the quiet village of Palena does not have Futaleufú's infrastructure, its late-January **Rodeo de Palena** showcases the local *huaso* culture and it's gaining popularity as a destination for outdoor enthusiasts. Palena is also the starting point for the Sendero de Chile trail section that runs through Reserva Nacional Lago Palena to the hamlet of Lago Verde (see box, p.358).

ARRIVAL AND INFORMATION
PALENA

By bus Buses Transaustral (☏ 67 524100) and Cumbres Nevadas (☏ 09 7496 0881) run between Futaleufú and Palena several times weekly; Buses Transaustral also runs to Chaitén twice weekly.

Tours Guiado Don Emir (☏ 65 741263) is a recommended horseriding tour operator offering excursions along the Sendero de Chile and Ruta Patrimonial Río Palena.

ACCOMMODATION AND EATING

Rincón de la Nieve B&B Alto Palena, Km20 ☏ 65 741221, ✉ rincondelanieve@gmail.com. Near Palena, this brightly painted, wood-shingled farm gives you a taste of gaucho life, courtesy of the enterprising Casanova family, who can organize multi-day horseback riding expeditions. Hearty home-made meals are a treat. CH$16,000
Río Palena Lodge Sector La Balsa ☏ 67 325220, ⊛ riopalena.com. This small, exclusive fly-fishing lodge caters to just six guests and offers all-inclusive packages which incorporate dry land activities: the terrain around the lodge is ideal for horseback riding and hiking, and there's rafting to be enjoyed on the nearby rivers. Cuisine is international gourmet, paired with a wide range of Chilean wines. 7-day full board CH$2,390,000 (US$4995) per person

Futaleufú

Sitting on the Río Futaleufú, near its confluence with the Rio Espolón, and surrounded by forested, snowy peaks, Futaleufú more than earns the grandiose slogan – "A landscape painted by God" – coined by its early inhabitants. With its big "explosion waves" and massive "rodeo holes", the Río Futaleufú is regarded by many professional rafters and kayakers as one of the most challenging whitewater rivers in the world, with sections of

SENDERO DE CHILE: FROM PALENA TO VILLA LA TAPERA

A section of the Sendero de Chile stretches for over 100km from the village of Palena to the hamlet of **Villa La Tapera**, passing through some spectacular scenery along the way; some sections are best tackled with local guides, as it crosses terrain where the trail is not very well marked. The first section runs through endemic forest of the **Reserva Nacional Río Palena**, skirting the beautiful Lago Palena, a popular fly-fishing destination, and finally arriving at the village of **Lago Verde**, by its namesake lake. From Lago Verde, the track leads south; having been used for generations by gauchos to move livestock from one place to another, it's not difficult to follow, passing through alternating landscapes of Patagonian steppes, covered in *coirón*, and thickly forested *lenga* and *coigüe* valleys, boxed in by the surrounding mountains.

Halfway to Villa La Tapera, the trail climbs to the **Portezuelo Los Contrabandistas** (1,355m), which offers a spectacular view of the nearby mountains and their glaciers. The final section of the trail crosses Río Cisnes before arriving at Villa La Tapera, a small village reachable by dirt road from an eastbound turn-off from the Carretera, north of Coyhaique but before the westbound turn-off towards Puerto Cisnes. There are several basic *refugios* along the trail and it's possible to camp wild.

the river known as "Hell" and "The Terminator". A number of Chilean and US operators offer **rafting** trips down the river, a body of water which runs through a basalt gorge known as the *Gates of Hell*, and boasts over forty class IV–V rapids.

An attractive little town, Futaleufú serves as a popular summer base primarily for rafting, though there is still a shadow hanging over it in the form of the Spanish energy corporation ENDESA, which has plans to construct a dam and to build a hydroelectric plant on the river; the plan currently faces concerted opposition by locals, tour operators and environmentalists.

ARRIVAL AND DEPARTURE

FUTALEUFÚ

By bus Buses Transaustral (☎ 67 721360) runs to Esquel, Argentina, several times weekly, and also Osorno and Puerto Montt via Argentina, departing on Mon at 8am; more frequently in peak season (12–14hr). Buses Becker (☎ 67 721360) runs to Coyhaique (Sun 8am; 12hr), Buses

Altamirano (☎ 67 721453) run's to La Junta (Mon, Wed & Fri; 3hr), while Cumbres Nevadas (☎ 67 721208) serves Palena (Mon, Wed & Fri; 1hr 30min). Most buses depart from the corner of Prat and Balmaceda, while some stop by the post office on the Plaza de Armas.

INFORMATION AND TOURS

TOURIST INFORMATION
Tourist office O'Higgins 536, south side of the Plaza de Armas (summer daily 9am–8pm in summer; closed the rest of the year; ☎ 65 721370). The helpful tourist office dishes out maps of local walks. Note that the Banco Estado, situated along with the post office on the Plaza de Armas, doesn't accept Visa, so bring plenty of cash.

TOUR OPERATORS
Earth River Expeditions ☎ 800 6432784, ⓦ www .earthriver.com. With four camps along the river, this long-established, highly praised operator allows

whitewater enthusiasts to combine aquatic activity with rock climbing, mountain biking, horseback riding, canyoning and more.
Expediciones Chile Mistral 296 ☎ 65 721386, ⓦ exchile.com. Experienced operator that specializes in multi-day rafting and kayaking on the Futa, though day excursions are also possible.
Futaleufú Explore O'Higgins 772 ☎ 65 721527, ⓦ futaleufuexplore.com. Established American–Chilean outfit that runs multi-day rafting and kayaking trips, as well as multi-activity "Week of Adventure" from its own luxury riverside camp. All-inclusive packages only.

ACCOMMODATION

Cabañas Frontera Patagónica 5km south of town ☎ 65 721320. This Dutch–Chilean-owned complex consists of several handsome four- and five-person cabins with wood-burning stoves, with breakfast included and fishing, kayaking and rafting trips available. Cabins from <u>CH$65, 000.</u>

Cara del Indio 4km from Puente Futaleufú ☎ 65 196 4239, ⓦ caradelindio.cl. This riverfront adventure camp makes a great base for whitewater enthusiasts, who can choose between camping, staying in a basic *refugio* or sharing one of the fully equipped *cabañas*. The on-site restaurant serves Chilean favourites, such as *cazuela* (stew) and if there's a group of you, you can opt for barbecued Patagonian lamb. Camping CH$3000 per person, *refugio* CH$3000, cabin CH$25,000

Hospedaje Adolfo O'Higgins 302 ☎ 65 721256, ✉ pettyrios@hotmail.com. This is a standout family-run budget choice, with comfortable rooms (some en suite) with creaky wooden floors, good breakfast and reliable hot showers. CH$20,000

Hotel Río Grande O'Higgins 397 ☎ 65 721320, ⓦ pachile.com. Favoured by rafting gringos, this hotel with its chic-rustic decor is still one of the most popular places to stay. The carpeted rooms are bright and comfortable, the bar makes a good hangout spot and the multilingual owners operate the Patagonia Adventure Centre, which can arrange anything from rafting adventures to multi-day, multi-activity programmes. CH$53,000

Lodge El Barranco Bernardo O'Higgins 172 ☎ 65 721314, ⓦ elbarrancochile.com. The owners of this lodge on the outskirts of town go out of their way to be helpful when organizing horseback riding and rafting excursions. The attractive wood-panelled rooms have comfortable new beds with crisp linens and the on-site bar and restaurant is one of the very best in town. CH$100,000

EATING

Burger stand Pedro Aguirre Cerda, next to the Telefónica Sur. If you happen to be passing through Futa during the off-season, this is one of the very few places open and the huge burgers are supremely satisfying. Daily 7–11pm.

Martín Pescadór Balmaceda 603 ☎ 65 721279. One of the best restaurants in town, serving the likes of grilled salmon with honey and ginger, carpaccio and inventive meat dishes in a mountain lodge living room-style atmosphere, with a fire roaring on colder days. The wine list is extensive. Daily 7–11.30pm.

Scorpion's Gabriela Mistral 265 ☎ 09 7718 8749. This informal restaurant lets you choose between several simple but well-prepared meat and seafood dishes daily. Daily 6pm–1am.

Sur Andes Pedro Aguirre Cerda 308 ☎ 65 721405. Real coffee, freshly squeezed juice and good vegetarian options contribute to the popularity of this café, which also offers good omelettes and hefty burgers. Daily 9.30am–11pm.

Raul Marín Balmaceda

Around 75km south of the crossroads settlement of Villa Santa Lucía – where the road to the Futaleufú Valley branches off from the Carretera Austral – a westbound, 53km-long gravel road leads splits off from the Carretera, running along the banks of Río Palena to **Raúl Marín Balmaceda** – a fishing village with the most attractive setting along the whole of the Carretera Austral. The cluster of houses, hiding behind greenery along several streets, sits on an island in the river delta, reachable by car ferry (an additional 21km from the road's end) and boasting attractive white sand beaches. The bay is full of marine life, such as seals and cormorants and it's possible to see dolphins and even blue whales if you do a boat excursion.

ARRIVAL AND DEPARTURE   RAUL MARÍN BALMACEDA

By bus Bus Gerardo Valenzuela (☎ 09 8197 8793) runs to Raúl Marín Balmaceda from Coyhaique (Sat 8am, returning Sun 10am). There may also be more frequent buses from La Junta; check at the La Junta tourist office.

By ferry The car ferry to and from the village runs several times daily (passengers free, cars CH$3000).

WHITEWATER RAFTING ON THE FUTA

Most people come to Futaleufú for the **whitewater rafting and kayaking**, though you needn't stop there: the area around Futa lends itself to a range of **outdoor activities**, including hiking, horse-trekking, mountain biking, fly-fishing, floating (drifting down a river on an inner tube) down the tamer Río Espolón, canyoning (abseiling down canyons) and canoeing. Expect to pay around CH$25,000 for a relatively simple run down the Río Espolón, CH$55,000 for a half-day excursion on the Río Futaleufú and CH$90,000 for a full day on the Futa, which includes tackling Class V rapids. A number of experienced local outfits offer these activities (see p.356).

8

DAMMED IF YOU DO...PATAGONIA SÍN REPRESAS!

Everywhere you look in Patagonia, you see Patagonia "Sín Represas!" stickers; graffiti on city walls testifies to the population's opposition to the controversial plan to tame two of the region's largest rivers, and *huasos* on horseback come out in protest, bearing defiant signs. The problem? HidroAysén, in conjunction with Spanish-owned ENDESA, formerly a state-owned enterprise given exclusive water rights by Chile's government over its rivers, proposes to put into action its plan to build **five massive dams** – two on Río Baker, three on Río Pascua – thus allegedly solving Chile's demand for vast amounts of hydroelectric energy, most of which would go up north to feed the country's mines. Chile's government supports this project, even though more than half of the population is against it. Though citizens of Patagonia who live off the land and environmentalists have traditionally not seen eye to eye, this proposal, which threatens traditional livelihoods and pristine wilderness alike, has brought them together.

THE ARGUMENTS FOR AND AGAINST

Besides irreversible scarring of the land, flooding of farmland and forest, and a massive blow to tourism, there are fears that once the transmission lines are in place, no Patagonian river will be safe. Some Chilean citizens do support the project for the jobs it will create and the energy it will provide, but the **counterargument** is that this energy could be obtained from wind, solar and dynamic geothermal sources instead. Though the dams have been approved, the battle is still being fought out in the courts and in the streets. A new proposal suggests sending HydroAysén power lines through Argentina but it remains to be seen what impact this problem will have on Patagonia's future. For more information, check out ⓦsinrepresas.com and ⓦwww.patagoniasinrepresas.cl.

ACCOMMODATION AND EATING

Fundo Los Leones ☎09 7898 2956, ⓦfundolosleones .com. You'll find this delightful retreat, reachable either by boat from the village or by charter planes, just on the outskirts of Raúl Marín Balmaceda. The wood-panelled, wi-fi-equipped cabins (sleeping 2) are bright, individually decorated and named after sea mammals, while the lodge offers a variety of boat trips and fishing excursions and there's an outdoor hot tub for relaxation. Meals extra. CH$90,000

Pension Los Dos Juanitos Costanera s/n ☎09 8743 2831. Snug family-run option on the waterfront; rooms share facilities and the lady of the house cooks fresh dishes at the restaurant. The bar is a bit of a gathering spot for locals. CH$20,000

Lago Verde

From La Junta (see p.359), a turn-off for the eastbound Ruta X-10 leads 74km southeastwards to **Lago Verde**, a neat little grid of streets near the northeast bank of the enormous blue-green expanse that is Lago Verde, near the Argentine border. The forests and rivers around Lago Verde are ideal for trekking, fly fishing and horseback riding; Patagonia Lago Verde (☎2 196 0057, ⓦpatagonialagoverde.com) offers a number of half-day and day-long expeditions which tend to combine two or more of the above activities with a traditional Patagonian meal.

ARRIVAL AND DEPARTURE   LAGO VERDE

By bus Transporte Bronco (☎09 9952 0907) runs from Coyhaique to Lago Verde (Wed & Sun – call ahead for times; returning Thurs & Mon 10am).

ACCOMMODATION AND EATING

Hospedaje y Camping El Miradór Camino a la Frontera ☎67 214031. True to its name, this family-run guesthouse and attached campsite en route to the border with Argentina (only 5km from Lago Verde) boasts great lake views. Campers have access to hot showers, rooms share bathrooms and home-cooked meals are an option. Camping CH$3000 per person, double CH$18,000

La Junta and Reserva Nacional Lago Rosselot

South of the turn-offs for Raúl Marín Balmaceda and Lago Verde, and just before the northern boundary of Parque Nacional Queulat, the Carretera Austral passes through **La Junta**, a collection of tin houses established in 1983 as one of General Pinochet's "new towns", and home to a controversial unauthorized monument to the dictator. La Junta is the access point to the **Reserva Nacional Lago Rosselot**, whose namesake lake has gained popularity with the fly-fishing set.

ARRIVAL AND INFORMATION   LA JUNTA

By bus Buses Altamirano (☎ 67 314143) runs to Coyhaique (Mon–Fri 5.30am; 7hr), while Transpore Terra Austral (☎ 67 314400) makes the same journey (daily 6am). Buses Becker (☎ 09 8465 2959) passes through at least twice weekly on the way to Futaleufú, and to Chaitén (Tues

around 3pm, returning the following day). Most buses depart from the plaza.
Tourist information Plaza de Armas (Summer Mon–Fri 9am–9pm, Sat & Sun 10.30am–7pm; shorter hours in winter; ☎ 65 721239).

ACCOMMODATION AND EATING

Espacio y Tiempo Hotel de Montaña Carretera Austral s/n ☎ 67 314141, ⓦ www.espacioytiempo.cl. With an appealing rustic interior, friendly staff and just nine spiffy rooms, this wood-and-stone mountain lodge is a favourite with anglers and allows easy exploration of the Río Palena watershed on horseback. The on-site restaurant serves good Chilean staples, and the bar is well stocked. **CH$76,000**
Hospedaje Valle El Quinto Diego Portales s/n ☎ 09 97713805, ⓔ javiera34@live.cl. Located half a block

south of the plaza, this family-run guesthouse offers bright rooms with colourful bedspreads and shared facilities. Lunch and dinner available on request. **CH$22,000**
Mi Casita de Té Antonio Varas at Patricio Lynch ☎ 67 314206. A good, inexpensive spot for meals, with friendly Eliana serving solid Chilean standards such as *lomo a lo pobre* (cut of meat with fried egg on top and French fries on the side) and grilled fish. Mon–Sat 12.30–3.30pm & 7–10.30pm, Sun 12.30–3.30pm.

8

Parque Nacional Queulat and around

CH$3500, payable only if you enter the Sector Ventisquero Colgante

With stunning, rugged scenery and its namesake hanging glacier, **PARQUE NACIONAL QUEULAT** is one of the region's biggest attractions. Located south of La Junta, it features a vast expanse of virgin forest, towering granite peaks and rumbling glaciers, and is divided into three sectors. The Carretera Austral enters the park's northern boundary 15km north of the village of Puyuhuapi and crosses its southern limit 55km further south, just beyond the Portezuelo de Queulat pass. The park's main entrance lies 2.5km along a signposted turn-off from the Carretera Austral, 22km south of Puyuhuapi.

Sector Angostura

Beyond Puyuhuapi, in the northern sector of the park, a track pulls off the road to the Conaf *guardería*, on the shores of the long, thin **Lago Risopatrón**. The lake, flanked by steep mountains jutting abruptly out of its deep-blue waters, is a lovely spot, and the **camping** area (see p.360) near the Conaf hut is one of the prettiest along the entire road. By the *guardería*, the **Sendero Laguna Los Pumas** (14km return; 5hr) starts with a steep ascent, climbing to 1100m. From the plateau at the top, you get sweeping views onto surrounding mountains and out to the fjord. The trail then descends through a pass, leading to the shimmering Laguna Los Pumas, bordered by a sandy beach.

Sector Ventisquero Colgante

By far the most popular sight in the park and accessible from the park's main entrance, is the incredible **Ventisquero Colgante**, or "hanging glacier". Wedged between two peaks, forming a V-shaped mass of blue-white ice, the glacier indeed seems to hang suspended over a sheer rock face. Long fingers of ice feed two thundering waterfalls that plummet 150m down to a glacial lake. From the parking area by the Centro de Información Ambiental (see p.360), follow the signposted 250m **Sendero Miradór Panorámico** to a spectacular viewpoint. If you cross the suspension bridge over the river and turn right, you will find the 600m **Sendero Laguna Témpanos**, which leads to its namesake lake through dense native forest, from where you get excellent views of the glacier.

Left of the bridge, the steep **Sendero Ventisquero Colgante** climbs 3.2km to a higher viewpoint. Another trail, the 6km **Sendero Valle Río Ventisqueros**, starts at the same car park and follows the southern bank of the Río Ventisquero Valley, passing through evergreen forest and numerous viewpoints overlooking the Ventisquero Colgante before ending up at a beautiful beach. Allow five hours for a return trip and consult the rangers regarding trail conditions.

Sector Portezuelo Queulat

Just beyond the southern entrance to the park, there's a short trail leading west to a mighty waterfall, the 40m-high **Saltos del Cóndor**. Five kilometres beyond, the Carretera Austral narrows and zigzags its way down the steep **Cuesta de Queulat**, through sheer-sided mountains crowned with glaciers. A signposted 2km trail, **Sendero Bosque Encantado** (2hr), makes for an easy but exhilarating hike (3hr 30min return), branching off to the left from the road just before the Portezuelo de Queulat, and leading 1.7km through moss-covered ancient trees before ending at the Río Cascadas.

From here, follow the river up the hill for another 800m, and you'll arrive at its source – a jade-green lake at the foot of a granite cliff, topped by a glacier and streaked by waterfalls. Just beyond the Portezuelo de Queulat pass is Sendero Padre García, leading 200m down to the **Salto Padre García**, a powerful waterfall dropping 30m into the Río Queulat.

ARRIVAL AND INFORMATION

PARQUE NACIONAL QUEULAT

By bus From Coyhaique, you can get any northbound bus that goes to Puyuhuapi or beyond, or any Coyhaique-bound bus from any destination north of Parque Nacional Queulat to drop you off by the entrance to the park, though it can be difficult to hitch a ride out.

By organized tour Several tour companies run day-trips to the Ventisquero Colgante from Coyhaique during the summer months (see p.365).

National park information The Centro de Información Ambiental (daily: April–Nov 9am–6pm; Dec–March 9am–8pm; CH$3500), with its detailed displays on the park's flora and glacier, is located at the main entrance, 2.5km along a signposted turn-off from the Carretera Austral, 22km south of Puyuhuapi.

ACCOMMODATION

Camping Angostura Sector Angostura. Beautiful campsite on the shores of Lago Risopatrón near the Conaf ranger hut; each site comes with its own picnic table and *fogon*. Note that the hot water is erratic. CH$3500 per person

Camping Ventisquero Sector Ventisquero Colgante. Though the ground is rocky and hard, the 10 camping sites are attractive and come equipped with picnic tables and *fogones* (barbecue areas). You'll need to make use of the firewood to get over the freezing cold showers. CH$3500 per person

Fiordo Queulat Ecolodge Carretera Austral Norte Km 192 ☎67 233302, ⓦqueulatlodge.com. South of

Puyuhuapi, this quiet retreat consists of six comfortable 2-person cabins orbiting the main lodge, itself with roaring fireplace. A bit expensive for what it is, but does it offer sea kayaking, trekking in Parque Nacional Queulat and fly-fishing. CH$115,000 (US$240)

El Pangue Lodge Carretera Austral, Km 240 ☎67 526906, ⓦelpangue.com. In a tranquil, secluded setting north of Puyuhuapi, near Lago Riopatrón, this attractive lodge is a good base for trekking, fly-fishing and horseback riding, among other activities. 4 days/3 nights full board CH$1,572,000 (US$3250) per person

Puyuhuapi

Squatting at the head of the narrow Ventisquero fjord, surrounded by steep, wooded hills, **PUYUHUAPI**, founded in the 1930s by four young German immigrants from

Sudetenland who married Chilean women, is a great place to break your journey along the Carretera Austral in either direction – not only for the wild beauty of its setting, but also for its proximity to the **Termas de Puyuhuapi** and its convenience as a base for exploring **Parque Queulat**. Puyuhuapi's unmistakably Teutonic look, with its steep-roofed chalets and well-tended gardens, offers a pleasing contrast to the utilitarian "villages" installed along the Carretera in the 1980s after the completion of the road.

Termas Ventisquero

Dec–Feb 9am–11pm • CH$12,000 • ☎ 67 325228,• ⓦ termasventisqueropuyuhuapi.cl

The town's premier attractions are the **Termas de Puyuhuapi** – an upmarket hot springs resort (see p.361). A cheaper alternative to the plush *termas* is the more easily accessible **Termas Ventisquero** 6km south of town along the Carretera, with two simple outdoor pools fed by thermal springs (temperature tends to vary), a beautiful view and a decent café serving sandwiches and *kuchen*.

ARRIVAL AND INFORMATION

PUYUHUAPI

By bus Puyuhuapi is served by a daily bus to La Junta courtesy of Buses Terra Austral (☎ 67 325119) while Buses Becker (☎ 67 721248) passes through en route to La Junta and Chaitén (Tues & Sat respectively; northbound buses pass between 2pm and 7pm, while southbound ones tend to arrive around 7.30am and between 3 and 5pm).

Tourist information Avenida Übel (Mon–Sat noon–2pm & 3–9pm; ⓦ puyuhuapi.org). This small but helpful tourist office is located in the centre of town.

ACCOMMODATION

Casa Ludwig Otto Uebel 202 ☎67 325220, ⓦ casaludwig.cl. The most popular option with international travellers, this delightful yellow chalet has comfortable rooms, polished wooden floors, excellent breakfast, a library and great views. It's run by a charming lady who speaks English and German and is a wealth of information on the area. CH$24,000

Hostal Augusto Grosse Camilo Henriquez 4 ☎67 325238, ✉ hostalaugustogrosse@gmail.com. Finally, an excellent choice for backpackers! The rooms at this hostel may not be the largest, but the beautiful wooden furniture was all lovingly made by the owner himself and guests can use the kitchen. Breakfast costs an extra CH$1000. CH$18000

Hostería Aonikenk Hamburgo 16 ☎67 325208, ⓦ aonikenkpuyuhuapi.cl. An ultra-helpful hostess presides over this collection of rooms and *cabañas* (sleeping up to 5) with something to suit everyone, from compact doubles to fully equipped cabins with balconies. Meals are served in the cheery dining area of the main house, and there's a lounge area upstairs for chilling out. Double CH$24,300, cabin CH$40,000

EATING

Café Rossbach Av. Ubel 450 ☎ 67 325203. Opposite the carpet factory, this café serves German-influenced dishes, including mouth-watering *kuchen* made with wild berries. Often closed during the off-season. Daily 11am–3pm & 7–10.30pm.

Cocinería Real Gabriela Mistral 8 ☎ 09 76525613. A favourite with locals, this red-shingled establishment is the best place in town for catch-of-the-day fish dishes. Daily noon–4pm.

Termas de Puyuhuapi

Day visit CH$15,000 for outdoor pools, CH$25,000 for use of the indoor pool; round-trip boat ride (free to guests) CH$10,000 • ☎ 67 325103 or 2 225 6489, ⓦ patagonia-connection.com • Boat departs from a signposted wooden jetty 15km south of Puyuhuapi four times daily Dec–March (call for updated schedule), less frequently off-season (10min)

The luxurious thermal baths, lodge and spa at ★ **TERMAS DE PUYUHUAPI** enjoy a fantastic location, marooned on the edge of a peninsula on the opposite side of the fjord from the Carretera Austral. You don't need to be an overnight guest to visit, but you should phone ahead to book.

The thermal baths used to be a handful of ramshackle cabins that were transformed into a series of low-lying, beautifully designed buildings made of reddish-brown *alerce* timber and lots of glass by the East German shipbuilding magnate Eberhard

8

Kossman in the late 1980s. Apart from its spectacular location, the main reason to come here is to soak in the steaming **hot springs**, channelled into three outdoor pools reached by a short walk through the forest. Two of the pools are large enough to swim in, and sit right on the edge of the fjord, while the third one, containing the hottest water, is a small pond enclosed by overhanging ferns and native trees. There's a state-of-the-art **spa**, specializing in a range of treatments and massage, whirlpools, a gym with an excellent view, a large indoor pool, a cold water pool, a children's pool and two Jacuzzis.

FLY-FISHING AND LODGES ON THE CARRETERA AUSTRAL

Aysén is the most exciting fly-fishing region in Chile and is internationally renowned, drawing serious anglers, including a number of Hollywood stars. The **season** varies slightly according to the area, but in general lasts from October or November to May. You need a **licence** to fish (CH$10,000), widely available in sport-fishing shops. For more info, contact the **Servicio Nacional de Pesca** at Victoria 2832, Valparaíso (☎32 281 9100, ⊛sernapesca .cl). A number of first-class fishing lodges have sprung up around the region; most lodges are of an extremely high standard, and charge US$450 – 12,000 per person for a seven-night package including accommodation, fishing guide, all food and an open bar. Below, we have listed the pick of the bunch.

Cinco Ríos Lodge Km 5, Camino a Balmaceda ☎67 244917, ⊛cincorios.cl. On the banks of the Río Simpson, a short drive from Coyhaique, this luxurious lodge with owners from Montana caters to up to twelve guests and offers gourmet takes on Chilean dishes as well as an extensive wine list. There's easy access to an astounding twelve rivers, such as Paloma, Blanco and Nireguao, as well as countless creeks and the small Pollux, Frio and Castor lakes. Guests fish mainly for trout, along with king and coho salmon, accessed by a combination of wading and floating. Open Oct–April.

Futa Lodge Near Futaleufú ☎800 628 1447, ⊛angleradventures.com/FUTA. North American Jim Repine spent many years guiding in Alaska before coming down to the Futaleufú river valley. With guest capacity of six, and excellent food and wine, this is a small, intimate, relaxing lodge, especially geared towards couples. Rainbow and brown trout are most prevalent, with driftboat fishing and wading right at the front door. Friendly owners organize horseback riding and whitewater rafting excursions for non-fishing guests. Open Nov–April.

Heart of Patagonia Lodge 11km from Puerto Aysén ☎67 233701, ⊛angleradventures.com /HeartofPata. A remodelled 1930s home on the banks of the Río Simpson, this intimate American-owned place caters to international guests and there's easy access to nearby Río Simpson and Río Manihuales. The fishing is mainly for rainbow and brown trout, though Atlantic and king salmon also make an appearance. The restaurant serves good Chilean food and there are

hiking and horseback riding options for non-fishing guests. Open mid-Oct to mid-April.

Nomads of the Seas ☎2 414 4600, ⊛www .nomadsoftheseas.com. Taking a unique approach to fly fishing, this exciting new operator bases all its fishing itineraries out of its 150-foot luxury mothership, complete with a helicopter and its own fleet of jet boats, which enable it to penetrate little-explored corners of Aysén for an experience of unparalleled diversity. Non-fishing guests can engage in whale- and bird-watching and there's an on-board spa available to all, as is the gourmet Chilean cuisine. Open mid-Oct to April.

El Patagón Lodge South of Futaleufú and Palena ☎65/212030, ⊛yankeewaylodge.com. Owned by the Yan Kee Way Lodge on Lago Llanquihue (see p.305), this remote lodge is located amid temperate rainforest, with great access to the area's trout-filled streams and lakes. The four rough-hewn wooden cabins house a total of eight guests; the restaurant is superb and the hot tub on the Río Figueroa an added plus. Ten-day horseback riding/fishing expeditions also on offer. Open Oct–April.

Patagonia Baker Lodge Puerto Bertrand ☎67 411903, ⊛pbl.cl. The place for fly-fishing enthusiasts, sitting on the waterfront of the world-renowned Río Baker, which is teeming with brown and rainbow trout as well as good-sized salmon. De-luxe rooms have electric heating and private bathrooms as well as a stunning view of the Río Baker. The lodge also boasts two halls with open fireplaces and a gourmet restaurant. Horseback riding, boat trips along Río Baker and bird-watching excursions also on offer. Open late Oct to April.

ACCOMMODATION AND EATING

Puyuhuapi Lodge & Spa Bahía Dorita ☎ 67 325103, ⓦ patagonia-connection.com. If you're looking both for seclusion and a good soak, then this elegant lodge – all shingles and glass – offers a happy marriage of the two. The pricier rooms hang right over the lakefront and the restaurant serves delicious three-course meals made with fresh local produce, even if they fall short of gourmet cuisine. The hotel also offers 3-night packages which include a catamaran cruise to Laguna San Rafael (see p.368). **CH$130,000 (US$272)**

Puerto Cisnes

A small, quaint fishing village in a dramatic setting at the mouth of Río Cisnes, **PUERTO CISNES** sits at the end of a 35km side road that branches west from the Carretera Austral, just beyond the southern limit of Parque Nacional Queulat. Formerly a solitary sawmill, set up by a German pioneer in 1929, Puerto Cisnes is also the access point to the little-visited Parque Nacional Isla Magdalena, a 1580-square kilometre expanse of densely forested mountains and pristine rivers with hot springs, very little infrastructure and home to such fauna as the *pudú* and the *güiña* (wildcat). Negotiating passage to the island is expensive (around CH$120,000 for up to ten people) but worth it.

ARRIVAL AND DEPARTURE   PUERTO CISNES

By bus Buses Terra Austral (☎ 67 346757) runs daily to Coyhaique (Mon–Fri 5pm, Sat & Sun 4pm), while Buses Sao Paolo (☎ 67 255726) departs for Puerto Cisnes from Coyhaique (daily 4pm, returning 5.30am).

By boat Naviera Austral (☎ 67 346757, ⓦ www.navieraustral.cl) ferries stop in Puerto Cisnes en route to Quellón and Puerto Chacabuco. The trip to the Isla Magdalena across the Canal Puyuhuapi costs around CH$120,000; contact Víctor Cea González (☎ 09 7967 0738) or Luís Méndez (☎ 67 346417 or 09 9698 3707).

ACCOMMODATION AND EATING

Cabañas y Restaurante El Guairao Prat 353 ☎ 67 346473. Near the bridge that links the two halves of the village, this place offers two-storey motel-style en-suite rooms with satellite TV. Its restaurant is also the best place to eat; try the local speciality of *puyes*, similar to whitebait and absolutely delicious, while reading the framed story of the owner's life on the wall. **CH$30,000**

Hospedaje Bellavista Séptimo de Línea 112 ☎ 67 346408, ⓦ tourbellavista.cl. This popular family-run B&B is a good bet for arranging trips to Isla Magdalena. The rooms are simple but cheery and the hostess is very helpful. **CH$20,000**

Coyhaique and around

After the smattering of small villages scattered along the Carretera Austral, Aysén's lively regional capital, **COYHAIQUE**, can be a welcome change. The city's fifty thousand inhabitants make up half the region's population, and it's the only place along the Carretera that offers a wide range of services, from pharmacies and banks to laundries and car-rental outlets. It's also a good launch pad for some great **day-trips** (see p.367).

Plaza de Armas

Coyhaique's most unusual feature is its large, five-sided **Plaza de Armas**, from which the main streets radiate like a spider's web; even with map in hand, travellers often find themselves wandering around in circles (or pentagons). During the day, on the southwest corner with Paseo Horn, the small **Feria de Artesanos** sells jewellery and leather goods, while just across the plaza on the corner with Montt, the **Galería Artesanal de Cema Chile** stocks a wide range of handicrafts, including knitwear, weavings, wooden carvings and ceramics.

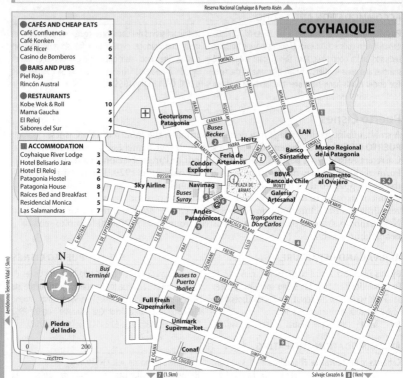

CAFÉS AND CHEAP EATS
Café Confluencia	3
Café Konken	9
Café Ricer	6
Casino de Bomberos	2

BARS AND PUBS
| Piel Roja | 1 |
| Rincón Austral | 8 |

RESTAURANTS
Kobe Wok & Roll	10
Mama Gaucha	5
El Reloj	4
Sabores del Sur	7

ACCOMMODATION
Coyhaique River Lodge	3
Hotel Belisario Jara	4
Hotel El Reloj	2
Patagonia Hostel	6
Patagonia House	8
Raíces Bed and Breakfast	1
Residencial Monica	5
Las Salamandras	7

COYHAIQUE

Museo Regional de la Patagonia and around

Eusebio Lillo at Baquedano • Mid-Dec to Feb daily 8.30am–8pm; March to mid-Dec Mon–Fri 8.30am–1.30pm & 2.15–5.30pm • CH$2000

At the junction of Montt with Baquedano, the city's main thoroughfare, the **Monumento al Ovejero**, a large sculpture of a shepherd and a flock of sheep, commemorates Aysén's pioneer farmers. Almost opposite the monument, stands the majorly refurbished **Museo Regional de la Patagonia**, where an informative collection of black-and-white photographs vividly captures the "Wild West" frontier atmosphere during the opening up of Aysén a century ago. There are also engaging displays on the regional geology and natural history, which include some stuffed specimens and petrified wood samples, and a separate photo exhibit dedicated to those who built the Carretera Austral.

ARRIVAL AND DEPARTURE
COYHAIQUE

BY PLANE

Sky and LAN flights to and from Santiago, Puerto Montt and Punta Arenas land at the Aeropuerto de Balmaceda, 55km south of Coyhaique, and are met by minibuses that take passengers to their hotels for CH$4000. Charter flights over the San Rafael glacier with Aerotaxis del Sur and Transportes Aéreo Don Carlos, as well as local flights to Villa O'Higgins, Cochrane and Chile Chico, take off from the Aeródromo Teniente Vidal, 5km west of town.

Airlines Aerotaxis del Sur (☎67 330726, ⊛aerotaxisdelsur .cl); LAN, Parra 402 (☎600 526 2000, ⊛lan.com); Transportes Aéreo Don Carlos, Subteniente Cruz 63 (☎67 231981); Sky

Airline, Prat 203 at Dussen (☎67 240827, ⊛skyairline.cl).
Destinations (airport) Puerto Montt (2 daily; 1hr 15min); Punta Arenas (5 weekly; 1hr 45min); Santiago (2 daily; 3hr).
Destinations (aerodrome) Chile Chico (2 weekly; 40min); Cochrane (2 weekly; 1hr); San Rafael glacier (daily in season; 2hr); Villa O'Higgins (2 weekly; 1hr 30min).

BY BUS

Most buses pull in at the central terminal on the corner of Lautaro and Magallanes, though a few arrive at, and depart from, their respective company offices. Companies are listed after the destinations they serve.

Destinations Ancud (Mon & Fri 4pm; 20–28hr; Buses Queilén ☎67 240760); Castro (Mon & Fri 4pm; 20–28hr; Buses Queilén ☎67 240760); Chaitén (Tues 8am; 12hr; Buses Becker, General Parra 335 ☎67 232167, ⓦbusesbecker .com); Cochrane via Villa Cerro Castillo, Puerto Tranquilo and Cruce El Maitén (1–2 daily, 9am & 9.30am; Don Carlos, Subteniente Cruz 63 ☎67 231981; Buses Sao Paolo ☎67 255726); Comodoro Rivadavia, Argentina (Mon & Fri, 8–9am; 9hr; Transaustral ☎67 232067); Futaleufú (Sat 8am; 12hr; Buses Becker, General Parra 335 ☎67 232167, ⓦbusesbecker.com); Lago Verde (weekly; Transportes Bronco, Monrreal 697 ☎09 9952 0907); La Junta (1–2 daily, 3pm & 4pm; Buses Becker, General Parra 335 ☎67 232167, ⓦbusesbecker.com; Buses Altamirano ☎67 314143); Osorno (Mon & Fri 4pm; 20–28hr; Buses Queilén ☎67 240760; Transaustral ☎67 232067); Puerto Aysén (every 30min 7am–8.30pm; fewer on weekends; Buses Sao Paolo ☎67 255726; Buses Syray, Prat 265 ☎67 238387); Puerto Bertrand (Buses Acuario 13 ☎67 255143; Buses Aguilas Patagonicas ☎67 211020); Puerto Cisnes (2 daily; 4hr; Buses Sao Paolo ☎67 255726; Buses Terra Austral ☎67 254335); Puerto Ibáñez (1 daily; 2hr 30min; Miguel Acuña, Moraleda at Carrera ☎67 251579; Buses Carolina ☎67 219009);

Puerto Montt (Mon & Fri 4pm; 20–28hr; Buses Queilén ☎67 240760; Transaustral ☎67 232067); Puyuhuapi (Buses Becker, General Parra 335 ☎67 232167, ⓦbusesbecker .com); Raúl Marín Balmaceda (weekly; Bus Gerardo Valenzuela ☎09 8197 8793).

BY FERRY

Navimag, Horn 47 (☎67 233306 ⓦwww.navimag.com), runs to Puerto Montt from nearby Puerto Chacabuco (see p.367) frequently during summer, less often in winter. Naviera Austral Horn 40 (☎67 210727, ⓦwww.navieraustral. cl) connects Puerto Chacabuco with Quellón via Puerto Cisnes and Raul Marín Balmaceda (see p.357, 363).

BY CAR

To make the most of the surrounding area, you may need to rent a car; reserve in advance, particularly in peak season, or else you'll be left with the most expensive options. For driving along the Carretera Austral, a 4WD is advisable but not strictly necessary (see p.351). Reputable car rental companies include Traeger, Baquedano 457 (☎67 231648, ⓦwww.traeger.cl); Hertz, General Parra 280 (☎67 245780, ⓦhertz.cl); and Varona, Ogana 799 (☎67 216674, ⓦvarona.cl).

INFORMATION AND TOURS

TOURIST INFORMATION

Conaf Los Coigües s/n (Mon–Fri 8.30am–noon & 3–5pm; ☎67 212225). For more on Aisén's national parks and reserves, visit Conaf's Oficina Patrimonio Silvestre.

Sernatur Bulnes 35 (Jan & Feb Mon–Fri 8.30am–8.30pm, Sat & Sun 11am–6pm; March–Dec Mon–Fri 8.30am–5.30pm; ☎67 270290, ⓦsernatur.cl). You can pick up an excellent glossy publication on the city and the region at this ultra-helpful Sernatur office.

TOUR OPERATORS

The adventure companies listed below are established, experienced and come highly recommended.

Andes Patagónicos Horn 48 ⓦap.cl. A good bet for arranging half-day and full-day **tours** to the nearby lakes (see p.367), to see local rock art and to Reserva Nacional Cerro Castillo (see p.370), among other destinations, as well as multi-day trips to the Northern and Southern Ice Fields.

Condor Explorer Dussen 357 ☎67 573634, ⓦcondorexplorer.com. Specializes in mountaineering excursions to the San Lorenzo Massif and Cerro Castillo, as well as the challenging 10-day Aysén Glacier Trail. Day-trips include short hikes in the area and ski treks in winter.

Geoturismo Patagonia Balmaceda 334 ☎67 573460, ⓦgeoturismopatagonia.cl. Long-standing operator offering a variety of excursions, from historical city tours of Coyhaique and horseback riding in the area to kayaking on the Río Paloma and aerial tours of Laguna San Rafael.

Salvaje Corazón ☎67 211488, ⓦsalvajecorazon.com. This recommended new operator, run out of *Patagonia House* (see p.366), offers expeditions to the Southern Icefields, trekking in the San Lorenzo Massif, photo safaris across Patagonia, fly fishing in Aysén and guided road trips along the Carretera Austral.

ACCOMMODATION

HOTELS AND B&B

Hostal Belisario Jara Francisco Bilbao 626 ☎67 234150, ⓦwww.belisariojara.cl. Run by a warm and welcoming family, this distinctively decorated, elegant B&B has airy wood-panelled en-suite rooms, each individually decorated. Though only a 5min walk from the plaza, you're far enough from the road to get a good night's sleep. CH$55,000

Hotel El Reloj Av Baquedano 828 ☎67 231108, ⓦelrelojhotel.cl. Located in a former sawmill and with a

hunting lodge ambiance, this hotel boasts spotlessly clean rooms with polished wooden floors and sloped ceilings, decorated in muted tones. Some of the rooms are a little dark, but the excellent on-site restaurant makes up for it. CH$80,000 (US$170)

⭐ **Raíces Bed and Breakfast** Av Baquedano 444 ☎67 210490, ⓦraicesbedandbreakfast.com. This B&B has some of the most attractive rooms in town – wood-panelled, full of light, decorated in whites and creams with

8

woollen accents (the owner sells high-quality knitwear). The breakfast is above par. **CH$60,000**

Residencial Monica Lillo 664 **☎** 67 234302. Friendly, family-run guesthouse with basic breakfast, frilly bedspreads and a house full of plants. En-suite private rooms are windowless. **CH$16,000**

LODGES

Coyhaique River Lodge Km10 Camino a Coyhaique Alto **☎** 67 219710, **ⓦ** coyhaiqueriverlodge.com. A short drive from the city, this new fly-fishing lodge run by two brothers sits on a 40-acre property with fabulous mountain views. Besides fishing, activities on offer include horseback riding, mountain biking, trekking, birdwatching and even traditional weaving and cooking classes, after which guests retire to one of the eight comfortable rooms or unwind on the terrace with a pisco sour. **CH$120,000 (US$250)**

★ **Patagonia House** Qunita 18 Julio **☎** 67 211488, **ⓦ** patagonia-house.com. Set on a hillside above Coyhaique, the large panoramic windows of this boutique three-storey lodge offer splendid views of the Coyhaique Valley. The four rooms make great use of natural light, Doña Rosa cooks up a gourmet's dream in the kitchen and the attention that Ruth, the owner, gives her guests is difficult to fault. **CH$58,000**

HOSTELS

Patagonia Hostel Lautaro 667 **☎** 09 6240 6974, **ⓦ** www.patagonia-hostel.com. Given that it's the only proper backpacker/cyclist hostel in town, with only 10 beds, it's little wonder this place is always booked up. The beds and bunks are large and comfortable, with a personal reading light above each one; the lounge encourages socializing and the young, energetic owners run their own tour agency and can assist with kayaking trips and more. Dorm **CH$10,000**, double **CH$26,000**

Las Salamandras Carretera Teniente Vidal, Km 1.5 **☎** 67 211865, **ⓦ** www.salamandras.cl. Set in a wood by a river 1.5km along the road to Teniente Vidal, this hostel, popular with backpackers and cyclists, offers the use of a kitchen, ample common spaces, mountain-bike rental and a range of excursions, including one to Parque Nacional Queulat and cross-country skiing trips. Camping **CH$6000**, dorm **CH$8500**, double **CH$20,000**

8 | EATING AND DRINKING

CAFÉS AND CHEAP EATS

Café Confluencia 21 de Mayo 548 **☎** 67 245080. This trendy, smoker-friendly café serves dishes as diverse as *ajis rellenos* (stuffed hot peppers), tacos and Spanish-style *tortilla*. The selection of teas and coffees is extensive and much appreciated, and the evening tipple to accompany the live weekend music includes the signature mint pisco sours. Daily 10am–11pm, Fri & Sat 10am–2am.

Café Konken Prat 340. This café is so tiny, there isn't even any room to sit down, but that doesn't stop customers from filing in for the excellent freshly ground coffee, giant smoothies and fresh fruit juices. Daily 10am–6pm.

Café Ricer Horn 48 **☎** 67 244917. Just off the plaza, this bright and cheerful café attracts a lot of gringos, partly for its vegetarian dishes, though the Chilean standards tend to be better than anything that sounds more adventurous. There's a more upscale restaurant upstairs, decorated early 1900s knick-knacks and evocative photographs of the early pioneers. Daily 10am–11.30pm.

Casino de Bomberos Parra 365 **☎** 67 244917. Slightly hidden away, Coyhaique's firemen's canteen is usually packed, lively and one of the best places in town for simple Chilean dishes, with excellent-value set meals. Daily noon–3.30pm & 7–11pm.

RESTAURANTS

Kobe Wok & Roll Lillo 557 **☎** 67 210585. The Vietnamese/Thai/Japanese menu at this cheerful new restaurant might be a bit ambitious, the masaman curry may be unlike any masaman curry you've ever tasted and the ratio between amount of sauce and amount of noodles may be off, but the staff are super-friendly and chef gets full marks for brave experimentation. Tues–Sun noon–3pm & 7–11pm.

★ **Mamma Gaucha** Horn 47 **☎** 67 244917, **ⓦ** mammagaucha.cl. At this trattoria-meets-Patagonia, efficient staff serve you wood-fired pizzas, baked Camembert with calafate berry jam, vast salads and imaginative desserts (try the blueberry *crème brulée*), all under the watchful eye of Mamma, looking down from the large black-and-white photos. The only downside is that the drinks machine that makes the signature mint lemonades sounds like an industrial drill. Daily 12.30–11.30pm.

★ **El Reloj** Av Baquedano 828 **☎** 67 244917. Given the quality of the dishes, the restaurant inside its namesake hotel provides some of the best value for your peso in town, all served in a small, sophisticated dining room by professional waiting staff. Start with a tart pisco sour, proceed to the ceviche, served with a shot of *leche de tigre* (or "tiger's milk" – the lemon juice, salt and fish juices in which the fish was marinated) and follow it up with leg of lamb with rustic mash. Daily 1–4pm & 7–11pm.

Sabores del Sur 12 de Octubre 308 **☎** 67 210801. A local favourite, *Sabores* offers an inexpensive *menú* of fresh fish and meat dishes. All the Chilean standards are well executed and service is friendly. Mon–Sat 12.30–3.30pm & 7.30–11pm, Sun 12.30–3.30pm.

BARS AND PUBS

Piel Roja Moraleda 495 **☎** 67 244917. An excellent spot for a beer and snack, this lively pub with a quirky interior serves good burgers and *quesadillas*. Strut your stuff on the dance floor of the adjacent disco or bond over a beer at the upstairs bar. Daily 6pm–4am.

Rincón Austral Sargento Aldea 128 ☎ 67 231714. This new resto-bar delights with its extensive choice of beers and mixed drinks and the food menu complements it well: choose from *tablas* (mixed platters) to share, *crudos*, carpaccio and nicely grilled steaks, among other dishes. Daily 12.30–4pm & 8pm–midnight.

DIRECTORY

Banks and exchange The following banks have ATMs: Banco Santander, Condell 184, Banco de Chile, Condell 298, and BBVA, Condell 254. *Cambios* include Turismo Prado de la Patagonia at 21 de Mayo 417 and Emperador at Freire 171.

Hospital The regional hospital is at Jorge Ibar 168 ☎ 67 219100.

Internet At the *centro de llamados* at Horn 51. Most accommodation options now offer wi-fi.

Laundry Lavandería All Clean, General Parra 55.

Outdoor equipment Condor Explorer, at Dussen 357, has a wide selection of camping, fishing and mountaineering gear, plus outdoor clothes.

Post office Cochrane 202, near Plaza de Armas.

Telephone Try the *centro de llamados* at Horn 51.

Reserva Nacional Coyhaique

5km north of Coyhaique • Daily: April–Nov 8.30am–5.30pm; Dec–March 8.30am–9pm • CH$1800 • Any bus from Coyhaique towards Puerto Aysén; to be dropped off near the entrance

About a 45-minute walk from Coyhaique, the **RESERVA NACIONAL COYHAIQUE**, huddled at the foot of towering Cerro McKay, is an easily accessible slice of wilderness, featuring areas of native forest, a couple of lakes and fantastic views down to Coyhaique and the Río Simpson valley. **Sendero Los Leñeros** leads almost 2km from the *guardería* by the entrance through native *lenga* and *ñire* trees to **Laguna Verde**.

From here, you pick up with a jeep track which, if you follow it north for a couple of hundred metres, will take you to the trailhead of **Sendero Las Piedras**, the best (and steepest) hike in the reserve, leading 13km up to and across a ridge, and giving breathtaking views for miles around; allow four hours to complete. After descending at the other end, a side path branches off to **Lago Venus**, an attractive lake 1km beyond, reached by walking through dense native forest. Alternatively, keep on going another couple of hundred metres and you'll join up with **Sendero El Chucao**, which leads 2.6km back to the *guardería*.

West of Coyhaique

From Coyhaique, a paved section of the Carretera Austral runs west towards the coast, to the former port of Puerto Aysén, 65km away – a small town you have to pass through on the way to the even more nondescript Puerto Chacabuco, the gateway to Parque Nacional Laguna San Rafael. Along the way you pass through the highly picturesque Reserva Nacional Río Simpson and pass a turn-off for the north section of the Carretera Austral.

Reserva Nacional Río Simpson

Road to Puerto Aysén, Km 37 • Daily: April–Oct 8.30am–5.30pm; Nov–March 8.30am–9pm • CH$1000 • Any bus from Coyhaique towards Puerto Aysén; ask to be dropped near the entrance

The scenic route holds fast to the Río Simpson as it rushes through the **Reserva Nacional Río Simpson**, sandwiched between tall, craggy cliffs. Thirty-seven kilometres out of Coyhaique, a small wooden sign by the road points to the reserve's Conaf office. The reserve's main attractions are conveniently located right by the road: 1km on from the Conaf office, you'll pass the **Cascada de la Virgen**, a tall, graceful waterfall that drops in two stages, separated by a pool of water with a shrine to the Virgin Mary next to it. A further 8km east thunders another waterfall, the **Velo de la Novia**, or "bride's veil", so named for its diaphanous spray.

8

Puerto Aysén

Formerly a port for shipping cattle, **Puerto Aysén** literally became a backwater when its harbour silted up, forcing commercial vessels to use nearby **Puerto Chacabuco** from 1960. Still, Puerto Aysén makes a marginally more attractive overnight base before or after a journey to the San Rafael glacier than Puerto Chacabuco (see p.368).

ARRIVAL AND DEPARTURE   PUERTO AYSÉN

By bus Buses Acuario 13 (☎67 240990) has hourly departures daily for Coyhaique, just off the main street, while Buses Suray (☎67 336231) has at least two hourly departures daily from Eusebio Ibar 630, half a block from the main Sargento Aldea, to neighbouring Puerto Chacabuco, as well as half-hourly departures to Coyhaique.

ACCOMMODATION AND EATING

Patagonia Green Bilbao 626 ☎67 336796, ⓦpatagoniagreen.cl. The best hotel in town sits amid lush gardens across the bridge and 500m to the east of Puerto Aysén. The six cheery rooms are large and comfortable, each with a small balcony. There are several satellite cabins for up to 5 people, each equipped with satellite TV and wi-fi, and the on-site restaurant serves fine takes on Chilean dishes, accompanied by an extensive wine list. Double ‾CH$54,000‾, cabin ‾CH$52,000‾

Puerto Chacabuco

Fifteen kilometres west of Puerto Aysén, the busy port of **PUERTO CHACABUCO** sits dramatically on a natural harbour enclosed by craggy, jagged peaks brushed with snow. In contrast, the road is lined with ugly fishmeal processing factories emitting a nauseating smell of fish. Your only reason for coming here would be to take a boat to the Laguna San Rafael glacier or to catch a Navimag or Naviera Austral ferry.

ARRIVAL AND DEPARTURE   PUERTO CHACABUCO

BY BUS
Buses Suray run to Puerto Aysén (every 30min daily 7.30am–8pm; CH$800).

BY FERRY
Chacabuco is the arrival and departure point for several

Naviera Austral ferries (ⓦwww.navieraustral.cl).
Destinations Laguna Puerto Montt via Puerto Cisnes and Raúl Marín Balmaceda (2–4 weekly; 24hr); Quellón (1–3 weekly; 20hr); San Rafael (ferry Dec–March 2 weekly; 16hr; catamaran several weekly in season; 5hr).

ACCOMMODATION AND EATING

Hotel Loberías del Sur JM Carrera 50 ☎67 351115, ⓦwww.catamaranesdelsur.cl. Just uphill from the port, the only upmarket option in Puerto Chacabuco looks impressive from the outside, and amenities include a gym, sauna and a good restaurant with a focus on seafood. The rooms, however, while clean, are rather tired and overpriced for what they are, though staying at the hotel does give you free access to the attractive, private 2.5 square kilometre nature reserve nearby

(ⓦwww.parqueaikendelsur.cl). ‾CH$72,000 (US$150)‾
Residencial El Puerto O'Higgins 80 ☎67 351147. The friendly proprietress is the only plus at this worn cheapie, popular with truck drivers. Rooms do not have locks (in fact, some don't even have windows that open, though they do have ashtrays) and beds are saggier than an old lady's bosom, but the place is clean and is pretty much your only budget option if you don't wish to splurge on a morning taxi from Puerto Aysén. ‾CH$8000‾

Laguna San Rafael

From Puerto Chacabuco, a 200km boat ride through the labyrinthine fjords of Aysén brings you to the dazzling San Rafael glacier, spilling into the broad Laguna San Rafael. The journey is a spectacle in itself, as boats edge their way through channels hemmed in by precipitous cliffs dripping with vegetation, passing the odd sea lion colony along the way. After sailing down the long, thin Golfo de Elefantes, the boat enters the seemingly unnavigable Río Témpanos, or "Iceberg River", before emerging into the Laguna San Rafael. Floating in the lagoon are dozens of **icebergs**, fashioned by wind

VISITING THE SAN RAFAEL GLACIER

The glacier is currently accessible *only* by boat or plane. **Flights** from Coyhaique in five-seater planes, offered by **Transportes Aéreo Don Carlos** (Subteniente Cruz 630 ❶67 232981) and **Aerotaxis del Sur** (❶67 330726, ⓦaerotaxisdelsur.cl), last ninety minutes each way and cost CH$150,000–170,000 per person, and usually require the full quota of five passengers. During high season two companies run weekly day-trips to the glacier in a high-speed **catamaran** (4 or 5hr each way): *Hotel Loberías del Sur*'s own **Catamaranes del Sur** (❶2 231 1902, ⓦwww.catamaranesdelsur.cl; CH$220,000) and **Patagonia Connection** (❶2 225 6489, ⓦpatagoniaconnex.cl); the latter's trips are combined with a two-night stay at the *Termas de* hotel *Puyuhuapi* (see p.361) and one night in Puerto Chacabuco; rates start from around US$1980/3360 for single/double occupancy.

All trips include three meals and operate an open bar – it is now a tradition to drink a whisky or cocktail containing "thousand-year-old ice cubes" chipped from an iceberg. The downside to catamaran trips is that you only get three hours or so at the glacier compared with the multi-day cruises. For a more leisurely visit, you could opt for a multi-day cruise from either Puerto Chacabuco or Castro with **Navimag** (Puerto Montt ❶65 432360; Coyhaique ❶67 233306, ⓦwww.navimag.com; cruises all year round; 5 days, 4 nights return journey from Castro from US$2700 for B-type cabin, US$3300 for AAA-type cabin), or else for the far more luxurious **Skorpios**, from Puerto Montt (Santiago ❶2 477 1900, ⓦskorpios.cl; 6-day/5-night journey from US$3150/4200 single/double occupancy; cruises Sept–April only).

and rain into monumental sculptures, with such a vibrant electric-blue colour that they appear to be lit from within.

8

San Rafael glacier

Sailing around icebergs akin to icy phantoms, you approach the giant **San Rafael glacier** at the far end of the lagoon. Over 4km wide, and rearing out of the water to a height of 70m, it really is a dizzying sight. While the cruise boat keeps at a safe distance, you'll be given the chance to get a closer look from an inflatable motor dinghy – but not too close, as the huge blocks of ice that calve off into the water with a deafening roar create dangerous waves. What you can see from the boat is in fact just the tip of the glacier's "tongue", which extends some 15km from its source.

The glacier is retreating fast, however, frequently by as much as 100m a year. Early explorers reported that in 1800 the glacier filled three-quarters of the lagoon, and archive photographs from the beginning of the twentieth century show it as being far longer than it is today. It is estimated that by the year 2030, the glacier will be gone.

Parque Nacional Laguna San Rafael

CH$6000, payable only if you land

Almost half of the 4.2 million-acre **Parque Nacional Laguna San Rafael** is covered by the immense ice field known as the **Campo de Hielo Norte**; it feeds eighteen other glaciers on top of the San Rafael Glacier and contains over 250 lakes and lagoons. The 4058-metre **Monte San Valentín**, the highest peak in the southern Andes, towers over the frozen plateau. A handful of visitors who opt to fly over the glacier touch down here with barely enough time to take the 7km trail from the Conaf *guardería* to a breathtaking viewpoint platform over the sprawling, icy tongue (allow around 2hr up and slightly less coming down).

| ARRIVAL AND DEPARTURE | PARQUE NACIONAL LAGUNA SAN RAFAEL |

By plane Coyhaique-based Aerotaxis del Sur and Transportes Aéreo Don Carlos offer charter flights in 5-seater planes (see box, p.369).

Reserva Nacional Cerro Castillo

57km south of Coyhaique along the Carretera Austral • April–Nov 8.30am–5.30pm; Dec–March 8.30am–9pm; CH$1500 • Take any southbound bus from Coyhaique

About an hour's drive south of Coyhaique, the Carretera Austral crosses the (un-signed) northern boundary of the **RESERVA NACIONAL CERRO CASTILLO**, a 445,000-acre protected area that's home to the elusive *huermúl* deer. Spread out below you is a broad river valley flanked by densely forested lower slopes that rise to a breathtaking panorama of barren, rocky peaks. Dominating the skyline is the reserve's eponymous centrepiece, **Cerro Castillo**, whose needlepoint spires loom over the valley like the turrets of a Transylvanian castle. Further down the road, by Laguna Chaguay, you pass the *guardería* on your left, which has a basic **camping** area (see p.370). Just south of Reserva Nacional Cerro Castillo, Villa Cerro Castillo (see p.372) is the ending/starting point for the **Sendero Cerro Castillo.**

Sendero Cerro Castillo

57km south of Coyhaique along the Carretera Austral • CH$1500 • Take any southbound bus from Coyhaique

Part of the Sendero de Chile, the rewarding 40km Sendero Cerro Castillo, which takes about three days to complete, starts at Km75, branches right (west) from the road 6km south of the *guardería*, and follows the Río La Lima upstream to a 1450m pass on the east side of Cerro Castillo (2300m) through *coigüe* and *ñire* forest. On the way, you pass the stunning **Laguna Cerro Castillo**, at the foot of a glacier suspended from the mountainside, before descending to the village of **Villa Cerro Castillo** (see p.372). Note that the trail is very poorly marked; you should buy an IGM map in advance in Coyhaique and get more detailed route advice from Conaf, whose staff should be informed before you set off. It may be easier to start at the Villa Cerro Castillo trailhead and hike the trail in reverse order.

ACCOMMODATION	RESERVA NACIONAL CERRO CASTILLO
Camping Laguna Chaguay This Conaf-maintained campsite at the start of the Sendero Cerro Castillo (with six other basic campsites spaced out along the trail) has	basic sites and access to hot showers. Camping CH$4000 per person

Around Lago General Carrera

Just beyond the southern boundary of **Reserva Nacional Cerro Castillo**, a 31km side road shoots southeast from the Carretera Austral to the tiny village of **Puerto Ibáñez**, on the northern shore of **Lago General Carrera**. This lake, encircled by rocky, sharp-peaked mountains, is the second largest in South America, and stretches east into Argentina. Regular ferries connect Puerto Ibáñez with the sunny, cherry-growing town of **Chile Chico**, on the opposite shore, making this an attractive alternative to following the Carretera Austral around the lake. From Chile Chico, a 128km road skirts the lake's southern shore, joining the Carretera just beyond the village of **Puerto Guadal.**

Puerto Ibáñez

Sitting in a green, fertile plain, divided up by rows of soldier-like poplars, in sharp contrast with the barren hills around it, **PUERTO IBÁÑEZ** is a shrinking village. Once an important port, connecting Coyhaique with Chile Chico and the remote *estancias* on the Lago General Carrera's southern shore, it fell into decline with the construction of the Carretera Austral bypass.

Chile Chico

Sitting on the southern shore of Lago General Carrera, the small agricultural town of **CHILE CHICO** is a sunny place with an attractive Plaza de Armas, lined with apricot trees and pines, and is famous for its fruit festival at the end of January, as well as Chile's best cherries. The town was settled by farmers who crossed over from Argentina in 1909, causing a conflict known as the "Chile Chico war" when they refused to hand over land to the concessionaires given grants by the government. The new settlement depended entirely on Argentina until a road was built between Coyhaique and Puerto Ibáñez in 1952, after which Chile Chico's orchards became Coyhaique's main source of fresh fruit. You get a great view of the town and the lake from the hill viewpoint opposite the dock, and Chile Chico makes a good base for the exploration of the **Reserva Nacional Jeinemeni.**

Reserva Nacional Jeinemeni

52km southwest of Chile Chico • CH$1500 • Accessible by 4WD only

This seldom-visited nature reserve covers a vast area of 1610 square kilometres and is home to guanaco, vizcacha (a cross between a bunny and a squirrel), the puma and a smaller forest cat, among others. There are several trails here: a 6km steep uphill hike to the Cueva de los Manos – a cave with Theuelche cave paintings; the Sendero Escorial del Silencio, an ascent of 1650m passing five viewpoints along the way with sweeping views of the park; the two-day Sendero La Leona, which connects the park to Valle Chacabuco; and, for a view of hanging glaciers, the Sendero Estero Ventisqueros (30km return). Trips to the park are run by Expeditions Patagonia, O'Higgins 416 (☎09 9968 5768, ⊛expeditionspatagonia.com).

Villa Cerro Castillo

Looping around Lago General Carrera along the Carretera Austral offers spectacular panoramas of the grey-and-pink mountains west of the road, plus a few glimpses of the Campo de Hielo Norte (see p.375). Nine kilometres on from the turn-off to Puerto Ibáñez, you pass **Villa Cerro Castillo**, a rather bleak pioneer settlement whose sole draw is the rugged hiking around Cerro Castillo (see p.370).

Monumento Nacional Manos de Cerro Castillo

Dec–April only • CH$1000

Just across the bridge outside the town, a signed 2km track leads steeply uphill to **Monumento Nacional Manos de Cerro Castillo**, a dense collection of over one hundred handprints, in three separate panels and some belonging to children, at the foot of a sheer basalt rock face. The images, mostly negative prints against a red background, are thought to have been left by the Tehuelche people between five thousand and eight thousand years ago.

Puerto Río Tranquilo

Some 25km south of the turn for Puerto Murta, a tiny cattle-farming community, you'll reach **Puerto Río Tranquilo**, a picturesque lakeside hamlet with basic services. A number of operators run boat trips across the lake to **Capilla de Mármol** ("Marble Chapel"), an impressive limestone cliff looming out of the water, streaked with blue-and-white patterns and gashed with caves which can be entered by boat. Try *Excursiones Maran-Atha* (☎66 479614 or 09 8752 0735; CH$25,000); ask for Lenin.

Cruce El Maitén

Thirty-five kilometres south of Puerto Tranquilo lies the outlet of **Lago General Carrera**, which drains into the adjacent Lago Bertrand. Shortly afterwards, you'll reach **Cruce El Maitén**, a fork in the road; the left road leads northeast along the southern edge of Lago General Carrera to Puerto Guadal, a picturesque little village with an excellent stretch of beach.

Puerto Bertrand

Twenty-five kilometres south of Cruce El Maitén you arrive at the charming little village of **Puerto Bertrand**, sitting near the head of the turquoise Río Baker. Patagonia Adventure Expeditions (☎09 8182 0608, ⓦadventurepatagonia.com) offers multi-day trekking, fishing, horseriding and kayaking trips in the pristine wilderness around the village.

ARRIVAL AND DEPARTURE

PUERTO IBÁÑEZ

BY BUS

Miguel Acuña, Moraleda at Carrera (☎67 251579) and Buses Carolina (☎67 219009) run minibuses to Puerto Ibañez from Coyhaique, timed to coincide with the arrival and departure of the ferry to Chile Chico. Book in advance to be picked up from your place of residence.

BY FERRY

The *El Pilchero* ferry to Chile Chico is operated by Mar del Sur, Coyhaique (☎67 231255). The ferry sails five times weekly (the schedule is subject to change, so it's best to call them in advance; 2hr 30min; passengers CH$5500, vehicles CH$28,000). Check times well ahead; reservations are a must. Be prepared for a rough ride as strong winds often whip up large waves.

CHILE CHICO

BY BUS

Buses Ale, Rosa Amelia 880 (☎09 9085 2550), run to Cochrane (7hr) via Puerto Guadál, Cruce El Maitén and Puerto Bertrand (Wed & Sat 1pm, returning Thurs & Sun 10am), and to Puerto Tranquílo (Tues & Fri 1pm, returning Wed and Sat 10am). There are up to 5 minibus departures daily to Los Antiguos, across the Argentine border

AROUND LAGO GENERAL CARRERA

(CH$4000), with onward connections to destinations along the Ruta 40; most bus services leave from in front of the Via Entel call centre at O'Higgins 426.

BY FERRY

Mar del Sur on the pier in Chile Chico (☎67 411864) runs ferry services across the lake to Puerto Ibañez (Mon 8am, Tues 3pm, Thurs 1pm, Fri 3pm & Sun noon; 2hr 30min; passengers CH$4000, vehicles CH$24,000). Check times well ahead because they are subject to change; reservations are a must. When buying your ticket in Chile Chico it's a good idea to buy an onward minibus ticket to Coyhaique (CH$5000).

BY PLANE

There are charter flights to Coyhaique (CH$36,000) with Transportes Aeréo Don Carlos at O'Higgins 265 (☎67 411490).

VILLA CERRO CASTILLO

BY BUS

Buses Miguel Acuña and Buses Carolina travelling between Coyhaique and Puerto Ibáñez, and Buses ALE running between Coyhaique and Cochrane, all stop next to La Cocina de Sole along the main street of Villa Cerro Castillo, amounting to at least two departures daily each way.

INFORMATION

Chile Chico O'Higgins, at the corner of Lautaro (Mon– Fri 9am–5pm; ☎67 411123, ⓦchilechico.cl). You can pick up a town map at the Oficina de Turismo on the main street.

ACCOMMODATION AND EATING

CHILE CHICO

Casa Quinta No Me Olvides Camino Internacional Chacra 3-A ☎09 8833 8006. Popular with backpackers, with seven basic, good-value rooms and space to camp in the large orchard. Camping CH$3500 per person, double CH$16,000
Café Loly y Elizabeth González 25 ☎09 9085 5091. Facing the plaza, and serving basic meat and fish dishes, as well as *empanadas*, this is the only place open on Sun. Daily 12.30–3.30pm & 7–10.30pm.

Hostería de la Patagonia Camino Internacional Chacra 3-A ☎67 411337, ⓔhdelapatagonia @gmail.com. A charming, Belgian–Chilean-owned house with comfortable en-suite rooms, a boat converted into lodging for up to five people, good home-cooked food and outdoor excursions on offer, tucked away in a large garden on the eastern edge of town. Double CH$24,000, boat CH$45,000

8

AROUND CRUCE EL MAITÉN AND PUERTO GUADÁL

★ **Un Destino No Turistico** Camino Laguna La Manga, Km1 ☏09 8756 7545, ⊛destino-noturistico .com. Sustainability is the watchword at this eco-hostel and campsite: these guys recycle and reuse anything they can and grow their own organic food. There's a sun cooker in the guest kitchen and even the shower runs on solar power. Even if you're not staying here, they're happy to show you their energy-saving techniques (CH$3500). Camping CH$4500 per person, dorm CH$9000, double CH$22,000
Terra Luna Lodge Camino a Chile Chico, Km 1.5 ☏67 431263, ⊛terra-luna.cl. Two kilometres along the road to Puerto Guadal, this lodge specializes in multi-activity programmes which couple kayaking, trekking, cross country skiing and mountaineering with relaxation in the on-site outdoor hot tubs and sauna. You can stay in either one of the lodge's comfortable doubles, a fully equipped cabin or a more basic *refugio*. Refugio CH$35,000 per person, double CH$60,000, cabin CH$77,000

PUERTO BERTRAND

Green Baker Lodge Camino a Cochrane, Km 3 ☏2 196 0409, ⊛greenlodgebaker.com. This attractive wooden lodge on the bank of Río Baker caters primarily to anglers with seven comfortable *cabañas* and a mini-hotel. Non-fishing guests can enjoy horseback riding, rafting on the Río Baker and ice trekking, among other adventures. Double CH$55,000, *cabañas* CH$45,000
★ **Hacienda Tres Lagos** Km 274 ☏67 411323, ⊛haciendatreslagos.com. In an idyllic location on the banks of Lago Negro, this hacienda boasts sumptuous, modern rooms with plenty of light, iPod docks, satellite TV, wi-fi and a restaurant serving gourmet takes on Patagonian cuisine. Trilingual guides lead kayaking, trekking, horseback riding and fly fishing excursions and relaxation options include outdoor hot tubs and Jacuzzi at the lakeside spa and telescopes for stargazing. Double CH$149,000 (US$312)

PUERTO TRANQUILO

Campo Alacalúf Valle Exploradores ☏67 234150, ⊛campoalacaluf.com. In the nearby Valle Exploradores, along a very basic dirt road leading towards Parque Nacional Laguna San Rafael, this secluded, German-owned rustic house offers a handful of rooms and home-cooked meals. Camping CH$4000 per person, double CH$28,000
Hostal El Puesto Lagos 258 ☏2 196 4555, ⊛elpuesto.cl. Specializing in multi-activity itineraries which include hiking on the San Valentín glacier and kayaking to the Capillas de Mármol, this boutique lodging option consists of three beautiful, light en-suite rooms with crisp linens and two fully equipped cabins, for 5 and 8 people, respectively. Double CH$65,000, cabin CH$55,000

VILLA CERRO CASTILLO

La Cocina De Sole Carretera Austral ☏09 8726 7082. Just by the main road passing through the settlement, this diner consists of two buses fused together, with owner Soledad cooking up great burgers and other simple, satisfying dishes. Daily noon–8pm.
Residencial La Querencia O'Higgins 460 ☏09 9503 0746. Rather basic guesthouse with spic-and-span rooms which are not terribly well lit. Attached restaurant serves good Chilean standards. CH$15,000

DIRECTORY

CHILE CHICO
Banks and exchange There is a single ATM at Banco Estado at O'Higgins and Baquedano; it only accepts MasterCard.

Internet Internet cafés and call centres are found along O'Higgins.

South of Lago General Carrera

South of the great lake, a gravel road winds its way along the river towards **Cochrane**, the last settlement of any size and the gateway to the **Reserva Nacional Tamango**. Beyond Cochrane, the road snakes its way through a dense carpet of evergreens and giant *nalca*. After just over 100km south, you come to the embarcadero de Río Vagabundo, the launching spot for boats to the tiny, remote hamlet of **Caleta Tortel**, also reachable by the gravel road that forks west from the Carretera. Further south, at Puerto Yungay, a car ferry crosses Fiordo Mitchell and a precarious road leads to the Carretera's final stop – tiny **Villa O'Higgins.**

Cochrane

The last major stop on the Carretera Austral, the ranching settlement of **COCHRANE** lies 50km south of Puerto Bertrand. The town's paved, orderly grid of streets spreading out from the neat Plaza de Armas, and array of limited services, make this a prime spot to rest up after the wildness of the Carretera Austral.

ARRIVAL AND DEPARTURE

COCHRANE

By bus There is no central bus terminal, but buses depart from the northwest corner of the Plaza. Buses Acuario 13 (☎67 522143) runs to Villa O'Higgins (Thurs & Sun 9am; 6–7hr; CH$12,000) and Tortel (Tues 5pm; 3hr). Buses Aldea (☎8 180 1962) also runs to Tortel (Tues, Thurs, Fri & Sun 9.30am; 3hr; CH$6000), while Buses ALE (☎67 522242) serves Chile Chico via Puerto Bertrand and Puerto Guadal (Thurs & Sun 10am; 6hr; CH$13,000). Buses Don Carlos (☎67 522150) and Buses Sao Paolo (☎67 522143) run services to Coyhaique (1–2 daily except Sun 8.30/9am; 7hr; CH$13,000).

INFORMATION AND TOURS

TOURIST INFORMATION

Tourist information Plaza de Armas (Mon–Sat 9am–1pm & 2.30–8pm; ⓦwww.cochranepatagonia.cl). You'll find a helpful information kiosk on the plaza during the summer months.

Conaf Río Nef 417 (Mon–Fri 10am–5pm; ☎67 522164). This is a good place for information on the nearby Reserva Nacional Tamango and it may also be possible to arrange guided walks in the reserve.

TOUR OPERATORS

Patagonia Adventure Expeditions ☎67 411330, ⓦadventurepatagonia.com. This Cochrane-based operator does multi-day expeditions to seldom-visited destinations such as the "Ice to Ocean", an eleven-day trip that involves hiking, rafting and horseback riding, as well as shorter rafting trips on the Río Simpson, Río Paloma or Río Mañihuales, and also horse trekking.

ACCOMMODATION

Hotel Ultimo Paraíso Lago Brown 455 ☎67 522361, ⓦhotelultimoparaiso.cl. As close as you get to paradise in Cochrane, this bungalow is split into six spacious wood-panelled rooms with wood-burning stoves and cable TV. Breakfast is included and in summer there's a restaurant for guests only. **CH$60,000**

Latitud 47 Sur Lago Brown 564 ☎08 829 0956, ⓔlatitud47sur_patagonia@hottmail.com. The rooms with private bathrooms inside this hunter's house,

decorated with antlers and other assorted paraphernalia, boast the best power showers in Aisén, as well as fridges and microwaves, while the cheaper ones with shared facilities are more modest. **CH$20,000**

Residencial Sur Austral Prat 334 ☎67 522150. Overseen by the friendly proprietress, the 17 rooms inside this large house all have cable TV and heating, and there's a fully equipped *cabaña* for you and five of your closest friends. Double **CH$25,000**, *cabaña* **CH$45,000**

EATING AND DRINKING

Ada's Café Restaurant Teniente Merino 374 ☎09 8399 5889. Cochrane's big splurge, this family run restaurant really delivers when it comes to perfectly cooked steaks and standard fish dishes. Mains from CH$5500. Daily 7–11pm.

Café Tamango Esmeralda 464 ☎09 9158 4521. Just off the main square, this light and bright café dishes up hearty

burgers, more-ish crêpes with sweet fillings and even fresh fruit juice. Mon–Sat 9am–8.30pm.

Nacionpatagonia Steffens at Las Golondrinas. Adorable little café with hospitable owners serving real coffee – a rarity in Chile! – as well as sandwiches and delicious home-made cakes. Daily 10am–11pm.

DIRECTORY

Banks and exchange There's a Banco Estado on the Plaza which doesn't accept Visa cards (and some foreign

cards in general), so bring plenty of cash.
Internet There's an internet café along Colonia.

Reserva Nacional Tamango

CH$4000; possible to arrange guided walks for around CH$50,000 for up to six people with the Conaf office in Cochrane (see p.376)

Reserva Nacional Tamango, 6km east of town, sits on the banks of **Lago Cochrane**, a skinny, twisting lake that straddles the Argentine border. The eight rewarding trails from the entrance vary in difficulty and range from 40 minutes to five hours; the best lead to Laguna Tamanguito, Laguna Elefantina and up Cerro Tamango (1,722m) for excellent views of Campo de Hielo Norte to the west and the nearby lakes; bring windproof clothing. The reserve is notable for its population of around eighty *huermúl* (native deer); if you're lucky, you may spot one, particularly along the Sendero Los

---

ESTANCIA VALLE CHACABUCO

Cochrane is an ideal base for those wanting to visit and volunteer for the ambitious conservation project **Estancia Valle Chacabuco** (🌐 conservacionpatagonica.org), a 173,000-acre plot of land purchased by Kristine Tompkins (see box, p.353) in 2004 through the non-profit foundation Conservación Patagónica. The aim is to restore the heavily damaged grasslands and wetlands in Valle Chacabuco, just east of the Carretera Austral, home to diverse fauna such as the endangered *huemúl*, as well as guanacos and the four-eyed Patagonian frog, and turn it into a national park.

Conservación Patagónica welcomes applications from **volunteers** able to commit for at least three weeks; the work involves land restoration, such as dismantling wire fences, and the project takes place between October and May. The first campsite of the future national park, **Los Alamos**, opened in late 2011; it's located several kilometres away from the park headquarters, near the park entrance, and has hot showers and cooking shelters (CH$5000 per person). Those wanting greater comfort can stay at the beautiful stone eco-lodge, built from local materials and featuring handcrafted wooden furniture and excellent local cuisine; there is no set price: instead, you make a donation to the foundation.

Huemules from the ranger station to Refugio El Húngaro (5km; 2hr). It's possible to walk to the park entrance from Cochrane by taking Pasaje 1 north and then east from San Valentín and Colonia.

Caleta Tortel

Visitors fall in love with Tortel as soon as they see this scattering of houses on forested slopes surrounding a pale emerald bay. Located at the mouth of the Río Baker between the northern and southern ice fields and a logging spot for a lumber company, Tortel soon grew into a scattered settlement of quaint wooden houses, each with its own jetty and linked by a network of walkways and bridges made of fragrant cypress (slippery when wet). There are no streets here, and even the fire engine is a boat. Tortel is in some ways more isolated than the rest of the settlements along the Carretera Austral; there is only one direct phone line to the municipality, with extensions to everywhere else, though landlines are coming soon.

Isla de los Muertos

Put on the map when Britain's Prince William worked on an Operation Raleigh project here before going to university, Tortel is also renowned for a mysterious incident (see box, below) that gave its name to a nearby island, the **Isla de los Muertos**. You can visit this morbid but beautifully unspoiled place on a forty-minute boat-trip from Tortel (CH$50,000 for up to six passengers).

Glaciers around Caleta Tortel

Also within easy reach by boat are two glaciers: Ventisquero Steffens, which originates in the northern ice field (3hr north by boat; speedboat CH$220,000; *lancha* CH$250,000), and Ventisquero Jorge Montt, an enormous bluish ice-wall that comes from the southern ice field (5hr by *lancha*; CH$280,000; 2hr by motorboat; CH$250,000), best done in a group, as the trip is charged per vessel.

DEATH IN THE FOREST

Caleta Tortel's nearby island assumed its grisly moniker after dozens of employees involved in a timber-felling scheme a century ago, suddenly died in **unexplained circumstances**. Officially the cause was an epidemic of some kind, possibly scurvy, but rumours suggested they were poisoned, maybe deliberately so that the company didn't have to pay their wages.

ARRIVAL AND INFORMATION

By bus Buses stop in the car park in Rincón Alto, the upper section of the village, next to the tourist kiosk. Bus Aldea (☎8 180 1962) runs from Caleta Tortel to Cochrane (Tues, Thurs, Fri & Sun 3pm; 3hr; CH$6000), while Buses Acuario 13 (☎67 522143) makes the same journey (Wed 4pm). Services to Villa O'Higgins consist of a weekly minibus (Sun; Jan & Feb only) operated by El Mosco (see p.378) and three weekly buses (Tues, Fri & Sun; 3hr 30min) operated by Robinson Crusoe (see p.378).

CALETA TORTEL

Tourist information In the car park at the upper entrance to the village (daily 10am–6pm in peak season). A very helpful tourist information kiosk with detailed brochures on Tortel and the Carretera Austral. Also, check out ⦿ tortelturismo.blogspot.com.

Tour operators Enquire at the Municipality about boats to Isla Los Muertos, Ventisquero Steffens and Ventisquero Jorge Montt.

ACCOMMODATION AND EATING

Tortel is divided into three sections: Rincón Alto, Rincón Bajo and Rincón Base, as well as Playa Ancha, with a free camping ground with no facilities. To book accommodation, call the municipality (☎67 211876) or the public phone (☎67 234815) and cite the radio phone number for each lodging option.

Hospedaje Brisas Del Sur Sectór Playa Ancha ☎171. Fourteen sparkling, simple rooms with shared bathrooms, colourful bedspreads and sea views, presided over by hospitable Señora Landeros. Meals available on request. CH$20,000

Hospedaje Hielo Sur Sectór Rincón Bajo s/n ☎161. Wood-shingled guesthouse run by friendly Señora Ortega;

compact rooms share facilities and home-cooked meals available on request. Boat trips can be arranged. CH$20,000

Lodge Entre Hielos Sectór Rincón Bejo s/n ☎2 196 0271, ⦿ entrehielostortel.cl. Beautiful wooden lodge uphill from the boardwalk, decorated in neutral tones with pleasing woollen detail in the six plush rooms. The restaurant serves fine Patagonian cuisine with emphasis on local ingredients and staff organize boat trips and glacier hikes. CH$67,000

★ **Sabores Locales** Sectór Rincón Bajo. The indomitable Martiza cooks up large portions of ultra-fresh fish dishes and is a great source of local info. There are plans to open a hostel, too. Mon–Sat noon–3.30pm & 7–10pm, Sun noon–3.30pm.

DIRECTORY

Banks and exchange There are no banks or ATMs, so you have to bring plenty of cash.

Internet There is internet inside the library in Sector Base, near the municipality.

Puerto Yungay

Jan & Feb 3 ferries south daily 10am, noon & 6pm; March–Dec 2 ferries daily each way; return trips one hour later; double-check timetable locally; 45min • Free

Villa O'Higgins is reached via the very final – and particularly spectacular – 100km stretch of the Carretera beyond the small military camp of Puerto Yungay, 20km beyond the turn-off to Caleta Tortel, where you must cross the Fiordo Mitchell via ferry. If driving, confirm departure times in Cochrane and arrive early to guarantee a space. Here the Carretera Austral narrows to a single lane, ribboning its way around hairpin bends as the terrain becomes even hillier, with sheer drops on the side of the track revealing spectacular vistas of glacial rivers cutting through endless forest, and distant mountains shrouded in mist.

Villa O'Higgins and around

Tiny **VILLA O'HIGGINS** was built on a simple grid, with the Carretera Austral running along the western side all the way down to the Bahía Bahamondez on the enormous glacial **Lago O'Higgins**, 7km away.

Most of the earliest settlers – who came at the beginning of the twentieth century, when it was most easily accessible from Argentina – were British. The first Chilean settlers did not arrive until the 1920s, and the town wasn't officially founded and given its present name until 1966. Until 1999, this cluster of wooden houses huddled against a sheer mountain face was reachable only by a small prop plane from Coyhaique or by boat from Argentina but is now on the verge of being connected to Argentina's Ruta

40, which will make travel between the two countries considerably easier if you have your own vehicle. Cosmopolitan Villa O'Higgins is not, but it is a triumphant finishing point for cyclists "doing" the Carretera Austral, as well as a springboard for reaching some of the area's more remote glaciers.

ARRIVAL AND DEPARTURE
VILLA O'HIGGINS

By bus Buses Acuario 13 (☎ 67 522143), leaving from the small Supermercado San Gabriel on Calle Lago O'Higgins (buy your ticket in advance in the supermarket), runs to Cochrane (Mon & Fri 8am; 7hr; CH$12,000), arriving in O'Higgins the day before. In Jan and Feb, the owner of the hostel *El Mosco* hostel (see below) runs weekly transfers to Tortel (Sun 4pm), while Robinson Crusoe (see below) also makes the journey three times weekly (Tues, Fri & Sun 8am; CH$15,000).

By plane Transportes Aéreos Don Carlos (☎ 67 231981) operates a twice-weekly flight between Cochrane and Villa O'Higgins (Mon & Thurs; 1hr 15 min; CH$36,000 one way).

INFORMATION AND TOURS

TOURIST INFORMATION
Tourist information On the plaza (summer only; Mon–Fri 9am–5pm; ⓦ villaohiggins.com). The staff at the small tourist office are very helpful and provide plenty of information on the town and all its surrounding area.

TOUR OPERATORS
Hielo Sur On a nameless side street off the west end of Calle Mosco ☎ 67 431821, ⓦ www.hielosur.com. Hans Silva has up-to-date timetables for the Lago O'Higgins crossing and organizes boat trips to the Ventisquero O'Higgins (see p.379) and Ventisquero Chico (CH$35,000), as well as single and multi-day hikes and horseback riding excursions.

ACCOMMODATION

For a village of around five hundred people, there are quite a few accommodation options, most of which consist of basic, family-run guesthouses. There are also several campsites with basic facilities, popular with cyclists. Food options are limited to three small grocery stores and a couple of restaurants, though most lodgings serve meals on request.

Camping Los Ñires Hernan Merino s/n ☎ 67 431811, ⓔ campinglosnires@gmail.com. The pick of the village's campsites, this one is spacious and tree-lined with a cooking hut for campers and hot showers, though the ground can be muddy. CH$3000 per person.

Hospedaje Patagonia Río Pascua 191 ☎ 61 431818. Friendly, family-run guesthouse just off the Plaza with simple but clean rooms and shared facilities. The lady of the house is happy to provide home-cooked meals, which are not terribly memorable but perfectly adequate. CH$16,000

El Mosco Carretera Austral Km 1240 ☎ 67 431819, ⓦ patagoniaelmosco.com. The town's only hostel is well-geared towards backpackers; campers can use the hot showers, cosy common room and kitchen; the dorms are spacious; and there are doubles upstairs for those wishing to splurge. José the Spaniard is a one-man show who runs a minibus to meet the boats (see p.379) and runs transfers to Tortel in summer. Breakfast CH$3000 extra. Camping CH$5000 per person, dorm CH$8000, double CH$28,000

★ **Robinson Crusoe Patagonia Lodge** Carretera Austral Km 1240 ☎ 67 431821, ⓦ robinsoncrusoe.com. The only high end option, this beautiful wooden lodge is distinguished by its 12 spacious, light-filled, centrally heated rooms, a high-ceilinged lounge and an attic full of books and maps of the area. Buffet breakfast is included, the outdoor hot tubs are great for a post-hike soak and there's glacier ice for your cocktails on excursion days to the glacier. CH$119,000 (US$215)

EATING

Restaurante Entre Patagones Carretera Austral 1 ☎ 67 431810, ⓦ entrepatagones.cl. The large dining hall fills up nightly with locals and travellers; food varies from the likes of noodle soup and spaghetti bolognese to Patagonian favourites such as *asador patagónico* (spit-roasted lamb) and hearty *cazuela* (stew). Mon–Sat 7.30–11pm, Sun 1–3.30pm.

DIRECTORY

Banks and exchange Since there are no banks or ATMs, you'll have to bring plenty of cash with you. If you've just crossed the border from Argentina and have a surplus of Argentine pesos but no Chilean currency, you can change a limited amount of cash on the *Quetru* boat (see p.379); also, Jorge from *El Mosco* acts as an unofficial money-changer.
Internet The library, on the east side of the plaza, has several computers with internet connections. Villa O'Higgins is now covered with a free wi-fi network, but connections tend to be slow.

ARGENTINA THE HARD WAY: THE EL CHALTÉN CROSSING

The crossing between Villa O'Higgins and Argentina's El Chaltén is still remote and challenging, yet more and more hardy travellers are prepared to take the boat, followed by a strenuous hike over the border and then another lake crossing. The sixty-passenger *Quetru*, connected to Villa O'Higgins by a private minibus run by the owner of *El Mosco* (CH$2000), leaves Bahía Bahamóndez at 8.30am (Jan & Feb Mon, Wed & Sat; Dec Wed & Sat; Nov & March Sat only; CH$40,000) and arrives at the hamlet of **Candelario Mancilla** at around 11am. Just beyond the dock a signposted dirt track leads uphill from the main dirt road to the only accommodation option – a **campsite** with no facilities apart from drinking water obtained from a stream and two or three basic rooms available in the owner's house (CH$6000 per room). Get your passport stamped by **Chilean border control** further up the main road before you set off for Argentina.

TO THE BORDER

Beyond, a gravel road winds uphill through patches of woodland to the international border; on the way, you will have to ford the shallow, glacial **Río Obstáculo**. Beyond the border, marked by signs welcoming you into Chile and Argentina, the 7.5km stretch of trail to the **Argentine Gendarmería** (no set hours) on the banks of the **Lago del Desierto** becomes a narrow, muddy footpath snaking its way through hilly forest and scrubland; cyclists have to push and sometimes carry their bikes. After getting stamped into Argentina, you can either pitch a tent at *Camping Lago del Desierto* (CH$2500), stay in the basic **cabaña** run by the gendarmes, catch the motor launch *Viedma* across the lake (daily 1.30pm, 4.45pm & 6.30pm; 30–45min; CH$10,000, bicycles CH$5000 extra) or hike the remaining 15km (5–7hr) along a steep, thickly forested path on the left side of the lake, emerging at the *guardería* by the pier on the south side.

Minibuses to **El Chaltén** meet the arriving motor launches, the last one leaving for town at 7.45pm (CH$5000). While it is possible to complete the border crossing in a day, particularly if coming the other way from El Chaltén to Villa O'Higgins (since the last part of the hike is all downhill), boat schedules are weather-dependent, so you must pack enough food for several days. To book a guide and packhorses (CH$20,000 per packhorse), visit ⓦ villaohiggins.com. Rumours abound that there are plans to build a road on the Argentinian side to connect it to the border, perhaps as early as 2013, so the time to do the crossing is now.

Glaciers around Villa O'Higgins

A footpath from Calle Lago Cisnes runs through Parque Cerro Santiago up to a *mirador* that offers an excellent view of the village; from here, the path continues on towards the ice "tongue" of the **Ventisquero Mosco**, the nearest hanging glacier, though the trail is sometimes impassable. Several glaciers, including Ventisquero O'Higgins, spill into Lago O'Higgins from the massive Campo de Hielo Sur – a titanic ice cap that blocks any further progress southwards for the Carretera. These can be visited by boat.

From here, in the spring and summer months (November–March), a cross-lake ferry travels to the Argentine side, from where it's possible to walk to Argentina's El Chaltén along a route that's become very popular with intrepid hikers and particularly with bikers (see box, above). The boat crosses over to the hamlet of Candelario Mansilla – the starting point for the rewarding 7km Sendero de Chile hike that climbs steeply through *lenga* forest to the Dos Lagunas pass, where you get sweeping views of the O'Higgins, Chico and Pirámide glaciers, before descending to the *refugio* by Lago O'Higgins' Brazo Sur. You can arrange to be picked up here by the boat that runs tours to the glaciers.

8

Southern Patagonia

385 Chilean Patagonia

408 Into Argentina: Parque Nacional Los Glaciares

GAUCHOS, PARQUE NACIONAL TORRES DEL PAINE

9

Southern Patagonia

Patagonia lies tucked away right at the southernmost tip of the Americas – indeed of the world's landmass, not counting Antarctica. While the very name holds a fascination for many travellers, the reality can be harsh: the place is cursed by a persistent wind, the *Escoba de Dios* (God's Broom); trees grow horizontally here, sculpted by the gales; winters are long and summers short. Geographically ill-defined, "Patagonia" usually refers to the narrow triangle of land south of a line between Puerto Montt, in Chile, and Argentina's Península Valdés, while in Chile the term is usually reserved for **SOUTHERN PATAGONIA**, where the Andes take a last, dramatic breath before plunging into the ocean.

While much of Argentine Patagonia is flat rolling **pampa**, the land rises in the western sliver of land shared by both countries; it is said that people on both sides of the border think of themselves as Patagonians first, and Chileans or Argentinians second, united by a common ranching culture that has long been in decline. These days, large numbers of Chileans and non-Chilean visitors alike come to Patagonia not to farm but to hike – in the country's most famous and stunning national park, **Parque Nacional Torres del Paine**, a massif crowned with otherworldly granite towers, and accessed from the superbly located gateway town of **Puerto Natales.** Others come to follow in the footsteps of the region's famous travellers: navigator Ferdinand Magellan, naturalist Charles Darwin and author Bruce Chatwin; to gaze at the region's many spectacular **glaciers**; or to visit the **penguin colonies** from the lively provincial capital of **Punta Arenas** – a port city sitting on the shore of the stormy Magellan Strait.

Since the whole of this region is physically cut off from the rest of Chile by two vast ice caps, the only links with territory to the north are by air, water or through **Argentina**. The last option allows you to visit some of the latter's finest landscapes, including the **Parque Nacional Los Glaciares**, where the **Fitz Roy Massif**, near the tiny town of El Chaltén, offers incredible hiking and climbing opportunities, while **Glaciar Perito Moreno**, accessible from the tourist hub of El Calafate, is visually arresting, not to mention the most accessible of all South American glaciers.

Brief history

Chilean Patagonia, the site of the some of the continent's oldest human habitation, was originally populated by Tehuelche hunter-gatherers, who stalked roaming guanacos in the interior, and the sea-faring Kawéscar who dove naked for shellfish in the frigid waters around the southern fjords. The first European to discover the area was **Ferdinand Magellan**, a Portuguese navigator who sailed through the strait now bearing

Punta Arenas orientation p.385
Magellan, pioneer of global
  exploration p.387
It's a dog's life p.388
The strange case of the giant
  sloth skin p.400
Fire in the park p.401

Beyond the W: Torres del Paine
  alternatives p.406
Refugios in Torres del Paine p.408
Visiting estancias p.411
Trekking in Parque Nacional
  Los Galciares p.412

Highlights

❶ Cemetery at Punta Arenas Visit this moving – and beautiful – memorial to the pioneers from Britain and Spain, Croatia and Italy. **See p.389**

❷ Penguins at Isla Magdalena Watch the birds' comic antics on this island sanctuary – the second largest colony of Magellanic penguins in South America. **See p.394**

❸ A boat trip to exquisite glaciers Sail up the fjord from Natales to see the frozen flows of Balmaceda and Serrano. **See p.399**

❹ Hiking Parque Nacional Torres del Paine Set aside at least a few days to trek through

Chile's most popular, spectacular park – an unforgettable experience. **See p.400**

❺ Glaciar Perito Moreno Admire Argentine Patagonia's most spectacular glacier from afar, take a boat right up to its face or go ice-hiking on its surface. **See p.411**

❻ Laguna de Los Tres Complete the most demanding and scenic of hikes in the Fitz Roy mountain range of Argentina's Parque Nacional Los Glaciares. **See p.412**

HIGHLIGHTS ARE MARKED ON THE MAP ON P.384

9

his name. Spanish colonization attempts failed catastrophically and no European tried to settle the place again for another two hundred and fifty years.

The nineteenth century

The voyages of the *Beagle*, from 1826 to 1834, the second one bearing young Charles Darwin, renewed interest in the area, prompting continued Chilean and Argentine

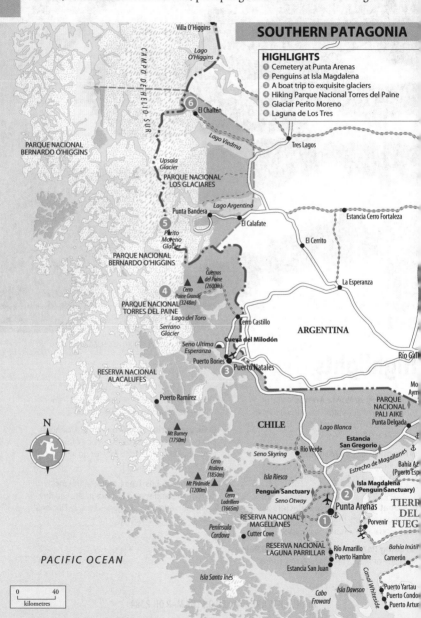

SOUTHERN PATAGONIA

HIGHLIGHTS
1. Cemetery at Punta Arenas
2. Penguins at Isla Magdalena
3. A boat trip to exquisite glaciers
4. Hiking Parque Nacional Torres del Paine
5. Glaciar Perito Moreno
6. Laguna de Los Tres

Villa O'Higgins

CAMPO DE HIELO SUR

Lago O'Higgins

6 El Chaltén

Lago Viedma

Tres Lagos

PARQUE NACIONAL BERNARDO O'HIGGINS

Upsala Glacier

PARQUE NACIONAL LOS GLACIARES

Punta Bandera — Lago Argentino

El Calafate

Estancia Cerro Fortaleza

5 Perito Moreno Glacier

El Cerrito

PARQUE NACIONAL BERNARDO O'HIGGINS

La Esperanza

Cuernos del Paine (2600m)

4 Cerro Paine Grande (3248m)

PARQUE NACIONAL TORRES DEL PAINE

Lago del Toro

Serrano Glacier

Cerro Castillo

ARGENTINA

Seno Ultima Esperanza

Cueva del Milodón

Puerto Bories

3 Puerto Natales

Río Gal

RESERVA NACIONAL ALACALUFES

Puerto Ramírez

Mo Aym

PARQUE NACIONAL PALI AIKE
Punta Delgada

N

Mt Burney (1750m)

CHILE

Lago Blanca

Estancia San Gregorio

Río Verde

Seno Skyring

Estrecho de Magallanes

Bahía A (Puerto Esp

Cerro Atalaya (1850m)

Mt Pirámide (1200m)

Isla Riesco

Isla Magdalena (Penguin Sanctuary)

Cerro Ladrillero (1665m)

Penguin Sanctuary

2

TIERRA DEL FUEG

Seno Otway

Punta Arenas

Península Cordova

Cutter Cove

1

Porvenir

RESERVA NACIONAL MAGALLANES

PACIFIC OCEAN

RESERVA NACIONAL LAGUNA PARRILLAR

Río Amarillo
Puerto Hambre

Bahía Inútil

Camerón

Estancia San Juan

Canal Whiteside

Isla Santa Inés

Cabo Froward

Isla Dawson

Puerto Yartau
Puerto Condo
Puerto Artur

0   40
kilometres

attempts to colonize the area. In the 1870s the two narrowly avoided war over the territory, not for the last time. From 1849, Punta Arenas was boosted by sea traffic en-route to the California Gold Rush; while it didn't last long, the introduction of sheep farming created sprawling **estancias** (ranches) and brought great wealth to their owners in the late nineteenth century.

Southern Patagonia today
Wool has now been replaced by **oil**, commercial salmon farming and tourism as the region's main resources. The Chileans call the area the province of **Magallanes**, in the explorer's honour; it has its own flag and is one of the least inhabited areas in Chile.

Chilean Patagonia

Chilean Patagonia can be divided up into four distinct areas: **Punta Arenas** and its surroundings; **Puerto Natales** and the unforgettable **Torres del Paine National Park**; the broad expanse of frigid grassland between the two towns, stretching to the Atlantic coast and taking in the desolately beautiful **Parque Nacional Pali Aike**; and the remote, hardly visited **islands** of the Pacific coast.

Punta Arenas

Seen from the air, **PUNTA ARENAS**, 3090km south of Santiago, is a sprawling patchwork of galvanized tin roofs struggling up from the shores of the Magellan Strait. On the ground, however, the city looks much more substantial and modern, especially in the centre where glass and concrete office buildings have replaced the ramshackle wooden houses, paid for in part by the oil.

Brief history
Punta Arenas started life 60km south of where it is today, at a place called **Fuerte Bulnes**, the first Chilean settlement along the Magellan Strait. It was founded in 1843 by Captain John Williams, a seaman from Bristol in the service of the Chileans, with the aim of forestalling any other country's attempts at colonization. In 1848 the new settlement moved to a more suitable location to the north, named by an English sailor "Sandy Point", loosely translated into "Punta Arenas" in Spanish. Punta Arenas blossomed in the nineteenth-century sheep boom, when thriving immigrant communities from Croatia, Germany and elsewhere sprang up and left their marks.

Plaza Muñoz Gamero
The tranquil **Plaza Muñoz Gamero**, featuring shady pathways under magnificent hundred-year-old Monterey cypresses, teems with strolling families and vendors selling souvenirs from their carts. In the middle rises an imposing **monument to Ferdinand Magellan**. Below Magellan sits a Tehuelche Indian - one of only two references to the now extinct people that you'll find in the city (see p.389). If you touch (some say kiss) the indian's toe, polished gold, tradition has it that you'll return to Punta Arenas. The two blocks of Magallanes running from the square's northeast corner are all that remains of the city's oldest original street, originally named Calle María Isabel.

PUNTA ARENAS ORIENTATION

The city has four main streets; the north–south axes are **Avenida Manuel Bulnes** and **O'Higgins**, the east–west are **Avenidas Independencia** and **Colón**. Contained within them, the compact centre of town is focused around the central **Plaza Muñoz Gamero**.

9

Conaf, Zona Franca (3km), Ferry Terminal (5km), Transbordadora Austral Broom Ferry (5km), ▲ 🟦 ① (15km) & Airport (20km)

CAFÉS AND CHEAP EATS
Café Tapiz — 7
Kiosko Roca — 8
Lomit's — 2

PUBS AND BARS
Pub Olijoe — 10
Sky Bar — 11
La Taberna del
  Club de la Unión — 4

RESTAURANTS
Brocolino — 6
Hotel José Nogueira — 3
La Luna — 5
La Marmita — 1
Remezón — 12
San Telmo — 13
Sotito's Bar — 9

ACCOMMODATION
La Casa Escondida — 1
Dreams — 11
Hospedaje Independencia — 12
Hospedaje Magallanes — 2
Hostal Calafate — 5
Hostal La Estancia — 6
Hostal Al Fin del Mundo — 10
Hotel José Nogueira — 9
Hotel Patagonia Pionera — 7
Ilaia — 8
Imago Mundi — 3
Tragaluz — 4

Cementerio Municipal

ANGAMOS

AVENIDA MANUEL BULNES

MAIPÚ

Museo Salesiano

SARMIENTO DE GAMBOA

Santuario María Auxiliadora

CROACIA

CROACIA

AV ESPAÑA

▲ 🟦 ③ (100m)

Turismo Aomikenk — 2

MEJICANA

MEJICANA

A SANHUEZA

CHILOÉ

Sala Estrella
Unimark Supermarket

MAGALLANES

BORES

SAMPAIO

NAVARRO

O'HIGGINS

CARRERA PINTO

CARRERA PINTO

▲ ⑦ (250m) & ⑧ (1.5km)

Buses Fernández/
El Pinguino

Pullman Bus

Río de las Minas

Central de Buses

Buses Pacheco

6

AVENIDA COLÓN

JORGE MONTT

Bus Sur

LAN

JOSÉ MENÉNDEZ

2

Aerovías DAP

Castillo Millward

St James

@ Futura Internet

COMAPA

Palacio Sara Braun

WALDO SEGUEL

Museo Regional Braun Menéndez

Parque Pinguino Rey office

Buses Ghisoni, Queilen, Techni & Austral
ⓘ

Hertz

Autoservicio Lavasol

PEDRO MONTT

Iglesia Matriz

PLAZA MUÑOZ GAMERO

Banco Santander

Museo Naval y Marítimo

5

10

6

Mirador Cerro de la Cruz

FAGNANO

7

ROCA

8

Whalesound

Sky Airline

9

ERRÁZURIZ

10

11 11

Frieda Lange & Co. Heritage Tours

A SANHUEZA

CHILOÉ

NOGUEIRA

21 DE MAYO

NAVARRO

COST

Port

▲ 🟦 ⑫ & Arka Patagonia (100m)

BALMACEDA

Magellan Strait

AV INDEPENDENCIA

PUNTA ARENAS

0 — 200 metres

▼ Fantástico Sur Expeditions (1.5km)

⑫ & ⑬ (150m) ▼

▼ Fuerte Bulnes (51km)

Palacio Sara Braun

Plaza Muñoz Gamero • Tues–Fri 10.30am–1pm & 5–8.30pm, Sat 10.30am–1pm & 8–10pm , Sun 11am–2pm • CH$1000

Around the plaza rise several grand houses dating from the wool boom, but the only one you can visit is the **Palacio Sara Braun**, on the northwestern corner, designed by a French architect, Numa Mayer, for Sara Braun, widow of the great sheep baron José Nogueira. While it is now divided between the *Club de la Unión* and the *Hotel José Nogueira*, visitors can stroll through the elegant, period furniture-lined rooms of the *Club de la Unión* section, and marvel at the opulence of the frescoes.

Museo Regional Braun Menéndez

Magallanes 949 • May–Sept Mon & Wed–Sat 10.30am–5pm; Oct–April Mon–Sat 10.30am–5pm, Sun 10.30am–2pm • CH$2000, free Sun and holidays

Half a block north of the square sits the **Palacio Braun Menéndez** – the former family residence of the marriage that united the two wealthiest and most powerful families in Punta Arenas, and now housing the **Museo Regional Magallanes**. The beautifully preserved private quarters of this early twentieth century family home offer a window onto a wealthy middle-class lifestyle achieved by few who came to Patagonia in search of it: a dining room, bedrooms and sitting room lavishly decorated and filled with superb French art nouveau furnishings.

Permanent exhibition

Several rooms are devoted to a permanent exhibition detailing the colonization of Patagonia and Tierra del Fuego, with pioneer articles, historical photos and bilingual

---

MAGELLAN, PIONEER OF GLOBAL EXPLORATION

Fernoã Magalhães, known to English-speakers as **Ferdinand Magellan**, was born in about 1480 in northern Portugal, and had an adventurous early life: in his 20 he saw service with the Portuguese fleets in their wars against the Muslims of the Indian Ocean, and by 1515 he was a veteran of the campaigns in Morocco. In 1516, after being refused a rise in his pension by the king of Portugal, Magellan took his services to the Spanish crown.

Those days were the beginning of European exploration, prompted mainly by the desire to seek out **new routes** to the East and its valuable **Spice Islands** (the Moluccas of Indonesia). Magellan believed that the answer lay to the west, under or through the newly discovered American continents, and he asked the king of Spain, Carlos I, to fund his search. Charles agreed, eager to prove that the Spice Islands lay in the half of the New World that the pope had just assigned to Spain.

THROUGH THE STRAITS TO THE PACIFIC

On September 20, 1519, Magellan sailed west as admiral of a fleet of five ships. They crossed the Atlantic Ocean, and started to search the coast of South America for the elusive passage. It was a long and hard hunt, and not all Magellan's fleet believed there was a strait: on Easter Day 1520, Magellan had to quash a mutiny by his Spanish captains. But on October 21, 1520, his flagship, the *Trinidad*, finally rounded Cabo Virgenes and entered the **strait** that now bears his name. Thirty-six days later the open seas of an ocean were sighted; they named the new ocean **"the Pacific"** for its calmness after the storms of the strait, and set out across it, not expecting it to be so wide.

BACK TO SPAIN

They sailed for four months without seeing land. When Magellan himself was **killed** in a fight with the natives of Mactán Island, the fleet didn't turn back; petrified of attempting to go through the straits at the bottom of South America for a second time, they took the longer route round the Cape of Good Hope. Three years after they'd set out, just one of Magellan's original five ships finally limped back to Spain. It was loaded with spices (cloves and nutmeg) and manned by only eighteen of the original crew, men wasted and half-dead. The voyage's chronicler said he could not imagine the journey ever being repeated.

9

displays on the maritime and farming history of the region, as well as the region's **native tribes** – the Kawéscar (Alacalúf) and the Selk'nam (Ona). Dusty old account books and documents reveal that the founding families controlled not only the sheep trade, but an immense range of other commercial activities. In effect, they *were* the city.

Museo Naval y Marítimo

Pedro Montt 981 • March–Nov Tues–Sat 9.30am–12.30pm & 2–5pm; Dec–Feb Mon–Fri 8.30am–6pm, Sat 10am–6pm • CH$1500

One and a half blocks east of the plaza, three blocks north of the port, sits the engaging **Museo Naval y Marítimo** with a focus on Punta Arenas' naval history and the exploration of the southern waters. The ground floor features a collection of minutely detailed scale models of ships associated with the town's history, including Sir Ernest Shackleton's *Endurance*, as well as a block of Antarctic ice, while upstairs you can play around in the area decked out as a ship, complete with nautical equipment, maps, charts and interactive displays.

Castillo Millward

España 959

In the nineteenth century when sterling was still a widely accepted currency, a leading member of the community was one **Charles Milward**, great-uncle of the author **Bruce Chatwin**. Chatwin wrote his celebrated part-travelogue, part-fiction, *In Patagonia,* about his trip here to learn more about Milward, ex-sea captain and adventurer, and the man who helped discover a chunk of a deep-frozen prehistoric ground sloth in the Cueva del Milodón (see p.399).

Milward's old house, a red brick tower with gothic windows, is now owned by the local daily newspaper, *El Pinguino*, and not open to the public. It was here, in 1914, that the famous explorer Sir Ernest Shackleton stayed and planned the rescue of his stranded crew after his ship, the *Endurance*, was crushed by ice in the Antarctic.

Mirador Cerro La Cruz

Across Avenida España, and a block along Fagnano, some steps lead up to the **Mirador Cerro la Cruz**, where you can enjoy a sweeping view of the city's multicoloured roofs and the wind-whipped Magellan Strait.

Museo Salesiano Maggiorino Borgatello

Av Manuel Bulnes • Tues–Sun 10am–12.30pm & 3–5.30pm • CH$2000

Seven blocks north of the plaza, this worthwhile museum covers local flora, fauna, geology and the evangelization of the natives of southern Patagonia and Tierra del Fuego by the Salesian religious order. The exhibits suggest that the missionaries acted as mediators between the locals and the settlers, failing to point out the evangelizers' roles in the demise of native culture.

IT'S A DOG'S LIFE

One thing many visitors notice when they arrive in Punta Arenas (and other large Chilean cities) is the large number of **stray dogs** on the streets. Most tend to be tame – many of them being abandoned pets – but there are occasional incidents of dog bites, car accidents and attacks on wildlife, not to mention sickness, injury and starvation on the part of the dogs, exacerbated by the city's large stray population.

The Chilean federal and local governments do not regularly provide animal control services, so it's up to NGOs such as the *Corporación de Defensa de los Derechos de los Animales* (☎ 09 8929 7697, ⓦ www.chileautral.com/perros) to gather up strays, nurse them back to health, neuter them and try to find them a new home. This **animal shelter**, with its population of around one hundred dogs, twenty cats and the occasional horse, welcomes volunteers and can be visited at Km 9.5, Ruta 9, just outside Punta Arenas.

9

The best displays among the natural history samples vividly depict the daily life of the Kawéscar Indians and the weapons they used for hunting and fishing. Another choice exhibit is the unparalleled collection of photographs of the region and its inhabitants, taken by the Italian mountaineering priest, Alberto de Agostini, who spent many years among the native people of Patagonia and Tierra del Fuego.

Cementerio Municipal
Av Bulnes • Daily: summer 7.30am–8pm; winter 8am–6pm • Free

Two blocks north of the Museo Salesiano lies the city's magnificent **Cementerio Municipal**, which covers four city blocks. Crisscrossed by a network of footpaths lined with immaculately clipped cypresses, this eclectic necropolis reflects the turbulent history of Patagonia. The monumental tombs of the city's ruling families – some made of the same Italian marble as Michelangelo's *David* and elaborately engraved with the English and Spanish names – mingle with the Croatian and Scandinavian names of immigrant labourers, etched on more modest gravestones.

A monument depicting a **Selk'nam Indian** is surrounded with plaques conveying the gratitude of those whose wishes it granted. See if you can spot the onion-domed crypt of the Braun family – one of the city's founding dynasties – and the simple gravestone of Charles Milward.

ARRIVAL AND DEPARTURE PUNTA ARENAS

BY PLANE
Most travellers arrive at the user-friendly Aeropuerto Presidente Ibañez, 20km north of town. Scheduled LAN and Sky Airlines flights leave Punta Arenas for Coyhaique (Balmaceda), Puerto Montt and Santiago. In summer, Aerovías DAP runs flights to Porvenir (CH$38,000 one way), Puerto Williams (CH$52,000 one way) and Antarctica (CH$1,400,000 (US$2895)/CH$1,900,000 (US$3929) for full day/overnight stay; Nov–March only). Taxis to the centre charge CH$10,000, minibuses CH$4000 and Buses Fernández (☎61 221429) runs airport transfers for CH$3000; they all meet incoming flights. Buses heading to Puerto Natales also stop at the airport.

Airlines Aerovías DAP, O'Higgins at Menéndez (☎61 616100, ⓦdap.cl or dapantartica.cl); LAN, Menéndez at Bories (☎61 241100, ⓦwww.lanchile.cl); Sky Airline, Roca 935 (☎61 710645, ⓦskyairline.cl).

Destinations Antarctica (several monthly Nov–March only; full day excursion); Balmaceda (several daily; 1hr); Porvenir (2–3 daily except Sun; 12min); Puerto Montt (2 daily; 2hr); Puerto Williams (summer 1 daily except Sun; winter 3 weekly; 40min–1hr 20min); Santiago (several daily; 4hr).

BY BUS
Each bus company has its own terminal in the centre of Punta Arenas; all are within five blocks of the main Plaza Muñoz Gamero. Buses Tecni Austral, Buses Pacheco and Bus Sur serve Ushuaia via Río Grande; book ahead in peak season. Bus Sur, Buses Fernández and Buses Pacheco go to Puerto Natales. Bus El Pinguino, Buses Ghisoni and Buses Pacheco serve Río Gallegos with connections to Buenos Aires and Los Antiguos, as well as Río Grande in Argentina.

Buses Queilén and Pullman run to Osorno, Puerto Montt, Ancud and Castro. Buses for anywhere north of Puerto Natales travel through Argentina. Bus journeys to Ushuaia involve a 40min ferry crossing and there are no meal stops along the way, so bring food with you. Central de Buses, Colón and Magallanes (☎61 245811) sells tickets for various bus companies.

Companies Bus El Pingüino, Sanhueza 745 (☎61 221812); Bus Sur, Menéndez 552 (☎61 614224, ⓦbus-sur .cl); Buses Fernández, Sanhueza 745 (☎61 242313, ⓦwww .busesfernandez.com); Buses Ghisoni/Quellen Bus, Navarro 971 (☎61 223205); Tecni Austral, Navarro 975 (☎61 613422); Buses Pacheco, Av Colón 900 (☎61 242174, ⓦwww.busespacheco.co.cl); Pullman, Av Colón 568 (☎61 223359, ⓦwww .pullman.cl).

Destinations Ancud and Castro via Puerto Montt & Osorno (several weekly 7.30/9.30am; 34–36hr); Puerto Natales (16 daily; 3hr); Río Gallegos, Argentina (1–2 daily; 5–7hr); Río Grande, Argentina (1–2 daily; 8hr 30min); Ushuaia, Argentina, via Río Grande (daily 7/8am; 12–14 hr).

BY FERRY
The ferry terminal at Tres Puentes, 5km north of town, is a shortish *colectivo* (CH$800) or taxi ride (CH$3000) from downtown, along the Natales road to the north. Transbordadora Austral Broom ferries, Juan Williams 6450 (☎61 728100, ⓦwww.tabsa.cl), serves Porvenir in Tierra del Fuego and Puerto Williams on Isla Navarino, as well as the Primera Angostura crossing between Punta Delgada on the Patagonian mainland and Bahía Azul (Puerto Espora) in Tierra del Fuego. Timetables are weather-dependent; if taking a car to Porvenir, book a space in advance.

9

Destinations Porvenir (1 daily except Mon; 2hr 30min–4hr; passenger CH$5500, car CH$34,900); Primera Angostura (every 45min 8.30am–11pm in summer, less often in winter; 20min; passenger CH$1600, car CH$13,900); Puerto Williams (Nov–March weekly on Wed; 28hr; Pullman seat US$186, berth US$258).

INFORMATION AND TOURS

TOURIST INFORMATION
You will see helpful blue-and-yellow plaques around the city next to historical monuments, each explaining the significance of the site (in Spanish only).
Conaf Bulnes 309, fourth floor (Mon–Thurs 8.30am–5pm, Fri 8.30am–4pm; ☎ 61 238554). A good place to pick up information on the area's national parks and reserves.
Parque Pingüino Rey office Navarro 975 (☎ 61 613420 ☜ pinguinorey.cl). The best place for information regarding the potential King penguin colony in Tierra del Fuego (see p.421).
Sernatur Navarro 999 (Mon–Fri 8.30am–6pm, Sat 10am–6pm; ☎ 61 241330, ☜ puntaarenas.cl). Offers lots of information on the city and the region.

TOUR OPERATORS
Most tour companies offer trips to the Seno Otway penguin colony (CH$14,000), Fuerte Bulnes (CH$15,000) and Parque Nacional Pali Aike (CH$50,000). Below are reputable operators offering standard and specialized excursions.
Arka Patagonia Manuel Señoret 1597 ☎ 61 248167, ☜ arkapatagonia.com. Runs multi-day trips around Punta Arenas, Puerto Natales and Torres del Paine, and can help arrange adventures further afield – sailing around Cape Horn and to Antarctica.
Fantastico Sur Expeditions Armando Sanhueza 579 ☎ 61 6157931, 800 656 1806 (USA), 800 680 0640 (UK), ☜ fsexpeditions.com. Experienced, high end operator with a focus on nature, photography and birdwatching tours in Patagonia and beyond. Runs trips to see King penguins in Tierra del Fuego (see p.421).
Frieda Lange & Co. Heritage Tours Errázuriz 950 ☎ 61 613991, ☜ flacotours.com. This excellent newcomer on the scene is the only operator to focus on Punta Arenas itself, offering engaging bilingual 2hr historical tours of the city as well as excursions to Fuerte Bulnes.
Kayak Agua Fresca ☎ 09 9655 5073, ☜ kayakaguafresca.com. Highly recommended outfit specializing in half- and full-day kayaking and marine life viewing trips on the Strait of Magellan. Full day excursions include a traditional Patagonian barbecue.
Turismo Aonikenk Magallanes 570 ☎ 61 221982, ☜ aonikenk.com. Intrepid operator offering multi-day hiking excursions – Torres del Paine, Cabo Froward and the Dientes de Navarino as well as local day-trips to the penguin colonies (including the one in Tierra del Fuego) and more adventurous options, such as a three-week horse trek along old pioneer routes or Tierra del Fuego trek to Estancia Yendagaia. Tailor-made trips possible.
Whalesound Navarro 1191 ☎ 61 223725, ☜ whalesound.com. Responsible operator offering study-based kayaking trips to the Coloane Marine Park and multi-day humpback whale-watching trips Dec–May (2 day, 1 night, all-inclusive trip US$900).

ACCOMMODATION

HOTELS AND B&B
★ **La Casa Escondida** Parcela 26, Sector Ojo Bueno ☎ 61 223023, ☜ lacasaescondida.com. The family-run "Hidden House" makes a wonderful retreat from the bustle of the city. Located 15km north of Punta Arenas, it consists of adorably rustic rooms and cabins with handmade furniture, down comforters and guest sauna. Traditional Patagonian barbecue and evening meals available on request and prices include airport transfer and breakfast. ‾CH$33,000‾
Dreams O'Higgins 1235 ☎ 61 204648, ☜ mundodreams.com. It may be part of a chain and its shiny seafront structure probably suits Dubai better than Punta Arenas, but *Dreams* is indisputably the city's most modern luxury hotel. Its rooms and suites come equipped with king-sized beds and every convenience you'd expect, and other perks include a lofty swimming pool with sea views, massage spa, international restaurant, swanky bar (see p.392) and casino. And if you don't know how to gamble, their special TV programme will teach you. ‾CH$155,600‾
Hospedaje Magallanes Magallanes 570 ☎ 61 228616, ☜ aonikenk.com. Just four simple doubles on offer (ideal for couples) at this family home which you'll share with the gregarious German–Chilean couple behind Turismo Aonikenk (see p.390), their two kids and two friendly dogs. The owners make you feel like part of the family, throw the occasional impromptu barbecue and give discounts to Germans from Leipzig (no one's claimed the 10% off yet apparently). ‾CH$20,000‾
Hostal Calafate Magallanes 926 ☎ 61 241281, ☜ calafate.cl. In its new incarnation, this boutique B&B has relocated to a refurbished 1920s house with ten spacious, centrally heated rooms with welcome touches of colour and down comforters on the beds. The buffet breakfast includes home-made bread and owners organize tours to various attractions in the area. ‾CH$30,000‾
★ **Hotel José Nogueira** Bories 959 ☎ 61 711000, ☜ hotelnogueira.com. The city's most atmospheric stay, this lovely hotel boasts a prime location on the plaza, inside the Palacio Sara Braun, former home to the city's most

powerful family. Some rooms are a little small but very stylish; the service is excellent service and the restaurant is first rate. CH$103,000 (US$215)

Hotel Patagonia Pionera Arauco 786 ☎61 222045, ⓦhotelpatagoniapionera.cl. An introduction to colonial history without the discomforts suffered by the colonists themselves, this beautifully restored mansion is run by the descendants of Patagonian pioneers. The rooms are anything but colonial: they come equipped with power showers, cable TV and an American-style buffet breakfast. CH$62,000

Ilaia Carrera Pinto 351 ☎61 223592, ⓦilaia.cl. At this small boutique hotel, the emphasis is on the rejuvenation of body and spirit. Rooms are decorated in soothing pastel shades, TVs are absent (though wi-fi is not) and you can take part in hatha yoga, reiki and meditation. Nourishment at breakfast consists of home-made muesli, flatbread, fruit and yogurt. CH$57,000

★ **Tragaluz** Mejiucana 1194 ☎61 613938, ⓦtragaluzpatagonia.com. This delightful B&B is as much of a joy to look at as it is to stay in. The Chilean–American owners have put enormous thought and effort into finding every single antique and piece of art that makes this place part-home and part-art gallery; each individually decorated en-suite room represents one of the elements, as does the solitary apartment. Double CH$40,000, apartment CH$50,000

HOSTELS

Hospedaje Independencia Independencia 374 ☎61 227572, ⓦchileaustral.com/independencia/camping.html. Friendly young owners allow camping in the yard and can rent out equipment and organize tours of the area. Dorms and rooms are too small to swing a cat but the warmth of the owners and generous inclusive breakfast makes us for this. Camping CH$2000 per person, dorm CH$5000 per person, double CH$10000

Hostal La Estancia O'Higgins 765 ☎61 249130, ⓦestancia.cl. Many travellers end up using Carmen and Alejandro's wonderful *hostal* as a home away from home, so don't be surprised if it's constantly booked up! This restored 1920s house features high-ceilinged dorms and bright rooms with cable TV, as well as excellent breakfast, and the hospitable owners are always on hand to assist. Note that there's a nineteen percent discount if paying in US dollars or Euros. Dorm CH$12,000, double CH$30,000

Hostal Al Fin del Mundo O'Higgins 1026 ☎61 710185, ⓦalfindelmundo.cl. This friendly hostel has spartan but clean rooms, which vary in size, and a dorm (with beds rather than bunks) in a central location. Perks include free breakfast, internet and wi-fi, kitchen use, pool table, book exchange and a comfy lounge with massive TV; all facilities are shared. Dorm CH$11,000, double CH$30,000

★ **Imago Mundi** Mejicana 252 ☎61 613115, ⓦimagomundipatagonia.cl. Environmentally conscious travellers and outdoor junkies alike flock to this popular little hostel run by a brother–sister team. There are just nine cosy bunk beds in two en-suite rooms, as well as a double room, an on-site climbing gym for pros and beginners alike, an excellent café (full board is possible) and an attached cultural centre that often features live music. Dorm CH$10,000, double CH$25,000

EATING AND DRINKING

CAFÉS AND CHEAP EATS

Café Tapiz Roca 912 ☎09 7769 3359. This wood-shingled café has been drawing locals and travellers alike with its hearty sandwiches (try the smoked salmon with capers and cream cheese), real coffee and excellent home-made cake selection. The carrot-and-orange juice is pricier than elsewhere but it's not watered down and will give you that vitamin boost you've been lacking. Mon–Sat 10.30am–6pm, Sun 11am–5pm.

Kiosko Roca Roca at Navarro. To get at this hole-in-the-wall's specialities – banana milk, *choripan* (mini grilled sandwich with chorizo) or *choripan con queso* (the same but with cheese) – you have to push through the rows of locals propping up the bar. But it's worth it. Daily 8am–4pm.

Lomit's José Menéndez 722. Locals and travellers alike pack this American diner-style burger and hot dog joint and it's a good spot for striking up a conversation with fellow diners. But in the name of all that is holy, why are there no French fries??? Daily 10am–2.30am.

RESTAURANTS

★ **Brocolino** O'Higgins 1049 ☎61 710479. A must-stop for gourmets, this excellent restaurant may not look like much from the outside (or even on the inside), but its gregarious chef Hector whips up such delights as "Aphrodisiac soup", using the freshest local fish and *centolla* (king crab), and sweetbreads in a champagne sauce. All dishes are imaginative, well executed and reasonably priced. Mains CH$5500–9000. Daily 1–3pm & 7–11.30pm.

Hotel José Nogueira Bories 959 ☎61 248840. The location – in a beautiful vine-draped winter garden inside one of the city's most splendid mansions – is just as impressive as the food, an expert blend of well-executed international and Patagonian dishes. Steak in crab sauce and the Patagonian lamb are inspired choices. Mon–Sat 12.30–3pm & 7.30–11pm, Sun 1–3.30pm.

La Luna O'Higgins 1017 ☎61 228555. Pasta, fish and seafood dishes served against the backdrop of bright blue and yellow decor and Latin rhythms. The food isn't exceptional, but the pisco sours are generous and the service is friendly, as testified to by scrawls on the wall left by contented customers. Daily 1–3pm & 7–10.30pm.

★ **La Marmita** Plaza Sampaio 678 ☎61 222056. One of the city's most beloved restaurants has expanded without sacrificing either ambiance or quality. The pisco sours are the best in town, the service attentive and it's difficult to go wrong with the likes of *cancato* (steamed salmon parcel) with quinoa, the ceviche or the courgettes stuffed three different ways. Daily 12.30–3pm & 6.30–11.30pm.

Remezón 21 de Mayo 1469 ☎61 241029. You may well have encountered Patagonia's fauna – guanaco, beaver, hares – in the wild. Now how about an even closer encounter…on your plate? The chef at this posh, native-themed restaurant conjures up some of the most imaginative dishes in town using local ingredients; for best results, go for game (mains CH$7500–10,000). Mon–Sat 1–3pm & 7.30–11.30pm, Sun 1–3.30pm.

San Telmo 21 de Mayo at Boliviana ☎61 223529, ⓦsantelmorestaurante.cl. This Argentinian restaurant unsurprisingly specializes in meat, in particular generously portioned, nicely aged, expertly cooked steak. There are fish and pasta options available for the less carnivorously inclined, but meat is the star here. Tango shows some evenings. Daily 12.30–3.30pm & 7.30–11.30pm; closed Mon outside peak season.

Sotito's Bar O'Higgins 1138 ☎61 243565. The bare brick walls and starched linen of this local institution's tablecloths conjure up an elegant New York or London brasserie. You won't find any deviation from the standards – *machas a la parmesana* (razor clams with parmesan), *merluza a la plancha* (grilled hake) – but what they do, they do very well indeed. Mon–Sat 1–3pm & 7.30–11.30pm, Sun 1–3.30pm.

BARS AND PUBS

Pub Olijoe Errázuriz 970 ☎61 223728. All leather and wood panels, this English-style pub is one of Punta Arenas' established watering holes. Apart from the good selection of beers, try *Glaciar*, the potent house special, consisting of pisco, milk, curacao and *horchata* (milky, sweet rice drink originally from Valencia in Spain). It may take a while to catch the barman's eye. Daily from 6pm–late.

Sky Bar O'Higgins 1235 ☎61 204648. Occupying a lofty spot inside the *Dreams Hotel* (see p.390) this luxury glass-and-chrome bar has a wide selection of spirits and cocktails, sushi on the menu and views of the Magellan Strait (only in the smokers' half, though; non-smokers get a view of Punta Arenas instead). Daily 7pm–3am.

La Taberna del Club de la Unión Plaza Muñoz Gamero 716 ☎61 241317. In the basement of the Palacio Sara Braun, this atmospheric former gathering spot for the city's most powerful men, decorated with black-and-white maritime photographs, is now a gathering place for travellers swapping travel yarns or to nurse a whisky. Daily 7pm–3am.

DIRECTORY

Banks and exchange Most of the banks, including BBVA and Banco Santander, are clustered around the plaza, especially on its eastern side, and numerous *cambios* are found on Pedro Montt and Navarro; try Sur Cambio de Moneda, Navarro 1070.

Car rental Europcar at the airport, O'Higgins 964 (☎61 202720, ⓦwww.europcar.cl); Hertz, O'Higgins 931 (☎61 613087, ⓦhertz.cl). Reserve in advance in peak season.

Hospital Hospital Regional, Angamos 180, between Señoret and Zenteno (☎61 244040).

Internet All accommodation options reviewed offer free wi-fi; some also offer free internet. Otherwise, try Futura Internet, Menéndez 787.

Laundry Most accommodation options offer laundry service. Otherwise, try Autoservicio Lavasol, O'Higgins 969.

Pharmacy There are several well-stocked pharmacies along Bories.

Post office Bories 911.

Reserva Forestal Magallanes

Daylight hours • Free • To get here, you can walk, cycle, join a tour or take a taxi (around CH$8000)

The pretty **RESERVA FORESTAL MAGALLANES**, 196 square kilometres of protected Magellanic forest, lies just 8km west of Punta Arenas. The nature reserve has two entrances, both of which provide wonderful views back over the city, across the Magellan Strait and towards Tierra del Fuego.

A road to the north of Punta Arenas leads to the reserve's main entrance; you can embark on several hikes here, including the two-hour loop of **Sendero Mirador**, which crosses the ski area and offers panoramic views of the Strait and Tierra del Fuego beyond, and the **Sendero de Chile Tramo Bocatoma-Las Minas** (3km, 1hr), both of which meander through native *coigüe*, *lenga* and *ñirre* trees. The **Sendero Las Lengas** (3.5km, 1hr) leads to the **ski centre**, the site of the reserve's second entrance, also accessible from the road to the south. There's also a mountain bike circuit, and a short trail from the top of the road that winds through the reserve, leading to the gorge known as the **Garganta del Diablo** (Devil's Throat), with sweeping views of Punta Arenas and Tierra del Fuego.

Puerto Hambre

Forty-eight kilometres from Arenas along the beautiful, mostly paved main road that skirts the shore, you'll see a large **white obelisk** – a monument to the "navel of Chile": the country's geographical centre, which takes into account Chilean Antarctic territory right down to the South Pole. The road to the left of the obelisk leads 2km south to **Puerto Hambre** ("Port Famine"). One of the first two Spanish colonies on the Magellan Strait, Puerto Hambre is the site of the ambitious 1584 colony founded by Pedro Sarmiento de Gamboa – "Ciudad del Rey Don Felipe" – which ended in the starvation of most of its 337 colonists. Two remaining men were rescued by English privateer Thomas Cavendish, one of whom then died on board the ship. All that's left is a plaque, a concrete dolmen and the ruins of a church, sitting forlornly on a little promontory.

Fuerte Bulnes

Nov to mid-April daily 8.30am–8pm • CH$1000 • There's no public transport here, though most tour companies run half-day tours from Punta Arenas to Fuerte Bulnes and Puerto Hambre

The road to the right of the obelisk near Puerto Hambre leads to **Fuerte Bulnes**, a 1940s reconstruction of the first Chilean settlement in the area. Fuerte Bulnes was founded in September 1843 (and named after President Manuel Bulnes) by a boatload of sailors from Chiloé who arrived in the *Goleta Ancud*, captained by one John Williams. They came to pre-empt colonization from Europe, and only just made it: a few hours after they arrived, a French warship, the *Phaeton*, turned up and planted the tricolour on the shore. After Williams protested, the French moved off and annexed Tahiti in the Pacific instead. The location was less than ideal for a settlement owing to a lack of drinking water and pasture land, which prompted Williams to move the colony to the site of present day Punta Arenas.

The fort

The restored fort comprises a number of old cannons, sturdy log cabins, a gaol building, a lookout tower, and a small wooden **chapel**, adorned inside with gifts and supplications left by visitors, giving it a shrine-like atmosphere. There are plans to make the fort into a historical park and to build a museum on site.

Cabo Froward

Ninety kilometres south of Punta Arenas lies **CABO FROWARD**, the southernmost mainland point on the continent, marked with an enormous cross, erected in honour of the 1987 visit by Pope John Paul II. The cape can be reached via a starkly picturesque two-day wild hike along the weather-beaten cliffs by any reasonably fit individual. The 50km trail is reasonably well signposted in places, but this is a challenging hike that requires you to ford or even swim across several narrow but deep rivers along the way (having your gear in a waterproof canoe bag is best). You can either join a guided expedition with Erratic Rock (see Puerto Natales tour operators, p.397) or with a hiking partner (it is not advisable to go it alone), taking all necessary supplies with you, as well as a good map: *SIG Patagon* and *Trekking Chile* maps of the Cabo Froward trail are practically identical.

ARRIVAL AND DEPARTURE

CABO FROWARD

By bus To get to the trailhead, you'll either need to find out the timetable for the

twice-weekly municipal bus that runs past Fuerte Bulnes or arrange a lift.

ACCOMMODATION

There are very basic camping facilities en route, as well as a rustic *refugio* (bring own bedding).

Hostería San Isidro ☎ 09 9349 3862, ⓦ hosteriafarosanisidro.cl. The southernmost guesthouse on the South American continent, located at the hilltop San

Isidro lighthouse, halfway along the trail, with six bright, centrally heated doubles. Great location for kayaking, trekking or wallowing in the on-site hot tubs. **CH$65,000**

Monumento Natural Isla Magdalena

The *Melinka* passenger ferry, operated by Turismo COMAPA (Magallanes 990, ☎ 61 200200, ⓦ www.comapa.com), departs 5pm every other day in season (Dec–Feb) and costs CH$25,000

One of the largest penguin colonies in southern Chile, **MONUMENTO NATURAL ISLA MAGDALENA** is home to more than 120,000 Magellanic penguins. The small island, just one square kilometre in size and topped by a pretty red lighthouse, lies 35km northeast of Arenas, two hours away by boat. The penguins dig their burrows under the tufts of grass covering the 15m-high cliffs.

In October each year, the birds migrate back here and find their mate – they're monogamous and remain faithful to one partner all their lives. The female lays two eggs in the nest and when the chicks hatch, in November, both parents nurture the young, one adult remaining with the chick, the other going fishing. In late January, the chicks shed their baby feathers and get ready for their first trips into the ocean. By the end of March the penguins have returned to sea again.

Viewing

You can get very close to the birds as they half hide in the waving grass, and lounge by the sea. If they start to cock their heads from side to side, it's a sign that you're disturbing them. The five-hour round-trip detailed above, which includes one hour on the island, is worth it for the scenic ride alone, as you may well spot black-and-white Commerson's dolphins and other marine mammals.

Seno Otway penguin colony

Nov–March 8am–7pm • CH$6000 • There is no public transport, but many tour agencies run half-day tours daily (CH$16,000)

An hour's drive north of Punta Arenas, across open pampa, lies the small **Seno Otway penguin colony**. Hosting around five thousand or so Magellanic penguins at its peak, the nesting ground is best seen in the morning before 10am or evening after 5pm, before or after they go fishing. The breeding site is fenced off and you're not allowed on the beach, but ramshackle beachfront hides strung along an 1800m walkway that runs between the penguin burrows let you watch the birds frolic in the frigid waves just a few metres away.

Parque Nacional Pali Aike

Oct–April daily 9am–6pm • CH$2000 • There's no public transport here, though several companies run full-day tours from Punta Arenas

Eleven kilometres beyond the turning for the ferry (see p.389) is the small town of Punta Delgada, from which a good gravel road heads 28km north to Chilean Patagonia's seldom-visited **PARQUE NACIONAL PALI AIKE**. The park's entrance looms up out of the barren rolling plains, green roof first; the sight explains its Tehuelche Indian name, meaning "desolate place of bad spirits". There's a strange magic to the otherworldly volcanic formations that dot the heath and the small lagoons ringed by white tidemarks; this seemingly barren place is home to a surprising amount of smaller wildlife – from well-camouflaged lizards and owls, which may be mistaken for rocks, to the guanacos feeding on the hardy *coirón*.

Cueva Pali Aike and around

From the *guardería*, the main gravel road runs north to the remote, picturesque **Laguna Ana**, where you can occasionally spot flamingos, and the start of the park's longest hike: a 9km (2hr 45min) **walk** across flat, windy, exposed terrain to **Cueva Pali Aike**, a 17m-deep cave in a tall ridge of congealed lava. It was excavated by the famous archaeologist Junius Bird in 1937, and was found to contain evidence of prehistoric inhabitation, including bones of a *milodón* and the *Onohippidium*, an extinct American horse, dating from nine thousand years ago.

An 8km gravel road branches off from the main one, heading east to the cave via the starting point for the park's other two hikes: a 1700m (30min) wander through the largely flat old lava beds to the volcano rim of the **Crater Morada del Diablo** ("Dwelling of the devil"), followed by a 2000m (45min) ascent through the fields of jagged volcanic rock to the **Pozos del Diablo** ("The devil's wells") – dozens and dozens of somewhat sinister craters; sturdy footwear is a must.

Puerto Natales and around

Chilean Patagonia's second city, **PUERTO NATALES**, 250km north of Punta Arenas, is the gateway to the **Parque Nacional Torres del Paine**, and a useful base for visiting the nearby **Cueva del Milodón**, the glaciers of the **Parque Nacional Bernardo O'Higgins**, and, across the border in Argentina, the **Parque Nacional Los Glaciares**. Natales is also a good transport hub, home to the terminal of the **Navimag** ferry from Puerto Montt in the Lake District, and linked to Punta Arenas, Torres del Paine and Argentina by regular bus services.

Enjoying a stunning location at the edge of the pampa, Puerto Natales sits on the lovely Seno Ultima Esperanza ("Last Hope Sound"), fringed by tall peaks, with the powerful wind stirring up waves on the turquoise channel where the remnants of a wooden pier bedecked with cormorants stretch into the distance. The channel's name comes from the 1557 explorer, Juan Ladrilleros, who came upon it when he was at the end of his tether while searching for the western entrance to the Magellan Strait. He found the strait, but almost all his crew died in the attempt.

Plaza de Armas

Natales centres on the newly spruced-up **Plaza de Armas**, which has an old **locomotive engine** formerly used in the nearby Puerto Bories abattoir as its centrepiece – an evening magnet for lovers and drunken teenagers.

Museo Histórico Municipal

Bulnes 285 • Mon–Fri 9am–7pm, Sat 10am–1pm & 3–6pm • CH$1000

A couple of blocks west of the plaza you'll find the small but well-laid-out **Museo Histórico Municipal**, with attractively laid-out bilingual exhibits on the region's European settlement, natural history, the Milodón's cave and the native Aonikenk and Kawéshkar tribes, illustrated with black-and-white photos. A room is dedicated to the region's first settler, a rather fierce-looking German called Herman Eberhard; look out for his ingenious collapsible boat that turns into a suitcase.

| ARRIVAL AND DEPARTURE | PUERTO NATALES |

BY PLANE

There's a tiny airport just north of Puerto Natales with some flights to Santiago with Sky Airline (Manuel Bulnes 682;

📞 61 410646, 🖥 skyairline.cl) during peak season, though flights are often rerouted to Punta Arenas airport instead or cancelled altogether. Taxis meet arriving flights.

9

BY FERRY

The Navimag ferry terminal is on Pedro Montt 308, five blocks west and one block south of the Plaza de Armas (☎61 411421), with departures to Puerto Montt once a week during summer, less often in winter (70hr). For more details see box, p.311.

BY BUS

There's no main bus terminal, so each bus pulls in outside its company's offices, all within a few blocks of the Plaza de Armas. Punta Arenas-bound buses may stop at the Punta Arenas airport on the way; inform the driver when you board the bus. Services to El Calafate and Torres del Paine only operate Oct–April.

Companies Buses Cootra, Baquedano 244 (☎61 412785) runs to El Calafate; Buses Fernández, Ramírez 399 (☎61 411111, ⓦwww.busesfernandez.com) serves Punta Arenas; Buses Pacheco, Ramírez 224 (☎61 414800, ⓦwww.busespacheco.com) runs to Punta Arenas, Ushuaia, Río Grande, Río Gallegos and Castro via Puerto Montt and Osorno; Bus Sur, Baquedano 668 (☎61 410784, ⓦbus-sur.cl) runs to Punta Arenas, El Calafate and Ushuaia; Turismo Zaahj, Arturo Prat 236 (☎61 411355, ⓦwww.turismozaahj.co.cl), Buses JBA Patagonia, Prat 258 (☎61 410242) and Buses Gómez, Prat 234 (☎61 411971 ⓦusesgomez.com) run to Torres del Paine; while Turismo Zaahj also serves El Calafate.

Destinations Castro via Puerto Montt and Osorno (1 weekly; 38hr); El Calafate, Argentina (2 daily; 5hr); Parque Nacional Torres del Paine; (6 daily; 3hr 30min; departures around 7–8am & 2–3pm); Punta Arenas (hourly; 3hr); Río Gallegos, Argentina (3 weekly; 5hr); Ushuaia, Argentina (3 weekly; 12hr).

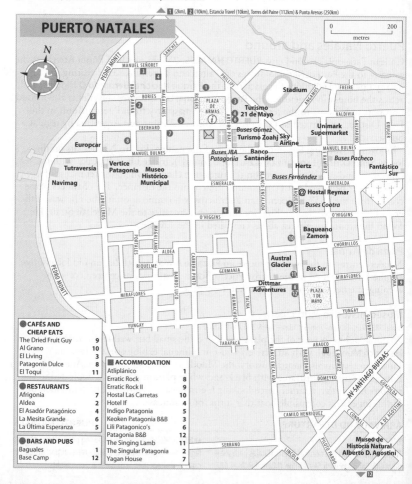

INFORMATION AND TOURS

9

TOURIST INFORMATION

A brand new Sernatur office on the Plaza de Armas was due to open at the time of writing. Visitors heading to Torres del Paine National Park (see pp.400–407) shouldn't miss the daily 3pm informative talk at Base Camp, next door to Erratic Rock (see p.397), where experienced local trekkers will give you the lowdown on what to expect and how best to tackle the park.

TOUR OPERATORS

Standard tours run by every one of the dozens of tour operators in town include a half-day-trip to the Cueva del Milodón (CH$8000; see p.399); a day-trip to the Argentine town of El Calafate and Parque Nacional Los Glaciares (from CH$55,000, park entrance extra), mainly to witness the Glaciar Perito Moreno (see p.411); and a day-trip to Torres del Paine (CH$40,000, park entrance extra). Below are outfits offering more specialized activities.

Austral Glacier Baquedano at Miraflores ☎ 61 411983, ⊛ australglacier.com. If you're looking to arrange onward travel, both in Chile and in neighbouring Argentina, helpful, bilingual Carla can help you plan your itinerary and book all your tickets (with no commission charge).

Baqueano Zamora Baquedano 534 ☎ 61 613531, ⊛ baqueanozamora.cl. Horse-trekking in Torres del Paine (CH$25,000/45,000 for half-/full-day-trip) arranged by this longstanding operator; they also run a ranch and a hotel in, and near, the park, respectively.

Dittmar Adventures Miraflores 604 ☎ 61 614201, ⊛ dittmaradventures.com. Experienced local mountain guide David runs trekking trips to Torres del Paine and beyond,

as well as kayaking – both day-trips and multi-day-trips – on Lago Dixon and Río Serrano. Once-in-a-lifetime cycling trips along the Carretera Austral can be organized for groups.

Erratic Rock Baquedano 719, ☎ 61 410355, ⊛ erraticrock.com. Experienced operator offering advice on trekking in Torres del Paine (see p.400), as well as running multi-day trekking and climbing trips – to Torres del Paine, the wilderness around Cabo Froward (see p.393; summer only) and to different parts of Tierra del Fuego.

Estancia Travel Puerto Bories 13B ☎ 61 412221, ⊛ estanciatravel.com. Highly recommended horseriding trips, from half-day rides to the Cueva de Milodón to multi-day expeditions.

Fantastico Sur ⊛ fsexpeditions.com. Acclaimed Punta Arenas-based operator offering guided walks and treks in Torres del Paine as well as the annual 11-day Patagonian wildlife-watching trip (the Torres del Paine leg focuses on puma-watching).

Turismo 21 de Mayo Eberhard 560 ☎ 61 614420, ⊛ turismo21demayo.cl. Organizes sailing excursions to see the Balmaceda and Serrano Glaciers in Parque Nacional Bernardo O'Higgins on their private cutter, 21 de Mayo, and combo sailing day-trips that include a tour of Torres del Paine. Multi-day adventures include yachting, horseriding and a stay at the Estancia Perrales.

Tutravesia Manuel Bulnes 47 ☎ 61 415747, ⊛ tutravesia.com. This established kayaking outfit offers multi-day-trips for beginner and advanced kayakers alike – from a gentle paddle along the Río Serrano to the spectacular 4-day Ice Route, which ends in a lake filled with icebergs.

ACCOMMODATION

HOTELS & B&B

★ **Altiplánico** Huerto Familiar 282 ☎ 61 412525, ⊛ altiplanico.cl. This waterfront hotel just north of Natales is best described as "elegant bunker". The two-storey adobe building encases spacious, contemporary rooms with warm touches of colour, soft sheepskins on the beds and huge windows offering great views of the Strait. **CH$130,000 (US$270)**

Hostal Las Carretas Galvarino 745 ☎ 61 414584, ⊛ portalmagallanes.com/lascarretas/. Cheerful B&B particularly popular with travelling couples and offering spacious rooms, all decked out in creams and reds, with central heating that you'll appreciate in the off-season, and cable TV. The on-site restaurant does a mean Patagonian barbecue. **CH$25,000**

★ **Hotel If Patagonia** Magallanes 73 ☎ 61 410312, ⊛ www.hotelifpatagonia.com. The light-filled atrium of this excellent mid-range hotel puts you in mind of an M.C. Escher work, leading up as it does to a rooftop terrace with superb views of the Last Hope Sound. There's solar power, the rooms are bright with warm touches of woven art and

the superior doubles have Jacuzzis. **CH$97,100**

Indigo Patagonia Ladrilleros 105 ☎ 61 413609, ⊛ indigopatagonia.com. Its unique decor hiding plush, airy rooms, decorated in neutral tones with warm accents, Natales's plushest hotel puts an emphasis on eco-friendly practices such as organic composting. Looking out over Last Hope Sound from one of its three rooftop hot tubs is nothing short of wonderful, and spa packages are bliss, post-trekking. **CH$120,000 (US$250)**

Keoken Patagonia B&B Manuel Señoret 267 ☎ 61 413670, ⊛ keokenpatagonia.com. Friendly, centrally located and family-run B&B with several compact, centrally heated rooms with comfortable beds, and a guest lounge with a fireplace to curl up in front of. **CH$55,000**

Patagonia B&B Prolongacion Av España, Huerto 82B ☎ 61 414517, ⊛ patagoniabedandbreakfast.cl. The brightly painted rooms at this family-run B&B are spacious and inviting, the buffet breakfast is excellent and the welcoming owners can help to arrange tours. On the outskirts of town, a 10min walk from the main square. **CH$35,000**

9

★ **The Singular Patagonia** Puerto Bories ☎ 61 722030, ⓦ thesingular.com. Located by the water in Puerto Bories, a 10min drive north of Natales, this five-star hotel has drawn nothing but praise from guests. The ultra-modern rooms come with floor-to-ceiling windows for that panoramic view of Last Hope Sound; the food served is an excellent blend of Patagonian and international; and full-board packages include tailor-made excursions such as horseriding, trekking, sailing and wildlife watching. B&B option also available. B&B CH$316,000 (US$660), full board CH$555,000,00 (US$1160)

HOSTELS

★ **Erratic Rock** Baquedano 719, ⓦ erraticrock.com. The self-styled "burnt-out hippie from Oregon" got it exactly right: the atmosphere is laidback, with hostel cats wandering in and out, but the rooms are spick-and-span. Bill's early morning breakfast – one of the best in town – provides the hikers heading to Torres del Paine with nourishment while the daily 3pm talk provides them with all the information needed. Dorm CH$9000, double CH$25,000

Erratic Rock II Zamora 732 ☎ 61 414317, ⓦ erraticrock2 .com. An upmarket offshoot of the original hostel, this warm, family-run guesthouse is a popular option with couples and older travellers wanting a quiet stay with all the creature comforts. The en-suite doubles have cable TV, the bathrooms

sparkle and breakfast is ample. CH$35,000

Lili Patagonico's Arturo Prat 479 ☎ 61 414063, ⓦ lilipatagonicos.com. This brightly painted backpacker favourite has a cavernous dining and lounge area and nice extras such as an indoor climbing wall, good breakfast and pre-Torres del Paine briefing. The owners organize half- and full-day-trips into the surrounding area. More expensive doubles come with their own bathroom. Dorm CH$8000, double CH$20,000

★ **The Singing Lamb** Arauco 779 ☎ 61 410958, ⓦ thesinginglamb.com. Very popular with international travellers of all ages, this hostel is a cut above the rest: a dorm with comfortable beds rather than bunks, attractive guest lounge, showers with an area where you can dry off and book exchange. Susan, the indomitable Kiwi owner, wakes her guests up on time so that they can fill up on fresh porridge, home-made bread and jam and scrambled eggs before going off to Torres del Paine. Dorm CH$11,000

Yagan House O'Higgins 584 ☎ 61 414137, ⓦ yaganhouse.cl. Excellent beds with down comforters, warm red-and-cream decor, eco-friendly practices and a guest lounge with a roaring fire distinguish this popular yet quiet hostel. The owners throw a great Patagonian barbecue and the only downside is that there are no lockers. Dorm CH$10,000, double CH$25,000

EATING AND DRINKING

Natales has an extensive eating scene, more imaginative than that of most other Patagonian towns because of the influx of international travellers, and with something for every budget. For self-caterers, the widest range of groceries is found at the well-stocked Unimark **supermarket** on Bulnes between Baquedano and Ramírez.

CAFÉS AND SNACKS

Al Grano Baquedano 553 ☎ 61 413108. The mains at this laidback café-lounge are best avoided as they taste like something cooked by a culinary-challenged bachelor, but it's a good place to nurse a real coffee and a portion of one of their divine cakes (the triple chocolate hits the spot!) while hunched over a laptop or a good book. Daily noon–10pm.

★ **El Living** Arturo Prat 156 ☎ 61 413609. Not just an excellent vegetarian restaurant, but also the town's most popular café-lounge, playing chilled-out tunes and featuring the best book exchange in town. Smoothies, sandwiches, salads and real coffee stand out, and the proprietress makes excellent cakes; the only drawback is that it seems to close too early (apart from Thurs, when the Navimag ferry comes in). Daily specials from CH$5500. Closed April to November. Daily 11am–10pm; until 11.30pm Thurs.

Patagonia Dulce Barros Arana 233 ☎ 61 413609. For home-made chocolate, cookies, excellent *kuchen* and home-made ice cream, head to this gingerbread-house-like café. They say that if you eat *calafate* berries, you'll return to Patagonia; you can find out if the same is true of *calafate*-flavoured ice cream. Mon–Sat 10–6pm, Sun 11am–3pm.

El Toqui Baquedano 699 ☎ 09 9401 3486. Soups, salads and big chunky sandwiches are the order of the day at this corner café – a new backpacker favourite. Daily noon–9pm.

The Dried Fruit Guy Baquedano 443. This shop is *the* place to stock up on trail mix and all manner of dried fruit before heading to Torres del Paine. Mon–Sat 10am–8pm.

RESTAURANTS

★ **Afrigonia** Eberhard 343 ☎ 61 413609. In a new, bigger location, Natales's most imaginative restaurant serves delectable African–Patagonian fusion dishes. Standout dishes include *ceviche* with mango, Patagonian lamb and spicy seafood curry with *wali* (rice with almonds and raisins). Service is excellent, though in high season, come early, or be prepared for a leisurely dinner. Mains from CH$7000. Daily 12.30–3pm & 7.30–11.30pm.

★ **Aldea** Barros Arana 132 ☎ 61 414027, ⓦ aldearestaurant.cl. The menu at this new, intimate, vegetarian-friendly spot changes daily according to the whim of the chef and consists of just a few beautifully executed dishes. Choose from the likes of hare loin with *platano* puree and vegetable tajine, and finish off with a sublime *arroz con*

9

leche. Mains CH$6000–7000. Daily 12.30–3pm & 7–11pm.

El Asadór Patagónico Arturo Prat 158 ☎61 413609. The signature *asado Patagonico* – lamb roasting on a spit in the barbecue pit by the window – acts as a magnet for the carnivorously inclined. The expertly grilled steaks at this established *parrilla* are just as good; if you have a dainty appetite, bring a friend, as the portions are ample. Daily 12.30–3pm & 7.30–11pm.

La Mesita Grande Eberhard 508 ☎61 413609. Hordes of hungry hikers stage a daily invasion of the best pizzeria in Patagonia, drawn by the generous portions of superb thin-crust pizzas (from CH$5500), home-made pasta and sumptuous desserts (including sweet pizza with *dulce de leche*). The two long wooden tables make for a communal dining experience and encourage mingling. Daily 12.30–3.30pm & 7–11.30pm.

La Última Esperanza Eberhard 354 ☎61 413626. With its white linen tablecloths, this restaurant may be formal-looking, but the seafood and fish on offer is reasonably priced and the portions plentiful. It gets particularly busy on Sundays in the off season when it's one of the few places open. Mains from CH$5500. Daily noon–3pm & 7–11pm.

BARS AND PUBS

Baguales Bories 430 ☎61 411920, ⓦwww .cervezabagules.cl. If the one thing that would make your Patagonian hiking experience complete is returning to a cosy microbrewery serving ample platters of fiery Buffalo wings, quesadillas, tacos and other assorted Tex-Mex food, accompanied by a home-made light or dark brew, then you're in luck: look no further than this new Californian–Chilean pub on the Plaza de Armas. Beers CH$2000; mains from CH$5000. Daily noon–late.

Base Camp Baquedano 719 ☎61 411920. Next door to the most popular hostel in town, this lively pub (which doubles as an equipment rental centre) is often full to the brim with pre- and post-Torres hikers, contentedly drinking beer and eating their way through large portions of inexpensive daily specials. Expect occasional performances by local bands, themed nights and spontaneous barbecues. Daily noon–1am.

DIRECTORY

Banks and exchange There's an ATM in Banco Santander, Manuel Bulnes 598, or Banco de Chile, Manuel Bulnes 544. There are several *cambios* along Blanco Encalada and Bulnes; try Mily at Blanco Encalada 266.

Camping equipment Try Erratic Rock, Baquedano 732, or La Maddera, Bulnes at Prat, which also sells all manner of equipment, including fuel canisters.

For car rental, try Europcar, Manuel Bulnes 100 (☎61 414475, ⓦwww.europcar.cl) and Hertz, Blanco Encalada 353 (☎61 414519, ⓦhertz.cl).

Hospital Hospital Puerto Natales, Ignacio Carrera Pinto 537 ☎61 411582.

Internet All accommodation options reviewed offer free wi-fi; some offer free internet also. Otherwise, try the internet café at *Hostal Reymar*, Baquedano 420.

Laundry ServiLaundry, Arturo Prat 357 ☎61 412869; promises to do your laundry within 2 hours.

Pharmacy Farmacia Puerto Natales, Esmeralda 701.

Post office Eberhard 429.

Cueva del Milodón

Cave Summer daily 8am–9pm; winter daily 8.30am–6pm **Museum** Daily 8am–8pm • CH$4500

From Natales, a bumpy 150-kilometre gravel road runs through flat Patagonian scrubland to Torres del Paine national park, with the **Cueva del Milodón** a standard stop after 21km. The cave itself is pretty impressive – 30m high, 80m wide and 200m deep. In 1895, the German settler Herman Eberhard, who owned the land bordering the cave, discovered a large piece of skin from an unidentifiable animal, which was eventually traced to a giant sloth called a milodón. This creature was thought to be long extinct, but the excavated skin looked so fresh that rumours began to circulate that it might still be alive. An expedition was mounted (see box, p.400), though no live sloth was ever found. On site there is a good **Museo de Sitio** with detailed information on the milodón and a life-size plastic replica of the creature.

The Balmaceda and Serrano glaciers

To the northwest of the Cueva del Milodón, the Seno Ultima Esperanza continues on for about 100km until it meets the Río Serrano, which, after 36km, arrives at the **Balmaceda** and **Serrano glaciers**. A boat trip here (see p.397) is one of the most beautiful in the entire area. It takes seven hours and you pass a colony of cormorants

9

THE STRANGE CASE OF THE GIANT SLOTH SKIN

In 1900 an **expedition** sponsored by London's *Daily Express* arrived to investigate the rumours of a **giant sloth** in a cave near Puerto Natales, but no live creatures were found. The skin, it turned out, was so well preserved because it had been deep-frozen by the frigid Patagonian climate. Shortly after the 1900 expedition an unscrupulous gold prospector together with **Charley Milward** (see p.388) dynamited the cave's floor, uncovering and then selling the remaining skin and bones. Two pieces made their way to Britain: one to the Natural History Museum in London, and the other to Charley Milward's family, the very same which was to fire the imagination of a young **Bruce Chatwin**.

---

and a slippery mass of sea lions. The glaciers themselves make an impressive sight, especially when a chunk of ice the size of a small house breaks off and crashes into the water. They form the southern tip of **Parque Nacional Bernardo O'Higgins** (see p.395), the largest and least visited national park in the whole of Chile. The east of the park is almost entirely made up of the Campo de Hielo Sur (the Southern Ice Field); the west comprises fjords, islands and untouched forest.

Parque Nacional Torres del Paine

Summer CH$15,000, winter CH$5000 • ☎ 02 953 8782, ⓦ torresdelpaine.com

Nothing really prepares you for your first sight of **PARQUE NACIONAL TORRES DEL PAINE**. The **Paine Massif**, the unforgettable centrepiece of the park, appears beyond the turquoise lakes long before you get close to it. The finest views of the massif are from the south bank of Lago Nordenskjöld, whose waters act as a great reflecting mirror. If driving through the park, take the southern entrance to constantly have the best views in front of you.

The centrepiece is made up of the twin peaks of **Cerro Monte Almirante Nieto** (2668m and 2640m). On the northern side are the soaring, unnaturally elegant **Torres del Paine** ("Paine Towers"), the icon of the park, and further west the sculpted, dark-capped **Cuernos del Paine** ("Paine Horns"). To the west of the park is the broad ice river of **Glaciar Grey**, and on the plains at the mountains' feet, large herds of **guanacos** and the odd *ñandú* (rhea) still run wild; you're more likely to spot these than the park's more elusive fauna: pumas and the rare *huemúl* deer.

In January and February the park is crammed with holidaymakers, so the best months to visit are October, November and December or March and April. Although in winter (June–Sept) temperatures can fall to -10°C (14°F) or even lower, freezing lakes and icing over trails, the small numbers of visitors, lack of wind and often clear visibility can also make this another good time to come – just wrap up warmly.

Hiking routes

This may not be the place to taste true wilderness, but there are still plenty of places to lose the crowds. The two most popular hikes are the "**W**", so-called because the route you follow looks like a "W", up three valleys, taking you to the "stars" of the park – Las Torres, Valle del Francés and Glaciar Grey, and the "**Circuit**", which leads you around the back of the park and encompasses the "W"; allow seven to ten days for the "Circuit" and at least four for the "W".

The Circuit

The best way to tackle the "Circuit" is anticlockwise, as it also means you'll have excellent views of Glacier Grey in front of you rather than behind you when you come to tackle the most challenging part of the hike – the Paso John Gardner.

Hostería Las Torres to Las Torres

From *Hostería Las Torres*, go southwest along the foot of the massif. Just after a bridge, the track veers to the north up Valle Ascencio along a dirt trail strewn with scree; after a relatively steep two-hour climb it's possible to spend the first night at the *Refugio y Camping Chileno*. From *Chileno*, the trail continues up and down exposed inclines (beware of sudden gusts of wind), and then through *lenga* brush, crossing a stream, to the wooded *Campamento Torres*; allow ninety minutes. Campamento Torres is a free campsite by another stream at the foot of the track up to the **Torres** themselves. You can camp overnight here, leave your gear and then tackle the knee-popping 45 minute climb up uneven boulders in order to reach Las Torres just before daybreak. If the weather is clear you are treated to a stunning postcard view across Laguna Torres up to the three strange statuesque towers that give the park its name – **Torre Norte Monzino** (2600m), **Torre Central** (2800m) and **Torre Sur D'Agostini** (2850m), at their most gorgeous when bathed in the first rays of the sun.

Campamento Torres to the Valle del Silencio

An alternative trek from *Campamento Torres* is to press on north for an hour or so, guided by cairns, to the *Campamento Japonés*, a climbers-only campsite. At *Japonés* you'll find the beautiful **Valle del Silencio** that heads west. It's much less visited than the Torres and a great place to escape the crowds.

Hostería Las Torres to Refugio Lago Dickson

From *Hostería Las Torres*, *Campamento Serón* is an easy four-hour walk northwards up and down gentle inclines and vast fields. From *Campamento Serón*, it's a five- or six-hour hike to *Refugio Dickson*, with a flat trail along the Río Paine, which then climbs steeply uphill as you pass a small horseshoe-shaped lagoon. The trail meanders on west, with sweeping views of Lago Paine on your right-hand side, ducking into patches of vegetation and crossing several streams. A boggy section of the trail is partially covered with wooden boardwalks. Finally, the trail descends steeply to *Refugio Lago Dickson* in its scenic setting at the southern end of iceberg-flecked Lago Dickson.

Refugio Lago Dickson to Campamento Los Perros

Campamento Los Perros lies a four-hour hike from *Dickson* southwest along a largely uphill trail that snakes through dense forest for most of the way. You cross two bridges over large glacial streams and pass a pretty waterfall, before emerging at an exposed,

---

FIRE IN THE PARK

On December 27, 2011, a **fire** that was started by human negligence in the southern section of **Torres del Paine** quickly spread, exacerbated by the bone-dry conditions and strong winds. The Chilean government has been criticized for its slow and inadequate response; by the time the blaze was finally brought under control, over 130 square kilometres of forest had been destroyed. An Israeli tourist was detained on suspicion of accidentally causing the fire; he denied responsibility and there is some evidence that pressure may have been put on him to make a confession.

Sadly, the incident has exacerbated the anti-Israeli sentiment among some Patagonians, and the suspect was subjected to racial abuse as he was led to court. However, the majority of Puerto Natales citizens have responded in a constructive manner; in a bid to protect the park from future damage, there will now be **compulsory talks on park safety** at the Laguna Amarga entrance to Torres del Paine, as well as volunteer patrols in the park. It remains to be seen whether the Chilean government will fund a permanent ranger patrol.

On January 4, 2012, the Chilean government reopened eighty percent of the park to visitors; at the time of writing, Refugio Grey, Paine Grande Lodge, and the Guardas, Paso, Carretas, Italiano and Británico campsites were closed but to reopen in expected course.

9

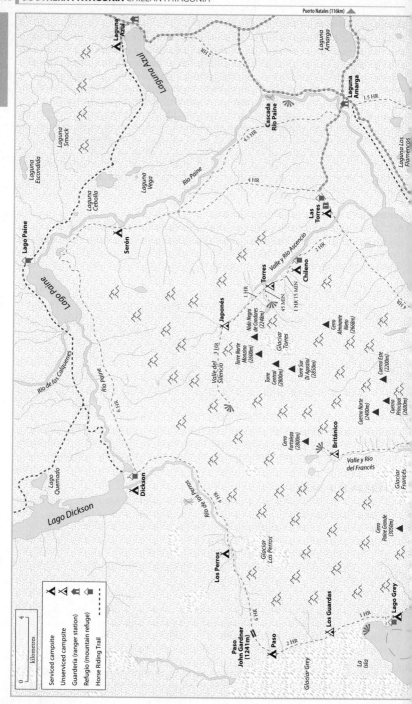

Puerto Natales (116km)

Laguna Azul

Laguna Amarga

Laguna Los Flamencos

Laguna Smock

Laguna Escondida

Cascada Río Paine

Laguna Vega

Río Paine

Laguna Cebolla

3 HR

4.5 HR

1.5 HR

4 HR

Las Torres

Lago Paine

Serón

Lago Paine

Valle y Río Ascencio

2 HR

Chileno

Torres

1 HR

4 HR

Japonés

45 MIN

1 HR 15 MIN

Río de los Calafquenes

Río Paine

6 HR

3 HR

Nido Negro de Cóndores (2240m)

Cerro Almirante Nieto (2668m)

Valle del Silencio

Torre Norte Monzino (2600m)

Glaciar Torres

Guerno Este (2200m)

Torre Central (2800m)

Torre Sur DI Agostini (2850m)

Guerno Norte (2400m)

Guerno Principal (2600m)

Lago Quemado

Cerro Fortaleza (2800m)

Británico

Valle y Río del Francés

Dickson

Glaciar Francés

Lago Dickson

Río de los Perros

4 HR

Glaciar Los Perros

Cerro Paine Grande (3050m)

Los Perros

Los Guardas

Lago Grey

1 HR

Paso John Gardner (1241m)

6 HR

Paso

2 HR

Glaciar Grey

La Isla

0 — 4
kilometres

X Serviced campsite
X Unserviced campsite
▮ Guardería (ranger station)
▮ Refugio (mountain refuge)
---- Horse Riding Trail

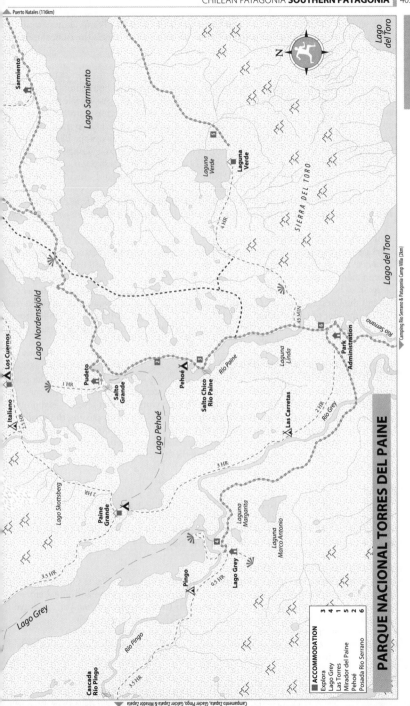

▲ Puerto Natales (116km)

Lago del Toro

Lago Sarmiento

Sarmiento

Laguna Verde

Laguna Verde

5

SIERRA DEL TORO

Lago del Toro

Lago Nordenskjöld

Los Cuernos

Italiano
2.5 HR

1 HR

Pudeto

Salto Grande

Pehoé

Salto Chico
Río Paine

Río Paine

2

3

Río Serrano

Park Administration

6

45 MIN

Laguna Linda

Las Carretas

Lago Pehoé

3 HR

2 HR

Río Grey

2 HR

Lago Skottsberg

Paine Grande

Laguna Margarita

Laguna Marco Antonio

Lago Grey

3.5 HR

Pingo

Lago Grey

0.5 HR

Río Pingo

Cascada Río Pingo

Río Pingo

3.5 HR

PARQUE NACIONAL TORRES DEL PAINE

▼ Campamento Zapata, Glacier Pingo, Glacier Zapata & Mirador Zapata

▲ Camping Río Serrano & Patagonia Camp Villa (2km)

■ ACCOMMODATION	
Explora	3
Lago Grey	4
Las Torres	1
Mirador del Paine	5
Pehoé	2
Posada Río Serrano	6

9

rocky section, which treats you to a fabulous view of Glaciar Los Perros above a round lagoon, before continuing to a patch of forest which partially shields the campsite from icy blasts of wind.

Across Paso John Gardner

The weather has to be in your favour before you start on a three-hour climb to the top of **Paso John Gardner** (1241m). It is too dangerous to cross the pass in gale-force wind; several hikers have lost their lives this way. From *Los Perros* you cross a stream using a rickety wooden bridge, followed by an hour's trudge through ankle-deep mud. Above the tree line, it's a straightforward uphill slog along the rock-strewn slope before reaching the exposed pass. The reward for all this is the sudden, staggering view over the icy pinnacles of **Glaciar Grey**, more than 7km wide at its largest point, and the vast immaculate expanse of the **Campo del Hielo Sur** – over ten thousand square kilometres of ice cap and one of the largest ice fields outside the poles.

On the other side of the pass crude steps descend steeply into *lenga* forest. It takes a couple of hours from the top of the pass to reach the small and basic *Campamento Paso*.

Campamento Paso to Refugio Lago Grey

Faster trekkers can press on down to the extremely basic, unserviced (except for a toilet) *Campamento Los Guardas*, two hours' trek away. In two places, you will have to ascend or descend along metal ladders attached to vertical slopes; they are often in various stages of disrepair, so be very careful. From *Campamento Los Guardas*, it's a further hour's descent through the forest to *Refugio y Camping Lago Grey*; the campsite is beautifully sited on the beach at the foot of Glaciar Grey, while the brand new *refugio* building is just uphill from it. It's possible to catch a boat to *Hotel Lago Grey* in summer; the boat sails alongside the glacier before making its way along the length of the lake (CH$36,000).

Refugio Lago Grey to Paine Grande Lodge

From *Refugio y Camping Lago Grey*, the path runs alongside the lake, before the largely exposed trail almost doubles back on itself, climbing steeply, after which it runs mostly uphill through the **Quebrada de los Vientos** ("Windy Gorge"), with several viewpoints from which to admire the lake. It then ducks into some *ñire* glens, passing the small Laguna Los Patos on the right-hand side, and descends to the *Paine Grande Lodge* and campsite, situated on the bank of the stunning glacial Lago Pehoé, three and a half hours later. From here you can continue along the "Circuit"; this is also the ideal place to start the "W".

The "W"

Like the "Circuit", it's best to do the "W" anti-clockwise, leaving the steepest hike to Las Torres until last, by which time you will have consumed most of your supplies. The first leg of the "W" is the hike there and back from *Paine Grande Lodge* to Glaciar Grey, described above. You can leave your gear at the lodge.

Paine Grande Lodge to Valle Francés

Take the signposted trail that runs along the southern side of the Paine Grande massif along Lago Skottsberg and a couple of smaller lagoons on the right-hand side, before crossing a suspension bridge across Río Francés to *Campamento Italiano*; you can leave your gear here before heading north up the Valle del Francés.

It's a rather steep two-hour hike with great views of the **Glaciar Francés** to *Campamento Británico*. It takes another hour through enchanted-looking *lenga* woods to the viewpoint from which you can admire **Paine Grande**, the massif's highest peak at 3050m, to your west, and the **Cuernos del Paine**, a set of incredibly carved towers capped with dark rock peaks, guarding the entrance to the valley to the southeast.

FROM TOP HIKERS, PARQUE NACIONAL TORRES DEL PAINE (PP.400–407); PUNTA ARENAS (PP.385–392)

9

> ## BEYOND THE W: TORRES DEL PAINE ALTERNATIVES
>
> There is more to Torres del Paine than just the "Circuit" and the "W"; numerous shorter hikes can be just as spectacular.
>
> ### MIRADOR LAGO GREY AND MIRADOR FERRIER
>
> From the Lago Grey ranger station near *Hotel Lago Grey*, a short trail leads through the forest to the lake's vast windswept beach, where you can watch house-sized chunks of bluish ice bobbling on the pale waters. To the left of the beach, by the jetty, a fairly steep unmarked trail skirts around the cliff before giving you an unobstructed view of Glaciar Gray. The most spectacular viewpoint of them all, **Mirador Ferrier**, lies a stiff two-hour hike up from behind the ranger station. From up there, you get a jaw-dropping vista over the park's many lakes, their colours ranging from aquamarine to greyish white. At the top, you make your way through forest before emerging among exposed rocks; bring warm clothes as the icy wind can be ferocious.
>
> ### LAGUNA AZUL
>
> There's a three-and-a-half-hour signposted walk from the *guardería* at Laguna Amarga to **Laguna Azul**, a secluded and little-visited lake in the northeast. From there, a mostly gentle four-hour trail leads past Laguna Cebolla to **Lago Paine**. It used to be possible to hike to Lago Dickson and cross the narrowest part of the lake to *Refugio Dickson*, but the boat is no longer functioning, though if you are on horseback, you can wade across Río Paine and continue along this trail to a viewpoint overlooking Glaciar Dickson.
>
> ### MIRADOR ZAPATA
>
> Another seldom-trod path takes you up to **Mirador Zapata**, a steep six-to seven-hour climb from *Guardería Lago Grey* at the southern tip of Lago Grey, itself a four-and-a-half-hour walk from the park administration building, rewarding you with views of the ice cap and the magnificent Glaciar Pingo. *Campamento Pingo* is half an hour into the trek, and **Campamento** *Zapata* an hour and a half from the *mirador*, making it an ideal overnight stop.

Valle del Francés to Refugio Los Cuernos

After you descend, from the foot of the valley, it's a mostly steep downhill ascent (allow two and a half hours) along the pale blue waters of the icy Lago Nordenskjold to the newly refurbished *Refugio y Camping Los Cuernos*, which nestles in a clearing in the shadow of Los Cuernos.

Refugio Los Cuernos to Hostería Las Torres

From *Los Cuernos*, it takes an easy four hours to reach the *Hostería Las Torres*, as the trail runs along gentle inclines through low shrubbery and then along green hills. If the water is high, you may have to wade across a glacial stream along the way. Shortly before reaching the *Hostería Las Torres*, you will see the signposted trail leading up Valle Ascencio (see p.401), and depending on whether or not you have already paid a visit to the park's last highlight, you either head uphill, or complete your trek up ahead.

ARRIVAL AND DEPARTURE
PARQUE NACIONAL TORRES DEL PAINE

BY BUS

The only entrance to the park for those coming by bus from Natales (twice daily; 3hr) is 117km from the town at Laguna Amarga, where you pay the park fee at the Conaf station. From here, minibuses meet bus arrivals from Natales for the transfer to *Hostería Las Torres* (CH$2000). The buses from Natales continue along Lago Nordenskjöld for another 19km to the *guardería* at Pudeto, the departure point for the catamaran to *Paine Grande Lodge*. The bus continues beyond here, past *Hostería Pehoé, Camping*

Pehoé and *Hotel Explora*, opposite Salto Chico, to reach the Park Administration 18km further on, where there's a visitor centre, a *refugio*, a grocery store and a *hostería*.

BY CAR

Driving up from Puerto Natales, you have a choice: to reach the southern entrance of the park, take a turn-off towards the Milodón Cave from the main road; this route is picturesque, but features numerous blind turns, loose gravel and numerous potholes. The main road from Natales continues to the park's north entrance via a newly paved road to Cerro Castillo; from there, it's a compacted gravel road to the Laguna Amarga entrance. A few kilometres before Laguna Amarga, you can turn off towards Lago Nordenskjöld.

GETTING AROUND

BY CATAMARAN
From the *guardería* Pudeto, a Hielos Patagónicos catamaran (@ 61 411380; mid-Nov to mid-March daily 9.30am, noon and 6pm; first half of Nov and second half of March noon and 6pm; Oct and April noon; CH$12,000 one-way, CH$19,000 return; tickets sold on board) runs across Lago Pehoé. Return trips from *Paine Grande Lodge* are 30min after the arrival times and are met by buses heading back to Puerto Natales. From the park administration there are daily buses to Puerto Natales, the latest leaving at 6.30pm.

BY CAR
The gravel road that runs through the park is reasonably well maintained. Take the bends slowly as loose gravel is a hazard. Watch out for buses and Explora minivans which tend to drive fast and in the middle of road.

INFORMATION

Tourist information The Park Administration Centre at the park's southern entrance (Dec–Feb daily 8.30am–8pm; @ 61 691931) has detailed displays on the park's fauna and flora. However, all the *guarderías* provide information about trail conditions and you'll be given a basic trail map when you pay your entrance fee.

Climbing To climb in the park, you'll need to get a permit from the Park Administration Centre; it costs CH$65,000 and covers any ascent.

Park rules Follow park guidelines regarding lighting fires (human negligence in 2005 and in 2011 led to the destruction of a large chunk of the park) and carry *all* your rubbish back to Puerto Natales, including toilet paper.

ACCOMMODATION

You'll find several different types of accommodation in the park: unserviced (free) campsites, serviced campsites and *refugios* as well as rather expensive *hosterías* and hotels.

HOSTERÍAS AND HOTELS
Explora @ 61 411247, @ explora.com. The most extravagant and exclusive five-star hotel in the park, this sleek white building overlooks Lago Pehoé, with incredible views from every room. A boardwalk leads down past nearby Salto Chico to the lakeside swimming pool and open-air hot tubs. The restaurant serves excellent fusion cuisine and you can choose from 25 different tours with knowledgeable bilingual guides, from day treks to horseriding. Explora only offers 4–8-night all-inclusive packages. 4-night double CH$262,200,000 (US$5480)
Hostería Lago Grey @ 61 410172, @ turismolagogrey .com. Sitting amid some beech trees, this *hostería* has beautiful views of Lago Grey and a number of good hiking trails nearby. However, the location is rather isolated from the rest of the park unless you have your own wheels, and meals (except breakfast) are not included in the price. A boat run by the *hostería* makes a 3hr return trip twice daily (9am and noon) to Glaciar Grey. CH$158,000 (US$330)
Hostería Pehoé @ 61 411390, @ pehoe.com. Connected to the mainland by a pedestrian bridge and featuring the most picturesque setting in the whole park, this bungalow-style hotel sits on a small island in the Lago Pehoé, looking out to the highest peaks of the Paine Massif. The rooms, however, are unremarkable and overpriced for what they are; snag rooms 36–38 for the best views. CH$160,000
Hostería Las Torres @ 61 363636, @ lastorres.com. Convenient location at the foot of Cerro Paine, beautiful, comfortable (though compact) rooms and a good restaurant (open to non-guests as well) make this a good, though overpriced, choice. Numerous excursions available in the all-inclusive package, such as horseriding trips of varying length and guided treks. There's also a spa in which to pamper yourself. CH$120,000 (US$250)
★ **Patagonia Camp** @ 2 334 9255, @ patagoniacamp .com. The most unusual lodging option in the park, this collection of luxury yurts offers the ultimate glamping (glamorous camping) experience overlooking Lago del Toro. The yurts are bright, and warm, the showers and bathtubs are excellent and there are skylights for stargazing. All-inclusive 3- or 4-night stays only. 3-night double CH$1,703,000 (US$3,560)
Posada Tercera Barranca @ 61 613531, @ baqueanozamora.cl. Located near Laguna Azul, this ranch, housed in an attractive old structure on the site of an old *estancia* established by pioneers back in the day, has just seven comfortable, centrally heated rooms. Run by Baqueano Zamora (see Puerto Natales tour operators, p.397), it's a good base for horseback riding excursions; if there are enough guests, the chef prepares a traditional lamb barbecue. CH$75,000

CAMPSITES AND REFUGIOS
Most campsites tend to be open Oct–April, though the ones on the Circuit open later in the season. **Unserviced**

REFUGIOS IN TORRES DEL PAINE

Refugios are usually open from September to May and are generally closed by the weather during the rest of the year. Six of them are run by two Puerto Natales-based companies, Fantástico Sur (Esmeralda 661, ☎61 614184, ⓦfantasticosur.com) and Vertice Patagonia (Ladrilleros 209, ☎61 412742, ⓦverticepatagonia.cl); these are well equipped, offer full board or hot meals on demand, as well as equipment rental, and charge around CH$25,000 for a bunk bed, CH$6000 to camp or around CH$6000/8000/10,500 for breakfast/lunch/dinner. Discounts are available if you pay in US dollars; foreigners are exempt from IVA (tax). In peak season, book *refugio* beds in advance. Conaf also operates a number of free *refugios* throughout the park (Zapata, Pingo, Laguna Amarga) though these are very basic and frequently in a poor state of repair.

campsites including *Japonés* (climbers only), *Italiano*, *Británico*, *Los Guardas* and *Paso* on the Torres del Paine Circuit are free and are basically just a flat patch of land and a *fogón* (some have toilets). All the **serviced campsites** are listed below. If camping, take your own food (the small shops attached to *refugios* and campsites have a limited selection and are overpriced); drinking water, however, can be collected from most streams. Bring a sturdy waterproof tent – enough to withstand the Patagonian wind – and all necessary camping equipment. It is possible to rent tents and sleeping bags from most *refugios* (see box, above) but the costs will add up. Wild camping isn't permitted.

Campamento Los Perros (Vértice Patagonia). Last campsite before the John Gardner pass, situated in a wooded area, with a small food shop, cold showers and a cooking hut. CH$4500 per person

Campamento Serón (Fantástico Sur). Partially shaded campsite beside the Río Paine with picnic tables, cold showers and a small shop in a pleasant meadow setting at the bottom of the massif's northeast corner. CH$4000 per person

Camping Lago Pehoé ☎61 266910, ⓦcampingpehoe .com. Attractive campsite on the eastern edge of turquoise Lago Pehoé, complete with a restaurant, hot showers, a shop, *fogones* for barbecues, and shelters for tent sites. You can also stay in one of the geodomes on offer. Camping CH$8,000 per person or CH$45,000 for a 2-person geodome tent

Camping Río Serrano ⓦcampingchile.com. South of the park administration building, this campsite with cold showers is on a bend in the Río Serrano and accessible from the road. It's possible to organize excellent horseriding tours from here and Patagonian barbecue can be arranged for groups. CH$4500 per person

Refugio y Campamento Dickson (Vertice Patagonia). On the shores of Lago Dickson on the northern part of the Circuit, this is the most remote refuge in the park; the staff are friendly and there's a well-stocked shop. The campsite has basic facilities only. Camping CH$3500 per person, refugio CH$15,000 per person

Refugio y Campamento Grey (Vertice Patagonia). A popular *refugio* in a new location near Lago and Glacier Grey; book meals in advance. Beachside campsite includes hot showers and a small on-site grocery store. Camping CH$3500 per person, refugio CH$15,000 per person

Refugio y Campamento Paine Grande (Vertice Patagonia). This modern structure has a scenic location and a café, restaurant and small store within the lodge. You can camp in the adjoining grassy fields and there are separate toilets and hot showers, as well as a cooking hut for campers. Camping CH$4500 per person, refugio CH$24,900 per person

Refugio y Campamento Las Torres (Fantástico Sur). Near the entrance to the park and the *Hostería Las Torres*, this *refugio* is split between two buildings and has comfortable bunks, a small shop and gear rental. Hearty meals are served in the large dining room. Campsite has hot showers, picnic tables and fire pits. Camping CH$5000 per person, refugio CH$20,000 per person

Refugio y Camping Chileno (Fantástico Sur). A popular stop halfway along the Valle Ascencio, this refugio offers kitchen privileges after certain hours as well as hot meals. Camping CH$5000 per person, refugio CH$20,000 per person

Refugio y Camping Los Cuernos (Fantástico Sur). A newly refurbished *refugio* in a clearing beneath the Cuernos del Paine, on the northern shore of Lago Nordenskjöld, with a cafeteria and campsite with semi-sheltered spots and hot showers. Camping CH$6000 per person, refugio CH$20,000 per person

Into Argentina: Parque Nacional Los Glaciares

The vast majority of travellers to Patagonia don't limit themselves to the Chilean side alone. Just over the easily crossed border lies Argentina's most spectacular national park – **Parque Nacional Los Glaciares** – home to two of the region's star attractions. The first

9

is the craggy blue face of the **Glaciar Perito Moreno** – regularly cited as one of the world's natural wonders, and situated near the tourist hub of **El Calafate**. The second is the trekkers' and climbers' paradise of the **Fitz Roy mountain range** in the north of the park, accessed from the relaxed little town of **El Chaltén**.

El Calafate

EL CALAFATE is the centre of the tourist network in the deep south of mainland Argentine Patagonia, whose proximity to Glaciar Perito Moreno makes it one of the most popular destinations in Patagonia and, indeed, in all of Argentina. The town is also a transport hub with onward connections to numerous Argentinian destinations and its compact size makes it easy enough to navigate on foot. You'll find most restaurants, along with an ATM, internet cafés and tour agencies, along Avenida Libertador, the main thoroughfare.

Glaciarium

6km from El Calafate along Ruta 11, en route to the Perito Moreno glacier • Sept–April 9am–8pm; May–Aug 11am–8pm • AR$80 • Ⓦ glaciarium.com • Hourly transfers from the car park in front of the Santa Cruz Province Touristic Bureau, 1 de Mayo between Libertador and Roca (AR$25 return)

El Calafate's main attraction is this superb new interactive museum dedicated to glaciers – an invaluable introduction for anyone about to visit the Perito Moreno glacier. The illuminated displays in the strategic semi-gloom of this vast building answer any questions you may have about glaciers – what they are, how they are created, the main features of different types of glaciers and where they are found. An extensive section is dedicated to the research of Patagonian ice fields and the video presentations – including a 3D documentary on the Parque Nacional Los Glaciares and one on environmental issues facing our planet – are particularly worthwhile. End the visit with a drink at the on-site *Glacio Bar Branca* – the first Icebar in Argentina.

ARRIVAL AND DEPARTURE   EL CALAFATE

BY AIR
El Calafate is linked by frequent Aerolíneas Argentinas (Ⓦ www.aerolineas.com.ar) and LADE flights to Buenos Aires, Ushuaia, Bariloche, Puerto Madryn and Esquel, among other Argentine destinations. Aeropuerto El Calafate (☎ 02902 491220) is located 17km east of town along Ruta 11. Airport shuttles Cóndor (☎ 02902 491655) and Manuel Tienda León (☎ 02902 493766) meet incoming flights.

BY BUS
Buses to and from Puerto Natales and various Argentine destinations arrive at the hilltop bus station along Av Roca, one block above the main street, Av Libertador, to which it's connected by a flight of steps. **Companies** Bus Sur/Cal Tur (☎ 02902 491842) serves Puerto Natales and El Chaltén; Chaltén Travel

(☎ 02902 491833) runs to El Chaltén and up Ruta 40 to Bariloche via Los Antiguos; TAQSA (☎ 02902 491843) and Interlagos (☎ 02902 491179) run tours to the Perito Moreno glacier and have services to Río Gallegos, with onwards connections to major Argentine destinations.
Destinations El Chaltén (4 daily; 5hr); Perito Moreno glacier (4 daily, typically around 7am and 3.30pm; 1hr 15min); Puerto Natales (1 daily; 5hr); Río Gallegos (5 daily, 4hr).

BY CAR
Numerous car rental companies include Adventure Rent a Car, Av Libertador 290 (☎ 02902 492595); Europcar, Av Libertador 1741 (☎ 02902 493606) and Hertz at the airport (☎ 02902 492525).

INFORMATION AND TOURS

TOURIST INFORMATION
Tourist information The helpful tourist kiosk is situated at the bus terminal (daily: April–Oct 9am–8pm; Nov–March 8am–10pm; ☎ 02902 491090, Ⓦ elcalafate.gov.ar or losglaciares.com) and can help track down accommodation.

National park information Parque Nacional Los Glaciares office, Libertador 1302 (Mon–Fri 8am–6pm, Sat & Sun 10am–7pm; ☎ 02902 491755). Has a useful map of the park, sells fishing licences and will give you the latest information on campsites near the glacier.

9

BAFT (Backpacking Free Travel) Gregores at 9 de Julio (daily 9am–7pm; w baftravel.com). Excellent information centre aimed at backpackers and staffed by an energetic young team who can help book accommodation and onward travel. In the lounge area you can look through guidebooks, have a coffee, use the free wi-fi and pick up maps of the area.

TOUR OPERATORS

Virtually every tour agency in El Calafate runs day-trips to the Perito Moreno glacier, allowing around four hours at the ice face. For more specialized excursions, try the established operators listed below.

Cabalgata en Patagonia Av Libertador 4315 ☎ 02902 493278, w cabalgataenpatagonia.com.

Highly recommended horseriding outfit, specializing in everything from 2hr rides with a panoramic view of Lago Argentino to 5-day *huaso* (cowboy) expeditions with pack animals, as well as tailor-made trips.

Hielo y Aventura Av Libertador 935 ☎ 02902 492094, w hieloyaventura.com. Runs the excellent Mini-Trekking and Big Ice excursions which allow you to hike on the Perito Moreno glacier itself. No prior experience required.

Overland Patagonia Av Libertador 587 ☎ 02902 491792, w glaciar.com. Ice-hiking on Glacier Viedma and guided treks/camping trips in El Chaltén, as well as "alternative" tours of Glaciar Perito Moreno, run by the *Hostel del Glaciar Libertador*.

ACCOMMODATION

America del Sur Puerto Deseado 153 ☎ 02902 493525, w americahostel.com.ar. Besides the all-you-can-gobble nightly barbecue, this lodge has great lake views, a busy atmosphere (don't expect any sleep before midnight) and the bathrooms really benefit from the underfloor heating on those crisp mornings. Dorm **ARS95**, double **ARS390**

Casa de Grillos B&B Los Cóndores 1215 ☎ 02902 491160, w casadegrillos.com.ar. This informal B&B, with rooms decorated in individual styles and a fully-equipped cabin (sleeping up to four) out back, makes for a peaceful and comfortable stay. Double **ARS313**, cabin **ARS478**

★ **EOLO – Patagonia's Spirit** Ruta 11, Km 23 ☎ 02902 492042, w eolo.com.ar. The main draws of this luxurious lodge, set amid a 7400 acre property, are isolation, incredible views of Lago Argentino, Torres del Paine and Valle Anita, and all manner of creature comforts – from indoor swimming pool and sauna to gourmet

Patagonian cuisine. Late Sept to late April only. 7-day full board only (transfers included in price). **ARS3218 (US$740)**

I Keu Ken Hostel Pontoriero 171 ☎ 02902 495175, w patagoniaikeuken.com.ar. Cosy hostel with an excellent hilltop location (15min walk from bus station), super-friendly staff and an atmosphere of camaraderie among the international guests. On the weekends, the owners throw an excellent barbecue. Dorm **ARS80**, double **ARS360**

Miyazato Inn Edigio Feruglio 150 ☎ 02902 491953, w interpatagonia.com/miyazatoinn. This Japanese *ryokan*-meets-Patagonian B&B has only five rooms, all of which are attractive and centrally heated. While recent construction is encroaching on the tranquility of the location, the warmth and local knowledge of the owner makes up for it. Engish and Japanese spoken. **ARS391**

EATING AND DRINKING

CAFÉS AND BARS

Borges & Alvarez Libro-bar Av Libertador 1015 ☎ 02902 491464. This cross between a cosy library and a microbrewery is one of the liveliest bars in town and good not just for the home brew but also for its extensive selection of whiskies and other sprits. Daily 10am–3am.

Viva La Pepa Amado 833 ☎ 02902 491880. Colourful little café serving all manner of sweet and savoury crêpes (try the special with home-made blueberry ice cream) as well as large, imaginative sandwiches (chicken with apple and blue cheese) – ideal as a packed lunch if you're going on an all-day excursion the following day. Daily 10am–11pm.

RESTAURANTS

★ **Casimiro Biguá** Av Libertador 963 ☎ 02902 492590. With formally attired waiters and a Patagonian barbecue pit in the window, this is one of the town's classiest and best-loved steakhouses. You can order

unusual (at least for Argentina) sides such as sweet potato chips or grilled vegetables to go with the grilled meats, and their made-to-share plate of Patagonian appetizers, such as smoked trout and deer salami, is superb. Daily 11.30am–4pm & 6pm–1am.

Pura Vida Av Libertador 1876 ☎ 02902 493358. A 15min walk or a short taxi ride along the main street, this Frida Kahloesque A-frame cabin is a godsend for vegetarians, though meat eaters can also enjoy the likes of the *carbonada en calabaza* (pumpkin stew served in a gourd), vegetable lasagne and excellent home-made bread. Mon, Tues & Thurs–Sun 7.30pm–midnight.

★ **La Tablita** Rosales 28 ☎ 02902 491065. This vast *parilla* fills up in the evenings with crowds seeking some of El Calafate's best steak, spit-roasted lamb and other meaty delights, such as *mollejas* (sweetbreads). The portions are sizeable and the meat is done to perfection. Reservations highly recommended. Daily noon–3.30pm & 7.30pm–midnight.

9

VISITING ESTANCIAS

El Calafate is a prime location for a day-trip to an **estancia** (ranch) in the surrounding area for an introduction to rural life in the pampas. Choice locations include:

Estancia Alta Vista 35km from El Calafate ☎02902 491247. Part of the near 183,000 acre *Estancia Anita*, established in the 1930s by Croat immigrants, this lodge offers participation in sheep shearing, tailor-made horse treks, hiking, birdwatching and fishing on the property, as well as a traditional barbecue and dance show.

Estancia Cristina Av Libertador 1037 ☎02902 491133, ⓦ estanciacristina.com. The most popular of the *estancias* neighbouring El Calafate, this ranch is located on the north side of Lago Argentino, near the Upsala glacier. Multi-activity days include tours of the property, combined with visits to the glacier, 4WD trips to the Miradór Upsala and treks through the Cañadon de los Fóciles – a marine fossil site. Overnight stays and meals available at the lodge.

Glaciar Perito Moreno

49 km from El Calafate along Ruta 11 • Daily day-trips to the glacier run by all tour agencies in El Calafate • Admission AR$85; boat trips AR$55

At the southern sector of the **Parque Nacional Los Glaciares** you'll find one of Argentina's leading attractions, the **GLACIAR PERITO MORENO**. The vast glacier – 30km long, 5km wide and 60m high – sweeps down off the ice cap in a great curve, a jagged mass of crevasses and towering, knife-edged obelisks of ice (seracs), almost unsullied by the streaks of dirty moraine; it's marbled in places with streaks of muddy grey and copper sulphate blue, while at the bottom the pressurized, de-oxygenated ice has a deep blue, waxy sheen.

When it collides with the southern arm of Lago Argentino, vast blocks of ice, some weighing hundreds of tonnes, detonate off the face of the glacier with the report of a small cannon and come crashing down into the waters of Canal de los Témpanos (Iceberg Channel) below. One of the world's few advancing glaciers, Perito Moreno periodically blocks off Lago Argentino, causing the waters to build up until they burst through the dam, creating a spectacular ice arch. The glacier tends to be more active in sunny weather and in the afternoon. You can admire it from a series of boardwalks or take one of the hourly boats up close to the face of the glacier for a greater appreciation of its vastness.

Parque Nacional Los Glaciares

Daily 9am–8pm in peak season, shorter hours rest of the year • ☎ 02962 493004, ⓦ elchalten.com

The northernmost section of Argentina's **Parque Nacional Los Glaciares** contains the **FITZ ROY MASSIF**, boasting some of the most breathtakingly beautiful mountain peaks on the planet. Two concentric jaws of jagged teeth puncture the Patagonian sky, with the 3445m incisor of **Monte Fitz Roy** at the centre.

El Chaltén

The base for **trekking** in this area is **EL CHALTÉN**, which has expanded considerably since it was established in 1985. It has an excellent infrastructure for a town of four hundred, and a cosmopolitan ambiance.

ARRIVAL AND DEPARTURE   EL CHALTÉN

By bus All buses stop at the national park information centre before arriving at the large new bus terminal at the south end of town. In peak season, buy your bus ticket out of town in advance, as demand outstrips supply. You have to return to El Calafate for all onwards connections to most other Argentine destinations.

Companies Chaltén Travel (☎02962 493092), Taqsa

(☎02962 493068) and Caltur (☎02962 493079) all run to El Calafate.

Destinations El Calafate, Argentina (up to 6 daily, less frequently off season; 3hr 30min; departures typically around 8am, 1pm and 6pm).

By car From El Calafate, head east along Ruta Nacional 11 for 30km, then turn left on Ruta 40 north, then northwest

9

TREKKING IN PARQUE NACIONAL LOS GLACIARES

One of the beauties of this park is that those with limited time can still make worthwhile **day hikes**, using El Chaltén as a base, and thus not have to lug around heavy rucksacks. For those who enjoy sleeping in the wild, there are free basic campsites at Laguna Torre, Laguna Capri, Laguna Toro and Poincenot, with Río Blanco reserved for climbers only.

LAGUNA DE LOS TRES AND AROUND

The most popular day hike takes you to the stunning **Laguna de Los Tres**, with Monte Fitz Roy looming directly behind it (8hr return). If you make it this far, go around the corner to take in the equally spectacular Laguna Sucia. From Poincenot, the last hour's scramble up is steep and rocky and if it's too windy, you'll have to detour to Piedras Blancas. Again, from Poincenot, you can take the Laguna Madre e Hija trail (2hr 30min) to connect with the other popular day hike to Laguna Torre to view Cerro Torre (4hr from El Chaltén).

SHORT WALKS

For short hikes, from the north end of town, it's an hour's walk to Chorillo del Salto (waterfall). From the national park information centre, take the Los Condores or Las Aguilas trails; even if you don't see condors or eagles, you will get a panoramic view of El Chaltén and the plains stretching towards El Calafate.

HIKES AROUND LAGO DEL DESIERTO

If you exhaust your hiking options in the immediate vicinity of El Chaltén, take the Lengas transfer to the nearby Lago del Desierto (daily at 8.30am & 3pm; AR$80; reserve in advance) and do the day hike to the icy expanse of Glaciar Huermúl, among others, or even take on the challenging border crossing to Chile's Villa O'Higgins (see box, p.377).

onto Ruta 23. The road is now completely paved and the 220km drive shouldn't take more than three hours.

By boat If you wish to take the most direct route possible to Chile on foot or by bike, you'll need to take the boat across Lago del Desierto (2–3 daily Nov–March; AR$150) and then hike to Lago O'Higgins to catch a boat to Villa O'Higgins (see box, p.377).

INFORMATION AND TOURS

TOURIST INFORMATION

Conaf 800m before the village (daily 9am–8pm in peak season, shorter hours rest of the year; ☎02962/493004, ⓦelchalten.com). Climbers *must* register here, as should anyone planning to stay at the Laguna Toro *refugio* and campsite to the south. Visitors are given an informative talk on hiking in the park and receive trail maps.

Tourist office Inside the bus terminal. Has a selection of brochures on the area's attractions and accommodation options.

TOUR OPERATORS

Parque Nacional Los Glaciares has more to offer than just trekking. Those looking for alternative adventure activities

can try the following reputable operators.

Casa de Guías de Montaña San Martín 310 ☎02962 493118, ⓦcasadeguias.com.ar. These certified guides specialize in mountain ascents and rock climbing. Good levels of physical fitness essential.

Patagonia Aventura San Martín 56B ☎02962 493110, ⓦpatagonia-aventura.com.ar. Specializes in excellent ice-trekking and ice-climbing trips to the nearby Glaciar Viedma. Previous experience not necessary.

Walk Patagonia Antonio Rojo 62 ☎02962 493275, ⓦwalkpatagonia.com. This energetic Argentinian–British husband and wife team organizes anything from tailor-made treks with an emphasis on local fauna, flora and history to onward travel all over Argentina.

ACCOMMODATION

Albergue Aylen Aike Trevisan 125 ☎02962 493317. Not only can you get great home-made cake here, but this hostel has nicer dorms than its competitors, with colourful bedspreads, good mattresses and down comforters, as well as a spot to gather by the fire with fellow guests. Dorm **AR$90**

Albergue Patagonia San Martín 392 ☎02962 493019, ⓦpatagoniahostel.com.ar. Unlike the other, more impersonal hostels in town, this compact traveller favourite is distinguished by the attentiveness of its multilingual staff and absence of dorms. Nice extras include book exchange and bikes for rent and the cosy lounge/dining area encourages mingling. AR$320

Estancia La Quinta ☎ 02962 493012, ⓦ estancialaquinta.com.ar. This historic *estancia*, 2km south of El Chaltén, is a hotel in a former ranch rather than a working ranch, with accommodation, rather than activities, as its principal function. Run by a descendant of the original pioneer, the place gives guests access to private hiking trails on the property, as well as a library full of books on Patagonia and the founder's tiny hut – now a small museum. Buffet breakfast is included and the resident chef cooks Patagonian specials using local produce. Open Oct–April. AR$739

Hostería Senderos Perito Moreno 35 ☎ 02962 493336, ⓦ senderoshosteria.com.ar. At this lodge attractive lodge, the attentive staff go out of their way to be helpful, the spacious rooms have comfortable king-size beds (some with views of Fitz Roy) and prices include an American-style buffet breakfast. The wine bar has an excellent selection of Argentine wines. AR$661

Hostería Thiamalu Lago del Desierto 99 ☎ 02962 493136, ⓦ thiamalu.com.ar. Ideal for families, small groups and couples, this friendly B&B features several bright, heated en-suite rooms, super-friendly staff and a good breakfast, which includes freshly baked bread. Credit cards accepted. AR$360

EATING AND DRINKING

El Bodegón Cervecería San Martín 564 ☎ 02962 493109. One of the most sociable spots in town, with locals and hikers perching on rough-hewn wooden seats to knock back pints of bock or pilsner (brewed onsite) or tuck into stew, pizza or pasta. Daily 11am–midnight or later.

Domo Blanco San Martín at Ricardo Arbilla. Some of the best ice cream in town, as well as unusually imaginative sandwiches for Patagonia (duck with hoisin sauce, smoked salmon). Daily 11am–9pm.

Estepa Cerro Solo 86 ☎ 02962 493069. Another

consistently creative and popular choice, dishing up lamb with calafate berries, wild boar steak and delectable pumpkin ravioli. Daily 12.30–3pm & 7.30–11pm.

Ruca Mahuida Lionel Terray 55 ☎ 02962 493018. Famous for some of most imaginative dishes in town, this adorable log cabin restaurant titillates the taste buds with the likes of spinach pasta with cognac and wild mushrooms, smoked trout and *yerba mate parfait* with vanilla sauce. Reservations recommended in the evenings. Daily noon–3pm & 7.30–11pm.

DIRECTORY

Banks and exchange El Chaltén has one ATM at the bus station but don't rely on it; bring plenty of cash to cover your stay. If planning on crossing the border to Chile's Villa O'Higgins (see p.377) and travel up the Carretera Austral, stock up on plenty of Chilean pesos, as most places will not accept credit cards and you may not find a working cash machine before reaching Coyhaique (see pp.363–67).

Camping equipment Pick up any camping gear that you're missing at Camping Center, San Martín 56, or Patagonia Hikes, Lago del Desierto at Rojo.

Hospital Puesto Sanitario (☎ 02902 493033) deals with medical emergencies.

Internet Most accommodation options now offer free wi-fi and internet and there's an internet café along Av Güemes between Av Viedma and Río de las Vueltas, though connections are slow, particularly in the evenings.

Laundry Wash your dirty camping gear at the *lavandería* on the corner of Lago del Desierto and Av Güemes.

9

Tierra del Fuego

418 Chilean Tierra del Fuego

426 Argentine Tierra del Fuego

CROSSING THE BEAGLE CHANNEL

Tierra del Fuego

At the bottom end of the South American continent, and split between Chile and Argentina, Tierra del Fuego ("Land of Fire") holds nearly as much fascination for travellers as Patagonia, from which it is separated by the Magellan Strait. In fact, it was Magellan who dreamed up the dramatic and somewhat unlikely name, after sighting dozens of fires lit by the native Yámana. Though comprising a number islands, it's more or less the sum of its most developed part, the Isla Grande, the biggest island in South America. Argentina possesses the easternmost half of Isla Grande, plus Isla de los Estados (Staten Island) and a smattering of tiny islets to the south; the rest is Chilean territory.

10

On the **Chilean side**, you'll find the isolated main town of **Porvenir**, which huddles on the Magellan Strait. Flat plains cover much of northern and central Isla Grande, but further south, the countryside becomes less barren, with thick woodland and crystalline rivers near little **Camerón** stretching southeast towards a number of exquisite lakes, including **Lago Blanco**, and the densely forested 2000m peaks of the Cordillera Darwin in the far south. South of Isla Grande, across the Beagle Channel, lies **Isla Navarino**, home to the tiny **Puerto Williams**, the southernmost permanently inhabited settlement in the world, plus one of the most challenging hiking trails in South America, the **Los Dientes Circuit**. Beyond Navarino is **Cabo de Hornos** (Cape Horn), the land's end of the Americas, accessible only by sea or air.

In the Argentine sector, the leading attraction is the well-known city of **Ushuaia** on the south coast of **Argentine** Tierra del Fuego. It is *the* base for visiting the **Beagle Channel**, rich in **marine wildlife**, the lakes, forests and tundra of nearby **Parque Nacional Tierra del Fuego**, the historic **Estancia Harberton**, and, of course, **Antarctica**. It is also Tierra del Fuego's main tourist destination, with winter skiing and summer trekking high on the list of activities. Also in Argentine Tierra del Fuego, you'll find the scenic **Lago Fagnano**; from the lake to the 2985m **Paso Garibaldi**, the gateway to Ushuaia by road, you'll travel through patches of low, transitional, lichen-festooned **Fuegian woodland**.

Ushuaia in particular gets very busy between December and February; however, in March and April the countryside is daubed with the spectacular autumnal colours of the southern beech, while spring (Oct to mid-Nov), the shoulder season, is also a great time to visit.

Exploring Tierra del Fuego on four wheels p.420
King penguins in Tierra del Fuego p.421
The Yámana, the Selk'nam and the Kawéskar p.423

Los Dientes de Navarino circuit p.425
How the Cape found its Horn p.427
Sailing to Cape horn p.428
Winter sports around Ushuaia p.435

PARQUE NACIONAL TIERRA DEL FUEGO

Highlights

❶ Porvenir and around Visit Chile's Fuegian capital and explore the harsh land around it, which includes gold mine remains and a potential king penguin colony. **See p.419**

❷ Isla Navarino Fly or sail to Puerto Williams, the most southerly town on earth or tackle one of the toughest hiking circuits in South America – the Dientes de Navarino. **See pp.422**

❸ Cape Horn Even if you don't kayak around it, consider rounding the tip in a ship or viewing its harsh beauty from the air. **See pp.426**

❹ Boat trip along the Beagle Channel Spot sea lions and penguins, cormorants and albatrosses, and maybe even killer whales. **See p.434**

❺ Winter sports at Ushuaia Zip down the slopes of the winter sports resort dramatically located at the end of the world or go sledging with huskies. **See p.435**

❻ Parque Nacional Tierra del Fuego Explore this fascinating and little-visited chunk of jagged mountains, beech forest, bogs, tundra and beautiful coast on foot or in a 4WD. **See p.436**

HIGHLIGHTS ARE MARKED ON THE MAP ON P.418

Chilean Tierra del Fuego

Chilean Tierra del Fuego can roughly be divided into two distinct areas, separated by the largely inaccessible Cordillera Darwin and the Beagle Channel: the largely flat and dusty plain that accounts for much of the northern and central Isla Grande, centred around **Porvenir**, the largest of Chile's Fuegian settlements; and Isla Navarino, with its picturesque town of Puerto Williams and Cape Horn just beyond.

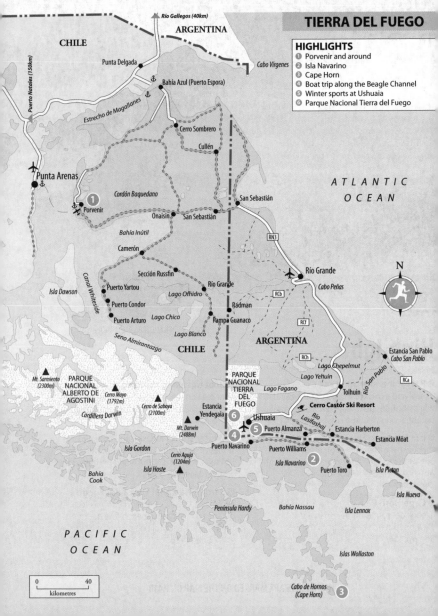

TIERRA DEL FUEGO

HIGHLIGHTS

1. Porvenir and around
2. Isla Navarino
3. Cape Horn
4. Boat trip along the Beagle Channel
5. Winter sports at Ushuaia
6. Parque Nacional Tierra del Fuego

Porvenir

A collection of brightly painted corrugated iron houses set in a narrow bay of the same name, **PORVENIR** (optimistically meaning "future") gives off the impression of order stamped on nature, with neat topiary leading down the main street, Philippi, from an immaculate Plaza de Armas, overflowing with native vegetation. The seafront Parque del Recuerdo sports a curve of flagpoles, the painted skeleton of a steam engine, the mounted stern of a boat and a statue of a Tehuelche man – a rare reminder of a culture made extinct by the gold rush. The harbour, meanwhile, teems with all manner of sea birds, such as cormorants and kelp geese, and a twenty-minute walk along the coast takes you to **Cerro Mirador**, from where you get an excellent view of the town.

10

Porvenir cemetery

Esmeralda at Damian Riobo · Daily 8am–6pm

Porvenir started life in 1883 as a police outpost during the Fuegian gold rush and has since been settled by foreigners: first came the British managers of sheep farms, and then refugees from Croatia after World War II. You can read the history of the town in the names of the dead at the **cemetery** four blocks north of the plaza, a smaller version of Punta Arenas' Cementerio Municipal (see p.389). Here English names mingle with Spanish and Croatian ones and grand marble tombs intermix with modest stone slabs amid meticulously pruned cypresses.

Museo de Tierra del Fuego Fernando Cordero Rusque

Padre Mario Zavattaro 402 · Mon–Thurs 8am–5pm, Fri 8am–4pm · CH$1000

On the north corner of the plaza, with a 1928 Ford-T parked outside, this intriguing museum ushers you into the harsh world that shaped Porvenir into its present entity. A mixture of evocative black-and-white photos, dioramas and period objects introduce the visitor to the Fuegian gold rush, the lives of the now-extinct Tehuelche and the conquest of Patagonia by Europeans. The Selk'nam skulls and mummies are a standout exhibit.

ARRIVAL AND INFORMATION

PORVENIR

By plane The aerodrome sits 5km north of town. Taxis charge around CH$4000 to take you to Porvenir; Aerovías DAP runs a cheaper door-to-door shuttle. DAP's office, in the same building as Tabsa on Calle Señoret, sells plane tickets to Punta Arenas (twice daily departures Mon–Sat: around CH$36,000; maximum 10kg luggage).

By ferry Ferries from Punta Arenas arrive at Bahía Chilota, 5km to the west of Porvenir along the bay. A taxi costs CH$3000 and a *colectivo* CH$1000. Purchase ferry tickets from Tabsa on the seafront at Calle Señoret s/n (Mon–Fri 9.15am–12.15pm & 2.30–6.30pm, Sat 9am–12.15pm; ☏ 61 580089). If that's shut, note that the restaurant at Bahía Chilota sells ferry tickets an hour before departure (Tues–Sat 2pm & Sun 5pm; check times well ahead).

By car The turn-off for Porvenir is 16km south of the Punta Delgada ferry crossing (see p.389). The gravel road has a few potholes, but the section near Porvenir is newly paved.

Tourist information At the time of writing, the tourist office (☏ 61 580094, ✉ muniprovenir@terra.cl) was due to move to the building across the courtyard from the museum.

ACCOMMODATION

Hostería Los Flamencos Teniente Merino 1253 ☏ 61 580049. Located at the far western end of Teniente Merino, this comfortable yellow lodge enjoys harbour views and has comfortable rooms and a decent restaurant. CH$34,000

★ **Hostería Yendegaia** Croacia 702 ☏ 61 581919, ⊚ hosteriayendegaia.com. Large, attractive, creaky wooden house run by congenial owners happy to organize tours. The spacious rooms have high ceilings, cable TV and wi-fi, and breakfast is the best in town. CH$38,000

Hotel Barlovento John Williams 2 ☏ 61 681000, ⊚ hotelbarlovento.cl. On the outskirts of town, not only does Porvenir's plushest hotel give you access to a unique gym and indoor football field, but the staff are among the friendliest in town, the rooms are spacious, centrally heated and tastefully decorated in neutral tones, and the restaurant is good by Chilean standards (steer clear of the more ambitious items, though). CH$75,000

Hotel España Croacia 698 ☏ 61 580760, ⊚ hotelespana.cl. This deceptively large old building run by a friendly, formidable woman, features large, centrally heated rooms with TV. Prices include breakfast and the downstairs restaurant serves bargain set lunches and good à la carte seafood dishes, such as the ever popular *palta Porvenir* (avocado stuffed with king crab). CH$25,000

10

EATING AND DRINKING

Club Croata Señoret 542 ☎ 061 580053. Though there's a Croatian coat of arms above the doorway, there is nothing Croatian about the menu at this grand old gentlemen's club: the focus is mainly on fresh fish and seafood and the house special is the *trilogia austral*: crêpes with *centolla* (king crab), oysters and mussels. Mains from CH$5500. Mon–Sat 12.30–3.30pm & 7–11pm, Sun 1–3.30pm.

Hotel Rosas Croacia 698 ☎ 061 580088. Generous portions of well-prepared seafood and fish dishes are to be had at this informal restaurant popular with locals. The lunchtime set menu is a bargain at CH$4500. Daily 12.30–3pm & 7–11pm.

Restaurant La Chispa Señoret at Riobo ☎ 061 580054. Though rather quiet when we visited, *La Chispa* (inside the historic fire station) is popular with locals who come for the no-nonsense grilled fish and other home cooking. Mains from CH$4000. Mon–Sat noon–3pm & 7–10.30pm, Sun 12.30–3.30pm.

DIRECTORY

Banks The Banco Estado ATM on the corner of Philippi & Croacia does not accept Visa cards, only Mastercard and Maestro.

Hospital Carlos Wood between Av Manuel Señoret and Guerrero (☎ 61 580034).

Internet Several of the reviewed accommodation options offer either free wi-fi or free internet access.

Post office On the plaza at Philippi 176.

Around Porvenir

The exploration of Porvenir's environs is more about the journey itself rather than a specific destination: it's about driving the island's virtually empty roads and taking in the rolling pampas, the lakes teeming with birdlife, and the rusting hulks of old machinery that hint at Tierra del Fuego's gold rush past.

Cerro Sombrero

The first 20km out of Porvenir heading north is lined with large shallow lakes, ranging in colour from turquoise to sapphire and often adorned with dazzling pink flamingos. A dusty 86km later you reach the turning to the right that leads to Chilean Tierra del Fuego's other town, **CERRO SOMBRERO**, a small oil settlement looming up out of the moonscape, snugly ensconced on the top of a small flat hill.

Bahía Azul

Ferry: summer every 45min 8.30am–11pm; less often in winter; 20min

Forty-three kilometres north of Cerro Sombrero (139km from Porvenir), the **ferry** that crosses the Primera Angostura departs from a place known locally as **BAHÍA AZUL**, but usually marked "Puerto Espora" on maps. During the crossing, if you're lucky, you may see schools of black-and-white Commerson's dolphins leaping out of the water alongside the ferry.

EXPLORING TIERRA DEL FUEGO ON FOUR WHEELS

Visitors with their own vehicles get far more out of a trip to Chilean Tierra del Fuego than those limited to Porvenir and its environs. Cars can be rented in Punta Arenas and brought over to the island on the car ferry. Most of the roads are unpaved and moderately potholed, but can be tackled without a 4WD if driving carefully – with the exception of the coastal road south of Camerón to Puerto Arturo, which is for 4WDs only, and the stretch of road between Onaisín and Cerro Sombrero if it has been raining.

Fuegians rely only on themselves and on each other when it comes to breakdowns and all motorists will stop should you come to grief, but given the low traffic volume on most roads, you should come prepared with a sleeping bag, food, water, a torch, warm clothes and – most importantly – a spare tyre and all necessary equipment. Always stop to help other motorists in need and plan your journey carefully: there are only two petrol stations – one in Porvenir and the other in Cerro Sombrero. If you wish to head south to Lago Blanco, you must take a spare canister of petrol with you.

KING PENGUINS IN TIERRA DEL FUEGO

A number of **king penguins**, whose colonies have previously not been found further north than the South Georgia islands and Antarctica, may have made Chile's Tierra del Fuego their home. The sixteen or so penguins have stayed on a beachfront piece of private land for the whole of 2011, raising hopes that they may create a new colony. The location, 15km south of the crossroads with the turn-off for Onaisín along the coastal road, is to be accessed via Estancia San Clemente, and *not* the neighbouring Estancia Tres Hermanos. The two estancias own land next to one another, and Estancia Tres Hermanos has been letting visitors cross its territory, some of whom have subsequently trespassed on the San Clemente land and frightened the penguins by getting too close to them.

The owners of San Clemente are working together with a Punta Arenas-based interest group (see p.391) keen to study the penguins' behaviour. Visitors coming by car will see the sign for **Parque Pinguino Rey** and the CH$12,000 entry fee must be paid at the trailer. Penguin-viewing tours are run by several companies from Punta Arenas (see p.391) though it makes for a very long day trip.

10

The Baquedano Hills

A little-used road heads east from Porvenir across the **BAQUEDANO HILLS**, where most of the region's gold was discovered. It starts with a beautiful view, 20km outside Porvenir, looking back down to the town and across the strait to Punta Arenas. All around, the landscape bears the reminders of the gold that was mined here – where the road crosses the Río del Oro (Gold River), you'll see the rusting remains of an original dredge. You'll also pass rudimentary grass shelters belonging to a few individuals who still hope to find gold here. After a steep descent, you come to the main Porvenir–San Sebastián road, and after another 84km of rolling pampas beneath a leaden sky you reach the **San Sebastián frontier** (see p.421). Ten kilometres southeast of San Sebastián lies "Las Onas" hill, the site of the oldest inhabited place on the island, estimated to be 11,880 years old.

Bahía Inútil

The prettiest road is the one that follows the coast, starting along the northern shore of **Bahía Inútil**, a wide bay that got its name by being a useless anchorage for sailing ships. After 99km you reach a crossroads; turn south, and a little past the village of Onaisín you pass a little **English cemetery**. The gravestones have inscriptions in English that suggest tragic stories: "killed by Indians", "accidentally drowned" and "died in a storm".

The coast road then skirts around the south of Bahía Inútil, giving beautiful views across to **Isla Dawson**. It passes the occasional small cluster of bare fishermen's huts; when the tide's out, you can see an ancient way of catching fish – underwater stone *corrales* (pens) built by the Selk'nam Indians to trap fish when the tide turned. Just before the village of Camerón, the road turns inland and leaves the bay, while a dirt track carries on south along the coast, passing the sawmills at Puerto Yartou, the beginning of Río Condor, which is excellent for salmon fishing, and ends at Puerto Arturo, a small stockbreeding settlement.

Camerón and around

CAMERÓN was once a Scottish settlement with a thriving sheep farm, built on either side of the Río Shetland, but nowadays all that's left are some neat little workers' houses and a large shearing shed. From here, the land begins to lose its Patagonian severity, and as you travel inland you'll see dense forest. Some 20km later, the road forks north to San Sebastián, and south to a place called Río Grande, where an iron bridge crosses the river. You are now surrounded by Magellanic forest, occasionally interspersed with open grassland, where you are likely to see roaming guanacos.

10

Lago Blanco and beyond

Twenty-one kilometres further lies **Lago Blanco** itself, majestic and brooding, surrounded by steeply forested hills and snow-covered mountains, where you'll find plenty of wilderness in which to trek, fish and camp.

From Lago Blanco the road continues further south, past Lago Deseado, currently ending just beyond the majestic Lago Fagnano, part of Parque Nacional Tierra del Fuego. The Chilean government has big plans for Tierra del Fuego, which include building a completely new settlement on the shores of the lake, thus providing easier access to the natural attractions on the Argentinian side.

Estancia Yendegaia

Another one of Doug Tompkins' conservation projects (see p.353), Estancia Yendegaia is a four-hundred-square-kilometre swathe of native Fuegian forest, snow-tipped crags and icy waters, sitting by the Beagle Channel amid the Cordillera Darwin. Originally a cattle ranch, this piece of land has been turned into a nature reserve. It is currently managed by the **Fundación Yendegaia** (T61 241197, W theconservationlandtrust.org) and the project's ultimate goal is to donate the land to Chile's national park system. Estancia Yendegaia's location directly between Chile's Parque Nacional Alberto de Agostini and Argentina's Parque Nacional Tierra del Fuego bridges the gap between the two. The only way to reach it is either on foot – Turismo Aonikenk (see p.391) sometimes runs expeditions here – or on horseback; since there is no visitor accommodation, camping wild is the only option.

There is an ongoing controversial project to pave the horse trail that runs south from Lago Fagnano to Estancia Yendegaia, ostensibly to connect the rest of Tierra del Fuego to Puerto Williams by regular ferry and to give visitors easier access to the southern fjords and to Argentina's Parque Nacional Tierra del Fuego (see pp.436–437). The construction of the road is due to be completed by 2020.

CROSSING THE ARGENTINE BORDER

Via San Sebastián Note that there are two San Sebastiáns, one being the Chilean border post (daily: April–Oct 8am–10pm; Nov–March 24hr) with a fast-food stall and not much else, and the other being a fully fledged village further on in Argentina.

ACCOMMODATION AND EATING   AROUND PORVENIR

Aldea Tierra del Fuego 8 miles south of Puerto Yartou along the coastal road, en route from Camerón towards Puerto Arturo T61 581894 or 613061, W aldeatierradelfuego.com. This fly-fishing centre consisting of several fully equipped cabins, specializes in multi-day all-inclusive fishing trips as well as other adventure excursions around Tierra del Fuego. Half board CH$75,000 (US$154), full board CH$85,000 (US$175).

Estancia Camerón Lodge Near Camerón T61 215029, W estanciacameronlodge.com. This cosy lodge, built of native wood and stone overlooking the Río Grande, was designed with serious anglers in mind; Lu, the host, is an extremely knowledgeable fishing guide, the four rooms are comfortable and centrally heated and the cuisine

emphasizes fresh local produce. Open Jan to mid-April; price includes land/air transfer from Punta Arenas or Río Grande, Argentina, as well as all meals, lodging, fishing licences and guided angling excursions. 7-day package CH$1,693,000 (US$3500) per person; CH$242,000 (US$500) per additional day

Tierra del Fuego Lodge East of Lago Blanco, overlooking Río Rasmussen T2 196 0624, W tierradelfuegolodge.cl. This "high end rustic" fishermen's retreat consists of two fully equipped cabins and a guest duplex. Visitors can expect a mixture of international and Patagonian cuisine as well as packed lunches to take on fishing excursions in season (mid-Oct to mid-April). 7-day package (2-person minimum) CH$1,815,000 (US$3750) per person

Isla Navarino

Apart from compact **Puerto Williams** and the even tinier fishing village of **Puerto Toro**, **ISLA NAVARINO**, the largish island to the south of Isla Grande, is an uninhabited wilderness studded with barren peaks and isolated valleys. Navarino is dominated by a dramatic range of peaks, the **Cordón Dientes del Navarino** through which weaves a 70km hiking trail called the **Los Dientes Circuit**. What has spoiled some of the landscape, especially the woodland, however, is the devastation brought about by feral **beavers**, imported from Canada for fur-farming in the 1940s by the Argentine military – a project that misfired most spectacularly and to which there is still no solution.

ARRIVAL AND DEPARTURE   ISLA NAVARINO

By plane Aerovías DAP has frequent flights from Punta Arenas to Puerto Williams (summer Mon–Sat 10am; winter less frequent; around CH$56,000 one-way), a spectacularly beautiful journey when the weather is good, and like flying through bumpy grey soup when it isn't.

By boat The new Transbordadora Austral Broom ferry, *Yaghan*, departs Punta Arenas Wed 6pm and returns from Puerto Williams Sat 10pm (28–36hr; Pullman seat US$186, berth US$258). COMAPA (ⓦ comapa.com) also runs a four-day luxury cruise on the *Mare Australis* and the *Via Australis*

(ⓦ australis.com), from US$1420 per person for the cheapest cabin, dropping anchor in Isla Navarino's Wulaia Bay. From Ushuaia, Ushuaia Boating (see p.430) runs daily Zodiac boats in summer. In windy weather, the journey is hair-raising, and if the wind is too strong, the boats don't sail at all. There are plans to start a regular ferry service between Ushuaia and Puerto Williams, but they have not yet been realized. You might also be able to catch a ride on a private yacht from Ushuaia's Yacht Club.

10

Puerto Williams

PUERTO WILLIAMS nestles in a small bay on the north shore of Isla Navarino, 82km due east and slightly south of Ushuaia along the Beagle Channel. Although Ushuaia loudly proclaims its "end of the world" status, it suffers from geographical envy when it comes to tiny Puerto Williams, home to just over two thousand people. Originally founded as a military outpost, it's officially the capital of Chilean Antarctica. The compact, windblown settlement has a somewhat desolate quality to it even in the height of the brief summer, but the people are exceptionally warm and welcoming and you get a real sense of a close-knit community, brought together by isolation from the rest of Chile. Most businesses are concentrated in the **Centro Comercial**, by the Plaza O'Higgins.

The seafront

The seafront Avenida Costanera, leads you past a rusted hulk of a half-sunken barge loaded with *centolla* traps towards the indigenous community of **Villa Ukika**. From the bright-red x-shaped pier that juts into the channel's cold blue waters, you get a wonderful view of the town against a backdrop of the forest-covered jagged peaks of **Los Dientes** beyond.

THE YÁMANA, THE SELK'NAM AND THE KAWÉSKAR

The harsh lands of Tierra del Fuego and Isla Navarino were originally home to three tribes, the **Yámana (Yaghan)**, the **Selk'nam (Ona)** and the **Kawéscar (Alacalúf)**. The latter inhabited the Magellan Strait and the western fjords, and the former two resided on and around Isla Navarino. The Yámana and the Kawéskar were both "Canoe Indians", who relied on their catch of fish, shellfish and marine animals, while the Selk'nam were hunter-gatherers who subsisted almost entirely on a diet of guanaco meat.

Though dismissed by European explorers as savages (Charles Darwin famously commented that the "Canoe Indians" were "among the most abject and miserable creatures I ever saw"), and now largely culturally extinct, the tribes had complex rituals. The Selk'nam, for example, performed a sophisticated **male initiation ceremony**, the *Hain*, during which the young male initiates, or *kloketens*, confronted and unmasked malevolent spirits that they had been taught to fear since their youth, emerging as *maars* (adults). Father Martín Gusinde was present at the last *Hain* ceremony in 1923, and managed to capture the event in a series of remarkable photographs, copies of which circulate as postcards today.

10

Museo Antropológico Martín Gusinde

Aragay at Gusinde • Oct–March Mon–Thurs 9am–1pm & 2.30–7.18pm, Sat & Sun 2.30–6.30pm; April–Sept Mon–Thurs 8am–1pm & 2.30–6.18pm, Sat 2.30–6.30pm • ⓦ www.museoantropologicomartingusinde.cl • Donations

In a smart new blue building with a skeleton of a whale by the entrance, this excellent museum, named after a clergyman and anthropologist who spent a great deal of time among the native tribes of Tierra del Fuego, you'll find a host of beautifully presented displays on the history, fauna and flora of the area. These include exhibits on Yámana life, complete with artefacts, photographs and accounts of their legends; an obligatory stuffed Fuegian fauna section; and maps that chart the exploration of the region, from the days of the Fuegian Indians, through the gold rush, to the commercial shipping of today. The spiral staircase is decorated with stunning close-ups of local wildlife and there is free internet and wi-fi at the little café.

Villa Ukika

A five-minute coastal walk east from Puerto Williams' new ferry ramp brings you to the hamlet of **Villa Ukika**, home to the last remaining descendants of the Yámana people. The only object of note here is the replica of a traditional dwelling – the **Kipa-Akar** (House of Woman) – which is uninhabited; in summer it's open to visitors who can purchase traditional handicrafts – from miniature canoes to whalebone harpoons.

ARRIVAL AND DEPARTURE   PUERTO WILLIAMS

By plane On arrival at the tiny Aeródromo, you're met by a transfer van (CH$2000). Aerovías DAP has its office at the Centro Comercial Sur 151 (⊕61 621114); double-check flight departure times here.

Destinations Punta Arenas (Nov–March 1 daily except Sun; otherwise 3 weekly; 40min–1hr 30min).

By boat Coming from Punta Arenas, you'll arrive at the new ferry ramp on Av Costanera. Zodiac boats from Ushuaia disembark at Puerto Navarino on the east side of the island,

where you pass through Chilean customs before an hour's ride in a minibus to Puerto Williams. The Transbordadora Austral Broom office at Costanera 435 (⊕61 621015, ⓦ tabsa.cl) sells tickets for the Punta Arenas-bound ferry. A minibus picks up passengers at their *hospedaje* to take them to Puerto Navarino in time to catch a boat to Ushuaia (weather permitting).

Destinations Punta Arenas (1 weekly on Sat; 36hr); Ushuaia (summer 1 daily; 45min–1hr).

INFORMATION AND TOURS

TOURIST INFORMATION

Tourist information Inside the Municipalidad on O'Higgins (Mon–Fri 8.30am–1pm & 2–5pm; ⊕61 412125). The helpful tourist information desk offers brochures on Puerto Williams and Cape Horn, but not maps of the Dientes de Navarino circuit.

TOUR OPERATORS

SIM Expeditions Casilla 6 ⊕61 621150, ⓦ simexpeditions.com. This intrepid German–Venezuelan operator runs highly recommended 2–3 week sailing trips to Cape Horn, South Georgia and Antarctica.

Turismo Akainij Austral 22 ⊕061 621173, ⓦ turismoakainij.cl. The owners of *Hospedaje Akainij* can

arrange anything from day hikes to Caleta Eugenia to multi-day treks to Lago Windhond, horseriding excursions and boat trips to Cape Horn and beyond.

Turismo Aventura Shila O'Higgins, opposite the municipality building ⊕09 7897 2005, ⓦ turismoshila .cl. The shop stocks basic maps of the Dientes de Navarino and camping equipment is available for rent. Owner Luís Tiznado organizes hiking in the Dientes de Navarino and fishing excursions to Lago Windhond, Lago Navarino and Laguna Rojas.

Victory Adventure Expeditions Teniente Muñoz 118 ⊕61 621010, ⓦ victory-cruises.com. Sailing expeditions around Cape Horn, along the Beagle Channel and even to Antarctica in schooner-style ships.

ACCOMMODATION

With the exception of *Hotel Lakutaia*, in an isolated location next to the airport, **accommodation** in Puerto Williams consists of private rooms and dorms inside family homes. Jan–March is peak season for hikers, so booking in advance is wise. Phoning is best, as most hostel owners do not have instant access to email.

HOTELS AND GUESTHOUSES

Hospedaje Akainij Austral 22 ⊕61 621173,

ⓦ turismoakainij.cl. Cosy en-suite rooms with down comforters, a cheerful living room filled with plants and friendly owners happy to arrange a plethora of excursions (see p.424) make this an ideal midrange guesthouse to base yourself in. CH$28,000

Hostal Paso McKinlay Piloto Pardo 213 ☎ 61 621124, ⓦ hostalpasomckinlay.cl. Though you can touch the walls of the corridor with both elbows if you stand with your hands on your hips, the six centrally heated rooms at this friendly guesthouse are bright, comfortable and come equipped with cable TV and intermittent wi-fi. Bikes available for rent. CH$30,000

Hotel Lakutaia ☎ 61 621721, ⓦ lakutaia.cl. Near the airport and 2km west of Puerto Williams, the island's only hotel attracts active, well-heeled tourists with its multi-day wilderness excursions around the island, which include heli-fishing, guided hikes in the Dientes de Navarino and helicopter flights over Cape Horn. Rooms are comfortable and the restaurant is decent; guests may also stay without participating in the all-inclusive programmes. CH$121,000 (US$250)

HOSTELS

Refugio El Padrino Av Costanera 276 ☎ 061 621136 or 09 8438 0843, ⓔ ceciliamancillao@yahoo.com.ar. A snug backpacker haven, this colourful hostel has a sign on the door inviting you to let yourself in and decide if you wish to stay. Most do; Cecilia, the owner, may not speak much English, but her genuine warmth transcends language barriers. Dorm CH$10,000

Residencial Pusaki Piloto Pardo 222 ☎ 061 621116, ⓔ pattypusaki@yahoo.es. A perpetual traveller favourite with a warm family atmosphere and excellent home-cooked food. Even if you are not staying here, you can arrange to come for dinner, provided you give Patty a couple of hours' warning; *centolla* night is best. Dorm CH$8500, double CH$25,000

10

EATING AND DRINKING

The best option for self-caterers is the well-stocked Supermercado Simón y Simón on Piloto Pardo, where you can buy delicious bread, *empanadas* and decent wine. For those who wish to do their bit for the environment, Cecilia of *Refugio El Padrino* (see p.425) can organize a beaver-eating experience at a family home or else she can ask Rosita, a local famous for her home cooking, to provide a group meal.

LOS DIENTES DE NAVARINO CIRCUIT

Many travellers come to Puerto Williams to complete the **Los Dientes de Navarino Circuit** challenge, a strenuous four- to seven-day hike in the Isla Navarino wilderness, where there is no infrastructure whatsoever, and you are faced with unpredictable weather as well as the rigours of the trail. This is for experienced hikers only and not to be attempted alone.

THE TRAIL

Follow Vía Uno west out of town; the trail starts behind the statue of the Virgin Mary in a grassy clearing. The road leads uphill to a waterfall and reservoir, from where a marked trail climbs steadily through the *coigüe* and *ñire* forest. It is a two-hour ascent to **Cerro Bandera**, a *miradór* with a wonderful view of the town, the Beagle Channel and the nearby mountains; this climb is definitely worthwhile, even if you're not doing the circuit. The rest of the trail is not well marked; there are 38 trail markers (rock piles) spread out over the 53km route, which entails crossing four significant passes and negotiating beaver dams in between.

Once past the starkly beautiful **Laguna El Salto**, you can either cross a fairly steep pass and make a detour to the south, to the remote expanse of Lago Windward, or head west to **Laguna de los Dientes**. Continue west past Lagunas Escondido, Hermosa and Matrillo before reaching the particularly steep and treacherous descent of **Arroyo Virginia**; beware of loose rocks. The trail markers end before Bahía Virginia, and you have to make your own way over pastures and through scrubland to the main road. The trail officially finishes 12km out of town, behind a former *estancia* owned by the MacLean family, which has been developed into a *centolla*- and shellfish-processing factory. From here you can follow the main road back to Puerto Williams or hitch a lift.

MAPS AND ESSENTIALS

The best map is the *Tierra del Fuego & Isla Navarino* satellite map by Zagier & Urruty Publications, available in Ushuaia in conjunction with GPS. Make sure you have plentiful food and water supplies (water on the island is not drinkable owing to the giardia carried by the beavers), sunscreen and warm and waterproof outdoor gear, and inform people in town of your plans before leaving.

10

Mikalvi Av Constanera. Docked at the west end of the Costanera and run by the congenial owner of *Hostal Yagan*, this ex-Navy supply ship with a markedly "old salt" atmosphere, flags of different countries covering the walls and a well-stocked bar often plays host to an eclectic mix of hikers, Antarctic explorers, international yachtsmen and local navy personnel. Nov–March Mon–Sat 9pm–2am; shorter opening hours rest of the year.

La Pica de Castór Centro Comercial. Red brick walls hung with black-and-white photos and friendly staff dishing out hearty home-style cooking, such as roast chicken with mash and peas, attract locals and travellers alike. In spite of the neon sign in the window, this place is *not* open 24 hours. Daily 12.30–3pm & 7–11pm.

La Trattoria de Mateo Centro Comercial. Mellow reggae on the stereo, cheery lime green decor and chef Mattías's imaginative creations make this the nicest place to eat in town. Mains from CH$4500. Mon–Sat 1–3pm & 7–11pm.

DIRECTORY

Banks Banco de Chile, located down a narrow passageway from the Centro Comercial towards the seafront, has an ATM.

Internet Some guesthouses have somewhat reliable, though excruciatingly slow, internet. Your best bet is one of the brand new computers at the museum (see p.424).

Post office The post office is located in the Centro Comercial.

Parque Etnobotánico Omora

Daylight hours · Donation · ⓦ omora.org

Near the start of the Los Dientes trail, 3km west of Puerto Williams, is the entrance to the experimental part-state, part-private enterprise **Parque Etnobotánico Omora**, named for the world's southernmost hummingbird. The park plays an educational and environmental role, protecting the *ñire* and *lenga* forest by, among other things, encouraging locals to cull beavers for their meat. Native birds, including the red-headed Magellanic woodpecker (*lana*) and the ruffed-legged owl (*kujurj*), are monitored, along with other endangered species of flora and fauna and plants along the trails, and labelled in Latin, Spanish and Yaghan.

Puerto Toro

On the east side of the island lies **Puerto Toro**, a tiny fishing post inhabited by around seventy *centolla* fishermen and their families, complete with a school for all seven children and a police station. It is reachable only by boat; visitors can come here on a day-trip by taking the monthly ferry (see p.424) from Puerto Williams.

Cabo de Hornos (Cape Horn)

Directly south of Isla Navarino lies a cluster of islands, part of the **Cabo de Hornos biosphere reserve** – a staggering five million hectares of native forest, tundra, glaciers, fjords and tall black cliffs. This pristine marine habitat is set aside for strict conservation only; overnight stays are not permitted.

Argentine Tierra del Fuego

Argentina possesses the easternmost, more developed, half of **Isla Grande**. Way down south lies **Ushuaia**, meaning "westward-looking bay" in the indigenous Yámana tongue. The continent's southernmost town, with a stunning mountain-backed location on the **Beagle Channel**, it makes for an ideal base from which to explore the wilds of southern Isla Grande.

HOW THE CAPE FOUND ITS HORN

In January 1616, the cape was christened Hoorn by the Dutchmen **Willem Schouten** and **Jacob Le Maire** who passed by aboard the *Unity*, in honour of another ship of theirs that got shipwrecked off the coast of Argentina. In time, the Spanish changed the name to **Cabo de Hornos**, which was corrupted in turn to Cape Horn.

ROUND THE HORN BY SEA AND AIR

For centuries the treacherous icy waters surrounding the islands of Cape Horn captured the imagination of sailors and adventurers, not least because they constitute the biggest ship graveyard in the Americas: on old nautical maps, the waters around the islands are littered with tiny pictures of sunken ships. Today, Cape Horn still presents a sizeable challenge for experienced sailors and travellers alike, many of whom, having come this far south, can't resist going all the way round.

SIM (see p.424) and Victory Adventure Expeditions (see p.424) are good places to enquire about **sailing trips**. Weather permitting, you disembark on a shingle beach, climb a rickety ladder and visit the tiny Chilean naval base, lighthouse and chapel; a statue of an albatross overlooks the stormy waters beyond. Aerovías DAP (see p.389) and the local flying clubs run fairly expensive (around CH\$500,000 per small chartered plane) half-hour flights from both Punta Arenas and Puerto Williams that do a loop and return without landing. These air excursions treat you to incredible views of Isla Navarino and the Darwin peaks. As always, weather is a vital factor.

Ushuaia

Dramatically located between the mountains and the sea, **USHUAIA** tumbles down the hillside to the wide, encircling arm of land that protects its bay from the southwesterly winds and occasional thrashing storms of the icy **Beagle Channel**. San Martín is the town's main thoroughfare, and most visitors without their own transport stick to the compact grid of streets in Ushuaia's centre.

Brief history

In 1869, Reverend Waite Stirling became Tierra del Fuego's first white settler when he founded his **Anglican mission** among the Yámana here. Stirling stayed for six months before being recalled to the Falklands Islands to be appointed Anglican bishop for South America. Thomas Bridges, his assistant, returned to take over the mission in 1871, after which time Ushuaia began to figure on mariners' charts as a place of refuge in the event of shipwreck. In 1896, in order to consolidate its sovereignty and open up the region to wider colonization, the Argentine government used a popular nineteenth-century tactic and established a **penal colony** here, eventually closed by Perón in 1947.

Museo del Fin del Mundo

Maipú 175 • Daily 9am–8pm • AR\$30

Along the seafront you'll find this small museum, with exhibits on the region's native peoples – the Yámana, Selk'nam, Alakalúf, and the arrival of the missionaries. There's a thorough section on bird life, complete with dozens of stuffed specimens, and a rare example of the Selk'nam–Spanish dictionary written by the Salesian missionary, José María Beauvoir. The ghostly figurehead of the *Duchess of Albany*, a ship wrecked on the eastern end of the island in 1893, looks on overhead.

Museo Marítimo & Museo del Presidio

Yaganes at Gobernador Paz • Daily 10am–8pm • AR\$70

The star attraction within the town itself is undoubtedly the imposing former **prison**, built by convicts between 1902 and 1920 and home to the **Museo Marítimo & Museo del Presidio**. Its exhibits, ranging from Antarctic wildlife and exploration of the last continent to everyday life in the prison and its most notorious inhabitants, are arranged inside the cells along three of the five wings that radiate from the central chamber like spokes from a half-wheel. Most engaging are the scale models of famous ships from the island's history; spot a ship made entirely out of matchsticks by one of the inmates. The most celebrated prisoner to stay here was early twentieth-century anarchist Simón Radowitzsky, whose miserable incarceration and subsequent brief escape in 1918 are recounted by Bruce Chatwin in *In Patagonia*.

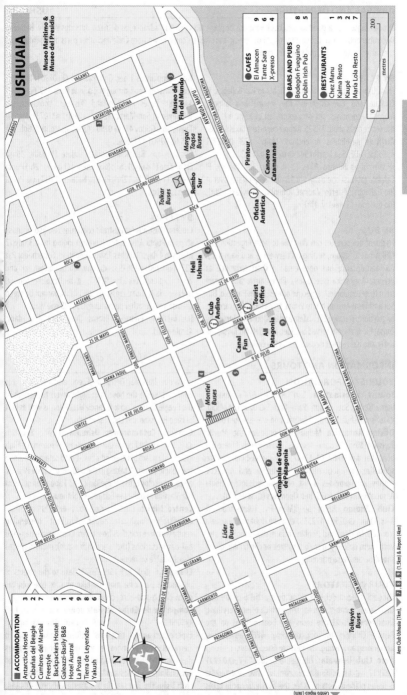

USHUAIA

Museo Marítimo & Museo del Presidio

Museo del Fin del Mundo

Marga/Taqsa Buses

Tolkar Buses

Rumbo Sur

Piratour

Canoero Catamaranes

Oficina Antártica

Heli Ushuaia

Club Andino

Tourist Office

Canal Fun

All Patagonia

Montiel Buses

Compañía de Guías de Patagonia

Líder Buses

Tolkeyén Buses

Aero Club Ushuaia (1km), ▼ 7, 8, 9 (1.5km) & Airport (4km)

▲ Centro Hípico (3km)

N

ACCOMMODATION

Antarctica Hostel	3
Cabañas del Beagle	2
Cumbres del Martial	7
Freestyle	5
Backpackers Hostel	1
Galeazzi-Basily B&B	4
Hotel Austral	9
La Posta	8
Tierra de Leyendas	6

Yakush	6

● CAFÉS

El Almacen	9
Tante Sara	6
X-presso	4

● BARS AND PUBS

Bodegón Fueguino	8
Dublin Irish Pub	5

RESTAURANTS

Chez Manu	1
Kalma Resto	3
Kaupé	2
María Lola Resto	7

0   200

metres

10

10

ARRIVAL AND DEPARTURE   USHUAIA

In peak season it's a good idea to book your bus or plane ticket well in advance, as demand outstrips supply. Between December and March, Ushuaia forms a "bottleneck" as travellers come down from Chile and other parts of Argentina and then attempt to get out the way they came.

BY PLANE

From Ushuaia there are frequent flights to Río Gallegos, El Calafate and Buenos Aires. The international airport, Malvinas Argentinas, sits 4km southwest of town; a taxi to the centre costs about AR$25. Airport departure tax is AR$35.
Airlines Aerolineas Argentinas, Maipú 823 ☎02901 436586; LADE, San Martín 542 ☎02901 421123.
Destinations Buenos Aires (2–4 daily; 3hr 30min); El Calafate (at least one daily; 2hr 15min, longer if stopover at Río Gallegos); Puerto Madryn, Argentina (5 weekly; 2hr); Río Gallegos (5 weekly; 1hr).

BY BUS

Frequent bus services run via Chile to both Argentine and Chilean destinations, setting off between 5 and 8am daily. All long-distance bus rides entail a short *ferry* ride at Primera Angostura (see p.389). Buses arrive and depart from their companies' respective offices. Buses Pacheco, Bus Sur and Tecni Austral run to Punta Arenas, Bus Sur carrying on to Puerto Natales; El Calafate and Bariloche are served by Taqsa; Río Grande is served by Lider, Montiel and Taqsa; the latter also has regular departures for Río Gellegos.

Bus companies Líder, Gob. Paz 921 (☎02901 436421); Tecni Austral; book through Tolkar at Roca 157 (☎02901 431408). Buses Pacheco and Bus Sur: book through Tolekeyen at San Martín 1267 (☎02901 437073); Marga/Taqsa, Gob. Godoy 41 (☎02901 435453); Montiel, Gob. Paz 605 (☎02901 421366).
Destinations Bariloche via El Calafate (1 daily; 36hr); El Calafate (1 daily; 18hr); Río Gallegos (1 daily; 12hr) Punta Arenas (1–2 daily; 12hr); Puerto Natales (1 daily via Punta Arenas; 15hr).

BY FERRY

Cruceros Australis (ⓦaustralis.com) runs two luxury cruise ships to Punta Arenas, the journey ranging from 3 days/2 nights to 4 days/3 nights. Ushuaia Boating, Gobernador Paz 233 (☎02901 436193, ⓦushuaiaboating.com.ar) and Zenit Explorer (☎01 486161, ⓦzenitexplorer.com.ar) operate daily boat crossings to Isla Navarino between themselves (weather permitting; US$125 one way).
Destinations Puerto Williams (Nov–April 1–2 daily; 45min–1hr).

INFORMATION AND TOURS

TOURIST INFORMATION

Tourist information San Martín 674 (Mon–Fri 9am–10pm, Sat & Sun 9am–8pm; ☎02901 424550, ⓦturismoushuaia.com). A helpful and well-stocked office.
Oficina Antartica Maipú 505, opposite the Muelle Turístico (Mon–Fri 8am–4pm and on weekends if there is a boat that day; ☎02901 421423). This ultra-helpful office specializes in information on Antarctica and Antarctic cruises and provides a list of approved International Association of Antarctica Tour Operators (ⓦiaato.org).
Club Andino Fadul 50 (Mon–Fri 10am–noon & 3–8.30pm; ☎02901 422335, ⓦwww.clubandinoushuaia .com.ar). Trekking and climbing information office; register with them before you make any trek or climb. Skiing and snowboarding also offered.

TOUR OPERATORS

Ushuaia is Tierra del Fuego's outdoor activity centre and there are a number of companies which offer everything from conventional city tours and boat outings on the Beagle Channel to rock climbing, 4WD adventures, horseriding and diving. The best are listed below.
Aero Club Ushuaia Luis Pedro Fique 151 ☎02901 421717, ⓦaeroclubushuaia.com.ar. Two spectacular 6-seater plane circuits on offer: the half-hour circuit takes

in Parque Nacional Tierra del Fuego and the Faro Les Eclaireurs, while the hour-long flight covers the length of the Beagle Channel up to Estancia Harberton as well as part of Lago Fagnano and Lago Escondido.
Canoero Catamaranes Ushuaia Muelle Turístico ☎02901 433893, ⓦcatamaranescanoero.com.ar. High quality, standard 5hr trips on a two-tiered catamaran along the Beagle Channel, taking in the bird life of Isla de Pájaros, a sea-lion colony, the Magellanic and Papua penguins of Isla Martillo and the Les Éclaireurs lighthouse.
Centro Hípico Ruta 3, Km 3021 ☎02901 443996, ⓦcentrohipicoushuaia.com.ar. Excellent horseriding centre with free transfers from town. Choose from half- and full-day excursions (the latter with *asado*); multi-day trips also available on request.
Chimango ☎02901 1560 5673. Take to the streets of Ushuaia as part of a morning bike tour, or else join the night-biking-and-barbecue combo.
Compania de Guías de Patagonia San Martín 628 ☎02901 437753, ⓦcompaniadeguias.com.ar. Experienced agency that runs multi-day trekking trips in Tierra del Fuego, arranges ice- and rock-climbing and offers dives in the Beagle Channel as well as sailing and horseriding excursions and last minute trips to Antarctica.
Heli Ushuaia San Martín at Laserre ☎02901 444444,

W heliushuaia.com.ar. Scenic helicopter circuits (7–45min), the shortest covering the city highlights, and the other three taking in various combinations of natural highlights around Ushuaia. Recommended.
Piratour Muelle Turístico ☎ 02901 424834, ✉ info@ piratour.com.ar. The only boat company authorized to offer a walk with the Magellanic penguins on Isla Martillo, which allows you to see the birds from up close.
Tierra ☎ 02901 1548 6886, W tierraturismo.com. Highly professional outfit specializing in 4WD trips in the surrounding area, combined with navigation in Zodiac boats on Lago Escondido and superb *asados* (barbecues).

ACCOMMODATION

Ushuaia offers a good range of hotels and hostels, most on the first four streets parallel to the bay, with the more exclusive options up in the foothills or further out of town along the waterfront. December to February is peak season for Antarctica-bound travellers and backpackers alike, so book all **accommodation** well in advance.

10

HOTELS AND B&BS

Galeazzi-Basily B&B Gob Valdéz 323 ☎ 02901 423213, W avesdelsur.com.ar. This guesthouse, run by the warm and hospitable Frances and Alejandro, is an excellent place to meet fellow travellers without sacrificing comfort or privacy. Besides the two doubles there are two fully equipped *cabañas* which sleep up to 4 people. Double **AR$280**, cabin **AR$500**

Hotel Austral 9 de Julio 250 ☎ 02901 422223, W hotel -austral.com.ar. This compact hotel boasts a central location two blocks uphill from the bay and its 10 rooms are light, bright, and come equipped with queen-sized beds, cable TV and wi-fi. Excellent mid-range choice. **AR$450**

Tierra de Leyendas Tierra de Vientos 2448 ☎ 02901 446565, W tierradeleyendas.com.ar. Southwest of the centre, this small boutique hotel gives you two choices of views: the sea or the mountains. Besides the splendid location, the de-luxe rooms all come with Jacuzzis and the on-site restaurant serves a buffet breakfast (included in the price) and fusion dishes. Airport pickup available. **AR$858 (US$198)**

LODGES AND CABINS

★ **Cabañas del Beagle** Las Aljabas 375 ☎ 02901 432785, W www.cabanasdelbeagle.com.ar. These three luxurious split-level cabins, lovingly constructed from local stone and wood by the indomitable Alejandro, are a perfect retreat from the downtown hustle and bustle. Each cabin sleeps up to four people and comes equipped with underfloor heating, enormous fireplace, kitchenette and bathtub, and your attentive hosts are always on hand to make your stay more comfortable. **AR$1083 (US$250)**

Cumbres del Martial Luis F. Martial Km5 ☎ 02901 424779, W cumbresdelmartial.com.ar. At this secluded mountain lodge, you can reside either in one of the six luxurious rooms, complete with king-sized beds and state-of-the-art bathrooms, or retreat with your loved one to one of the four de-luxe split-level cabins, built out of native wood and stone and equipped with large fireplaces. The restaurant focuses on local produce and fondues and non-guests can also stop by the Tea House for a wide range of tea and sumptuous cakes. Double **AR$1127 (US$260)**, cabin **AR$1647 (US$380)**

HOSTELS

Antarctica Hostel Antartida Argentina 270 ☎ 02901 435774, W antarcticahostel.com. Popular, secure hostel with guests socializing in the split-level cavern-like lounge and dining area. Book exchange and board games are a nice touch and breakfast includes cereal, eggs and fresh juice. Dorm **AR$85**, double **A$270**

Freestyle Backpackers Hostel Gob Paz 866 ☎ 02901 432874, W ushuaiafreestyle.com. Some of the best showers in town, a proper games room with billiards, impromptu barbecues for guests and a fab view of the bay distinguish this firm backpacker favourite. Dorm **AR$90**

La Posta Perón Sur 864 ☎ 02901 444650, W laposta -ush.com.ar. A flat 30min walk (or AR$15 cab ride) from downtown, this lovely family-run hostel has facilities more akin to a hotel than a backpacker joint. The comfy beds have down comforters, the bathrooms sparkle and Lucas the owner is a treasure trove of local knowledge. Dorm **AR$85**, double **AR$270**

Yakush San Martín at Piedrabuena ☎ 02901 435807, W hostelyakush.com.ar. Central hostel with compact dorms (with large lockers), large guest kitchen, underused lounge with book exchange and super-friendly, welcoming staff. Popular with a mix of local and international backpackers. Dorm **AR$80**, double **AR$240**

EATING AND DRINKING

Ushuaia is crammed with eateries and **restaurants** of all kinds – many run-of-the-mill, all-you-can-gobble affairs, but with a few dazzling exceptions. Self-caterers will find all they need at one of two supermarkets in town: La Anónima on the corner of Gob. Paz and Rivadavia and another at San Martín and Onas, or else at one of the gourmet shops along San Martín.

10

CAFÉS

El Almacen Ramos Av Maipú 749 ☎02901 424317. At this half-museum, half-café and bakery, the surroundings are as a much of a draw as the hearty soups, sandwiches and cakes. See if you can spot the porcelain chamber pots and the harlequin doll peeking out of an antique chest. Daily noon–10pm.

Tante Sara San Martín at Fadúl ☎02901 423912. Aunt Sara must be a busy woman, judging from the perpetually full interior of this spacious, shiny café. Expect a potpourri of pastas, salads, sandwiches and dish-of-the-day deals, which include such standards as lasagne and goulash. Good stop for coffee, too. Daily 11am–11pm.

X-presso San Martín at Laserre Grab a cupcake, quiche, good coffee, salad or hefty sandwich at this spacious modern café which shares the premises with Heli Ushuaia (see p.430). Daily 9.30am–6pm.

ANTARCTICA – THE REMOTEST CONTINENT

Every year, over 30,000 visitors converge on Ushuaia with one goal in mind: **to reach Antarctica**, one of the remotest and most beguiling destinations on earth. Formerly considered one of the greatest challenges for explorers and navigators, Antarctica is now within reach of anyone prepared to part with a large sum of money in exchange for the opportunity to board an **Antarctic cruise** and gaze at floating mountain-sized "ice cathedrals" and glaciers spilling from pristine mountains; to observe killer and minke whales, elephant and leopard seals and an immense wealth of birds, ranging from Emperor, King and Macaroni penguins to albatross and Antarctic terns; and even to dive the frigid waters.

The journey is not without risks: in January 2011, the MV *Polar Star* struck an un-surveyed rock and passengers were transferred to another vessel for the return journey. Such incidents are, however, rare: the ships used for these cruises tend to be ice breakers or at least have ice-strengthened hulls, and even the yachts come equipped with auxiliary engines, making them perfectly suitable for the task. The **Antarctic tourist season** runs from November until mid-March and cruises tend to last between 10 and 21 days. Typical destinations include the Antarctic continent, the South Georgia Islands and the Falkland Islands.

CHOOSING A CRUISE

When choosing the length of the cruise, you must bear in mind that the crossing of the Drake Passage alone lasts at least two days one-way. You also have to take into consideration the activities on offer, which depend on the capacity and facilities of your ship. These typically include lectures on environmental issues and shore excursions by Zodiac boat, which last half a day; some cruises may also offer kayaking, scuba diving and trekking. Ships vary in capacity – from thirteen to five hundred passengers – and comfort (most offer a range of cabin categories); the very adventurous with time on their hands can also opt for **multi-week yacht journeys**. The smaller the ship and the fewer the passengers, the more shore landings there are per passenger, though at the same time, smaller vessels are more vulnerable to the elements, making the notoriously stormy Drake Passage crossing even rougher.

PRICES

Cruise prices start from US$3350 (the last-minute bargain price) and go up into six figures; all depends on the length of the trip and the level of comfort you require. Since most cruises tend to sell out, those trying to get a last-minute bargain need to have weeks of free time at their disposal and even that may not guarantee substantial savings.

AGENCIES

Agencies in Ushaia offering last-minute bookings include **All Patagonia** at Juana Fadúl 60 (☎02901 433622, ⊛allpatagonia.com), **Canal Fun at 9 de Julio 118** (☎02901 437395, ⊛canalfun.com) and **Rumbo Sur** at San Martín 350 (☎02901 422275, ⊛rumbosur.com.ar). Otherwise, the following companies are members of IAATO (International Association of Antarctica Tour Operators; ⊛iaato.org), specializing in safe and environmentally responsible travel to Antarctica: **Aberkrombie & Kent** (⊛abercrombiekent.com), **Aurora Expeditions** (⊛auroraexpeditions.com.au), **Heritage Expeditions**,(⊛heritage-expeditions.com), **Lindblad Expeditions** (⊛expeditions.com); **Quark Expeditions** (⊛quarkexpeditions.com), and **SIM Expeditions** (see p.424).

RIGHT YACHTS ANCHORED AT PUERTO WILLIAMS (P.423)

10

RESTAURANTS

Chez Manu Luis F. Martial 2135 ☎ 02901 431253, ⓦ chezmanu.com. A stiff hike or a short taxi ride uphill, this fine establishment rewards you both with spectacular views of the bay and with chef Emmanuel's creations combining traditional French cuisine with Fuegian ingredients. It's difficult to go wrong either with the home-smoked fish, the Patagonian lamb or the trout with almond crumble. Daily 12.30–3pm & 7.30–11.30pm.

★ **Kalma Resto** Antártida Argentina 57 ☎ 2901 425786, ⓦ kalmaresto.com.ar. We have a distinct suspicion that up-and-coming chef Jorge might be some kind of mad genius. Who else would combine olive oil with chocolate, edible flowers with *centolla* (king crab) or oranges with perfectly grilled *merluza negra* (black hake)? Yet it all works, with spectacular results. Dinner only outside the Dec–Feb peak season. Tues–Sun 1–3pm & 7.30–11.30pm.

★ **Kaupé** Roca 470 ☎ 02901 422704, ⓦ kaupe.com. ar. This stylish, well-established hilltop restaurant still holds its own against the newcomers thanks to the efforts of chef Ernesto who works wonders with *centolla* and

merluza negra dishes and the extensive wine list. Non-pescetarians can opt for steak flambéed in cognac whereas seafood lovers can splash out on the "Del Mar" tasting menu. Reservations recommended. Mon–Sat 1–3pm & 7.30–11.30pm, Sun 1–3.30pm.

María Lola Resto Deloqui 1048 ☎ 02901 421185. Uphill from the bay, this shiny, modern establishment distinguishes itself with its excellent service and its Mediterranean-inspired cuisine that uses local ingredients to great effect. The seafood pasta is excellent. Mon–Sat 1–3pm & 7.30–11.30pm, Sun 1–3.30pm.

BARS AND PUBS

Bodegón Fueguino San Martín 859 ☎ 02901 431972. Central spot popular with travellers tempted by the home-brewed beer, melt-in-your-mouth lamb, exotic meat dishes such as wild boar steak and a wide range of wine. Daily 12.30–3.30pm & 7.30–11.30pm.

Dublin Irish Pub 9 de Julio at Deloqui ☎ 02901 430744. This traveller favourite draws Guinness drinkers by the dozen. Lively spot for meeting people and the occasional performance by local bands. Daily 8pm–late.

DIRECTORY

Banks and exchanges ATMs at most banks, most of which are along San Martín, as is the main *casa de cambio*, at no. 788.

Car rental Alamo Rent a Car, Belgrano 96 ☎ 02901 431131; Hertz, San Martín 409 ☎ 02901 437529; Patagonia Sur Rent a Car, 9 de Julio 423 ☎ 02901 440385. Rental rates, including insurance, start at AR$220 per day.

Hospital The regional hospital is at Maipú and 12 de Octubre; ☎ 02901 423200.

Internet All accommodation options reviewed offer either free wi-fi or free internet access. Otherwise, try one of several *locutorios* along San Martín.

Pharmacy Several pharmacies are located along San Martín.

Post office San Martín at Godoy.

Around Ushuaia

While Ushuaia's museums will satisfy your curiosity about the town's history, and its restaurants will tickle the taste buds of any traveller coming from small-town Tierra del Fuego, those seeking Ushuaia's greatest attractions should look beyond the city limits, towards the nature trails of Parque Nacional Tierra del Fuego, the fauna inhabiting the spectacular Beagle Channel, the historic Estancia Harberton and the snow-covered slopes of Cerro Castor.

Cerro Martial and Glaciar Martial

Chairlift April–Oct 10am–4pm daily • AR$35

Seven kilometres northwest of Ushuaia lies the hanging **Glaciar Martial**, with magnificent views of the Beagle Channel and Isla Navarino from the top. To get here, walk or take one of several buses (four companies offering ten daily departures between 8.30am and 6pm; AR$20) from the corner of Maipú and Fadul up to the *Hotel Del Glaciar*, and then climb or take the **chair lift** from behind the hotel. The climb takes two hours without the chair lift. Beware of loose rocks on the steep middle section of the trail.

Beagle Channel

Boats depart from Ushuaia's Muelle Turístico; several companies run tours of the channel (see p.430).

No visit to Ushuaia is complete without a journey on the **BEAGLE CHANNEL**, the majestic, mountain-fringed sea passage to the south of the city. Most **boat trips** start

WINTER SPORTS AROUND USHUAIA

To ski at the end of the world, come sometime between June and early September (though not in July if you wish to avoid the holidaying crowds) and head for **Cerro Castór** (full-day tickets AR$200), the only Alpine ski resort in the area, located 26km away from Ushuaia along the RN3 and boasting powder snow as well as 24km of ski runs. The fifteen slopes feature a good mix of slopes catering to beginners, advanced and everything in between and you can rent skis, boards and cross-country skis at the resort; equipment costs between AR$40 and AR$100 a day. Ask at the tourist office about transport to and from Ushuaia. If cross-country skiing is your passion, you won't want to miss the annual **Marcha Blanca** (Ⓦmarchablanca .com), the ski marathon that symbolically recreates General San Martín's crossing of the Andes.

If you have your own transport there are a couple of other nearby attractions: **Nunatak Adventure** (❶02901 430329, Ⓦnunatakadventure.com) runs a host of winter activities from the Tierra Valle Mayor centre, 20km from Ushuaia, which include cross-country skiing, short husky sledding trips, and Snow Cat safaris. In the same valley you'll come across the **Valle de Lobos** (❶015 612319, Ⓦwww.gatocuruchet.com.ar), 18km out of Ushuaia. This breeding centre for seventy or so huskies (husky rides available in the winter (open for visits in the summer) is part of owner Gato Cruchet's dream to take part in Alaska's challenging 1800km Iditarod race; he was the first South American contestant to do so.

10

and finish in Ushuaia, and you can enjoy the best views of town looking back at it from the straits. Most tours visit Les Eclaireurs Lighthouse – previously thought to be the Lighthouse at the End of the World from Jules Verne's namesake novel. Other popular destinations include Isla de los Pájaros, Isla de los Lobos, Estancia Harberton, the penguin colony on Isla Martillo and Parque Nacional Tierra del Fuego. The main draw of these excursions is the chance to spot the **marine wildlife** that lives along the channel, including albatrosses, giant petrels, skuas, cormorants, South American terns and Magellanic penguins; resident sea mammals are sea lions, Peale's dolphins, minke whales and, if you're lucky, killer whales. Tours returning by land from Estancia Harberton stop by the **árboles banderas** – trees bent sideways by the fierce Patagonian wind, known as the *Escoba de Díos* (God's Broom).

Estancia Harberton

Estancia Daily mid-Oct to mid-April 10am–7pm; entry by guided tour (daily at 11am, 1.30pm, 3pm and 5pm) only • AR$45pm • Ⓦestanciaharberton.com. **Museo Acatushún** Daily 10am–7pm • AR$20 • Ⓦacatushun.com

Eighty-five kilometres east of Ushuaia along the scenic RC-j lies the first ranch to be founded in Tierra del Fuego, **ESTANCIA HARBERTON**, an ordered assortment of whitewashed buildings on the shores of a sheltered bay. The estancia was built in 1886 by the Reverend Thomas Bridges, author of the Yámana–English dictionary, and served as a voluntary refuge for groups of Yámana, Selk'nam and Mannekenk. Its location was immortalized in the *Uttermost Part of the Earth*, the evocative memoir written by Thomas's son Lucas.

It is now run as a museum by his great-grandson, Tommy Goodall, and bilingual tours of the grounds include sampling and identification of local flora and viewing the estancia's cemetery. If you're staying as a guest at the estancia, you can take part in a number of tours, including trekking in the Harberton and Cambaceres Peninsulas (see website for more details) and full-moon barbecues. If you come to Harberton by boat, you stop at Reserva Yécapasela on Isla Martillo, also known as **Penguin Island**, along the way, home to Magellanic and Gentoo penguins and a large shag colony; only Piratour customers are allowed to disembark on the island (see p.430).

Museo Acatushún

Tommy Goodall's wife, Nathalie, is a renowned biologist who oversees the impressive marine mammal museum, **Museo Acatushún**. Exhibits focus on marine birds and mammals, with over four thousand specimens, the pride and joy of the collection being the rare Hector's beaked whale. You can wander around the museum by yourself, learning about the behaviour and anatomy of the animals, or you can take one of the excellent tours in English.

ARRIVAL AND DEPARTURE   ESTANCIA HARBERTON

By bus Daily buses run from the corner of Maipú and 25 de Mayo in Ushuaia, departing at 9am and coming back around 3pm; the return fare is AR$260.

By boat Several tour companies (see p.430) run boat tours of the Beagle Channel, which include a stop at Estancia Harberton.

ACCOMMODATION AND EATING

Estancia Harberton ⓦestanciaharberton.com (reservations by Skype or email). It's possible to stay on the estancia itself, in semi-rustic but comfortable accommodation, inside either the *Old Shepherd's House* or the *Old Cook's House*. Visitors can choose either half board (which includes the cost of some activities) or full board.

Half-board <u>AR$300</u>, full board <u>AR$400</u>
Mánacatush Estancia Harberton. Incredibly popular with visitors, this café serves hearty soups as well as afternoon tea with large helpings of cake and home-made jams. Daily 11am–6.30pm.

Parque Nacional Tierra Del Fuego

Daily 8am–8pm in summer; reduced hours in winter • Summer AR$85; rest of the year AR$35

The **PARQUE NACIONAL TIERRA DEL FUEGO**, a mere 12km west of Ushuaia, protects 630 square kilometres of jagged mountains, intricate lakes, southern beech forest, swampy peat bog, sub-Antarctic tundra and verdant coastline. The park stretches along the frontier with Chile, from the Beagle Channel to the **Sierra de Injugoyen** north of Lago Fagnano, but only the southernmost quarter is open to the public, accessed by the RN-3 from Ushuaia.

The park is broken down into three main sectors: Bahía Ensenada and Río Pipo in the east; Lago Roca further to the west; and the Lapataia area to the south of Lago Roca, which includes Laguna Verde and, at the end of RN-3, Bahía Lapataia on the Beagle Channel. Here you may see **birds** such as Magellanic woodpeckers, condors, torrent ducks, steamer ducks, upland geese and buff-necked ibises, and **mammals** such as guanacos, the rare sea otter, Patagonian grey foxes and their larger, endangered cousin, the native Fuegian fox once heavily hunted for its pelt. The park offers several relatively unchallenging though beautiful **trails**, ideal for short excursions or day hikes.

Bahía Ensenada and Senda Costera

The small **BAHÍA ENSENADA**, 2km south of the crossroads by the Tren del Fin del Mundo train station, is where you'll find the jetty for boats (no fixed schedule) to Lapataia and the Isla Redonda. It's also the trailhead for one of the most pleasant walks in the park, the highly recommended **Senda Costera** (7km; 3hr). The not-too-strenuous route takes you through dense coastal forest of evergreen beech, winter's bark, and *lenga* while affording spectacular views from the Beagle Channel shoreline. On the way, you'll pass grass-covered mounds that are the ancient campsite **middens** of the Yámana.

Cerro Guanaco

Another recommended, if tiring trek, is the climb up **CERRO GUANACO** (8km; 3hr), the 970m-high mountain ridge on the north side of Lago Roca. Take the Hito XXIV path from the car park at Lago Roca and after ten minutes you'll cross a small bridge over a stream. Immediately afterwards, the path forks: to the left, **Senda Hito XXIV** runs along the northeastern shore of Lago Roca to an obelisk that marks Argentina's border with Chile (5km; 1hr 30min). To the right, **Senda Cerro Guanaco** runs right up the slope to the summit of its namesake peak.

The path up the forested mountainside is steep but not hazardous, but after rain you're sure to encounter some slippery tree roots and muddy patches, especially during the boggy part of the trail. The view from the crest to the south is memorable: the tangle of islands and rivers of the Archipiélago Cormoranes, Lapataia's sinuous curves, the Isla Redonda in the Beagle Channel, and across to the Chilean islands, Hoste and Navarino, separated by the Murray Narrows.

| ARRIVAL AND INFORMATION | PARQUE NACIONAL TIERRA DEL FUEGO |

By bus Frequent daily buses (20min) run from Ushuaia's waterfront between 8am and 7pm (AR$60).

By train The gimmicky but fun narrow-gauge tourist railway of El Tren del Fin del Mundo (regular AR$155, first class AR$240, premium AR$310; ⊛ trendelfindelmundo .com.ar) departs from a station 8km west of Ushuaia,

reachable by taxi. The 4.5km trip to the park takes 40min and the one way/return ticket costs are the same.

Park office (Daily 8am–8pm in summer; reduced hours in winter.) Offers a map of the park in exchnge for your entrance fee; if you're planning to come back the following day, let the staff know, and you won't have to pay the park fee twice.

Easter Island and the Juan Fernández Archipelago

440 Easter Island

456 The Juan Fernández Archipelago

MOAI, AHU TONGARIKI, EASTER ISLAND

Easter Island and the Juan Fernández Archipelago

Chile's two remote island territories, enchanting Easter Island and the virtually unknown Juan Fernández Archipelago, are collectively referred to as the Islas Esporádicas ("Far Flung Isles"). Both are national parks and have been singled out by UNESCO for special protection. Neither is easy to get to, and most travellers never do, but those who make the journeys will find their efforts and expenditure richly rewarded with a set of tantalizingly enigmatic statues and one of the world's most precarious ecosystems, respectively.

11

Lost in the vastness of the ocean, tiny **Easter Island** (or, in Spanish, Isla de Pascua) remains a world unto itself, its closest inhabited neighbour being Pitcairn Island, 2250km northwest. Spanning just 23km at its longest stretch, the island is triangular, with low-lying extinct volcanoes rising out of each corner. Scattered between these points are dozens of **moai**, the intriguing monolithic stone **statues** that have made the island universally famous.

Much closer to the mainland, at a mere 675km west of Valparaíso, but still relatively unknown, the **Juan Fernández Archipelago** is, ironically, far more difficult to reach. With their sharp, jagged peaks, coated in lush, deep-green foliage, the islands boast a topography that is among the most spectacular in Chile.

The archipelago's largest and only permanently inhabited island – **Isla Robinson Crusoe** – started out as a pirates' refuge. In 1709 it was brought to public attention when Scottish seaman Alexander Selkirk was rescued from its shores after being marooned there for more than four years - a story was used as the basis for *The Adventures of Robinson Crusoe* (see p.459). Today the Juan Fernández Archipelago, badly affected by a tsunami triggered by the 2010 earthquake (see p.457), remains an adventurous destination, well off the beaten track.

Easter Island

One of the most remote places on earth, tiny **EASTER ISLAND** is home to 5000 or so people. Around half are indigenous (who generally refer to themselves as Rapa Nui; mainland Chileans call them *pascuenses*), with the rest being mainly *continentales* (mainland Chilean immigrants). The Rapa Nui have fine-boned Polynesian features and speak their own Polynesian-based language (also called Rapa Nui) in addition to Spanish.

Where did the Rapa Nui come from? p.443
Rongo Rongo p.444
Outdoor activities and tours p.446
Rongo Rongo: Easter Island's mysterious script p.444
Easter Island festivals p.448
Parque Nacional Rapa Nui essentials p.449

The Moai of Easter Island p.453
The myth of the "Long Ears" and the "Short Ears" p.455
The Birdman ceremony p.456
The 2010 tsunami p.457
Alexander Selkirk p.459
Boat trips from San Juan Bautista p.460

TAPATI RAPA NUI FESTIVAL, EASTER ISLAND

Highlights

❶ Tapati Rapa Nui festival Discover the mysterious roots of Easter Island's ancient culture at its carnival (late Jan/early Feb), featuring everything from traditional dancing and singing to hurtling down volcanic slopes on banana trunks. **See p.448**

❷ Ahu Tongariki Fifteen impeccably restored *moai* (giant statues) line up to be admired against a backdrop of green cliffs and roaring waves. **See p.450**

❸ Rano Raraku This mighty mountain at the heart of Easter Island is where the *moai* were

quarried – and some, too big to move, never left the rock where they were hewn. **See p.450**

❹ Orongo Imagine the mindboggling rituals of the Birdman cult as you gaze out at craggy islets in a sapphire-blue ocean or inwards to a reed-filled crater at one of the island's most breathtaking natural sites. **See p.456**

❺ Juan Fernández flora and fauna Frolic underwater with fish and sea lions, watch the antics of hummingbirds and observe dozens of endemic species of plant on this treasure island of unique (and painfully fragile) wildlife. **See p.456**

HIGHLIGHTS ARE MARKED ON THE MAPS ON P.442 & P.458

EASTER ISLAND

HIGHLIGHTS
1. Tapati Rapa Nui festival
2. Ahu Tongariki
3. Rano Raraku
4. Orongo

N

Poike Peninsula

Ana o Keke

Maunga Puka Tikei (400m)

Ahu Ature Huki
Ahu Nau Nau
Anakena
Conaf Guarderia
Ovahe
Ahu Te Pito Kura
Bahía La Pérouse

Iko's Ditch

Ahu Tongariki
Rano Raraku
Conaf Guarderia
Camino de los Moai

Ahu Hanga Tetenga

Ahu Akahanga

Ahu Vaihu

Terevaka (510m)

Ahu Te Peu

Ahu Akivi

Ana Kakenga
Ana Te Pahu
Museo Antropológico
TAHAI
Ahu Ko Te Riku
Ahu Tahai
Ahu Vai Uri
Ahu Tautira

Puna Pau

Hanga Roa

Ana Kai Tangata

Ahu Vinapu

Rano Kau

Conaf Guarderia
Orongo

Motu Kau Kau
Motu Iti
Motu Nui

PACIFIC OCEAN

Site with moai

0 — 1 — 2

Virtually the entire population lives in the island's single settlement, **Hanga Roa**, and most islanders make their living from tourism, which has been growing steadily ever since an airstrip was built here in 1968.

The key points of interest are found within **Parque Nacional Rapa Nui**, which comprises much of the island. Highlights include **Rano Kau**, a huge volcanic crater and site of the ceremonial village of **Orongo**; the **Rano Raraku** quarry, where almost all the *moai* were carved; and the largest *ahu* (platform) on the island, **Ahu Tongariki**, which boasts fifteen *moai*. Archeological treasures aside, Easter Island has much to offer outdoor enthusiasts, from diving in waters with arguably the best visibility in the world to surfing major waves off the island's south coast.

Easter Island is two hours behind mainland Chile. The weather is fairly constant year-round, with an average temperature of 23°C (73°F) in January and February, and 18°C (64°F) in July and August. Late January and early February is the busiest time, as the islanders stage the annual **Tapati Rapa Nui festival**.

Brief history

11

Easter Island was "discovered" and named by Dutch naval commander **Jacob**

WHERE DID THE RAPA NUI COME FROM?

The islanders' oral history claims that Easter Island's original colonizer was **Hotu Matu'a**, a great *ariki henua* (chief) who lived possibly in Polynesia or the Marquesas. It had been revealed to Hotu Matu'a's tattooist in a dream, that an island with craters and fine beaches awaited his master. The chief dispatched a reconnaissance party to find this promised land, following some time later with his family and fellow colonists. He arrived on Anakena beach, just as his wife was giving birth to their first son.

As *ariki henua*, Hotu Matu'a was not a political leader, but a revered and important person with great supernatural qualities (*mana*). Accordingly, he and his home were *tapu* (sacred and untouchable), and so Hotu Matu'a and his family lived at Anakena while the rest of his party dispersed around the island. Their families eventually grew into eight separate kin-groups, and as time passed, these groups became more sophisticated and stratified.

THOR HEYERDAHL AND THE SOUTH AMERICAN THEORY

Central to any discussion of Easter Island's settlement are the controversial theories of **Thor Heyerdahl**, the Norwegian explorer-archeologist whose widely publicized expeditions and books generated enormous interest in the island. Heyerdahl was convinced the island had been colonized by South American settlers and, in 1948, he proved, spectacularly, that such a voyage was possible when he and five companions successfully sailed a traditional balsa raft (the *Kon Tiki*) from Peru to an island east of Tahiti.

He backed up his theory with some persuasive but highly selective details, concentrating on the fact that Pacific winds and currents move in a westward direction; the presence in Polynesia of the sweet potato, indisputably of South American origin; the resemblance between the stonework of some Easter Island platforms and certain types of Inca masonry; and the ancient Peruvian custom of artificially extending the ear lobes, just like the islanders at the time of European contact. He failed to explain, however, the total absence of South American pottery and textiles in Polynesia, and the fact that no trace of any indigenous South American language had been found there.

WHAT THE EXPERTS SAY

The view of most experts is that Easter Island was colonized by Polynesians from the west – an opinion backed by linguistic evidence, physical anthropology and the proliferation on Easter Island of Polynesian plants. Which part of Polynesia these settlers came from is still open to debate, though the **Marquesas** is thought the most likely.

As for the date of the settlers' arrival, all we can be sure of is that they were constructing *ahu* (ceremonial platforms) by 800 AD. No one knows for sure if this culture developed in complete isolation, or if another wave of colonists arrived later, as suggested in some of the oral traditions.

Roggeveen on Easter Sunday, 1722. In the absence of any written records left by the islanders, Roggeveen's **log** is the earliest written account of the island. His party spent only a single day on land, long enough to observe the "particularly high erected stone images". After their departure, it was another 48 years before Easter Island was revisited, this time by Spanish commander **Felipe González**, who mapped the island and claimed it for King Carlos III of Spain during a six-day stay.

Four years later, **Captain Cook** anchored here in the hope of restoring the health of his scurvy-ridden crew. He, too, observed with incredulity the "stupendous figures", though he noted that some lay strewn on the ground, toppled from their platforms. Later visitors reported an increasing number of **fallen statues**, and by 1825 all of the *moai* on Hanga Roa bay had been destroyed.

The arrival of the slave traders

In 1805, the island was raided by the first of the **slave traders**, when an American schooner captured 22 men and women to be used as seal hunters on the Juan Fernández Islands. After three days at sea, the prisoners were allowed onto the deck, whereupon they promptly threw themselves overboard and drowned in a desperate attempt to swim back to the island. Between 1862 and 1864, Peruvian sailors captured over two thousand five hundred islanders, who were shipped off to work as slaves in the guano mines.

After many of the islanders had died from disease and the appalling conditions in the mines, the Bishop of Tahiti finally managed to persuade the Peruvian government to repatriate the remaining prisoners – most of whom died on the voyage home. Tragically, the sixteen who made it back infected the rest of the islanders with smallpox and TB, reducing the population to around one hundred. Critically, the loss of life was accompanied by the loss of a crucial part of the island's culture and collective memory, for the last *ariki henua* (high chief), *moari* (keepers of sacred knowledge) and *tangata rongo rongo* (specialist readers) were among those who perished.

Missionaries and plantations

A certain degree of stability came when the first missionary, **Eugène Eyraud**, arrived in 1864 and set to converting the islanders to Christianity, a mission fully accomplished by the time of his death, four years later. The peace was disrupted, however, when a French plantation owner, **Jean-Baptiste Onésime Dutrou-Bornier**, bought up large tracts

---

RONGO RONGO: EASTER ISLAND'S MYSTERIOUS SCRIPT

In 1864, French missionary **Eugène Eyraud** wrote of "tablets or staff of wood covered with hieroglyphics" that he'd found in the islanders' homes. This was the first the outside world had heard of *ko hau motu mo rongo rong* or "lines of script for recitation". The *rongo rongo* tablets remained firmly beyond the grasp of the scholars who came to study them, for none of the islanders knew how to read them. Almost one hundred and fifty years later, no one has succeeded in deciphering them.

The script consists of tiny, tightly packed symbols carved in straight lines across the wooden boards. The symbols, which include representations of people, animals, birds and plants, are upside down on each alternate line. Late nineteenth-century oral testimonies suggest the tablets contained records of genealogies, myths, wars, deaths and religious hymns.

POPULAR THEORIES

Some modern scholars believe the script was developed after the first European contact, inspired by the written documents the Spaniards made the chiefs sign in 1770; others believe it is only one of four written languages in the world to have developed entirely independently of outside influence. The most widely accepted theory is that the symbols were **mnemonics** for use in recitals and chanting.

Today, only 29 *rongo rongo* tablets remain in existence, all of them spirited off to overseas museums in Santiago, Rome, London and Washington, D.C.

of land and proceeded to run the island as his personal ranch, paying the islanders a pittance for their hard labour and resorting to violence when they wouldn't cooperate. When the missionaries opposed Doutrou-Bornier's exploitation, he attacked their missions, forcing them to flee the island. He dealt a further blow to the island's slowly recovering population by sending all but a hundred islanders to Tahiti to work on his partner's plantation, before finally being murdered in 1877 by the oppressed islanders.

Chile's annexation

The **Chilean government** acquired first Doutrou-Bornier's lands, and then most of the remaining land on the island, leaving only the village of **Hanga Roa** in the possession of the islanders. Then, on September 9, 1888, the Chilean Navy – apparently with the islanders' consent – officially **annexed** Easter Island, declaring it Chilean territory. Chile subsequently leased it to Williamson Balfour, a British wool-trading company, which virtually governed the island according to its own needs and interests.

In 1953, the company's lease was revoked and the Chilean Navy stepped in to resume command, though the islanders were given no say in the running of the island. It was not until 1964, that they were allowed outside Hanga Roa (let alone off the island), and granted full citizenship and the right to vote.

The drive towards autonomy

Since the return to democracy, the management of some local affairs, including education, which is now bilingual, has been transferred to the islanders. However, many continue to call for greater autonomy and even secession, expressing concern over the pace of development, the impact of the growing tourist industry and the increasing numbers of mainland Chileans settling on the island. At the time of writing, legislation was set to be passed in the Chilean parliament to give the Easter Island authorities greater powers to regulate tourist numbers (and potentially levy a visitor charge).

ARRIVAL AND DEPARTURE   EASTER ISLAND

BY PLANE

LAN, currently the only airline serving Easter Island, has six to seven weekly flights from Santiago, two weekly from Lima, Peru, and one to two weekly from Papeete, Tahiti. Return flights from Santiago often cost in excess of US$1200 if booked from outside Chile; cheaper deals are generally available if you buy your ticket at a LAN office in Chile, via a Chilean travel agent, or in conjunction with a long-distance LAN flight. Mataveri airport is on the southern edge of Hanga Roa, about 1km from the centre. The LAN office is at Atamu Tekena and Pont (☎ 32 210 0279, ⊕ lan.com).

GETTING AROUND

The easiest way to get around is via a guided tour (see box, p.446), though some of the cheaper ones can feel a bit crowded and rushed.

By car or motorbike Many travellers hire a car (from around CH$30,000/day), motorbike (from around CH$20,000/day) or even a quad bike (from around CH$25,000/day) to explore the island. Book a vehicle as soon as you can after arrival (or even before). Outlets include Insular Rent a Car, Atamu Tekena s/n (☎ 32 210 0480, ⊕ rentainsular.cl), and Oceanic Rent a Car, Atamu Tekena s/n (☎ 32 210 0985). Note that there is no car insurance on the island.

By bike or on foot You can visit some sites on a mountain bike or on foot, though walking around the whole island would present quite a challenge. Several stores on Atamu Tekena have bikes for hire (generally CH$10,000–15,000/day).

Hanga Roa

Hanga Roa has been the island's only residential sector since the 1860s, when Catholic missionaries relocated the islanders here to facilitate their conversion. Its long, sprawling streets are lined with single-storey houses and fragrant eucalyptus trees, giving the place the unfinished feel of a recently settled frontier town.

OUTDOOR ACTIVITIES AND TOURS

There are innumerable ways to explore Easter Island's beautiful sites and terrain – from horseriding and scuba diving to kayaking and ziplining.

Cabalgatas Pantu (☎ 32 210 0577) offers horseback tours of the west and north coasts, including the ascent of Maunga Terevaka, the island's highest point, as well as traditional Rapa Nui meals. Piti Pont (☎ 32 210 0664 or 09 9574 0582), a renowned guide, also runs various horseriding excursions. A day trip with either costs around CH$40,000. The established Orca Diving Centre (☎ 32 255 0877 or 32 255 0375, ⓦ www.seemorca.cl) and Mike Rapu Diving Centre (☎ 32 255 1055, ⓦ mikerapu.cl), both with offices on the *caleta*, offer a range of scuba-diving trips (CH$25,000–50,000). Hare Orca, next to the Orca Diving Centre, rents out surfboards (CH$10,000/day), boogie boards (CH$7500/day), kayaks (CH$7500–12,500/day) and snorkelling gear (CH$5000/day); the shop can put you in touch with surfing instructors. There is also a zipline on the island, run by Mar'ari Canopy (☎ 09 9507 2540), near the road to Anakena.

GUIDED TOURS

Aku Aku Turismo at Av Tu'u Koihu s/n (☎ 32 210 0770, ⓦ akuakuturismo.cl), and Kia Koe Tour, Atamu Tekena s/n (☎ 32 210 0282, ⓦ kiakoetour.cl), both offer bilingual archeological tours (around CH$30,000–35,000 for a full day, CH$20,000 for a half day). ★ Haumaka Archaelogical Tours on Puku Rangi Uka s/n (☎ 32 210 0274, ⊖ haumakatours@gmail.com) offers excellent, small-group tours of the island's sites in English, French and German, with extremely well-informed and friendly guides. Taura'a Tours, Atamu Tekena s/n (☎ 32 210 0463, ⓦ tauraahotel.cl), also offers small-group trips.

Atamu Tekena is the main road, lined with small supermarkets, souvenir shops, internet cafés, restaurants and tour agencies. Most of the action is centred around the Caleta Hanga Roa harbour, overlooked by Ahu Tautira, the only *moai* in the town proper. Restaurants stretch from here along oceanside Policarpo Toro, parallel to Atamu Tekena. East–west Te Pito O Te Henua connects the two, ending at the church, where islanders still congregate every Sunday morning. Just south of the pier lies tiny Playa Pea, where a rock pool safe for swimming is cordoned off from the stretch of ocean popular with surfers and body boarders.

INFORMATION

HANGA ROA

Tourist office Sernatur, Tu'u Maheke and Policarpo Toro (Mon–Fri 8.30am–1.30pm & 2.30–5.30pm; ☎ 32 210 0255, ⊖ ipascua@sernatur.cl).

Conaf has a small booth at the airport, a larger office at Mataveri s/n, on the outskirts of Hanga Roa (Mon–Fri 9.30am–5pm; ☎ 32 210 0236, ⓦ conaf.cl), and a visitors' centre at Orongo.

ACCOMMODATION

Accommodation on Easter Island is more expensive than on the mainland, though there are some budget options. As many places don't accept credit cards, you should bring plenty of cash with you; US dollars are widely accepted. It's a good idea to arrange your accommodation beforehand during busy times such as Tapatai (see p.448). Most hotels offer a free airport pick-up (and generally greet you with a garland of flowers), and include breakfast in the rates.

HOTELS AND GUESTHOUSES

Aloha Nui Guest House Av Atamu Tekena s/n ☎ 32 210 0274, ⊖ haumakatours@gmail.com. Run by the couple behind the excellent Haumaka Tours (see box, above), this tastefully decorated guesthouse has six clean and comfortable en suites, a tropical garden, and a well-stocked library filled with books, music and pieces of artwork. CH$51,000

★ **Explora Posada de Mike Rapu** 5.6km from Hanga Roa; reservations ☎ 2 395 2800, ⓦ explora.com. The most luxurious hotel on the island, and one of the most memorable places to stay in Chile, the eco-friendly Explora has elegant, contemporary en suites with all the creature comforts you'd expect. There's also a wonderful pool, Jacuzzi and spa, delicious food and drinks, and expert guides to help you explore the island. Rates include full board and two daily excursions. Three-night programme CH$1,600,000 (US$3225) per person

Hotel Iorana Ana Magaro s/n ☎ 32 100608, reservations ☎ 2 695 2058, ⓦ ioranahotel.cl. Although the rooms are significantly overpriced, the secluded location, looking down to the ocean, is unbeatable. As well as a regular outdoor pool, there's a "natural" pool enclosed by rocks and filled with seawater. It's a 15min walk from town. **CH$108,000 (US$212)**

Hotel O'Tai Av Te Pito Te Henua s/n ☎ 32 210 0250, Ⓦ hotelotai.com. The lush flower-filled garden at this hotel is a real highlight, as is the appealing pool. The rooms are clean and well kept: all have private bathrooms, indigenous artwork on the walls, fridges, safes and patio doors; superior ones also come with a/c. **CH$72,000**

★ **Hotel Taura'a** Av Atamu Tekena s/n ☎ 32 210 0463, Ⓦ www.tauraahotel.cl. This highly recommended hotel boasts spacious, airy a/c rooms and an attractive garden. English and French are spoken, and the congenial owners run a good tour agency. Free wi-fi access. **CH$74,000**

CABINS

Mana Nui Inn Tahai s/n ☎ 32 210 0811, Ⓦ mananui.cl. Boasting a peaceful location away from the town centre and great sea views, Mana Nui Inn is a good mid-range option. There is a choice of rooms and cabins with kitchenettes sleeping up to seven; all have private bathrooms, TVs, fridges and fans. Guests can also use the kitchen, barbecue and laundry facilities. Doubles **CH$55,500**, cabins **CH$60,000**

Residencial Chez Cecilia Av Atamu Tekena s/n ☎ 32 210 0499, Ⓦ rapanuichezcecilia.com. A range of economical accommodation is on offer here, including cosy en-suite rooms, cabins that sleep up to six and have kitchens and fridges, and camping spots in the garden. Numerous activities can be arranged too. Doubles **CH$36,000**, cabins **CH$60,000**, camping **CH$5000** per person

Te'ora Tupina Apina s/n Ⓦ rapanuiteora.com. This friendly, good-value Canadian-run place has, amid its gardens, a handful of delightful, spotlessly clean cabins; all come with kitchenettes, private patios and sea views. A laundry service (CH$5000 per load) is also available. **CH$40,000**

HOSTELS

Residencial Kona Tau Avareipua s/n ☎ 32 210 0321, Ⓔ konatau@entelchile.net. Hostelling International-affiliated hostel in a large and friendly family home, with comfortable dorms, as well as simple en-suite rooms and a mango-strewn garden. Close to the airport but somewhat inconvenient for the rest of town. Dorms **CH$17,500**, doubles **CH$50,000**

CAMPSITES

Camping Mihinoa Pont s/n ☎ 32 255 1593, Ⓦ mihinoa .com. Large campsite with an excellent ocean view, run by a friendly family. Showers, kitchen facilities, dining room, wi-fi access and car, scooter and bike hire all available; the lack of shade is the only drawback. The adjoining guesthouse has basic rooms and a five-bed dorm; it's also possible to rent tents (CH$500/person). Camping **CH$5000** per person, dorms **CH$7000**, doubles **CH$15,000**

11

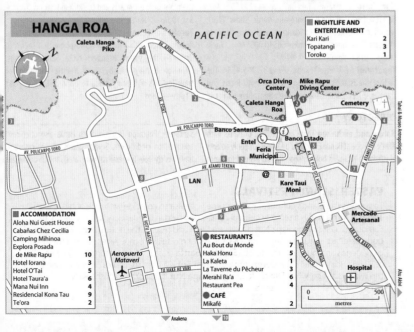

EATING AND DRINKING

Hanga Roa offers a good selection of cafés and restaurants, though prices are significantly higher than on mainland Chile. The **seafood** is a highlight, and keep an eye out for Mahina beer, produced by the island's first microbrewery.

CAFÉS

Mikafé Caleta. This tiny café, with just a handful of tables outside, serves delicious home-made ice cream (from CH$1500) – don't miss the *lúcuma* meringue flavour – as well as cakes, muffins, pastries and great coffee. Mon–Sat 9am–1.30pm & 4.30–9pm.

RESTAURANTS

Au Bout du Monde Av Policarpo Toro s/n ☎ 32 2552 060, ⓦ restaurantauboutdumonde.com. A Belgian chef is at the helm at this restaurant, and the inventive menu features some excellent food such as prawn pesto salad, smoked salmon pate, and chocolate mousse. There's live music and dance in the evenings. Mains CH$8000–15,000. Mon & Wed–Sun 1–2.30pm & 7–10.30pm.

Haka Honu Av Policarpo Toro ☎ 32 255 1677. This super-friendly, open-fronted restaurant has a breezy location looking out to sea. Excellent fish and seafood is on offer, including *pastel de jaiba* (crab gratin), ceviche, seafood salad and fish and chips. Mains CH$9000–14,000. Daily 10.30am–11pm.

★ **La Kaleta** Caleta ☎ 32 255 2244. *La Kaleta's* wooden deck, right on the water, is a wonderfully romantic place for a meal, particularly around sunset. The menu is strong on seafood – try the octopus carpaccio or the scallops topped with Parmesan – and dishes are beautifully presented. Mains CH$6000–13,000. Daily 12.30–3.30pm & 7.30–11pm.

Merahi Ra'a Te Pito O Te Henua s/n. This low-key joint is *the* place for large servings of expertly prepared fish and the local speciality of *rape rape* (spiny lobster), as well as melt-in-your-mouth tuna ceviche. Mains CH$6000–25,000. Daily except Thurs noon–10pm.

Restaurant Pea Policarpo Toro s/n, next to Playa Pea. In a lovely seafront location, particularly appealing in the early evening, *Restaurant Pea* serves tasty fish and seafood *empanadas* (around CH$1500–2000) that are ideal for a snack or light meal, as well as decent mains (around CH$9000). Daily except Wed noon–3pm & 7–11pm.

La Taverne du Pêcheur Te Pito O Te Henua s/n ☎ 32 210 0619. The food is undoubtedly good at this restaurant – notably the steaks, which come direct from Argentina, the lobster dishes and the desserts, such as the blueberry melba. However, prices are high and the service leaves a lot to be desired. Mains CH$5000–39,000. Mon–Sat noon–3pm & 6–11pm.

NIGHTLIFE AND ENTERTAINMENT

Kari Kari Av Atamu Tekena s/n ☎ 32 210 0767. Entertaining traditional dance-and-music show (1hr), featuring talented young dancers and musicians in elaborate costumes. Entry from CH$10,000. Mon, Tues, Thurs and Sat 9pm.

Topatangi Av Atamu Tekena s/n ☎ 32 255 1554. The pick of the island's clubs, popular with both locals and travellers, *Topatangi* has a pub-like atmosphere earlier in the night before live acts and DJs kick in later on. Thurs–Sat 10pm–4/5am.

Toroko Av Policarpo Toro s/n, near the cemetery. Popular disco with a mellow atmosphere that seems to draw all the young islanders on a Saturday night; although it may initially seem a little daunting for travellers, it's a friendly place to hang out. Thurs–Sat 11pm–4/5am.

DIRECTORY

Banks and exchange There are a couple of banks with ATMS: the one at Banco Estado, Tu'u Maheke s/n, only accepts Mastercard; Visa-card holders should head instead to Banco Santander, Policarpo Toro s/n. Both banks also offer cash advances on credit cards. Several places change cash and travellers' cheques (generally at poor rates), and US dollars are

---

EASTER ISLAND FESTIVALS

To witness the island's culture at its best, time your visit to coincide with one of the festivals. **Tapatai Rapa Nui** is a ten-day cultural celebration held in late January or early February. Famous for celebrating Rapa Nui culture, tradition and history, the festival features dancing, body painting, statue carving, choral recitals, surfing displays, canoe races, re-enactments of old legends and huge *curanto* feasts. **Semana Santa** (Easter week) features lively celebrations at Hanga Roa's church. The **Ceremonia Culto al Sol** is a feast that takes place on June 21 for the winter solstice, while **Día de la Lengua Rapa Nui**, a celebration of the Rapa Nui language, is held in late November.

widely accepted. It's worth bringing a stash of pesos/dollars with you from the mainland, just to be on the safe side.

Hospital Hospital Hanga Roa on Simón Paoa s/n (☎ 32 210 0183), southeast of the church, has basic medical facilities.

Internet access Hare PC, Av Akamu Tekena, charges CH$1200/hr.

Post office Av Te Pito Te Henua, opposite *Hotel O'Tai* (see p.447). You can get a novelty Easter Island stamp in your passport here.

The southeastern circuit

The loop formed by the 16km southern coast road and the 30km paved road from Anakena to Hanga Roa lends itself to a convenient sightseeing route that takes in some of the island's most impressive sights – including **Vinapu**, **Ahu Tongariki**, **Rano Raraku** and **Anakena**.

Vinapu

From Hanga Roa, follow Avenida Hotu Matu'a down to the southern coast road then turn right, just after the white oil containers, and you'll reach **VINAPU**, the site of two large *ahus*, with *moai* lying in fragments behind the platforms. Anyone who's seen Machu Picchu or other Inca ruins will be amazed by the similarity of the masonry of Vinapu's main *ahu*, made of huge, mortarless blocks of stone "fitted carefully to one another without a crack or a hole". Close to this platform, known as Vinapu I, is another *ahu*, Vinapu II, whose stonework is vastly inferior to its neighbour.

Thor Heyerdahl's theories

Thor Heyerdahl's expedition was the first to excavate the site and, with radiocarbon dating, concluded that the precisely carved Vinapu I was among the earliest built on the island, and that Vinapu II was a much later construction, suggesting that the island's first settlers imported the highly specialized stone-carving techniques of Peru, and that later platforms were built by "far less capable architects, who were no longer masters of the complicated Inca technique". Modern archeologists, however, believe that this impressive masonry is simply a perfected example of a style developed locally on Easter Island, and more recent radiocarbon tests have given Vinapu I a new date of 1516 AD, and Vinapu II a date of 857 AD – the reverse of Heyerdahl's sequence.

Sites along the southern coast

South from Vinapu on the coast road, the first site you pass is **Vaihu**, where eight tall statues lie face-down on the ground, their red stone topknots strewn along the coast. Three kilometres further along, **Ahu Akahanga** presents an equally mournful picture of a row of fallen *moai*; according to some oral traditions, it's also the burial place of Hotu Matu'a. Further up the coast, **Ahu Hanga Tetenga** is the site of the tallest *moai* (9.94m) ever transported to a platform.

PARQUE NACIONAL RAPA NUI ESSENTIALS

There is a CH$30,000 fee to enter **Parque Nacional Rapa Nui**, which covers most of the island's archeological sites. If you buy your entry permit from the Conaf kiosk at the airport just after you land, you'll get a fifteen percent discount. Permits are also available from the Conaf office on the outskirts of Hanga Roa (see p.446) and at the Orongo visitors' centre; most hotels and travel agencies will also purchase them for you. Along with the permit, you'll receive leaflets warning you not to touch or interfere in any way with the *moai* or the other archeological sites. These rules are not to be taken lightly: an idiotic Finnish tourist was arrested, fined and banned from Chile for three years after chipping off the earlobe of a *moai* in 2008.

Just beyond Ahu Hanga Tetenga, the road forks. The left-hand branch (**Camino de los Moai**) leads to the quarry of Rano Raraku. It's thought to have been the main roadway along which the statues were transported from the quarry. The right-hand branch continues up the coast to the magnificent Ahu Tongariki.

Ahu Tongariki

The fifteen colossal *moai* lined up on **AHU TONGARIKI** make a sensational sight. This was the largest number of *moai* ever erected on a single *ahu*, which, at 200m long, was the largest built on the island. It was totally destroyed in 1960 when a massive tsunami, triggered by an earthquake in Chile, swept across this corner of the island, dragging the platform blocks and the statues 90m inland – a remarkable distance, given that the statues weigh up to 30 tonnes each.

Restoration

In November 1988, Sergio Rapu, a former Governor of Easter Island, was being interviewed for a **Japanese television programme**, and said that if they had a crane they could save the *moai*; a Japanese man watching the show decided to act and a committee was set up in Japan. The restoration of the *ahu* involved Chilean archeologists Claudio Cristino and Patricia Vargas, a group of forty islanders, specialists from the Nara Institute of Japan and recognized international experts in stone conservation. The project took five years and was finally completed in 1995.

Rano Raraku

Daily: summer 9am–8pm; winter 9am–6pm • Your entry permit will be checked at the ranger's office here

North of Tongariki, **RANO RARAKU** rises from the land in a hulking mass of volcanic stone. This crag is where almost all of the island's statues were produced, carved directly from the "tuff" (compacted volcanic ash) of the crater's outer slopes. The first surprise, on approaching the crater from the car park, are the dozens of **giant heads** sprouting from the ground. They are, in fact, finished *moai* brought down from the quarry, which were probably placed in shallow pits (that gradually built up) until they could be transported to their *ahu*. One of them bears an image on its chest of a three-masted sailing ship, suggesting that they were carved after European contact.

Among this mass of shapes, still attached to the rock face, is **El Gigante**, the biggest *moai* ever carved, stretching over 20m from top to bottom. Experts believe that it would have been impossible to transport, let alone erect.

The east end of the trail culminates in the kneeling, round-headed **Moai Tukuturi**, the only one of its kind, discovered by Thor Heyerdahl's expedition in 1955. To the west, the trail winds its way up between wild guava trees into the crater itself, with several dirt paths running through knee-high shrubbery alongside the large reed-strewn, freshwater lake. If you follow the trails all the way up to the crater's eastern rim (avoid treading on the toppled *moai* right at the top) you are rewarded with unparalleled views of the bay and Ahu Tongariki in the distance.

The Poike Peninsula

East of Rano Raraku, the seldom-visited **POIKE PENINSULA** is a green, gently rounded plateau bound steep cliffs. You can walk round the edge of the peninsula in about four hours, but there's no shade and no path.

Ana o Keke

Poike's main interest lies in the myths and legends associated with it. One tells of the **cave of the virgins**, Ana o Keke, where a number of young girls were confined for months on end so that their skin would remain as pale as possible. Access to Ana o Keke is treacherous, however, and should only be attempted with a guide.

Iko's Trench

More famous than Ana o Keke is the myth of the battle of the **"Long Ears" and "Short Ears"** (see box, p.454). This battle is supposed to have taken place in the 3.5km-long ditch separating the peninsula from the rest of the island, known as Ko te Ava o Iko, or "Iko's ditch".

Ahu te Pito Kura

From the southern coast, the road turns inland, cutting past the Poike Peninsula, and leads directly to Ovahe and Anakena. On the way, look out for **Ahu te Pito Kura**, down by Bahía La Pérouse (signposted). This is the site of **Paro**, at 9.8m tall probably the largest *moai* successfully erected on a platform. Paro is thought to have been one of the last *moai* to be moved and erected, and is estimated to weigh a staggering 90 tonnes. No one has attempted to restore and re-erect the giant, which still lies face down before its *ahu*, surrounded by rubble.

Ovahe

Further north from Paro, **Ovahe** is a tiny, secluded and exquisitely beautiful beach, its white sands lapped by crystal-clear waters at the foot of a large volcanic cliff, very popular with locals who come here to picnic, swim and snorkel. It's best earlier in the day, before the cliff blocks the afternoon sun.

Playa Anakena

A little further up the coast from Ovahe, **Playa Anakena** is much larger, and presents a picture-postcard scene of powdery golden sands fringed by swaying palm trees, great for an afternoon of swimming or sunbathing. Several snack stands offer drinks and sandwiches, though they're not always open, so bring some food and water with you.

Anakena

ANAKENA has a special place in Rapa Nui oral history, which holds it to be the landing site and dwelling place of Hotu Matu'a, the island's first colonizer (see p.443). It's also home to the splendid *moai* of **Ahu Nau Nau**, which were so deeply covered in sand until their restoration, led by local archeologist Sergio Rapu Haoa in 1978, that they were largely protected from the effects of weathering.

Ahu Ature Huki

Just up the hillside by the beach you'll find the squat and rather corpulent *moai* of **Ahu Ature Huki**. This was the first *moai* to be re-erected on the island in the experiment carried out by Thor Heyerdahl in 1955, when twelve strong islanders showed they could raise a 25-tonne statue in eighteen days (see p.452).

The northern circuit

Although the triangle formed by Vinapu, Tongariki and Anakena contains the densest concentration of sites, the western and northern parts of the island are also well worth exploring. Attractions include the impressive *moai* of **Tahai** and **Ahu Akivi**, plus a network of underground **caves**.

Tahai and around

If you walk north from the *caleta* past the cemetery, taking the road that hugs the coast, after about ten minutes you'll reach the ceremonial centre of **TAHAI,**, composed of three *ahus*, a favourite spot for viewing colourful sunsets. The first, **Ahu Vai Uri**, supports four broad, squat *moai*, two of which have badly damaged heads, and the stump of a fifth statue. In front of the *ahu* is the outline of a flattened esplanade, presumed to have been used as a ceremonial site.

11

Archeological remains suggest some individuals – possibly chiefs and priests – used to live near these ceremonial sites, in several locations on the island, in stone, oval houses called *hare paenga* that looked like an upturned canoe. You can see the foundations of one of these houses near Ahu Vai Uri. The second platform is **Ahu Tahai** itself, topped by a lone, weathered *moai*. Finally, **Ahu Ko Te Riku** is the site of a well-preserved *moai* fitted with white, glinting eyes and a red topknot.

Museo Antropológico Sebastián Englert

Tues–Fri 9.30am–12.30pm & 2–5.30pm, Sat & Sun 9.30am–12.30pm • CH$1000 • ☎ 32 255 1020, ⓦ museorapanui.cl

About 500m further north of Tahai, set well back from the coastal path, the excellent **Museo Antropológico Sebastián Englert** is not to be missed. It gives a thorough introduction to the island's geography, history, society, **birdman cult** and the origins and significance of the *moai*. The well-labelled displays are in Spanish, with English handouts, and include an evocative collection of black-and-white photographs of islanders from about 1915 onwards, a rare female *moai* and replica *rongo rongo* tablets.

Dos Ventanas Caves

On the coastal road, around 3km north of Museo Antropológico, you reach the point where you're opposite two little islands out at sea. A stone cairn by the left-hand side of the road signals a track down towards the cliffs; it's not easy to spot. At the end of the

---

THE MOAI OF EASTER ISLAND

The enduring symbol of Easter Island always has been the *moai*. A **Neolithic statue cult** on this scale would impress in any location, but the fact that it developed in total isolation on a tiny island in the middle of the Pacific almost defies belief. There are some four hundred finished statues scattered around the island, and almost as many in the quarry, in varying stages of completion. The *moai* range in height from 2m to about 20m, and though styles evolved over time, all are carved in a **highly stylized** manner. Their bellies are gently rounded, and their arms are held tightly by their sides, with their strange, long-fingered hands placed across their abdomens. Their heads are long and rectangular, with pointed chins; prominent, angular noses; and thin, tight lips.

FUNCTION AND FORM

According to the islanders' assertions, which are consistent with widespread Polynesian tradition, these figures represented important **ancestors**, and were erected on the ancestral land of their kin-groups, which they would watch over and protect with their *mana* (almost all the *moai* face inland). Archeologists have proposed tentative dates of around 1000 AD for the carving of the early statues, and around the **fifteenth century** for the bulk of the statues, when production peaked. Rano Raraku's unfinished statues demonstrate how their forms were chiselled out of the rock face until they were attached to it by just a thin keel running down their spine. When all was completed but their eye sockets, they were freed from their keel and slid down the quarry's slope, then temporarily erected in a pit until they were transported to their *ahus*.

TRANSPORTATION

The island's oral histories offer no clues as to how the **20 to 25-tonne statues** were moved, claiming the statues' *mana* enabled them to walk short distances each day until they reached their platforms. Modern theories have included horizontal and vertical swivelling, but since it was established in the 1980s that the island was once densely covered by trees, it's been assumed that they were dragged on wooden sledges or on top of rollers.

RAISING THE MOAI

How the statues were **erected** onto their platforms in the absence of any type of machinery is another enigma, though in 1955, Thor Heyerdahl challenged the island's mayor to raise a fallen, 25-tonne statue at Anakena Beach and, under the mayor's supervision, twelve islanders raised the statue in eighteen days, using two levers and slipping layer after layer of stones

track, a tiny opening in the ground is the entrance to a pitch-black passage (take a torch), which continues 50m underground to the adjoining Ana Kakenga (**DOS VENTANAS CAVES**). Both caves are flooded with light streaming in from the "windows", or gaping holes, that open out of the cliff wall. Prepare for a rush of adrenaline as you approach the edges, as both drop vertically down to a bed of sharp rocks and pounding waves many metres below.

Ahu Te Peu

About 1km further up the coast from the Dos Ventanas Caves is **AHU TE PEU**. The *moai* that once stood on the *ahu* still lie flat on the ground, left as they were during the period of warfare. Scattered around are the remains of many boat-shaped *hare paenga*, including one that's 60m long. It's thought this was the site of the village of the Miru clan, the direct descendants of Hotu Matu'a.

At Ahu Te Peu, most people join up with the inland road and head back to Hanga Roa via Ahu Akivi. You can, however, continue north, either heading up the gentle volcanic cone of **Terevaka**, where you'll be rewarded with fine views across the island from its 510m summit, the highest point of the island (no path; 1hr up), or else follow the coastline round to Playa Anakena (4–5hr on foot; sunscreen is absolutely essential and you must take plenty of water). On the way, you'll pass many fallen *moai*, none of them restored, as well as the ruins of stone houses and chicken pens.

11

underneath the horizontal statue. Little by little, it was raised on the bed of stones until it was level with its platform; at this point, the layers of pebbles were placed only under its head, until the statue was nearly vertical and could be slipped into place. Archeologists agree this method is highly likely to have been used to raise the statues. In contrast, no one has been able to demonstrate how the large, heavy "topknots" were placed on the raised statues' heads – a monumental feat, achieved only with a crane in modern times.

THE STATUE-CARVERS

Easter Island society was based around independent clans, or **kin-groups**, each with its own high-ranking members. The statue-carvers were highly revered members of a privileged class who were exempt from food production and were supported by farmers and fishermen. Such a system must have involved a great deal of economic cooperation, which appears to have been successfully maintained for hundreds of years.

THE BEGINNING OF THE END

Then, in the later stages of the island's prehistory, the system collapsed, and the island became engulfed by warfare. Archeological records reveal a sudden, dramatic proliferation of obsidian **weapons** during the eighteenth century, as well as the remains of violently beaten skulls, and evidence of the widespread use of caves as refuges. Archeologists have also found possible evidence of cannibalism – something featured prominently in the island's oral traditions. The most dramatic testimony of this period, however, is provided by the hundreds of fallen statues littering the island, deliberately toppled as enemy groups set out to desecrate each other's sacred sites.

SO WHAT WENT WRONG ON EASTER ISLAND?

It seems likely the seeds of social collapse lay in the extremes the statue cult was taken to by the islanders. As the impulse to produce *moai* required more and more hands, the delicate balance between food distribution and statue-carving was destroyed. This situation was profoundly aggravated by the growing scarcity of food brought about by overpopulation, and deforestation, following centuries of logging for boat-building, fuel consumption and statue-transportation. This must have had a catastrophic effect on the islanders' ability to feed themselves: deep-sea fishing became increasingly difficult, and eventually impossible, owing to the lack of wood available for new canoes, and even land cultivation was affected, as the deforestation caused soil erosion. In this climate of encroaching deprivation, the Easter Island civilization descended into anarchy, dragging its majestic monuments with it.

THE MYTH OF THE "LONG EARS" AND THE "SHORT EARS"

An oft-repeated oral tradition has it that the island's population, in the time just before the toppling of the statues, was divided into two principal groups, the **"Short Ears"** and the **"Long Ears"**. In fact, the whole myth is based on a mistranslation. It seems the two clans were really the *Hanau eepe* ("short and stocky") and the *Hanau momoko* ("tall and slim"); the strange mix-up came from mistranslating *eepe* – short and stocky – as "ear" (*"epe"* in Rapa Nui).

The "Long Ears", who saw themselves as more aristocratic, were extremely domineering, and the "Short Ears" resented them intensely. The "Short Ears" rebelled when forced to clear rocks off the land, forcing the "Long Ears" to retreat to the **Poike Peninsula**. Here they dug deep ditches, and filled them with branches and grass, intending to force their enemies inside and set them alight. However, a "Short Ears" woman who was married to one of the "Long Ears" alerted her people, and allowed them to surround their enemies while they were sleeping. When they attacked, the "Long Ears" ran straight into their own ditch, which was set alight. Most of the "Long Ears" burned to death, but three escaped. Two of them were caught and executed, but one, **Ororoina**, was allowed to live, and went on to father many children – whose descendants, to this day, are proud of their *Hanau momoko* heritage.

11

Inland to Puna Pau

From Hanga Roa, heading up the inland road to Ahu Akivi (first left from the paved road to Anakena) you'll pass a signed track branching left to **PUNA PAU**, a low volcanic crater made of rusty-coloured rock, known as *"scoria"*, where the islanders carved the **pukao** – the cylindrical "topknots" worn by up to seventy of the *moai* standing on *ahu*. No one knows for sure what these cylinders represented, though suggestions include topknots (of hair) and feather headdresses. Up in the quarry, and along the track to the top, you can see thirty or so finished *pukao* lying on the ground.

Ahu Akivi

On the inland road north of Puna Pau, you'll find **AHU AKIVI**, whose seven *moai* are the only ones to have been erected inland, and the only ones that look towards the sea. It's been discovered that they are oriented directly towards the rising summer solstice, along with several other *ahu*, suggesting that solar positions were of significance to the islanders. The Ahu Akivi *moai* were raised in 1960 by William Mulloy and Gonzalo Figueroa, two of the archeologists recruited by Heyerdahl in 1955, both of whom devoted their careers to Easter Island.

Te Pahu Caves

From Ahu Akivi, the road turns towards the coast, where it meets Ahu Te Peu. On the way, a second path branches left from the main road, leading towards the **ANA TE PAHU CAVES**. If you clamber down, you'll see some tall bamboo trees growing in a magical underground garden, along with sweet potatoes, taro, avocados, lemons and sugarcane. This cave is connected to another huge cave (once used as a dwelling) by a long lava tube.

South of Hanga Roa: Rano Kau

South of Hanga Roa, a dirt road climbs steeply past a *mirador* offering an excellent view of Hanga Roa up to one of the most awe-inspiring spots on the island – the giant crater of the extinct **RANO KAU** volcano, and the ceremonial village of **ORONGO**, perched high on its rim. The dull waters of the volcano's reed-choked lake contrast sharply with the brilliant blue of the Pacific, stretching as far as the eye can see, visible where a great chunk of the crater wall is missing. Just before you reach Orongo, a path disappears into the lush vegetation around the crater's edge; it is possible to follow this around the crater as a leisurely day's walk, but bring plenty of water.

FROM TOP RANO KAU, EASTER ISLAND (P.454); FISHERMAN HOLDING LOBSTER, ISLA ROBINSON CRUSOE (P.457)

Orongo

Daily: summer 9am–8pm, winter 9am–6pm • Car or taxi from Hanga Roa (10min), or on foot (1hr)

Orongo, just beyond the Conaf visitors' centre (where national park entry permits are available), consists of the partially restored remains of some 48 low-lying, oval-shaped huts made of thin stone slabs, each with a tiny entrance just large enough to crawl through (don't try). A few steps from the houses, on the face of some basalt outcrops looking out to sea, you'll find a dense group of exquisitely carved **petroglyphs** depicting curled-up human figures with birds' heads and long curved beaks. These images honour an important annual ceremony dedicated to the **cult of the birdman**. A great deal is known about this ceremony, as it was practised right up to 1878.

The Juan Fernández Archipelago

The **JUAN FERNÁNDEZ ARCHIPELAGO** is made up of three islands and numerous rocky islets. The archipelago is named after **João Fernandes**, the Portuguese sailor who discovered it on November 22, 1574, while straying out to sea to avoid coastal winds and currents in an attempt to shorten the journey between Lima and Valparaíso. The more easterly of the two main islands was originally called **Más a Tierra** ("Nearer Land"), while the other, 187km further west, was known as **Más Afuera** ("Farther Out").

Brief history

João Fernandes made a brief attempt to colonize the three uninhabited islands, introducing vegetables and goats, which multiplied in great numbers (the third, smallest, island was later known as Goat Island, officially as Isla Santa Clara). These were still flourishing when British buccaneers started making occasional calls here to stock up on water and fresh meat between their raids on the mainland.

Following Alexander Selkirk's much-publicized rescue (see p.459) buccaneers began calling at the islands more frequently, prompting the Spanish Crown to take official possession of the archipelago in 1742, building a series of forts around Más a Tierra. The island was then used as a **penal colony** for many years, and it wasn't until the mid-nineteenth century that a mixture of Chilean and European colonizers formed a permanent settlement. In 1966, with an eye on the islands' potential as a tourist destination, the Chilean government changed Más a Tierra's name to **Isla Robinson Crusoe**, while Más Afuera became **Isla Alejandro Selkirk**, seasonal home to lobster fishermen and very difficult to reach.

THE BIRDMAN CEREMONY

The Birdman ceremony took place annually at the September **equinox**, when the chiefs of the various kin-groups assembled at Orongo to compete. The aim was to find the first egg laid by the sooty tern (a migratory bird) on Motu Nui, the largest of three islets sitting opposite Orongo, 2km out to sea. Each chief would choose a representative, or *hopu*, who would scale down the sheer cliff to the ocean and swim through shark-infested waters to the islet. It could take several weeks for the egg to be found; meanwhile, the chiefs would remain in Orongo, where they participated in ritual dances, songs and prayers.

Once the egg was finally found, its discoverer would bellow the name of his master, and then swim back to the island with the egg tucked into a headband. The victorious chief now became the new *tangata manu*, or **birdman**. The new birdman would first have all the hair shaved off his head; he would then live in strict seclusion for a whole year in a sacred house at the foot of Rano Raraku, eating only certain foods, and forbidden to bathe or cut his nails. His kin-group, meanwhile, was endowed with a special, high status, which was often taken as an excuse for members to dominate and bully their rival groups.

THE 2010 TSUNAMI

In the early hours of February 27, 2010, a **tsunami** triggered by the 8.8 magnitude **earthquake** on mainland Chile struck the Juan Fernández Archipelago. A wave of around 20m in height swept 300m into Isla Robinson Crusoe, destroying much of San Juan Bautista and killing sixteen people. A mix-up between the Chilean Navy and the tsunami alert services meant that the islanders received no official warning, and the death toll would have been much higher but for a 12-year-old girl: awake at night, Martina Maturana spotted the fishing boats bobbing violently in the harbour, and ran from her home to ring the emergency bell in the town square to warn the island's six hundred or so inhabitants.

Following the disaster, the island's population fell by about a third, as many people left for the mainland. Islanders, angry at the lack of official warning, launched a court case against the government. Meanwhile, **rebuilding** attempts - the tsunami destroyed the island's library, town hall, civil registry office, museum, cultural centre, naval offices, post office, school and every single shop, as well as many homes and hotels – are ongoing.

To compound matters, on September 2, 2011, 21 passengers were killed after an air force plane crashed into the sea after twice failing to land in windy conditions on the island. Among those killed was TV presenter Felipe Camiroaga, who had been making a film on the reconstruction efforts.

Although the island is still getting back on its feet, it is possible to visit – and the money you spend will certainly help the rebuilding efforts. Most hotels remained closed at the time of research, but many plan to reopen – check the latest situation ahead of your visit.

11

Today, only a few hundred tourists make it out here each year, arriving mainly between October and March, when the climate is warm and mostly dry, and the sea is perfect for swimming.

Isla Robinson Crusoe

Twenty-two kilometres long, and 7km at its widest point, **ISLA ROBINSON CRUSOE** is the archipelago's only permanently inhabited island. Most of the islanders – some of them descendants of the Swiss Baron de Rodt and his compatriots who settled the island at the end of the nineteenth century – live in the little village of **San Juan Bautista**, on the sheltered Bahía Cumberland. The main economic activity is trapping **lobsters**, and one of the highlights of a stay here is accompanying a fisherman out to haul in his catch (and later sample it).

Lobsters aside, the island's two principal attractions are the sites associated with **Alexander Selkirk** and the richness of its flora and fauna. Of the 146 plant species that grow here, 101 are endemic or unique to the island (the second highest proportion in the world after Hawaii), which is both a national park and a UNESCO World Biosphere Reserve. Most prolific, and stunning, is the luxuriant rainforest that covers the island's higher slopes.

The local fauna also comprises numerous endemic species, such as the **Juan Fernández fur seal**, which is making a comeback after being hunted to near-extinction in the eighteenth century, and the Firecrown hummingbird, as well as sea birds, such as the giant petrel. Meanwhile, diving at various sites around Isla Robinson Crusoe is an excellent way to appreciate the wealth and diversity of its abundant underwater life. **Mosquitoes** abound, so be sure to bring plenty of repellent.

San Juan Bautista

Huddled by the shores of Bahía Cumberland, at the foot of a green curtain of mountains, **SAN JUAN BAUTISTA** is the island's only settlement. A spread-out village with a few dirt streets lined with simple wooden houses, and an unfinished look to it, for most people, "El Pueblo" is just a base from which to explore the island's interior and the coast. That said, there are several curious historical relics here.

11

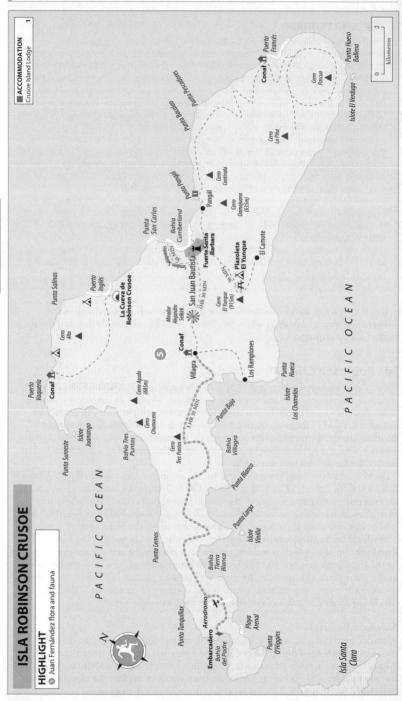

ISLA ROBINSON CRUSOE

HIGHLIGHT
⓺ Juan Fernández flora and fauna

ACCOMMODATION
Crusoe Island Lodge   1

ALEXANDER SELKIRK

Daniel Defoe's story of Robinson Crusoe, the world's most famous literary castaway, was inspired by the misadventures of the real-life Scottish mariner **Alexander Selkirk**, who was marooned on Isla Robinson Crusoe (then Más a Tierra) in 1704 while crossing the Pacific on a privateering expedition. Unlike Crusoe, who was shipwrecked, Selkirk actually asked to be put ashore following a series of quarrels with his captain. The irascible sailor regretted his decision as soon he was deposited on the beach with a few scanty supplies, but his cries from the shore begging to be taken back onboard were ignored. Selkirk spent four years and four months on the island, with only his Bible and dozens of wild goats for company. During that time he was transformed into an extraordinary athlete, as he hunted the goats on foot, and a devout Christian.

Following his **rescue** by a British ship in 1709, however, Selkirk reverted to his buccaneering ways, joining in attacks on Spanish vessels all the way home. Back in Fife, the former castaway became something of a celebrity and threw himself into a life of drink and women. Fourteen years after his rescue, Selkirk finally met his end when he took up the seafaring life once more, set off on another privateering expedition, and died of fever in the tropics.

11

Fuerte Santa Barbara

Fuerte Santa Barbara, a small stone fort, is perched on a hillside just north of the plaza. Heavily restored in 1974, it was originally built by the Spanish in 1749 in an attempt to prevent buccaneers from using the island as a watering point.

Cuevas de los Patriotas

A short walk north of the fort takes you to the **Cuevas de los Patriotas**, a group of seven fern-covered caves allegedly inhabited by 42 independence fighters who were banished to Más a Tierra after the Battle of Rancagua in 1814.

Punta San Carlos

Down on the shore, follow the path to the north end of the bay and you'll reach the cliffs of the **Punta San Carlos**, embedded with unexploded shells fired by British warships at the German *Dresden* during World War I. The Germans surrendered, but sank their ship rather than let it go to the British, and the wreck still lies 70m under the sea, in Bahía Cumberland. Nearby you'll find the graves of the naval battle's casualties in the island's **cemetery**, next to the lighthouse.

Casa de la Cultura and El Palillo

At the **Casa de la Cultura**, there are some interesting historic **photos**, primarily of the World War I incident. The building was badly damaged in the tsunami, however, and was closed at the time of research. At the southern end of the bay, a 5min walk from the village, the small rocky beach of **El Palillo** is good for swimming and diving.

Hikes on Isla Robinson Crusoe

There are numerous good hikes around the island, though some are not marked; you will need local guides for all of those in the eastern half of the island, as well as between Bahía Inglés and Puerto Vaquería. Some destinations are reached by boat with a local fisherman, who can drop you off in the morning and pick you up at the end of their day's work.

Sendero Salsipuedes

Excellent short hikes from San Juan Bautista include the fairly steep **Sendero Salsipuedes** ("Get out if you can"), which leads from the village's Calle La Pólvora through pine and eucalyptus forest up to the *mirador* overlooking Bahía Cumberland from the northwest side. Allow an hour's roundtrip and beware of loose scree. The views of San Juan Bautista spread out below are excellent. From here, though, landslides render it dangerous to navigate.

BOAT TRIPS FROM SAN JUAN BAUTISTA

A fifteen-minute boat ride from the village is **Puerto Inglés**, where you'll find a mock-up of the cave where Selkirk took refuge and a good camping spot. Other boat destinations include **Puerto Vaquería**, west of Bahía Inglés, a popular spot to snorkel with seals; **Puerto Francés**, in the eastern part of the island, where there are ramparts overlooking the sea, built by the Spanish to deter French pirates; and **Playa Arenal**, the island's only sandy beach with warm, transparent waters, which lies 2hr 30min by boat through islets and seal colonies, just south of the airstrip.

Plazoleta El Yunque

A sometimes muddy 3km trail leads from the village (continuing from Calle Lord Anson; 1hr 30min return) through native forest to **Plazoleta El Yunque**, a lookout point and an attractive shaded campsite with picnic tables at the foot of Cerro El Yunque, the island's tallest mountain (915m). The nearby stone ruins are the remains of the house of Hugo Weber, the "German Robinson Crusoe", who spent twelve years living as a hermit here after escaping from the *Dresden* in 1915. From the campsite, the pleasant trail loops through native vegetation, including giant *nalca* (rhubarb) and ferns, before finishing back at the campsite. From the Plazoleta, it is possible to make the steep ascent through thick native forest to **El Camote**, a peak offering spectacular views of the island, though this requires a guide.

Cerro Centinela

A 45min walk south of San Juan Bautista, and then a 362m hike up a trail, takes you to the top of **Cerro Centinela**, which offers expansive views of Bahía Cumberland and Bahía El Pangál. From here, an unmarked trail zigzags its way along the coast to Puerto Francés, a route only to be attempted with a knowledgeable local.

The cross-island hike

The island's **best hike** runs from the airstrip to San Juan Bautista, via the Mirador Alejandro Selkirk; bring plenty of water and allow at least five hours. Arrange to be dropped off by a fisherman at the Bahía del Padre, the launching place for the boat that picks you up from the airstrip, and home to a large colony of fur seals. Outside breeding season, they are not dangerous and you can swim and snorkel with them. The largest fur seal colony lies at **Bahía Tierra Blanca**, the first bay you come to along the trail.

Follow the road uphill and take the well-marked trail running from the airstrip. The path skirts the zigzagging coastline, with turquoise bays appearing around every corner, the barking of sea lions echoing from below and the landscape gradually changing from arid desert-like hills with their vividly multicoloured soil to steep pasture land to jagged mountains covered in dense endemic vegetation. For the most part, it's wide enough to take a vehicle, ascending very gradually until you reach **Villagra**, a couple of houses with a corral for animals, where the rodeo is held in February.

Mirador Alejandro Selkirk

At Villagra, the cross-island track divides; take the rocky footpath overgrown with vegetation, which climbs steeply uphill until it reaches the **Mirador Alejandro Selkirk**, the famous lookout point where, according to a disputed story, Selkirk lit his daily smoke signals and scoured the horizon for ships. Here you'll be rewarded with stunning panoramic views of most of the island. Note the two metal memorial plaques set in the rocks, one donated by the officers of HMS *Topaze* in 1868, the other by one of Selkirk's descendants in 1983, pledging to remember his forefather "Till a' the seas gang dry and the rocks melt i' the sun".

If you don't have time to do a cross-island hike, you can reach the *mirador* from the village, though it's a steeper climb (around 90min); the path starts north of the plaza.

ARRIVAL AND DEPARTURE

ISLA ROBINSON CRUSOE

BY PLANE
Getting to Isla Robinson Crusoe is an adventure in itself, involving a bumpy flight on a seven-seater plane. Two airlines serve fly to the island (usually twice weekly): ATA (☎ 2 275 0363, ⓦ aerolineasata.cl) and LASSA (☎ 2 273 5209, ⓔ lassa@terra.cl), both based at Aeródromo Tobalaba, Av Larraín 7941, in Santiago's eastern suburb of La Reina. Both firms have a 10-kilo luggage allowance and charge around CH$550,000 (US$1100) return. It is a bit cheaper to organize a charter flight, if you can get a group of at least six together; contact Santiago FBO (☎ 2 674 4000, ⓦ santiagofbo.cl) for details. Flights are weather-dependent, so be prepared to spend an extra day or two on the island in case of inclement weather. The little airstrip is 13km from San Juan Bautista; a speedboat (included in the price of your flight) transfers you to the village; it can be a rough ride.

BY BOAT
Transmarko (☎ 09 6157 7480, ⓔ catherine.espinoza @transmarko.cl) has irregular services from Valparaíso; the journey takes 40–45hr, and the boat spends 5–7 days on the island, before returning. A return ticket, including full board, costs CH$154,500 (US$300). There is also a monthly navy supply boat from Valparaíso, which spends around 72 hours on the island; a one-way ticket costs around CH$30,000. You can try and book passage with the Comando de Transporte at the Primera Zona Naval, Plaza Sotomayor 592, Valparaíso (☎ 32 250 6354), but bear in mind that departure dates change monthly, and preference is given to islanders.

11

INFORMATION AND TOURS

Tourist information The Municipalidad (☎ 32 270 1045, ⓦ comunajuanfernandez.cl) and Conaf (Santiago ☎ 2 663 0125, ⓦ conaf.cl) can provide information on the island, and give you the latest on the rebuilding process, though note that, at the time of writing, neither office had a fixed location. National park entry permits (necessary for most of the activities on the island) cost CH$3000, and are valid for a week. Crusoe Island Lodge (see below) offers a range of activities, including hikes, historical tours, fishing trips (including for lobster), diving, surfing and birdwatching.

ACCOMMODATION

The tsunami destroyed or badly damaged virtually all of the island's hotels and guesthouses (and with them, most of the eating options). As of early 2012, few were operating, though a couple of private homes were taking in guests. Some hotels – including *Hostería Refugio Náutico* (☎ 09 7483 5014, ⓦ islarobinsoncrusoe.cl) – plan to reopen, but for many others the situation is unclear. Unless you're planning to stay at *Crusoe Island Lodge*, contact the island's Municipalidad (see p.461), the airlines ATA or LASSA, or a travel agency to check the latest developments.

Crusoe Island Lodge 3km east of the village ☎ 32 275 1077, ⓦ islarobinsoncrusoe.cl. This stylish lodge has a wonderful location, in a tranquil spot overlooking a bay. The modern en suites – constructed from recycled materials and local wood – have wonderful sea views from their balconies. There's an excellent restaurant, plus a pool, spa, wi-fi access and plenty of activities to keep you busy. Rates include breakfast; full-board deals available too. CH$103,000 (US$203)

DIRECTORY

Banks and exchange There are no banks or *cambios* on the island, so bring plenty of cash with you; bear in mind that poor weather may delay your flight by a day or two.

Hospital The Posta Rural, Vicente Gonzáles s/n, deals with minor medical emergencies; anyone requiring serious treatment has to be flown to the mainland.

Isla Alejandro Selkirk

Travellers to Isla Robinson Crusoe with plenty of time and energy to spare may consider attempting to reach the even more remote and ruggedly mountainous **Isla Alejandro Selkirk**. During the October to May lobster season, it is home to around forty to fifty people, as well as a small team of conservationists and some feral goats. Bring all necessary food and gear with you, including a tent.

ARRIVAL AND DEPARTURE

ISLA ALEJANDRO SELKIRK

By boat An irregular supply boat (roughly 17hr; around CH$60,000), as well as fishermen, ply the waters between Isla Robinson Crusoe and Isla Alejandro Selkirk. Contact the Municipalidad about passage; if you don't arrange a return trip, you may find yourself marooned for some time.

CHILEAN PRESIDENT SEBASTIÁN PIÑERA EMBRACING A MINEF
AT COPIAPÓ

Contexts

463 History

488 Landscape and the environment

493 Chilean music: nueva canción

500 Books

505 Chilean Spanish

History

Enveloped by the Andes, the Atacama Desert and the Pacific Ocean, Chile has evolved almost as an island, relatively undisturbed by the turbulence that has raged through much of South America's history. Though inhabited by indigenous groups for millennia, the country's actual recorded history dates from the sixteenth-century arrival of the Spaniards. The colonial society that emerged and the ensuing struggle for independence resemble that of the whole continent, but from its early days as a republic, Chile took on its own political shape, distinct from that of its neighbours. With its largely ordered, constitutional model of government, and a healthy respect for the law, Chile earned itself the sobriquet "the England of South America" in the nineteenth century, which is why it was so surprising that it returned to the attention of the outside world with the repressive military regime of General Augusto Pinochet in the 1970s and 1980s. Today, with democracy firmly back in place, Chile is an outward-looking nation boasting political and economic stability, albeit with some serious social inequalities and unresolved political legacies lurking beneath the surface.

The Ice Age and beyond

Chile's anthropological record, like that of all the Americas, began when the first groups of Asians crossed the land bridge connecting Siberia to Alaska before the end of the last Ice Age, when the sea level was 70–100m lower than it is today. Archaeologists are unable to tell us exactly when this **first migration** occurred, but it's generally thought to have been between 25,000 and 40,000 years ago.

What *is* known is that by 12,000 BC the descendants of these people, supplemented by further waves of migration from Asia, had spread down the whole of North and South America as far as the southern tip of Patagonia. While some devoted themselves to fishing, the majority were probably nomadic hunters living off the animals that inhabited the region at the time – mastodons (prehistoric elephants), mammoths, giant armadillos and wild horses. When the last Ice Age came to an end around 11,000 BC, the climate changed abruptly and many of these animals became extinct. The hunters were forced to adapt, supplementing their diet by gathering fruits and seeds. Eventually this led to the deliberate cultivation of foodstuffs and the domestication of animals; along with these incipient agricultural practices came more stable communities and important developments, such as pottery and burial customs. Slowly, distinct cultural groups emerged, shaped by their very different environments and the resources available to them.

12,500 BC	5000 BC	1463
Carbon dating places the first inhabited site in South America just outside Puerto Montt.	Mummification technique developed by the Chinchorro people, involving replacing internal organs with mud and vegetable fibres.	Inca Emperor Pachacuti's warriors conquer a huge swathe of Chile up to the Río Maule.

The pre-Columbian cultures

In the absence of written records, archeologists have had to piece together information about Chile's **pre-Columbian cultures** from what these groups have left behind, principally funerary offerings found in burial sites and domestic objects left in former dwelling places. The strata in which the remains are buried (plus the use of radiocarbon dating) indicate the chronology in which these developments took place. However, variations in Chile's geography from north to south present unequal conditions for the preservation of artefacts and have led to a far greater knowledge of the cultures of the north than of the south.

Mummies and hallucinogens: El Norte Grande

More is known about the pre-Columbian cultures of Chile's Norte Grande – the Far North – than of any other part of the country. The extreme dryness of the Atacama Desert preserved archaeological remains for thousands of years. One of the earliest groups of people to leave its mark was the **Chinchorro culture**, a collection of nomadic fishing communities that lived along the desert coast some 8000 years ago. By 5000 BC, the Chinchorro had developed the practice of **mummifying their dead** (see box, p.210) – two thousand years earlier than the Egyptians. Their technique, which involved removing internal organs and tissues and replacing them with vegetable fibres and mud, survived for 4000 years and is the oldest known in the world.

By around 500 BC, life in El Norte Grande was based largely on agriculture, supplemented by fishing in the coastal areas, and herding llamas and alpacas in the Andean highlands. Although vast tracts of the region are taken up by barren desert, a number of oases provided fertile land where agricultural communities were able to dedicate themselves to the cultivation of maize, beans, squash, chillies and potatoes. They lived in permanent dwellings, usually consisting of circular huts surrounding a shared patio, and often with a cemetery nearby.

Among the most important (and longest-lasting) of these early agricultural groups was the **San Pedro culture** (also known as the Atacameño culture), which settled along the salt-flat oases around San Pedro de Atacama around 500 BC. They produced ceramics, textiles and objects in copper and stone, along with delicately carved wooden snuff tablets and tubes used for inhaling hallucinogenic substances – a custom probably introduced by the **Tihuanaco culture** around 300 AD. This latter was a powerful religious state based near the southern shores of Lake Titicaca in present-day Bolivia, and its influence extended over most of northern Chile and much of Peru for many centuries. The Tihuanaco impact was most visible in the spread of its ceramics and textiles, often decorated with images of cats, condors and snakes, which probably had religious significance. The Tihuanaco also fostered an active trading system, encouraging the exchange of goods between regions, bringing about increased social stratification, with those at the top controlling the commercial traffic.

Sometime between 900 and 1200 AD, the Tihuanaco culture declined and collapsed, for reasons unknown today. The regional cultures of the Norte Grande were then free to reassert their individual authority and identity, expressing their independence with a series of *pukarás* (fortresses) dotted around the altiplano. This period of *desarrollo regional* ("regional development"), as it is known, was halted only by the arrival of the Inca in the late fifteenth century.

1520	1535	1535–1880
The first European to reach Chile, Ferdinand Magellan sails through the strait now named after him.	The first Spanish venture into Chile under the command of Diego de Almagro ends in failure.	The Arauco War: the Mapuche resist all attempts at conquest from their stronghold south of the Río Bíobío.

Llamas and ceramics: El Norte Chico

Around 300 AD, when the peoples of the Norte Grande had been living in fixed agricultural communities for several centuries, those of the Norte Chico were just beginning to abandon their lives of hunting and gathering, and turn to cattle herding and farming. The resulting **El Molle culture** was composed of communities that settled along the river valleys between Copiapó and Illapel, where they developed a system of artificial irrigation to cultivate maize, beans, squash and possibly cotton. They also herded llamas, a practice recorded in numerous petroglyphs, and produced the first ceramics of the Norte Chico. Between 700 and 800 AD the El Molle culture declined and was replaced by a new cultural group known as **Las Animas**, which probably originated in the Argentine highlands. The changes introduced by this culture included rapid developments in metalworking; new, more decorative, styles of pottery, and – most curiously – the custom of ritual sacrifice of llamas.

Towards 1000 AD, the important **Diaguita culture** appeared in the Norte Chico, dominating the region over the next five centuries until the Spanish invasion. The Diaguita tended to live in large villages along the river valleys, presided over by a chief and a shaman. Each valley was divided into two sections: a "lower" section, towards the coast, which was ruled by one chief, and a "higher" section, towards the mountains, ruled by another. Their economy was based on agriculture, herding, mining and metalworking, and was supplemented by fishing on the coast, aided by the invention of inflated sealskin rafts. The Diaguita's greatest achievement, however, was their outstandingly fine pottery, characterized by intricate white, black and red geometric patterns.

Burial urns and mud huts: central Chile

The first agricultural groups to settle in central Chile were the **El Bato** and **Llolleo** peoples, from around 300 AD. The El Bato group occupied the zone between the Río Choapa (near Illapel) and the Río Maipo (south of Santiago); its highly polished monochrome pottery indicates that it was strongly influenced by the El Molle culture from the Norte Chico. The Llolleo settlements were spread along the coastal plains between the Río Aconcagua (just north of Santiago) and the Río Maule (near Talca). One of the most striking characteristics of this culture was their custom of burying their dead under their own houses, with small children buried in clay urns.

Later, around 900 AD, the **Aconcagua** emerged as the dominant culture in Central Chile; these people lived in houses made of branches and mud and dedicated themselves to growing beans, maize, squash and potatoes; they also developed far more specialized ceramics than had previously existed in the region.

Nomads and hunters: Araucania

While relatively little is known about the development of the cultures of the south of Chile, owing to a paucity of archaeological remains, it's generally agreed that the first group to adopt cultivation was the **Pitrén culture**, around 600 AD. This comprised small family groups spread between the Bío Bío and Lago Llanquihue, where they grew maize and potatoes on a small scale, as well as hunting and gathering. They also produced ceramics, often decorated with zoomorphic and anthropomorphic images, which they usually buried with their dead.

1541	**1553**	**1554**
Conquistador Pedro de Valdivia reaches the Mapocho Valley and founds the city of Santiago de Nueva Extremadura on February 12.	Lautaro, a young Mapuche chief, kills Pedro de Valdivia in a particularly gruesome manner during the Battle of Tucapel.	The first vines are brought to Chile by conquistadors, marking the beginning of wine production.

Around 1000 AD a new community, known as **El Vergel**, emerged in the region between Angol and Temuco. Its economy combined hunting and gathering with the cultivation of potatoes, maize, beans and squash, and it is likely that its people were the first to domesticate guanacos. Other practices these people brought to the region included burying their dead in ceramic urns, which they decorated with red and white paint. They also developed a very beautiful style of pottery, now known as Valdivia pottery, characterized by parallel zigzag lines and shaded triangles.

Sometime in the fourteenth century a group of nomadic hunters called the *moluche* ("people of war") arrived from Argentina and occupied the land between the Itata and Toltén rivers. They absorbed the existing Pitrén and El Vergel cultures to form a new entity called **Mapuche** ("people of the land"). While engaging in fishing, hunting and gathering, their lifestyle was based principally on herding and farming – labour was divided between the sexes, with men responsible for preparing the fields, and women for sowing and harvesting. The basic social unit was the family clan, or "lov", which were

LA LUCHA DE MAPUCHE

The **Mapuche**, or "people of the land" from "che" (people) and "mapu" (of the land), have been in constant conflict with invaders since the arrival of the Spanish, a conflict that continues today. Though they have put up the bravest resistance out of all the indigenous people of the Americas, the Mapuche have nevertheless seen their original homeland of over 100,000 square kilometres shrink to just 5000 square kilometres. While Chile's left-wing governments tried to address the **land issue**, any improvements made between 1965 and 1973 were reversed by Pinochet's government, which went a step further by signing into law an anti-terrorist act aimed squarely at any Mapuche attempts to assert themselves and pursue their rights, punishing crimes such as arson with excessively long prison sentences and worse.

While some progress has been made in the dispute over their historical **ancestral territory** (known as *Wallmapu*) since the return of democracy, many Mapuche feel that the concessions made by the Chilean government fall far short and that their lands are under constant threat from powerful business interests. Today, the Mapuche lead a largely marginalized existence in Chile's Lake District; living mostly in cities – Temuco in particular – or rural *reducciones* (settlements) and making a living from small-scale agriculture and selling handicrafts. Though their language, *Mapundungun*, is no longer outlawed as it was under Pinochet, there is nevertheless constant pressure to assimilate.

Though not as actively endorsed by the Chilean government as under Pinochet, police persecution of Mapuche communities (and those sympathetic to the Mapuche cause, such as foreign journalists) has nevertheless been brought to the attention of various human rights organizations in recent years. **Clashes** between the Mapuche and the police are commonplace and abuses have ranged from harassment, such as tear gas grenades thrown into Mapuche houses, to holding the likes of 12-year-old Luis Marileo – accused of belonging to an "illegal terrorist organization" – in a detention centre and shooting 17-year-old Alex Lemun in the head during a violent eviction. In January 2012, indigenous Mapuche activists were accused of deliberately starting forest fires in the Biobío region, leading President Sebastian Piñera to invoke an **anti-terror law** to pursue those responsible; when coming home after attending the funeral of a fire fighter who died in the forest fire, one of the Mapuche leaders found his house had been deliberately burnt down.

For more information on the Mapuche's ongoing struggle check out ⓦmapuche-nation.org.

1561	1593	1598
Governor Don García Hurtado de Mendoza sent from Peru to subjugate the natives in central Chile.	The first Jesuit order arrives in Chile and sets about converting locals and appropriating large amounts of land.	The Great Uprising removes all Spanish presence south of the Río Biobío and the river becomes the Spanish–Mapuche frontier.

independent from each other and autonomous. Its isolation meant the Mapuche culture didn't develop any further until forced to unite in the face of the Spanish invasion.

Canoe fishermen and hunters: the far south

The narrow channels, fjords, impenetrable jungles and wild steppes of the far south have never encouraged communities to settle in one place. Accordingly, the peoples that inhabited this region led a more primitive lifestyle than those further north – they could not adopt agriculture as their main economy, and so maintained their tradition of hunting and fishing in nomadic groups. Groups like the **Selk'nam** and the **Tehuelche** hunted guanaco and rhea on the Patagonian steppes, and lived in temporary wigwam-like structures covered in guanaco skins. The **Yámana** and **Chono** people hunted seals, otters, birds and gathered shellfish in their canoes, constantly moving from place to place. None of the Patagonian or Fuegian groups produced ceramics, manufacturing instead bows, arrows, lassos, baskets and warm skin capes. Their understanding of the world was rich in mythology and symbolism – the Selk'nam, for instance, believed that many birds and animals were spirits that had once been human; they also practised elaborate initiation rites marking the passage from boyhood into manhood, involving physical tests and secret ceremonies. Unlike the other native peoples of Chile, these groups were never incorporated into Spanish colonial society, and their lifestyles remained virtually unchanged until the twentieth century, when the clash with seal hunters and sheep farmers led to their disappearance.

The Inca conquest

While the native peoples of Chile were developing relatively simple communities based on agriculture, herding and fishing, a great civilization was emerging further to the north – that of the **Inca**. This people arrived in Cusco around 1200 AD and by the fifteenth century had developed a sophisticated and highly organized society that boasted palaces, temples and fortresses of great architectural sophistication. In 1463, the Inca emperor, Pachacuti, initiated a period of massive **expansion** that saw the conquest of lands stretching north to modern-day Quito and south as far as the Río Maule in Chile, where its progress was halted by the fierce resistance of the Mapuche.

The Inca effect

The impact of the Inca in Chile was considerable: they constructed a breathtaking network of roads connecting conquered territory to the capital of the empire in Cusco (later very useful to the Spanish conquistadors), and forced the subjugated peoples to pay tribute to the Inca ruler and to use **Quechua** as their official language. While the Inca tolerated indigenous cults, they required their subjects also to adopt the **cult of the sun**, a central tenet of the Inca religion. Sun worship usually took place at altars built on high mountain peaks where the sun's first rays were received; it sometimes involved human sacrifice, but more commonly animals or objects like silver figurines were offered as substitutes. Remains of Inca worship sites have been found on numerous mountains in Chile, the most famous being Cerro El Plomo, near Santiago, where the frozen body of a small child, undoubtedly offered as a sacrifice, was discovered in 1954. The Inca occupation of Chile spanned a relatively short period of time – about seventy

1600s	Late 1600s	1759–88
The *encomienda* system is established, which involves parcelling out land to settlers and using natives as slaves.	Owing to the decimation of the native population, mestizos are used as hacienda labourers.	Charles III takes the Spanish throne and lifts trade restrictions in order to increase Chile's revenue and then tax it.

years in the Norte Grande and perhaps just thirty in Central Chile. It was interrupted first by civil war in Cusco, caused by the struggle between two rivals over succession to the throne. Then, in 1532, the Spanish arrived in Peru, marking the beginning of the end of the Inca empire.

Enter the Spanish

It was while seeking a westward route to Asia across the Atlantic that **Christopher Columbus** inadvertently "discovered" the Americas in 1492. His patron, Queen Isabella of Spain, supported him on two further expeditions, and sent settlers to colonize the Caribbean island of Hispaniola (site of today's Haiti and Dominican Republic). It gradually became apparent that the islands were not part of Asia, and that a giant landmass – indeed a whole continent – separated them from the East. After colonizing several other islands, the explorers and adventurers, backed by the Spanish Crown, turned their attention to the mainland, and the period of conquest began in earnest.

The conquest of Peru and venture into Chile

In 1521 **Hernán Cortés** defeated the great **Aztec Empire** in Mexico and then in 1524 **Francisco Pizarro** and his partner **Diego de Almagro** set out to find the rich empire they had been told lay further south. After several failed attempts, they finally landed on the coast of **Peru** in 1532, where they found the great **Inca Empire** racked by civil war. Pizarro speedily conquered the empire, aided by advanced military weapons and tactics, a frenzied desire for gold and glory and, most significantly, the devastating effect of Old World diseases on the indigenous population. Within a few years, Peru was firmly in Spanish hands.

Diego de Almagro was entrusted with the mission of carrying the conquest further south to the region named **Chile**, spoken of by the Peruvian natives as a land rich in gold and silver. In 1535, Almagro and his four hundred men set off from Cusco and followed an Inca road down the spine of the Andes as far as the Aconcagua Valley, suffering extreme deprivation and hardship along the way. To make matters worse, the conquistador found none of the riches the Peruvians had spoken of. Bitterly disappointed, Almagro returned to Cusco, where his deteriorating relations with Pizarro led to armed combat and death at the hands of Pizarro's brothers.

Colonization of Chile and clashes with the Mapuche

Three years later, **Pedro de Valdivia** (one of Pizarro's most trusted officers) was granted license to colonize Chile. Owing to its lack of gold and the miseries of the first expedition, Chile was not an attractive destination, and so it was with just ten compatriots, a group of native porters and his mistress, Inés Suarez, that Valdivia set off from Cusco in 1540. Almost a year later, having picked up 150 extra men en route, Valdivia reached the Río Mapocho in the Aconcagua Valley, where he founded **Santiago de la Nueva Extremadura** on February 12, 1541. The new "city" was hastily put together, with all the trappings of a colonial capital, including church, prison, court and *cabildo* (town council), which elected Valdivia as governor. It was a humble affair, regularly attacked and destroyed by local Picunche, but the new colonists were determined to stay and did not return to Peru.

1767	1777–78	1810
Believing them to be too powerful, the Spanish Crown expels the Jesuits from Chile and other Spanish colonies.	Chile's first general census indicates that the country's population consists of 259,646 inhabitants.	A national junta is established to govern Chile in place of the deposed King Ferdinand VII.

Over the next decade, Valdivia attempted to expand the colony, founding the cities of **La Serena** in the north in 1544 and **Concepción** in the south in 1550, followed by a handful of other centres in the south. It was here that the Spaniards faced the fierce resistance of the **Mapuche** (known by the Spanish as the Araucanians), who successfully prevented the spread of colonization south of the Bío Bío River, thereafter known as **La Frontera**. It was in a confrontation with the Mapuche that Valdivia met his death in 1553, at the hands of the famous chief **Lautaro**. The details of Valdivia's execution are believed to be particularly grisly – some versions claim he was forced to swallow molten gold, others that he was lanced to death by a crowd of warriors, one of whom sliced through his breast and ripped out his heart.

In the panic caused by Valdivia's death, the southern colonists retreated to Santiago, leaving only Concepción as a garrison outpost, occupied mainly by soldiers guarding La Frontera. A new governor – Don García Hurtado de Mendoza – was dispatched from Peru, and by the time his term of office ended, in 1561, the natives in the central region had been subjugated, though the south would remain a no-go area for another three centuries.

Colonial society

The new colony was a marginal, isolated and unprofitable addition to Spain's empire in the Americas, which revolved around the viceroyalties of Mexico and Peru. The need to maintain a standing army to guard La Frontera, and the absence of large quantities of precious metals to fund it, meant that Chile ran at a deficit for most of the colonial period. Administratively, it was designated a "**captaincy-general**", ruled by a governor with the help of an *audiencia* (a high court, whose function included advising the governor). All high officials were sent from Spain as representatives of the king, whose authority was absolute, and whose instructions were communicated via the *Consejo de Indias* (Council of the Indies). Chile, however, received little attention and, enclosed within the mighty barriers of the Atacama desert and Andean cordillera, was more or less left to its own devices.

Haciendas and encomiendas

Growth was very slow, amounting to no more than five thousand settlers by 1600. Most of these lived from the farming of land handed out by the governor in grants known as **mercedes de tierra**, spreading over the valleys near Santiago and in the Central Valley. At the same time, large "grants" of indigenous people were given to

---

THE LIE OF THE LAND

In theory, the land-owning *encomenderos* of the colonial system were supposed to look after the wellbeing of their charges and convert them to Christianity in exchange for tribute (by means of work) offered to the Spanish Crown. In reality, the system simply provided the colonists with a large **slave workforce** that they could treat however they pleased, which was often appallingly. From the very beginning, then, the *mercedes de tierra* and *encomiendas* established a pattern that was to dominate Chile's rural society until modern times: namely, large estates owned by seignorial landlords at the head of a dependent, disempowered workforce.

1818	1821	1826
José de San Martín liberates Santiago and Bernardo O'Higgins becomes "supreme director" of the new Chilean republic.	Spanish troops around Valdivia are defeated by British privateer Thomas Cochrane who sails in under a Spanish flag.	The remaining troops on the island of Chiloé surrender, marking the end of the Spanish presence in Chile.

the colonists in what was known as the **encomienda** system – the *encomienda* being the group of natives allocated to an encomendero as a force of effectively slave labour (see box, p.469).

During the **seventeenth century** this pattern became more clearly defined with the emergence and economic dominance of the **hacienda**. Enclosed within thick, protective walls, haciendas were self-sufficient, self-contained entities, whose buildings – arranged around numerous courtyards – comprised workshops, wine *bodegas*, dairies, a chapel and the *casa patronal*, the landowner's home. Initially the workforce was provided by *encomiendas*, but, with tragic inevitability, the indigenous population rapidly decreased through exposure to Old World diseases. In its place there sprang up a new generation of **mestizos**, the result of miscegenation between the Spanish colonists (almost exclusively male in the early years) and indigenous women.

In time, a more or less homogeneous *mestizo* population came to make up the bulk of the Chilean workforce, presided over by a ruling, land-owning elite made up of **peninsulares** (Spaniards born in Spain) and **criollos** (those of Spanish blood born in the colony). Most *mestizos* were incorporated into the haciendas either as peons or as **inquilinos** – labourers allowed to farm a small plot of land in return for year-round service (a practice that continued until the twentieth century).

The rise of the Catholic Church

Along with the haciendas, the other main shaping force in Chilean society was the **Catholic Church**. From the colony's earliest days, missionaries from most orders poured into Chile and embarked on a zealous programme of conversion in the farthest flung corners of the territory, which further helped to decimate the native population through the introduction of European-borne diseases. The missionaries' success was rapid and set the seal on the "pacification" of the Indians, who were less likely to cause trouble if they could be incorporated into the Hispanic culture and their sense of separate identity diminished. The Catholicism that emerged wasn't an altogether orthodox version, as many indigenous elements of worship – such as ritual dancing and sacrificial offerings – were incorporated into this new religion, and even now survive in Chile's more remote communities, especially in the north. Nonetheless, both *indígenas* and *mestizos* embraced the symbolic elements of the Catholic faith with enthusiasm, and several cults sprang up around supposedly miraculous icons, such as the **Cristo de Mayo** in Santiago, believed to have bled real blood after an earthquake in 1647.

The most influential element of the Church was the **Jesuit order** (Compañía de Jesús), which arrived in Chile in 1593 and quickly established itself as one of the colony's largest landowners (see box, p.470).

THE RISE AND FALL OF THE JESUITS

In a paternalistic arrangement, the **Jesuits** gathered hundreds of indigenous families to their **missions**, where they were fed, clothed, converted, taught Spanish and instructed in a diverse array of skills from weaving to glass manufacturing. As a result, the order's numerous **workshops** were the most productive and profitable in the country, as was the case throughout Spanish America – until the Jesuits were suddenly **expelled** from the Spanish Empire in 1767, when the Crown was persuaded that they had become too powerful to tolerate.

1833	1834–35	1848–58
Diego Portales is the architect of Chile's first Constitution, which grants enormous powers to the president.	Charles Darwin sails along Chile's coast in the HMS *Beagle* and seizes three Fuegian natives.	The port of Valparaíso becomes a crucial supply stop for ships en route to California during the California Gold Rush.

Expansion of trade

The reign of **Charles III**, from 1759 to 1788, brought great changes to the colony. The most progressive of the Bourbon monarchs (who had replaced the Habsburg dynasty in Spain in 1700), the king set about improving the management of the American colonies and increasing their productivity, so as to augment revenues. Among his reforms was the relaxation of the stifling trade restrictions that had hampered economic growth throughout much of Spanish America. Suddenly, the colonies were able to trade freely with each other and with Spain. There was no overnight miracle, but Chilean trade did expand considerably, particularly with neighbouring Río de la Plata (future Argentina).

At the same time, imports soared, and the need to pay for them in gold or silver stimulated a small **mining boom** in the Norte Chico. Settlements sprang up around the mining centres, and some, such as Copiapó, Vallenar and Illapel, were granted official city status. All in all, there was an emerging spirit of change and progress, which gave a sense of empowerment to Chile's *criollos*, who had always been barred from the highest colonial offices. But while Chile's commercial horizons were widening, the king's administrative shake-ups – which involved sending a number of *intendants* to the colonies to tighten up administration and eradicate abuses of local power – were experienced as unwanted interference. The resulting tension would soon find a more focused channel.

The struggle for independence

Chile entered the **nineteenth century** with a burgeoning sense of its own identity. The *criollo* elite (Chile-born Spanish), while fiercely loyal to the Spanish king, was becoming increasingly alienated from the *peninsulares* dispatched from Spain to administer the colony, and the gap between them was widening with each successive generation. *Criollo* aspirations of playing a more active role in government (and thus of looking after their own interests, not just the Crown's) were given a sudden, unexpected opportunity for fulfilment when Napoleon invaded Spain in 1808 and deposed Ferdinand VII. **Local juntas** sprang up in Spain's main cities to organize resistance to Napoleon, and they were soon followed by a number of locally elected juntas in the American colonies. In Chile, over four hundred leading citizens gathered in Santiago on September 18, 1810, and elected a six-man **junta**, made up of Chileans. It must be stressed that the junta's initial objective was to "preserve the sovereignty of Ferdinand VII" in the absence of legitimate authority, and few entertained thoughts of independence at this stage. The junta did, however, go on to implement several far-reaching reforms: trade was liberalized; a Congress was elected; and the *real audiencia* (royal court) was replaced by a tribunal with Chilean judges.

The first stirrings of independence

Soon, a minority of *criollos* began to seek a far greater degree of autonomy for the colony, and whispers of independence grew. This small tide was given dramatic impetus in November 1811, when **José Miguel Carrera**, a member of one of the wealthiest and most influential *criollo* families in Chile, seized power, dissolving Congress and appointing himself head of a new, more radical, junta. His actions were swift and bold,

1860	1865	1879–84
Orelie Antoine de Tounens, an eccentric Frenchman, befriends Mapuche leaders and is crowned King of Araucanía.	A wool boom heralds a prosperous new era in Patagonia after the introduction of sheep from the Falklands brings wealth.	Chile goes to war with Bolivia and Peru in the War of the Pacific and emerges victorious.

and included the creation of a Chilean flag and the drafting of a provisional constitution that declared all rulings issued outside Chile to be illegitimate. Greatly alarmed, the viceroy of Peru – where the colonial machinery remained intact – sent troops in early 1813 down to the old-guard strongholds of Chiloé and Valdivia to prepare for an assault on Santiago. In response, Carrera charged down to confront them with Chilean troops (whose generals numbered one Bernardo O'Higgins, the son of a former viceroy of Peru), and war was effectively declared. Loyalties were now thrown sharply into focus with the **Royalists** on one side, made up of Spaniards and pro-Spanish Chileans, and the **Patriots** on the other, made up of *criollos* who supported some form of self-government.

The liberators: Bernardo O'Higgins and José de San Martín

When Carrera's military leadership did not produce impressive results, the junta voted to replace him with **Bernardo O'Higgins**, who proved far more adept at holding off the Royalist forces. In July 1814, the power-hungry Carrera returned to Santiago and overthrew the government once more, reinstating himself at its head and causing considerable upheaval. In October of that year, Royalist troops, taking advantage of the chaos, began to advance on Santiago and, after a showdown at Rancagua (see box, below), ultimately won out.

The victory coincided with the defeat of Napoleon in Spain and the restoration of Ferdinand VII, who immediately set out to crack down on all insurgent elements in his American colonies. In Chile, some forty Patriot *criollos* were exiled to the Juan Fernández Islands, where they were to live in caves, and every reform instigated by the junta was reversed. The Spanish Crown's attempt to turn back the clock and revert to a centralized, interventionist colonial government was felt as repressive and authoritarian by *criollos* throughout the continent.

Just as the great general **Simón Bolívar** was preparing anti-Spanish campaigns in Venezuela that would liberate the northern half of the continent, **José de San Martín**, the Argentine general, was drawing plans for South American emancipation from his base in Mendoza, near the Chilean border. San Martín knew that independence could never be assured until the Spanish were ejected from their heartland in Peru, which he planned to achieve by first liberating Chile, from where he would launch a naval attack on Lima.

The final push

With O'Higgins in command of the Chilean division, San Martín's army scaled the cordillera over four different passes in February 1817. On the twelfth, Patriot forces surprised the Spaniards and defeated them at the Battle of Chacabuco, just north of

---

THE DISASTER OF RANCAGUA

As Royalist troops neared Santiago in the autumn of 1814, **Bernardo O'Higgins** mounted a desperate and heroic defence at Rancagua, but promised reinforcements never arrived and the Patriots were overwhelmingly defeated. The "**Disaster of Rancagua**", as it is known, marked the end of **La Patria Vieja** (the name given to the fledgling independent nation) and its leaders fled across the Andean border to Mendoza in Argentina, as the Royalist troops marched triumphantly into the capital.

1881–83	**1883–1909**	**1888**
The last big Mapuche uprising is defeated in the "Pacification of Araucanía"; Mapuche children enslaved.	Gold is discovered in Tierra del Fuego, prompting mass immigration by fortune seekers and abuse of the native Selk'nam population.	Chile claims Easter Island; the island is turned into a sheep farm and islanders are confined to Hanga Roa.

Santiago. The Royalists fled to the south, and the Patriots entered the capital in triumph. Fighting continued after Royalist reinforcements were sent from Peru, but when San Martín inflicted devastating losses on their army at the Battle of Maipú in April 1818, the Patriot victory was complete, setting the final seal on Chilean independence. Leadership of the new country was offered to San Martín, but he declined – instead, the job went to Bernardo O'Higgins, who was elected Supreme Director by an assembly of Chile's leading *criollos*.

O'Higgins' immediate task was to put together a national navy with which to clear the southern coast of remaining Royalist troublemakers and launch the seaborne attack on Peru. A flotilla was equipped and placed under the command of a British admiral, **Lord Thomas Cochrane**, who successfully captured Callao, the port of Lima, in 1820. With the colonial nerve centre effectively toppled, the days of the Spanish Empire in the Americas were numbered.

The building of a nation

The transition from colony to republic was not smooth. In its first thirteen years of independence, Chile got through five constitutions and eleven changes of government, marked by continual tussles between **Liberal** and **Conservative** factions. Then, in 1829, the Conservatives, with the support of the army, imposed an authoritarian-style government that ushered in a long period of political stability, making Chile the envy of Latin America. The chief architect of the regime was **Diego Portales**, who never stood for presidency, preferring to run the show from various cabinet posts. Convinced that Chile could only move forward under a strong, centralist government able to maintain rigorous order, Portales designed, in 1833, the **Constitution** that was to underpin Chilean government for 92 years. It granted enormous powers to the president, allowing him, for instance, to veto any legislation passed by Congress, and protecting him from impeachment until his term of office had expired (two five-year terms were allowed). Portales was not, however, without his detractors, and in 1837, in protest at the government's invasion of Peru (which had been forcibly annexed by the Bolivian president), he was brutally gunned down by political opponents. This atrocity led to increased support for the government, which went on to defeat the Peru–Bolivia Confederation – to the great pride of Chilean citizens.

Growth and prosperity

The growing self-confidence of the nation, together with the political and social stability within it, created conditions that were favourable to growth. Between the 1830s and 1870s international trade took off rapidly, with hugely increased wheat exports fuelled by the Californian and Australian gold rushes, and, more significantly, **a silver- and copper-mining boom** in the Norte Chico. At the same time, advances in technology and communications saw railways, roads, steamships and telegraphs opening up the country. Its populated territory expanded, too: a government programme encouraged Europeans to come over and settle the lakeland region of the south, which was duly cleared and farmed by some four thousand German immigrants. Meanwhile, Santiago and Valparaíso were being transformed – with avenues, parks, palaces and mansions, and an ever-expanding population.

1890–91	1904	1907
Civil war erupts when Congress revolts over President José Manuel Balmaceda's wealth redistribution reforms, resulting in 10,000 deaths.	Neftalí Ricardo Reyes Basoalto, better known as Pablo Neruda, is born on July 12.	The Chilean army massacres over five hundred saltpetre miners, their wives and children in Iquique.

Rise of the Liberals

In time, the nation began to tire of the authoritarian model of government established by Portales, and the influence of Liberal politics began to gain ground. In 1871 the election of **Federico Errázuriz Zañartu** as president marked the beginning of twenty years of Liberal government. Many of the Liberals' reforms were aimed at reducing the undiminished power of the Church: they legalized free worship in private places; they introduced civil cemeteries, where persons of any faith could be buried; and they instituted civil marriages and registries. The Liberals also went some way towards reducing the individual power of the president, and giving Congress a stronger role in government. The breath of fresh air and sense of optimism produced by these reforms suffered a deathblow, however, when a world recession between 1876 and 1878 sent copper and silver prices tumbling and brought wheat exports to a virtual halt, plunging Chile into economic crisis.

The War of the Pacific

Rescue was at hand in what at first appeared to be yet another calamitous situation. Ever since the 1860s, when two enterprising Chileans started exploiting the vast nitrate deposits of the Atacama desert, Chilean capital and labour had dominated the region's growing **nitrate** industry (see box, p.195). Most activity took place on the pampas around Antofagasta, which Chile had formally acknowledged as Bolivian territory in 1874 – following lengthy border disputes – in exchange for an assurance from Bolivia that export tariffs would not be raised for 25 years. Many of Chile's most prominent politicians had shares in the nitrate companies, so when Bolivia flouted its agreement by raising export taxes in 1878 – directly hitting shareholders' pockets – they were up in arms, and determined to take action.

With tension mounting, Chilean troops invaded Antofagasta in February 1879 and soon took control of the surrounding coastal strip. Within two weeks Chile and Bolivia were at war, with Peru drawn into the conflict on Bolivia's side within a couple of months. It soon became clear that success would depend on **naval supremacy** – Bolivia did not have a navy, leaving Peru and Chile pitted against each other, and fairly evenly matched. Following a series of early losses, Chile secured an overwhelming maritime victory in August 1879, when it captured Peru's principal warship, the *Huáscar*. The

ARTURO PRAT - A NAVAL TRAGEDY

Nothing has captured the Chilean imagination like the heroic, and tragic, efforts of **Arturo Prat** in the Battle of Iquique. On the morning of May 21, 1879, the *Esmeralda* – an old wooden boat under Prat's command – found itself under attack from Peruvian artillery on one side, and from the ironclad warship, the *Huáscar*, on the other. The two vessels could not have been more unevenly matched: the *Huáscar* boasted 300lb cannon, while those of the *Esmeralda* were only 40lb. When the *Huáscar* rammed the *Esmeralda*, Prat refused to give in, instead leaping aboard the enemy's vessel, sword in hand, determined to fight to the end. The gesture was futile, and Prat was killed on the warship's deck, but the commander's dignity and self-sacrifice have made him Chile's favourite national hero, in whose honour a thousand avenues and squares have been named.

1914	1924	1925
The creation of the Panama Canal deals a huge blow to Chile's economy. Punta Arenas goes into decline.	President Arturo Alessandri appoints military figures to key cabinet positions and puts pressure on Congress to pass social reform laws.	The new Constitution is drafted, restoring authority to the president, and incorporating welfare measures to quell protests.

coast was now clear for the invasion of Peru's nitrate territories, and the emphasis shifted to land fighting. Casualties were heavy on both sides, but by June 1880 Chile had secured control of these areas with a resounding victory at El Morro, Arica.

With the nitrate fields theirs, the Chilean government would doubtless have been happy to bring the war to a close, but the public was clamouring for blood: it wanted Peru brought to its knees with the capture of Lima. In January 1881 Peru's humiliation was complete when Chilean troops occupied the capital. Peru was still not ready to give up, though, and the war dragged on for two more years, exhausting both sides and resulting in heavy human loss. Eventually, Peru accepted defeat, sealed by the **Treaty of Ancón** in October 1883 (an official truce with Bolivia was not signed until April the following year).

By the conclusion of the war, Chile had extended its territory by one-third, acquiring the Peruvian province of Tarapacá, and the Bolivian littoral (thus depriving Bolivia of sea access). Its new, nitrate-rich pampas yielded enormous, almost overnight wealth, refilling government coffers and restoring national confidence.

Civil war

With the nitrate industry booming in earnest, by 1890 export taxes were providing over fifty percent of government revenue. With national confidence running high and the economy in such good shape, the government's position looked unassailable. Within a short time, however, cracks began to appear in the constitutional framework, expressed by mounting tension between the legislature (Congress) and the executive branch (chiefly the president).

The conflict came to a dramatic head under the presidency of **José Manuel Balmaceda** (1886–91), a Liberal but autocratic leader who believed passionately in the president's right to run a strong executive branch – an approach jarringly at odds with the political trend of the previous couple of decades. One of the unifying objectives of the various Liberal parties was the elimination of electoral intervention, and when Balmaceda was seen to influence Congressional elections in 1886, many Liberals were outraged and withdrew their support. Equally polarizing was the president's determination to insist on his right to pick and choose his cabinet, without the approval of Congress – whose response was to refuse to pass legislation authorizing the following year's budget until Balmaceda agreed to appoint a cabinet in which they had confidence.

Neither side would give way, and as the deadline for budget approval drew close, it became obvious that Balmaceda would either have to give in to Congress's demands, or act against the Constitution. When he chose the latter option, declaring that he would carry the 1890 budget through to 1891, Congress revolted, propelling the two sides into war. Balmaceda held the army's support, while Congress secured the backing of the navy. Operating out of Iquique, where they established a junta, Congress was able to use nitrate funds to recruit and train an army. In August that year, its troops landed near Valparaíso, where they defeated Balmaceda's army in two long, bloody battles. The president, whose refusal to give in was absolute, fled to the Argentine embassy, where he wrote poignant farewell notes to his family and friends before shooting himself in the head.

1927–31	1931	1938–46
General Carlos Ibañez passes far-reaching agrarian, industrial and educational reforms before being ousted on a wave of Great Depression-related discontent.	Mountaineering priest Alberto de Agostini is the first man to cross the Patagonian Ice Fields.	The unionized labour movement lends its support to the Popular Front – a coalition of socialists, communists and radicals.

The Parliamentary Republic

The authoritarian model of government established by Diego Portales in the 1830s, already undermined over the previous two decades, had now collapsed. Taking its place was a system – dubbed the **Parliamentary Republic** – based on an all-powerful legislature and an extremely weak executive. Now it was Congress who imposed cabinets on the president, not the other way round, with frequent clashes and constantly shifting allegiances seeing cabinets formed and dissolved with breathtaking frequency – between 1891 and 1915 the government got through more than sixty ministries. This chronic instability seriously hampered government action, although, ironically, the one arena where great progress was made was the public works programme vigorously promoted by Balmaceda, which saw rapid construction of state railways, roads, bridges, schools, hospitals, prisons and town halls.

Industrial development and unrest

All this was taking place against a background of momentous social and economic change that the government, bound up with its continual infighting, seemed scarcely aware of. One of the by-products of the nitrate industry was increased **industrialization** elsewhere in Chile, as manufacturing stepped up to service increased production in the north. This, combined with the growth of railways, coal mining, education, construction and banking, saw a period of rapid **social diversification**. A new group of merchants, managers, bureaucrats and teachers formed an emerging middle class, while the increasingly urban workforce – usually living in dire poverty – formed a new working class more visible than its counterpart on the large rural estates.

It was in the nitrate fields of the north that an embryonic **labour movement** began to take root, as workers protested against the appalling conditions they were forced to live and work in. With no political representation to voice these grievances, **strikes** became the main form of protest, spreading from the mining cities of the north to the docks of Valparaíso. The government's heavy-handed attempts to suppress the strikes – reaching a peak of brutality when almost two hundred men, women and children were shot dead in Iquique, in 1907 – were symptomatic of its inability to deal with the social changes taking place in the country. When the nitrate industry entered a rapid decline with the outbreak of World War I in 1914, leaving thousands of workers unemployed and causing inflation to soar, Chile's domestic situation deteriorated further.

Military intervention

The first leader committed to dealing with the republic's mounting social problems was **Arturo Alessandri**, elected in 1920 on the strength of an ambitious reform programme. The weakness of his position, however, in the face of an all-powerful and obstructive Congress, prevented him from putting any of his plans into action, and after four years hardly anything had been achieved. Then, in 1924, a strange set of events was set in motion when an army junta – frustrated by the lack of government action – forced the cabinet to resign and had Alessandri appoint military men to key cabinet positions. The president appeared quite willing to accommodate the junta, which used its muscle to ensure that Congress swiftly passed a series of social reform laws, including legislation to protect workers' rights. After several months, however, the relationship

1945	1947	1960
Gabriela Mistral – poet, educator and diplomat – is the first Latin American to win the Nobel prize for literature.	Chile establishes its first permanent Antarctic research station – Captain Arturo Prat Base – on Greenwich Island.	The tsunami caused by the Great Chilean Earthquake, the most powerful ever recorded (9.5 on the Richter Scale) devastates Valdivia.

between the president and his military cabinet began to unravel and Alessandri fled to Argentina in exile.

More drama was to follow when, on January 23, 1925, a rival junta led by Colonel **Carlos Ibañez** staged a coup, deposed the government and invited Alessandri to return to Chile to complete his term of office. With Ibañez's weight behind him, Alessandri set about redrafting the Constitution, with the aim of restoring authority to the president and reducing the power of Congress. This was achieved with the **Constitution of 1925**, which represented a radical departure from the one of 1833, incorporating protective welfare measures among other reforms. Despite this victory, however, tensions between Ibañez and Alessandri led to the president's resignation. The way was now clear for the military strongman, Ibañez, to get himself elected as president in May 1927.

Boom to bust

Ibañez's presidency was a curious contradiction, at once highly autocratic, with severe restrictions on freedom of expression, and refreshingly progressive, ushering in a series of badly needed reforms promoting agriculture, industry and education. His early years were successful, bringing about improvements in living standards across all sections of society, and stimulating national prosperity. But when the Wall Street crash of 1929 sparked off a worldwide Depression, Chile's economy collapsed virtually overnight, producing deep social unrest. Faced with a wave of street demonstrations and strikes, Ibañez was forced to resign in July 1931. The task of restoring stability to the nation fell to the old populist, Alessandri, who was re-elected in 1932.

The rise of the multi-party system

Military interference in government affairs was now at an end (for a few decades, at least), and the country settled down to a period of orderly political evolution, no longer held back by a weak executive. What emerged was a highly diverse multi-party system embracing a wide spectrum of political persuasions. After 1938, the government was dominated by the **Radical Party**, a centre-right group principally representing the middle classes. Radical presidents such as Pedro Aguirre Cerda, Juan Antonio Ríos and Gabriel González Videla took an active role in regenerating Chile's economy, investing in state-sponsored steelworks, copper refineries, fisheries and power supplies. In the 1950s, left-wing groups gained considerable ground as the voting franchise widened, but old-guard landowners were able to counter this by controlling the votes of the thousands of peasants who depended on them for their survival, thus ensuring a firm swing back to the right. Nonetheless, it was by a very narrow margin that the socialist Salvador Allende was defeated by the Conservative Jorge Alessandri (son of Arturo) in the 1958 elections, causing widespread alarm among the wealthy elite. As the next election approached in 1964, the upper classes, with the discreet backing of the USA (still reeling from the shock of the Cuban missile crisis), threw all their efforts into securing the election of **Eduardo Frei**, the candidate of the rising young **Christian Democrat Party**.

From right-wing to left

In power, Frei turned out to be a good deal more progressive than his right-wing supporters could have imagined, initiating – to their horror – bold **agrarian reforms**

1964	**1964**	**1970**
Easter Island citizens, the Rapa Nui, are finally granted Chilean citizenship and given the right to vote.	Christian Democrat Eduardo Frei elected president; he initiates far-reaching social and economic reforms.	Salvador Allende becomes the first democratically elected Marxist president in the world, winning by a tiny margin.

that allowed the expropriation of all farms of more than 180 hectares. The other memorable achievement of the Frei administration was the "Chileanization" of the **copper industry**, which had replaced nitrates as the country's dominant source of revenue, and which was almost exclusively in the hands of North American corporations. Frei's policy gave the state a 51 percent stake in all the major copper mines, providing instant revenues to fund his social reform programme. These included the introduction of a minimum wage and impressive improvements in education, and made Frei's government popular with the working classes, though his reforms were unable to keep pace with the rush of expectations and demands. At the same time, Conservative groups became increasingly alarmed at the direction in which Frei was steering the country, prompting Liberals and Conservatives to join forces and form the new **National Party**, aimed at putting a check on reform. As Chile approached the 1970s, its population grew sharply polarized between those who clamoured for further social reform and greater representation of the working class, and those to whom this was anathema and to be reversed at all costs.

Salvador Allende's rise to power

On September 4, 1970, **Salvador Allende** was elected as Chile's first socialist president, heading a coalition of six left-wing parties, known as the **Unidad Popular** (UP). His majority, however, was tiny, and while half the country rejoiced, full of hopes for a better future, the other half feared a slide towards communism. Allende was passionately committed to improving the lot of the poorest sectors of society, whose appalling living conditions had shocked him when he had encountered them in his training as a doctor. His government pledged, among other things, to nationalize Chilean industries, to redistribute the nation's wealth, to increase popular participation in government, and to speed up agrarian reform, though there were disagreements as to how fast these changes should be made.

Within a year, over eighty major companies had been nationalized, including the copper mines, which were expropriated without compensation. The following year, radical agrarian reform was enforced, with over sixty percent of irrigated land – including all haciendas with more than 80 hectares – taken into government hands for redistribution among the rural workforce. In one fell swoop, the *latifundia* system that had dominated rural Chile for more than four hundred years was irrevocably dismantled.

In the short term, Allende's government was both successful and popular, presiding as it did over a period of economic growth, rising wages and falling unemployment. But it wasn't long before strains began to be felt. For a start, government expenditure soon exceeded income by a huge margin, creating an enormous deficit. The looming economic crisis was dramatically accelerated when the world copper price fell by some 27 percent, cutting government revenue still further. Inflation began to rise uncontrollably, with wages unable to keep pace, and before long food shortages became commonplace.

The cracks appear

Part of the UP's failure stemmed from the sharp divisions within the coalition, particularly between those who, like Allende, were in favour of a measured pace of reform, and those pressing for rapid, revolutionary change. The internal disunity led to

1970–73	1973	1973
Allende's radical reforms – the nationalization of industry and land redistribution – are crippled by overspending and uncontrollable inflation.	Military coup led by Augusto Pinochet overthrows Allende's government on September 11; Allende dies during the siege of La Moneda.	Pablo Neruda dies on September 23; thousands of mourners defy Pinochet by mourning in the streets.

THIS DARK AND BITTER MOMENT: ALLENDE'S LAST STAND

Refusing a safe passage to exile, Salvador Allende ordered his soldiers to drag away his daughter (who wanted to remain with him in the besieged presidential palace) and, in an emotional **speech** broadcast live on radio, vowed that he would never give up, and that he was ready to repay the loyalty of the Chilean people with his life. In this unique moment of history, citizens heard their president declare "I have faith in Chile and in its destiny. Other men will overcome this dark and bitter moment…You must go on, safe in the knowledge that sooner rather than later, the great avenues will open once more, and free men will march along them to create a better society…These are my last words, but I am sure that my sacrifice will not be in vain." Shortly afterwards, the signals were cut short, and jets began to drop their bombs. At the end of the day, Allende was found dead in the ruins of the palace, clutching a submachine gun, with which, it is widely believed, he had killed himself.

a lack of coordination in implementing policy, and an irreversible slide towards political chaos. Making matters worse were the extremist far-left groups outside the government – notably the Revolutionary Left Movement, or **MIR** – which urged the workers to take reform into their own hands by seizing possession of the haciendas and factories where they worked.

Opposition to the government rose sharply during 1972, both from political parties outside the coalition (such as the Christian Democrats, who had previously supported Allende) and from widening sectors of the public. Panic was fuelled by the right-wing press and reinforced behind the scenes by the CIA, who, it later emerged, had been given a US$8 million budget with which to destabilize the Allende government. Strikes broke out across the country, culminating in the truckers' stoppage of October 1972, which virtually paralysed the economy. By 1973, with the country rocked by civil disorder, it was clear to all that the government could not survive for much longer. On the morning of September 11, 1973, tanks rolled through the capital and surrounded the presidential palace, La Moneda, marking the beginning of the **military coup** that Chile had been expecting for months, and the end of both Salvador Allende's reign and his life (see box, above).

The Pinochet years

The military coup was headed by a four-man junta of whom **General Augusto Pinochet**, chief of the army, quickly emerged as the dominant figure. Although Chile had seen military intervention in government affairs on two occasions in the past, these had been the exception to a highly constitutional norm. Nothing in the country's political history prepared its people for the brutality of this operation. In the days and weeks following the takeover, the Caravan of Death – a Chilean army death squad – travelled the length of Chile, executing 97 people. At least seven thousand people – journalists, politicians, socialists, trade union organizers and so on – were herded into the national football stadium, where many were executed; tens of thousands more were tortured. Curfews were imposed, the press was placed under the strict control of the junta, and military officers were sent in to take charge of factories, universities and other seats of socialist support. Before long, Congress had been dissolved, opposition parties and trade unions banned, and over thirty thousand Chileans had fled the country.

1973	1973–89	1976–81
In September and October, the Caravan of Death army death squad travels the length of Chile, murdering Pinochet's opponents.	Pinochet dissolves Congress, indefinitely suspends all political parties and rules by decree; thousands are tortured and 3065 killed.	The rapid growth of Chile's free-market economy, spurred on by elimination of price controls, is dubbed the "Chilean Miracle".

Death and the free market

At the same time as his henchmen were murdering the opposition (see box, below), General Pinochet saw his mission – and it was one in which he was supported by a sizeable portion of the population – as being that of rescuing Chile from the Left and, by extension, from the economic and political chaos into which it had undoubtedly fallen. To achieve this, he planned not to hand the country over to a right-wing political party of his approval, but to take it into his own hands and rule it himself. His key strategy was to be the adoption of a radical **free-market economy**, which involved a complete reversal of Allende's policies and a drastic restructuring of government and society. In this he was influenced by a group of Chilean economists known as "the Chicago boys", who had carried out postgraduate studies at the University of Chicago, where they'd come into contact with the monetarist theories of Milton Friedman. Almost immediately, price controls were abolished, government expenditure was slashed, most state-owned companies were privatized, import tariffs were reduced, and attempts were made to liberalize investment and attract foreign capital.

Such measures would take time to work, and called for a period of intense austerity. Sure enough, unemployment soared, wages plummeted, industrial output dropped, and the lower and middle classes became significantly poorer. At the same time, as Pinochet strove to reduce the role of the state in society, social welfare became increasingly neglected, particularly health and education. By the late 1970s, the economy was showing signs of growth and inflation was finally beginning to drop – from an annual rate of 900 percent in 1973 to 65 percent in 1977 and down to a respectable 9.5 percent in 1981. Soon, there was talk of the Chilean "economic miracle" in international circles. The boom did not last, however, and in 1982, Chile found itself, along with much of Latin America, in the grip of a serious **debt crisis** which swept away the previous advances: the country was plunged into recession, with hundreds of private enterprises going bankrupt and unemployment rising to over 30 percent. It wasn't until the late 1980s that the economy recovered and Pinochet's free-market policies achieved the results he sought, with sustained growth, controlled inflation, booming, diversified exports and reduced unemployment. This prosperity, however, did not benefit all Chileans, and 49 percent of Chile's private wealth remained in the hands of 10 percent of its population.

STATE-SPONSORED TERROR

Pinochet's free-market experiment had only been possible with the tools of ruthless repression at his disposal. His chief instrument was the secret police known as the **DINA**, which carried out surveillance on civilian (and even military) society, brutally silencing all opposition. Although the wholesale repression that followed the coup diminished in scale after the first year, regular "disappearances", torture and executions continued throughout Pinochet's regime. The regime was actively, if clandestinely, supported by the US, through the CIA, which even helped with the elimination of dissidents. In the absence of any organized political opposition, only the Catholic Church spoke out against the government's human rights violations, providing assistance and sanctuary to those who suffered, and vigilantly documenting all reports of abuse.

1980	1982	1982
Controversial new constitution passed, in spite of many voters abstaining in protest, giving Pinochet extended powers and an eight-year term.	Isabel Allende's debut novel, *The House of the Spirits*, is published, giving her international prominence.	Chile's economy suffers during the worldwide economic recession but bounces back again by the late 1980s.

The beginning of the end

Pinochet held the country in such a tight, personal grip – famously claiming "there is not a leaf that stirs in Chile without my knowing it" – that it doubtless became difficult for him to conceive of an end to his authority. The Constitution that he had drawn up in 1980 – ratified by a tightly controlled **plebiscite** – guaranteed him power until 1988, at which point the public would be given the chance to either accept military rule for another eight years, or else call for elections.

From the mid-1980s, **public protest** against Pinochet's regime began to be voiced, both in regular street demonstrations and with the reformation of political opposition parties (still officially banned). Open repression was stepped down as international attention became increasingly focused on the Chilean government's behaviour, and the US (a major source of foreign investment) made clear that it favoured a return to democracy. In this climate, the opposition parties were able to develop a united strategy in their efforts to oust the dictator. As the referendum in which Chile would decide whether or not to reject military rule drew closer, the opposition forces banded together to lead a highly professional and convincing "no" campaign. Pinochet remained convinced of his own victory, and with control of all media, and the intimidation tactics of a powerful police state at his disposal, it is easy to see why. But when the plebiscite took place on **October 5, 1988**, 55 percent of the nation voted "no" to continued military rule.

Pinochet goes quietly

After sixteen years in power, the writing was on the wall for Pinochet's dictatorship. Much to everyone's surprise, he accepted his defeat without resistance and prepared to step down. But the handover system gave him one more year in power before democratic elections would be held – a year in which he hastily prepared **amnesty laws** that would protect both himself and the military from facing any charges of human rights abuses levied by the new government, and that would make his constitutional model extremely difficult to amend. A year later, on December 14, 1989, the Christian Democrat Patricio Aylwin, at the head of a seventeen-party centre-ground coalition called the **Concertación de los Partidos por la Democracia**, became Chile's first democratically elected president in seventeen years.

Return to democracy

The handover of power was smooth and handled with cautious goodwill on all sides, including the military. **Patricio Aylwin** was in the fortunate position of inheriting a robust economy and an optimistic public. Yet he faced serious challenges, including the need to channel substantial funds into those areas neglected by the previous regime while sustaining economic growth, and to address human rights abuses without antagonizing the military and endangering the transition to democracy.

Pinochet's **economic** model was barely contested, and was vigorously applied in an effort to promote "growth with equity" (the Concertación's electoral slogan). Foreign investment poured into the country and exports continued to rise, keeping economic growth at high levels and allowing Aylwin to divert resources into health and education. He was also felt to be making genuine efforts to alleviate the problems faced by the poorest members of society.

1988	1989	1990
Fifty-six percent of the population vote against Pinochet's continuing presidency in the plebiscite, leading to a democratic election.	The first free elections since 1970 result in a victory for moderate Christian Democrat Patricio Aylwyn.	Pinochet steps down but not before obtaining immunity from prosecution for himself and his cronies in the military.

JUSTICE FOR SOME

One of the new Patricio Aylwin government's first actions was the establishment of a **National Commission for Truth and Reconciliation** to investigate and document the abuses committed by the military regime. The commission's 1991 report confirmed 2279 executions, disappearances and deaths caused by torture, and listed a further 641 suspected cases. Although compensation was paid to the families of the victims, the few attempts made to bring the perpetrators to justice were unsuccessful, owing to the protective **amnesty laws** passed by Pinochet before he relinquished power.

By 1995, however, with courts finally willing to find ways of getting round Pinochet's amnesty laws., there were breakthrough convictions of six former *carabineros*, two former DINA (secret police) agents and most significantly, of General Manuel Contreras and Brigadier Pedro Espinoza, both sentenced to **life imprisonment** in "Punta Peuco", a jail built purposely for high-profile human rights criminals. Several more cases resulted in prison sentences for violators, though the government controversially approved measures aimed at imposing a time limit on human rights investigations, which some claimed were dragging on excessively. In spectacular circumstances, former secret police chief **Manuel Contreras**, who had already served part of an earlier life sentence, was arrested in early 2005 on fresh charges – he allegedly tried to shoot the officers who went to his house to detain him.

Return of Eduardo Frei (Jr)

After a successful four-year term, the Concertación was in 1993 once again elected to power, headed by the Christian Democrat **Eduardo Frei** (son of the 1964–70 president). Frei's policies were essentially a continuation of his predecessors', with a firmer emphasis on tackling human rights issues (see box, above) and eradicating severe poverty. His success was mixed. His National Programme for Overcoming Poverty, established in 1994, was seen as inconsistent and ineffective. In its last couple of years, Frei's government ran into unexpected problems. First, the Asian economic crisis of 1998 had serious repercussions on the Chilean economy, hitting exports, foreign investment (much of which came from Southeast Asia) and the value of the peso, which has been sliding gradually ever since. At the same time, the unresolved tensions over lack of justice for Pinochet erupted afresh when the general retired from his position of commander-in-chief of the army in early 1998 but immediately took up a seat in Congress as a life senator. More controversy followed later the same year as he was dramatically thrust into the international spotlight following his arrest in a London hospital on October 16, following a request for his **extradition** to Spain to face charges of murder and torture (see box, opposite).

The rise of the left

In December 1999, the first round of presidential elections left two front-runners neck and neck in the second round: the Concertación's candidate, socialist **Ricardo Lagos**, a former education minister under Aylwin who had famously voiced criticism of Pinochet in the late 1980s, and **Joaquín Lavín**, who had served under the general and was standing on a firmly right-wing platform. Lagos pulled off an eleventh-hour victory on January 16, 2000, beating his opponent narrowly – by 51 to 49 percent.

1998	2000	2000
Pinochet arrested in Britain – the first former head of state arrested on the principle of universal jurisdiction.	Ricardo Lagos, a moderate leftist, is elected president – one of several leftist leaders in South America at the time.	Pinochet is released on medical grounds and sent back to Chile, disappointing those demanding justice for his victims.

Social and land reform

Determined to continue with his predecessors' overhaul of two main areas of social policy, namely **health and education**, the highly popular Lagos implemented an ambitious programme based on reforming the state. A push towards universal free medical care initiated by Lagos has now mostly been achieved, with free treatment for low-income earners and people over 60, and with the rest paying a contribution dictated by their earnings. Hospitals and other services, mostly in a pitiful state after years of neglect, were improved, too. After compulsory schooling, shortened to the bare

WILL HE OR WON'T HE: THE PINOCHET AFFAIR

On October 16, 1998, justice finally caught up with Augusto Pinochet, arrested in a London hospital after Spain had requested his extradition. The arrest provoked strong reactions in Chile: families of Pinochet's victims rejoiced euphorically; supporters of the general were outraged, burning British flags in the streets; while the government, in a difficult position, denounced the arrest as an affront to national sovereignty and demanded Pinochet's immediate return to Chile – whereupon, they claimed, his alleged crimes would be dealt with in the Chilean courts. After a protracted and complex legal battle, during which the British judiciary ruled both in Pinochet's favour and against him, in April 1999 Britain's Home Secretary, **Jack Straw**, announced that proceedings could go ahead. They again got bogged down, this time over whether the former dictator was fit to stand trial.

Straw finally decided to send Pinochet back to Chile in early March 2000, just before Ricardo Lagos was sworn in at La Moneda. There was an international outcry when he was welcomed back with pomp and circumstance by the armed forces, and Congress granted all former heads of state **lifelong immunity** from prosecution. Even Lagos expressed support for such a move, to quell any stirrings in the military. Yet the former dictator was stripped of his immunity in June and faced charges for kidnapping opponents before Christmas 2000. At the beginning of 2001 he was judged mentally fit for trial, and, at the end of January Chilean judge **Juan Guzmán** ordered Pinochet's house arrest. But within months the case fizzled out yet again, and in July 2001 all charges against Pinochet were dropped after a Santiago court decided he was, after all, unfit to stand trial. Nevertheless, like the former tyrant himself, the case would not lie down and die. Further appeals and counter appeals meant that the affair dragged on for one more year. Finally the country's Supreme Court ruled, in early July 2002, that Pinochet was indeed unfit to stand trial on mental-health grounds. He responded by resigning as life senator from Chile's Congress and was reported as saying that he did so "with a clear conscience", unleashing a furore among his opponents.

CORRUPTION CHARGES

Spectre-like, Pinochet returned to the fore once more amid a **financial scandal** in 2005. Though the ex-dictator had always claimed that, unlike many of his peers, his only interest was the wellbeing of his country and not of his pocket, it transpired that he and/or his relatives had creamed off tens of millions of dollars in murky wheeling and dealing, and carefully stashed the laundered booty in US bank accounts, one of them at Riggs; cooperation with the US financial authorities revealed the existence of the funds, a very generous nest egg for his family. In February 2005, the Riggs Bank donated $8 million to a pension fund set up for the families of three thousand victims of human rights abuses under the general's regime. In June of the same year, the courts decided that he was fit to stand trial to answer the corruption charges yet mortality was to intervene before any sentence could ever be passed (see p.485).

2004	2005	2006
In spite of being a predominantly Catholic country, Chile finally legalizes divorce; courts are flooded with thousands of cases.	Constitutional reforms fully restore democracy, dispensing with military commanders and senators-for-life (non-elected senators) such as Pinochet.	In January, Chile elects its first female president, Michelle Bachelet, to lead the centre-left Concertación coalition.

minimum by Pinochet, was dramatically lengthened, plans to recruit more teachers, improve their training and raise their salaries were implemented. **Divorce** was finally legalized in late 2004 (leaving only Malta and the Philippines divorce-free), despite opposition by the Church, which has said it will do all it can to obstruct the new, democratically enacted law – but abortion remains utterly taboo.

Lagos also tried to tackle the thorny issue of **indigenous peoples' rights**, handing back large tracts of land to the Mapuche and others early on in his presidency. This backfired somewhat, with emboldened *indígenas* demanding even more of their land back, resulting in some ugly clashes with the police in early 2002, when demonstrators tried to block the construction of a new road through land claimed by the Mapuche; there have been several similar incidents in recent years.

Trouble abroad

International relations, in particular with the country's neighbours, were decidedly rocky as Lagos headed towards the end of his term of office. His dismissive remarks plus chauvinistic Chilean media coverage following the arrest of two young Chileans accused of defacing an ancient wall in the Inca city of Cusco, did little to smooth relations with **Peru**, Chile's traditional rival to the north. Chile's refusal to negotiate a guaranteed ocean access for landlocked **Bolivia**, meanwhile, further soured relations with another long-time foe. And **Argentina**'s decision to prioritize its domestic gas demand, at the risk of cutting supplies to Chile, increased trans-Andean tensions.

South America's first female president

From March 2006, Chile had a woman president, socialist **Michelle Bachelet**, elected by a comfortable margin in the second-round run-off on January 15 of that year. She had stood against charismatic businessman and current president Sebastián Piñera, of the centre-right National Renewal Party, in the *balotaje* (decisive second round). Furious at his decision to run and split the right-wing vote, Lavín supporters likened Piñera, billionaire owner of the TV channel Chilevisión, and president of LAN, the national airline, to Italy's Silvio Berlusconi. Bachelet, by contrast, was a physician who'd gone into exile in Australia and East Germany in the 1970s after her father, a moderate Air Force general, was assassinated under Pinochet. In her victory speech she said that a **feminine touch** was needed to smooth international relations and promised to work for greater friendship between Chile and its neighbours, particularly Argentina.

A woman's work

Michelle Bachelet's election as Chile's first female head of state also made her the first woman to be directly and democratically elected in South American history. Indeed, one of outgoing President Lagos' stated aims had been to reduce the acute **gender inequality** in the country, and he appointed Chile's first female ministers for defence (Bachelet herself) and foreign affairs (her erstwhile rival in the presidential race, Soledad Alvear). The number of women in the principal judicial bodies has also gone up while the House of Deputies had two woman speakers at the beginning of the millennium and during Bachelet's presidency the Cabinet of Chile had an equal number of male and female ministers.

2006	2007	2010
Pinochet dies without ever standing trial for his crimes and is denied a state funeral. Bachelet does not attend.	The DNA of a Polynesian chicken is found at the Mapuche settlement of El Arenal, suggesting new human migration theories.	On February 27, a powerful earthquake damages Concepción and the resulting tsunami devastates the island of Juan Fernández.

Criticized during the campaign for her vague policies and indecision, Bachelet nevertheless started her presidency with a strong mandate, a supportive parliament and many expectations. She promised a new, participatory style of government that would continue pro-market economic policies begun under the dictatorship of Augusto Pinochet, but with an accent on empowering ordinary Chileans. The fact that she was detained and tortured, along with her mother, in the early Pinochet years before her family was allowed to leave the country, enhanced her popularity on the left; but her **progressive stance** on delicate issues such as divorce, human rights and religion (she is a professed agnostic) and the fact that she is separated from her husband and did not marry the father of her third child, put off many traditional voters even in her own camp. All that said, she was staunchly opposed to abortion and gay marriage (but not to some kind of official recognition of same-sex couples).

Although Bachelet enjoyed 62 percent approval shortly after taking office, it didn't take long for the inherited hangovers from the previous administrations to reassert themselves: labour protests, social unrest from students complaining about the poor quality of public education and a botched overhaul of Santiago's transport caused her public standing to plummet. During the first two and a half years of her presidency, Chile's economy ticked along nicely, thanks largely to Asian demand delivering booming revenues for Chile's chief export, copper. But amid the **global financial crisis** that took hold in mid-2008, the price of copper halved in the space of four months.

Diplomatic manoeuvres

Bachelet aimed to focus foreign policy on improving **international relations** with Chile's neighbours. In a move seen as a chance to improve strained ties between Bolivia and Chile, Bachelet made a rare trip to **Bolivia** in 2007 for talks with President Evo Morales and the president of Brazil in La Paz. There they agreed ambitious plans to

---

JUSTICE DENIED: THE DEATH OF PINOCHET

Chile was once more convulsed with polarized passions following **Pinochet's death** from a heart attack in December 2006, symbolically enough on International Human Rights' Day. At the time of his death, he was under house arrest and facing trial over charges in Chilean courts relating to one financial enquiry and five human rights cases. In October 2006, an appeal court had dropped corruption charges brought against his wife and five children who had been accused of sending state funds illegally to foreign bank accounts in the US. They say that for Chileans there's no middle ground on Pinochet – they either love him or hate him. This never appeared so true than in the days following his death. While jubilant opponents danced in the centre of the capital, his supporters mourned outside the military hospital where he died, loving the man they insisted had saved the country from Marxism and put Chile on the path of strong economic growth.

Bachelet **refused to authorize** the type of state funeral normally granted to former presidents, saying it would be "a violation of my conscience" to do so and did not attend. Instead, he was allowed only military honours as a former head of the Chilean army. For many, there is still anger and frustration that the former dictator never faced trial for his crimes. Though it may be little solace, in the words of Uruguayan writer Mario Benedetti: "Formal justice may remain incomplete, but history has judged him and condemned him."

2010	2010	2011
Sebastián Piñera comes to power in January's elections in the first democratic victory for Chile's right-wing movement since Pinochet's coup.	In August, the collapse of a copper-gold mine leaves 33 miners trapped underground for 69 days.	Seven cyclists are arrested in Santiago over participation in Chile's first Naked Bike Ride.

build a highway linking the Atlantic and Pacific coasts of South America from Santos in Brazil to Iquique in Chile, one that promises to be economically advantageous for all parties. However, though the countries might appear friendlier towards each other, the territorial dispute still rumbles on. The same old tensions continued to shape relations between Chile and **Argentina**; when President Cristina Fernández de Kirchner, a friend of Bachelet, was elected, diplomatic relations improved, though the two countries had still not formally agreed on border issues. In 2007, however, during one of South America's coldest winters, Argentina cut supplies of natural gas along pipelines to Chile, a move that led inevitably to frostier relations between the two. Bachelet was keen to emphasize Chile's long-term energy option of diversifying its energy supplies thereby reducing future dependence on Argentina for fuel.

In 2009, Bachelet and Fernández signed the Maipú Treaty of Integration and Cooperation, and Argentina's assistance after Chile's earthquake of 2010 was followed by Piñera's visit to Argentina and his expression of deep commitment to good relations between the two countries. The only fly in the ointment remains the disputed demarcation of the limit of the Southern Ice Field (a closed issue as far as Chile is concerned). Relations with **Peru** meanwhile, soured in 2008 when it filed a lawsuit at the International Court of Justice in a bid to settle the long-standing dispute over maritime boundaries; a verdict is due to be reached in no less than seven years.

A new decade, natural disaster and a swing to the right

In spite of Michelle Bachelet's efforts, the Chilean public was growing disillusioned with the centre-left coalition amid allegations of incompetence and large-scale corruption. By 2009, the main opposition to Bachelet's governing party, the right-wing Alliance for Chile coalition, gained ground in local elections. It won mayoral contests in a number of key cities so that, for the first time, the right had more mayors in office than the ruling coalition. Led by billionaire businessman **Sebastián Piñera** – who narrowly lost to Bachelet in 2006 – the Alliance finally translated these gains into success at the January 2010 presidential poll, winning 52 percent of the vote.

While Piñera inherited his share of problems, he doubtless didn't anticipate the global media frenzy Chile would find itself at the centre of after suffering two major disasters within months of his taking office. On Saturday, February 27, 2010, a powerful **earthquake** – 8.8 on the Richter scale – occurred off the coast of Chile, causing particular destruction in the coastal city of Concepción and affecting the southern half of the country. The death toll numbered 525, with a countrywide blackout and half a million homes rendered uninhabitable. An attendant **tsunami** compounded the misery, wreaking havoc in south-central Chile and causing over twenty deaths on the tiny

WOMEN'S RIGHTS IN THE NEW CHILE

In a country with fewer **women** in the workforce than anywhere else in Latin America, Bachelet promised to champion the woman's cause and, in her first year, delivered not only the breast-feeding law but also set up hundreds of nurseries and shelters for victims of domestic violence. By presidential decree, and to the disgust of the Catholic Church, she made the **morning-after pill** available free to girls as young as 14.

2011	2011
The ALMA telescope – the most complex in the world – begins its quest to study the "Cosmic Dawn".	Forest fire in Torres del Paine National Park, caused by human negligence, sparks anger at the government's slowness of response.

island fishing community of San Juan Bautista alone – an immeasurable loss for a community of only six hundred people. Half of the country was declared a "disaster zone" and Piñera's government came under criticism for its inadequately fast response in dealing with the aftermath. Mobs of post-earthquake looters converged on supermarkets in Concepción to steal electrical goods as well as food, necessitating deployment of a special force of *carabineros* wielding water cannon and tear gas. A prison riot in Concepción, meanwhile, required the intervention of the armed forces, and prison escapees in Chillán wreaked havoc further south.

Chile's annus horibilis continued later that year when, on August 5, a major cave-in was reported at the 121-year-old San José copper-gold mine near the town of Copiapó, trapping 33 men (who came to be known as "Los 33") 700m underground. Given the mine's troubled history, it was originally thought that the miners would not survive or would not be found in time. However, seventeen days after the accident, with successful exploratory drilling having pinpointed the trapped miners' location, president Piñera himself held up a note for the jubilant public to see: "*Estamos bien en el refugio, los 33.*" In the wake of the criticism directed at the Chilean government for its handling of the earthquake and tsunami, Piñera cut short official business especially to visit the mine and was there to greet the miners when they were freed through international efforts, thus giving a much-needed boost to his government's ratings.

Economy, education and Piñera's prospects

While the Chilean economy has remained relatively stable throughout the economic crisis which has affected much of the world, the growing **student unrest** has exploded in a series of protests, some of them violent, over the high price and poor quality of state education. Thus far, their demands for free university education have gone unanswered. When it comes to indigenous rights, there has been escalating unrest as well (see box, p.466), and on the environmental front Piñera's government has come under heavy criticism for their environmentally unfriendly decision to approve plans for five major hydroelectric dams in Patagonia (see box, p.358). By the elections of 2013, it remains to be seen whether Chile will grow disillusioned with so-called "change" and whether the pendulum will swing left yet again.

2011–12

Chilean Education Conflict: thousands of students stage demonstrations, and occupy universities and school in protest against expensive, inadequate education.

Landscape and the environment

One of South America's smaller countries, Chile is roughly the same size as France and Britain combined – but stretched over the equivalent distance of Vancouver to Panama. This strange sliver of a country, on average just 180km across, spans 4350km from the desert of the north to the subantarctic ice-fields in the south, and encompasses almost every kind of natural habitat along the way.

Geography

Geographically, Chile is divided into a number of latitudinal **zones**, each of which shows clear differences in climate, vegetation and fauna. These zones only tell part of the story, though, with Chile's three principal landforms – the Andes, the central depression and the coastal range, running the length of the country – all having a significant impact on the local ecology. The **Andes**, in particular, straddles all of Chile's disparate regions. Characterized by precipitous slopes with ravines cut deep into the rock, at points the range acts as a great, impenetrable wall dividing Chile from neighbouring Argentina and Bolivia. Scores of **volcanoes**, many topping 6000m, line these borders, where episodic eruptions and seismic activity are everyday realities. The country's highest peak, Ojos del Salado (6893m), is also the world's highest active volcano; Aconcagua (6959m), the globe's tallest peak outside the Himalayas, lies a few kilometres over the Argentine border.

Desert and volcanoes: Norte Grande

In the far north, the **Norte Grande** region stretches from the Peruvian border over 1000km south to the Copiapó river valley. Covering the central depression between the Andes and the coastal range lies the **Atacama Desert**, thought to be the driest place on earth. Surprisingly, the desert is unusually temperate, owing to the moderating influence of the Humboldt Current, a cold-water sea current just off the coast. While thick fog banks, known as *camanchaca*, accumulate along the coast where the cold water meets the warm air, a high-pressure zone prevents the cloud from producing rain and moving inland.

A search for wildlife is a pretty fruitless activity in these barren northern wastes. The frustrated ornithologist A.W. Johnson remarked that the desert was "without doubt one of the most completely arid and utterly lifeless areas in the whole world". It's a very different story, however, up in the Andes bordering the Atacama, where a high plateau known as the **altiplano** is home to a diverse wildlife population and an otherworldly landscape of volcanoes, lakes and salt flats.

Mining and exotic fruit: Norte Chico

The semi-arid **Norte Chico**, bounded roughly by the Copiapó Valley and the Aconcagua Valley, just north of Santiago, forms a transitional zone, where the inhospitable northern desert gives way to scrubland and eventually forests further south, as precipitation levels increase. The heat of the sun here is tempered by air humidity, making the land suitable for irrigation farming. The crops of tobacco and cotton that predominated in the colonial era have since been replaced by more lucrative exotic fruits, such as papaya and *cheirimoya*. Throughout the north mining has also long been prevalent, thanks to the high levels of nitrates, copper, silver and other minerals in the soil.

Grapes and non-native trees: Central Valley

Beyond Santiago, the region known as the **Central Valley** extends south to the Bíobío river. Mineral-rich earth coupled with warm dry summers and short humid winters have provided ideal conditions here for growing grapes, peaches, pears, plums, mangoes, melons and apricots. As the country's primary agricultural zone, as well as a major centre of industry, it is no surprise that this region is home to around eighty percent of the country's population, almost half based in the capital.

Towards the southern end of the Central Valley, forests signal a marked increase in precipitation levels. Systematic **afforestation**, begun over a hundred years ago in Arauco province, has seen the introduction of a variety of foreign trees, such as eucalyptus and Australian myrrh. No species has flourished as well as the radiata pine, however, which far exceeded the rate of development normal in its native California; concern is mounting that its success is damaging Chile's fragile endemic forest habitats.

The Lake District, Patagonia and Tierra del Fuego

In the **Lake District**, between Temuco and Puerto Montt, precipitation reaches 2300mm a year, allowing luxuriant native forests to predominate over the rolling foothills of the coastal range. To the east, azure lakes, remnants of the last glacial age, are backed by conical, snowcapped **volcanoes**. Among the many volcanoes still active, both Villarrica and Llaima have erupted ten times in the last hundred years. On May 2, 2008, the Chaitén volcano, situated further south on the mainland across from Chiloé, began erupting for the first time in nine thousand years; a huge column of smoke and ash rose into the sky, coating the land around the volcano and reaching into neighbouring Argentina.

Beyond Puerto Montt, the central depression submerges into the sea, while the tops of the coastal mountains nudge through the water in a mosaic of **islands** and **fjords**. It is here, in this splintered and remote region, that continental Chile finally runs out of dry land: the Carretera Austral, the highway that runs south from Puerto Montt, is cut short after 1000km by two massive ice fields, the largest in the southern hemisphere outside Antarctica. **Southern Patagonia** is a mostly inhospitable place, with continual westerly winds roaring off the sea and dumping up to seven metres of snow, sleet, hail and rain on the western slopes every year. Even so, the glaciated scenery, with its perfect U-shaped valleys and rugged mountains, has an indisputable grandeur. In stark contrast, the monotonous grasslands of the Patagonian pampa, which lies in the rain shadow on the eastern side of the Andes, describe the beginning of a quite different habitat.

Tierra del Fuego ("Land of Fire") is an archipelago separated from mainland Chile by the Magellan Strait. Mountains and forests dominate the south of the region, while the north hosts little more than windswept grasses. From Cape Horn, South America's southernmost point, Antarctica is a mere 1000km away.

Flora

Extraordinary diversity of altitude, latitude and precipitation inevitably leads to an extraordinary diversity of flora. Only humid tropical forest fails to feature in Chile's rich and varied ecology. The tropical area in the far north is stricken with aridity too severe to support most plant life, except at higher altitudes, where **xerophytes** ("dry growers"), such as **cacti**, begin to appear. Ninety percent of Chile's vascular plants are from the cactus family, many of them endemic and endangered. On the altiplano, **tough grasses** and **brush** associated with minimal rainfall support the herds of grazing alpaca.

Central Chilean flora

Moving south towards Central Chile, where the climate is more balanced and water less scarce, **sclerophyllous** ("rigid leaf") shrubs and trees feature leathery leaves that help them retain water. As rainfall increases towards the south, these plants begin to blend with **temperate rainforests**. In the heavily populated areas of this central region, such woodlands have suffered widespread deforestation as land has been cleared for farming and housing, and only patches remain. In Parque Nacional La Campana near Santiago, for example, stands the last forest of endangered **Chilean palm** (*Jubaea chilensis*), sole reminder of a time when millions of the trees covered the area, favoured as they were for the flavour of their sap.

Temperate tree species and Patagonian flora

Further south the **temperate rainforests** have fared a little better, constituting almost a quarter of this type of habitat worldwide. Over 95 percent of the fifty tree species found here are endemic, including the **araucaria** (*Araucaria araucana*), known in English as the **monkey puzzle**, Chile's national tree, and rare **southern beeches** (*Nothofagus*) – principally *coïgue*, *ñire*, *raulí* and *lenga* – which vie for sunlight, towering up to 40m into the air to break clear of the canopy. The **alerce**, or **Chilean false larch** (*Fitzroya cupressoides*), a relative of the North American sequoia, takes several hundred years to reach maturity and can live for four thousand years, providing the loggers don't get there first. The tree is best seen in the areas around Puerto Montt.

In Chilean Patagonia, **evergreen beeches** (*Nothofagus betuloides*) grow in the sheltered areas bordering the great fields of ice, while their **deciduous** cousins *Nothofagus pumilio* and *antarctica* prefer the drier eastern flanks of the Andes. Where the canopy is broken, dazzling scarlet *embothrium*, yellow *berberis* bedecked with mauve berries, and deep-red *Pernettya* emblazon the ground. Rare **orchids** and pink **oxalis** interweave in a tapestry of colour. Such brilliant displays are impossible on the coastal Magellanic **moorland**, where high levels of precipitation drown all but the sphagnum **bog** communities and **dwarf shrubs**. Here, the wind-beaten **Magellanic gunnera** grows only a few centimetres high, a tiny fraction of what its relatives are capable of in the Valdivian rainforest. Meanwhile, the rain shadow effect on the eastern Patagonian steppe supports little more than coarse tussocks of *festuca* grasses.

Environmental issues

The slow destruction of Chile's environment was set in motion by the Spanish in the sixteenth century, though it wasn't until the early twentieth century, with widespread settlement and increased industrialization, that the scale reached damaging levels. Today, although Chile has suffered less environmental degradation than most other countries with comparable resources, there are few habitats that have not been affected in some way by human activity, and it's debatable whether the government is prepared to prioritize future protection over financial exploitation – the current issue over damming Patagonia's rivers (see box, p.358) is a case in point.

Pollution

There was little interest in environmental issues in Chile until large-scale disruption caused by the appalling **smog in Santiago**, considered by Greenpeace to be the third most polluted city in Latin America, mobilized public concern. Most years the capital's schools are suspended for days on end and people are warned to stay indoors as a dense cloud of toxic gases hangs over the capital, caught between the two surrounding mountain ranges. The problem is worsened in dry weather, when the concentration of contaminated air is not dissolved by rain. Pressure from the urban middle class has forced the government to introduce (many say weak) measures to lessen air pollution in Santiago and has encouraged politicians to include environmental elements to their policies.

The most important **new environmental law**, following a guarantee in the 1980 Constitution that all Chileans have "the right to live in an environment free of pollution", is the Environmental Act of 1994, which has standardized procedures for assessing environmental damage, while encouraging public involvement by allowing citizens to bring charges against violators, even if they have not been directly affected by them. One successful application of this new law occurred in 1997, when the Chilean Supreme Court overturned a government-approved project involving the logging for woodchips of centuries-old, endangered forests of native *lenga*, a cherry-like beech found in Tierra del Fuego.

Forests under threat

Chile's precious **temperate rainforests** have been threatened for many years by intensive logging and the introduction of harmful foreign species, with large tracts razed in the free-for-all scramble to colonize remote areas. The worst damage occurred in the prewar years, but illegal clearance is still common today. The *alerce*, an evergreen with a life span of four thousand years, has been a target of international campaigning as it continues to be logged because of the high commercial value of its wood, despite a law passed in 1976 making it illegal to cut live *alerces*. Yet landowners burn the trees or strip their bark to kill them first, thus evading the hands of the law. Many thousands of hectares of *alerce* forest are wiped out in this manner every year.

Meanwhile in the central regions native trees have been wiped out to make space for the commercial planting of more profitable foreign species. In many areas the practice has left only islands of indigenous forest in an ocean of introduced eucalyptus and radiata pine. The result is genetic isolation of both flora and fauna, leaving many mammals with distinct ecological needs imprisoned in small pockets of native woodland. The few thin strips that connect such pockets are the only way for many species to maintain communication with the rest of their population. If these corridors are destroyed, countless endemic organisms face extinction.

Mining

In the north **mining** is a major cause of environmental concern. Chuquicamata, near Antofagasta, is the biggest open-pit copper mine in the world and it continues to grow. Now visible from space, the giant pit has effectively swallowed up the town that grew with it, as 600,000 tons of rock are dug up every day, spewing arsenic-rich dust into the air. Workers at the mine and their families have now been relocated from Chuquicamata to nearby Calama. The plume from the smelting works carries 200km to San Pedro de Atacama, a pre-colonial village in the east. The country's mines consume vast quantities of water, often contaminating it in the process. In tandem with agricultural irrigation, reckless water usage is taking its toll on wildlife, as animals find the search for drinking places increasingly difficult. Even the human population has been put out, relying in some northern villages on an ingenious invention that turns fog into drinking water.

Overexploitation of resources

Overexploitation of the land and sea has brought further problems. Incompetent or negligent farming, either through overgrazing or the clearing of vegetation, has resulted in extensive **desertification**, particularly in the north. Meanwhile, careless practices in the fishing industry are upsetting the fragile balance of Chile's **marine life**. A leaked government report shows that some fish stocks were depleted by as much as 96 percent between 1985 and 1993. On a global level, many believe human-induced climate change to be a leading cause of the **El Niño phenomenon**, which has badly damaged Chile's fisheries, agriculture and marine species (see box, p.492). Moreover, the large hole in the ozone layer over Antarctica has put many people, especially in Patagonia, on guard against the harmful ultraviolet rays that seep through it. Chile has been more effective than most Latin American countries in its opposition to the damage brought about by the excesses of unfettered capitalism, and awareness of the delicacy of the country's habitats and its unique species is growing. However, environmentalists continue to bemoan the lack of concerted pressure, claiming that many merely respond occasionally and emotionally to images churned out in the media rather than pushing consistently for action and reform.

THE EL NIÑO EFFECT

Nature's footnote to the end of the millennium, the **1997–98 El Niño** wreaked havoc with global climate patterns and brought chaos to the world. In parts of Chile, Peru and Ecuador, floods and landslides engulfed people and animals, houses, farms and factories, while torrents swept away bridges, roads and railways. Elsewhere, severe droughts scorched the earth, drying up forests and bushland and creating the tinderbox conditions that sparked off raging fires. Clouds of poisonous smoke billowed into the atmosphere, affecting seventy million people in Southeast Asia, while millions of others risked starvation following widespread crop failure. As the Pacific countries affected by El Niño picked up the pieces, conservative estimates of the cost of reparation put it at around US$20 billion.

In Chile, **flooding** was the worst it had been for a decade, as eighty thousand people were made homeless in June 1998 alone. The warm coastal water associated with El Niño drove fish stocks to cooler places, crippling the fishing industry and killing millions of marine animals. But while some watched their crops and livestock drown, the rains also filled irrigation basins that had been at a critically low level for years, and water surges saved the hydroelectric companies from having to ration their power output. In the Atacama Desert, freak rainfall woke up the barren soil, causing it to burst into blossom. A relatively mild El Niño in early 2002, meanwhile, meant that while the ski season was one of the best in the last ten years, torrential rains in central Chile left fifty thousand people homeless and killed nine. The last El Niño episode occurred in 2009, bringing with it an unusually cold and wet summer which affected Chile's busiest tourist season.

THE METEOROLOGY BEHIND THE MAYHEM

The El Niño phenomenon is no new thing and it occurs roughly every five years or so. Records document such events over four hundred years ago, but it was only in the 1960s that the Norwegian meteorologist Jacob Bjerknes identified the processes that lead to such an event. He saw that the El Niño (meaning "the Little Boy" or "the Christ Child", a name given by Peruvian fishermen to the body of warm water that would arrive around Christmas) was intimately connected to extremes in the so-called **Southern Oscillation**, a feature where atmospheric pressure between the eastern equatorial Pacific and the Indo-Australian areas behaves as a seesaw, one rising as the other falls.

In "normal" years easterly trade winds blow west across the Pacific, pushing warm surface water towards Indonesia, Australia and the Philippines, where the water becomes about 8°C warmer and about 50cm higher than on the other side of the ocean. In the east, the displacement of the sea allows cold, nutrient-rich water, known as the Humboldt or Peru Current, to swell up from the depths along the coast of South America, providing food for countless marine and bird species.

An El Niño event occurs when the trade winds fall off and the layer of warm water in the west laps back across the ocean, warming up the east Pacific and cooling the west. Consequently, air temperatures across the Pacific begin to even out, tipping the balance of the atmospheric pressure seesaw, which further reduces the strength of the trade winds. Thus the process is enhanced, as warm water continues to build up in the eastern Pacific, bringing with it abnormal amounts of rainfall to coastal South America, while completely starving other areas of precipitation. The warm water also forces the cold Humboldt Current and its microorganisms to deeper levels, effectively removing a vital link in the marine food chain, killing innumerable fish, sea birds and mammals. Meanwhile, the upset in the Southern Oscillation disturbs weather systems all around the world, resulting in severe and unexpected weather.

EL NIÑO AND GLOBAL WARMING

Since 1980 or so, El Niño-Southern Oscillation (ENSO) events seem to have become stronger, longer and more frequent, leading many to suggest that human activity, such as the warming of the earth's atmosphere through the **greenhouse effect**, could well be having an influence. If this is true, failure to cut emissions of greenhouse gases may in the end cost the lives and livelihoods of millions of people across the world, though some schools of thought suggest that perhaps the stronger El Niño events occur only during the initial stage of global warming and that they will become weaker as the ocean becomes warmer. More research is required to provide a definitive answer.

Chilean music: nueva canción

Chile has produced a wide range of music genres, from cueca to bolero, but none has been so important and influential as **Nueva Canción**, the "New Song" movement that developed in Chile in the 1960s, along with parallel movements in Argentina, Uruguay and also Cuba. A music rooted in the guitar traditions of the troubadour, the songs could be love lyric or chronicle, lament or call to action, and, as such, they have played a part in Latin America's political and cultural struggles. It was brought to international attention, above all, through the lyrical songs of Chilean theatre director and singer-songwriter Víctor Jara, who was murdered for his art by Pinochet's thugs during the 1973 coup d'état, while groups like Inti Illimani were forced into exile. In an extract taken from the *Rough Guide to World Music*, Jan Fairley looks at the history and legacy of this music of "guitar as gun".

Pity the singer…

Nueva canción as a movement spans a period of over thirty years, from the early 1960s, when its musicians became part of the political struggle to bring about change and reform in their own countries. As a result of their activities, many of their number were arrested or forced into exile by dictatorships which through murder, torture and disappearance wiped out so much of a generation. The sense of a movement grew as the musicians involved met one another at festivals in Cuba, Nicaragua, Peru, Mexico, Argentina and Brazil, visited each other's countries, and occasionally sang each other's songs. At the end of the 1990s, with the return to democracy on the continent, the singers continued to pursue their careers in different ways, while maintaining long-term friendships and exchanges.

The 1960s was a time of politics and idealism in South America – far more so than in Europe or North America. There was a stark challenge presented by the continent's obvious inequalities, its inherited power and wealth, its corrupt regimes, and by the denial of literacy and education to much of the population. It is within this context that *nueva canción* singers and writers must be understood. With voice and guitar, they composed songs of their own hopes and experiences in places where many of those involved in struggles for change regularly met and socialized.

It is a music that is now, in some ways, out of date, though its spirit, in keeping with the 1960s rhetoric of guitar as gun and song as bullet, is, in other ways, entirely appropriate to the current climate of global upheaval, given the Arab Spring and other protest movements around the world. These particular songs, though – poems written to be performed – are classic expressions of the years of hope and struggle for change, their beauty and truth later nurturing those suffering under dictatorship, and those forced into exile. They are still known by heart by audiences throughout the continent and exiled communities in Europe.

Nueva canción was an expression of politics in its widest sense. It was not "protest song" as such. The musicians involved were not card-carrying members of any international organization and were often independent of political parties – although in the early 1970s the Chilean musicians were closely linked with the Popular Unity government of Salvador Allende, the first socialist president and government to be legitimately elected through the ballot box.

What linked these and other musicians of the movement was an ethical stance – a commitment to improve conditions for the majority of people in Latin America. To that end they sang not only in concerts and clubs but in factories, in shanty towns, community centres and at political meetings and street demonstrations. People in protest the world over have joined in the Chilean street anthems *El Pueblo Unido Jamás Sera Vencido* (The People United Will Never Be Defeated) and *Venceremos* (We Will Win).

Yupanqui and Violeta Parra

The roots of the *nueva canción* movement lie in the work of two key figures, whose music bridged rural and urban life and culture in the 1940s and 1950s: the Argentine **Atahualpa Yupanqui** (1908–92) and the Chilean **Violeta Parra** (1917–67). Each had a passionate interest in his or her nation's rural musical traditions, which had both an Iberian and Amerindian sensibility. Their work was in some respects paralleled by the Cuban Carlos Puebla.

Atahualpa Yupanqui spent much of his early life travelling around Argentina, collecting popular songs from itinerant *payadores* (improvising poets, Chile's indigenous rappers) and folk singers in rural areas. He also wrote his own songs, and during a long career introduced a new integrity to Argentine folk music – and an assertive political outlook which ultimately forced him into exile in Paris.

Violeta Parra's career in Chile mirrored that of Yupanqui. She travelled extensively, singing with and collecting songs from old *payadores* and preserved and popularized them through radio broadcasts and records. She also composed new material based on these rural song traditions, creating a model and repertoire for what became *nueva canción*. Her songs celebrated the rural and regional, the music of the peasant, the land-worker and the marginalized migrant.

Musically, Parra was also significant in her popularization of **Andean or Amerindian instruments** – the armadillo-shelled *charango*, the *quena* (bamboo flute) and panpipes – and in her enthusiasm for the **French chanson** tradition. She spent time in Paris in the 1960s with her children Angel and Isabel, where they met Yupanqui, Edith Piaf and the flautist Gilbert Favre, who was to found the influential Andean band, Los Jaivas, and with whom Violeta fell in love. Returning to Buenos Aires, she performed in a tent in the district of La Reina, which came to be called the Carpa de La Reina (The Queen's Tent). However, with a long history of depression, she committed suicide in 1967.

Parra left behind a legacy of exquisite songs, many of them with a wry sense of humour, including the unparalleled *Gracias a la Vida* (Thanks to Life), later covered by Joan Baez and a host of others. Even her love songs seem informed by an awareness of poverty and injustice, while direct pieces like *Qué dirá el Santo Padre?* (What will the Sainted Pope Say?) highlighted the Church's responsibility to take action. As Parra wrote (in the form she often used in her songs) in her autobiography:

I sing to the Chilean people
if I have something to say
I don't take up the guitar
to win applause
I sing of the difference there is
between what is certain
and what is false
otherwise I don't sing.

The movement takes off

Nueva canción emerged as a real force in the mid-1960s, when various governments on the continent were trying to effect democratic social change. The search for a Latin

American cultural identity became a spontaneous part of this wider struggle for self-determination, and music was a part of the process.

The first crystallization of a *nueva canción* ideal in Chile emerged with the opening of a crucial new folk club. This was and is the legendary crucible of *nueva canción*, the **Peña de los Parra**, which **Angel and Isabel Parra**, inspired by the Paris *chanson* nightclubs, opened in downtown Santiago in 1965. Among the regular singer-songwriters who performed here were Víctor Jara and Patricio Manns. Their audiences, in the politically charged and optimistic period prior to the election of Allende's government, were enthusiastic activists and fellow musicians.

Víctor Jara

The great singer-songwriter and theatre director **Víctor Jara** took *nueva canción* onto a world stage. His songs, and his life, continue to reverberate, and he has been recorded by rock singers like Sting, Bruce Springsteen, Peter Gabriel and Jackson Brown, and (memorably) by the British singer Robert Wyatt. All have been moved by Jara's story and inspired by his example.

Jara was born into a rural family who came to live in a shanty town on the barren outskirts of Santiago when Víctor's father died; he was just 11. His mother sang as a *cantora* for births, marriages and deaths, keeping her family alive by running a food stall in the main Santiago market. It was from his mother and her work that Jara gained his intuitive knowledge of Chilean guitar and singing styles.

He began performing his songs in the early 1960s and from the beginning caused a furore. During the government of Eduardo Frei, for example, his playful version of a traditional piece, *La Beata* – a send-up of the desires of a nun – was banned, as was his accusatory *Preguntas por Puerto Montt* (Questions for Puerto Montt), which accused the minister of the interior of the massacre of poor landless peasants in the south of Chile. Working with Isabel Parra and the group **Huamari**, Jara went on to create a sequence of songs called *La Población*, based on the history and life of Santiago's shanty-town communities. His great gift was a deceptively simple and direct style applied to whatever he did.

One of his best-loved songs, *Te recuerdo Amanda* (I remember you, Amanda), is a good example of the simplicity of his craft. A hauntingly understated love song, it tells the story of a girl who goes to meet her man, Manuel, at the factory gates; he never appears because of an "accident", and Amanda waits in vain. In many of his songs, Jara subtly interwove allusions to his own life with the experiences of other ordinary people – Amanda and Manuel were the names of his parents.

Jara's influence was immense, both on *nueva canción* singers and the Andean-oriented groups like **Inti Illimani** and **Quilapayún** (see opposite), whom he worked with often, encouraging them to forge their own new performance styles. Enormously popular and fun-loving, he was nevertheless clear about his role as a singer: "The authentic revolutionary should be behind the guitar, so that the guitar becomes an instrument of struggle, so that it can also shoot like a gun." As he sang in 1972 in his song *Manifiesto*, a tender serenade which with hindsight has been seen as his testimony, "I don't sing just for love of singing, but for the statements made by my guitar, honest, its heart of earth, like the dove it goes flying…Song sung by a man who will die singing, truthfully singing his song."

Like many Chilean musicians, Jara was deeply involved with the Unidad Popular government of Salvador Allende who, in 1970, following his election, had appeared on an open-air stage in Santiago surrounded by musicians under a banner saying "There can be no revolution without song". Three years later, on September 11, 1973 – along with hundreds of others who had legitimately supported the government – Jara was arrested by the military and taken to the same downtown stadium in which he had won the First Festival of New Chilean Song in 1969. Tortured, his hands and wrists broken, his body was found with five others, riddled with machine-gun bullets,

PLEGARIA AUN LABRADOR (PRAYER TO A LABOURER)

Stand up and look at the mountain
From where the wind comes, the sun and the water
You who direct the courses of the rivers
You who have sown the flight of your soul
Stand up and look at your hands
So as to grow
Clasp your brother's, in your own
Together we will move united by blood
Today is the time that can become tomorrow

Deliver us from the one who dominates us
through misery
Bring to us your reign of justice and equality

Blow like the wind the flower of the canyon
Clean like fire the barrel of my gun
Let your will at last come about here on earth
Give to us your strength and valour so as to fight
Blow like the wind the flower of the canyon
Clean like fire the barrel of my gun

Stand up and look at your hands
So as to grow
Clasp your brother's, in your own
Together we will move united by blood
Now and in the hour of our death
Amen.

Víctor Jara

dumped alongside a wall of the Metropolitan Cemetery; his face was later recognized among a pile of unidentified bodies in one of the Santiago mortuaries by a worker. He was just 35.

DISCOGRAPHY

Nueva canción has had a raw deal on **CD** – it peaked in the decades before shiny discs – and for many classics, you'll need to search second hand stores for vinyl. If you travel to Chile, you can also obtain **songbooks** for the music of Víctor Jara (the Fundación Víctor Jara publishes his complete works), while most other songs of the period are featured in Clásicos de la Música Popular Chilena Vol 11 1960–1973 (Ediciones Universidad Católica de Chile).

Compilations

Music of the Andes Despite the title, this is essentially a nueva canción disc, with key Chilean groups Inti Illimani, Quilapayún and Illapu to the fore. There is also an instrumental recording of Tinku attributed to Víctor Jara.

Ilapu

With a track record stretching back over 25 years, and a big following in Chile, this band play's Andean instruments – panpipes, quenas and charangos – along with saxophones, electric bass and Caribbean percussion. Their music is rooted in the north of the country where most of the band hails from.

Sereno This enjoyable collection gives a pretty good idea of what Illapu have got up to over the years and includes strongly folkloric material, as well as dance pieces influenced by salsa, romantic ballads and the earlier styles of vocal harmony.

Inti Illimani

The foremost Chilean "new song" group, who began as students in 1967, bringing the Andean sound to Europe through their thousands of concerts in exile, and taking European influences back home again in the late 1980s. The original band, together for thirty years, featured the glorious-voiced José Séves.

Lejan'a The focus is on Andean themes in this celebration of their thirtieth anniversary and their original inspiration.

Arriesgaré la piel A celebration of the music the Intis grew up with, from creole-style tunes to Chilean cuecas, most lyrics by Patricio Manns with music by Salinas. This was the final album to be made with the core of the original band before Séves left.

Grandes Exitos A compilation of seventeen songs and instrumental pieces taken from the band's thirty-year history.

Jara left behind a song composed during the final hours of his life, written down and remembered by those who were with him at the end, called as a poem of testimony *Estadio Chile* (Chile Stadium). It was later set a cappella to music as *Ay canto, que mal me sales*, by his friend and colleague Isabel Parra.

Exiles and Andean sounds

After Pinochet's coup d'état anything remotely associated with the Allende government and its values came under censorship, including books and records, whose possession could be cause for arrest. The junta issued warnings to musicians and folklorists that it would be unwise for them to play *nueva canción*, or indeed any of the Andean instruments associated with its sound – *charangos*, panpipes and *quenas*.

It was not exactly a ban but it was menacing enough to force the scene well underground – and abroad, where many Chilean musicians lived out the junta years in exile. Their numbers included the groups Inti Illimani and Quilapayún and later Illapu (see p.495), Sergio Ortega, Patricio Manns, Isabel and Angel Parra, and Patricio Castillo. They were not the only Latin Americans forced from their country. Other musician exiles of the 1970s included Brazilian MPB singers Chico Buarque, Caetano Veloso and Gilberto Gil; Uruguay's *nueva canción* singer Daniel Viglietti; and Argentina's Mercedes Sosa.

Quilapayún
This key Chilean new-song group worked closely in their early years with Víctor Jara and in 1973 – the year of the coup – they split into multiple groups in order to get their message across on as many stages as possible. They co-authored, with Sergio Ortega, the street anthem *El Pueblo Unido Jamás Sera Vencido* (the People United Will Never Be Defeated). Although they disbanded in the late 1990s, their influence lives on.
Santa María de Iquique Chilean composer Luis Advis's ground-breaking Cantata, composed for Quilapayún, tells the emblematic and heroic tale of the murder of unarmed nitrate workers and their families in 1907.

Víctor Jara
The leading singer-songwriter of his generation, Víctor Jara was murdered in his prime by Pinochet's forces in September 1973. His legacy is an extraordinary songbook, which can be heard in his original versions, as well as a host of Latin and western covers.
Manifesto Reissued to mark the 25th anniversary of his death, this is a key disc of *nueva canción*, with *Te recuerdo Amanda*, *Canto libre*, *La Plegaria a un Labrador* and *Ay canto*, the final poem written in the Estadio Chile, before his death. Includes Spanish lyrics and English translations.
Vientos del Pueblo A generous 22-song compilation that includes most of the Jara milestones, including *Te recuerdo Amanda* and *Preguntas por Puerto Montt*, plus the wonderful revolutionary romp of *A Cochabamba me Voy*. Quilapayún provide backing on half the album.
Víctor Jara Complete This four-CD box is the definitive Jara, featuring material from eight original LPs. Plane has also released an excellent single-disc selection of highlights.
La Población Classic Jara: a project involving other musicians, but including most of all the lives and experiences of those celebrated here, who lived in various shanty towns (*poblaciones*) including the one where Jara himself grew up.

Violeta Parra
One of South America's most significant folklorists and composers, Violeta Parra collected fragments of folklore from singers, teaching them to the next generation and influencing them with her own excellent compositions. Parra's songs have also been superbly recorded by Argentinian Mercedes Sosa.
Canto a mi América An excellent introduction to Parra's seminal songs.
Las Ultimas Composiciones A reissue of Parra's 1965 release which turned out to be her last as well as latest songs ("*Ultimas*" means both in Spanish).

In Chile, the first acts of musical defiance took place behind church walls, where a group of musicians who called themselves **Barroco Andino** started to play baroque music with Andean instruments within months of the coup.

It was a brave act, for the use of Andean or Amerindian instruments and culture was instinctively linked with the *nueva canción* movement. Chilean groups like **Quilapayún** and **Inti Illimani** wore the traditional ponchos of the peasant and played Andean instruments such as panpipes, bamboo flutes and the *charango*, and the maracas and shakers of Central America and the Caribbean. That these were the instruments of the communities who had managed somehow to survive slavery, resist colonialism and its aftermath had a powerful symbolism. Both the "*los Intis*" and "*los Quilas*", as they became familiarly known, worked closely with Víctor Jara and also with popular classical composers Sergio Ortega and Luis Advis.

European exile

In 1973 both groups travelled to Europe as official cultural ambassadors of the Allende government, actively seeking support from governments in Europe at a time when the country was more or less besieged economically by a North American blockade, its economy being undermined by CIA activity. On September 11 when General Pinochet led the coup d'état in which Salvador Allende died, the Intis were in Italy and the Quilas in France. For the Intis, the tour ("the longest in history", as Intis member Jorge Coulon jokes) turned into a fifteen-year-and-fifty-four-day European exile for the group, an exile which put *nueva canción* and Amerindian music firmly on Europe's agenda of Latin American music.

The groups were the heart and soul of a worldwide Chilean (and Latin American) solidarity movement, performing almost daily for the first ten years. Both also recorded albums of new songs, the Intis influenced by their many years in Italy, creating some beautiful songs of exile, including the seminal song *Vuelvo*, with key singer-songwriter and musician **Patricio Manns**.

The impact of their high-profile campaigning against the military meant that the Intis were turned back on the airport tarmac long after politicians and trade union leaders were repatriated. They eventually returned on September 18, 1988, Chile's National Day, the day of one of the biggest meetings of supporters of the "No" vote to the plebiscite called by Pinochet to determine whether he should stay in office. Going straight from the airport to sing on a huge open-air stage and to dance the traditional *cueca* (Chile's National Day dance), the group's homecoming was an emotional and timely one. Though their line-up has somewhat changed over the years, the two groups are still going strong today: they've joined forces as Inti+Quila though various collaborative efforts over the last few years, including a tour of South America and Europe and a release of a CD and DVD of their joint concerts.

The Andean instruments and rhythms used by Quilapayún (who disbanded in the 1980s) and Inti Illimani have been skilfully used by many other groups whose music is equally interesting – groups like **Illapu**, who remained popular throughout the 1980s (with a number of years in forced exile) and 1990s, and who released their most recent album, *Vivir Es Mucho Más*, in 2006.

The future and legacy

Times have changed in Chile and in Latin America generally, with revolutionary governments no longer in power, democracy restored after dictatorships, and even Pinochet dead and buried. The *nueva canción* movement, tied to an era of ideals and struggle, and then the brutal years of survival under dictatorship, would seem to have lost its relevance.

Its musicians have moved on to more individual concerns in their (always poetic) songwriting. But the *nueva canción* form, the inspiration of the song as message, and the rediscovery of Andean music and instruments, continues to have resonance and influence. The more recent generation of singers inspired by the history of "new song" includes **Carlos Varela** in Cuba, **Fernando Delgadillo** in Mexico, El Salvador's **Cutumay Camones**, Nicaragua's **Duo Guardabarranco** and the Bolivian singer **Emma Junaro**.

And there will be others. For Latin America, *nueva canción* is not only music but history. As the Cuban press has said of the songs of Silvio Rodriguez: "We have here the great epic poems of our days." Or as the Dominican Republic's merengue superstar Juan Luis Guerra, put it, "They are the master songwriters – they have influenced everyone."

Books

Unfortunately, a number of the best and most evocative books written on Chile have long been out of print, but we include some of them – mainly travel narratives or general accounts – below (marked by o/p in the parentheses after the title), as they can often be found in public libraries or on the internet. Modern publications are inevitably dominated by analyses and testimonies of the Pinochet years, much of which makes compelling reading. There are relatively few up-to-date general histories of Chile in English, with those available focusing more on the academic market than the general reader. Chilean fiction, meanwhile, is not very widely translated into English, with the exception of a handful of the country's more famous authors. Its poetry, or more specifically the poetry of its famous Nobel laureate Pablo Neruda, has been translated into many languages and is widely available abroad.

TRAVEL: GENERAL INTRODUCTIONS

Stephen Clissold *Chilean Scrapbook* (o/p). Beautifully and evocatively written, taking you from the top to the bottom of the country via a mixture of history, legend and anecdote.
Augustin Edwards *My Native Land* (o/p). Absorbing and vivid reflections on Chile's geography, history, folklore and

literature; particularly strong on landscape descriptions.
Benjamin Subercaseaux *Chile: A Geographic Extravaganza* (o/p). This seductive, poetic meander through Chile's "mad geography" is still one of the most enjoyable general introductions to the country, if a little dated.

TRAVEL: NINETEENTH- AND EARLY TWENTIETH-CENTURY

John Arons and Claudio Vita-Finzi *The Useless Land* (o/p). Four Cambridge geography students set out to explore the Atacama Desert in 1958 and relate their adventures along the way in this highly readable book.
Charles Darwin *Voyage of the Beagle*. This eminently readable (abridged) book contains some superb, evocative descriptions of nineteenth-century Chile, from Tierra del Fuego right up to Iquique.
Maria Graham *Journal of a Residence in Chile During the Year 1822* (o/p). *The* classic nineteenth-century travel narrative on Chile, written by a spirited, perceptive and amusing British woman.
Che Guevara *The Motorcycle Diaries*. Comic, picaresque narrative taken from the diaries of the future revolutionary as he and his friend, both just out of medical school, travelled around South America – including a large chunk of Chile – by motorbike.
Auguste Guinnard *Three Years Slavery Among the*

Patagonians. This is the account of Guinnard's capture and often brutal enslavement by Tehuelche Indians at war with the European colonizers in 1859, his surprising enlightenment and eventual escape.
Bea Howe *Child in Chile* (o/p). A charming description of the author's childhood in Valparaíso in the early 1900s, where her family formed part of the burgeoning British business community.
W.H. Hudson *Idle Days in Patagonia*. Drawn by the variety of fauna and the remarkable birdlife, the novelist and naturalist W.H. Hudson travelled to Patagonia at the tail-end of the nineteenth century and wrote this series of charming, gentle observations.
George Musters *At Home with the Patagonians*. Remarkable account of time spent living with the Tehuelche Indians at the end of the nineteenth century that explodes the myth of the "noble savage" and provides a historically important picture of their vanishing way of life.

TRAVEL: MODERN AND CONTEMPORARY

Tim Burford *Chile and Argentina: The Bradt Trekking Guide*. Fantastically detailed account of how to access and climb the Andes from Atacama to Tierra del Fuego. Plenty of trail maps and practical advice.

★ **Bruce Chatwin** *In Patagonia*. The cult travel book that single-handedly enshrined Patagonia as the ultimate edge-of-the-world destination. Witty and captivating, this is essential reading for visitors to Patagonia, though unfortunately concentrates far more on the Argentine side.

Ariel Dorfman *Desert Memories*. Vivid depiction of desert life gleaned from Dorfman's travels through Chile's Norte Grande, which weaves past and present, memoir and meditation, history and family lore to provide an engaging chronicle of modern Chile.

Toby Green *Saddled with Darwin*. One hundred and sixty-five years after Charles Darwin embarked on the journey that produced the most radical theory of modern times, Green set out to retrace his footsteps on horseback. The result is an epic journey across six countries, including Chile, which paints an incisive portrait of change across the southern section of the continent.

Alistair Horne *Small Earthquake in Chile*. Wry description of a visit to Chile during the turbulent months leading up to Pinochet's military coup, written by a British journalist.

Brian Keenan and **John McCarthy** *Between Extremes: A Journey Beyond Imagination*. Five years after Keenan and McCarthy were released from captivity in Beirut, the pair set off to fulfil a dream they'd shared as hostages to journey

down the spine of Chile, from Arica to Tierra del Fuego. This account of their journey, told in alternating narratives, is as much a homage to their friendship as it is a description of the landscapes and people of Chile.

John Pilkington *An Englishman in Patagonia* (o/p). A fun-to-read and sympathetic portrayal of Patagonia and its people. Includes some wonderful black-and-white photographs.

Rosie Swale *Back to Cape Horn* (o/p). An extraordinary account of the author's epic 409-day journey on horseback from the Atacama Desert down to Cape Horn – which she'd last visited while sailing around the world ten years previously in 1972.

★ **Patrick Symmes** *Chasing Che*. The author undertakes an epic motorbike trip through South America – including hundreds of miles of Chile – following the route taken by a young Che Guevara back in 1952, as chronicled in *The Motorcycle Diaries* (see below). A great mix of biography, history, politics and travel anecdotes, this is a sharply written and highly entertaining read.

HISTORY, POLITICS AND SOCIETY: GENERAL

Leslie Bethell (ed) *Chile Since Independence*. Made up of four chapters taken from the *Cambridge History of Latin American History*, this is rather dry in parts, but rigorous, comprehensive and clear.

Nick Caistor *In Focus: Chile*. Brief, potted introduction to Chile's history, politics and society, highlighting the social problems bequeathed by Pinochet's economic model.

★ **Simon Collier and William Sater** *A History of Chile, 1801–1994*. Probably the best single-volume history of Chile from independence to the 1990s; thoroughly academic but enlivened by colourful detail along with the authors' clear fondness for the country and its people.

John Hickman *News from the End of the Earth: A Portrait of Chile*. Written by a former British ambassador to Chile, this concise and highly readable book makes a good (if conservative) introduction to Chile's history, taking you from the conquest to the 1990s in some 250 pages.

Brian Loveman *Chile: The Legacy of Hispanic Capitalism*. Solid analysis of Chile's history from the arrival of the Spanish in the 1540s to the 1973 military coup.

Sergio Villalobos *A Short History of Chile*. Clear, concise and sensible outline of Chile's history, from pre-Columbian cultures through to the past decade, aimed at the general reader with no prior knowledge of the subject. Available in Santiago.

HISTORY, POLITICS AND SOCIETY: THE PINOCHET YEARS

★ **Andy Beckett** *Pinochet in Piccadilly: Britain and Chile's Hidden History*. A fascinating political travelogue that connects the past to the present as it explores the relationship between the two nations.

Sheila Cassidy *Audacity to Believe* (o/p). Distressing account of the imprisonment and horrific torture of a British doctor (the author) after she'd treated a wounded anti-Pinochet activist.

★ **Pamela Constable and Arturo Valenzuela** *A Nation of Enemies*. Written during the mid- to late 1980s, this is a superb look at the terror of everyday life in Chile at that time and the state apparatus used to annihilate free thinking and initiative. Essential reading if you want to understand contemporary Chile.

Marc Cooper *Pinochet and Me: A Chilean Anti-Memoir*. First-hand account of life under Pinochet in the early days of the coup, written by a young American who served as Allende's translator and barely escaped the death squads.

Followed up by accounts of his periodic visits to Chile over the next quarter century.

John Dinges *The Condor Years: How Pinochet and His Allies Brought Terror to Three Continents*. Exhaustively researched book that examines the creation and use of international hit squads by the Pinochet regime. The chilling accounts of multinational agreements to execute "enemies of the state" are recreated by author Dinges, an internationally recognized investigative reporter and professor at Columbia University.

Paul Drake (ed) *The Struggle for Democracy in Chile*. Excellent collection of ten essays examining the gradual breakdown of the military government's authority. The pieces, which offer contrasting views in support of and opposition to the regime, were written in 1988, during the months around the plebiscite.

Diana Kay *Chileans in Exile: Private Struggles, Public Lives*. Although written in a somewhat dry, academic style, this is nonetheless a fascinating study of Chilean exiles in

Scotland, with a strong focus on women. The author looks at their attempts to reconstruct their lives, their sense of dislocation, and the impact exile has had on their attitude to politics, marriage and the home.

Hugh O'Shaughnessy *Pinochet: The Politics of Torture*. Covering everything from the arrest of Pinochet in London to Pinochet's secret plans to distribute sarin nerve gas to Chilean consulates abroad, this book provides an overview of the most influential man in Chilean politics from 1973 to 1998.

Patricia Politzer *Fear in Chile, Lives Under Pinochet*. Award-winning account of the lives of Chileans during the dictatorship, and another insight into the repressive apparatus used to subdue Chileans.

Grino Rojo and John J Hasset (ed) *Chile, Dictatorship and*

the Struggle for Democracy. A slim, accessible volume containing four essays written in the months approaching the 1988 plebiscite, in which the country would vote to reject or continue with military rule. Contains contrasting analyses of the impact of the dictatorship on the country and its people.

Jacobo Timerman *Chile: Death in the South* (o/p). Reflections on the Pinochet years by an Argentine journalist, written thirteen years into the military regime. Particularly compelling are the short personal testimonies of torture victims that intersperse the narrative.

Thomas Wright and Rody Oñate *Flight from Chile: Voices of Exile*. Detailed and affecting account of the exodus after the 1973 coup, when over 200,000 Chileans fled their homeland.

SPECIAL-INTEREST STUDIES

George McBride *Chile: Land and Society* (o/p). A compelling and exhaustively researched examination of the impact of the hacienda system on Chilean society, and the relationship (up to the mid-twentieth century) between landowners and peasants.

Colin McEwan, Luis Borrero and Alfredo Prieto (eds) *Patagonia: Natural History, Prehistory and Ethnography at the Uttermost End of the Earth*. Brilliant account of the "human adaptation, survival and eventual extinction" of the native peoples of Patagonia, accompanied by dozens of haunting black-and-white photographs.

★ **Nick Reding** *The Last Cowboys at the End of the World:*

The Story of the Gauchos of Patagonia. A brutally honest and at times brutal look at the end of the gaucho era in Patagonia. Excellent exploration of how in the mid-1990s the gaucho culture crashed headlong into the advance of modern society.

William Sater *The Heroic Image in Chile* (o/p). Fascinating, scholarly look at the reasons behind the near- deification of Arturo Prat, the naval officer who died futilely in battle in 1879, described by the author as "a secular saint".

Richard W Slatta *Cowboys of the Americas*. Exhaustively researched, highly entertaining and lavishly illustrated history of the cowboy cultures of the Americas, including detailed treatment of the Chilean *huaso*.

CHILEAN WOMEN

Marjorie Agosin (ed) *Scraps of Life: Chilean Arpilleras: Chilean Women and the Pinochet Dictatorship*. A sensitive portrayal of the women of Santiago's shanty towns who, during the dictatorship, scraped a living by sewing scraps of material together to make wall hangings, known as *arpilleras*, depicting scenes of violence and repression. The *arpilleras* became a symbol of their protest, and were later exhibited around the world.

Jo Fisher *Out of the Shadows*. Penetrating analysis of the emergence of the women's movement in Latin America,

with a couple of chapters devoted to Chile.

Elizabeth Jelin (ed) *Women and Social Change in Latin America*. A series of intelligent essays examining the ways women's organizations have acted as mobilizing forces for social and political change in Latin America.

Alicia Partnoy (ed) *You Can't Drown the Fire: Latin American Women Writing in Exile*. Excellent anthology bringing together a mixture of short stories, poems and essays by exiled Latin American women, including Veronica de Negri, Cecila Vicuña, Marjorie Agosin and Isabel Morel Letelier from Chile.

FICTION

Marjorie Agosin (ed) *Landscapes of a New Land: Short Fiction by Latin American Women*. This anthology includes four short stories by Chilean women authors, including the acclaimed Marta Brunet (1901–67) and María Luisa Bombal (1910–80). Overall, the book creates a poetic, at times haunting, evocation of female life in a patriarchal world. Also edited by Agosin, *Secret Weavers: Stories of the Fantastic by Women of Argentina and Chile* (o/p) is a spellbinding collection of short stories interwoven with themes of magic, allegory, legend and fantasy.

Isabel Allende *The House of the Spirits*. This baroque, fantastical and best-selling novel by the niece of Salvador

Allende, chronicles the fortunes of several generations of a rich, landowning family in an unnamed but thinly disguised Chile, culminating with a brutal military coup and the murder of the president.

★ **Isabel Allende** *Of Love and Shadows*. Set against a background of disappearances and dictatorship, including a fictional account of the real-life discovery of the bodies of fifteen executed workers in a Central Valley mine.

★ **José Donoso** *Curfew*. Gripping novel about an exiled folk singer's return to Santiago during the military dictatorship, by one of Chile's most outstanding twentieth-century writers. Other works by Donoso translated into

English include *Hell Has No Limits*, about the strange existence of a transvestite and his daughter in a Central Valley brothel, and *The Obscene Bird of Night*, a dislocated, fragmented novel narrated by a deaf-mute old man as he retreats into madness.

Ariel Dorfman *Hard Rain*. This complicated, thought-provoking novel is both an examination of the role of the writer in a revolutionary society, and a celebration of the "Chilean road to socialism" – not an easy read, but one that repays the effort. Dorfman later became internationally famous for his play *Death and the Maiden*, made into a film by Roman Polanski. Dorfman has also written an account of the effort to prosecute Pinochet in *Exorcising Terror: The Incredible Unending Trial of Augusto Pinochet*.

Alberto Fuguet *Bad Vibes* (o/p). Two weeks in September 1980 as lived by a mixed-up Santiago rich kid. A sort of Chilean *Catcher In the Rye* set against the tensions of the military regime.

Luis Sepúlveda *The Name of a Bullfighter*. Fast-paced, rather macho thriller set in Hamburg, Santiago and Tierra del Fuego, by one of Chile's leading young novelists.

Antonio Skármeta *The Postman*, formerly *Burning Patience*. Funny and poignant novel about a postman who delivers mail to the great poet Pablo Neruda. Neruda, in turn, helps him seduce the local beauty with the help of a few metaphors. It was also made into a successful film, *Il Postino*, with the action relocated to Capri. Also by Skármeta, *I Dreamt the Snow Was Burning* is a tense, dark novel evoking the suspicion and fear that permeated everyday life in the months surrounding the military coup, while *Watch Where the Wolf is Going* (Readers International) is a collection of short stories, some of them set in Chile.

POETRY

Vicente Huidobro *The Selected Poetry of Vicente Huidobro*. Intellectual, experimental and dynamic works by an early twentieth-century poet, highly acclaimed in his time (1893–1948) but often overlooked today.

Gabriela Mistral *Selected Poems*. Mistral is far less widely translated than her fellow Nobel laureate, Neruda, but this collection serves as an adequate English-language introduction to her quietly passionate and bittersweet poetry, much of it inspired by the landscape of the Elqui Valley.

Pablo Neruda *Twenty Love Poems and a Song of Despair; Canto General; Captain's Verses*. The doyen of Chilean poetry seems to be one of those poets people love or hate – his work is extravagantly lyrical, frequently verbose, but often very tender, particularly his love poetry. Neruda has been translated into many languages, and is widely available.

Nicanor Parra *Emergency Poems*. Both a physicist and poet, Parra pioneered the "anti-poem" in Chile during the 1980s: bald, un-lyrical, often satirical prose poems. A stimulating read.

BIOGRAPHY AND MEMOIRS

Fernando Alegria *Allende: A Novel*. Basically a biography, with fictional dialogue, of Salvador Allende, written by his former cultural attaché, who was busy researching the book while the president died in the coup. Also of note by Alegria is *The Chilean Spring*, a fictional diary of a young photographer coming to terms with the coup in Santiago.

Isabel Allende *My Invented Country – A Nostalgic Journey Through Chile*. A memoir that is an enthralling mix of fiction and biography and which describes her life in Chile up until the assassination of her uncle, president Salvador Allende. She provides a very personal view of her homeland and exhaustively examines the country, its terrain, people, customs and language.

Ariel Dorfman *Heading South, Looking North*. Memoir of one of Chile's most famous writers, in which he reflects on themes such as language, identity, guilt and politics. Intelligent and illuminating, with some interesting thoughts on the causes of the Unidad Popular's failures.

★ **Joan Jara** *Victor: An Unfinished Song* (o/p). Poignant memoir written by the British wife of the famous Chilean folksinger Víctor Jara, describing their life together, the *nueva canción* movement (see p.493) and their optimism for Allende's new Chile. The final part, detailing Jara's imprisonment, torture and execution in Santiago's football stadium, is almost unbearably moving.

R.L. Mégroz *The Real Robinson Crusoe* (o/p). Colourful biography of Alexander Selkirk, who spent four years and four months marooned on one of the Juan Fernández Islands, inspiring Daniel Defoe to write *The Adventures of Robinson Crusoe*.

Luis Muñoz *Being Luis*. Account of a childhood spent growing up in 1960s–70s Chile that reflects recent history and leads to Muñoz's development as a left-wing activist, his arrest and torture by the military regime and eventual exile to England.

Pablo Neruda *Memoirs*. Though his occasional displays of vanity and compulsive name-dropping can be irritating, there's no doubt that this is an extraordinary man with a fascinating life. The book also serves as a useful outline of Chile's political movements from the 1930s to the 1970s.

PACIFIC ISLANDS

Paul Bahn and John Flenley *Easter Island, Earth Island* (o/p). Richly illustrated with glossy photographs, this scholarly but accessible book provides an up-to-date and comprehensive introduction to the island's history and archeology. Interestingly, it also suggests that Easter Island could be a microcosm representing a global dilemma – that of a land so despoiled by man that it could no longer support its civilization.

Sebastian Englert *Island at the Centre of the World* (o/p). Based on a series of lectures broadcast to the Chilean Navy serving in Antarctica, this is perhaps the clearest and most accessible (though now somewhat dated) introduction to Easter Island, written by a genial German priest who lived there for 35 years from 1935.

Thor Heyerdahl *Aku Aku* (o/p). This account of Heyerdahl's famous expedition to Easter Island in 1955 makes a cracking read, with an acute sense of adventure and mystery. Dubious as the author's archeological theories are, it's hard not to get swept along by his enthusiasm. In contrast, his *Reports of the Norwegian Archeological Expedition to Easter Island and the East Pacific* is a rigorous and respected documentation of the expedition's findings.

Alfred Métraux *Easter Island* (o/p). Key study of Easter Island's traditions, beliefs and customs by a Belgian anthropologist, based on exhaustive research carried out in the 1930s. Métraux's *The Ethnology of Easter Island*, published in periodical format.

Catherine and Michel Orliac *The Silent Gods: Mysteries of Easter Island* (o/p). Pocket-sized paperback, densely packed with colour illustrations and surprisingly detailed background on the island's explorers, statues, myths and traditions.

★ **Katherine Routledge** *The Mystery of Easter Island*. Recently back in print, this compelling book chronicles one of the earliest archeological expeditions to the island, led by the author in 1914. Routledge interviewed many elderly islanders and recounts their oral testimonies as well as the discoveries of her excavations.

★ **Diana Souhami** *Selkirk's Island*. This gripping account of the misadventures of Alexander Selkirk – the real life Robinson Crusoe, who spent four years marooned on a Chilean Pacific island – includes some vivid and evocative descriptions of what's now known as Isla Robinson Crusoe. Deservedly won the Whitbread Biography Award in 2001.

Ralph Lee Woodward *Robinson Crusoe's Island* (o/p). There's a good deal more drama to the Juan Fernández islands' history than the famous four-year marooning of Alexander Selkirk, all of it enthusiastically retold in this lively book.

FLORA AND FAUNA

Sharon R. Chester *Birds of Chile*. First-rate, easy-to-carry guide with over 300 colour illustrations of the birds of mainland Chile.

Claudio Donoso Zegers *Chilean Trees Identification Guide/ Arboles Nativos de Chile*. Handy pocket guide to Chile's main native trees, with commentary in Spanish and English. Produced for Conaf (Chile's national parks administration), and part of a series that includes *Chilean Bushes*, *Chilean Climber Plants* and *Chilean Terrestrial Mammals*. It may be available in Conaf's information office in Santiago.

Chilean Spanish

To get by in Chile, it's very helpful to equip yourself with a bit of basic Spanish. It's not a difficult language to pick up and there are numerous books, cassettes and CD-ROMs on the market, teaching to various levels – *Teach Yourself Latin American Spanish* is a very good book-cassette package for getting started, while for an old-fashioned, rigorous textbook, nothing beats H. Ramsden's *An Essential Course in Modern Spanish*, published in the UK by Nelson.

The snag is that Chilean Spanish does not conform to what you learn in the classroom or hear on a cassette, and even competent Spanish-speakers will find it takes a bit of getting used to. The first thing to contend with is the dizzying **speed** with which most Chileans speak; another is **pronunciation**, especially the habitual dropping of many consonants. In particular, "s" is frequently dropped from the end or middle of a word, so *dos* becomes *do*, *gracias* becomes *gracia*, and *fósforos* (matches) becomes *fohforo*. "D" has a habit of disappearing from past participles, so *comprado* is *comprao*, while the "gua" sound is commonly reduced to *wa*, making the city of Rancagua *Rancawa*. The *–as* ending of the second person singular of verbs (*estás*, *viajas*, and so on) is transformed into *–ai*: hence *¿cómo estás?* usually comes out as "comehtai"; the classic *"¿cachai?"* ("get it?") is the second person singular form of the slang verb *cachar*, meaning to understand.

Another way in which Chilean differs from classic Castilian Spanish is its borrowing of words from indigenous languages, mainly Quechua, Aymara and Mapuche, but also from German (*kuchen*, for cake) and even English ("plumber" in Chile is inexplicably *el gasfiter*). Adding to the confusion is a widespread use of **slang** and **idiom**, much of which is unique to Chile. None of this, however, should put you off attempting to speak Spanish in Chile – Chileans will really appreciate your efforts, and even faltering beginners will be complimented on their language skills.

Pronunciation

The rules of **pronunciation** are pretty straightforward and, once you get to know them, strictly observed. Unless there's an accent, words ending in d, l, r, and z are **stressed** on the last syllable, all others on the second last. All **vowels** are pure and short.

A somewhere between the "a" sound of back and that of father.

E as in get.

I as in police.

O as in hot.

U as in rule.

C is soft before E and I, hard otherwise: *cerca* is pronounced "serka".

G works the same way, a slightly guttural "h" sound (between an aspirate "h" and the ch in loch) before e or i, a hard G elsewhere – *gigante* becomes "higante".

H is always silent.

J is guttural: *jamón* is pronounced "hamón".

LL sounds like an English Y: *tortilla* is pronounced "torteeya".

N is as in English unless it has a tilde (ñ) over it, when it becomes NY: *mañana* sounds like "manyana".

QU is pronounced like an English K (the "u" is silent).

R is rolled, RR doubly so.

V sounds more like B, *vino* becoming "beano".

X is slightly softer than in English – sometimes almost SH – except between vowels in place names where it has an "H" sound – for example México (Meh-Hee-Ko).

Z is the same as a soft C, so *cerveza* becomes "serbessa".

On the following page we've listed a few essential words and phrases, though if you're travelling for any length of time a dictionary or phrase book is obviously a worthwhile investment. If you're using a **dictionary**, bear in mind that in Spanish CH, LL, and Ñ count as separate letters and are traditionally listed in a special section after the Cs, Ls, and Ns respectively, though some new dictionaries do not follow this rule.

WORDS AND PHRASES

The following should help you with your most basic day-to-day language needs; a menu reader and list of slang terms follows on.

BASICS

yes, no	sí, no	open, closed	abierto/a, cerrado/a
please, thank you	por favor, gracias	with, without	con, sin
where, when?	dónde, cuándo	good, bad	buen(o)/a, mal(o)/a
what, how much?	qué, cuánto	big	gran(de)
here, there	aquí, allí	small	pequeño/a, chico
this, that	este, eso	more, less	más, menos
now, later	ahora, màs tarde	today, tomorrow	hoy, mañana
		yesterday	ayer

GREETINGS AND RESPONSES

Hello, Goodbye	Hola, adiós (ciao/ chau)	Do you speak English?	¿Habla (usted) inglés?
		I (don't) speak Spanish	(No) Hablo español
Good morning	Buenos días	My name is…	Me llamo…
Good afternoon	Buenas tardes	What's your name?	¿Cómo se llama usted?
Good evening/night	Buenas noches	I am English	Soy inglés(a)
See you later	Hasta luego	…Irish	…irlandés (a)
Sorry	Lo siento/discúlpeme (perdón)	…Scottish	…escocés (a)
		…Welsh	…galés (a)
Excuse me	Con permiso/perdón	…American	…norte-americano(a)
How are you?	¿Como está (usted)?	…Australian	…australiano (a)
I (don't) understand	(No) Entiendo	…Canadian	…canadiense
Not at all/You're welcome	De nada	…New Zealander	…neozelandés (a)

ACCOMMODATION AND TRANSPORT

I want	Quiero…	How do I get to…?	¿Por dónde se va a ?
I'd like	Quisiera…	Left, right, straight on	Izquierda, derecha, derecho
Do you know…	¿Sabe ?		
I don't know	No sé	Where is…?	¿Dónde está…?
There is (is there?)	(¿) Hay (?)	the bus station	el terminal de buses
Give me…	Deme…	the train station	la estación de ferrocarriles
…(one like that)	(uno así)		
Do you have…	¿Tiene ?	the nearest bank	el banco más cercano
…the time	…la hora	the post office	el correo
…a room	una habitación	the toilet	el baño
…with two beds/double bed	…con dos camas/ cama matrimonial	Where does the bus leave from?	¿De dónde sale el bus para ?
…with private bath	con baño privado	Is this the train for Santiago?	¿Es éste el tren para Santiago?
It's for one person (two people)	es para una persona (dos personas)	I'd like a (return) ticket to…	Quisiera un pasaje (de ida y vuelta) para…
For one night (one week)	para una noche (una semana)	What time does it leave (arrive in…)?	¿A qué hora sale (llega en)?
It's fine	Está bien		
How much is it?	¿Cuánto es?	How long does the journey take?	¿Cuánto tiempo demora el viaje?
It's too expensive	Es demasiado caro		
Don't you have anything cheaper?	¿No tiene algo más barato?	What is there to eat?	¿Qué hay para comer?
		What's that?	¿Qué es eso?
Can one…?	¿Se puede ?	What's this called in Spanish?	¿Como se llama esto en español?
…camp (near) here?	…acampar aquí (cerca)?		
Is there a hotel nearby?	¿Hay un hotel aquí cerca?		

USEFUL TRANSPORT VOCABULARY

Ticket	Pasaje	**Non-4WD**	Tracción single or dos por dos (2x2)
Seat	Asiento		
Aisle	Pasillo	**Unlimited kilometres**	Kilometraje libre
Window	Ventana	**Insurance**	Seguro
Luggage	Equipaje	**Damages excess**	Deducible
Left luggage	Custodia	**Petrol**	Bencina
Car	Auto	**Petrol station**	Estación de bencina
Car rental outlet	Rentacar	**Jerry can**	Bidon
To rent	Arrendar	**Highway**	Carretera
4WD	Doble tracción or cuatro por cuatro (4x4)	**Pick-up truck**	Camioneta

CHILEAN ROAD SIGNS

Danger	Peligro	**No overtaking**	No adelantar
Detour	Desvío	**Dangerous bend**	Curva peligrosa
Slippery surface	Resbaladizo	**Reduce speed**	Reduzca velocidad
		No hard shoulder	Sin berma

NUMBERS AND DAYS

1	un/uno/una	**50**	cincuenta
2	dos	**60**	sesenta
3	tres	**70**	setenta
4	cuatro	**80**	ochenta
5	cinco	**90**	noventa
6	seis	**100**	cien(to)
7	siete	**101**	ciento uno
8	ocho	**200**	doscientos (as)
9	nueve	**201**	doscientos (as) uno
10	diez	**500**	quinientos (as)
11	once	**1000**	mil
12	doce	**2000**	dos mil
13	trece	**first**	primer(o)/a
14	catorce	**second**	segundo/a
15	quince	**third**	tercer(o)/a
16	dieciséis	**Monday**	lunes
17	diecisiete	**Tuesday**	martes
18	dieciocho	**Wednesday**	miércoles
19	diecinueve	**Thursday**	jueves
20	veinte	**Friday**	viernes
21	veintiuno	**Saturday**	sábado
30	treinta	**Sunday**	domingo
40	cuarenta		

FOOD: A CHILEAN MENU READER

BASICS

Aceite	Oil	**Mermelada**	Jam
Ají	Chilli	**Miel**	Honey
Ajo	Garlic	**Mostaza**	Mustard
Arroz	Rice	**Pan**	Bread
Azúcar	Sugar	**Pimienta**	Pepper
Huevos	Eggs	**Sal**	Salt
Leche	Milk		
Mantequilla	Butter	**SOME COMMON TERMS**	
		A la parrilla	Grilled

A la plancha	Lightly fried
A lo pobre	Served with chips, onions and a fried egg
Ahumado	Smoked
Al horno	Oven-baked
Al vapor	Steamed
Asado	Roast or barbecued
Asado al palo	Spit-roasted, barbecued
Crudo	Raw
Frito	Fried
Pastel	Paste, purée, mince
Picante	Spicy hot
Pil-pil	Very spicy
Puré	Mashed (potato)
Relleno	Filled or stuffed

MEALS

Agregado	Side order
Almuerzo	Lunch
Cena	Dinner
Comedor	Dining room
Cuchara	Spoon
Cuchillo	Knife
Desayuno	Breakfast
La carta	The menu
La cuenta	The bill
Menú del día	Fixed-price set meal (usually lunch)
Once	Afternoon tea
Plato vegetariano	Vegetarian dish
Tenedor	Fork

MEAT (CARNE) AND POULTRY (AVES)

Bistec	Beef steak
Carne de vacuno	Beef
Cerdo	Pork
Chuleta	Cutlet, chop (usually pork)
Churrasco	Griddled beef, like a minute steak
Conejo	Rabbit
Cordero	Lamb steak
Escalopa Milanesa	Breaded veal escalope
Filete	Fillet steak
Jamón	Ham
Lechón, cochinillo	Suckling pig
Lomo	General term for steak of indiscriminate cut
Pato	Duck
Pavo	Turkey
Pollo	Chicken
Ternera	Veal
Vienesa	Hot-dog sausage

OFFAL (MENUDOS)

Chunchules	Intestines
Guatitas	Tripe
Lengua	Tongue
Patas	Feet, trotters
Pana	Liver
Picante de conejo	Curried rabbits' innards
Riñones	Kidneys

FISH (PESCADO)

Albacora	Albacore (a small, white-fleshed tuna)
Anchoveta	Anchovy
Atún	Tuna
Bonito	Pacific bonito, similar to tuna
Ceviche	Strips of fish marinated in lemon juice and onions
Congrio	A large, superior member of the cod family known as conger eel
Corvina	Sea bass (not the same as Chilean sea bass, which is under boycott)
Lenguado	Sole
Merluza	Hake
Reineta	Similar to lemon sole
Salmón	Salmon
Trucha	Trout
Vidriola	Firm-fleshed white fish from the Juan Fernández archipelago

SEAFOOD (MARISCOS)

Almeja	Clam, cockle
Calamar	Squid
Camarón	Prawn
Centolla	King crab
Choro, chorito	Mussel
Erizo	Sea urchin
Langosta	Lobster
Langosta de Isla	Spiny lobster de Pascua
Langosta de Juan	Crayfish, rock lobster Fernández
Langostino	Crayfish, red crab
Loco	Abalone
Macha	Razor clam
Mariscal	Mixed shellfish, served chilled
Mejillones	Mussels
Ostiones	Scallops
Ostras	Oysters

Paila marina	Thick fish and seafood stew
Picoroco	Giant barnacle with a single crab-like claw
Piure	Scarlet-red, kidney-shaped animal with hair-like strands that lives inside a shell
Pulpo	Octopus

VEGETABLES (VERDURAS)

Aceitunas	Olives
Alcachofa	Artichoke
Cebolla	Onion
Champiñón	Mushroom
Choclo	Maize, sweetcorn
Chucrút	Sauerkraut
Espinaca	Spinach
Lechuga	Lettuce
Palmito	Palm heart
Palta	Avocado
Papa	Potato
Papas fritas	Chips (French fries)
Poroto verde	Green, French, runner bean
Tomate	Tomato
Zapallo	Squash

SOUPS AND STEWS

Caldillo	Vegetables cooked in meat meat stock; between a stew and a soup
Caldo	Quite bland, simple meat stock with loads of added salt
Charquicán	Meat stew with lots of vegetables
Chupe	Thick fish stew, topped with butter, breadcrumbs and grated cheese
Crema	Creamy soup thickened with flour or egg yolks
Zarzuela	Seafood stew (like bouillabaisse)

SALADS (ENSALADAS)

Ensalada chilena	Tomatoes, shredded onion and vinaigrette
Ensalada primavera	Hard-boiled eggs, sweetcorn, peas, carrot, beetroot
Ensalada rusa	Diced vegetables and peas mixed in a thick mayonnaise
Ensalada surtida	Mixed salad
Palta reina	Avocado filled with tuna

SANDWICHES (SANWICHES)

Ave mayo	Chicken and mayonnaise
Ave sola	Chicken
Barros jarpa	Ham and melted cheese
Barros luco	Beef and melted cheese
Churrasco solo	Griddled beef, like a minute steak
Completo	Hot dog, sauerkraut, tomato, mayonnaise
Diplomático	Beef, egg and melted cheese
Especial	Hot dog with mayonnaise
Hamburguesa	Hamburger

FRUIT (FRUTAS)

Albaricoque	Apricot
Cereza	Cherry
Chirimoya	Custard apple
Ciruela	Plum
Durazno	Peach
Frambuesa	Raspberry
Frutilla	Strawberry
Higo	Fig
Limón	Lemon
Lúcuma	Native fruit often used in ice cream and cakes
Manzana	Apple
Membrillo	Quince
Mora	Mulberry
Naranja	Orange
Pera	Pear
Piña	Pineapple
Plátano	Banana
Pomelo	Grapefruit
Sandía	Watermelon
Tuna	Prickly pear
Uva	Grape(s)

DESSERT (POSTRES)

When fruit is described as being "in juice" (*al jugo*) or "in syrup" (*en almíbar*), it will be out of a tin.

Flan	Crème caramel
Helado	Ice cream
Kuchen	Cake
Macedonia	Fruit salad
Manjar	Very sweet caramel, made from condensed milk
Panqueques	Pancakes
Torta	Tart

DRINKS AND BEVERAGES

Note that, owing to the Chileans' compulsive use of the diminutive (*ito* and *ita*), you'll hardly ever be asked if you want a *té* or *café*, but rather a *tecito* or *cafecito*, which tends to throw people at first.

ALCOHOLIC DRINKS

Cerveza	Beer

IDIOM AND SLANG

As you travel through Chile you'll come across a lot of words and expressions that crop up again and again, many of which aren't in your dictionary, or, if they are, appear to have a different meaning from that given. Added to these day-to-day **chilenismos** is a very rich, exuberant and constantly expanding vocabulary of slang (*modismos*). Mastering a few of the most common examples will help you get by and raise a smile if you drop them into the conversation.

EVERYDAY WORDS AND EXPRESSIONS

Some of the words and expressions listed below are shared by neighbouring countries, while others are uniquely Chilean. As well as these peculiarities, we've listed a few other expressions you're likely to encounter very frequently.

Al tiro "right away", "immediately" – though this can mean anything up to several hours.
Boleta as Chilean law requires that customers must not leave shop premises without their *boleta* (receipt), you will frequently hear "*su boleta!*" yelled at you as you try to leave without it.
Calefónt (pronounced calefón) water heater; not a real Chilean word, but one you'll need every day if you're staying in budget accommodation, where you'll have to remember to light the *calefónt* with *fósforos* (matches) before you take a shower.
Carné identity card.
Cédula interchangeable with *carné*.
Ciao (chau) by far the most common way of saying "goodbye" among friends; in slightly more formal situations, *hasta luego* is preferred over *adiós*.
Confort (pronounced "confor") a brand name but now the de facto word for toilet paper (which is correctly *papel higiénico*).
De repente in Spain this means "suddenly"; in Chile it means "maybe", "sometimes" or "occasionally".
Flojo "lazy", frequently invoked by northerners to describe southerners and southerners to describe northerners.
Guagua (pronounced "wawa") baby, derived from Quechua.

Champán	Champagne	**SOFT DRINKS**	
Chicha (or sidra)	Cider	**Bebida**	Fizzy drink
Vino (tinto/blanco/ rosado)	Wine (red/white/rosé)	**(en lata/botella)**	(in a can/bottle)
		(de máquina)	(draught)
HOT DRINKS		**Jugo natural**	Juice (pure)
Café	Coffee	**Néctar**	Juice (syrup)
Descafeinado	Decaff (rarely available)	**Agua**	Water
Chocolate caliente	Hot chocolate	**Agua mineral**	Mineral water
Té	Tea	**(con gas)**	(sparkling)
Té de hierbas	Herbal tea	**(sin gas)**	(still)

Harto "loads of" (for example *harto trabajo*, loads of work); a more widely used and idiomatic alternative to *mucho*.

Listo literally "ready", and used as a response to indicate agreement, or that what's been said is understood; something like "sure" or "right".

Plata literally "silver" but meaning "money", used far more commonly than *dinero*, except in formal situations.

Qué le vaya (muy) bien "May everything go (very) well for you", frequently said when saying goodbye to someone you probably won't see again.

Rico "good", "delicious", "tasty", usually to describe food and drink.

Ya Chilean equivalent of the Spanish *vale*; used universally to convey "OK", "fine", "sure" or (depending on the tone) "Whatever", "Hmm, I see".

SLANG

The few examples we give below barely scrape the surface of the living, constantly evolving lexicon of Chilean slang – for a crash course, get hold of the excellent *How to Survive in the Chilean Jungle* by John Brennan and Alvaro Baboada, published by Dolmen and available in the larger Santiago bookshops.

Buena onda "cool!"

Cachar "to understand"; hence "*¿cachai?*", "are you with me?", scattered ad nauseam through conversations.

Cocido drunk.

Cuico yuppie (especially in Santiago).

Huevón literally "huge testicle", meaning something like "asshole" or "fucker", but so commonly and enthusiastically used it's no longer particularly offensive. More like "jerk" or "idiot".

Los pacos the police.

Pololo/a boyfriend, girlfriend.

¡Sale! emphatically used to mean, "bullshit!" or "not a chance!"

Sí, po abbreviation of *sí, pues*, meaning "yeah", "sure" ("po" is tacked onto the end of just about every phrase, hence "*no po*", "*no sé po*").

Taco traffic jam.

Small print and index

513 Small print

514 About the authors

516 Index

522 Map symbols

A ROUGH GUIDE TO ROUGH GUIDES

Published in 1982, the first Rough Guide – to Greece – was a student scheme that became a publishing phenomenon. Mark Ellingham, a recent graduate in English from Bristol University, had been travelling in Greece the previous summer and couldn't find the right guidebook. With a small group of friends he wrote his own guide, combining a highly contemporary, journalistic style with a thoroughly practical approach to travellers' needs.

The immediate success of the book spawned a series that rapidly covered dozens of destinations. And, in addition to impecunious backpackers, Rough Guides soon acquired a much broader readership that relished the guides' wit and inquisitiveness as much as their enthusiastic, critical approach and value-for-money ethos.

These days, Rough Guides include recommendations from budget to luxury and cover more than 200 destinations around the globe, as well as producing an ever-growing range of eBooks and apps.

Visit **roughguides.com** to see our latest publications.

Rough Guide credits

Editor: Brendon Griffin
Layout: Ankur Guha, Jessica Subramanian
Cartography: Katie Lloyd-Jones
Picture editors: Mark Thomas, Michelle Bhatia
Proofreader: Susannah Wight
Managing editor: Keith Drew
Assistant editor: Prema Dutta
Production: Rebecca Short
Cover design: Nicole Newman, Dan May, Ankur Guha
Photographer: Tim Draper

Editorial assistant: Eleanor Aldridge
Senior pre-press designer: Dan May
Design director: Scott Stickland
Travel publisher: Joanna Kirby
Digital travel publisher: Peter Buckley
Reference director: Andrew Lockett
Operations coordinator: Becky Doyle
Publishing director (Travel): Clare Currie
Commercial manager: Gino Magnotta
Managing director: John Duhigg

Publishing information

This fifth edition published September 2012 by
Rough Guides Ltd,
80 Strand, London WC2R 0RL
11, Community Centre, Panchsheel Park,
New Delhi 110017, India
Distributed by the Penguin Group
Penguin Books Ltd,
80 Strand, London WC2R 0RL
Penguin Group (USA)
375 Hudson Street, NY 10014, USA
Penguin Group (Australia)
250 Camberwell Road, Camberwell,
Victoria 3124, Australia
Penguin Group (NZ)
67 Apollo Drive, Mairangi Bay, Auckland 1310,
New Zealand
Penguin Group (South Africa)
Block D, Rosebank Office Park, 181 Jan Smuts Avenue,
Parktown North, Gauteng, South Africa 2193
Rough Guides is represented in Canada by Tourmaline
Editions Inc. 662 King Street West, Suite 304, Toronto,
Ontario M5V 1M7
Printed in Singapore by Toppan Security Printing Pte. Ltd.

© Andrew Benson, Melissa Graham, Anna Kaminski,
Shafik Meghji 2012
Maps © Rough Guides
No part of this book may be reproduced in any form
without permission from the publisher except for the
quotation of brief passages in reviews.
528pp includes index
A catalogue record for this book is available from the
British Library
ISBN: 978-1-40538-980-8
The publishers and authors have done their best to
ensure the accuracy and currency of all the information in
The Rough Guide to Chile, however, they can accept no
responsibility for any loss, injury, or inconvenience
sustained by any traveller as a result of information or
advice contained in the guide.
1 3 5 7 9 8 6 4 2

Help us update

We've gone to a lot of effort to ensure that the fifth edition of **The Rough Guide to Chile** is accurate and up-to-date. However, things change – places get "discovered", opening hours are notoriously fickle, restaurants and rooms raise prices or lower standards. If you feel we've got it wrong or left something out, we'd like to know, and if you can remember the address, the price, the hours, the phone number, so much the better.

Please send your comments with the subject line "**Rough Guide Chile Update**" to @ mail@uk.roughguides .com. We'll credit all contributions and send a copy of the next edition (or any other Rough Guide if you prefer) for the very best emails.

Find more travel information, connect with fellow travellers and book your trip on ⓦ roughguides.com

ABOUT THE AUTHORS

Andew Benson Andrew Benson splits his year between South America, based in Buenos Aires, and Europe and New York, where he works for UN agencies. He has co-authored or contributed to numerous Rough Guides, including Argentina, South America, France, Greece and Europe. He originally visited Chile in 1997 to realise a childhood dream of seeing the Easter Island moai in situ. Apart from that, he enjoyed pisco sours, the great outdoors and the sight of some of the world's driest, remotest and most breathtaking spots.

Melissa Graham first got hooked on Latin America while studying Spanish-American literature and history at Cambridge University. She has since travelled widely in Chile, Peru and Ecuador, and has co-authored *The Rough Guide to Ecuador* as well. These days she spends most of her time in London, where she lives with her husband and children.

Anna Kaminski Anna has been enamoured of this long, thin country ever since becoming hooked on Isabel Allende novels and Pablo Neruda's poetry while doing a degree on the history and literature of Latin America. Since then, she has travelled the entire length of Chile on several occasions – for research and pleasure – though it's the frozen south that entices her the most: she considers Patagonia her second home and finds herself returning year after year.

Shafik Meghji A travel writer, journalist, editor and photographer, Shafik Meghji is based in South London but has travelled extensively throughout Chile since his first visit in 2004. He also co-authors *The Rough Guide to Bolivia*, *The Rough Guide to India* and *The Rough Guide to Nepal*, and has updated Rough Guides to Egypt, Central America, Paris and the Baltic States.

Acknowledgements

Anna Kaminski I would like to thank my fellow authors and our long-suffering editor for having worked so hard on this edition, as well as all the people who assisted me during my travels, including: Fernando and Amory of Chepu Adventures – my 'Chilean parents'; Konrad and his huskies; Stefan and Jan in the Lake District; Martin and Britt in Ancud; Deb and Darren in Pucón; the good folk from Erratic Rock and David of Dittmar Adventures in Puerto Natales; Sebastian of Turismo Aonikenk in Punta Arenas; Parque Pinguino Rey in Tierra del Fuego; the exceptionally helpful tourist office in Coyhaique; Nicolás in Chaitén; Carolyn and the lovely Xic Dalí sisters at Puerto Varas; Zoë in El Chaltén; Graham for the chivalry and company during the border crossing and beyond; Diego, Leivi, Marceló and Cecilia in Puerto Williams; Jorge for the amazing meal in Ushuaia; and Traeger Rent-a-Car for not insisting I take a 4WD up the Carretera Austral.

Shafik Meghji Thanks to the many locals and travellers who helped out in big and small ways during the researching of this book. A special muchas gracias must go to: Brendon Griffin for his editing skills and support; Anna Kaminski, Janine Israel and Clemmy Manzo; Cath Collins in Santiago for her insight and company; Kristina Schreck for her help with hotel arrangements; Francisco Klimscha Bittig from Slow Travel; Laura Rendell-Dunn at Journey Latin America; Janak Jani in Valpo; Brian Pearson of Santiago Adventures; everyone at La Bicicleta Verde; Gemma Dunn at Cascada; Josefina Nahoe for a memorable tour of Easter Island; all the staff at Explora Posada de Mike Rapu; Jean, Nizar and Nina Meghji; and Sioned Jones for all her love and support.

Janine Israel Héctor Coto Gómez; Gustavo Carvallo; Veronica Morgado; the exceptional staff at M.I. Lodge; Todd Ericson; Consuelo Garcia; Franz Schubert and the staff at Casa Chueca; Frank at Costa y Cumbre Tours; Copiapó tourism; the wonderful people of Caldera; Aji Verde Hostel; Will and Carolina at Tumuñan Lodge; Vicente and Ruth at Mapuyampay; Jorge Rodriguez; the kindness of strangers; and my tireless editor.

Clemmy Manzo A very big thank you to: editor Brendon Griffin for his patience and guidance; Turismo Chile (Alejandra Saenz in particular); Victoria Coombes at Mango PR; Charlie from Latinorizons (Arica) for his kindness and time; Roberto from Doña Inés hostel (Arica) for her helpful tips and ´buena onda´; everyone at Sernatur but particularly Michael Arancibia, Aaron Baruch, Jessica Diaz, and the very helpful folk at both the San Pedro de Atacama and Iquique offices; the manager and all staff at the wonderful Hotel Kunza in San Pedro de Atacama; Space Obs (San Pedro de Atacama); Cosmo Andino (San Pedro de Atacama); Jacob Espinosa from Puro Vuelo for the unforgettable paragliding flight in Iquique; and per-haps the biggest thank you of all to Isabel from Hostel La Casona 1920 in Iquique for her kindess, enthusiasm and going out of her way to help me.

Readers' letters

Thanks to all the readers who have taken the time to write in with comments and suggestions (and apologies if we've inadvertently omitted or misspelt anyone's name):

Alejandro Aguirre, Emmanuelle Brault, Caroline Devoyer, Alet van't Eind, Scott Fitzgerald, Sebastian Elsinger, Oliver Fay, Paulina Cabañas Guerrero, Horiols Aqueveque Hoffens, Lani Imhof, Vicky Junik, Pat Kuta, Mark Lum-ley, Marco Muñoz, Nils Ohlendorf, Bill Penhollow, Daniela Pirola, Juliet Robinson, Ninfa Rojas, Daniel Silva, Joyce Snyder, Nadja Teich, Paolo Votino.

Photo credits

All photos © Rough Guides except the following:
(Key: t-top; c-centre; b-bottom; l-left; r-right)

p.1 Getty Images/John W Banagan
p.2 Alamy/Blaine Harrington III
p.4 Getty Images/John W Banagan
p.7 AWL Images/John Warburton-Lee (tr), Corbis/Fridmar Damm (b), Getty Images/Thomas Schmitt (tl)
p.11 Alamy/Foxphotoruins
p.12 Corbis/Momatiuk - Eastcott
p.13 SuperStock/Oliver Gerhard (b)
p.15 Getty Images/Matthias Clamer (tl)
p.16 Alamy/Oriol Alamany (tl)
p.17 AWL Images/Paul Harris (t)
p.18 Alamy/Emily Francoise (t), Getty Images/Martin Bernetti (b)
p.19 Corbis/Frank Krahmer (t)
p.20 Getty Images/Sven Creutzmann (b)
p.22 Getty Images/Design Pics (tr)
p.65 Alamy/David A. Barnes (b)
p.91 Alamy/James Quine (t), Corbis/Jon Hicks (b)
p.99 Alamy/Stefano Politi
p.115 Alamy/Bon Appetit (b), Brenton West (t)
p.139 Alamy/Megapress
p.257 Alamy/Fabian Gonzales

p.265 SuperStock/Aaron McCoy
p.299 SuperStock/Kordcom
p.317 Alamy/Robert Harding
p.341 Alamy/Robert Harding
p.344 Alamy/Imagebroker
p.371 Alamy/Novarc Images (b)
p.380 AWL Images/Paul Harris
p.405 Corbis/Jose Fuste Raga (b)
p.414 Alamy/LOOK Die Bildagentur der Fotografen
p.427 Alamy/Feargus Cooney (t), SuperStock/Ken Gillham (b)
p.433 Alamy/WorldFoto
p.438 4Corners/Ripani Massimo
p.441 Alamy/Bill Bachmann
p.455 Alamy/Svea Pietschmann (b), SuperStock/Ken Welsh (t)
p.462 Corbis/Government of Chile

Front cover Llama in Torres Del Paine, Getty Images /Ingo Arndt
Back cover Expedition in the Chilean Andes, Getty Images/Menno Boermans (t); Sunset at a Moai Quarry, Easter Island, Alamy/Jon Arnold Images (br)

Index

Maps are marked in grey

A

accommodation 30–32
  alternative 30
  cabañas 31
  camping 32
  casas de familia 31
  hospedajes 31
  hostels 32
  hotels 30
  prices 31
  refugios 32
  residenciales 31
Achao 329
addresses 29
adventure sports 10, 38–42
adventure tourism 38–42
Aguas Calientes 295
Aguas Calientes (Parque
  Nacional Volcán Isluga) 199
Ahu Akahanga 449
Ahu Akivi 454
Ahu Ature Huki 451
Ahu Hanga Tetenga 449
Ahu Te Peu 453
Ahu Tongariki 450
air passes 25
airlines 27
airport tax 25
Alcohuaz 149
Aldea Intercultural Trawupeyüm
 279
alerce trees 350
Allende, Salvador 478
Alma Observatory 175
altitude sickness 43
Alto del Carmen 153
Anakena 451
Ancud 319–321
Ancud 320
Andacollo 132
Angelmó 309
Angol 256
Antarctica 432
Anticura 297
Antillanca 296
Antofagasta 171–174
Antofagasta, Downtown ... 172
Argentine border crossing
  El Chaltén 379
  Puerto Varas 301
  San Sebastián 422
Arica 202–209
Arica 203
Arica tours 207

Arica's beaches 206
artesanía 45
ATMs 49
Aymara people 202
Azapa Valley 209

B

Bachelet, Michelle 484
Buchupureo 246
Bahía Azul 420
Bahía Ensenada 437
Bahía Inglesa 163
Bahía Inútil 421
Bahía Salada 163
Balmaceda, José Manuel
 475
Baños de Colina 89
Baños de Puritama 186
Baños Morales 189
Baquedano Hills 421
bargaining 45
Barrio Inglés 135
Beagle Channel 434
beavers 425
birdman ceremony 456
boat trips, San Juan Bautista
 460
Bolívar, Simon 472
Bolivian border crossing 200
books 500–504
buses
  to Chile 26
  within Chile 27

C

Cabo de Hornos 426, 427, 428
Cabo Froward 393
Cachagua 120
Cajón del Maipo 88–90
Cajón del Morado 90
Calama 176–178
Calama 176
Caldera 161–163
Caldera 162
Caleta Puelche 350
Caleta Tortel 376
calling cards 50
Camar 186
Camerón 421

Candelario Mancilla 379
Cañete 252
Cape Horn 426, 427, 428
Capilla de Mármol 372
Captain Cook 444
car rental 28
Cariquima 200
Carretera Austral 344–379
Carretera Austral, driving 351
Casa del Arte 248
Casablanca Valley Wine Route
 113
Castillo de San Pedro de
  Alcántara 290
Castro 330–334
Castro 331
Caulín 325
cell phones 50
Cementerio Municipal 389
Central Valley 216–261
Central Valley, the 220
Centro de Esquí Volcán Antuco
 255
Centro de Ski Pucón 281
Centro de Visitantes de las
  Iglesias de Chiloé 319
Cerro Castillo 370
Cerro Glaciar 434
Cerro Guanaco 437
Cerro Mamalluca observatory
 146
Cerro Martial 434
Cerro Paranal Observatory 175
Cerro Pintados 194
Cerro Sombrero 420
Cerro Tololo observatory 141
Cerro Unitas 168
Chaitén 354
Chañaral 164
Chanco 241
Chapa Verde ski centre 224
Chatwin, Bruce 388
Chepu 325
Chepu Valley 325
Chile Chico 372
Chilean music 493–499
Chilean Spanish 505–511
Chillán 242–244
Chillán 243
Chiloé 314–343
Chiloé 318
Chilote churches 321, 328
Chilote mythology 321
Chinchorro mummies 210
Chonchi 337

Choshuenco 286
Chug Chug geoglyphs 176
Chuquicamata 178
churches, Chilote 328
climate...............................39, 45, 46
Cocha Resbaladero 195
Cochamó 308
Cochiguaz 149
Cochrane 200, 374
colectivos 28
Collowara observatory 132
colonial Chile 468
Coñaripe 284
Concepción 247–250
Concepción..........................248
Concón 119
Constitución................................240
Copiapó 154–158
Copiapó 156
copper mine, El Teniente......223
Coquimbo 134–136
Corral...292
Cortés, Hernán...........................467
costs 45
Coyhaique 363–367
Coyhaique 364
crime 46
crossing the altiplano 200
Cruce El Maitén 372
Cucao 336
cueca 38
Cuernos del Paine 400
Cuesta de las Raíces 260
Cueva del Milodón....................399
Cuevas Volcánicas 282
culture and etiquette...............44
Curacautín........................260, 269
Curaco de Vélez.........................329
Curanipe 241
curanto..324
Curicó...........................231–233
Curicó....................................232
currency 49
cycling 29

D

Dalcahue.......................................327
dams in Patagonia 358
Darwin, Charles..........................423
dehydration 44
Del Pangue observatory.........146
Detif...338
Dichato..251
Dientes de Navarino.................425
disabilities, travellers with.......51
disabled access 51
discography..................................496

Dos Ventanas Caves.................452
drinking............................32–35
driving 28

E

earthquake, 2010 225
Easter Island 438–456
Easter Island.......................442
eating...............................32–35
El Abanico 255
El Calafate....................................409
El Chaltén 411
El Morro..204
El Niño..492
El Norte Chico.............122–165
El Norte Chico 126
El Norte Grande 166–215
El Norte Grande 170
El Tatio geysers 186
El Teniente...................................223
El Tren del Fin del Mundo
....437
El Volcán..89
electricity......................................46
Elqui Valley 143–150
Elqui, Hurtado & Limarí
Valleys, the......................130
email..48
embassies, Chilean abroad....47
Enqelga...198
Ensenada......................................305
entry requirements 46
environmental issues...........490
Estancia Harberton...................435
Estancia Valle Chacabuco.......376
Estancia Yendegaia 422
Estuario de Reloncaví 308
extensions, tourist card...........47

F

Faro Corona 325
ferries 29
Festival Costumbrista 333
festivals 35
festivals, Easter Island 448
Fitz Roy Massif 411
flights
from Australia, New Zealand and
South Africa.......................25
from the UK and Ireland............25
from the US and Canada...........25
round-the-world....................25
within Chile.............................27
flora 489
flowering desert 155

fly-fishing..............................40, 362
fly-fishing lodges 362
food 32–35
football...37
Frutillar...303
Fuerte Agüi 325
Fuerte Bulnes 393
Fuerte de Niebla 290
Fuerte Santa Barbara................459
Futaleufú......................................355

G

gay and lesbian travellers 47
geoglyphs 202
geography....................................488
giant sloth...................................400
Gigante de Atacama.................198
Glaciar Balmaceda....................399
Glaciar Perito Moreno.............411
Glaciar San Rafael.....................369
Glaciar Serrano 399
gold mining 154
González, Felipe........................444
Guallatire 214

H

Hacienda de Tiliviche..............201
Hacienda San Agustín de Puñal
....246
Hanga Roa....................445–447
Hanga Roa 447
health 43
hiking..39
history............................463–488
history, Easter Island
....443–445
hitching..29
Horcón..119
Hornopirén 350
horse racing................................37
horse-riding................................42
hot springs near Pucón..........278
Huáscar..249
Huasco valley, upper..............153
huaso...37
Huicha 338
Humberstone.............................193
Humberstone, James 201
Hurtado Valley...........................127
Hurtado..129
hypothermia 44

I

Iglesia Catedral............................138
Iglesia de San Marcos.............204
Iglesia de San Pedro................179
Iglesia San Francisco (Castro)
....331
insurance 47
internet 48
Iquique 187–193
Iquique 188
Isla Alejandro Selkirk...............461
Isla de los Lobos..........................121
Isla de los Muertos....................376
Isla Lemuy.......................................338
Isla Mechuque 329
Isla Navarino................. 422–426
Isla Negra..111
Isla Quinchao 329
Isla Robinson Crusoe ... 457–461
Isla Santa María 252
Isla Teja..288
Islotes de Puñihuil....................325
Isluga..199
Itata Valley.....................................244
itineraries.. 22

J

Jara, Victor......................................495
Juan Fernández Archipelago
.... 456–461

K

Kawéscar people 423
kayaking 28, 325
King penguins 421

L

La Herradura..................................135
La Junta...359
La Ligua 120
La Portada.......................................175
La Ruta del Vino del Valle de
   Colchagua 229
La Serena....................... 138–143
La Serena, downtown........ 137
La Serena's churches 138
La Silla observatory 141
La Tirana..198
Lago Blanco....................................422

Lago Calafquén...........................284
Lago Chungará.............................213
Lago Colbún..................................239
Lago del Desierto.......................379
Lago General Carrera 370
Lago General Pinto Concha...352
Lago Lanalhue..............................253
Lago Llanquihue......... 298–305
Lago Neltume................................286
Lago Panguipulli.........................285
Lago Pellaifa 284
Lago Pirehueico 286
Lago Puyehue 295
Lago Rapel 225
Lago Riñihue.................................286
Lago Todos Los Santos 307
Lago Todos Los Santos 306
Lago Verde 358
Lago Vichuquén...........................233
Lago Villarrica 271
Lago Villarrica & around ... 272
Laguna Chaiquenes....................349
Laguna del Negro Francisco ...160
Laguna Lejía 186
Laguna Margarita........................308
Laguna Miñeques........................186
Laguna Miscanti..........................186
Laguna San Rafael......................368
Laguna Santa Rosa....................160
Laguna Torca.................................233
Laguna Triángulo.........................349
Laguna Tuyajto............................186
Laguna Verde (El Norte Chico)
....160
Lagunas de Cotacotani 212
Lake District................. 262–313
Lake District, the................ 266
language 505–511
Las Campanas observatory ...141
Lebu...252
Lican Ray...284
Limarí Valley 127
Liquiñe..284
living in Chile 48
Llico...233
Longquimay 260
Los 33..159
Los Andes 90
Los Angeles 254
Los Vilos 121
Lota...252

M

Magalhães, Fernão.....................387
Magellan, Ferdinand 387
mail...49
Maitencillo 120

Mamiña 196
maps...49
Mapuche people 466
Maqui berry 319
marea roja 43
Matilla 196
media...35
medical resources 44
Melipeuco.......................................269
Mercado Fluvial...........................288
military coup, Pinochet............479
Mirador Alejandro Selkirk 460
Mistral, Gabriela..........................150
moai 452
mobile phones 50
money..49
Montegrande.................................147
mountain biking............................42
Museo Arqueológico (Arica)...209
Museo Arqueológico (La Serena)
....140
Museo Arqueológico Gustavo Le
   Paige...180
Museo de Arte Contemporaneo
   (Valdivia).....................................290
Museo de Colchagua 228
Museo de la Exploración R. A.
   Philippi 289
Museo de las Tradiciones
   Chonchinas.................................338
Museo Desierto de Atacama
....174
Museo Gabriela Mistral 145
Museo Histórico y
   Antropológico Maurice van de
   Maele 288
Museo Regional (Ancud) 319
Museo Regional de la Araucanía
....267
Museo Regional Magallanes
....387
mythology, Chilote 321

N

Naess, Arne.....................................353
**national parks, reserves and
   monuments**...........................42
   Monumento Natural Isla
      Magdalena..............................394
   Parque de Aguas Nevados de
      Chillán..245
   Parque Nacional Alerce Andino...349
   Parque Nacional Bernardo
      O'Higgins...................................395
   Parque Nacional Chiloé 334–337
   Parque Nacional Chiloé 335
   Parque Nacional Conguillío
....269–271
   Parque Nacional Fray Jorge 131

Parque Nacional Huerquehue.....278
Parque Nacional la Campana........94
Parque Nacional Laguna del Laja
....255
Parque Nacional Laguna San Rafael
....369
Parque Nacional Lauca 211–213
Parque Nacional Lauca 212
Parque Nacional Llanos de Challe
....154
Parque Nacional Los Glaciares
....408–413
Parque Nacional Nahuelbuta 256
Parque Nacional Nahuelbuta and
around 256
Parque Nacional Nevado de Tres
Cruces..159
Parque Nacional Pali Aike 394
Parque Nacional Pan de Azúcar
....164
Parque Nacional Puyehue
....295–298
Parque Nacional Puyehue 296
Parque Nacional Queulat....359–360
Parque Nacional Rapa Nui ..443, 449
Parque Nacional Tierra del Fuego
....436
Parque Nacional Tierra del Fuego
.... 436
Parque Nacional Tolhuaca............258
Parque Nacional Tolhuaca 259
Parque Nacional Torres del Paine
....400–407
Parque Nacional Torres del Paine
....402–403
Parque Nacional Vicente Pérez
Rosales 305–309
Parque Nacional Vicente Pérez
Rosales 306
Parque Nacional Villarrica ...280–283
Parque Nacional Villarrica
....280–281
Parque Nacional Volcán Hornopirén
....352
Parque Nacional Volcán Isluga
....197–200
Parque Nacional Volcán Isluga
and around 199
Parque Pumalín 352–354
Parque Tantauco...................340–343
Reserva Forestal Magallanes 392
Reserva Nacional Altos de Lircay
....237
Reserva Nacional Cerro Castillo....370
Reserva Nacional Coyhaique.......367
Reserva Nacional Federico Albert
....241
Reserva Nacional Jeinemeni.........372
Reserva Nacional Lago Rosellot
....359
Reserva Nacional Laguna Torca...233
Reserva Nacional las Vicuñas.......213
Reserva Nacional Malalcahuello-
Nalcas 260
Reserva Nacional Pampa del
Tamarugal 194
Reserva Nacional Pinguino de
Humboldt..................................185

Reserva Nacional Radal Siete Tazas
....234
Reserva Nacional Río de Los
Cipreses.....................................224
Reserva Nacional Río Palena........356
Reserva Nacional Río Simpson
....367
Reserva Nacional Tamango........375
Neruda, Pablo 72, 112
Nevados de Chillán...................244
newspapers 35
Ninhue...246
nitrate boom...............................195
nitrate pampa.............................176
nueva canción 493

O

O'Higgins, Bernardo................472
observatories near La Serena
....141
offsetting carbon footprint ...26
Ojos de Caburgua 277
Olmué..95
opening hours..............................49
Orongo...456
Osorno 293–295
Osorno 294
outdoor activities 38–42
Ovalle........................... 127–129
Ovalle................................ 128

P

palafitos 331
Palena...355
Pali Aike......................................394
Panguipulli..................................285
Papudo..120
Parinacota..................................212
Paro..451
Parque Etnobotánico Omora
....426
Parque Oncol 290
Parque Ross 230
parques nacionales............ 42, see
national parks
Parra, Violeta 494
Paso del Agua Negra...............148
Paso Garibaldi............................416
Patagonia, Argentine
....408–413
Patagonia, Chilean 385–408
Patagonia, Northern ... 344–379
Patagonia, Northern 348
Patagonia, Southern ... 380–413
Patagonia, Southern 384

Pedro de Valdivia......................137
Peine 186
Pelluhue 241
penguins 325, 394
Peninsula Lacuy........................325
Perito Moreno glacier 411
Petrohué.....................................307
Peulla 308
phones 50
Pica 194
Pichasca 129
Pichidangui 120
Pichilemu....................................230
Piedra del Aguila.......................258
Pinguineras de Puñihuil.........325
Pinochet, Augusto
..................................67, 479–481
Pinochet, arrest of....................483
Pinochet, death of....................485
Pisagua 201
pisco..152
Playa Aguas Blancas.................120
Playa Cocholgue........................251
Playa Grande 120
Playa Las Cujas 120
Plazoleta El Yunque 460
Poike Peninsula 450
police 47
Polloquere...................................215
Pomaire..90
Porvenir......................................419
post...49
press...35
public holidays............................49
Puchuldiza..................................198
Pucón 273–277
Pucón 274
Puerto Aysén.............................368
Puerto Bertrand........................373
Puerto Chacabuco 368
Puerto Cisnes 363
Puerto Hambre..........................393
Puerto Ibáñez 370
Puerto Montt.............. 309–313
Puerto Montt.................... 310
Puerto Montt, ferries................311
Puerto Natales............. 395–399
Puerto Natales 396
Puerto Octay.................... 304
Puerto Río Tranquilo................372
Puerto Toro................................426
Puerto Varas 298–303
Puerto Varas 300
Puerto Williams 423
Puerto Yungay...........................377
Pukará de Quitor.......................185
Puna Pau 454
Punta Arenas 385–392
Punta Arenas...................... 386
Putre..210

Puyehue hot springs 297
Puyuhuapi 360

Q

Quebrada de Jérez 186
Queilen 339
Quellón 339
Quemchi 327
Quicaví 329
Quintay 111

R

rabies 43
radio 35
rafting 38
Ralún 308
Rancagua 221–223
Rancagua 222
Rano Kau 454
Rano Raraku 450
Rapa Nui, origins 443
Raúl Marín Balmaceda 357
Reñaca 119
rental cars 28
Riñihue 286
Río Bío Bío 247
Río Cochiguaz 149
Río Copiapó Valley 158
Río Futaleufú 355
Río Maule 235
rodeo 37, 223
rongo rongo 444
Ruinas de Huanchaca 171
Ruta del Vino del Valle de
     Colchagua, La.....................229
Ruta del Vino del Valle del Maule
    238

S

Salar de Atacama 185
Salar de Surire 214
Salto de la Princesa 260
Salto del Huilo-Huilo 286
Salto del Indio 260
Salto del Laja 254
Salto del Torbellino 255
Salto las Chilcas 255
Salto Malleco 258
Saltos de Petrohué 307
San Alfonso 89
San Fernando 226

San Gabriel 89
San Javier 240
San José de Maipo 88
San José miners rescue 159
San Juan Bautista 457–461
San Pedro de Atacama
     178–183
San Pedro de Atacama 179
San Pedro, Around............. 184
San Rafael glacier 369
Sanctuario El Cañi 279
Santa Cruz 228
Santa Cruz 228
Santa Laura 194
SANTIAGO 52–87
Santiago 58–59
Bellavista 72
Santiago and around 56
Santiago, Downtown........... 62
Santiago metro 77
     accommodation 77–80
     airports 75
     arrival 75
     arts and entertainment 85
     banks 87
     Barrio Bellavista 71
     Barrio Brasil 69
     Barrio Concha y Toro 69
     Barrio Lastarria 67
     Barrio París-Londres 67
     Barrio Yungay 69
     Biblioteca Nacional 66
     bike rental 76
     bus terminals 75
     buses 76
     cambios 75
     car rental 75
     car rental 76
     Casa Colorada 61
     cathedral 60
     Cerro San Cristóbal 73
     Cerro Santa Lucía 66
     colectivos 76
     Correo Central 59
     currency exchange 87
     drinking 80–84
     eating 80–84
     Edificio Iñiguez 68
     embassies 87
     emergencies 87
     Estación Central 69
     Estación Mapocho 71
     Ex Congreso Nacional 61
     Fería Municipal La Vega 86
     gay Santiago 86
     history 57
     hospitals 87
     Huérfanos 64
     Iglesia San Francisco 67
     information 78
     internet access 87
     La Chascona 72
     Las Condes 74
     markets 86
     Mercado Central 70
     metro 76

Moneda, La..............................64
Museo Colonial 67
Museo de Arte Contemporaneo 71
Museo de Arte Precolombino 61
Museo de Arte Precolombino 61
Museo de Arte Sagrado.................60
Museo de la Memoria y los
     Derechos Humanos 70
Museo de Santiago 61
Museo del Huaso 69
Museo Histórico Nacional...........60
Museo Nacional de Bellas Artes....71
nightlife 84
Palacio Cousiño 68
Palacio de Bellas Artes 71
Palacios of the Alameda................68
Parque Bernardo O'Higgins 69
Parque Quinta Normal.................69
Paseo Ahumada 63
Peñalolén 74
Plaza de Armas 57
police 87
post offices 87
Providencia 74
shopping 86
shops 86
taxis 76
telephone centres 87
tour operators 78
train station 76
transport 76
Tribunales de Justicia 61
Universidad de Chile 68
Santuario Cuna de Prat 246
Santuario de la Tirana 196
Santuario de le Naturaleza
     Carlos Anwandter.................293
Selk'nam people 423
Selkirk, Alexander.....................459
Seno Otway penguin colony
    394
Sewell...................................223
shellfish poisoning 43
shopping 45
Sierra Velluda 255
Siete Lagos.................. 283–287
Siete Lagos 284
skiing 42, 90
Socaire 186
souvenirs 45
sports 36
statues, Easter Island...............452
study and work programmes... 48
sunburn................................. 44
surfing 42

T

Tahai 451
Talca 235–237
Talca 235
Tapati Rapa Nui festival...........441

taxis 28
Te Pahu 454
telephone numbers, emergency
.... 47
telephones 50
television 35
Temuco 264–269
Temuco 268
Tenaún 328
Termas de Cahuelmó 352
Termas de Panimávida 239
Termas de Puyuhuapi 361
Termas de Quinamávida 239
Termas de Socos 131
Termas de Tolhuaca 259
Termas del Flaco 227
Termas Geométricas 285
Tierra del Fuego 414–435
Tierra del Fuego 418
Tierra del Fuego, driving 420
time 50
tipping 45
Toconao 186
Tomé 251
Tompkins, Douglas 353
Tongoy 135
Torres del Paine 400–407
torture 67, 480
tourist entry card 47
tourist information 50
tours, Easter Island 446
trains
  to Chile 30
  within Chile 25
transport 25–30
travel insurance 47
travelling with children 51
trekking 411
Tricahue Parque 239
tsunami, 2010 457
Tulor 185
Túnel de las Raíces 260

U

Universidad Austral de Chile
....248
Ushuaia (Argentina) 428–434

Ushuaia (Argentina) 429
Ushuaia, winter sports 435

V

Vaihu 449
Valdivia 288–293
Valdivia 289
Valdivia, Pedro de 137
Valle de Aguas Calientes 245
Valle de la Luna 185
Valle del Encanto 129
Vallenar 151–153
Vallenar 152
VALPARAÍSO 96–111
Valparaíso 102–103
Valparaíso, Viña & the central
  coast 100
Cerro Alegre & Cerro
  Concepción 106
  accommodation 109
  arrival 108
  Congreso Nacional 108
  drinking 110
  eating 110
  entertainment 111
  funiculars 106
  information 108
  Sebastiana, La 106
  tours 109
  transport 108
Ventisquero Colgante 359
Ventisquero Mosco 379
Vertiente del Radium 197
Vichuquén 233
Victoria 259
Vicuña 144–146
Vicuña 144
Villa Allegre 240
Villa Cerro Castillo 372
Villa Cultural Huilquilemu 237
Villa O'Higgins 377
Villa Ukika 424
Villarrica 271
Viña del Mar 113–119
Viña del Mar 116
Vinapu 449
visas 46
Volcán Antuco 255

Volcán Chaitén 354
Volcán Chillán 245
Volcán Copiapó 160
Volcán Llaima 260
Volcán Longquimay 260
Volcán Ojos de Salado 160
Volcán Osorno 306
Volcán Parinacota 213
Volcán Tres Cruces 160
Volcán Villarrica 282
volcanic eruption 354
volunteering 48

W

War of the Pacific 474
websites 51
whitewater rafting 357
wildlife 9
wine tours 88, 232
working 48

Y

Yámana people 423
Yupanqui 494

Z

Zapallar 120

Map symbols

The symbols below are used on maps throughout the book

✈	International airport	◆	Reserve	🏠	*Guardería* (ranger station)	▨	Building
✈	Domestic airport	⛷	Ski area	⛪	*Refugio* (mountain lodge)	☗	Church
Ⓜ	Metro station	🍇	Vineyard	⛺	Campsite	☐	Market
★	Transport stop	∴	Ruins	🔭	Observatory	◯	Stadium
ⓘ	Information office	〰	Viewpoint	⚔	Battle site	▨	Park
✉	Post office	〜	Mountain range	⚓	Port	▨	Beach
🕓	Telephone office	▲	Mountain peak	— · —	Ferry	▨	Salt pan
@	Internet access	/|\	Volcano	- - - -	Footpath	▨	Glacier
✚	Hospital	◠	Cave	▭▭▭	Railway	▭+	Cemetery
🏛	Monument	⛲	Waterfall	⊪⊪⊪	Funicular railway		
◆	Point of interest	◊◊	Hot spring	●- -●	Cable car		

Listings key

◼	Accommodation
●	Eating and drinking
◼	Nightlife
●	Shop

ROUGH GUIDES

WE GET AROUND

ONLINE start your journey at roughguides.com

EBOOKS & MOBILE APPS

GUIDEBOOKS from Amsterdam to Zanzibar

PHRASEBOOKS learn the lingo

MAPS so you don't get lost

GIFTBOOKS inspiration is our middle name

LIFESTYLE from iPads to climate change

...SO YOU CAN TOO

BOOKS | EBOOKS | APPS

Start your journey at **roughguides.com**
MAKE THE MOST OF YOUR TIME ON EARTH™

WE KNOW THE LATIN AMERICA YOU'LL LOVE

For individual travel recommendations and unrivalled insight,
speak to the UK's Nº1 specialist in travel to Latin America

www.journeylatinamerica.co.uk ☎ 020 8622 8470